SERGEI PROKOFIEV

SERGEI PROKOFIEV

A BIOGRAPHY

BY

HARLOW ROBINSON

PARAGON HOUSE PUBLISHERS
New York

First paperback edition, 1988.

Published in the United States by

Paragon House Publishers
90 Fifth Avenue
New York, New York 10011

Reprinted by arrangement with Viking Penguin, Inc.

Grateful acknowledgment is made for permission to reprint the following material:

Excerpts from Prokofiev's letters to Fatima Samoilenko by permission of the Hough-
ton Library, Harvard University.
Excerpts from letters by Konstantin Balmont by permission of the Beinecke Rare
Book and Manuscript Library, Yale University, and Svetlana Shales Balmont.

Photographic acknowledgments:

Frontispiece, bust of Prokofiev by G. Derujinsky, and photographs 6, 7, 8, 9, 10,
11, 12, 15, 16, 17, 18, 19, 20, 21, 24 used by permission of the Paris Opera Library,
Bibliothèque Nationale; photographs 2, 23, 27, 28, 35, 36, 37, 39, 40 by Harlow
Robinson; photograph 13 by permission of Ming Tcherepnin; photographs 22, 26 by
permission of Boosey & Hawkes, Ltd.; photograph 25 by permission of Evgeny Pasternak; photographs 29, 30, 31 by M. Azadovsky, by permission of K. Azadovsky.

LIBRARY OF CONGRESS CATALOGING-IN-PUBLICATION DATA

Robinson, Harlow Loomis.
Sergei Prokofiev : a biography / by Harlow Robinson.—1st pbk. ed.
p.   cm.
Bibliography: p.
Includes index.
ISBN 1-55778-009-9 (pbk.)
1. Prokofiev, Sergey, 1891-1953.   2. Composers—Soviet Union—
Biography.   I. Title.
[ML410.P865R55 1988]
780'.92'4'—dc 19
[B]   87-21007

For my parents,
and for Robert Holley

It's no misfortune to be born in a duck's nest from a swan's egg.

SERGEI PROKOFIEV, "The Ugly Duckling"
(after the fairy tale by Hans Christian Andersen)

PREFACE AND

ACKNOWLEDGMENTS

never met Prokofiev in the flesh, but I have met him many times in his music. When I was about ten, my parents took the family to a performance of *Love for Three Oranges* by a community group at the local high school. It was the first opera I ever saw. What impressed me most deeply then was not so much the odd, jerking rhythms and violent harmonic contrasts (though I liked those, too), but the plump pieces of artificial citrus fruit—swollen to unnatural size—that rolled out on stage in Act II. When three princesses—each singing sadly about something—emerged from them, my curiosity turned to amazement. I turned with wide eyes to my brother, whose similar wonder was reflected in the same tiny lines of joyful concentration that furrowed his brow when he was reading his favorite books.

A few months ago—about twenty-five years after that first meeting—I met Prokofiev again, this time in *Romeo and Juliet* at the Maly Theater in Leningrad. Arriving ticketless at the theatre only moments before the curtain was to rise, I was uncertain whether I could get in. I approached the box office window, which had been made tiny to protect the little old ladies who sit behind it from abuse when they announce that the performance is (as usual) sold out. Suddenly a slip of paper was thrust into my hand and a small number of rubles specified. "Run," the *babushka* said as she took the diminutive bills, "or you'll be late." I sprinted up the staircase indicated by the anxious usher, opened a small door and found myself in the lavishly appointed box once occupied by the Tsar and his family. Suffusing the gold-velvet upholstery in a muted glow, the lights dimmed as I squeezed through to my seat in the front row—the best one in the house.

Though I have seen *Romeo and Juliet* many times in many theatres, and many performances better than the one I saw on that bitter January night in icy Leningrad, this *Romeo* was a special one. I felt that Prokofiev had wanted me to be there.

Between this *Oranges* and this *Romeo* came many other meetings with Prokofiev: in his symphonies and concertos, his ballets and operas, his suites and songs. Listening to this beguiling music made me want to know more about its creator, so I read whatever I could find (mostly in Russian). Very soon, I discovered that the peculiarly nomadic life Prokofiev led had largely eluded his biographers. Gaping lacunae yawned before me as I worked to follow the twisting route of his personal and artistic odyssey; it was like coming to the most important pages of a suspense novel only to find them torn out. Ultimately, I came to see that these gaps resulted both from logistic problems (Prokofiev rarely stayed in one place for long, dashing between America, Europe and the Soviet Union) and political bias.

It became clear to me that Prokofiev's life and music had been recounted and interpreted from two equally unsatisfying and incomplete points of view. One was the official Soviet version, propounded by generations of Soviet musicologists and writers, that insisted (at least until quite recently) upon regarding Prokofiev's decision to leave Russia in 1918 as the biggest mistake of his life. The other was the "Western" version, argued with particular vehemence by members of the Russian emigration, which has insisted on the opposite: that his decision to return to the Soviet Union in 1936 was the biggest mistake of his life. Unfortunately, Prokofiev's complicated personal life in the U.S.S.R. only contributed further to this political polarization. As in most things, of course, the truth—some of which, at least, I hope to illuminate in the pages that follow—lies somewhere in between these two extreme positions.

I have tried to provide a more complete and balanced portrait of this remarkably misunderstood genius, drawing extensively on Russian-language sources previously unavailable to the English-speaking audience. My goal is to encourage greater appreciation of Prokofiev's tart and tender music, presenting it as part of a wider human and historical struggle. Strong and mysterious bonds linked Prokofiev's art to his personality and to his national identity. The nature of these bonds, and the sources of the prolific talent from which music flowed so forcefully, with a nearly biological urgency, are my subject here.

My long pursuit of Prokofiev has led me to many places—New York, Paris, London, Moscow, Leningrad—and to many extraordinary people. Writing this book would not have been possible without their help. But most of all, I am deeply grateful for the cooperation, encouragement and inspiration I received on my research trips to the U.S.S.R., where I uncovered a great deal of new information that is appearing for the first time in this book. The generosity and erudition of the staff at the Central State Archives of Literature and Art in Moscow made the many hours I spent there rewarding and memorable. I am also grateful to the staff of the manuscript division of the Saltykov-Shchedrin Library in Leningrad, and to the many Soviet scholars, librarians, musicians and friends who eagerly shared with me their personal and musical memories of a man they obviously adored.

I would also like to acknowledge the help of the following institutions: Boosey and Hawkes Music Publishers, Ltd.; the British Museum; the Bibliothèque Nationale in Paris—particularly the music Division and the Library of the Paris Opera; Houghton Library of Harvard University; the Music Division of the Library of Congress; and the Slavonic Division and the Lincoln Center Library of the Performing Arts of the New York Public Library. My work was aided by generous and much appreciated grants from the International Research and Exchanges Board, the Fulbright-Hayes Program, the State University of New York Research Foundation and the American Council of Learned Societies.

While it would take many pages to list all those individuals who provided help and encouragement along the way, I would like to extend special thanks to Simon Karlinsky, Robert Hughes, Malcolm Brown, Michael Heim, Phillip Ramey, Edmund White, Jeff Langley, Ming Tcherepnin, Pyotr Souchinsky, the late Boris Schwarz, and to the surviving members of Prokofiev's immediate family: Mme. Lina Llubera-Prokofiev, Oleg Prokofiev and Sviatoslav Prokofiev. I must also thank the members of the Biography Seminar of the New York Institute for the Humanities, who offered support, criticism and a sense of humor at a crucial stage in my work. Maxine Groffsky, my resilient agent, provided advice and energy in formulating the project. With their intelligence and enthusiasm, my subtle editor, Amanda Vaill, and her efficient assistant, Giovanni Favretti, made the job of putting it together not only an education but an adventure.

Two final notes involve problems that are the curse of those who write about Russia in languages other than Russian. The first is transliteration. In the body of the text, I have chosen to use popularly accepted spellings of Russian names (e.g., Prokofiev, not Prokof'ev) and places, rather than transliterating according to the scholarly Library of Congress system. Where there were several possible popular spellings (as in the case of Koussevitsky), I have made an arbitrary choice. In the notes and bibliography, however, I have employed the Library of Congress system. If I have erred, it is on the side of accessibility and readability, and I happily accept that responsibility.

The second is dating. The Western calendar was adopted in the U.S.S.R. in 1918. In the nineteenth century, the Russian calendar (commonly referred to as Old Style) lagged behind the Western calendar (New Style) by twelve days, and in the twentieth century (until 1918) by thirteen days. In the interest of authenticity, I have chosen to use Old Style dates in Part I, since it is set for the most part in Russia and ends in early 1918. In those sections of Part I which take place in Europe, however, I have used New Style dates. In other words, when in Russia, Old Style; when in Europe, New Style. Don't despair: where there is potential for confusion, I have provided both.

All translations from the Russian and French are mine unless indicated.

Brooklyn, New York

CONTENTS

ILLUSTRATIONS FOLLOW PAGE 240.

SERGEI PROKOFIEV

MARCH 5, 1953

ergei Sergeevich Prokofiev was dead. When Dmitri Kabalevsky—
a minor composer and major bureaucrat—burst in on a meeting at
the Composers' Union to break the news, his colleagues responded
with resignation, not surprise. Prokofiev had been in and out of
hospitals for more than eight years. Informing the appropriate Communist Party official was Kabalevsky's next and more important errand;
Stalin's office would decide on the delicate wording of the official
announcement. Should Prokofiev be called an "outstanding" Soviet
composer, or, because of his suspicious Western connections and many
years spent abroad, merely "great"? Stalin and his advisers took as
much trouble over such decisions as they did over battle strategy.

But as Kabalevsky and the official were discussing such protocol,
the phone rang. The Kremlin was calling. Normally impassive, the
official flinched as he listened, at attention, to the nearly hysterical
voice crackling from the receiver. Suddenly white and still, he hung
up and faced Kabalevsky. "It's all over. Stalin has died. Do you
understand—Stalin! What will happen to us?" No decision on how to
announce Prokofiev's death would be made that day—March 5, 1953.

Kabalevsky ran the few blocks to Prokofiev's small apartment near
the Bolshoi Theater. Already quietly gathering were the composer's
second wife, Mira, his two sons by his first wife, Lina, and other
friends and musicians. Lina could not be there—she was serving the
fifth year of an eight-year sentence in a Siberian labor camp. Stunned
by more intimate grief, Prokofiev's mourners could barely absorb the
shattering and liberating news of the Great Leader's death. On a thin,
hard divan lay Prokofiev, his skin bluish from the effects of a cerebral
hemorrhage. Stalin—at least according to some official accounts—

died of the same cause at 9:50 P.M., only fifty minutes after the composer whose life he so often complicated. Stalin was seventy-three; Prokofiev died a month short of his sixty-second birthday.

Only a few hours before, Prokofiev, frail but still alert and enthusiastic, had been planning the move to his country house at Nikolina Gora for spring and summer; making arrangements for the copying of a new revision of the Fifth Piano Sonata originally written in Paris in 1923; working on the seemingly endless changes demanded by the bureaucrats in his last ballet, *The Stone Flower*; and talking with his chauffeur about one of his favorite writers, Anton Chekhov. With one eye on mortality, however, he was also putting his meticulously preserved manuscripts and papers in order. Mira would finish the job.

Under more normal circumstances, Prokofiev's death would have been celebrated with solemn ceremony and proud rhetoric. Despite their sporadic, arbitrary and often nonsensical attacks on his music, the Soviet cultural bureaucrats were forced to recognize Prokofiev's enormous talent and cultural significance—if only because of his international reputation and the popularity of his music abroad. The Soviet system has never been comfortable with geniuses like Prokofiev, who disprove the socialist myth that all men are created equal.

And yet judged by the standards of a theoretically Marxist society obsessed with production quotas, Prokofiev was a model worker who surpassed his norm with exemplary enthusiasm. Composer of seven symphonies (among them the "Classical" Symphony, perhaps the most frequently performed of all symphonies written in the twentieth century), seven ballets (including *Romeo and Juliet*, *Cinderella* and *The Prodigal Son*), seven operas, nine piano sonatas, five piano concertos, two violin concertos, eight film scores, dozens of spicy piano pieces— not to mention cantatas, oratorios and songs—Prokofiev was rewarded for his labor with numerous official honors, among them the coveted Stalin Prize. To his émigré rival and countryman Igor Stravinsky, Prokofiev was "the greatest Russian composer of today—*après moi*."

The closest to Prokofiev sat all night in his crowded apartment. No newspapers circulated during the next several days, so few people outside the immediate circle of family and friends learned of his death until some time later. (Characteristically, American newspapers reported Prokofiev's death before Soviet ones did, although even *The New York Times* published the story only on March 9.) On Friday, March 6, he lay in state at the Composers' Union, where a civil funeral was held, but only forty or fifty people could maneuver through the barricades to attend. David Oistrakh played the first and third movements of Prokofiev's unusually dark F Minor Sonata for Violin and Piano, begun soon after the composer's final return to the U.S.S.R. in 1936 and finished during World War II. Introspective, muscular and bitterly passionate, the piece had been written for Oistrakh—for his unique combination of virtuosity, discipline and passion that Prokofiev so admired. He once told Oistrakh that the rapid scale-like passages in the chilling first movement (*Andante assai*) should sound like "wind in a graveyard."

Lacking other funereal music by their perpetually optimistic colleague, his friends turned to Bach, whose transparent efficiency, logic and precision had always appealed to Prokofiev the chess-player. Flowers were nearly impossible to find, so pianist Sviatoslav Richter placed a pine branch on the coffin.

On Saturday the modest funeral procession took a long, circuitous route to Novodevichy Cemetery, passing roadblocks and detours. Impenetrable walls of trucks, tanks and soldiers surrounded the city center, forming a wide ring around the Kremlin's brick towers as Stalin lay in state in the Hall of Columns—once an assembly for aristocrats. Party leaders, isolated like Cardinals in the Vatican, met day and night to choose a successor to the brutal autocrat who had ruled Russia for nearly thirty years. At Novodevichy, between a forest of gilded onion domes and the frozen Moscow River, the ceremony at Prokofiev's gravesite was brief.

Prokofiev died as he had lived—buffeted by momentous historical events. Indifferent to ideology and politically unsophisticated, he had chosen to spend his last seventeen years in one of the most relentlessly ideological societies ever created. This was not the only irony of his remarkable career, which began in a Ukrainian village, led to St. Petersburg, New York and Paris, and ended with his controversial return to Moscow in 1936, on the eve of the terrible Stalinist purges. In Russia, he was regarded as a European, but in Europe as a Russian. Soviet officialdom criticized his music as too "difficult," an elitist attack on "proletarian" taste, while the Western avant-garde found it too old-fashioned. Optimist in a pessimistic era, *naïf* among cynics, Prokofiev strove to devote his life to his craft, but the bloody modern history of the homeland he could not abandon rarely gave him the peace to do so. He was not a political man, but politics and politicians profoundly affected his personal life and the evolution of his musical style.

Like other members of his generation—Vladimir Mayakovsky,

Marina Tsvetaeva, Kazimir Malevich, Boris Pasternak—Prokofiev lived in two centuries and two irreconcilable Russias, belonging to neither. Born twenty-six years before the Russian Revolution, he never understood completely what Lenin and the Bolsheviks had done to the country he loved, nor what his new Soviet patrons expected of him. This dialectic contributes to the special force and personality of his startling music—at once modern and traditional, nostalgic and mocking, lyrical and savage—and to its grotesque contradictions. His art resounds with the cruel and gentle ironies of his life.

PART ONE

CHAPTER 1

SERYOZHENKA

It was the devil's doing that I was born in Russia
with intelligence and talent.

—ALEXANDER PUSHKIN

To Prokofiev, childhood was a state of mind. Long after his own idyllic
boyhood, he continued to love children for their unfettered imagination, sense of play and inability to dissimulate. That he never
forgot what it meant to be a child, and how children think, is evident
in the playful but never condescending music he wrote for them, most
of all in the phenomenally successful *Peter and the Wolf*, written when
Prokofiev was a boy of forty-five.

So much did Prokofiev enjoy childhood—both personally and
aesthetically—that he devoted a six-hundred-page "autobiography,"
by far his largest literary attempt, solely to his first eighteen years.
Here, in an offhand, tongue-in-cheek style, he examines his early
education, adventures and music in rich and microscopic detail. Like
many remembrances of childhood recorded in adulthood, Prokofiev's
autobiography is romanticized and idealized; there are few rainy days
and even fewer scraped knees. Such unambiguously cheerful memories
inevitably arouse suspicion: why does the author need to believe that
his childhood was so happy? What darker memories lie repressed
below? It is only fair to note, however, that Prokofiev was always an
incurable optimist, even under the most difficult circumstances. More
than most people, he simply forgot the bad things.

The first part of the volume ("Childhood") was written between
1937 and 1939, and the second part ("The Conservatory") between

1945 and 1950. These were difficult times in the composer's life. No doubt he was tempted to escape insoluble adult problems—a broken marriage, war, failing health, the arrest and imprisonment of friends, bureaucratic interference in his music—in a lost childhood paradise.

But Prokofiev's playmates, relatives and teachers for the most part corroborate his description of a sunny and entertaining childhood, virtually free of obstacles to the happy unfolding of his musical talent. No tales here of childhood frustration and anger later avenged by artistic fame. His happy memories are very different, for example, from those of Igor Stravinsky, nine years Prokofiev's senior, who recalls his Russian childhood mainly as a time of tyranny, constraints and loneliness. Spoiled wholeheartedly by doting parents, Prokofiev accepted loving indulgence as reality. Later, he came to expect it from everyone.

Prokofiev had the good fortune to be born to parents who desperately wanted a baby. Ecstatic when he came into the world on April 11 (April 23, New Style), 1891, they called him Sergei, after his father, Sergei Alekseevich Prokofiev, who was already nearly forty-five. His mother, Maria Grigorevna Zhitkova Prokofiev, was thirty-four and had already borne two children—both daughters—who died in infancy. She had been waiting for a child to fuss over and educate, a companion in the remote Ukrainian village where her husband, an agronomist, managed an aristocrat's estate. When Sergei Sergeevich was born, the village was called Sontsovka, after the family that owned the estate; after the 1917 Revolution it was renamed Krasnoye—red—for the favorite color of the new owners.

Prokofiev's parents came to Sontsovka in 1878, only a year after they were married. Thirteen long years went by before Seryozhenka was born. Photographs show that he inherited his mother's face: long and oval-shaped, with thick protruding lips, a wide chin and deep-set sky-blue eyes. His hair was white-blond and straight. From his mother, too, at least in part, came his musical inclinations. She was a serious amateur pianist, and would practice up to six hours a day while pregnant with Sergei Sergeevich, attempting to maintain a link to the cultured urban life she had led before marriage. When her only child, still a toddler, revealed an instinctive love for the instrument, she was understandably pleased.

There is a bit of the Cinderella story in the history of his parents' courtship. Maria Grigorevna was descended from a family of serfs. Before the emancipation of 1861, her father served in the Petersburg household of the Sheremetevs, one of Tsarist Russia's richest families.

After the emancipation, he worked first as a free servant in the Winter Palace, the royal residence, and later as a scrivener. The life of the Zhitkovo family was impoverished, unstable and marked by tragedy—including the suicide of one of Maria's four teenage sisters.

Despite the difficulties, she demonstrated impressive energy and independence, taking aggressive advantage of the new educational opportunities for women and nonaristocrats. She attended high school in Moscow, where she met students from better social and economic backgrounds. (Maria always tended to think of herself, though, as a Petersburger rather than a Muscovite and preferred the capital's more Western cultural atmosphere.) Among her new friends were the daughters of Nadezhda Smirnova, Sergei Alekseevich Prokofiev's sister. Soon, she was spending a good deal of time at their house, where Sergei Alekseevich, uncle to Maria's new girlfriends, had also been living since his own parents' death from cholera when he was fourteen.

Ten years older than she, and a student at an agricultural academy, Sergei Alekseevich at first seemed to Maria a dry and forbidding character. Descended from a family of merchants and factory owners, he appeared to have a solid future ahead of him. He studied seriously and even single-mindedly, for the most part ignoring the tumultuous political events shaking Russia at the end of the nineteenth century. (Perhaps it was from his father that Sergei Sergeevich inherited his own indifference to politics, an attitude which would hurt him later on.) In the early 1870s, when student terrorist organizations proliferated wildly, threatening bombings and assassinations, Sergei Alekseevich was once asked to denounce his fellow students who were participating in the uprisings. He refused, and was punished by having his diploma withheld. Forever after, he pointedly avoided political involvement—and even political conversation—of any kind.

By the time Sergei Alekseevich graduated, bought a small estate in the Smolensk district and went off to make his farming fortune, he and Maria Grigorevna had become very important to each other. The thought that he might throw himself away on the lively but penniless daughter of peasants alarmed Sergei Alekseevich's relatives, who did nothing to encourage the relationship. But Maria's knowledge and wit, her sociability and energy appealed to Sergei Alekseevich, an intelligent but reserved person. In most ways his opposite, she did not hesitate to tease him for his excessive gravity.

Prokofiev—whose relationship with his mother was always exceptionally close—emphasizes in his autobiography that in spite of their economic-social pretensions, his father's family was in fact less refined and intellectually developed than his mother's, which had worked hard for its advancement. And in their future married life, too, Maria would most often take the lead in matters intellectual and cultural; Sergei Alekseevich remained in the background—a dutiful, aloof and somewhat colorless patriarch. Marrying Maria Grigorevna was the most rebellious act of his life.

Soon after their wedding in 1877, Sergei Alekseevich and Maria Grigorevna went to live on their land in the Smolensk district, deep in the Russian provinces southwest of Moscow. Life there was hard. Capital to buy farm machinery and construct buildings was what Sergei Alekseevich needed, but most of the money he had inherited from his parents had been lost in an investment scheme with a friend who had disappeared in China. Scrambling to make ends meet, the newly married couple was tempted by an interesting proposal from an old university friend. Dmitri Dmitrievich Sontsov owned two estates: he lived on one, but the other, far to the south in the fertile Ukraine, was run by an inefficient manager who never sent profits. Would Prokofiev, a trained agronomist who could put the place in order, be interested in taking over the manager's job at a higher salary?

After long deliberation—and further financial difficulties—Sergei Alekseevich and Maria Grigorevna agreed to the offer. The owner promised that Prokofiev could run Sontsovka as if it were his own property. In the spring of 1878, they made the journey to Sontsovka, having agreed on a trial period of three years, and remained until Sergei Alekseevich's death thirty-two years later. Prokofiev spent his first thirteen years in Sontsovka, and school vacations there until he was eighteen.

Sontsovka was remote from civilization; the nearest railroad station, on a rural branch line, was twenty-five miles away. Kiev and Kharkov and Odessa, the large cities of the Ukraine, were hundreds of miles distant, across the flat steppe stretching toward the Black Sea. To reach Moscow and St. Petersburg took days. Educated neighbors were few and far between.

Because Sergei Alekseevich was in complete charge of the Sontsovka estate, and Sontsov himself rarely visited, the Prokofievs were to some extent treated like local gentry. They lived in the manor house, a modest but comfortable one-story structure, and had servants who called Maria Grigorevna "Barynya"—"Mistress." After Sergei Sergeevich was born, the peasant boys he played with thought of him as a nobleman's son. And yet Sergei Alekseevich was accountable to Sontsov, and had to send monthly financial statements. Therefore the family found itself in the somewhat unusual—and not always comfortable—position of living like nobility while being constantly reminded that they were less than noble. Some of the neighbors, nobility by blood, treated the Prokofievs condescendingly, even when their estates were smaller and less productive. Snobbish and clannish, the Russian aristocrats regarded even prosperous merchant families like Sergei Alekseevich's as crude and unrefined, almost indistinguishable on the social scale from the peasants.

His family's ambiguous social position influenced the composer's later dealings with members of the Russian aristocracy, and with those who cultivated aristocratic pretensions—the impresario Sergei Diaghilev, for example. Aware of how hard his father worked to make a living from Sontsov's estate and how disappointed he must have been that he never owned his own property, Prokofiev always resented those who did not have to earn a living. Like his mother, he placed his faith in discipline, hard work and intellect—not in social class or possessions. Nor did Prokofiev inherit his father's belief that the wealthy had a social and moral responsibility to improve the lot of the less fortunate. In his own political views—as in most things—the composer took after his mother, and remained all his life suspicious of grand philanthropic gestures.

Before giving birth to Sergei Sergeevich, a healthy and rosy-cheeked baby, Maria Grigorevna had spent her time helping out at the local school, dispensing medicine to the sick, and playing the piano. "She had little musical talent," her son wrote many years later; "she acquired technique with difficulty, and her fingers had no cushion of soft skin in front of the fingernails. She was afraid to play in front of people. She did, however, have three virtues: stubbornness, passion and good taste. Mother achieved the best possible performance of the pieces she studied, regarding this work with love, and she was interested in serious music only. This played a significant role in the evolution of my own musical taste: from birth I heard Beethoven and Chopin, and I remember, at the age of twelve, consciously despising light music." Even with the diversion music provided, though, Maria Grigorevna often felt isolated in Sontsovka. Every winter she would escape to spend a few months with friends and family in St. Petersburg, feasting hungrily on intellectual conversation and cultural life. When her son was a little older, she would bring him along.

As usually happened on Russian estates far from urban centers, Seryozha's early education occurred entirely in the home. Maria Grigorevna was the single most important force in his intellectual and musical life until she died in 1924. Only his innate sense of independence and mischief saved Prokofiev from becoming a "mama's boy." As an only child, he was the center of attention, receiving not only his mother's affection, but that of servants, nursemaids and, later, tutors hired for his benefit. Maria Grigorevna did try to provide him with a balanced and relatively disciplined upbringing, and relied on her husband's spartan severity to offset her indulgent nature. Prokofiev and his father, who shows up surprisingly infrequently in his son's autobiography, had a distant relationship; neither was comfortable with emotional display.

Prokofiev is known as a *Wunderkind*, a reputation only partially deserved. It was only when he entered the Conservatory, at age thirteen, that he began to demonstrate his exceptional natural gifts to their full extent. As a baby he was intelligent, but not remarkably so. He did not compose symphonies before learning to walk. He did not even learn to play the piano until he was almost six, and did not master it in any significant sense until his adolescent years. But an acute sensitivity to and love for music did appear very early; he would sit quietly listening to his mother practice the piano even before he could speak. Exceptional, too, was his natural musical ear, which could identify fragments of music his mother played before he was six. Even before he had any clear understanding of notation, he wrote "pieces," and was fascinated with the concept of creating signs on a page that translated into sounds from a piano. Throwing his hands left and right on the keyboard, in imitation of his mother, he would sit at the piano and improvise.

Luckily, Maria Grigorevna never forced her son to study the piano. An instinctive pedagogue, she believed that the essential element at the beginning level was to develop love for and curiosity about the instrument. When he began to "compose" little pieces on notebook paper in a childish scrawl, and then ask her to play them, she yielded to his insistence to teach him about notation. With her help he wrote down his first composition, "Indian Gallop," inspired by newspaper stories about famine in India. Regular music lessons with his mother began at age seven. At first limited strictly to twenty minutes so as not to bore him, the lessons in elementary theory and piano were gradually extended to thirty minutes, and finally, at age nine, to an hour. By the time he was eight, Seryozhenka (as he was called as a child, later abbreviated to Seryozha) had composed several marches (three for four hands), plus waltzes, a polka and a rondo. Always the doting mother, Maria Grigorevna loved to show him off to relatives and friends, who, of course, were charmed. Never shy, he would oblige by performing his own pieces and the classics. By age nine he could play easy Beethoven sonatas and pieces by Mozart.

Mozart's parents wanted to create a musical professional, but Prokofiev's, at least initially, were intent on raising a well-rounded and "normal" boy. His father insisted on supervising rigorous study of academic subjects (with heavy concentration on mathematics and the sciences), perhaps preparing him for an engineer's career, and allowed him to play outside with the peasant boys. Bossy and used to getting his own way, Seryozhenka enjoyed commanding them to play roles in games he invented. Chess was also discovered early, by age seven, and it soon became—after music—his favorite pastime. Fascinated by the clear logic, the straight lines, the charts of moves, the mathematical problem-solving challenge, Prokofiev soon learned the rules and taught his companions—and the maid—how to play. Competition never intimidated him, even as a boy, and he always played to win. With his slender and delicate build he was less gifted for more physical pastimes, and the peasant boys were instructed not to play too roughly with him. Although he grew up in the country, he never worked in the fields and could not tell rye from barley. Flowers were more interesting to him; he would make long lists of their exotic Latin names.

To celebrate the new century, a century that would change the Russia into which their son had been born beyond their wildest imaginings, Prokofiev's parents took him to Moscow for the first time in January 1900. Sergei Alekseevich's sister still lived there, along with her daughters, Maria Grigorevna's former girlfriends. Seryozhenka was in a state of almost uncontrollable excitement at the prospect of traveling to Moscow by train; he studied train schedules, routes and equipment with a conductor's passion that lasted his entire life. Soon after they arrived in Moscow, then a chaotic mix of the rustic and the sophisticated, a lively city of burgeoning economic opportunity and industrial fortunes of fairy-tale proportions, the eight-year-old country cousin went to the theatre for the first time. It was love at first sight. He saw two operas—Gounod's *Faust* and Borodin's *Prince Igor*—and, at the Bolshoi Theater, one ballet—Tchaikovsky's *Sleeping Beauty*.

Of the three performances, it was, not surprisingly, the mephistophe-
lean mysteries of *Faust* that most stimulated his imagination.

As he recalled in his autobiography,

> They started playing the overture, and the curtain rose. There were
> books—lots of books—and Faust with a beard. He's reading from
> a thick volume and singing something, then he reads and sings again.
> But when does the devil come on? How slow it all is. Ah—there he
> is at last! But why is he dressed in a red suit, with a sword—why
> so fashionable? I thought somehow that the devil would be black,
> like a Negro, half-naked and maybe even with hooves. Later, when
> they began amusing themselves, I immediately recognized both the
> march and the waltz, which I had heard my mother play in Sontsovka.

Back in Sontsovka and still under the spell of his night at the
opera, Seryozhenka announced that he was going to compose one
himself. By early summer he had finished the first act of *The Giant*,
for which he wrote both libretto (in verse) and music, using characters
inspired by his loyal Sontsovka playmates.

In Act I, the heroine, Ustinya (Stenya), is sitting in the forest
reading a book. A giant appears and tries to catch her, but Sergeev
(the composer's alter-ego) and Egorov (his friend Egor) enter and scare
the beast away as Ustinya falls into a faint. Leaving, the heroes thought-
fully drop their calling cards so she will know who has saved her. The
next day, the giant reappears and eats Ustinya's lunch while she is
away at the post office. Something must be done, the indignant pro-
tagonists decide. They tell the king about the giant and, receiving his
royal blessing, engage the giant in combat in the forest, forcing him
to flee. Egor is wounded. Act III begins conventionally, with a celebration at Ustinya's house, but concludes unexpectedly with the king's
suicide, which causes the characters to grieve only briefly before breaking into triumphant song: "All hail our giant!"

Seryozhenka's father saw incipient revolutionary sentiments in the
strange political twist at the end, and tried to convince him to rewrite
it with a scene of reconciliation between the giant and the king. To
the composer's credit, he refused to yield to the censor.

A piece of juvenilia never intended to be taken too seriously,
The Giant nonetheless shows that at the age of nine, Prokofiev was
already able to conceive of a composition as an artistic whole and to
complete it with imagination, originality and a sense of style. Musical
tricks he had learned from *Faust*, and from his lessons with his mother,

found their way into the score, which breathes the same satirical spirit as his mature opera *Love for Three Oranges*. In *Oranges*, too, royal characters act in quirky fashion—the hero is an incurably hypochondriacal prince who can be cured only through laughter—and absurd touches of concrete reality (like the dropped calling cards) rub shoulders with the fantastic. Highly rhythmic waltzes and marches abound in *The Giant*; the few operas with which Seryozhenka was familiar at the time—*Faust, Eugene Onegin*, perhaps *Aida* and Meyerbeer's *The Prophet*—had them, too.

Like most children, Prokofiev loved fairy tales. What was unusual about him was that he very early began to see them in a theatrical—and sardonic—light. By the time Prokofiev composed *The Giant*, besides *The Sleeping Beauty*, he may have known of Tchaikovsky's other ballets (*Swan Lake* and *The Nutcracker* were performed in the capitals while Seryozhenka was growing up) and of Rimsky-Korsakov's many fairy-tale operas, which he would soon come to cherish: *The Snow Maiden, May Night, Sadko*. But if Tchaikovsky and Rimsky-Korsakov viewed fairy tales with a sweet childlike innocence, Prokofiev—even as a boy—regarded them with a caustic irreverence.

Despite its unromantic spirit, *The Giant* did not suffer for lack of praise and attention from family and friends. Seryozhenka's mother helped him with the musical notation, his tutor Louise (whom Maria had lured to Sontsovka from Paris) copied the score over neatly, and his sentimental Aunt Tanya, his mother's sister, to whom *The Giant* was dedicated, had the manuscript lavishly bound in red with gold lettering: "*The Giant*: an opera in three acts, a composition by Seryozhenka Prokofiev."

A year later, in summer 1901, on a visit to his aunt's country house, Prokofiev directed a domestic production. Aunt Tanya was cast as the Giant (if only for reasons of size), cousin Katya as Ustinya, cousin Shurik as Egorov, and Prokofiev as Sergeev. So intense was her son's excitement and anticipation over the impending performance that Maria Grigorevna feared he would fall ill. But the papered audience of relatives and friends was charmed with the piece, and praised its creator as the next Glinka. Such overwhelmingly positive early experiences as a performer help to explain why Prokofiev suffered little from stage fright in his adult life.

Nor was opera the only theatrical form at which he tried his hand. At Sontsovka his peasant companions—under his dictatorial direction—presented little plays with similarly fantastic themes. One year

Prokofiev received as a New Year's gift from his parents an assortment of masks—of a bear, a parrot, monkeys—that they thought he could use in these presentations. "In a little while I had some ideas, and in the summer I wrote four plays with roles for the masks I had received," he wrote in his autobiography. "This wasn't *commedia dell'arte* with improvisation, as we had been presenting up until then: the whole text was written out."

The first play was called *People*. It described a forest gathering of talking domestic animals who were discussing how to confront an approaching storm. Their discussion rapidly degenerated into a stubborn argument that ended with the appearance of humans who shot the animals dead. If the play has a moral, it seems to be: stick together, or your enemies will overpower you, or, guns have the last word.

Prokofiev's childhood fascination with wily beasts and supernatural spirits never disappeared: it is found in works from all periods of his artistic maturity, from *The Ugly Duckling* to *Love for Three Oranges* to *The Buffoon, Peter and the Wolf, Cinderella* and *The Stone Flower*.

In December 1901, Maria Grigorevna and Sergei Alekseevich took their son to St. Petersburg for the first time. He was ten. They strolled along the Imperial capital's broad avenues and arcades, admiring the city's formal and magnificent architecture, its brilliantly refined atmosphere—so different from Moscow's folksy informality. They also went to the Mariinsky Theater, upholstered in icy royal blue, to see Glinka's grand patriotic opera *A Life for the Tsar*, Alexander Dargomyzhsky's fairy-tale opera *Rusalka* (about a forest spirit), the then-popular but now-forgotten opera *Demon* by Anton Rubinstein (based on a romantic poem by Mikhail Lermontov), Verdi's *La Traviata* and Bizet's *Carmen* (Tchaikovsky's favorite opera and one of the most beloved foreign operas in the Russian repertoire even today). In these early years of the century, Russian opera and ballet were entering their most glorious era; small private companies began to compete artistically with the state-run, wealthy and conservative Imperial Theaters (like the Mariinsky, now called the Kirov, and the Bolshoi in Moscow). Pressed by the competition and responding to the great variety of new artistic movements, even the Imperial Theaters were taking more risks.

In 1901, a twenty-nine-year-old former law student named Sergei

Diaghilev was working at the Mariinsky, trying to shake that stodgy institution out of its artistic paralysis. His radical ideas and flamboyant manners led not long after to his expulsion from the staff and, indirectly, to his creation of an independent troupe. That troupe—eventually known as the Ballets Russes—and its founder would profoundly influence Prokofiev's career, though the boy from Sontsovka knew nothing of all that in the cold winter of 1901–1902. No doubt what his mother heard of Diaghilev did not please her.

From St. Petersburg, the family traveled on to Moscow. Here they made direct contact for the first time with the world of professional music. It happened that the son of their friends the Pomerantsevs was a student at the Moscow Conservatory. When Yury Pomerantsev met Prokofiev and discovered his talent and precocity, he suggested to Maria Grigorevna that the boy be introduced to Sergei Taneev (1856–1915). Taneev was a composer of well-respected, if academic, music, and a professor at the Moscow Conservatory, where he had studied with Tchaikovsky. Behind his quiet and self-effacing demeanor, Taneev was one of the most powerful figures on the Moscow musical scene. Like Rimsky-Korsakov in St. Petersburg, he worked tirelessly for the cause of Russian music and composers, encouraging budding talents. A surprisingly familial atmosphere reigned in the small world of Russian music—and in the entire world of Russian culture—and Taneev agreed to talk with the boy and his mother.

Of this first meeting with Taneev, which proved to be a turning point in his life, Prokofiev admits to remembering little except the chocolate that the professor immediately offered him. (Prokofiev always had a weakness for sweets.) Maria Grigorevna noticed the almost monastic atmosphere, the total dedication to the cause of art, evident in the piles of music, the quiet and the isolation. By now, Seryozhenka had begun a second opera, *Desert Islands* (a tale of shipwrecks and maritime heroism), which he played for Taneev, followed by an excerpt from the classic *Giant*. Impressed with the boy's natural talent and artistic poise, the professor recommended that he immediately begin studying harmony, theory and composition with a professional instructor, before bad habits developed.

So many of their gifted but haphazardly educated predecessors— Mussorgsky, Borodin, Glinka—had been denigrated as "amateurs" that professional Russian musicians like Taneev demanded rigorous technical training of the younger generation. Nikolai Rimsky-Korsakov (1844–1908), galvanized by Mussorgsky's undisciplined example, was similarly insistent (even obsessed by the notion) that composers who studied at the St. Petersburg Conservatory become fluent in the language, practice and history of their craft. What Russia needed now was musical engineers and technocrats, not wildly romantic dilettantes drowning in inspiration and vodka.

Taneev recommended that Prokofiev study with Yury Pomerantsev for the moment, at least as long as he was in Moscow. As for the future, Taneev suggested hiring a young composer to spend the summer at Sontsovka, where he could work with the boy systematically. Seryozhenka remained largely unaware of the significance of these discussions about his artistic future. While apparently enjoying his subsequent lessons with Pomerantsev, and Taneev's attention and chocolate, he was just as happy to play with toy soldiers or write down long lists of the numbers on the horse-drawn trolley cars that rumbled by their Moscow hotel room.

Returning to the harsh realities of life in Sontsovka, Maria Grigorevna and Sergei Alekseevich wondered how they could afford the recommended tutor-composer. Seventy rubles a month was for them a significant sum requiring careful planning and sacrifice, but their concern for their son's talent and future prevailed, as it always would. They wrote to Taneev, accepting his offer. After anxious consultation, Taneev and Prokofiev's parents chose a young composer of Belgian origin from Kiev: Reinhold Glière (1874–1956). When he arrived at Sontsovka in the summer of 1902, he was twenty-eight years old; his student was eleven.

Years later, recalling his two summers at Sontsovka, Glière, who eventually became the director of the Kiev Conservatory, was in the embarrassing position of having been overtaken long before in talent, fame and achievements by his erstwhile student. Today, Glière is remembered primarily for his ballet *The Red Poppy*, first staged in 1927 by the Bolshoi Theater. One of the first examples in ballet of what eventually became formalized as Soviet Socialist Realism, the subject is the awakening of revolutionary awareness in China. Whatever their later relationship, during the pleasantly quiet summers of 1902 and 1903, Glière and Prokofiev got along well. Glière understood that Prokofiev, for all his talent, ability and quickness to learn, was still a little boy who liked to play, tease, show off and invent games, which made it easier for them to work together.

"Very soft and affectionate, tenderly attached to his parents"— this was Glière's first impression of Prokofiev. Glière discovered, however, as he came to know this spoiled and indulged only child a little better, that he could be mischievous and assertive as well. The daily regimen during those summers was strictly set down and policed by Maria Grigorevna and her husband. Such discipline helped, perhaps, to instill in Prokofiev the passion for the absolute maintenance of a regular work schedule so characteristic of his adult years. Before breakfast, a swim in the river near the house, followed by breakfast and a lesson with Glière from ten to eleven. Next Prokofiev and his father worked on Russian and math. French and German lessons with his mother concluded the morning. After a bountiful country midday repast, he would play—at horseback riding, croquet, walking on stilts, chess—until the evening, when he and Glière would play four-hand piano arrangements of symphonies of Haydn, Beethoven, Mozart, Tchaikovsky and other classics. Sometimes Seryozhenka would accompany his teacher as he played Mozart violin sonatas.

His student's natural gifts impressed Glière as they worked on theory and harmony: "perfect pitch, a good memory, a marvelous harmonic sense, rich creative imagination." He clarified Prokofiev's vague understanding of the theoretical basis of composition and gave him exercises to complete. Cautious, conventional and long-winded in his own musical style, Glière provided a sensible creative super-ego for the boy's fertile fantasy. Prokofiev did not rebel against the imposition of form and structure on his innate creativity; music remained, as it had been since his earliest years, a wonderfully complex game. This playful relationship to music stayed with him for the rest of his life, and helps to explain both the strengths and weaknesses of his art.

Working systematically with Glière led to a sudden growth in the list of Seryozhenka's compositions. After Glière explained song form, Prokofiev produced a series of six *pesenky* ("little songs") for the piano, the first of almost seventy that he would write over the next six years. Glière also instructed him in the fundamentals of symphonic form and instrumentation. Intrigued by the exciting new possibilities, Prokofiev convinced his reluctant tutor to allow him to compose a real symphony. By the summer's end the piece—opening with an assertive, even cocky, nineteen-measure theme, rhythmic and imposing—was finished. Soon he started orchestrating it under Glière's supervision.

Music now assumed the leading role in Seryozhenka's life. His mother, supported silently by his father, spent even more time and money in developing and protecting what people who knew more than she did were telling her was her son's extraordinary natural talent.

Afraid to contradict Glière's teachings, Maria Grigorevna sat in on their piano lessons, anxious to provide continuity in his education after Glière returned to Moscow in the fall. Dreams of glittering opening nights lured the stage mother in Maria Grigorevna; she wanted to believe in her prodigy's brilliant future. Fortunately, her child was willing (and able) to go along with her ambitious plans, or he might have rebelled at the evening rituals of the Prokofiev household. Maria Grigorevna would ask Seryozhenka two questions: "So then what did you accomplish today?" and "Are you satisfied with what you accomplished?"

In fact, Prokofiev never expressed resentment over his mother's role in pushing him toward a musical career (though he never pushed his own children as hard as she pushed him), perhaps because Maria Grigorevna knew how to encourage his natural love of music and how to make his lessons seem like fun. She never turned them into drudgery, or a test of will between parent and child.

Fortunately, too, Maria Grigorevna was intelligent enough to realize her own limitations. As Prokofiev notes, Glière's arrival was important "not only because I grew stronger in harmony and learned about new aspects of musical technique, like form and instrumentation; but it was also important because I passed from my mother's hands, who, although she was a born teacher, was a dilettante and not a composer, into the hands of a professional. He dealt with music in a completely different way, and, even without noticing it, opened up new horizons to me."

After leaving Sontsovka in the fall, Glière continued his lessons with Prokofiev by correspondence. They met again in November in Moscow, where Maria Grigorevna and her son stayed for more than a month. Prokofiev also visited his mentor Taneev, who approved of his first attempt at a symphony but found Seryozhenka's harmonic language too conventional, a judgment that made both of them laugh in later years, when the dissonance and quirkiness of Prokofiev's harmonies regularly horrified and titillated audiences. Through Taneev and Glière, Prokofiev and his mother met various composers and musicians, who began to treat the eleven-year-old as a musical equal, making him feel welcome and important.

Evenings were spent at the opera and concerts. Among Russian performers then active were the pianist and composer Sergei Rachmaninoff, the virtuoso bassist Sergei Koussevitsky (later famous as conductor of the Boston Symphony), the pianist and composer Alexander Scriabin, and the operatic bass Fyodor Chaliapin. During November and December of 1902, Prokofiev heard several of them. One night, he saw Wagner's *Die Walküre* at the Bolshoi Theater, which he described, in a self-assured letter to his father (back in Sontsovka tending the farm) as a "terribly boring opera, without themes, without movement, but with a great deal of noise."

Despite such pronouncements, Prokofiev's musical assurance amazed everyone with whom he came in contact, but he remained in other ways underdeveloped. At age eleven, he still carried his doll "Sir" (*Gospodin*) with him everywhere, even to Moscow conferences with Glière. Physically he was small for his age, and his mother feared to let him learn how to ice skate without a teacher there to catch him.

Returning to snowbound Sontsovka by late January, after a few weeks in St. Petersburg, Prokofiev continued to compose. Because his pupil dealt reasonably well with symphonic form, Glière gave him a new assignment: a violin sonata. (That Glière was an accomplished violinist surely had something to do with the choice of instrument.) Seryozhenka finished it in five weeks. Later lost, the sonata was memorable enough to furnish a theme (from the first part, the *Allegro*) used ten years later as the main theme of his "Ballade for Cello," Op. 15. Along with the violin sonata, Prokofiev wrote more piano *pesenky* to complete the "First Series" of twelve by the end of 1902. Until 1907 he wrote twelve more each year for a total of five series.

Music of the composers his mother liked to play—Beethoven and Chopin—exerted a strong influence on these early piano pieces. Beethoven became much more important to Prokofiev's musical style than Chopin; one feels it throughout his career, especially in the First String Quartet, the First Violin Sonata, and some of the piano solo works. Even as a boy, Prokofiev was antisentimental, and unimpressed by Chopin's soft emotionality, despite its tremendous popularity in Russia at the time. "I was indifferent to his waltzes, and didn't value his nocturnes very highly. Probably his études and sonatas would have appealed to me more, but my mother didn't play them. It would especially irritate me when my mother would say: 'Why don't you compose something tender and melodic? Chopin's "Nocturnes" are so pretty!' "

Prokofiev's irritation did not prevent him from imitating Chopin in a few of his *pesenky* (and even in some of his early piano sonatas). Truly, the arpeggios and gently singing line did not suit the composer's natural talent for an aggressively staccato, percussive and spare sound. Even at age eleven, he showed a strong preference for strong irregular rhythms, jarring chromatic intervals and fierce velocity. One could explain this in part as a musical rebellion against his mother's fondness for conventional and sentimentally clichéd musical gestures. And yet his musical personality—"sharp and ringing, like the dripping of snow in spring"—was too deeply organic and spontaneous to be a mere reaction.

Numbers, counting, lists, collections and quantities of all sorts were, besides music, Prokofiev's passions through boyhood and youth. During that winter and spring of 1903, he spent much of his free time counting the exact number of measures in the score of Tchaikovsky's *Eugene Onegin* (around four thousand) and collecting stamps. (Glière sent him some foreign stamps from Moscow, prompting this confident reply: "Let me offer you a free seat in the first row at all my performances.") Sorting, arranging and listing exercised a strange and unceasing fascination over Prokofiev into middle age and beyond. Nothing entertained him (or calmed him) more thoroughly than to compose lists of his opus numbers (both completed and prospective), cities he had visited, or performances he had heard. He was obsessed with organization and categorization, which bespeaks a desire to control experience and to keep it at bay, to explain and arrange his feelings and, perhaps, to avoid confronting darker and more formless impulses. His obsession with systemitization helps to explain how he could accomplish so much; it also irritated his more casual friends, whose lateness for appointments was always recorded—and reported to them—in the precise number of minutes.

In April 1903, Seryozhenka turned twelve. Friends and family started calling him Seryozha, a name more befitting someone about to become a teenager. It was time to start thinking seriously about his education. Should they send the boy along to Moscow, more than two days' journey from Sontsovka by train, to enter the gymnasium? Should he live there with relatives so that his mother could come often to stay? Or should she go to live with him there permanently? This alternative attracted Maria Grigorevna, who found the long snowbound winters and cultural isolation of rural life difficult to bear. No matter where he went to study, Seryozha would have to pass demanding examinations, so his work on purely academic subjects intensified. His parents, particularly his pragmatic father, were not sure if they should send their only son to a conservatory. What if his talent proved insufficient, and he ended up as a mediocre musician with few financial possibilities? No decision was made for the moment, and Glière agreed to return to Sontsovka for the summer of 1903.

With a symphony and a sonata behind them, tutor and pupil decided to try another genre. Academic and systematic, Glière suggested a string quartet or sextet, which sounded boring to Prokofiev: he insisted on an opera. He had already finished two! Perhaps envious of his student's ambition and obvious natural gifts, Glière at first tried to discourage him, but finally suggested a rather dry and static subject, "The Feast During the Plague," a dramatic poem by Alexander Pushkin. Glière chose it partly because it lacked a love intrigue—supposedly unfathomable to a twelve-year-old—but the poem's mysterious fatalism and gloomily historical mood did not capture Prokofiev's imagination. Where were the dragons and wise-cracking royalty?

That he was not inspired by the abstract and symbolic characters was obvious in his decision to devote most of his energy to the overture, which was so long in comparison to the short opera that Prokofiev later compared it to a "big head on a little torso." To illustrate the plague ravaging the city, Prokofiev composed an evocative theme contrasting a strong dotted rhythm repeated on D by the right hand against sliding chromatic triplets by the left—unavoidable fate mingled with murky foreboding. Prokofiev was always adept at translating a visual image into a musical one, which helped when he came later to write film music.

From Glière, too, came the idea to keep a diary. When Prokofiev one day discovered his teacher recording the events of each day, he was fascinated. Here was another kind of list, offering unlimited opportunities for numerals, dates and times.

August 3, Sunday. I got up late. The day was rather hot. Before breakfast, Reinhold Morisevich [Glière] and I were joking and argued, so I challenged him to a duel. His second was Mlle. [the French governess], and mine was Nikita. We shot at each other in turn from a crossbow loaded with small rubber balls. Reinhold Morisevich hit me in the stomach and then grazed me on the shoulder and hand. I hit him in the left shoulder. Then Mlle. and Nikita shot at each other. Mlle. tried four times and hit Nikita once in the foot, but he—on the same number of tries—hit her once in the forehead, once in the stomach and once in the heart. We fought some more uninteresting duels. . . .

August 6, Wednesday. I sent a money order to Moscow for music paper. I wrote some charades and I'm turning them into poems to send to the editorial board of a magazine I receive. . . . We walked in the big garden and collected lots of oak-galls. . . .

August 9, Saturday. I got up early and immediately sat down to study with papa. Aunt Tanya left at three in the afternoon. Mama and I went to the station to see her off. On the way I chipped my upper left front tooth when we hit a bump. At Grishina we went to church. . . .

August 10, Sunday. I worked on the lessons that we missed yesterday. The doctor's family came. I started reading the French book *La quarantaine*. I was very tired.

After Glière went back to Moscow in mid-August, Seryozha did not stop composing. In addition to more *pesenky*, which became harmonically more complex without losing the same rhythmic playfulness, he worked on his first piano sonata (in B Major). The first two movements, quickly completed, were both precipitously fast—the first *presto*, beginning with a rapidly climbing line of staccato eighth notes, against sixteenths in the left hand; and the second *vivo*, in an unusual 3/8 meter. Many features characteristic of Prokofiev's nine mature sonatas appear in this youthful attempt: dynamic and compelling motion; insistently repeated bass lines (*ostinato*); a sharp, almost grating edge to the harmonic language, often created by means of repeated seconds and other dissonant intervals within a solidly tonal framework. Also present is the strong classical basis on which all of Prokofiev's piano sonatas stand—the clarity and security of form.

In October 1903, Prokofiev also turned to the art song (in Russian, *romans*) for the first time. He chose a sentimental religious poem by the Romantic poet Mikhail Lermontov (1814–1841): "The Branch of Palestine." In contrast to the aggressively irreverent style of his early piano pieces, Prokofiev's musical setting is "pretty" and lyrical, influenced by Tchaikovsky and Rachmaninoff—and by his father, who "advised me to penetrate to the meaning, which led me to succumb to sentimentality." Even as a mature artist, Prokofiev was not strongly drawn to the tradition of the conventional art song in verse so dear to Russian Romantic composers. Mussorgsky's acerbic, prosaic vocal settings ("Sunless," "Songs and Dances of Death") inspired him more deeply, as "The Ugly Duckling" and *The Gambler* demonstrate.

Seryozha and his mother, who continued to fret over his education, spent little time in Sontsovka in the winter of 1903–1904. In mid-November they traveled to Moscow, where they stayed a month. Returning briefly to Sontsovka to relieve her husband's loneliness, Maria Grigorevna left again with her son for more than two months in St. Petersburg. By the time they went home in late March, a decision had been made: Prokofiev would enter the St. Petersburg Conservatory in the fall.

Although most of the boy's musical contacts had been with the Moscow Conservatory (Taneev, Glière, Goldenveizer), Maria Grigorevna had her heart set on St. Petersburg. Her family—more interesting and amusing than the dour Moscow relatives—lived there; a higher and more influential level of society would be accessible to them in Petersburg than in Moscow; the Tsarist capital surely did not suffer from any shortage of musical talent or tradition. Aunt Tanya was especially anxious to have her dear sister and precocious nephew living nearby, and strongly influenced Maria Grigorevna's choice. She set about introducing them to the city's musical elite. Moscow might have Taneev, but St. Petersburg boasted the great Alexander Glazunov, inheritor of the Russian symphonic tradition. Glazunov was no less influential in the St. Petersburg Conservatory than Taneev was in the Moscow Conservatory, and an interview could be arranged.

Moscow and St. Petersburg had always cultivated different identities—economically (Moscow was a city of merchants and industrialists, Petersburg a city of bureaucrats and aristocrats); architecturally (Moscow was a jumble of styles, from Byzantine to Art Nouveau, while Petersburg was symmetrically classical and pure); intellectually (Moscow was more "Russian" and mysterious, Petersburg more Western and rational); and culturally. Moscow was at least four hundred years older than St. Petersburg, which was founded by Peter the Great at the beginning of the eighteenth century. Native Muscovites resented St. Petersburg for seizing the country's cultural and intellectual leadership, but they would take their revenge after 1917. Even today, Russians are divided into those who prefer Moscow and those who prefer St. Petersburg–Leningrad.

Tolstoy loved cozy, "organic" Moscow; Dostoevsky preferred artificial, cerebral St. Petersburg. Tchaikovsky, Rachmaninoff and Scriabin were Muscovites (by birth or association), while Rimsky-Korsakov, Mussorgsky and the other "Mighty Handful" composers (Cesar Cui, Mily Balakirev, Alexander Borodin) were men of St. Petersburg. So was Alexander Konstantinovich Glazunov (1865–1936). Best known as a composer (he wrote eight symphonies, though they are rarely performed today, even in the U.S.S.R.), Glazunov taught at the St.

Petersburg Conservatory for many years and became director in 1905, one year after Prokofiev entered. When Maria Grigorevna and her son first met Glazunov in early 1904, she found him more formal, drier and less encouraging than the fatherly Taneev. But Glazunov, who was famous for his efforts in encouraging young musicians, was struck by the boy's enormous natural talent (Seryozha played him an excerpt from *The Feast During the Plague*) and productivity. He tried to persuade her to enroll him at the Conservatory. Thrilled with Glazunov's proposal, Maria Grigorevna still felt compelled to voice her husband's more pragmatic considerations. What if he spent long years at the Conservatory only to discover he was insufficiently gifted? What if he ended up as a second-rate music teacher in the boondocks?

To his credit, Glazunov recognized Prokofiev's special gift. "If a child like yours—with such ability—shouldn't enter the Conservatory, then who should?" he asked. "If you prepare him to become a civil engineer, then he'll study music like an amateur and will never develop into the artist that he could be. And if he remains as involved with music as he is now, then he'll hardly give other studies the attention they would require for him to make a good career as an engineer." This eminently sensible analysis impressed Maria Grigorevna, especially since it advanced her own agenda: moving to St. Petersburg. For the moment, Glazunov found an aspiring composer, Mikhail Mikhailovich Chernov, an advanced student at the Conservatory, to work with Seryozha until they had to return to Sontsovka.

During the winter of 1903–1904, which saw the beginning of the disastrous Russo-Japanese War, Prokofiev often attended concerts, opera and the theatre. Among the operas he saw in St. Petersburg were Massenet's languid *Manon*, Rimsky-Korsakov's fairy tale *The Snow Maiden* and Gounod's operatic version of a Shakespeare tragedy that Prokofiev would reinterpret thirty years later: *Romeo and Juliet*. At this point, however, the heated passions of *Romeo and Juliet* appealed to him less than the icy fairy-tale world of *Snow Maiden*, which became one of his favorite operas. It did take him some time, though, to get used to Rimsky-Korsakov's subtly shimmering, carefully crafted, musical style. "I learned to love it later."

Another fairy-tale piece that impressed Seryozha was "March of the Trolls" by Edvard Grieg, which he heard in an orchestral version at a concert in St. Petersburg in early March. Like many of Russia's nineteenth-century composers, the Norwegian Grieg (1843–1907) was a nationalist; like them, he often turned to fairy tales for inspiration, most successfully in his music for Ibsen's play *Peer Gynt*. For some years after this first acquaintance with Grieg, Prokofiev remained fascinated with his music; Maria Grigorevna gave him Grieg's complete piano works on his thirteenth birthday a few months later. One can hear Grieg even in some of Prokofiev's mature music—most strongly the echo of the buffoonish "In the Hall of the Mountain King" from *Peer Gynt* in the grotesque march of *Love for Three Oranges*.

Dramatic activity was also intense in Moscow in the early years of the twentieth century. The Moscow Art Theater, founded only five years before by Konstantin Stanislavsky and Vladimir Nemirovich-Danchenko, was just entering its most glorious era. Soon it would revolutionize stage- and film-acting technique throughout the world. Prokofiev's parents took him to see the new Art Theater production (directed by Nemirovich-Danchenko) of Shakespeare's *Julius Caesar*, whose charms were lost on the twelve-year-old. "It was very good, but too long—from 7:30 to 12:30!"

All the concerts, operas, lessons (in music and languages) and social visits did not keep Seryozha from composing. He was already demonstrating that enviable ability to work on many different things at once no matter what the physical surroundings. Encouraged by a military friend of his parents, he turned for a while to marches: he composed four between January and May of 1904. (Indeed, Prokofiev remained all his life intrigued by the possibilities of this seemingly most hackneyed of genres.) He also wrote more *pesenky* (one for violin and piano), continued work on the piano sonata, and dashed off (originally he improvised them for friends at the piano) variations on a Russian song "Siskin, o siskin, where have you been?"

But the irrepressible creative power that had flowed from Seryozha since early childhood, before all these tutors and textbooks, occasionally demanded to be heard on its own terms. "I was sick of all the harmonies, counterpoint, accompaniments and little songs, with their symmetrically repeated measures. I felt like composing something grand in scale, so that nobody would be holding me by the coattails." Accordingly, he began sketching out a piece in "free composition," with five flats, thick and dissonant harmonies and a self-consciously "profound" complexity. Glière disapproved of such experiments, and the piece was left unfinished. Even as an adult, Prokofiev did not wander far from the realm of musical respectability. He might throw tantrums, but he remained a good boy. When he did rebel, it was within the limits of the established academic-musical rules; he never questioned or sought to change the rules themselves.

Returning to Sontsovka in late March, Prokofiev took with him a mass of new musical impressions, a collection of Schumann's symphonies arranged for piano four-hands that Glazunov had advised him to study and an idea for a new opera. It came from a polite society lady and literary amateur, Maria Grigorevna Kilshtett, an acquaintance of the Prokofiev family who found Seryozha irresistible. When she discovered he was searching for a new subject for an opera, she suggested a romantic fairy tale in verse, "Undine" ("The Water Nymph"). Originally published in German, it had been translated by Vasily Zhukovsky—the "Russian graveyard poet"—in 1837. Bubbling over with sylph-like water sprites and benign forest creatures, in the style of the Brothers Grimm, it belongs to the same world as *Swan Lake, The Snow Maiden* or *The Nutcracker*. It was also Prokofiev's first collaboration with a librettist.

As he prepared to leave his secure childhood nest for a new life in St. Petersburg, Seryozha worked on the music for Act I of *Undine*. Although the libretto's sweetly nostalgic and sentimental tone did not suit his sharp and irreverent approach to fairy tales, Prokofiev finished the piano score of Act I and had begun to orchestrate it by the end of the summer. Work on the opera continued sporadically for the next few years, as Seryozha's musical style underwent significant changes. As a result, *Undine* was a bit of a hodge-podge.

More interesting than *Undine* musically were the small *pesenky* he was composing during that same spring and summer. Particularly imaginative is the *Vivo* for piano dedicated to Prokofiev's father on his fifty-eighth birthday. Complex and at the same time transparent in the manner of his best piano pieces, it indicates that the composer was already an accomplished and daring pianist.

To his impending entrance into St. Petersburg Conservatory Prokofiev claims to have reacted "without special interest." Most of all he was glad not to be sent to a regular high school. He knew he would be teased there as a "new boy," and one who was unequipped to defend himself with his fists. "I wasn't strong and wasn't able to fight. I didn't have any practice, since Vasya was told to treat the master's son carefully. 'Peaches and cream,' my mother used to say affectionately as she looked at my face." Then, too, Prokofiev was fascinated with the big city—with electricity, telephones, streetcars and machines of all kinds. "I left Sontsovka without special regret, for in the final analysis, I didn't like it much. Just once, as we were leaving for the capital, I swallowed tears as we sat in the carriage; I tried to banish them with happy thoughts of the toy locomotive I was going to buy with the twelve rubles I had saved."

In the weeks before he and his mother left for St. Petersburg—his father, it was decided, would come to visit periodically—Seryozha had invented another game. It involved naval battles, and was inspired by the ongoing war between Japan and Russia. But by summer 1904, the war was no longer a game for the Tsarist government; it was growing into an embarrassment, a scandalous admission of what an anachronistic and toothless dinosaur Russia's once-feared military machine had become. The Japanese navy was proving a much more formidable enemy than Tsar Nicolas and his ever-changing advisers had expected. Unrest over the lackluster performance in combat fueled dissatisfaction with working conditions and heavy-handed censorship, particularly in the industrial centers of Moscow and St. Petersburg. The proliferating revolutionary groups gained new converts, profiting by the government's vacillation and insensitivity. By fall 1904, when Prokofiev and his mother took up permanent residence in the capital, the situation was explosive and the stage set for a full-scale uprising. It would be the first step down the road to the apocalyptic events of 1917. Prokofiev, entering the Conservatory on the eve of one crisis, the Revolution of 1905, and leaving it ten years later on the eve of another, World War I, saw the last glittering years of Imperial St. Petersburg.

But Seryozha remained blissfully, even dangerously, unaware of all that as he traveled with Maria Grigorevna to the capital in late August, diligently studying his train schedules and compiling new lists. The days of Romanov splendor and power were numbered, a world was on the brink of extinction, but Prokofiev's life and music were only beginning.

H A R M O N Y

A N D   R E V O L U T I O N

No, you will drown in blackest mire,
Damned city, foe of God!
And the swamp worms, tenacious worms,
Will devour your skeleton of stone!

—ZINAIDA GIPPIUS, "Petersburg"

or Seryozha, and even more for his mother—she was restless after twenty-six years of an isolated provincial existence—living in glamorous Petersburg was "a dream come true." Graceful broad avenues streaming with trolleys and carriages, store windows gleaming with the finest from Paris, London and Berlin, opening nights at the Imperial Mariinsky Theater, the imposing presence of Tsar Nicolas II and his multitudinous retinue—the realization that he could see all of this any day, every day, was intoxicating to a teenager with Prokofiev's imagination and energy. He was living in the classical and abstract city of the "white nights," where Pushkin wrote his poems, where Dostoevsky and his overwrought heroes wandered streets scoured by cold rain and wind from the Gulf of Finland, where Tchaikovsky saw the premiere of his *Sleeping Beauty*, where Mussorgsky died, almost unnoticed, from delirium tremens. Like Nikolai Gogol—one of his favorite writers—almost a century before him, Prokofiev had come from the Ukrainian heartland to make his name in the fantastic and forbidding Imperial capital. Cultural and intellectual center of the vast Russian Empire, it had become, just as Peter the Great had intended, one of the world's great cities.

When the starry-eyed Prokofievs arrived in late August of 1904,

St. Petersburg was on the threshold of one of its most glorious eras, a remarkable artistic and intellectual revival often called the "Silver Age." (The era of Pushkin and his contemporaries a century before is known as the "Golden Age.") For the next ten years, until the beginning of World War I, cultural life in Petersburg was extraordinarily rich, complex and varied. From this final explosion of Tsarist culture emerged, along with Prokofiev, an amazing number of artists who would have an immense impact on the course of twentieth-century Western culture: Sergei Diaghilev in dance and the visual arts, Igor Stravinsky in music, Vsevolod Meyerhold in theater, Andrei Bely in literature, Marc Chagall in painting.

Lavishly produced journals proliferated, enjoying brief but brilliant lives. They featured expensive color reproductions of work by Russian and European artists, poems by the rebellious new generation of writers, articles on Russian folklore and folk art and descriptions of cultural life in Paris and Munich. Perhaps the most famous of them, *The World of Art*, founded by Diaghilev and his associates, published its last issue a few months after Prokofiev arrived in St. Petersburg. Now Diaghilev turned his attention to other projects, increasingly involving music and theater.

These were years of startling contradictions, of bloody confrontations between police and mobs, of countless political and artistic manifestoes flying like snow through the damp cold air, of exquisite art exhibitions and soirées attended by bejeweled nobles, of intense hedonism and apocalyptic anxiety. Few described this atmosphere of hope and fear—arising from the unavoidable conflict between the new industrial and the old aristocratic Russia—more accurately or painfully than Anton Chekhov in his last play, *The Cherry Orchard*. It had its premiere in Moscow in early 1904, only six months before Chekhov died.

While the great old men of Russian literature were no longer producing novels—Dostoevsky and Turgenev were also dead and Tolstoy had turned to spiritual concerns—a new and very talented generation was emerging. Unlike the great late nineteenth-century authors, however, most of them were poets. Many, like Alexander Blok and Andrei Bely, were concerned with spiritual issues, with religion, mysticism and the world beyond, and not with the concrete and prosaic daily-life realism more typical of their literary predecessors. They tended to explore smaller, more intimate forms, often in complex language and elaborate symbols. The Russian Symbolist movement, profoundly affected by French Symbolism and the European avant-garde, was crystallizing; soon it would begin to dominate Russian literature almost until the Russian Revolution.

A similar process was occurring in Russian theatre. The realism espoused by Stanislavsky and Nemirovich-Danchenko at the Moscow Art Theater was being challenged by new stylization and nonrealistic ideas. Most important among these new theatrical thinkers was Vsevolod Meyerhold, who believed—in direct opposition to Stanislavsky—that a theatre production should not for a moment permit a spectator to forget that he is in a theatre. Eventually, through his theory of biomechanics, he would violently reject psychological realism in acting and production technique. In all fields of the arts, realism, dominant in Russian culture since the 1840s, was under assault.

Among certain connoisseurs and the younger generation of painters in St. Petersburg and Moscow, the French Impressionists were finding an audience, partly through the collections assembled by the Russian industrialists (particularly Sergei Shchukin) who were growing wealthy as Russia experienced an economic boom under belated capitalism. The music of Debussy, Wagner and Reger was being played in Russia for the first time. In its entire history, Russia had rarely been so strongly influenced by European culture as it was during the last few decades before the Russian Revolution. But even more important was the greater role Russian culture began to play in Europe, a process in which Prokofiev would eventually be a significant force.

During the eighteenth and nineteenth centuries, St. Petersburg had been the most progressive city in Russia, more innovative and fashionable than Moscow. To a certain extent this was still true in the early years of the twentieth century, but the "academic" climate of Petersburg, which had given birth to generations of tasteful but perhaps overly cautious artists, now rejected certain trends in art and culture that Moscow, more rough and ready, eagerly embraced. A telling example is the work of the French Impressionists and Post-Impressionists, which was for the most part admired by Muscovites but dismissed as unimportant by the leading artists of St. Petersburg. (Surprisingly, even Diaghilev and his circle did not appreciate the work of the Impressionist painters.) Similarly, it was not by mere coincidence that the then wildly daring composer Scriabin emerged from Moscow and the more academic Rimsky-Korsakov from Petersburg.

Even so, there was a great deal of cultural exchange between the two cities. Vsevolod Meyerhold, for example, began his career in Moscow with Stanislavsky and the Moscow Art Theater, but came later to do his first important work in Petersburg, where he also encountered Prokofiev.

All fields of the arts flourished in the last fifteen years of the Russian Empire, but it was perhaps in the visual arts that the list of talent is most impressive. Vasily Kandinsky, Marc Chagall, Kazimir Malevich, Mikhail Vrubel, Mikhail Larionov, Natalia Goncharova, Léon Bakst, Alexander Benois, Konstantin Korovin, Viktor Vasnetsov, Valentin Serov, Sergei Sudeikin and Kuzma Petrov-Vodkin were all active. So was Ilya Repin, leader of the Peredvizhniki ("The Wanderers"), a group of realist painters which Diaghilev loathed as depressingly civic and literal. Perhaps the strong "visuality" of early twentieth century Russian culture helps to explain why so many critics have commented on the "visuality" of Prokofiev's music—its unique ability to convey a pictorial image, to translate physical properties into the abstract language of music. "Seryozha was always interested in painting," writes his childhood friend Vera Alpers, "and we often went together to exhibitions of the Peredvizhniki, the *World of Art* and others." Prokofiev was more naturally visual than literary as a composer, as the great success of his ballet and film scores—and the difficulties he encountered with opera—seem to indicate. Presentation, not transformation, is at the heart of his talent and his aesthetic.

But Seryozha and his mother, tired from the long trip from Sontsovka, were more concerned with making a home for themselves than with examining the current state of Russian culture when they arrived in the capital. Maria Grigorevna's Petersburg relations helped their country cousins settle in. They found an apartment—where they would live for the next six years, until Sergei Alekseevich's death—on what was then called "The Square of the Protector" after the cathedral that stood at its center. (Today the cathedral is long gone, replaced by a children's playground, and the square, its lawns now dusty and lined with billboards, has been renamed after Ivan Turgenev.)

It was a handy location, on one end of the Ring Street (Sadovaya ulitsa, which has retained its name), not too far from the Petersburg Conservatory and the Mariinsky Theater. While not one of the city's most fashionable districts, it was respectable enough. "Our apartment on the Sadovaya was on the fifth floor and had five rooms. A front hall and a short hallway divided it into two halves: the windows of the dining room, living room and Mother's room faced the street; the windows of my room and Aunt Tanya's room faced the courtyard. There was also a kitchen and a bathroom. The price was seventy rubles a month, including firewood; of this amount Aunt Tanya paid twenty rubles. The apartment had its shortcomings: an unpresentable staircase without a doorman, and a dining room that wasn't where it should have been. My room was tiny." Soon after moving in, they bought a piano, decorated with fancy carved woodwork, at an auction.

Confronting Petersburg—a big, noisy city teeming with the drunk and the destitute as well as the fashionable—must have been daunting for Maria Grigorevna without her husband's support, but she was never one to yield to coquettish helplessness. Strong-willed, active and not easily intimidated, Maria Grigorevna pushed ahead single-mindedly in pursuit of Seryozha's advancement. Both she and Prokofiev coped with Sergei Alekseevich's absence by writing long and almost excru-ciatingly detailed letters home about their new life in Petersburg. It is from these, many of them reproduced in Prokofiev's autobiography, that we know so much about his early years at the Conservatory.

One senses that Maria Grigorevna welcomed the new separation and independence more than Sergei Alekseevich. In one of her first letters, cited by her son, she even used a description of Glazunov to tease her husband about his excessive emotional restraint. " 'I think that Glazunov is really good-hearted,' she wrote, 'but he is afraid to show his kindness, for fear that he will be taken advantage of. That's why he is restrained and doesn't say what he thinks. He reminds me of a certain person [a hint about Father], who is always holding himself back and afraid to be too generous with his attention, who always talks in a bored tone—coldly, as it were—but without conviction.' "

In fact, Glazunov—plump, reassuring and genteel—was the only musical contact Prokofiev and his mother had in these first years in Petersburg. He helped to guide Seryozha through the examination process at the Conservatory and spoke well of him to the powers-that-be. Not surprisingly, Seryozha, bearing his bulging folder of compo-sitions, made quite an impression on the Conservatory faculty, though his mother paced anxiously outside the exam rooms as though she feared some previously unrecognized flaw would send them both back to the muddy provinces. Apparently her son did not share her anxiety: "He was very indifferent to the fact that he was going to take an exam. In part that's fine, and probably just a trait of his character."

In her concern to do everything correctly, she brought Seryozha to the Conservatory two weeks early, while many of the professors were still on vacation. When the day finally arrived for the first set of examinations, in nonmusical subjects (French, German, geography, mathematics, theology), Prokofiev sailed through without difficulty. His father had prepared him well.

Just before the entrance exam in specialized musical theory, Glazunov introduced Prokofiev to Rimsky-Korsakov as "the little composer I told you about." It was Rimsky-Korsakov's opinion that mattered the most: he was the best-known of all the composer-teachers at the Conservatory, and one of the most dedicated to pedagogy. By then, Rimsky-Korsakov was at the height of his fame, having composed more than ten operas and having "edited" Mussorgsky's operas *Boris Gudunov* and *Khovanshchina*. He had taught Glazunov and Diaghilev, and was mentor to the young Stravinsky.

At the exam, Rimsky-Korsakov asked the boy to sightread, to recognize intervals and to play an excerpt from his new opera *Undina*. He did all this easily and without affectation; his only area of weakness was in singing. (He never did develop a good singing voice.) All the members of the examination jury, including the composer Anatoly Lyadov, were impressed with his natural talent and the long list of his compositions. Their only problem was how to schedule his classes: the advanced theory class conflicted with the academic subjects Seryozha's father was so worried about. Preliminary arrangements were made, and Prokofiev was assigned to Lyadov's section in Theory of Composition.

The social environment of the Conservatory was completely new to Prokofiev. He had never studied in a classroom situation with other students, and his social skills were primitive. No doubt he seemed immature—though very clever—to his classmates. He was a "tall, lively boy, very blond, with bright eyes, a rosy complexion and full prominent lips. His clothes and haircut were very much *comme il faut*." It was especially novel for him to be in regular contact with girls: the classes in academic subjects were mixed.

I responded with indifference to the presence of so many girls—my naivete in this area was total. Once, at home, I slipped two small rubber balls under my sweater, arranging them like a woman's breasts, and appeared like that in front of my mother.

"Well, well, it's early for you to be interested in such things," Mother said, wrinkling her brow. Removing the rubber balls, she threw them into the next room and shouted, "Catch!" I ran after the balls. I noted that my mother had said "early," but what was early and why it was early I couldn't understand. Another time I heard someone say about some pair: "They were both so good-looking that when they were out together all the girls looked at him, and all the young men looked at her." And I thought, why did all the young men look at her, and not at him?

Sheltered from contact with other children his own age as he grew up—with the exception of the peasant boys who regarded him as a distant master's son to be treated delicately—Prokofiev had little opportunity to learn the facts of life from his peers. Although he grew up on a farm, he knew remarkably little of biological and animal realities. Nor did he have any sisters or brothers to help him.

In his inexperience, Prokofiev tended to rely heavily on his mother's choice and assessment of playmates. She tried to steer him toward the "nice boys" with whose mothers she became acquainted during the hours she spent sitting in the hallways of the Conservatory. During his first weeks there, however, Prokofiev managed to strike up an acquaintance on his own with a boy three years older than he was, Potemkin (no relationship to the mutinous battleship that would burst into the headlines in the summer of 1905). Potemkin had a bad reputation with the school administration—reading between the lines of Prokofiev's autobiography, it seems that he was homosexual—and one of the administrators warned Prokofiev's mother that her son was associating with suspicious characters. Maria Grigorevna was beside herself.

" 'So who is it you're striking up a friendship with?' she shouted. 'I don't look after you for two weeks, and who knows who you end up with. . . . Did he say anything bad to you?' " She forbade him to have anything more to do with Potemkin, and Prokofiev complied with almost disturbing cold-heartedness.

Although I didn't understand why Potemkin was bad, my mother's anxiety won out. Potemkin turned out to be a secret leper whom one should avoid. At our next encounter I greeted him evasively and immediately disappeared, and during the breaks between classes I tried to remain out of his sight. For two days he followed me with his waddling gait and would say: "I don't understand what's happened to you. . . ." But I would slip away. That's how the acquaintance was broken off.

His mother's judgment on most matters—especially personal and social—reigned supreme for years to come. One of the ironies of Prokofiev's reputation as the "bad boy of Russian music," the *enfant terrible*, was that in fact he was obedient in the important things, and eager to please his parents, like many only children. This trait turns up in his later relations toward authority (both personal and political) and toward established musical conventions. His music might be filled with "wrong notes," but it was resolutely tonal all the same; he might fill sonatas with dissonances and shocking rhythms, but he still called them sonatas and wanted them to be considered as such. He stretched the limits of traditional musical forms with a mischievous glee, much as he tested the patience of his teachers.

From the start, Prokofiev excelled in his Theory of Composition class, even though his relationship with the teacher was frequently combative. Anatoly Lyadov, his composition instructor, was a distracted and lethargic character. The son of a conductor at the Imperial Opera and a student of Rimsky-Korsakov, Lyadov (1855–1914) regarded his pedagogic duties at the Conservatory as an unfortunate necessity in the performance of which he tried to expend as little energy and time as possible. In his own compositions, he was drawn to small-scale reworkings of Russian folk and liturgical sources. By the time Prokofiev encountered him, Lyadov was already in the twilight of his career, and had only ten more years to live.

In his composition class, Lyadov used the "Rimsky-Korsakov system," which emphasized the fundamentals. (Rimsky-Korsakov was terrified that the students would turn into undisciplined Mussorgskys.) The six students, who ranged in age from Prokofiev's thirteen to thirty, would prepare exercises that Lyadov would correct as they gathered around him at the piano. At first, Prokofiev admits, he tended to regard these exercises as unconnected to the music he had been writing all along for himself. "I saw the lessons in harmony as a boring obligation which was much less interesting to me, for example, than the classes in geography." Only gradually did the harmonic principles he was learning in the academic setting become incorporated in his own music, though he never lost the originality of his own style. He continued to write one sort of music for himself—which annoyed almost all of his Conservatory professors—and another for his lessons.

To a certain extent, this dichotomy between what he wrote for his teachers and what he wrote for himself never disappeared. His native feeling for music, and the sounds he had always heard in his head, burst academic bounds. The essence of his musical personality was formed very early—perhaps at birth; it was refined, but not changed, by his years at the Conservatory. One cannot study to become a genius.

Bored or not, Prokofiev began to take an intense and strange interest in the statistics of who was present and exactly how many mistakes each student in the class would make on a given day. Eventually he even drew up a chart on which he plotted the number of mistakes beside each student's name. He seemed to take little account of the feelings of those who made more errors than he did; some of them became irritated at this obnoxious upstart in their midst. Of Prokofiev's five classmates, one, Boris Asafiev (his later pseudonym as a music critic was Igor Glebov), was destined to make a significant career as a composer and writer, in part as an advocate of Prokofiev's music.

The slow pace of the class, as well as Lyadov's apparent indifference and frequent absence, irritated Maria Grigorevna more than her son, who could always find lots of other things to do with his time: compiling statistics about the naval maneuvers proceeding in the Pacific as the Russo-Japanese War dragged on, solving intricate chess problems, breaking an electromagnet by forcing too strong a current of electricity through it, continuing his Pushkinian narrative poem "The Count," playing with the electric-light switches in their apartment, and composing more *pesenky*, just as he had in Sontsovka.

In mid-October his father came for his first visit. Still concerned that Seryozha receive a well-rounded education in the event that he did not become a professional musician, he decided to remove him from the academic classes at the Conservatory, which he considered insufficiently rigorous. So Prokofiev stopped going to the classes that provided him with his only real social contacts with children his own age. He attended classes in composition, ear training and piano, but studied nonmusical subjects under his father's guidance—by correspondence when necessary. Again, he was mostly isolated, but by now he had grown used to that situation and does not seem to have resented the revision in his routine.

If Sergei Alekseevich had very definite ideas about his son's academic education, he was less sure about his religious instruction. Neither of Prokofiev's parents was particularly religious. This was more surprising in his mother's case, since she came from a very devout peasant family, and her sisters were faithful churchgoers. His father came from the less religiously inclined merchant class, and his education at the university—oriented toward science and technology—did nothing to strengthen his faith in Russian Orthodoxy. Maria Grigorevna's natural skepticism and cynicism, strengthened by the harsh reality of Russian provincial life and her own family's struggles, led her eventually to openly question and even mock church dogma, rather than to embrace it. Prokofiev inherited these skeptical sentiments from her. One should remember, too, that atheistic attitudes were almost universal among the progressive intelligentsia in Russia in the years leading up to the Russian Revolution.

As a teenager, Prokofiev went through a period when he felt almost guilty over this lack of family-centered religious life. He couldn't figure out, for one thing, why religion was unimportant if men and women had to be married in a church before they could have children. Characteristically, however, he kept his doubts and questions to himself: "Generally speaking, I was reserved in dealing with questions of the heart, and that trait showed up here, too; I waged the battle for religion internally, without sharing it or discussing it with anyone." One Sunday he went with his mother's sister, Tanya, who regularly attended church, to the cathedral on the square in front of their apartment. It was crowded, stuffy and the air was heavy with the smell of incense. Before he knew it, Seryozha had fainted and was coming to on the street outside.

"My fainting spell frightened me and cooled my desire for the church. At home we didn't talk about religion. So, gradually the question faded away by itself and disappeared from the agenda. When I was nineteen, my father died; my response to his death was atheistic. The same was true when I was twenty-two and I lost a close friend, who had written me a farewell note. I took this 'farewell' very bitterly, the farewell of a human consciousness that had departed finally and forever." The love of rationality, mathematical organization and logic characteristic of Prokofiev's personality and working methods stems in part, at least, from his rejection of emotional, irrational and religious explanations for the way the world works. Fuzzy promises of happiness in the world hereafter were alien to his uncompromisingly rational, disciplined, here-and-now nature.

Many years later, Prokofiev did for a while become intrigued with Christian Science, no doubt because the doctrine emphasized the power of the will over the weak flesh. Christian Science was a pragmatic faith that could help concretely during life on earth. Unlike so many Russian composers before him, Prokofiev never wrote a single explicitly religious setting—no requiems, vespers, choruses or pieces of the Russian Orthodox liturgy. The opera *The Fiery Angel* revolves around religious-spiritual issues, but it is fictional and uncomplimentary in its treatment of institutionalized religion.

St. Petersburg offered too many other attractions to the always inquisitive Prokofiev for him to spend time wondering about religion. As the autumn progressed, the concert season began. Two excellent series offered a wide variety of symphonic music: the concerts of the Russian Musical Society, founded in 1859 by Anton Rubinstein, and the concerts sponsored by the conductor Alexander Ziloti (1863–1945). Students from the Conservatory could sit in on the rehearsals. Prokofiev loved nothing better than to get the score and follow along as the rehearsals progressed; in this way he became familiar with orchestration, the symphonic repertoire, and how a conductor and orchestra work together. When he discovered that some of the older, more experienced Conservatory students would take the scores to be performed out of the library far ahead of the concert date, leaving none for him, he began to plan even farther ahead, checking out scores before anyone else could get to them. Neither could he resist the chance to gloat when the other students discovered that it was he who had beat them to it, and they tried to curry his favor so he would allow them to look on.

These rehearsals and concerts introduced Prokofiev to a wide variety of European and Russian composers: Glazunov, Berlioz, César Franck, Mozart. Prokofiev's music has often been compared to Mozart's in its transparency, lightness and directness, but surprisingly, Seryozha did not care much for Mozart's works. He wrote his father that Mozart's Mass in C Minor was "very boring and very long." Later, in his autobiography, he explained that he didn't come to love Mozart until many years later, "not finding in him the interesting harmonies and dramatic content that I was looking for in music. My antipathy to him was so strong that if anyone began to praise him, I would exclaim, 'But how can you love Mozart!' "

He also saw many operas. On a page of the diary that he maintained sporadically during these years, he recorded a list of "Operas which I have attended" between February 1904 and June 1905. There were forty-five of them. They included several by Wagner, whose operas were just coming into vogue in Russia—*The Flying Dutchman, Tann-*

häuser, Lohengrin, Das Rheingold, Siegfried and *Götterdämmerung*. And of course there were many by Russian composers: Rimsky-Korsakov, Dargomyzhsky, Tchaikovsky, Anton Rubinstein, Borodin, Glinka and Mussorgsky. Prokofiev was also present at the rehearsals for the premiere of Rimsky-Korsakov's fairy-tale opera *Kashchei the Immortal*, which turned into a great political event because of Rimsky-Korsakov's defense of the student uprisings in the winter of 1905.

But even as he listened to performances, Prokofiev's imagination never stopped working. Boats fascinated him almost as much as music, and he would imagine that the high, narrow, long Great Hall of the Petersburg Conservatory was a dry dock. Any minute a huge cruiser would sail in for cleaning.

If music, games, electricity and statistics were more than enough to keep Seryozha happy, Maria Grigorevna nonetheless realized the necessity of introducing her son to society. She was helped in this undertaking by her more highly placed relatives. In Sontsovka, the Prokofievs had been treated almost like aristocrats; in Petersburg they were ordinary middle-class provincials. They would dine every Sunday evening at Uncle Sasha's, where Seryozha would be instructed in table manners and the proper usage of society Russian. From his cousin Shurik, five or six years his senior, Prokofiev heard of the Imperial Gymnasium where Shurik studied. From his cousin Andrei, several years older than Shurik, he learned one evening that a young man could not go out to a fancy ball if he had cut himself while shaving. Maria Grigorevna and her son were aware that they did not belong to that higher stylish sphere. Once, a Sontsovka acquaintance came to visit and asked to be taken to visit the Raevskys. After consulting with Aunt Tanya, Maria Grigorevna decided it would be better not to bring "a profoundly provincial lady" into the "immaculately pressed society that gathered there." The Sontsovka acquaintance "was mortally offended and left Petersburg the next day, and this stupid incident left an unpleasant mark in our memory for a long time to come."

Seryozha's father was, of course, still in rural Sontsovka. In December Maria Grigorevna set off with Seryozha to spend the winter holidays there; this was a routine they would follow—winter, summer and sometimes Easter vacations in Sontsovka—until Sergei Alekseevich's untimely death in 1910. When they started back to Petersburg in early January, the country was on the brink of revolution. The failures of the Russian fleet in the Russo-Japanese War, the worst student strikes the country had ever seen, the rise of various Marxist factions dedicated to overthrowing the Tsarist regime, frequent assassinations and bombings, nearly constant peasant disturbances in the country-side—all these factors were creating a dangerous atmosphere of pervasive and volatile instability. Even the hermit Taneev asked Prokofiev, when he visited his mentor briefly as they passed through Moscow, how they could be returning to Petersburg "when there are such disturbances there." Prokofiev, no doubt repeating what his mother had told him, replied, "Well, you know they're saying it will start here tomorrow."

The Revolution of 1905 severely disrupted life at the Petersburg Conservatory for most of the next year. Classes were held sporadically or not at all, professors became deeply involved in political activity, performances were canceled or became raucous political events, the student body was polarized into factions opposing or defending the government. It was impossible to escape the impact of this "dress rehearsal" for the 1917 Revolutions, particularly in Petersburg, the seat of the government and the center of revolutionary activity. Even musicians, those usually most apolitical of artists, were affected. A feeling of impending disaster hung heavy over the country.

The streets of Petersburg were patrolled by soldiers, and windows smashed in rioting were boarded up when Maria Grigorevna and Seryozha returned. It was dangerous to go out at night, and Maria Grigorevna wouldn't allow Prokofiev out of the apartment by himself. Newspapers stopped publishing for a while. The railroads went on strike. The Grand Duke Sergei, second cousin and brother-in-law of Tsar Nicolas II, was shot by the terrorist organization "Will of the People." Excited and disturbed by these and other events, most of the students at the Conservatory declared a strike in February 1905. Their demands were a strange mixture of the idealistic and the petty: to expel a student who had supposedly fired upon striking workers, to stage an opera every month performed and directed entirely by students, to prevent the famous violinist and professor Leopold Auer (1845–1930) from striking his students on the head with a bow. The revolutionary contagion did not spread, however, to naive little Seryozha, who repeated his mother's thoughts on the unrest and devoted his energy to his usual pastimes. "My mother's point of view was as follows: we've left Father and come to Petersburg to study—so we should study, and not get involved in any funny business." Prokofiev did not.

By March, the Conservatory was in total chaos. Police, some on horses, surrounded the building to ensure that the few who wanted to could enter. Rimsky-Korsakov, the institution's most famous professor, was fired by the Conservatory administration after publishing a letter denouncing the administration's handling of the strike. Outraged, Lyadov and Glazunov resigned. This led the students to write a collective letter to the administration stating that they no longer wanted to study there and demanding the return of their official documents. Prokofiev was asked to sign and did so, but only after asking for and receiving his mother's permission. "This is such an unprecedented time in Russian history," Maria Grigorevna wrote to her husband. "Each day brings as much news as most years." They worried that their hard-earned bank accounts would be wiped out by rioting or bank failures.

For the moment, the Conservatory was empty. Prokofiev took lessons from Lyadov and Alexander Winkler, his piano teacher, at their homes. All the adjustments and political unrest contributed to a drop in Prokofiev's rate of composing during 1904–1905.

By Easter the situation in the Conservatory had improved little, and Lyadov told Prokofiev and his mother, who were planning to return to Sontsovka for the holiday, that there was no sense in coming back to Petersburg until autumn. Seryozha had a five-month summer vacation. Much of it, however, was spent preparing intensively for the examinations in academic subjects to be given in the fall. So diligent and demanding were his mother and father in drilling him that Prokofiev acquired a far greater command of languages, history and the social sciences than he would have gained in Petersburg. They would work for up to five hours each day, rewarding him for good work with pieces of chocolate. Despite the chocolate, he resented the regimentation. "What a nice thing a free summer would have been," he complained later.

Stilts were Prokofiev's new passion that summer. He would organize extravagant battles with the peasant children, imagining himself—inspired by reports of the battles of the Russo-Japanese War—as some great admiral at the head of his heroic fleet. Inside, his mother could barely control her panic, sure that he would fall, break his hands and end his chances for a career as a pianist. She and her husband were also worried that Prokofiev—who was, at fourteen, no longer a child—would start to find out about love and sex. When a visiting cousin struck up a more than purely platonic acquaintance with Egor, the peasant boy who had performed in Prokofiev's opera *The Giant*, Seryozha's parents tried to isolate him from the incident, and quickly sent the cousin away.

But they could not prevent him from discovering love in the books he was reading—by Gogol, Grigory Danilevsky and Turgenev. Turgenev's lyrical novel *Nest of Gentlefolk*, its atmosphere saturated with subtly repressed sexual passion, confused him so much that he blushed to the ears when his father asked him how he liked it. *Nest of Gentlefolk* was his favorite reading of the summer: he awarded it a "five" on a five-point scale, followed closely by Gogol's hilarious and satirical picaresque epic about nineteenth-century Russian provincial life, *Dead Souls*, which received a "five-minus." Prokofiev always needed to quantify his feelings—no matter whether for books, music or chess problems. It was hard for him to confront raw, unorganized experience, whether artistic or personal. Everything and everyone had a place on a rating scale.

Socially Prokofiev may have been underdeveloped, but intellectually he was the match of adults twice his age. That summer he made the first of many friends older than he, the local veterinarian, Vasily Morolev. When they sat down to play chess, Morolev, obviously overjoyed to discover such a clever young artist in the midst of the Ukrainian steppe, saw that he had encountered a formidable opponent, fluent not only in the practice but also in the theory and history of the game. Prokofiev also introduced Morolev, a serious amateur pianist, to some mazurkas (Op. 3) by the charismatic and mystically inclined Alexander Scriabin, who from this time on exerted an increasingly important influence on Prokofiev's music, especially his piano works. While the vague philosophical-spiritual realms to which Scriabin claimed to travel in his music were utterly foreign to Prokofiev's materialistic and ironic nature, he came to admire Scriabin as a technician, especially his shimmering, overloaded and experimental harmony.

This placid summer existence was interrupted sporadically, however, by the revolutionary turbulence Prokofiev and his mother had seen during the winter and spring in Petersburg. His father received an anonymous letter threatening him as an oppressor of the peasants. Alarm bells screamed as fires raged late into the night on the flat horizon, consuming bundles of hay gathered from the harvest. Eventually Sontsov sent five armed guards to patrol his property, which further irritated the peasants and placed Sergei Alekseevich in an even more dangerous position. Prokofiev's parents would send him off to bed, doing all they could to protect him from these unsettling events. Despite their perhaps misguided efforts to shelter him, Seryozha, always sensitive to his surroundings, was upset by the atmosphere of potential violence. For a while, he was unable to fall asleep without a sleeping pill.

CHAPTER 3

THE BAD BOY
OF RUSSIAN MUSIC

He jests at scars, that never felt a wound.

—SHAKESPEARE, *Romeo and Juliet*

Soon after he turned fourteen, Seryozha got his first pair of long trousers. They did not help him attain grace at the ballroom dancing lessons in which his mother enrolled him after they returned to St. Petersburg in the fall of 1905, however; he stumbled unhappily without ever learning the steps. Surprisingly, the remarkably strong and original sense of rhythmn so important to Prokofiev's music did not find its way to the composer's feet, which were destined to tread on many a partner's toes, including the ballerina Galina Ulanova's at the party after *Romeo and Juliet* more than thirty years later. Perhaps his own feeling of music and rhythm was so definite that it overwhelmed the conventional dance tunes which he disliked for their superficiality even then. Then, too, Prokofiev had little natural athletic ability, and a poorly developed sense of physicality. Uncomfortable and out of his element, Seryozha cut a clumsy and awkward figure among the golden youth of St. Petersburg, but his mother, engrossed in polite conversation with her friends along the sidelines, hardly noticed. He had suddenly grown taller and gawky, with long arms and legs, and his face was thinning to the profile of adulthood. But his awareness of sexuality lagged: he believed even now that "roosters laid bigger eggs than hens did."

Political events continued to disrupt life at the Conservatory, which closed and reopened sporadically. For ten days at the end of October, a nationwide strike virtually halted the economy and transportation, paralyzing the country. The strike forced the Tsar to make some concessions. Most important among them was the establishment of a Duma, a sort of parliament that would have the power to legislate; for the first time, the absolute power of Russian autocracy—bestowed upon the Tsar directly from God—would be legally regulated. The three-hundred-year-old Romanov dynasty had become a constitutional monarchy, at least in theory. It was only the first in a series of mishandled concessions that would lead to the Revolution.

Only the classes in academic subjects (Prokofiev didn't attend them anyway) were held regularly. Classes in performance were restored only in the spring of 1906, after Glazunov was appointed director of the Conservatory, leading to the return of his friends Rimsky-Korsakov and Lyadov. Through the autumn and winter, Prokofiev studied with Lyadov and Winkler at their homes. Since he had found the first year at the Conservatory far from taxing, he decided—at his mother's encouragement—to work on two specialities: piano and composition. (Still unsure if he could make it financially as a composer, she figured he could safely become some sort of pianist.) The number of hours he worked with Winkler accordingly increased; he tried to cure Seryozha of some of the careless habits that had crept into his piano playing over the years. Winkler found that Prokofiev was inconsistent, that "one measure would come out well, and the next poorly." But he was playing more now, and by the following summer his friend Morolev noticed that his technique had become authoritative and clearly articulated. The sloppiness was disappearing.

One of the pieces he prepared for Winkler was a Bach gavotte in B Minor, arranged by Saint-Saëns. Perhaps it was this piece that led to his lifelong love for the gavotte form, which shows up (grotesquely and comically reworked) in his "Classical" Symphony, his ballets and various piano works.

Lyadov's class had progressed to the study of counterpoint, conducted in the same desultory and "grumbling" manner. Later in the fall, Seryozha had his first class with Rimsky-Korsakov, a crowded course in instrumentation that apparently left little impression. At the end of the academic year in 1908, after two years of studying with Rimsky-Korsakov, Prokofiev "barely passed" an examination in orchestration. Only "five or six years later," after independent work, did Prokofiev feel he had really learned how to orchestrate effectively. He found the four-hand Schubert marches that Rimsky-Korsakov had them orchestrate "clumsy and uninteresting," and was not afraid to say so.

Unawed by Rimsky-Korsakov's great reputation and finding his classes boring, Seryozha would disagree—in front of his classmates—with the teacher's criticisms of his assignments.

Unlike Stravinsky, who called Rimsky-Korsakov "master" and professed a deep affection for him, Prokofiev never developed a strong relationship with the grand old man of Russian music, an original member of the legendary "Mighty Handful" and Mussorgsky's editor and friend. By all accounts, Rimsky-Korsakov was rather reserved and distant in personal relations, and did not know how to deal as well with children, perhaps, as the more indulgent Muscovite Taneev. "Capable, but immature," was Rimsky-Korsakov's official assessment of Prokofiev, who was already demonstrating his refusal to take anybody, or anything, too seriously. Famous people almost never intimidated him; he treated them the same way he treated everyone, sometimes to his own detriment.

Prokofiev and Rimsky-Korsakov also disagreed over the exciting new music of Scriabin, which was being performed with increasing frequency in St. Petersburg and abroad. Prokofiev went to every rehearsal for the premiere of Scriabin's Third Symphony ("The Divine Poem"), watching with amusement as Rimsky-Korsakov threw up his arms, horrified by the sensual, supercharged sounds. They affected the conscientious Salieri of Russian music "as though an electric current had been turned on in his chair." No doubt Rimsky-Korsakov's reaction only heightened Seryozha's interest in this "decadent," intriguingly romantic, even scandalous figure with grand mystical schemes of bringing the world to nirvana through music. By liking Scriabin, Prokofiev could be naughty. Many critics regarded Prokofiev's energetic, concrete, cleanly "classical" and strongly rhythmic musical style as a welcome antidote to (and rejection of) Scriabin's other-worldly, hyperromantic and rhythmically static idiom, but in fact Prokofiev's music (particularly in the early years) was profoundly influenced by Scriabin. From him, Prokofiev learned of new harmonic possibilities— particularly the juxtaposition and combination of supposedly incompatible intervals (fourths and thirds) and modes (major in one hand and minor in the other).

Despite his disagreements with Rimsky-Korsakov over modern music, Seryozha adored his teacher's operas. That season he saw *The Snow Maiden* ("one of his best," he wrote confidently to his father) at the Mariinsky, and the premiere of *The Tale of the Invisible City of*

Kitezh and the Maiden Fevronia. Rimsky-Korsakov's last and perhaps most ambitious opera, and perhaps his most Wagnerian, *Kitezh* is an ornate and epic tale of an ancient Russia still divided between its pagan past and Christian present. Magic flowers of paradise grow on stage, unusual folk meters and intonations abound, exciting Tartar raids on the defenseless people of the Russian forest bring a legendary past to life. Seryozha went to see *Kitezh* five times. It was the fairy-tale and supernatural elements in Rimsky-Korsakov's operas that Prokofiev loved most; they strongly influenced his own *Love for Three Oranges* (which shares a highly sardonic attitude toward royalty with Rimsky-Korsakov's *The Tale of the Golden Cockerel*) and his ballets *The Stone Flower* and *Cinderella.*

Joining Rimsky-Korsakov and Scriabin on concert programs as the third titan of post-Tchaikovsky Russian music was Rachmaninoff. Traditionally, Rachmaninoff and Prokofiev have also been regarded as emotional and aesthetic opposites, but Seryozha absorbed a great deal from some of Rachmaninoff's music. The "Russian" lyrical quality and plaintiveness so evident in the first movement of Prokofiev's Second Piano Concerto can certainly be traced to Rachmaninoff's own Second Piano Concerto, which Seryozha heard for the first time in the winter of 1905–1906. But unlike Rachmaninoff (and Scriabin), Prokofiev viewed the piano as a percussive instrument, and tended to exploit its mechanical personality rather than its ability to sing.

By now, Prokofiev's musical tastes were becoming quite definite, if eclectic. When Lyadov asked him at one of their lessons who his favorite composers were, Prokofiev replied with three: Tchaikovsky, Wagner and Grieg. "The first two are fine," said Lyadov, "but the last one is a bad influence." And in fact, as his own sense of craft matured, Prokofiev's infatuation with Grieg gradually faded. As for Tchaikovsky, Prokofiev then knew only his Symphony No. 2 and some chamber music. Surprisingly, when Lyadov showed his student the score of *Sleeping Beauty* (autographed by the composer as a present to Lyadov) as an example of good counterpoint, Prokofiev remained unmoved. "I didn't like all those ballet-style numbers," he said.

Wagner, on the other hand, was selected "out of snobbism. I had heard that his music was good, and that people in musical circles talked a lot about him, but I had heard neither *The Ring* nor *Tristan* and could figure out *The Meistersingers* only to a limited degree." The extravagant fairy-tale stories of the Ring Cycle—their monsters and river maidens—must also have appealed to Seryozha. Later, he asked for a score of *Die Walküre*—the opera he had dismissed as "terribly boring" five years earlier—as his New Year's present for 1907.

Many of Prokofiev's musical impressions were described in letters sent back to Sontsovka. Postal and train service was unreliable due to the continuing political unrest; Maria Grigorevna and Seryozha were afraid they would lose contact with Sergei Alekseevich, or, even worse, that he would be unable to make his scheduled trips to St. Petersburg. If he didn't come, they would also run out of butter, which was in short supply in the city but not in Sontsovka.

A fourteen-year-old intensely involved in his studies and games, Seryozha was unable to appreciate the enormous sacrifices his father was making to support two residences and keep him and his mother in St. Petersburg. Nor did Sergei Alekseevich, who was spending long dark winters and muddy springs alone in Sontsovka, try to make them feel guilty. If anything, since he saw his only child so rarely, Sergei Alekseevich found it hard to deny Seryozha anything he asked for. Both he and Maria Grigorevna always put their son's interests first. She would spend hundreds of rubles to buy Seryozha a piano, but stay home from her nephew's wedding because she didn't have a dress good enough to wear. Prokofiev's father would buy him any toy he wanted, and the best seats in the house at the opera whenever they went. It seems Seryozha was rarely, if ever, punished.

Prokofiev grew up, therefore, expecting attention, and feeling that he could do and say almost anything he wanted. That he was at the center of his family—without siblings to compete with—also fostered in him a certain lack of regard for other people's problems. He could be remarkably unsympathetic—even cruel—to those less fortunate, less talented or less interesting. Once, traveling on a train, he happened to sit across from a Jew "with a biblical appearance." The man was eating a chicken. When he had finished, he tried to throw the bones and garbage out the window, failing to notice it was closed. The trash landed on the man and on the floor. "He was horribly embarrassed and crawled around for a long while, gathering up the garbage, and I sat there, staring wide-eyed. It was rather disgusting, and I didn't know if I should help him or not."

On another occasion, at the Conservatory, he devised the "nice little game" of asking a fellow student who was "boring and evoked little sympathy in me" why he was playing with the second violins in the orchestra, and not with the first. When the timid object of his teasing blushed in confusion, Prokofiev repeated the question, louder, so that others could hear. But like most who enjoy teasing, of course, Prokofiev could not bear to be teased himself.

Compassion and empathy were never strong traits in his character, a fact which Soviet biographers have understandably ignored in their attempts to transform Prokofiev into a good socialist artist profoundly concerned over the fate of his fellow man. On his way home from the Conservatory, he used to enjoy watching family arguments in first-floor and basement apartments; he would even squat down on the sidewalk for a better view. Such voyeurism indicates a highly theatrical nature, but also a lack of human sympathy. Perhaps this same lack of identification with others also helps to explain Prokofiev's failure as a composer of noncomic opera. According to Nikolai Tcherepnin, a composer and Prokofiev's professor of conducting, Seryozha would sit on the staircase at the Conservatory and make fun of students as they entered. In his operas, he tends to distribute music to his characters from that same vantage point, laughing at them as they go by. Such an approach may work for the satirical *Love for Three Oranges* or *Betrothal in a Monastery*, but not for the tragic *Gambler* or *Semyon Kotko*. He found it difficult to enter into other lives.

This is not to say that he did not have any friends. He was demanding, however, and tended to cultivate those with whom he had professional interests in common, or whom he could dominate. One in the former category was Nikolai Miaskovsky (1881–1950), who joined Lyadov's class in the fall of 1906 and was to become Prokofiev's most important lifelong friend. While Prokofiev was younger than most of his fellow students, Miaskovsky was older: he was already twenty-five years old when he began at the Conservatory, almost exactly ten years older than Prokofiev. Like Rimsky-Korsakov, Miaskovsky remained for a long while in the military service, where he received training as an engineer, before turning to music professionally. In fact he was still a soldier during his first year at the Conservatory, before entering the reserves. When he did finally make the decision to study music, however, Miaskovsky proceeded with gravity and thoroughness.

By the time they met, Miaskovsky had composed considerably less than Prokofiev: songs to poems by Balmont, Baratynsky and Gippius, plus some piano pieces. Eventually, however, Miaskovsky became the "greatest Soviet symphonist," completing twenty-seven symphonies before his death in 1950. Reserved, shy, melancholic, pessimistic, sedentary and given to depressions, Miaskovsky was in many ways Prokofiev's opposite as a personality, which is, perhaps, why they developed such a long and close relationship. Miaskovsky, who never married, marvels, in the countless letters he wrote to Prokofiev over the years, at his younger friend's boundless optimism, energy and enthusiasm. For his part, Prokofiev seemed to find in Miaskovsky a source of quiet stability and advice, the older brother that he never had. Miaskovsky's opinion came to carry great weight with Prokofiev, even after he had become a celebrity in the West, although Miaskovsky's music does not seem to have strongly affected Prokofiev's.

It was Miaskovsky's respect for Prokofiev's enormous natural talent that first drew him to his precocious and often irritating classmate. They also shared an ambivalent attitude toward Lyadov, whom Miaskovsky later said he remembered "with admiration, gratitude, but also with horror." When Miaskovsky discovered that Prokofiev was an excellent pianist and sightreader, he proposed that they start reading through piano arrangements of scores he wanted to learn, like Beethoven's symphonies, Rimsky-Korsakov's "Scheherazade" and Max Reger's "Serenade." (Reger had conducted the "Serenade" in St. Petersburg shortly before, and Prokofiev was intrigued with the way the work "juxtaposed distant tonalities with such ease that one would think they were the tonic and dominant.") Their sessions of piano four-hands became an established tradition that continued throughout their relationship.

By the summer of 1907, Prokofiev and Miaskovsky were exchanging detailed letters with critiques of the music they were each composing. It was the start of a very long and deep professional correspondence, extending, with a few breaks, from 1907 to 1950. The hundreds of letters deal almost exclusively with technical musical matters, very rarely with the personal and emotional, although the Soviet compilers of the collected correspondence have heavily edited the letters and may well have omitted most personal references.

Miaskovsky—and all of Prokofiev's classmates—were surprised when they began to look closely at the music this often irritating little brat was writing for himself. Indeed, Miaskovsky provided much more encouragement at this crucial stage than any of Prokofiev's instructors at the Conservatory, most of whom were too uninterested (or overworked) to pay close attention to what he was writing, or who found his music irreverent, noisy and filled with the awful dissonant intervals they banned from students' homework assignments.

Seryozha still continued to write the small piano pieces—*pesenky*—he had been composing since childhood, but now he preserved them in a notebook, giving them individual titles and combining them into groups. The first set was sent as a present to Morolev, who had moved away to the Dnepr. Morolev told Prokofiev that, with the exception of "Reproach," in lilting, almost Mendelssohnian, 6/8 rhythm, the pieces "were rather bad little dogs ('*sobachky*') whose bite is very painful." Prokofiev liked the description, and hereafter referred to them as "little dogs." The manuscript did not survive.

Not all of Prokofiev's music was so sharp and unsentimental, however. He continued to work on *Undina*, realizing that in the course of its composition his style had undergone great changes as he matured technically. For the ending of Act V and the opera, he chose to use merely two chords, played *piano*, without a strong cadence and "without adornments." Morolev, whose tastes were decidedly more conventional, found this unsatisfying, but Prokofiev remained firm.

More sentimental yet was an art song for piano, violin solo and voice, set to gushing verses by the popular poet Aleksei Apukhtin ("The boat has cast off, the dawn has barely broken./A final greeting resounds in our ears. . . ."). It was never performed, but Prokofiev returned to the same poem three years later and wrote a new setting, one of the songs of his Op. 9. Another fragment written in 1907—a theme in one of the "little dogs"—later found its way into a mature work: it became the galloping second theme, announced by the unaccompanied soloist in dotted eighths and triplets, in the Piano Concerto No. 1.

Already apparent, then, in these adolescent experiments is Prokofiev's tendency to think in terms of separate themes rather than whole movements or whole works. (This is part of the reason he was able to write so successfully for film, which requires many different sharply defined themes associated with characters or emotional states.) If a theme did not work well in one context—and even if it did—Prokofiev would try it, most often unchanged, in another later on.

After a Sontsovka summer filled with rigorous study of academic subjects, picture-taking and letter-writing—"Intellectual pursuits led to a lessening of my contacts with my village acquaintances"—Prokofiev returned eagerly to St. Petersburg. His Conservatory routine altered slightly: he was now studying conducting with Nikolai Tcherepnin (1873–1945), and he returned to classes in academic subjects. Tcherepnin had been Prokofiev's instructor for score-reading during the previous spring and was regarded as one of the most influential conductors on the Russian musical scene. It was, in fact, Tcherepnin who conducted the first Paris seasons of Diaghilev's Ballets Russes, and who wrote the first full-length ballet score that Diaghilev's company performed during their first full season in Paris in 1909—*Le Pavillon d'Armide.*

When they began to work together, Tcherepnin told Prokofiev honestly that he had little natural talent for conducting, but that he believed in his potential as a composer and that he would need to be able to conduct his own music. Of all the instructors he had at the Conservatory, Prokofiev felt most positively about Tcherepnin, with whom he developed a warm father-son relationship. What he did not learn about orchestration from the severe Rimsky-Korsakov he made up with Tcherepnin. While he quickly understood that Tcherepnin was better at talking about conducting and composing than in doing them, Prokofiev respected his teacher for his advocacy of new music and his knowledge of the latest techniques and trends. "He talked about innovation in such a way that I felt almost old-fashioned."

It was from Tcherepnin that Prokofiev first learned about musical life in Europe, and became acquainted with the avant-garde in Russian culture. And although he never came to feel entirely comfortable on the conductor's podium, he absorbed enough from Tcherepnin to be able to conduct his own music around the world. From Tcherepnin, too, Prokofiev first learned to love Haydn and Mozart—"and that's where the 'Classical' Symphony eventually came from."

Conducting students also had more access to free passes for orchestral performances. Hearing Wagner's "Siegfried Idyll" sent Prokofiev into "ecstasy." His reaction to Rimsky-Korsakov's Piano Concerto was only slightly less enthusiastic. In fact Prokofiev loved this compact concerto—it lasts only thirteen minutes—for the rest of his life, and chose it as his graduation examination piece in the spring of 1909. Another evening he heard Glazunov's Seventh Symphony, which he found "put together, but not composed." Prokofiev's childhood infatuation with Glazunov's romantic symphonies was passing; he now found them "boring and nothing new." Despite his affection for his mentor Taneev, Seryozha also began to cast a more critical eye on his music, especially since Taneev wrote a great deal of chamber music. When

Taneev came to perform in Petersburg, however, Seryozha proudly turned pages for him on stage.

Claiming to prefer the "new" in music, Prokofiev might have been expected, then, to be interested in the work of Richard Strauss, who was just becoming known in Russia. Miaskovsky gave his friend a score of the opera *Salome* to look at, "saying that this was the very most modern of contemporary works." But Seryozha did not appreciate Strauss's ecstatic musical language, thick with strings; at this point he dismissed it as "all that scratching." Particularly early in his career, Prokofiev disliked hyperbole of any kind: he wanted it said briefly, with small forces and dynamic rhythm. Why use thirty violins when ten will do? Another possible reason for his lack of enthusiasm was that Strauss was too philosophically and musically static for Prokofiev, who valued movement above all else.

Wagner's creation of a mythological world peopled by giants and mermaids was much closer to Prokofiev's fairy-tale imagination than the decadent sexual obsession of many of Strauss's operas. He was enthralled with the Ring Cycle, which was produced in its entirety at the Mariinsky Theater in each of the three seasons from 1907 through 1910.

Returning to the classes in academic subjects after three years brought Prokofiev back into contact with Conservatory social life and gossip. He looked down on the other "academic" students, who responded in kind by calling him "professor" and "motor." Because Sergei Alekseevich had drilled his son more rigorously than the Conservatory teachers would have, Seryozha immediately moved to the head of the class, the final course in "scientific" subjects.

More interesting to him than the tedious lessons was the presence of girls in the class: they outnumbered the boys seventeen to three. Sheltered during the past few years from contact with his female peers, he viewed them as exotic creatures he was discovering for the first time. Henceforth, girls play a much larger role in his autobiography and correspondence. Two girls particularly intrigued him: Leonida Glagoleva ("slender, tall and 'as dark as the ace of spades' ") and Vera Alpers ("quiet, restrained, and 'pale as the day she was born' "). Both were studying to be pianists.

With Glagoleva he developed a playful, flirtatious and stylized relationship, reflected in ornately written letters—using a sort of short-hand, eliminating many vowels and substituting the Roman letter "i" for its Cyrillic equivalent—that sought unsuccessfully to mask his infatuation. Prokofiev always had a weakness for women with dark hair and eyes. With Alpers he was more sincere and direct, in matters both musical and personal, and they became lifelong friends. Toward Glagoleva he behaved like an awkward suitor; toward Alpers, like an affectionate brother. In his relations with the opposite sex Prokofiev received no help from his friend Miaskovsky, who exhibited little interest in women and once told Seryozha he had "no matrimonial tendencies."

Girls liked Seryozha better than boys did. When the class voted to select a committee to organize the Christmas Ball, Prokofiev received all the girls' votes, and none of the boys'. He found it difficult to understand why some of the intelligent girls were so attentive to one handsome but not very interesting boy. But Prokofiev attracted girls through his wit and intelligence; even the mysterious Glagoleva became more friendly after he explained Wagner to her. She also involved him in an elaborate masked ball that she gave with some of her fashionable friends. Dressed as a clown, Seryozha provided the piano accompaniment as Glagoleva and a male companion performed a Middle Eastern dance. Afterward, out of his element, Seryozha wandered uncomfortably among the brilliantly dressed guests. "Listen," Glagoleva told him, "I dressed you up as a clown, so you must act like a clown, and not a serious composer. Otherwise I'll give you a contrabass and you'll have to walk around with that." He tried to be more clownish, although he hated to be laughed at.

During 1907–1908, Prokofiev became much better known as a performer and composer, at least within the Conservatory and knowledgeable Petersburg musical circles. First he played a few of his piano pieces for a composers' group at the Conservatory. He chose a few of the piano pieces he had recently been writing, including two that were eventually placed in his mature Op. 3: "Skazka" ("Tale") and "Prizrak" ("Phantom"). "Skazka" is a rather lyrical, meditative piece while "Prizrak," marked *Presto tenebroso* and in 5/8 meter, drives over an insistent *ostinato* phrase in the bass—five eighth notes, falling, then rising: A–D–G sharp–D–A.

Seryozha already had the reputation around the Conservatory of being "unable to hear two right notes in succession. That's because his piano at home is out of tune and he's gotten used to it." Apparently, he enjoyed that reputation. The pieces he played for his fellow students, particularly "Prizrak," confirmed the legend, although he did refrain from playing "Shutka" ("The Joke"), which also ended up later in Op. 3, because he thought it was too "daring and irreverent." One can understand why he thought it was more shocking than the others: it is filled with the brittle staccato dissonances—especially tritones and seconds—and empty fourths that later made him famous as the "bad boy of Russian music." It is a brilliantly irrepressible, fresh and naughty little piece, overflowing with playful athletic energy and a desire to épater les bourgeois.

But far more important for Prokofiev's career was meeting and playing for the members of the Evenings of Contemporary Music. This influential circle of the non-Conservatory (even anti-Conservatory) Petersburg musical avant-garde had existed since 1901, when it was established by five young gentlemen, including the sensitive music critic Viacheslav Karatygin, the book collector Alfred Nurok and the "musician-dilettante" (as Soviet reference works like to identify him disparagingly) Walter Nouvel. The young Igor Stravinsky heard his music played for the first time at the Evenings; the circle also introduced the music of Schoenberg, Debussy, Ravel, Dukas, d'Indy and lesser-known works by Russian and European composers of the eighteenth and nineteenth centuries. By the time they encountered Prokofiev, Nurok and Nouvel were good friends and associates of Sergei Diaghilev. Nouvel had already helped to set up Diaghilev's first season of concerts in Paris in the spring of 1907 and would play a central role in the development of the Ballets Russes, as manager and artistic consultant.

Prokofiev's acquaintance and one-time tutor, Mikhail Chernov, brought him to one of the regular Thursday Evenings in early 1908 so that he might play his music. Like Diaghilev, Nurok, Nouvel and Karatygin were always on the lookout for new talent and sensations with which to surprise Petersburg. Shock value was an important part of their aesthetic. When Seryozha sat down and played his piano pieces—he chose the ones he had played for the Conservatory students, plus the daring "Shutka" and "Snezhok" ("Snowflakes"), a disarmingly simple piece structured entirely on gently falling seconds—they were instantly won over. Karatygin exclaimed that Prokofiev's music was a mixture of Reger, Mussorgsky and Grieg, and the "antithesis to Scriabin—and thank God that the antithesis has appeared!" They all noticed, as Stravinsky would later, that this gawky seventeen-year-old had "the instant imprint of personality."

No one had reacted so positively to the music he was writing, and Prokofiev was excited. They talked about when he could make his public debut in their concert series—sometime next fall. That appearance would launch Prokofiev's professional career.

It is difficult to overestimate the importance of Prokofiev's introduction to the Evenings of Contemporary Music. Discouraged by the conservative and lethargic climate at the Conservatory, he now saw that there was another world out there, containing knowledgeable people who appreciated what was different and antiacademic about him (that was, in fact, what they liked most about him). Even better, they could present his music to the world. Through them he would learn about the Western avant-garde, and eventually come to know Diaghilev.

The sometimes self-consciously artistic atmosphere surrounding Nurok and Nouvel was also new for the country boy from Sontsovka. One evening Nurok invited him to his apartment to discuss writing music for a pantomime he wanted to stage. Nurok's apartment reflected *fin-de-siècle* taste. "The walls were hung with photographs and drawings," Prokofiev wrote later. "Spying one among them that depicted a lion in the act of mounting a lioness, I was embarrassed to see the king of beasts in such a pose. I walked away from it. But then I approached it again: the lion's expression reflected concentration, and the lioness's jaw was thrown open in lust." Around this same time, Prokofiev stopped discussing certain things with his mother.

By now he was slightly more aware of sexuality, if not proficient in its practice. A surprising amount of space in Prokofiev's account of these years is devoted to a description of the attempts of a member of an all-male chess club he used to frequent to seduce him. One day—while an intense chess discussion was raging—Seryozha sat on this man's knee because "there were no empty chairs." Some of those present found his behavior questionable enough to report it to Prokofiev's cousin Andrei Raevsky, who of course told his mother, who told her sister Maria Grigorevna. She was so upset that she had a migraine attack. Not without embarrassment, she explained why it was wrong for him to sit on this man's knee "in view of his inclinations"— it was apparently his first "birds and bees" lecture. But something in the man's attentions continued to intrigue Prokofiev, for he goes on to describe the vicissitudes of their social relationship over the following months.

After passing his exams in the spring, Seryozha traveled with his mother and Aunt Tanya not to Sontsovka but to the exotic semitropical Black Sea coast. An old high school friend of Maria Grigorevna's had an estate in Sukhumi, a beautiful port and resort on the lush eastern shore. Prokofiev stayed for three weeks, intrigued by the atmosphere of luxury and refinement, and his mother even longer. Sergei Alekseevich worked alone in Sontsovka. While traveling back home from the Black Sea, Seryozha read in the papers of Rimsky-Korsakov's death; it was the end of an era in Russian music.

Before they parted in St. Petersburg, Seryozha and Miaskovsky had agreed they would both compose a symphony over the summer. As usual, Prokofiev set promptly and efficiently to work in Sontsovka, which he now found more boring than ever, while Miaskovsky, neurotic and indecisive, agonized and castigated himself. One can already recognize features of Prokofiev's mature aesthetic views in the letters he sent to Miaskovsky that summer. "I'm very disturbed by what you are writing me: why these *longueurs* of 120 pages? What can be worse than a long symphony? In my opinion, a symphony should ideally last twenty minutes, or thirty maximum. I am trying to write mine as compactly as possible: I'm crossing out even the slightest 'wordiness' with a merciless pencil." As a symphonist, Prokofiev for most of his life remained true to this conviction: his first four (mature) symphonies are all under forty minutes long, perhaps partly in reaction to the huge dimensions of the symphonies of Brahms, Mahler and Bruckner. Only the final three "Soviet" symphonies exceed forty minutes.

During the following year, Prokofiev—after overcoming many obstacles, including Glazunov's rising irritation with the transformation of his former favorite into a musical nuisance—managed to arrange a performance of this symphony (he did not assign it an opus number) at a closed rehearsal of the Court Orchestra. It proved to be a disillusioning but instructive experience, and Prokofiev abandoned the piece. Later, in 1917, he recycled the symphony's first movement (*Andante*) in the Piano Sonata No. 4, Op. 29.

Having completed the mandatory courses in harmony, counterpoint and fugue, Prokofiev and his classmates passed in the fall of 1908 into a course on the study of musical form taught by Iosif Vitol (1863–1948), a well-known Latvian composer. His teaching methods were less aggressive but not much more encouraging than Lyadov's:

"He just didn't pay attention to anything written in a new style." More enlightening, perhaps, than the Conservatory courses were the afternoons Prokofiev, Miaskovsky and their fellow student Boris Zakharov spent playing and listening to piano four-hand arrangements of works by Reger, Richard Strauss, Debussy, Rachmaninoff and Scriabin on a Steinway that Zakharov's wealthy father had bought him.

Prokofiev also renewed contact with Nurok, Nouvel and Karatygin soon after returning to Petersburg in the fall. One evening he played some new piano pieces he had written over the summer, plus his new symphony. The symphony met with a cold reception, but two of the new piano pieces delighted them and immediately received names— "Despair" ("Otchaianiia") and "Suggestion diabolique" ("Navazhdeniia"). Wonderfully exciting and insistent, of strong personality, they already contain some of the characteristic features of Prokofiev's mature style: an aggressive *ostinato* foundation (in "Despair," descending D–C sharp–C on eighth notes in 6/8 meter, heard alternately in the right and the left hand); the use of the piano as a percussive instrument; wildly fast tempos (*Prestissimo fantastico* in "Suggestion diabolique") building to crashing finales; and abrupt staccato splashes of seconds and other dissonant intervals. Both pieces eventually went into the mature Op. 4.

Prokofiev had developed into an excellent pianist by then, too, and could dispatch these pieces with impressive strength and *panache*. His "concrete," even metallic pianism was absolutely at the opposite pole from the gentle, barely audible Chopin-Scriabin salon tradition. "Suggestion diabolique" should be played, he said, "at breakneck speed, with a dry and assertive touch." He hated to hear other pianists smooth it out or slow it down. When a pianist friend of Nurok played it that way in his presence, Prokofiev told him in no uncertain terms that he didn't understand the music and should not attempt to perform it, mortally offending the young man—several years his senior—and nearly damaging his relationship with his new sponsors. All through his life, Prokofiev was mercilessly direct to performers who misinterpreted his music; he earned more than a few enemies that way.

"Suggestion diabolique" is also a good example of the "infernal" music that shows up throughout Prokofiev's career (*The Fiery Angel, Prodigal Son, The Gambler*). Its Russian title, "Navazhdeniia," which means an incantation or a seductive dance by supernatural powers intended to lure the innocent into evil, was provided by Nouvel. Immediately upon hearing it, he jumped up and exclaimed, "But that's some sort of incantation!" The best French translation they could come up with for this very Russian word was "Suggestion diabolique." Interest in the supernatural and the devil was, of course, very important in the Decadent movement then so strong in Petersburg; Scriabin's *Poème satanique* emerged in part from that obsession.

A few weeks before his eagerly awaited debut at the Evenings of Contemporary Music with "Suggestion diabolique," Seryozha played a very different sort of repertoire at a Conservatory recital: Chopin's Étude No. 1, Brahms's G Minor Rhapsody and an étude by Rubinstein. So strong was the personality of his playing—he was especially proud of the way he played staccato, with his hand held absolutely stiff— that even Anna Esipova, the prima donna of Petersburg piano teachers, took notice of him.

When December 18 arrived, Prokofiev was ready. His mother, and the Morolevs, who happened to be at that moment in Petersburg, were in the audience. So were a number of music critics. This was one of the formal concerts of the Evenings of Contemporary Music, and the hall in the Reformatorsky Institute on the banks of the Moika near the Nevsky Prospekt was filled. According to most accounts, Prokofiev scored the greatest success of the evening, playing the four pieces of Op. 4 (including "Suggestion diabolique"); the first piece— "Fairy Tale"—of Op. 3; "Snowflakes"; and a piece called "Supplication," subsequently lost. Some art songs by Miaskovsky and pieces by their teachers Vitol, Taneev and Tcherepnin filled out the program.

The spectators and reviewers were used to being surprised by Nouvel *et al.*, but the appearance of this "youth, not yet completely mature, dressed according to all the demands of reigning etiquette— etiquette, not fashion," who sat down at the piano "freely and boldly" to play his "exceptionally original" music, full of "extravagant combinations of sound" and "an enormous strength of fantasy," left most of them shouting for more. It was a brilliant debut, a gust of "fresh air" from the Russian steppe, primal and invigorating.

There were a few critics, of course, to whom this startling new voice was alien or even ugly. The harmonies "transgressed the borders of beauty." Others, including Winkler, found traces of the Decadent movement in Prokofiev's music. A certain few features—like his fondness for devilishness—were, perhaps, influenced by the Decadents, but in his overwhelmingly optimistic, "bright" and abrupt style, Prokofiev was more of a preacher against the hopeless gloom of decadence than its disciple. In the sense that Winkler and other conservative critics used it, the label "Decadent" had simply come to mean avant-garde.

One is tempted to expect adult behavior of an artist who achieves success and recognition at such an early age. And yet Seryozha was still a rather immature adolescent receiving a weekly allowance of five rubles; after his brilliant performances he would go to his mother's side and lay his head on her shoulder. He was "not used to denying himself anything." After another performance at about this same time, at the Conservatory, Vera Alpers watched as Prokofiev became "terribly upset—I was even afraid for him, thinking he might have some sort of nervous attack. He rushed off the stage and suddenly sat down on the stairs. He couldn't seem to get his breath, then he jumped up like he was crazy, slammed the door and left." Such energy seemed to rush through him after a performance; he was not notably anxious about facing an audience beforehand.

This same excess energy overflowed into everything Seryozha did. Sitting still was almost impossible for him; he always had to be doing something—playing chess in person or by correspondence, studying languages in the trolley, making lists of statistics. This frenetic level of activity seems to have been an attempt to avoid a confrontation with silence or his subconscious; he was never a particularly reflective individual.

Whatever the reasons behind his behavior, Seryozha—eccentric, abrupt, driven—"had come into fashion" among his Conservatory peers.

If his world was growing larger and more exciting, the classes at the Conservatory seemed petty and ever more boring. In Vitol's class the students all wrote one piano sonata. This was Prokofiev's sixth according to the childhood catalogue. The juxtaposition of major and minor—like Reger, as Miaskovsky observed—in the second theme of the first movement irritated Vitol, who was similarly offended by the "wild and teeth-gnashing" dissonances of an opera scene Seryozha produced; it was a revision of the final scene of *The Feast During the Plague*, written years before for Glière. The revision shows how Prokofiev's aesthetic had changed in five years. Originally, Prokofiev portrayed the priest presiding over the feast in a conventional "churchy" fashion, against organ-like chords. Now he felt, however, that the priest was in fact a raging medieval preacher, "foaming at the mouth as he denounced the feasting sinners." Accordingly, he filled the scene with dissonances and tried to write a very dramatic vocal line with few concessions to singability. This is the first evidence of the goal of dramatism in opera—to be attained, if necessary, by sacrificing the vocal line—that Prokofiev pursued throughout his career as an operatic composer.

His success outside the Conservatory was also leading Seryozha to become more demanding of his instructors. Fellow students who heard his piano playing advised him to abandon Winkler, who had nothing more to teach him, and begin studying with the legendary Esipova. At first he resisted, out of loyalty to Winkler, who, while uninspiring, had been for the most part supportive and gentle. Finally, however, he took Miaskovsky's advice—"When you have a goal in sight, don't stop to look at the corpses you have to walk over to get there"—and decided to change piano instructors. Winkler, disappointed, did not stand in the way, but demanded that Prokofiev pass his end-of-the-year examination, which he did brilliantly with a performance of the Rimsky-Korsakov Concerto, with Winkler accompanying in a piano arrangement. Released from further obligation, he began studying with Esipova the next autumn. But to remember Winkler—and assuage his guilt—he dedicated the four Études Op. 2, which he wrote during the summer, to his first real piano instructor. The fourth of these études—*Presto energico*—is a wonderfully quirky study in split octaves for the left hand, impudent and sassy.

Prokofiev had reached the age of eighteen. He received the official designation "free artist" after five years at the Conservatory, and began to act more independently. His mother and her opinions receive noticeably less mention in his autobiography and letters of this year. New friends helped him acquire some social graces, among them the selection and use of a new wardrobe; he chose a more stylish gray suit, a red tie and yellow shoes. (He always liked to wear bright colors.) At the end of the year, they moved into a new apartment, bigger and more elegant, with a doorman and carpeted stairway. Life was interesting and amusing, and the future seemed bright. The political situation was relatively calm, and the country's economy was booming.

Vera Alpers, who suffered from an acute crush on Seryozha, describes in her diary—with the full force of teenage passion and hyperbole—the day he left for Sontsovka. "What a night!," she wrote. "Seryozha has already gone to the station and in a half hour or so he'll be speeding to the countryside, to the smells of springtime, to the singing of nightingales! How lucky he is! The train rattles along, a fresh spring evening breeze caresses his face through the open window. Perhaps he is remembering the Conservatory, so far away, or, more likely, he is playing chess with one of his traveling companions."

This would be Prokofiev's last Sontsovka summer.

C H A P T E R   4

FREE ARTIST

What joy to be hot and shining!
What pleasure to consume the moments in flame!
I converse through light with those who shine.
I reign. I am in ecstasy. I burn.

— K O N S TA N T I N   B A L M O N T , "The Sunbeam"

hile Prokofiev had been irritating his Conservatory professors in
St. Petersburg, Diaghilev and his growing entourage of composers,
designers, dancers and musicians had been seducing audiences
in Paris. The Paris seasons that had begun modestly and eclect-
ically in 1907 were enjoying such success that Diaghilev, Nouvel and
their friends were full of even more ambitious plans for the future. In
the spring of 1908 they had staged Mussorgsky's *Boris Godunov* at the
Paris Opera with Chaliapin in the title role; the scenery was by Golovin
and Bénois, and the costumes by Bilibin. The combination of tortured
Russian intensity and folksy color was wildly successful, convincing
Diaghilev that there was a strong market for Russian art in the West.
He would continue for a while to export the best the Imperial Theaters
had to offer, until his own company was so strong that it no longer
needed their support, prestige and artists.

In 1909 the company tried its first ballet, Tcherepnin's *Le Pavillon
d'Armide*, which introduced the aloof and extraordinary Nijinsky to
Europe. Diaghilev had admired his performances at the Mariinsky
Theater in Petersburg—where *Le Pavillon* was first produced—and
persuaded him to participate in their enterprise. Tamara Karsavina—
"her dark, lustrous beauty seems the incarnation of Russia"—was his

partner. Alexander Benois designed the lavishly rococo sets, glowing with subtle "apple-green, rose-pink and turquoise blue," and Mikhail Fokine choreographed. The production exemplified what the Parisians loved in the Ballets Russes: the marriage of European taste and sophistication with Russian strength and mystery.

Once again, the evening—which also included the third (Polovetsian) act of Borodin's *Prince Igor* and short dances gleaned from the music of Tchaikovsky, Glazunov, Rimsky-Korsakov and Mussorgsky— was a triumph. Diaghilev was now more determined than ever to concentrate on ballet and choreography, and to deemphasize opera, a decision that would profoundly affect the careers of Stravinsky and Prokofiev. In the next season, he presented the first of many original ballet scores commissioned for the company: Stravinsky's *The Firebird*.

Several of Prokofiev's Conservatory professors were involved in the first seasons of the Diaghilev company: Tcherepnin, Rimsky-Korsakov, Glazunov, Lyadov. (As time went on, however, Diaghilev turned decisively away from these academic composers to Stravinsky and the French.) For the moment, however, Prokofiev himself appears to have known little of Diaghilev's activities and did not express a strong interest in ballet. As late as November 1912, he wrote to a friend, "I've heard something of Stravinsky's ballets, but for the moment the idea of writing my own does not interest me." He does not mention seeing any ballet performances in his letters or autobiography during these years: opera was his theatrical passion. This preference may have originated in part from the cautious Conservatory atmosphere. Most of the faculty members, despite their tentative involvement with Diaghilev's company in its early years, were reluctant to take ballet— an unworthy and lightweight genre—as seriously as opera. Prokofiev himself always seemed to view ballet as a more commercial and less substantial kind of music—a mistress rather than a wife. He would spend years writing operas without any promise that they would eventually be performed, but each of his ballets was written for a specific commission.

Even when he wrote more for himself than for his professors, Prokofiev still gravitated toward traditional forms: sonatas, symphonies and opera. By the summer of 1909, he had composed six piano sonatas, two symphonies, four operas and many piano pieces. Prokofiev regarded none of these youthful works as mature, however. Only beginning with some works of late 1909 did he start awarding opus numbers. But he did use a good deal of material from these early pieces later in reworked form. Thrift was always characteristic of Prokofiev as a composer: he could not bear to let good music (or any of his music, for that matter) go to waste.

During the summer of 1909, there was little for Prokofiev to do in Sontsovka but compose. His mother had remained in Petersburg, his father had been called on business to Kharkov, and his childhood playmates had all dispersed or were busy with their own lives. After a week he was ready to flee this "bear's lair. All day long I occupy myself with composing, the piano and chess." Practicing and learning more of Scriabin's music—the sonatas, especially the fourth, which he considered the best, and arrangements of the symphonies—left his fingers aching. He also read *The Devils*, a complex and frightening novel of revolutionary fanaticism by Dostoevsky, an author "for whom I don't always feel the greatest love," but who would provide the subject seven years later for his first full-length opera, *The Gambler*. And of course there was chess: he was carrying on nearly twenty games by correspondence. For occasional entertainment he would travel twenty-five versts (about fifteen miles) to visit the three "merry provincial" daughters of the local doctor, although they paled beside his more sophisticated Petersburg acquaintances.

So there was ample time for new compositions, and Prokofiev began work on an orchestral piece that would become the Sinfonietta Op. 5/48. He had heard Rimsky-Korsakov's "very pleasant, soft and appealing" Sinfonietta (Op. 31) at a concert the preceding January and may have wished to emulate it; perhaps more important, it appeared that his Conservatory friend Anatoly Kankarovich would be able to present its premiere in Voronezh, where he was conducting a series of summer concerts. In his characteristically trusting manner, Prokofiev took Kankarovich at his word and set methodically to work. It was the first time in his career he had ever been promised a performance as soon as he finished something. By late July he had nearly completed the five-part work, when he received a letter from his friend announcing that the deal in Voronezh was off due to his disagreements with the orchestra management.

Eventually, Prokofiev himself came to find the Sinfonietta—at least in its original form—a flawed work. It was first performed only in late 1915, and only after it had been reworked. But this revision, too, failed to satisfy the composer, and he rewrote it once again in 1929, giving it a new opus number, 48. (Now it is usually referred to as Op. 5/48.)

What is interesting about the 1909 version of the Sinfonietta, described in a feverish exchange of letters with Miaskovsky that summer, is how it presages Prokofiev's "neoclassical" style, particularly that of his first full-length symphony, the "Classical," composed seven years later. Just as he had told Miaskovsky the preceding summer, when they were writing full-length symphonies, Prokofiev was at this point more interested in a pared-down Mozartian scale and sound than in dense and swollen romanticism. (He was not rigorously consistent in this conviction, however: several works of this early period, particularly the opera *Maddalena* and the symphonic poem "Dreams," are, in fact, very romantic and lush.) Miaskovsky, who felt that interesting music had to be opaque, criticized his friend for what he called the Sinfonietta's "simplicities." To him, they were much less intriguing than the chromatic and rhythmic complexities of his piano pieces, which reflected both Prokofiev's "fiery temperament and the purely superficial technical merits without which music for me loses half of its value."

That Prokofiev's aesthetic views and self-confidence were already strong is clear from his reply to Miaskovsky, where he shrugs off the criticism as a reflection of his friend's depression, and makes no attempt to apologize for his "simplicity." Miaskovsky's own music never did aim for, or achieve, an impression of "simplicity." As has been proven time and again in music, simplicity only sounds easy.

Miaskovsky needn't have worried that Prokofiev was abandoning complexity, anyway. Four études (Op. 2) that he dashed off that same summer are full of thorny virtuoso problems for pianists—18/16 meter in the right hand and 4/4 in the left in Étude No. 2, three staffs to manage at once in No. 3, a wildly fast tempo with dizzying chromatic alterations in No. 4. This set, first performed in early 1910 in Moscow, is Prokofiev's first work with an opus number that is not a reworking of something composed earlier. Also written that summer was a mazurka in which, he wrote proudly to Vera Alpers, "both hands play in parallel fourths." Later, the mazurka, revised and dedicated to "Kolechka Miaskovsky," became the fourth of the Ten Pieces for Piano, Op. 12, completed in 1913.

At the end of the summer Seryozha traveled to Essentuki, a resort in the Caucasus, where his mother (she was now fifty-five) was taking a cure for her rheumatism. Apparently his parents spent little time together that year. His father, who had turned sixty-four, was still healthy but working hard at maintaining the Sontsov estate; his mother avoided spending time in the boring countryside. In the Caucasus, Prokofiev—uncharacteristically—allowed himself a complete vacation, leaving all his music, books "and even my chess set" behind. From Essentuki he traveled to other resorts in the Caucasus, including fashionable Kislovodsk (a mineral spa whose name means "sour waters"), the Saratoga Springs of pre-Revolutionary Russia. In years to come he would spend many vacations there. He found the "entire musical world" also recuperating from a damp Petersburg winter in the refreshing alpine air of Kislovodsk; among the luminaries were Glazunov and Seryozha's new piano teacher, Anna Nikolaevna Esipova.

Resting was never easy for Prokofiev, though, and he was happy to return to Sontsovka and start working again for a month, surrounded by a cousin and "a gaggle of aunts." From the almost-finished Sinfonietta he turned to composing a piano sonata in F Minor—the Sonata No. 1, Op. 1—the first of his nine sonatas composed over the next forty years. Dedicated to his old friend Morolev, with whom he had spent some days that summer near the Dnepr River, the sonata is surprisingly unadventurous and considerably less interesting than the following eight. Academic and imitative, it lacks the impudence, drive and freshness of the piano pieces with which he had made his debut. No doubt the conventional Morolev, who found Prokofiev's more rebellious music upsetting, loved it.

During the following winter, on February 21, 1910, Prokofiev gave the premiere of the Sonata No. 1 in his first Moscow appearance, at the thirteenth "Musical Exhibition" organized by the soprano Maria Deisha-Sionitskaya. A Bolshoi Opera star, Deisha-Sionitskaya sponsored these free recitals to introduce new chamber music by Russian composers. Works by Taneev and Glière were frequently on the program. For his Moscow debut, Prokofiev also played three of the four Études of Op. 2.

The sonata was the first of Prokofiev's scores to be published, by the Moscow firm of Jurgenson in 1911. Jurgenson was a family business, founded by Peter Jurgenson in 1861. The company had grown wealthy on Tchaikovsky's music, which the elder Jurgenson had the foresight to publish beginning with Op. 1. It took several letters of recommendation from Taneev and from the Petersburg musicologist Alexander Ossovsky to persuade the rather conservative Jurgenson to publish Prokofiev's rambunctious music, however. Jurgenson was Prokofiev's sole publisher until late 1916, although the company was interested almost exclusively in his piano pieces, which could be produced inexpensively.

Before he had finally convinced Jurgenson to make him a published composer, Prokofiev had also tried unsuccessfully to sell his music to two other firms: Bessel and the Russian Music Publishing House. Koussevitsky, widening his concert and publishing activities, had established the Russian Music Publishing House only recently, in March 1909, basing the firm in Berlin rather than in Russia because German law better protected composers' rights. The editorial board included Koussevitsky, Scriabin, Rachmaninoff, Medtner, Gedike, Ossovsky and N. G. Struve, although the votes of Scriabin, Rachmaninoff and Medtner carried the most weight. During its early years, the organization published music by Stravinsky (including the scores to *The Rite of Spring* and *Petrushka*) and Scriabin.

Despite Koussevitsky's interest in new music—he would eventually become one of Prokofiev's most important sponsors in Russia, Europe and America—the editorial board insistently rejected Prokofiev's music. Medtner, a Moscow composer known for his deeply philosophical song settings and densely written piano pieces, would join with his supporter Rachmaninoff to turn down unanimously "everything that contained the slightest hint of innovation," overriding Scriabin's more progressive views. Even as late as 1915, when Prokofiev was already famous in Russia, Rachmaninoff would insist that the Russian Music Publishing House should not publish "The Scythian Suite," which he considered "barbaric, impudently innovative and cacophonous music." Eventually, Koussevitsky circumvented Rachmaninoff's intransigence by publishing Prokofiev's music at Gutheil, another independent publishing concern he acquired in 1914. There, he operated without an editorial board.

Dealing with businessmen, publishers and money never intimidated or disgusted Prokofiev, which led other composers to both admire and envy him. He enjoyed devising business strategy and could drive a hard bargain, sometimes so aggressively that he alienated his patrons. Nor was he discouraged by rejection. His business energy also went toward setting up concerts of his music; he was notably persistent and thick-skinned in asking his friends and contacts to help him out. It was Glière who arranged his February 1910 appearance in Moscow with his Sonata No. 1 at the "Musical Exhibition" series concert. In this case, too, Prokofiev listed specific requirements, refusing to play the same pieces he had performed for the Evenings of Contemporary Music. "I strongly insist on playing my sonata, because it's just not at all interesting to me to play old stuff."

Apparently Prokofiev's Moscow debut was a success, at least judging from the review in the newspaper *The Russian Word*. Describing the composer admiringly as "still very young, even adolescent," the critic found in him "obvious talent and a completely serious attitude toward the business at hand. In all that he played there is a good deal of youthful bravado, but also solid preparation. Mr. Prokofiev turned out to be a good pianist as well."

While his Moscow performance was the most important appearance he made in 1910, he was also honing his conducting skills at Conservatory concerts back in Petersburg. Now that he was a "free artist," he had decided to continue studying at the Conservatory, working with Tcherepnin on conducting and with Anna Esipova on piano. He had also begun advanced composition study with Lyadov, but they did not get along well and the lessons soon stopped. Beginning in the fall of 1909, Prokofiev was on his own as a composer: Rimsky-Korsakov was dead, and Glazunov was uninterested. In the end, this was probably to Prokofiev's advantage, for his professors had for the most part objected to that which was most original about his music. To a certain extent, Miaskovsky took their place as Seryozha's mentor; he certainly offered more encouragement.

What Prokofiev concentrated on at the Conservatory during his second five years there, until his graduation in the spring of 1914, was performance, so that he might better present his music—on the piano and the podium—to the public. Under Tcherepnin's guidance he prepared and conducted many symphonic works at student concerts, beginning with Schubert's "Unfinished" Symphony in November 1909. Later, Prokofiev also ventured into opera, conducting excerpts from Verdi's *Aida* and finally, in March 1914, Mozart's *Marriage of Figaro*.

Despite all this practice, he still felt "constrained and uncomfortable" in the conductor's role, a judgment with which many observers concur. "Only after I graduated from the Conservatory, and Tcherepnin was no longer behind my back, did I attain freedom of movement with an orchestra." This constraint stemmed in part from Prokofiev's youth when he began working with Tcherepnin; when he would stand up on the podium, "it seemed like the orchestra was far away and my gestures didn't reach it." Consequently, Tcherepnin came to put Prokofiev once and for all in the category of those untalented for conducting. Clumsy and rather stiff, Prokofiev did not possess the natural physical ease and confidence that a good conductor needs to communicate his interpretation to the muscians. As an adult, Prokofiev would conduct many premieres of his orchestral works, but he never developed a love for the art of waving the baton. He was happy to have others more gifted—Koussevitsky or Samosud, for example—do the job.

If he felt uncomfortable and insecure as a conductor, he had no such doubts as a pianist. Leaving behind Winkler's approach of benign neglect, Prokofiev hoped to make faster progress under the legendary rigor of Esipova. But in the end he encountered the same sort of resistance from her that he had from Lyadov and Glazunov. His personality as a pianist was already so unique and strong that she wasn't quite sure what to do with him. She was one of those teachers who "wanted to fit all of her students into the same mold" and liked to work with malleable and "pleasant young people" submissive to her strong will. Instead of allowing Prokofiev, who was never malleable and prided himself on his individuality even at this young age, to develop and strengthen his independent style, which was his genius, she tried to make him conform to her ideal. In May 1910, after working with him for a year, Esipova reported that Prokofiev "has assimilated my method only to a limited extent. He is very talented, but rather crude." Nor did Seryozha, intent on finding a "new harmonic language," care for the heavy doses of Mozart, Schubert and Chopin that she wanted her students to swallow.

Their differing points of view led to numerous sharp disagreements. In early 1912 he began preparing for a piano competition on his own, without asking for Esipova's help. When she found out, she was deeply offended and demanded that he play the pieces for her. Predictably, she found that his willful interpretations differed from hers; since there was no time to relearn the pieces, he withdrew from the competition.

Pedagogues and Prokofiev rarely got along very well. He refused to become a "nice student" who behaved, performed and composed in a docile way that pleased the teacher. He was too idiosyncratic, definite and artistically self-confident to be a teacher's pet. Neither was he willing to conceal his knowledge and talent for the sake of ingratiating himself with the instructor—as his generally undistinguished grades throughout his Conservatory career seem to prove. And yet he was never so much a rebel as to reject the value and necessity of Conservatory training. Prokofiev might criticize, resist and try to outsmart his professors, but he still wanted the institutional stamp of approval and respectability. Later on, his attitude toward the Soviet government was similarly motivated: although uncomfortable with certain aspects of the system, he still wanted its official approval.

When Prokofiev's father came to Petersburg to visit in February 1910, he suddenly fell ill and had to be hospitalized. His condition was so serious that he was unable to return to Sontsovka to manage the estate. Characteristically undemonstrative, Prokofiev hardly mentions this illness in his autobiography and letters. It also had no apparent impact on his usual high level of activity; in late February he made his Moscow debut, and he continued to compose new works.

Among them were two songs (Op. 7) for women's chorus and orchestra to poems of the Russian Symbolist Konstantin Balmont (1867–1942), composed in the hope that they could be sung by a student choir recently organized at the Conservatory by Glazunov. Only one, "The White Swan," was ever performed, to piano accompaniment at a morning student recital conducted by Prokofiev. Later, in his autobiography, Prokofiev remarked that the songs were too difficult for the student choir, while his official Soviet biographer, Israel Nestyev, dismissed them as "too unusual." A glance at the manuscript, however, does not justify such an assessment; the melody line is clear and unchromatic, while the accompaniment proceeds in gentle arpeggios (the tempo marking is *andante molto*). The vocal style is melodic, unlike the declamatory idiom of "The Ugly Duckling" and *The Gambler*. Romantic, dreamy, even sentimental, the songs are very different from the insistent and aggressive piano pieces composed during the same period, and demonstrate another side of Prokofiev's musical personality, one that reappears in the opera *Maddalena*.

Prokofiev was not the only Russian composer who appreciated Balmont's fluid, sweetly musical poetry (which bears a strong resemblance to the poetry of Edgar Allen Poe, whom Balmont loved to translate) enough to set it to music. Rachmaninoff and Stravinsky also wrote songs to Balmont's verses. In the future, Prokofiev would turn repeatedly to Balmont as a literary source, and they would become friends in the early 1920s.

Another project that occupied Prokofiev during the months of his father's illness was "Dreams" (Op. 6), a "Symphonic Tableau" for large orchestra completed in early summer. It was dedicated to Scriabin, whose music (and messianic personality) continued to intrigue him; the choice of the title was inspired by the title of Scriabin's first orchestral piece, "Reverie." Prokofiev had also been working on a piano arrangement of the first part of Scriabin's Symphony No. 3 ("The Divine Poem"), which he had shown to the composer on a visit to Scriabin's fashionable Petersburg quarters in February 1910. "Dreams" did not enjoy much success with conductors (who for the most part refused to perform it) or with audiences. Despite its title and dedication, Prokofiev wrote later, " 'Dreams' reveals little influence of Scriabin."

By the summer of 1910, Prokofiev's father was in even graver condition. For the first time since moving to St. Petersburg six years earlier, Seryozha and his mother stayed on in the city after the end of the academic year, instead of returning to Sontsovka as they always had in the past. Eventually, Sergei Alekseevich underwent two operations, and the doctors found cancer of the liver, which amounted to a death sentence. On July 1, Prokofiev wrote Morolev that "Papa's health is for the moment no better, and there has been no change." And yet Seryozha was not sorry to remain in the city; Sontsovka bored him.

He divided his time that summer between Petersburg and the countryside nearby, where he stayed with friends, particularly Boris Zakharov, whose wealthy family owned a seaside villa in Terioki. Glagoleva, with whom he was still infatuated, lived nearby. He also went several times to visit Vera Alpers at her family's dacha in Pavlovsk, where a town and park surround the English-style palace built by Tsar Pavel, son of Catherine the Great. A military band gave concerts in Pavlovsk in the summertime, in the midst of lush English gardens filled with gazebos, statues and monuments.

But such carefree summer pastimes were interrupted on July 23, when Seryozha's father died, only two weeks after his sixty-fourth birthday. (Prokofiev would live almost exactly as long as his father: he died a month short of his sixty-second birthday.) Sergei Alekseevich, who had worked so hard to provide the means to develop his son's musical talent—so hard, perhaps, that he undermined his health— did not live to see and enjoy the rewards for his sacrifices.

Prokofiev's response to his father's death was muted and undemonstrative—in keeping with the stiff-upper-lip relationship they had always maintained. After the burial on July 27, Prokofiev and his mother traveled to Sontsovka, where they spent a month straightening out their business affairs and planning for the permanent move to St. Petersburg. From Sontsovka, less than two weeks after the funeral, Prokofiev wrote Miaskovsky a letter that expresses nearly as much concern about the attitudes of various conductors toward his new music as it does over his father's death. He does not mention his mother, or her response to her husband's death. Miaskovsky wrote back in similarly stoic language: "You know that I love you with all my soul so it makes no sense to talk about my sympathy for your grief. You should be sure of it anyway."

The death of Sergei Alekseevich must have significantly influenced the financial situation of Prokofiev's mother, although there is no evidence that their life became more difficult. What does seem clear is that Prokofiev's mother did not burden him with her financial worries; perhaps her Petersburg relatives helped them out. Prokofiev's working routine was apparently unaffected, and his productivity did not decline significantly during the following months. He did begin to concentrate on larger works, however—the First Piano Concerto, an opera (*Maddalena*), the Second Piano Sonata. As an adult, too, Prokofiev tended to channel emotional difficulties into his work, increasing his rate of activity to avoid confronting uncomfortable issues. At the same time, his attitudes toward friends and colleagues—at least judging by correspondence—mellowed to some extent after his first real experience with death. The mockery and teasing became a little less sharp.

If Prokofiev found it difficult to express his feelings verbally and emotionally over his father's passing, he did express them musically. While in Sontsovka in August, he worked on a small orchestral piece ("A Symphonic Sketch for Small Orchestra"), which he eventually called "Autumn" (Op. 8). "I don't know if you'll like it or not, but then it's the sort of piece that doesn't have any pretensions about trying to please anyone," he wrote to Miaskovsky.

In his autobiography, Prokofiev says that the "gloomy" atmosphere of the work originated in his interest in Rachmaninoff's music, particularly *Isle of the Dead* (composed and first performed in Moscow in 1909) and the Second Symphony (first performed in St. Petersburg in early 1908). The similarities between "Autumn" and Rachmaninoff's style of the time are, indeed, so strong—abundant suspensions, drooping *legato* melody, a mournful, lyrical and even sentimental mood— that one could easily think Rachmaninoff had written it. No other piece by Prokofiev sounds so "soft," so completely Romantic, or so completely lacking in "Prokofievian" features (strong rhythm, hollow-sounding orchestration, playfulness). Later, "Autumn" was twice rewritten, in 1915 and in 1934, when it assumed its final performing version.

What drew Prokofiev into this uncharacteristically elegiac frame of mind seems to have been his father's death. It must have made him reflect—if only briefly—on his own mortality and the inevitable passage of time. As he remarked a few years later, after a performance of "Autumn": "The critics wrote about gentle rain and falling leaves, and they quoted poems. Not one of them figured out, though, that it reflects an internal world, not external. This kind of 'autumn' can come in spring and in summer."

C H A P T E R   5

O U T   I N   T H E   W O R L D

Don't listen to our laughter, listen to the pain behind it.

— A L E X A N D E R   B L O K

To recover from the emotional and physical strain of reorganizing their lives, Prokofiev and his mother spent a few quiet weeks in the clear air of the Caucasus before returning to St. Petersburg in late September. They stayed again in the luxurious Sukhumi villa owned by the Smetsky family, Maria Grigorevna's friends from high school days. Surrounded by semitropical vegetation and warmth, looking out at the Black Sea, Prokofiev "lazily scribbled" some ideas for the piano concerto he had been thinking about writing since the previous spring.

Ideas for this piece—the first of his five piano concertos, it would win him wide recognition—continued to come to him when he arrived back in St. Petersburg. But perhaps because of his father's death and the need to establish some financial independence, getting his music published now became his first priority. He put the piano pieces of the Opuses 3, 4 and 12 in order and showered Jurgenson and Koussevitsky with aggressive letters. The form rejection he received from the Russian Musical Publishing House inspired him to announce indignantly to Miaskovsky that he didn't need those stuffy editors anyway. He had sold his "bicycle and a photograph" and would use the proceeds to publish his music himself—"without any of those various sons of Ivan." The rejection did not sap his creative energy: besides the concerto, two solo songs with piano accompaniment were in the works.

Now came the inevitable period of consolidation and hard work after his early successes; now he had to prove he had staying power. In two important ways he was better equipped than many composers to publicize his own music: he could perform it on the piano and, if necessary, conduct it. One evening in late November, he displayed both these skills at a Conservatory concert. Conducting, he led the world premiere of his "Dreams"; at the piano, he performed his First Piano Sonata. "The sonata was especially successful—the general opinion was that I played it brilliantly. Unfortunately there was a Scriabin concert on the same day, and all the critics rushed over to hear that." The receipts from the Conservatory concert went into a scholarship fund established in the name of Leo Tolstoy, who had died at the age of eighty-two only a few months before.

Prokofiev also maintained his connection with the Evenings of Contemporary Music series, making two important appearances in the 1910–11 season. In late December St. Petersburg heard his four Études (Op. 2) for the first time. The audience liked them so much, and the invigorating way that he played, that they applauded "after each étude." Pleased, the members of the series also asked him to give the Russian premiere of three piano pieces ("Klavierstucke" Op. 11) written in 1909 by Arnold Schoenberg—an impressive tribute to Prokofiev's skill as a pianist. In fact, Prokofiev was the first to perform Schoenberg (on March 28, 1911) in Russia—ironic in light of his later indifference to Schoenberg's methods and music. Although Prokofiev never became a disciple of Schoenberg's twelve-tone system—he avoided joining any circles or identifying himself with any movements—he must have been intrigued by the new harmonic language of Schoenberg's music, just as he was by Scriabin's. From his early years, Prokofiev was catholic in his musical curiosity, even if his interest in a particular composer or method was most often short-lived.

Along with the Schoenberg pieces, Prokofiev played his Op. 3— "Fairy Tale," "Joke," "March" and "Phantom." The last three of the pieces were being heard in public for the first time.

Through the Evenings of Contemporary Music, Prokofiev also met other avant-garde composers, artists and writers. One of these was Igor Stravinsky, who by early 1911 was basking in his celebrity as the creator of the score for *The Firebird* and would within a few months follow up his first success with *Petrushka*. He was closely involved with the organizers of the Evenings, since they were working together with Diaghilev on the Ballets Russes productions.

According to Stravinsky, he and Prokofiev had first met earlier, in 1906–1907. They did not come to know each other well, however, until after Prokofiev graduated from the Conservatory in 1914 and began to collaborate with Diaghilev. (Soviet musicologists for a long time obscured or distorted Prokofiev's personal and musical relationship with Stravinsky, who left Russia before the Revolution and then "subordinated his art to the demands of Western snobs.") Prokofiev remembers that they first encountered each other around 1912 in Petersburg, on which occasion Stravinsky played the introduction to *The Firebird* on the piano. Never one to conceal his reactions, Prokofiev told Stravinsky that "there was no music in the introduction, and if there was any, it came from *Sadko*" (*Sadko* was one of Rimsky-Korsakov's most popular operas). Stravinsky was not amused. Prokofiev's lack of social diplomacy was only one of the factors that complicated the difficult and mercurial relationship between the two composers.

Both Stravinsky and Prokofiev wrote songs to poems by the same poet—Balmont—in 1911, neatly demonstrating that despite their differences, their music and aesthetic sprang from similar sources. Stravinsky chose two poems ("The Dove" and "The Forget-me-not Flower"), which he set in a spare and understated style reminiscent of his "Three Japanese Lyrics"; Prokofiev used Balmont's "There Are Other Planets" for one of the two songs in his rather romantic Op. 9. Written at the height of Balmont's popularity, "There Are Other Planets" is full of the atmospherically mystical bombast and sing-song rhythm for which he became famous—and infamous.

> There are other planets,
> Where the melodious winds are softer,
> Where the sky is paler,
> Where changing colors
> Flow and ebb in streams,
> Caressing as they change,
> Laughing.

Balmont's heavily perfumed verses, in incantatory dactylic meter, led Prokofiev to write a surprisingly—for him—rhetorical setting (*Andante misterioso*), emphasizing the dactylic meter literally, in 6/8, and with rolling Mendelssohnian arpeggios in the left hand. Harmonically, "There Are Other Planets" is thick and a little overcomposed, under the influence of Rachmaninoff and Scriabin. Only with "The Ugly Duckling" in 1914 and the Akhmatova songs in 1916 would Prokofiev's mature song-writing style—with an uncluttered sound, a more declamatory vocal line and a marvelous transparency—emerge. While he was at the Conservatory he was still strongly influenced by more conventional *romansy*; his early songs do not possess the spontaneous originality of his adolescent piano music. Significantly, the Op. 9 songs were performed for the first time only in 1914. Either the composer himself doubted their value, or he was unable to convince anyone to perform them.

But Prokofiev realized better than most that writing music was only part of being a successful composer. As soon as the Conservatory classes ended in early May, he threw himself into self-advertising. Finally convincing Jurgenson in Moscow to publish his First Sonata was a major achievement. The publisher asked him what kind of cover he wanted, and Prokofiev replied, "something like the cover on Stravinsky's 'Pastorale' " (a vocalise composed in 1907). From his first steps as a recognized composer, Prokofiev was fated to be compared— and even to compare himself—to Stravinsky.

Prokofiev did have some help in trying to make a name for himself: Miaskovsky was in Moscow in May for performances of his music, and loyally used the opportunity to praise his younger friend. He so enthusiastically described to the conductor Konstantin Saradzhev (1877–1954) and the critic-editor Vladimir Derzhanovsky (1881–1942) how brilliantly talented and prolific Prokofiev was that by early June, Saradzhev had agreed to perform "Dreams" and "Autumn" in his summer concerts, and, even before hearing it, to perform the as yet unfinished Piano Concerto No. 1 the following summer. Like Nouvel and Nurok, Derzhanovsky and Saradzhev were always on the lookout for new talent to present at the concerts they organized in Moscow's Sokolniki Park. Derzhanovsky, who had studied at the Moscow Conservatory, also ran his own weekly journal, *Music (Muzyka)*, which promoted contemporary music. Miaskovsky became a regular contributor, often praising Prokofiev's new compositions. In turn, Prokofiev wrote a few reviews praising Miaskovsky's work.

Although "Dreams" (performed under Saradzhev on July 1) and "Autumn" (conducted by Aleksandr Medtner, the composer Nikolai's brother, on July 19) were not especially successful with the Moscow audiences and critics, they were interesting enough to convince Derzhanovsky that Prokofiev was a composer of promise. "The reception for 'Dreams' was not so bad, but not so good either, because my name is still too little known in Moscow. And those who do know who I am had all gone off to their summer houses," Seryozha wrote to his mother.

The collaborative friendship with Derzhanovsky that began in 1911 lasted for the next thirty years: Prokofiev came to rely heavily on his judgment, knowledge and influence. Even orthodox Soviet observers have had to admit that "despite his erroneous views"—advocacy of the formalist works of Schoenberg and Stravinsky, criticism of musical realism, a preference for sophistication, indifference to socialist revolutionary movements—"Derzhanovsky was a sincere and sensitive man who tried to encourage gifted young Russian musicians." If anything, it seems that Prokofiev was more accepted by, and more comfortable with, the members of the Sokolniki Circle than he was with the more effete impresarios of the Evenings of Contemporary Music. Prokofiev even stayed at Saradzhev's apartment in July when he was in Moscow for the performance of "Autumn."

Suddenly, Prokofiev's music was being performed more than ever before—and in professional settings. Prokofiev's old friend Kankarovich (for whom he had originally composed the Sinfonietta) conducted "Dreams" at Pavlovsk in early July, and a few weeks later Glière conducted "Autumn" there as well. All these concerts meant lots of traveling: from Petersburg to Sukhumi—two thousand miles—to join his mother in early June, from Sukhumi to Moscow for the performance of "Dreams," from Moscow to Petersburg for the Pavlovsk concert, back to Moscow for the second Sokolniki concert, and finally from Moscow to the Caucasus resort of Kislovodsk, where his mother was staying, in late July. Prokofiev, always an avid voyager, did not seem to mind such a schedule. No doubt he would have loved the era of the jet-set musician.

Even during the quieter periods of this busy summer—in June and in August—Prokofiev did not stop to catch his breath. He was working "fiercely"—no less than five hours a day—on a new project: an opera.

Maddalena belongs to the same sphere of mystical decadence as "Dreams" and the Op. 9 songs. Based on the play "Maddalena" written sometime in the first decade of the twentieth century by "Baroness" Magda Gustavovna Liven, a St. Petersburg "society lady more charming than talented," the opera describes a doomed sexual triangle in a hyperromantic fifteenth-century Venetian setting. Strongly influenced by Oscar Wilde, Liven, of whom very little is known, wrote plays and short stories with titles like "Voices of the Night" and "Astorre Trinei." Her *Maddalena* bears a strong resemblance to Wilde's unfinished one-act verse drama *A Florentine Tragedy*. How Prokofiev happened upon this unlikely and obscure source is not clear, but once he did, he set it to music with uncommon speed. By the end of the summer, he had finished the four scenes of the one-act opera (about forty-five minutes in length) in piano-vocal score. On the last page he wrote, "I finished this on August 31, 1911, in Kislovodsk." He was hoping to get *Maddalena* staged at the Conservatory opera studio.

How much Liven wrote of the libretto, and how much Prokofiev himself contributed, is not clear, but since he was composing in Kislovodsk, and makes no mention of collaborating with the author, most likely he wrote the libretto himself. (Prokofiev wrote the libretti for all his major operas.) It unfolds melodramatically, in a highly romanticized, nearly poetic style (e.g., "Their passion is as perishable as rose petals"). Indeed, the *Maddalena* text comes very close to the kind of sentimental, conventional "libretto language" Prokofiev mocked only a few years later.

Similarly, the plot, heavy with overheated *Sturm und Drang*, is antipathetic to Prokofiev's later striving for operatic realism and satire. Maddalena is a cruel "fatal woman" who takes pleasure in destroying the two men who love her—her husband, Genaro, an artist (tenor), and his friend Stenio, an alchemist (baritone). After rapturously expressing her love for her husband in Scene 2, she turns around and encourages Stenio to fight a duel with him in Scene 4. Both men perish, which leads Maddalena to exclaim, reveling in her sexual power, "Alone, alone, I am free and alive! Which one of you did Maddalena love? Maybe neither one."

Coups de théâtre abound: a gust of wind reveals Maddalena standing behind a curtain, where she has been listening voyeuristically as Stenio tells Genaro of his passionate love for a woman who demands anonymity—of course, she is Maddalena. Thunder and lightning crash as the opera opens, climaxing noisily as the tension of the drama increases. The first scene is calm, lyrical and atmospheric; the dramatic and musical excitement gradually intensifies, rising in an unbroken arc.

If the literary antecedents for *Maddalena*, perhaps the most unabashedly romantic piece Prokofiev ever wrote, are works by Oscar Wilde and Balmont, the musical antecedent is—despite Prokofiev's earlier dismissal of his music as "all that scratching"—Richard Strauss. (Strauss, of course, had also turned to a play by Wilde for the libretto of his scandalous *Salome*, first produced in 1905.) After looking at

Maddalena, Miaskovsky wrote to Derzhanovsky: "One can feel that his talent has matured. The volcanic quality of his temperament is amazing. . . . The opera is reminiscent of Richard Strauss in the tension of its style, but it doesn't exhibit Strauss's bad taste. There's only one problem—despite its dramatic quality, such a work is unlikely to be staged at the Conservatory. I have never encountered more difficult vocal parts, and there is not the slightest chance that the venerable powers-that-be would approve it."

Particularly Straussian are the set-piece—a richly harmonized gondoliers' chorus—in Scene 1, and Maddalena's soaring, supple vocal line, rising above thick orchestral accompaniment. And yet Prokofiev's language here is more percussive and biting than Strauss's, particularly as the dramatic tension rises.

Just as Miaskovsky predicted, *Maddalena* did not have an easy road to the stage. Perhaps because it was too difficult for student performers, it was never performed at the Conservatory. Only the first scene was ever orchestrated, in June 1912. ("It's not a full score, but a jewel, a chocolate with expensive *liqueur* inside," he told Miaskovsky.) Partially revised (and dedicated to Miaskovsky) in 1913, *Maddalena* was scheduled to be produced at the Free Theater in St. Petersburg, but the theatre closed down before it could be staged. Subsequent attempts to produce *Maddalena* in Russia were equally unsuccessful, and the full score remained uncompleted.

The lushly romantic musical and dramatic style of *Maddalena* is all the more surprising when one recalls that in the same year, Prokofiev wrote the antiromantic, "footballish" First Piano Concerto, the nasty Toccata Op. 11 and the sardonic Ten Pieces for Piano Op. 12. His style was still uncertain and shifting, particularly in his choice and setting of literary texts. Impressionable and easily influenced, he was seduced by the popularity of the Decadent and Symbolist movements. *Maddalena* does, however, prefigure *The Gambler*, Prokofiev's first full-length opera, written five years later, in several aspects: both focus on a destructive "fatal woman," both trace a rising line of dramatic tension reflected in the orchestration and vocal line, both present expressionistically exaggerated and hysterical emotions. What separates *Maddalena* from *The Gambler*, "The Ugly Duckling" and *Love for Three Oranges* is its smoother vocal line; in *Maddalena*, one does not sense the Mussorgskian presence that hovers over the other three works.

As Prokofiev became more sure of himself as a composer, the Conservatory ceased to occupy a central position in his life. Lyadov and Glazunov had written him off as an impudent rebel who did not want to be taught; he regarded them as unimaginative and old-fashioned. Esipova thought him demanding, arrogant and inflexible, and he found her lessons for the most part unenlightening. While he was her student, however, Prokofiev did learn a number of piano concertos on which he later depended to earn his living: Beethoven's No. 5, Rubinstein's No. 4, Tchaikovsky's No. 1, and Rachmaninoff's Nos. 1 and 2. These last two he called "wonderfully charming, epecially the second." But Rachmaninoff's Third Piano Concerto was "dry, difficult and unappealing."

Tcherepnin remained Prokofiev's closest friend, mentor and supporter in the Conservatory milieu. It was while working with Tcherepnin on a Berlioz score that Prokofiev came to the idea of writing his own full orchestral scores "in C"—that is, a transposed score in which the parts for all instruments are written down as they actually sound to the conductor (or, as they would be played on the piano). Why not simplify, he asked in his characteristic rage for clarity? He eliminated the tenor clef and used only three clefs—soprano, bass and alto—believing this system was more logical, simple and efficient. The transposing instruments in the orchestra (clarinets, trumpets, English horns, French horns, saxophones) would play from transposed parts while the conductor worked from a score in C. Prokofiev used this system throughout his career (so have some other composers, including Samuel Barber), but it never caught on universally the way he thought it might.

If Prokofiev received little support from the Conservatory luminaries, neither did they hinder him. By February 1912, he had two published works to his credit—the First Sonata and the Op. 3 piano pieces—and was going over the proofs for the Op. 2 piano pieces. He had also completed his First Piano Concerto, begun more than a year before in Sukhumi. Those who had looked at the score were highly complimentary, including the French critic Calvocoressi, who promised to bring news of Prokofiev to Paris and set up a performance for him there. All this activity and the wretched Petersburg climate—freezing, windy and damp, like London but twenty degrees colder—took its toll on Prokofiev's health: in late March he came down with pleurisy, which kept him in bed for several weeks. It also prevented him from seeing the Fokine-Diaghilev production of Schumann's *Carnaval* at the Mariinsky.

By the time he had recovered, Prokofiev had to start preparing for his first important appearances with an orchestra—two performances of his Piano Concerto No. 1, the first for Derzhanovsky's Moscow Sokolniki series in late July, and the second at Pavlovsk outside Petersburg ten days later. Most of the six weeks he spent in Essentuki, in the Caucasus, in June and July, was devoted to learning his concerto, which "by the way, is not at all easy, and I have to play it well. They say the hall in Moscow is bursting with people—up to six thousand listeners—and since it will be my first appearance with an orchestra I'll have to know it cold." Besides practicing, he began orchestrating *Maddalena*, corrected copies of the Sinfonietta and the concerto, and worked on a few of the piano pieces eventually gathered into Op. 12. His reputation was growing so quickly that he even had to turn down a proposed performance of the Sinfonietta—"otherwise I won't be able to get any work done during August." For recreation he was playing tennis for four hours each day in ninety-degree heat and working on a sunburn.

Saradzhev, who had conducted "Dreams" the previous summer, conducted again when Prokofiev played the premiere of his remarkable First Piano Concerto in Moscow on July 25. Prokofiev was up late the night before, after angry rehearsals with the orchestra which didn't play the way he wanted. But even though he went to bed "tired and bad-tempered," the performance the next day went well. The critics were split in their verdict; predictably, some found the unusual structure, driving rhythm and ecstatic mood of the concerto unsettling and tasteless, while others hailed it as the dawn of a new musical era. By now Prokofiev was almost used to such strongly contrasting reactions, and even seemed to enjoy them. His own appraisal of the performance was positive—and he was usually harder on himself than most critics.

Saradzhev knew all the tempos perfectly. The music was right in my fingers. The orchestra was faking it at times and was on a slightly lower level. I was told that the concerto sounds good from an instrumental point of view, and that the orchestra didn't once obscure the piano part. The audience responded with considerable enthusiasm—there were many curtain calls and three encores: the "Gavotte" (from Op. 12) and the fourth Étude of Op. 2 twice. I didn't have anything else prepared. I am satisfied. It was not difficult to play with an orchestra—it was even extremely pleasant.

Played without pause, the concerto is, in a sense, in one movement, though it is episodic rather than developmental, and does not follow traditional sonata-allegro form. Lasting only a little over fifteen minutes—much shorter than any of his subsequent piano concertos—the First Concerto reflects Prokofiev's early striving (revealed also in the "Classical" Symphony and the First Violin Concerto) for brevity and economy. The piece is dedicated to Tcherepnin, who had always encouraged Prokofiev to be original and innovative. What surprised audiences and critics was the abrupt and explosive rhythm and form, and the shining metallic quality to the piano and orchestral sound. This was something very different from the dreamy, rhythmically flaccid concertos of Rachmaninoff and Scriabin.

The concerto's trademark is the recurring introductory section—an ecstatically affirmative line rising two octaves and played in open octaves in both hands. He called this massive thrice-repeated introductory episode "the three whales that hold the concerto together"; it is a thrilling statement of Prokofiev's optimistic, forceful and "Scythian" aesthetic. Some observers who found the often repeated opening five-note phrase (dotted eighths followed by three quarter notes) excessively aggressive and energetic dubbed it a "hit on the head" ("*po cherepu*").

On August 3, Prokofiev repeated the concerto at Pavlovsk, under Alexander Aslanov, who was less careful about the tempi. The orchestra was not as well prepared as in Moscow, but the performance "didn't go too badly." There, too, it provoked both wild cheers and outraged catcalls. The First Concerto established Prokofiev as a bold new force that had to be reckoned with; whether they liked him and his music or not, critics and audiences now knew who he was.

Soon after the Pavlovsk performance, Prokofiev made the long journey back to the Caucasus, to Kislovodsk, where he joined his mother for a month at her favorite resort. It was warm and bright in the mountains; he used the time to complete his Second Piano Sonata, begun in the late winter. "Every morning I go to the drugstore to work. There is a good upright piano there, the room is comfortable, no one bothers me and it doesn't smell of medicine." By August 28 he had finished the sonata, numbered Op. 14.

Considerably more ambitious than his First Piano Sonata, the Second is more than twice as long and has four movements rather than one. It was written easily and quickly, and is not especially difficult to play. But the musical texture is rich and varied, full of the sudden contrasts characteristic of Prokofiev's piano music: the contrast between simple harmony and complex rhythm, between hazy impressionistic writing and "concrete" transparency, between seemingly incompatible tonalities and dynamic levels. The second theme of the first movement, in waltz time, is the kind of broad, open (in octaves) melody found in many of his subsequent sonatas and symphonies. The third movement (*Andante*), in highly chromatic G sharp minor, slips into an infernal realm, murky and dark, but the concluding movement, another 6/8 gallop that slows down momentarily to allow the first movement waltz theme to pass by, returns to the real world of hard shining surfaces.

Prokofiev's first four sonatas—composed before he left Russia in 1918—are all in minor keys, no doubt because the minor mode provided more opportunities for the chromatic alterations so important in his early music. His last five sonatas are all in major keys.

Also composed around the same time as the Second Sonata were the Toccata Op. 11, the "Ballade" for Cello and Piano Op. 15, and the Ten Pieces for Piano Op. 12. The Toccata—marked *Allegro marcato* and almost four minutes long—is a marvelously acerbic and biting exercise, jumping with harsh dissonances and making extravagant demands on the performer. Perhaps for this reason, it was not performed in public for the first time until early 1916, by the composer.

The ten short pieces of Op. 12 suggest, for the most part, a less aggressive creator. They also reveal for the first time Prokofiev's love for dance forms: of the ten pieces, four are dances ("Gavotte," "Rigaudon," "Allemande" and "Mazurka") and one is a march. Of these, only the grotesquely awkward "Allemande" mocks the form; the others are surprisingly affectionate and polite in tone. But all of the dances bear the strong mark of a modern composer: the remarkable "Mazurka" is written completely in open fourths in both hands. The other five are "Prelude," "Legend" and "Capriccio," and, to complete the cycle, "Humorous Scherzo" and "Scherzo." (Prokofiev also wrote two other versions of the "Humorous Scherzo," one for a quartet of bassoons, and another for voice with orchestra.) These ten pieces had been written over the preceding six years, beginning in 1906.

Like most of the piano pieces of Op. 12, the "Ballade" for Cello originated in a childhood composition. In early 1903, Seryozhenka wrote a violin sonata for Glière; it was the main theme of the first movement that Prokofiev later used for the melody of the "Ballade," which is similar to "a two-part sonata in form." He wrote this cello piece at the urging of Nikolai Ruzsky, to whom it is dedicated, a "very nice person, a wealthy businessman who played the cello well and loved to organize chamber groups." They had become friends, and occasionally played chamber music together.

By fall of 1912, on the strength of his well-publicized summer appearances, Prokofiev felt he could ask his publisher Jurgenson for higher fees. He demanded one hundred rubles for the Toccata Op. 11, arguing that his Petersburg supporters thought it a fine piece. In the end, Prokofiev accepted the seventy-five rubles that Jurgenson offered. A month later, in November, he sent Jurgenson the completed Second Sonata, demanding a fee of two hundred rubles and warning at the outset that he would accept no less. He received the two hundred. During the winter of 1913 Prokofiev also met Koussevitsky in Moscow, apparently for the first time. Koussevitsky did not promise to publish his music—that would happen a few years later—but he was encouraging, and invited Prokofiev to conduct a concert in his regular series the following season.

Seryozha happily shared the triumphs and disappointments of this exciting year—the real start of his professional career—with one of the closest friends he ever made: his fellow Conservatory student Maksimilian (Max) Shmitgoff. Max, one year younger than Prokofiev, was a pianist; they had been friends since 1909. Prokofiev respected Max for his intellectual precocity: even at age fifteen, he had been familiar with Schopenhauer, and could more than hold his own with Seryozha at word games. Max and Seryozha usually spent most of their summer vacation together, both in the countryside outside Petersburg and in the Caucasus. As often happens with adolescents, their relationship was intense and consuming. "At that time I was not always myself, but half-Max. His influence on me was enormous," Prokofiev later wrote with unusual feeling to Max's sister, Ekaterina Shmitgoff.

On April 26, 1913, shortly after his twenty-second birthday, Prokofiev received a note from Max, who was in Terioki, outside Petersburg on the Finnish Gulf. "Dear Seryozha, I'm writing to tell you the latest news—I have shot myself. Don't get too upset and take it with indifference, for in truth it doesn't deserve anything more than that. Farewell. Max. The causes are unimportant." By the time Prokofiev received the letter, Max was already dead, having shot himself in the deep Finnish forest.

Max's death shocked Prokofiev, affecting him much more deeply

than his father's death three years earlier. In memory of their friendship, Prokofiev dedicated four pieces to Max: the just-completed Piano
Sonata No. 2; the "Allemande" of the Op. 12 piano pieces; the Second
Piano Concerto, which he was completing at the time of Max's suicide
and fragments of which Max had been the first to hear; and the Fourth
Piano Sonata, composed in 1917 but based on themes dating from
1908–1909, when he and Max first became friends. "I was very close
to him, and now . . . I feel completely alone," Prokofiev wrote to an
acquaintance. He had been able to share more with Max, a fellow
musician and soul-mate, than with anyone else he had ever known—
including Miaskovsky. No one else took Max's place. Perhaps this
very painful experience of losing the closest friend he had ever made
intensified the attitude of emotional distance which was to a large
extent natural in Prokofiev. Perhaps, too, he felt some vague feelings
of guilt over Max's suicide. In an attempt to remain close to Max, he
corresponded frequently with his sister Ekaterina in the following years.

    Weirdly, Prokofiev received one more letter from Max, a month
after his suicide. It came out of a joke they had thought up together.

> This is how it happened: in the winter we had decided to begin a
> correspondence with a certain interesting young lady with whom we
> were not acquainted. We asked her to write to the post office, to the
> Bearer of Chinese Currency. But since we didn't receive any letters
> in response, we tried to verify if letters addressed to the Bearer of
> Chinese Currency were in fact reaching their destination. Max wrote
> a letter to that address. We forgot to fetch the letter, so yesterday,
> passing by chance by the post office, I went to inquire—for old
> times' sake—if there were any letters for the Bearer of Chinese
> Currency. They gave me one letter, dated April 3. It was full of all
> sorts of nonsense, written so the envelope wouldn't be empty.

CHAPTER 6

BATTLE OF THE PIANOS

From childhood I was trained for battles!
All in the sweep of the steppe is mine!
And my voice sounds in perfect harmony
With the deafening cry of war.

— VALERY BRYUSOV, "Scythians"

The summer of 1913 was the last peaceful summer for the old Russia, a final interlude of calm before a bloody decade of war and revolution. Superficially, the country appeared to be thriving: agricultural and industrial production had increased dramatically since the Revolution of 1905, almost doubling the national income between 1900 and 1913, while the population rose by forty-five million people in the twenty years before the Russian Revolution. Fed by large amounts of foreign capital—some of it American—Russian industry was booming as never before, creating a new class of wealthy capitalists. Peasants flocked into Petersburg, Moscow and other industrial centers to work in the new factories. While Tsar Nicolas II was an uninspiring and ineffectual leader, some of his advisers, particularly Pyotr Stolypin, the prime minister, managed to enact imaginative and desperately needed economic reforms.

Despite the real progress, however, enormous problems still plagued the Russian Empire. The gap between the wealthy few and the millions of desperately poor was deep and wide; the striking inequalities in Russian society created an environment favorable to the spread of revolutionary ideas, particularly as the growing urban proletariat gained a better understanding of its power and possibilities. Expectations rose with dramatic speed and force. Russia had finally entered the modern industrial era, but too late and too precipitously. Strikes were chronic: they involved 887,000 workers in 1913 alone. Political radicalism flourished on both ends of the spectrum, and various socialist parties, Lenin's Bolsheviks among them, were gradually gaining a committed following. The terrorism that had disrupted Russian political life since the end of the nineteenth century continued unabated: Stolypin was shot to death by a revolutionary agent in 1911.

Culturally, too, this was a turbulent and exciting time in Russia. The literary influence of Symbolism—particularly as practiced by the poets Alexander Blok, Andrei Bely and Valery Bryusov—was waning, and two new movements emerged: Acmeism and Futurism. Acmeism, whose most famous exponents were the poets Anna Akhmatova and Osip Mandelshtam, sought verbal clarity and transparency and turned away from the complex and sometimes vague language of the Symbolists, overloaded with religious-philosophical "significance." Futurism, led by the irrepressible Vladimir Mayakovsky, declared war on bourgeois culture in its 1912 manifesto, "A Slap in the Face of Public Taste," denouncing realism and literary decorum and proclaiming the need to invent a new vocabulary and language to convey the concerns of the twentieth century. Mayakovsky, originally trained as a painter, also loved to act out his assault on philistinism: he traveled around Russia wearing a bright yellow blazer, sometimes with vegetables stuck in the buttonholes, declaiming his shocking and intentionally "ugly" poems.

Writers also collaborated with painters and actors and musicians; Wagnerian ideas stimulated Russians to find their own *Gesamtkunstwerken*. Two of Mayakovsky's Futurist colleagues, the poets Velimir Khlebnikov and Aleksei Kruchenykh, collaborated in 1913 with the Cubist painter Malevich and the violinist-critic-painter-composer Mikhail Matyushin in staging *Victory over the Sun*, a performance piece written in "trans-sense" language ("I eat dog/ And white feets/ Fried meat cake/ Croaked potato/ Space is limited/ Print to be silent/ Zheh Sheh Cheh") that describes the capture of the sun and a dark vision of the future. Scriabin was experimenting with synaesthesia and had abandoned key signatures in his search for a transcendental music. Wagner's operas were enjoying tremendous popularity, while Meyerhold was staging Strauss's *Elektra* at the Mariinsky.

Many aspects of this brilliant artistic ferment intrigued and influenced Prokofiev, who had a large cultural appetite and tended to respond quickly—if not always profoundly—to what was going on around him: he often reflected artistic trends like a mirror, without absorbing them. Never did he align himself with any one artistic movement—he could be called, at various times, a Symbolist, an Acmeist, a Futurist and a Realist. Symbolism affected him directly in his fondness for Balmont's poetry and in his choice of Bryusov's novel *The Fiery Angel* as the subject for an opera; Acmeism in his use of Akhmatova's poems and his work with the Acmeist poet Sergei Gorodetsky on the scenario for *Ala and Lolly*; and Futurism in his friendship with Mayakovsky and certain works written between 1917 and 1930 (the Second Symphony, the ballet *Le Pas d'acier*). Realism came later, in the 1930s.

Much of what was happening culturally in Russia in the years just before the Great War was, of course, also happening in Europe. A great deal of it—like Symbolism and Futurism—had come from there. Eager to see the sources for himself, Prokofiev made his long-awaited first trip to Europe in the summer of 1913. At the age of twenty-two, he would see the fragile Old World for the first and last time. A year later, when he would return to Europe for a second time, it would already be a threatened and uncertain civilization.

Maria Grigorevna and her son traveled to Europe together—to France, England and Switzerland. Leaving Petersburg on May 30, they went first to Paris, where they stayed for a week, living in a pension on the Boulevard Malesherbes. Prokofiev wrote to Miaskovsky: "Dear Kolechka, Today I arrived in Paris and am enjoying it greatly. Up until now I had always thought of it either as a dot on a geographic map of Europe, or as the city in whose middle stands the Eiffel Tower. As a matter of fact it is much more interesting." Prokofiev's long love affair with Paris, which would last for more than thirty years, had begun. "The liveliness of the French people, the tempo of their life and their general level of culture is fascinating," he wrote to his mentor Tcherepnin. "I'm glad that I've managed to come abroad, for it has widened my horizons in many ways." He visited Versailles and the Louvre, which he found "interesting, educational, but a little dry."

Being in Paris in June of 1913 also proved to be an important musical experience for Prokofiev: he saw Diaghilev's Ballets Russes for the first time. Already a fixture of Parisian cultural life, acclaimed and chic, the company was presenting yet another spectacular season— and for the first time in the grandiose setting of the Théâtre des Champs-Élysées. The most important event of the ambitious 1913 season was the sensational and scandalous premiere of the Stravinsky-Nijinsky *The Rite of Spring* on May 29 (New Style), when the bejeweled audience split into warring factions, simultaneously disgusted and excited by the "biological" music and choreography. "People shouted insults, howled and whistled, drowning the music. There was slapping and even punching." Prokofiev missed all that by only a few weeks, but he did see Stravinsky's *Petrushka*, Ravel's *Daphnis and Chloe*, the Schumann-Fokine *Carnaval* (orchestrated by Rimsky-Korsakov, Glazunov, Tcherepnin and Arensky), Rimsky-Korsakov's *Scheherazade* and Florent Schmitt's *Tragedy of Salome*.

Prokofiev's evaluation of what he had seen and heard reveals jealousy and a certain immaturity. Surprisingly, in a letter to Tcherepnin he mistakenly identifed the composer of *Daphnis and Chloe*— which "left me cold"—as Debussy (not Ravel), and complained that he found it difficult "to come to terms with the seeming abundance of water" in what he thought was Debussy's score. "As a rule, when Debussy illustrates poetic episodes they come out nicely, with poetic effectiveness, but in dealing with action or dramatic movement he is impotent and unimaginative." (Prokofiev met Debussy a few months later, in November, when he came to Petersburg at Koussevitsky's invitation.) He liked *Carnaval* better, although he criticized the production for its lack of fantasy in staging Schumann's "aromatic and evocative" musical scenes.

As for Stravinsky, Prokofiev could not—or did not want to— appreciate fully his talent and significance. "*Petrushka* is highly entertaining, lively, gay, witty and interesting," he wrote to Miaskovsky, never a great fan of Stravinsky's music.

> Using lots of movement and screeching, the music illustrates the smallest details of the action very well—just as the action on stage illustrates very successfully the smallest phrases in the orchestra. The instrumentation is marvelous, and, where it calls for it, extremely amusing. But now for the main thing: is there any music in the ballet or not? Yes and no. Unquestionably, not a single place in the ballet has really good music; a large part of it is modernistic *remplissage*. [Prokofiev uses this French word, meaning "filler," writing it in Cyrillic letters.] But where does he use *remplissage*? And when is *remplissage* permissible—if it is permissible at all? It seems to me that one can use it in the perfunctory or boring sections of an unsuccessful scenario.

But how about Stravinsky? Even at the most interesting moments, in the liveliest spots in the action, it is not music that he writes, but something brilliantly illustrating that moment. If this is not *remplissage*, then I don't know what is. And if he can't compose music for the most important spots, and merely fills them in with whatever comes along—then he is musically bankrupt. Stravinsky may be breaking through a new doorway, but he is breaking through it with the small, very sharp little knife of the quotidian—and not with the big axe which would earn him the status of a titan.

When Prokofiev was writing his autobiography years later, he apologized for his negative first impression of the "new music" written for the Ballets Russes, including Stravinsky's. "The material in these ballets was so 'different' that I simply didn't recognize it as material—something which also often happens, no doubt, among audiences hearing my music for the first time."

From Paris, Prokofiev went on to London, where he eagerly saw the sights, including Windsor Castle, but "suffered from not knowing the language"; he would learn English well only a few years later. When he returned to France, there was a new English tennis racket in his baggage. Maria Grigorevna had always liked mineral spas, so after a few more days in Paris they spent the next two weeks in the Auvergne, at the Grand Hôtel des Sources in Royat, where she took baths and drank the water. Annoyed to be so far from Paris, surrounded by aging invalids, Prokofiev channeled his frustration into work, spending at least four hours each day learning his Second Piano Concerto, which "has turned out to be incredibly difficult and mercilessly tiring." He was scheduled to perform it later in the summer in Pavlovsk. He was also writing out the piano score for the new concerto, going over proofs and "pouring out new opus numbers so they can be sent along to Jurgenson." Before returning to Russia in mid-July, full of new impressions and "exhausted after my back-breaking work," Prokofiev gathered "strength and repose in a pleasure trip through beautiful Helvetia [Switzerland]."

Due to a change in his concert schedule, Prokofiev found himself with a chunk of free time when he arrived back in Russia. Since he was determined to visit the Black Sea coast that summer, he abruptly left for Gurzuf, in the Crimea, only a few days after returning from abroad. On the way, he stopped in Moscow to confer with Derzhanovsky about future appearances, and to play him some of *Maddalena*. Derzhanovsky liked the opera well enough to hold out the possibility of a performance later in the year.

In Gurzuf, near the historic city of Sevastopol, he stayed for three weeks with the wealthy Meshchersky family. Meshchersky was an engineer and director of an important machine-building firm. Prokofiev had met the Meshcherskys and their artistic daughters—dabblers in Cubism and other fashionable avant-garde movements—several years earlier in Petersburg. He began pursuing Nina Meshchersky, his first real girlfriend, soon after they met. Accustomed to more stylish and cultivated friends, Nina at first found Prokofiev awkward, odd and affected. While other young men who visited their home wore uniforms of the most prestigious military and administrative institutions, Prokofiev appeared in striped gray trousers, with a handkerchief in his pocket and Guerlain cologne on his skin. Because of his eccentricities and foppishness, Nina and her girlfriends at first called him "The Martian." As time passed, however, Nina fell under the spell of his raw talent, self-assurance and persistence; soon she had developed a serious crush on the family friend.

As a guest in the lively Meshchersky household in Gurzuf in the summer of 1913, Prokofiev would join another house guest, the famous operatic tenor Ivan Ershov, in musical evenings. They were followed by luxurious feasts on the balcony. As always, Prokofiev worked: he practiced the new concerto for an hour a day and made a few corrections in *Maddalena*. But "very satisfied with my idleness," he also relaxed by swimming, hiking in the hills, racing in chariots pulled by fast Tartar horses, and playing tennis and billiards. "In a word," Nina Meshchersky later recalled, "it was a magical summer—flowers and cypresses, the moonlit path to the sea at night."

While Prokofiev was basking in the sunshine and flirting with Nina, Miaskovsky was stuck in rainy Petersburg, where he was spending his time taking care of tedious details involved with Prokofiev's upcoming appearance in Pavlovsk. Prokofiev, who avoided such things as much as possible, had persuaded his friend to check over the concerto's complicated orchestra parts and get them to the conductor. All his life, Prokofiev was able to enlist his friends and colleagues to take care of most of the busy work that came after a piece was written. He expected such help as his due.

Prokofiev's performance on August 23 at Pavlovsk is now part of Russian musical legend. Like Stravinsky's *Rite of Spring*, the fiery and ambitious Second Piano Concerto provoked strongly conflicting responses in the cultured audience gathered on the meticulously manicured lawns of Tsar Paul's English-style palace. It added to Prokofiev's reputation as the insolent creator of relentlessly "modern" music—a musical Mayakovsky. One writer for the *Petersburg Journal*, who signed himself "noncritic," left a description of the scandal.

> A youth with the face of a high school student appears on stage. This is Prokofiev. He sits down at the piano and starts either wiping off the keys or trying them out to see which ones produce a high or low sound. All this is done with a sharp, dry touch. The audience is uncertain. A few get upset. One couple rises and turns to the exit—"Music like that can drive you crazy!" Others leave their seats. The young artist concludes his concerto with a mercilessly dissonant combination of sounds from the brass. The scandal in the audience is now full-blown. The majority of them are hissing. Prokofiev bows impudently, and plays an encore. Exclamations resound all around: "The devil take all this Futurist music! We want to hear something pleasant! We can hear music like this from our cats at home." Another group—the progressive critics—are in ecstasy: "It's a work of genius!" "How innovative!" "What spirit and originality!"

One of the progressive critics was Karatygin, an intelligent and literate writer who had appreciated Prokofiev's talent when they were both involved with the Evenings of Contemporary Music five years earlier. Karatygin's review offered a serious musical analysis, pointing out the concerto's neoclassical features and linking them to Reger. As for the strong public reaction, Karatygin calmly predicted, "Ten years from now the audience will atone for yesterday's hissing with unanimous applause for the now famous composer with the European reputation." He was only four years off in his prediction: that scene would occur in 1927.

Listening to the Second Piano Concerto now, more than seventy years after its stormy premiere, it is difficult to understand why the piece provoked such strong reactions. But the Russian general musical public of 1913 was conservative and unadventurous—considerably more conservative than the European public at the time. True, there were many small avant-garde movements, but their impact was still limited. Then, too, Petersburg's cultural climate was even more conservative than Moscow's, and the Pavlovsk concerts (unlike the Evenings of Contemporary Music where the audience *expected* to hear something shocking and new) drew a particularly cautious public that wanted to enjoy unchallenging music in a pretty setting as they sipped champagne—rather like the summer music audiences at Tanglewood or Saratoga Springs.

More disturbing to Prokofiev than the public outrage at his new concerto was the resistance he encountered even among his senior colleagues. The respected conductor Alexander Ziloti returned the score of the concerto with this comment: "It will be very interesting to see what happens to you when you find yourself." Unfazed, Prokofiev retorted tartly in a note to Miaskovsky, "Can it really be that I jump so much from one extreme to the other in the Second Concerto that it's impossible to find my physiognomy? Or is the problem that his eyes are jumping from too much feasting on those empty-sounding French confections?"

Whatever Prokofiev's contemporaries thought about it, the Second Concerto clearly represented an important step forward in his musical development. Conceived on a large scale, and more than twice as long as the First Concerto, it was the most ambitious orchestral piece Prokofiev had written so far. Rambling and diverse in mood, it is much less unified than the First Concerto; it overflows with interesting ideas that threaten at any moment to crash through the boundaries of the form. The main theme of the first movement and the second theme of the fourth movement are both very "Russian" in mood—melancholy, lyrical and hollow. They are structured around the falling fourths found in Russian folk music and popularized in Rachmaninoff's piano concertos.

But the concerto is also bursting with music for the machine age, particularly in the second movement (*Vivace*), an infectiously optimistic episode of perpetual motion that moves with the relentless force and fluidity of a speeding locomotive. Later we hear clusters of dissonant chords massed in heavy orchestration, crashing awkwardly, pointing the way to "The Scythian Suite," *Seven, They Are Seven* and the Second Symphony. In the middle of the long and perversely difficult first-movement cadenza, Prokofiev placed this grandiose instruction: *Colossale*. As Karatygin noted, the concerto is fascinating precisely for the sharp contrast between the "nightmarishness" of the harmonies and the "enormous reserve of health, robustness and merriment which overflow from the music."

Today, the Second Concerto is performed infrequently, never having attained the popularity of the Third, or even of the First. This may be due to the extreme difficulty of the solo part, or to the concerto's fragmentary structure. Prokofiev believed that the First Concerto was more interesting for the orchestral ensemble, and the Second more interesting for the soloist. Later left behind in Prokofiev's apartment when he departed for America in 1918, the original orchestral score of the Second Concerto perished, apparently in a fire. Prokofiev wrote a new version in 1923 which became the standard performing edition.

After all the excitement of the summer, Prokofiev had to settle down to hard work—it was his final year at the Conservatory. His growing reputation as a composer and pianist and his controversial appearances outside the Conservatory did not greatly influence how Glazunov and Lyadov viewed Prokofiev; to them he was still a troublesome and boisterous character who rejected their aesthetic and wrote horribly dissonant music. It is hardly surprising, then, that his academic record in composition was mediocre. Prokofiev was fortunate, though, that Esipova, his piano instructor, was seriously ill during his last year at the Conservatory, leaving him to his own devices as he prepared for the final exams. She would die of cancer only a few months after he graduated. By now, Tcherepnin was his only active supporter among the Conservatory faculty.

To receive his diploma, Prokofiev had to prepare various conducting and piano performances. He conducted Beethoven's Seventh Symphony; excerpts from Verdi's *Aida*; Mozart's *The Marriage of Figaro* in a student production; and, at the graduation ceremonies, a piece by a fellow student. By the time he left the Conservatory in 1914, Prokofiev had become acquainted with a wide repertoire, even if he did not consider himself especially talented as a conductor. As a pianist, he gave three world premieres of his own music on January 23, 1914, in the small hall of the Moscow Conservatory—the Piano Sonata No. 2, several pieces ("Rigaudon," "Legend" and "Prelude") from the Op. 12 set, and the "Ballade" for Cello and Piano, performed by Evsei Belousov and Prokofiev. Once again, the critics were sharply divided in their opinions.

Prokofiev's student piano career ended at the St. Petersburg Conservatory, and with a brilliant flourish. He was determined to compensate for his unimpressive academic record by relying on his skill at the keyboard. Each year, the best students specializing in piano (those who had received an A + from all the judges in an obligatory competition) participated in a "battle of the pianos" at which they were expected to play a classical concerto. The winner—chosen by a jury—received the Anton Rubinstein Prize, a new Shreder piano, lots of publicity and the opportunity to play at the graduation ceremonies. Of the five students originally in the running, three played the Liszt Piano Concerto and one played the Saint-Saëns Concerto, but Prokofiev, as usual, decided to do something different. Taking advantage of Esipova's absence—for she would no doubt have insisted he play a classical piece—he decided to play his own First Concerto. His own concerto would show off his superior technique and clearly set him apart from the other contestants. He chose the First, and not the Second, since in the aftermath of the scandal at Pavlovsk the preceding summer, the Second "would have resounded too impudently within the Conservatory walls."

To further impress the judges, he had arranged with Jurgenson to provide published copies of the concerto. "When I came out on stage, I saw my scores spread out on twenty knees—an unforgettable spectacle for a composer who was just beginning to be published." Vladimir Drashnikov, a fellow student and future collaborator, accompanied him, playing the orchestral part in a piano arrangement. Prokofiev's most serious opponent was Nadezhda Golubovskaya, who would eventually become a professor of piano at the Leningrad Conservatory. After the contestants had performed, they played chess amicably as the jury debated. Following prolonged and stormy deliberations, the jury decided in Prokofiev's favor, infuriating Glazunov and the other older professors who had voted against this upstart troublemaker. Their votes were outweighed, however, by those of Esipova's former students, who felt they should stick up for one of their own, and by those of more progressively minded professors, like Tcherepnin.

Glazunov, Prokofiev's one-time mentor, was so disturbed by what had happened—the vote represented an embarrassing undermining of his authority—that he almost had to be pushed on stage to make the announcement. He made the award lethargically and unenthusiastically in a packed hall as the Prokofievites cheered and the anti-Prokofievites booed. A few weeks later, on May 11, at the official graduation ceremonies, Prokofiev performed the concerto again, with an orchestra conducted, appropriately, by Tcherepnin, without whose protection and encouragement he might not have been there.

Prokofiev's spectacular exit from the Conservatory exemplifies his love for the theatrical, the unexpected and the controversial. He left the institution where he had spent ten years—where he had learned his craft, honed his skills, made lifelong friends and offended his elders—very much on his own terms. He was still a bad boy, but a brilliant and assured one. Though he was grateful for the strong foundation he had built in his classes at the Conservatory, he could not forget the pettiness and pedantry of some of his instructors. He did not come to love the academic life through his experiences at the Conservatory, and would never become a teacher himself, despite numerous invitations.

By the spring of 1914, on the eve of war, the power of Prokofiev's genius, confidence and drive had grown and strengthened; it could no longer be checked by an outraged appeal to traditional standards of decorum and *bon ton*. Perhaps it was this final sweet victory over Glazunov—and others who disliked his style—that led Prokofiev to believe he was immune to official criticism. This attitude would prove dangerous later on, when he would encounter men much more ruthless and powerful than his gently melancholic professor.

CHAPTER 7

LET US BE

LIKE THE SUN

Le Roi-Soleil a dit: "L'état c'est moi." Vous, mon
cher Prokofiev, pourriez dire: "Le Soleil c'est moi."

—ARTHUR RUBINSTEIN

When Serbian patriots assassinated Archduke Francis Ferdinand, heir to the Hapsburg throne, on June 28, 1914, beginning the sad chain of events that would culminate in World War I, Prokofiev was alone in London. His mother had rewarded him for his successful completion of the Conservatory with a trip to Europe. The voyage would prove to be the start of his professional career as a composer and his collaboration with Diaghilev. He sailed to London by way of Stockholm, Copenhagen, Hamburg, Amsterdam and Flissinden, arriving in England on June 22 (New Style); the Ballets Russes was in the midst of its London season at Drury Lane, which included the ballets *Thamar, Daphnis and Chloe* and *Scheherazade.* His companions and guides in London were the Andreevs (Anna and Nikolai), St. Petersburg opera singers who often performed with Diaghilev's company.

Tcherepnin—"my benefactor and father"—had given Prokofiev some letters of recommendation to luminaries of the London musical world. One of these was Otto Kling, the representative in England for the publishing firm Breitkopf and Hartel, who provided a studio for Prokofiev to work in. There—every morning, despite the many distractions of a huge new metropolis—Prokofiev revised his Sinfonietta, which Ziloti had agreed to perform in one of his concerts the following season.

In the evenings, Prokofiev went to the ballet. If one year earlier he had been only a spectator at the Ballets Russes, this year—on the strength of his growing and appropriately controversial reputation in Russia—he suddenly became a potential participant. Nouvel, his friend from the Evenings of Contemporary Music, introduced Prokofiev to Diaghilev on July 3. Nearly twenty years older than Prokofiev (he was forty-two years old at the time of this first meeting), Diaghilev, impeccably groomed and impressively corpulent, presented a stark contrast to the fresh-faced youth from Sontsovka. Already, Diaghilev was one of the most influential forces in modern art, music and dance. One word from him could make or break a career. He was famous, successful and surrounded by the most creative people of his era. Wealthy patrons vied to support his projects.

One of these patrons was Misia Sert, who had become fascinated with Diaghilev after seeing his *Boris Godunov* in Paris in 1908. Ever since, she had been deeply involved in the running of the Ballets Russes, contributing extravagant sums from her husband's fortune to finance new productions. Sert, half-Polish and half-Belgian, also became one of Diaghilev's closest friends and advisers. She and Nouvel joined Diaghilev and Prokofiev for lunch on the day that this wild new composer was first introduced to the impresario. After lunch, Prokofiev entertained them with some selections from his recent compositions: *Maddalena*, the Second Piano Sonata and the Second Piano Concerto. *Maddalena* did not interest Diaghilev; it was melodramatic, old-fashioned and worst of all, opera, a form he and his disciples scorned. Similarly dismissed was Prokofiev's proposal for an opera based on Dostoevsky's short novel *The Gambler*.

For Diaghilev and his friends, the future lay in dance. Of all that they heard that afternoon, the powerful Second Piano Concerto intrigued them the most. Sert, not realizing that Prokofiev could understand French, exclaimed delightedly upon hearing its massively rugged and dissonant sound, "But he is some sort of *fauve!*" They discussed the possibility of staging it with choreography by Nijinsky. Such an unconventional approach confused the more literal Prokofiev, who still knew little of the dance world: to him, a concerto was a concerto, and not meant to serve as the background for "some sort of mimed scenes. It's just another new Diaghilev thing," he explained to his mother. But he was prepared, if necessary, to go ahead with it if he were the soloist—"it would make me an excellent career as a pianist." The possibility of staging dances to a suite of Prokofiev's piano pieces was also considered.

More attractive to all of them, however, and the variant they chose to pursue was a new ballet to be composed by Prokofiev, with choreography by Nijinsky. After a few meetings, they agreed upon a subject from Russian mythology and legend, to be written by the poet Sergei Gorodetsky with the composer, back in Petersburg. The piano score of what would later be called *Ala and Lolly* ("The Scythian Suite") would be ready by late November, and the full score by March. Even at the tender age of twenty-three, Prokofiev was not a romantic; he wanted to sign a contract and talk about money before making a commitment.

The impression Prokofiev made on Diaghilev and his associates was not entirely positive. His "insolence," arrogance, aggressiveness and untamed naivete both titillated and offended them. Prokofiev's abrupt and sometimes crude manners, his at times remarkable selfishness and his insensitivity toward other artists did not go unnoticed in this ultrasophisticated milieu and colored his relations with the Diaghilev circle forever after.

Being recognized by the impresario as a promising young artist also gave Prokofiev the opportunity to see many of the Ballets Russes performances. Tickets were virtually unavailable for the spectacular 1914 season, one that celebrated the end of an era—"the end of *la belle époque*, the end of *Art Nouveau*, the end of the *World of Art* movement, the end of empires." No doubt because the enormous possibilities that working for Diaghilev could bring were beginning to dawn upon him, Prokofiev's evaluations of what he saw and heard— in letters to Miaskovsky and Tcherepnin—are considerably more positive and measured than the cavalier criticisms tossed off a year earlier. Observing how the company worked also made Prokofiev realize that its six years of shared history had created definite insiders and outsiders. One of the insiders was Stravinsky, whose music Prokofiev had previously belittled. "Let it be said, by the way," he wrote to Miaskovsky in a rather chastened tone, "that foreign musicians are much more radical than ours. There are many among them who hail Stravinsky and who understand every detail of his music."

At Drury Lane, where seven Ballets Russes premieres were staged that summer, Prokofiev saw *The Firebird* for the first time and *Petrushka* for the second—he found both "very amusing and ingenious." London was also seeing the new Stravinsky offering of the season, *The Nightingale*, a delicate short opera based on the Hans Christian Andersen fairy tale and choreographed by Boris Romanov. *The London Daily News* called it a "triumph of staging," but Prokofiev was more concerned with the music, which he found full of "a lot of gratuitous intentional scratching that cheapens the moments when such scratching is really necessary. Its second deficiency (in comparison, for example, with *Petrushka*) is a pale sense of humor and less animation." Despite his reservations, however, Prokofiev must have loved the fairy-tale subject from Andersen—he may even have been influenced by Stravinsky's example when he turned to Andersen himself only a few months later, for "The Ugly Duckling."

Prokofiev and Stravinsky did not meet in London in the summer of 1914, for—ironically—Stravinsky was back in Russia at the family home in Oustilug, collecting material for *Les Noces*, his new ballet based on Russian peasant wedding ritual. It was Stravinsky's last trip to Russia for almost fifty years. Only a year later, the Austro-Hungarian army destroyed Oustilug, severing Stravinsky's physical connection to his homeland and confirming his status of expatriate.

Besides the Stravinsky productions, Prokofiev also saw a ballet version of Rimsky-Korsakov's opera *The Golden Cockerel* (the singers were in the pit, while dancers acted out the story in front of resplendent designs by Natalia Goncharova); *Midas*, a ballet with music by Rimsky-Korsakov's son-in-law Maximilian Steinberg and choreography by Fokine; *The Legend of Joseph*, by Richard Strauss and Fokine, which featured Leonid Massine, Diaghilev's new discovery and eventual lover, in his first major dancing role; and *Narcisse* by Tcherepnin and Fokine. Perhaps it was loyalty to his teacher that led Prokofiev to rate *Narcisse* above the others. As he left London in late July, encouraged by Diaghilev's parting comments, Prokofiev had good reason to believe that next year he would see his own ballet among those of Stravinsky, Tcherepnin and Ravel. In fact, however, he would have to wait seven frustrating years.

Prokofiev arrived back in Petersburg shortly before Germany declared war on Russia on August 1 (New Style). Mobilization claimed many of Prokofiev's friends, including Miaskovsky, who became a lieutenant and spent much of the war on the front lines. As the only son of a widow, Prokofiev was spared. He and his mother left the troubled capital—which lost its two-hundred-year-old Germanic name St. Petersburg and received the more patriotically Slavic title of Petrograd soon after the German declaration of war—for the more peaceful surroundings of the Caucasus. They spent more than a month there. Prokofiev stayed with the Meshcherskys, to whom he had written amusing letters from Europe, in Kislovodsk; his romance with Nina intensified. In the mornings he worked on the Sinfonietta; during the afternoons he and Nina took long walks. The piano lessons he had been giving Nina were discontinued, but they would occasionally sit down at the instrument together and he would ask her to play Mozart sonatas as he added an improvised accompaniment in the right hand. "It would come out marvelously—it was in an entirely new style. I think Mozart would have liked them," she wrote later.

The war seemed distant and unreal; only Miaskovsky's increasingly despairing letters, describing horrendous losses, disastrous retreats and spectacular disorganization in the Imperial Army, brought it closer. Prokofiev, along with most people of his class and education, did not grasp that the civilization in which he had grown up was on the verge of collapse, and joked to Miaskovsky about "finishing off the despicable descendants of Schubert." It was simply not in Prokofiev's nature to look at the world tragically. "All misfortunes are always followed by happiness, just as there is always sun after the rain," he wrote from Kislovodsk to Ekaterina Shmitgoff, whose mother had just died. "The advice I'm offering you might be immoral, but it is practical: the more light-heartedly you view the vicissitudes of fate, the easier it will be to survive them."

More important than the war to Prokofiev was getting to work on the ballet for Diaghilev. He had met with Gorodetsky in Petersburg, and they had worked out an initial plan for the scenario, but the poet was tardy in sending the finished product. Impatient, and unable to sit still for long, Prokofiev filled in the time by finishing his revision of the Sinfonietta for an upcoming Ziloti performance in Petrograd. Certain parts of the piece, particularly the *Intermezzo*, were almost completely rewritten from the original 1909 version. But even this project was upset by the war: the Hall of the Nobles, in which the Ziloti concerts were scheduled to take place, was turned into a hospital to house the growing number of soldiers wounded at the front. The premiere of the Sinfonietta occurred only one year later.

Back in Petrograd by late September, nearly broke and still waiting for Gorodetsky's scenario, Prokofiev began a small new piece, a setting for voice and piano of the Hans Christian Andersen fairy tale "The Ugly Duckling." The subject was suggested to him by Nina

Meshchersky, who also wrote the adaptation. "The main thing, of course, was to try to compose a text which would express the duckling's bitter loneliness. My text was ready in two weeks: I copied it over neatly and gave it to Prokofiev with the words, 'Here is my text—do with it what you will.'" Prokofiev also worked quickly: he completed his musical setting within two or three weeks and, "ecstatic" over what he had written, dedicated it to Nina.

The tale describes how a homely duckling, scorned by his barn-yard peers as ugly and clumsy, runs away to escape their ridicule. He spends a long and lonely winter in the wild, threatened by hunters and rejected by swamp ducks who warn him he could never hope to marry one of them. At last spring comes, and the ugly duckling notices he has grown wings. Flying to a lush garden, he sees three beautiful swans, and, even at the risk of their mockery, finds himself irresistibly drawn to the graceful creatures. He approaches, expecting abuse. But, glancing down at his reflection in the water, he joyfully realizes that he has become, like them, a beautiful swan. They welcome him with affectionate kisses. "How could he have dreamt of such happiness when he was an ugly duckling?"

Prokofiev's setting of this simple and bittersweet story is one of his most successful and spontaneously affecting illustrations of a literary text. About ten minutes in performance, "The Ugly Duckling" is "not just a song, but a large vocal fairy tale about twenty pages in length." The vocal line closely follows the intonation and imagery of the tale, in a style strongly reminiscent of Mussorgsky's narrative songs. There is no melody or any memorable tune, and the piano accompaniment is extremely restrained and transparent. The declamatory vocal line, never silent for more than three measures at a time, determines the musical direction. This emphasis on verbal intonation and texture points the way toward Prokofiev's early operatic style, particularly toward *The Gambler*, begun a year later. Brief, economical and fanciful, "The Ugly Duckling" is a piece that exploits Prokofiev's strengths as a composer—his instinctive understanding of the fairy-tale world, his special feeling for the absurd and ironic, his ability to translate and "visualize" the subtle thematic and dramatic changes in a verbal text into sharp musical images, his peculiar blending of the lyrical and the sarcastic.

But the wholeness, freshness and directness of "The Ugly Duckling" comes from another source as well—Prokofiev's identification (either conscious or subconscious) with the barnyard hero. Never known for being handsome, even at twenty-three Prokofiev was gangly and skinny, with narrow sloping shoulders and oversized arms that dangled at his side. His white-blond hair, large mouth and oversized lips had already earned him the nickname of "White Negro." While he dazzled his peers with his genius and piano virtuosity, he was socially awkward and very obviously "different."

Others also noted Prokofiev's emotional and physical resemblance to the homely protagonist of his new composition. Reviewing the first performance of "The Ugly Duckling," Boris Asafiev, who had known Prokofiev since Conservatory days, wrote (under his critical pseudonym Igor Glebov):

> The deficiency in "Ugly Duckling" is an unmotivated and undeveloped conclusion. It doesn't offer a psychological conclusion to all the mishaps; it doesn't resolve them in a single joyful stroke. Nor does it clearly outline the change in the ugly duckling's view of the world—for he has suddenly recognized himself as a swan. . . . For many people, Prokofiev is himself an ugly duckling. And who knows, perhaps that's why the ending of the tale is unsuccessful, because his transformation into a swan—the complete unfolding of his rich talent and self-knowledge—is still to come.

Prokofiev did not, however, consider "The Ugly Duckling" a confessional work, or even an especially important one—just something dashed off between projects. *Ala and Lolly*, the ballet for Diaghilev, was Prokofiev's first priority; no doubt he hoped it would make him rich and internationally famous. After several months, the "lazy" Gorodetsky finally produced a scenario, and Prokofiev started writing the music. Very aware of Stravinsky's head start with Diaghilev, he vowed to write something "intricate." Boris Romanov, also in Petrograd, worked with Prokofiev and Gorodetsky on the choreography.

Named after its hero and heroine, *Ala and Lolly* involved "the ninth century, idols, bulls in the sky and so on." Actually, Prokofiev was mistaken in telling Miaskovsky it took place in the ninth century; the setting was the nomadic Scythian Empire, which reached its height on the steppes of what is now southern Russia in 400 B.C. and then vanished mysteriously, leaving little behind but intricate objects of gold. Stravinsky's *Rite of Spring* and *The Firebird*, also set in the pagan Slavic past, were very much—even too much—in Prokofiev's mind when he was composing *Ala and Lolly*. Elements from both of Stravinsky's ballets turn up in Gorodetsky's story line, which also reflects the burgeoning interest in the "primitive" that was so important to visual artists of the time. Ala is the daughter of the sun god Veles; Lolly, a mortal hero, saves her from the enemy god (probably modeled on the evil Kashchei from *The Firebird*). As in Stravinsky's ballets, there are sacrifices, deliriously dancing monsters and a happy ending. Prokofiev worked quickly, for he had received a telegram from Diaghilev asking him to come to Rome—all expenses paid—with the completed piano score in a few months.

Many years later, in his autobiography, Prokofiev claimed that he had heard *Rite of Spring* in concert by then, although he didn't mention it in any letters at the time. He also admitted that he "didn't understand it," and that it was "entirely possible that I was searching for the same images in my own way" in *Ala and Lolly*. That Prokofiev's first ballet was a rather obvious imitation of Stravinsky did not escape Nurok and Nouvel, who heard the first sketches played by Prokofiev on the piano in late autumn in Petrograd. They were sufficiently doubtful about what he was composing that they conveyed their concern to Diaghilev, who insisted that Prokofiev come to Rome for consultations. But he continued to write the music quickly: by mid-January he had completed three-quarters of the score and had begun orchestrating it.

Prokofiev was eager to see more of Europe, and flattered that Diaghilev was willing to pay his way. The only difficult part about leaving Petrograd—which was becoming increasingly isolated as the War dragged on—was his concern for Nina Meshchersky. They had been meeting quietly for months. Impatient as always, Prokofiev now presented her with a virtual ultimatum: tell your parents about us, marry me and come with me to Italy. Nina, aware that her wealthy and snobbish parents considered the bohemian Prokofiev an inappropriate and unpromising husband, hesitated. When she finally announced his proposal, they responded with indignation, particularly since Prokofiev wanted her to leave for Italy within a few weeks. Unintimidated, Prokofiev had a bitter confrontation with Nina's father, who refused to give up his daughter to an "artist" with an uncertain financial future. After this argument, Prokofiev stopped coming to their house.

Nina was so distraught that she even attempted to elope with Prokofiev, but, like Natasha Rostova in *War and Peace*, was discovered and restrained by a family servant. Scandalized, Nina's mother took her away to Ekaterinoslav, and Prokofiev left for Europe alone. Nina and Prokofiev saw each other again only many years later, in Paris.

Characteristically, Prokofiev left no record of his romance with Nina Meshchersky, but he was never one to carry a torch. He liked to break things off abruptly and finally.

The War made it necessary to travel to Italy the long way around—via Rumania, Bulgaria and Greece. In Rome, Diaghilev welcomed Prokofiev with the style and manners for which he was famous. A gracious and accommodating host, the impresario showed him around Rome, Milan, Naples, Palermo, Sorrento and Pompeii, introducing him to Italian writers—including the Futurist Marinetti—and artists. The brash but naive young man from Petrograd was plainly dazzled. Reporters wanted to ask him questions and take his picture, and there were "dinners and lunches with various marquises, *Herzogs* and other important people." He was so impressed with all the fuss that he did not even argue when Diaghilev told him that *Ala and Lolly* was unsatisfactory. Such obsequiousness was not at all in Prokofiev's nature, but the glamor, power and resources of the Diaghilev organization were much more grand and intimidating than anything he had encountered. Here was a man who knew what he was doing. "The ballet needs major changes, to which I have agreed," he wrote to his mother on March 10 (New Style).

Ever the encouraging agent and diplomat, Diaghilev was gentle with Prokofiev, whom he later called "my second son." (Stravinsky was his "first son.") Diaghilev hid the intensity of his distaste for *Ala and Lolly* from the composer, but in a letter to Stravinsky, he expressed doubt over Prokofiev's musical future and potential. Dismissing the Gorodetsky scenario as a "Petersburg trifle appropriate for the Mariinsky Theater ten years ago, but inappropriate for us," Diaghilev observed:

Prokofiev says he is not looking for Russian effects—it's just music in general. It certainly is music in general, and very bad music at that. Since we must now start absolutely everything all over again from scratch, we should show him some kindness and keep him around with us for two or three months. I'm counting on your help. He is gifted, but what can you expect of him if the most cultured man he associates with is Tcherepnin, who impresses him with his *avant-gardism*? He is very easily influenced, and more appealing than it seemed after his first insolent appearance on the scene. I'll bring him to see you. He must change totally. Otherwise we will lose him forever.

Despite Diaghilev's fear that Stravinsky and Prokofiev would not get along because Prokofiev had so rudely criticized *Petrushka* a few years earlier, Stravinsky did spend time with Prokofiev in Italy that winter. A planned trip to Stravinsky's home in Switzerland did not take place, however. By now, Prokofiev had seen for himself how wildly successful Stravinsky's music was with European audiences, and how much Diaghilev had done to make Stravinsky's career. He wanted it, too. Eager to please his generous new patron, he deferred to the impresario's "first son," and even joined with Stravinsky in a four-hand piano performance of *Petrushka*, the piece he had ridiculed as devoid of music only eighteen months earlier. By the end of his Italian trip, Prokofiev felt that he and Stravinsky had become "very good friends—both in our shared composing sympathies and just because." This judgment proved premature.

To soothe Prokofiev's ego over the failure of *Ala and Lolly*, Diaghilev arranged a piano appearance for him—his first performance abroad—in a large hall in Rome on March 7 (New Style). He played his Second Piano Concerto and several solo pieces, including an étude from Op. 2 and three pieces from Op. 12. The audience was small but enthusiastic, and, just as in Pavlovsk, split into vocal factions, cheering and booing. The critical response was mixed, and included an observation not found in Russian reviews—that the concerto was neither modern nor traditional, that it "wandered between the old and the new." To find himself accused of being insufficiently modern was a new and disarming experience for Prokofiev: the provincial Russian critics, less familiar with the latest trends in European music, complained that he was years ahead of his time.

Still confident that Prokofiev had a future as a ballet composer, Diaghilev proposed that he discard *Ala and Lolly* and begin another. Prokofiev agreed and happily signed a generous contract for three thousand rubles. This time Diaghilev sat down himself with Prokofiev to work out a scenario, based on Russian folk tales from the famous collection edited by the ethnographer Alexander Afanasiev (1826–1871). They chose a series of tales about a buffoon, arranged in six scenes. The stories were colorful, violent and crude, intended to poke fun at human gullibility and venality. Complicated but graphic, the action of the ballet describes how a clever buffoon and his wife devise a scheme to outsmart seven other buffoons by selling them a magic whip that supposedly brings the dead back to life.

This absurd and nasty fairy tale was much more suited to Prokofiev's temperament and talents than the vaguely primitive narrative of *Ala and Lolly*. He always adored fairy tales, particularly satirical ones in which silly or ignorant people are outsmarted and made to look ridiculous. Moreover, this one was filled with opportunities for specific "physical" musical illustration. As Prokofiev was preparing to return to Russia, Diaghilev gave him this advice: "Write Russian music. You've all forgotten how to compose in Russian in that rotting Petersburg of yours." (In general, as Prokofiev later told Miaskovsky, the members of the Ballets Russes "abuse Petrograd with all their strength.") Diaghilev also chastised Prokofiev for his eclectic and unselective taste. "In art, you have to be able to hate—otherwise your own music will lose its personality."

The return trip to Petrograd was long and uncomfortable. The boat was crowded with many other Russians and Poles making the roundabout overland passage through Salonika and Bucharest, but Prokofiev joked about the hardships in a letter to Diaghilev. Meanwhile, the Russian army was rapidly running out of arms and ammunition, and commanders sent soldiers to the front unarmed, telling them to scavenge among the dead for weapons.

Prokofiev's obvious infatuation with Diaghilev and his troupe did not please the dour Miaskovsky, who was slogging through mud at the front and had little time or energy for music. Perhaps he was jealous of Prokofiev's new "friendship" with Stravinsky, and he was "not at all pleased" that Prokofiev had become "enamored of balletomania." As far as Miaskovsky was concerned, ballet music was a frivolous and inferior "applied art." Neither did Miaskovsky think that his own music would interest Diaghilev (he was probably right), and he rejected the idea of sending it to him as Prokofiev suggested. If "pathos, inspiration and internationalism" were, as Diaghilev declared, out of style, then Miaskovsky saw no point in showing his music—based on those principles—to the impresario. This was the first, but not the last, time that the differences in Russian and European taste would be pointed out to Prokofiev. But forgetting Diaghilev's warning about the need to be selective, he continued to compose simultaneously for both audiences.

The Buffoon, as the new ballet for Diaghilev came to be called, took most of Prokofiev's time in the spring of 1915. Originally, it was to have been completed in piano score by August 1915, and in full score by March 1916, for a production in Paris in May 1916. Prokofiev was intending to travel to Italy in late spring of 1915 for further consultation with Diaghilev and Stravinsky; they continued to send him affectionate telegrams in expectation of his arrival. In a letter to Stravinsky written on June 3, however, Prokofiev explained that he was "extremely sad" that he had to delay his trip until the end of June due to problems connected with his military status. In the end, he did not go abroad at all. Indeed, he did not leave Russia again for three more years—until May 1918—and *The Buffoon* was produced only in May 1921, more than six years after it was first conceived in Rome.

Prokofiev's decision to stay in Russia in 1915 was a turning point. It cut him off from Diaghilev, with whom he was just beginning to develop a working relationship, and from European musical life. It also delayed his premiere as a ballet composer. By the time Prokofiev saw Diaghilev again, the Ballets Russes had survived the War and Revolution, and undergone a fundamental change in staff and orientation; Stravinsky was more firmly established than ever as the principal composer and musical adviser; and Diaghilev was in the twilight of his career. With so much at stake, why did Prokofiev remain in Petrograd?

In his brief 1941 autobiography, Prokofiev explained:

> Diaghilev and I had agreed that I would go again to Italy so that we could work out the ballet with the choreographer. But at that time the passage through the Balkans closed, and it was terrible to travel through the North Sea [as Diaghilev advised him in one of his telegrams] because of the mines. But the main thing was that musical life in Petrograd exercised more of an appeal over me than the glittering perspectives abroad with which Diaghilev was trying to lure me—so I sent off the ballet manuscript with Sergei Grigoriev [Diaghilev's man Friday], who was going to see him in Rome.

There was surely more to the decision than these quasi-patriotic considerations. On May 7 (New Style), the *Lusitania* had been sunk, making travel significantly more dangerous. Prokofiev's mother—she had not been happy over his two recent European trips—must have been beside herself at the thought that he would go away at such a moment, when it was entirely possible that he would be unable to return for a long time, or even be killed. For him, too, the prospect of being stranded in Europe, where he still had few real contacts, and of abandoning his friends and sponsors in Russia, was full of uncertainty. Ziloti and Derzhanovsky were setting up concert dates; he had no similar European commitments. Characteristically, Prokofiev opted for security, and, in a letter to Miaskovsky on May 29, he explained without elaborating: "I am for the moment putting off my second voyage abroad for a number of reasons."

Numerous other members of Diaghilev's company faced a similar choice. By the summer of 1915, the Ballets Russes was reforming in Ouchy on Lake Geneva: Stravinsky, Massine, Natalia Goncharova, Mikhail Larionov and Bakst were there. The following year, they would make their first American tour.

Prokofiev did fulfill the terms of his contract with Diaghilev, although he sent him the six scenes of *The Buffoon* in piano score several months later than they had first agreed. After receiving the score in America, Diaghilev sent him fifteen hundred rubles. Nothing was done with *The Buffoon*, however, until 1920, when Prokofiev substantially revised it before its belated Paris premiere in May 1921. This 1920 version, published in 1922 by Gutheil, is the standard performing edition.

There were several reasons why *The Buffoon* did not make it to the stage in its original version in 1916. The company was homeless and in a difficult financial situation because of the War and could not afford to mount many new productions, the personnel was shifting due to the War and changes within the troupe, and Prokofiev was not present to work out the problems in the score. Diaghilev always preferred to have his composers on the spot in order to develop a project to its fullest potential.

Perhaps to distract himself from his second misfortune with a ballet score in six months, Prokofiev threw himself into other projects. Loathe to waste the rejected *Ala and Lolly*, he reconstructed it as the four-part "Scythian Suite," an orchestral work approximately seventeen minutes in length. The four sections follow the same general story line and in the same order as the ballet: "The Adoration of Veles and Ala," "Chuzhbog and the Dance of the Evil Spirits," "Night" and "The Procession of Lolly and the Funeral March of the Sun." In this, his first large orchestral piece (without piano soloist) since 1910, Prokofiev strove above all for interesting and unusual instrumental effects, influenced by Stravinsky's ballet scores. "The Scythian Suite" is scored for a big orchestra, heavy with percussion (two sets of cymbals, plus timpani, bass drum, triangle, tam-tam, tambourine and snare drum, chimes and xylophone), celesta, two harps, piano and enlarged brass sections. Accordingly, the orchestral sound is enormous, and harshly metallic.

"The Scythian Suite" sounds quite different from anything Prokofiev composed before it; only a few moments in the Second Piano Concerto obviously prefigure it. True, it is full of the harsh and bristling dissonances already familiar from the solo piano music, but in a more dense and overloaded texture piled heavily on top of booming, insistent rhythmic patterns and fiercely aggressive *ostinati*. (The rhythmic patterns are more square and less fluid, however, than the revolutionary polyrhythms of *The Rite of Spring*.) While strongly tonal, the suite plays ostentatiously with juxtapositions of incompatible keys. The impression it leaves is one of brute force, not grace; there is little of Prokofiev's typical humor, except perhaps in the heavy grotesquerie of "Chuzhbog and the Dance of the Evil Spirits."

The use of strange combinations and configurations of instrumental groups was one of Prokofiev's primary concerns in "The Scythian Suite." The result sounds like the product of a young composer who has just discovered the fascinating possibilities of the noises each instrument can make, and cannot resist showing off his knowledge. Where the orchestration of Rimsky-Korsakov and Stravinsky shimmers and glows, Prokofiev's lurches and heaves. Inevitably, critics compared the suite to Stravinsky's music. Karatygin, a loyal Prokofiev supporter, wrote that while Stravinsky was a "genuine master" as an orchestrator, Prokofiev was still only an "apprentice."

In fact, what Diaghilev seems to have disliked about the music that ended up as "The Scythian Suite" was that it was too imitative of Stravinsky, too crude and too self-conscious. He clearly did not think of it as a revolutionary work, at least not when compared to the music of Stravinsky or Ravel. The more conservative Petrograd audience that heard the premiere of "The Scythian Suite" on January 16, 1916, however, in a Ziloti concert conducted by Prokofiev found it disturbingly modern. Their response was a milder version of the scandal that had occurred at the first performance of its prototype, *The Rite of Spring*. "At the end, an incredible din resounded in the hall, similar to what happened after the first performance of the Second Concerto in Pavlovsk, except this time all of musical Petrograd was present." One of those most offended by "The Scythian Suite" was Glazunov, who made a great show of leaving the concert hall eight measures before the end.

Even the musicians were upset: the timpanist broke through the skin on his timpani, and the cellist complained to Prokofiev that he agreed to play only because he had a wife and three children to support. Interestingly, on this occasion, Ziloti, who had previously opposed Prokofiev's music, supported him, and even appeared amused by all the shouting. Because the suite presented unusual problems for the orchestra, Ziloti had even agreed to the unprecedented and generous number of nine rehearsals.

As usual, the conservative critics reviled Prokofiev as a musical hooligan, while Karatygin wrote an intelligent and laudatory review. He saw it as representing a new "impressionistic" line in Prokofiev's music, different from the neoclassicism of the piano works and linked to "modernist" music by composers like Stravinsky, Strauss and Schoenberg. What Prokofiev was using in "The Scythian Suite," wrote Karatygin, was a kind of "heterophony"—placing distinct and separate voices against a background without bringing the voices together in counterpoint. Miaskovsky was also present, and heaped praises upon the suite, declaring it "sumptuous, significant, vivid" and "one of your best compositions."

By now, the fiercely contradictory reviews and public reaction did not upset Prokofiev—he rather enjoyed them and profited by the publicity. In Russia, at least, "The Scythian Suite" served to perpetuate the legend of Prokofiev the idol-smasher, Futurist and *enfant terrible*. With the death of Scriabin in early 1915 and Stravinsky's move to Europe, Prokofiev had assumed the mantle of the most avant-garde Russian composer, even though by European standards he was considered almost conventional.

Akin to "The Scythian Suite" in their "search for a new harmonic language and for the means to express strong emotions" are the "Sarcasmes" (Op. 17), five piano pieces composed between 1912 and 1914. By turns reflective and sharply unsentimental, they are dotted with remarks like *tempestoso*, *ironico* and *precipitosissimo*. The fifth of the "Sarcasmes"—which jumps at the start between 2/4 and 3/8 meter, insolently contrasts tonalities between the right and left hands, and seethes with tritones, seconds, ninths and all manner of odd chromatic alterations—has a program that describes the entire cycle: "Sometimes we laugh maliciously at someone or something, but when we look closer, we see how pathetic and unfortunate is the object of our laughter. Then we become uncomfortable and the laughter rings in our ears— laughing now at us." Prokofiev believed that this last piece, and the darkly phantasmagoric one (*Smanioso*) that preceded it, were the most successful.

Predictably, Nurok and Nouvel loved all of them, for they reflected the same obvious striving for novelty and freshness that they had first discovered in Prokofiev's early piano pieces, and for which they had looked in vain in his ballet scores. Prokofiev performed the "Sarcasmes" for the first time on November 27, 1916, in Petrograd; as usual, they provoked widely differing responses. Jurgenson apparently liked them, for he paid Prokofiev five hundred rubles—one hundred for each piece—to publish the cycle.

It was difficult for Prokofiev to work on only one thing at a time; his concentration was enormous, but his attention span was short. He was happiest when he could spend a few hours of intense work on a project, and then switch to something else. In the summer of 1915, for example, he put "The Scythian Suite" together, rewrote "Autumn," worked on *The Buffoon*, polished the "Sarcasmes," started thinking about the opera *The Gambler*, and composed a new cycle of five songs.

His longest song cycle to date, the Op. 23 songs (he called them "Five Poems," not "Five Songs") are settings of poems by five different writers: "Under the Roof," by Valentin Goryansky; "The Gray Dress," by Zinaida Gippius; "Trust Me," by Boris Verin; "The Wizard," by Nikolai Agnitsev; and "In My Garden," by Konstantin Balmont. The choice of texts is eclectic and undiscriminating, and the poems—with the exception of the first two, both dealing with poor children and death—do not share a common central theme or image. Gippius and Balmont were famous poets of recognized quality who both belonged to the Decadent wing of Russian Symbolism; Goryansky and Agnitsev were popular satirical poets who contributed to the journal *The New Satyricon*; Verin was an embarrassingly sentimental dilettante.

The first two songs, "Under the Roof" and "The Gray Dress," resonate with a social awareness not found in any of Prokofiev's previous music. Their gloomy mood is surprisingly alien to the carefree Diaghilev aesthetic with which he had recently been so infatuated. Perhaps the depressing wartime atmosphere, and the increasingly insistent anti-Tsarist revolutionary socialist rhetoric flying around Petrograd, were partly responsible. Both songs are composed in a recitative-declamatory style strongly influenced by the Dargomyzhsky-Mussorgsky tradition (also characterized by social consciousness, usually expressed in satirical terms) that had already appeared in "The Ugly Duckling." The last three songs all concern love, and use more lyrical and romantically conventional imagery. Harmonically, however, they are not conventional: "In My Garden," for example, ends ambiguously, gently mixing the tonalities of A Minor and G flat Major.

If Prokofiev regretted not having gone to Europe to join Diaghilev, he had little time to think about it during the busy summer and fall of 1915. Besides maintaining a feverish pace of composition and revision, he was also performing, having finally broken through the prejudice most concert organizers had previously held against him. For the most part, however, they were more interested in programming old works (including the softly romantic "Dreams," uncharacteristic of Prokofiev's evolving dissonant style) rather than new ones. He also continued to perform his piano concertos and sonatas, and conducted the premiere of his revised Sinfonietta at a Ziloti concert in late October. His performing activity for the season came to a dramatic climax with his appearance as conductor for the riotous premiere of "The Scythian Suite" on January 16.

Prokofiev continued to meet the important artistic figures of his day. In late May he participated in an "evening" sponsored by the Moscow Art Theater, held at the Lawyers' Club. After Prokofiev played his Second Piano Sonata and some small pieces, Stanislavsky read some scenes from Griboedov's classical play, *Woe from Wit*; another actress read poems by the Symbolist poet Valery Bryusov, who was to be the source for the libretto of Prokofiev's opera *The Fiery Angel*; Chekhov's widow, the actress Olga Knipper, gave a reading; the legendary actor Ivan Moskvin read a Chekhov story; and Karatygin accompanied the singer Vasilenko in a Debussy song.

Recognition had not softened Prokofiev's straightforward manners and brutal frankness, however. He made little attempt to cultivate or flatter musical stars. At a concert in the fall of 1915 devoted to the memory of Scriabin, Rachmaninoff, with whom Prokofiev had recently become acquainted, played Scriabin's Fifth Piano Sonata. "When Scriabin played this sonata, it all floated upwards somewhere, but when Rachmaninoff played it, all the notes remained distinctly clear and resolutely earthbound," Prokofiev observed. The fanatic Scriabinites in the audience loudly expressed their displeasure with the flat interpretation, so Prokofiev thought he was paying the sensitive Rachmaninoff a compliment when he went backstage and told him, " 'You know, Sergei Vasilevich, you did play very well after all.' Rachmaninoff smiled crookedly. 'And did you think, perhaps, that I would play badly?' He turned away to someone else. With this, our good relations ended, although Rachmaninoff's rejection of my music and the irritation that it caused in him no doubt also played a significant role." Some years later, in America and Europe, Rachmaninoff and Prokofiev would develop a relationship of mutual respect, if not friendship.

Meanwhile, the War was bogging down in Europe. The influence of the mad monk Rasputin on Tsar Nicolas II had isolated him even from his loyal advisers and strikes were endemic, but Prokofiev seemed not to share the public mood of restlessness. Music was his life, and his fame was growing with every performance.

He was also full of new projects. The idea of writing an opera based on Dostoevsky's short novel *The Gambler* had never left his mind despite Diaghilev's dire predictions, so, with no other big projects in the works, and encouraged by the ballet-hater Miaskovsky, he set to it. But *The Gambler*, Prokofiev's first complete libretto and first completed full-length opera, was, like *Ala and Lolly* and *The Buffoon*, not fated to travel an easy road to the stage. The reasons were both musical and political.

Aware that Dostoevsky (1821–1881) had been strangely overlooked by both Russian and European composers, Prokofiev and Miaskovsky had since their Conservatory days talked of writing operas based on works by the great Russian urban realist *cum* philosopher. As late as early 1916, Miaskovsky was still considering writing an opera on Dostoevsky's novel *The Idiot*, although he never started the project. In choosing *The Gambler* for his opera, Prokofiev—who adapted the novel into a libretto himself—turned to a work in many ways uncharacteristic of the author. *"The Gambler* is the least Dostoevskian of all Dostoevsky's stories," he said later. Dostoevsky wrote this book in less than a month in late 1866, in the midst of finishing the first of his great works, *Crime and Punishment*. *The Idiot, The Possessed* and *The Brothers Karamazov* would follow over the next thirteen years.

What is "un-Dostoevskian" about *The Gambler* is chiefly its small size. Less than two hundred pages long, it also contains more dramatic action and less philosophical-religious argumentation than the more celebrated novels. Exterior description predominates over interior, and Dostoevsky provides little description of the thought processes and feelings of the main characters. "The subject of the story is as follows: a certain type of Russian abroad," Dostoevsky wrote in a letter in 1863. Aleksei Ivanovich, the first-person narrator and protagonist, "reassures himself with the thought that there is nothing for him to do in Russia and, consequently, there is bitter criticism of those in Russia who challenge our Russians living abroad to come back home. But the main thing is that all his vital juices, forces, impetuosity, daring have gone into roulette. He is a gambler and not a mere gambler . . . this story will without fail attract attention as a firsthand and most detailed portrayal of roulette gambling." Dostoevsky's own obsessive gambling had brought him to this theme; he spent much of the summer of 1863 at the tables in Baden-Baden, where he "lost his last penny." In the novel and opera, Baden-Baden becomes the fictional gambling spa of Roulettenberg.

Dostoevsky's prose is what first attracted Prokofiev to *The Gambler*. Much of the novel is written in dialogue, which could be left intact in the libretto. Retaining Dostoevsky's own words became, in fact, Prokofiev's main goal—even his obsession—in writing the scenario and music. "The orchestration will be transparent, so that each word will be audible—especially desirable in view of the incomparable Dostoevsky text. I feel that the convention of writing operas on rhymed texts is a completely absurd convention. In this case, Dostoevsky's prose is clearer, more incisive and more convincing than any verse." In fact, however, Prokofiev's "Scythian" style orchestration, heavy, brassy and full of brilliant pictorial effects—like the spinning of the roulette wheel created by the woodwinds and xylophone—frequently upstaged the text and plot in the opera's original version. "Encouraged by the interest provoked by the 'Scythian Suite,' I chose the most radical style possible for *The Gambler*. . . . One day my mother came into the room where I was composing and cried out in desperation: 'Do you have any idea what you are knocking out on that piano of yours?' We argued for two days."

Russian operatic precedents for a "literary" approach to opera existed in Dargomyzhsky (*The Stone Guest*) and, most important, in Mussorgsky. In his one-act experimental operatic setting of Nikolai Gogol's play *Marriage*, composed in 1868, just before he began work on *Boris Godunov*, Mussorgsky was fascinated with rendering the exact intonations of Gogol's idiosyncratic Russian, catching, in a sort of semi-melodic recitative, subtle nuances of character and speech. He completely rejected traditional set pieces—arias, duets, ensembles—and sought a kind of continuous musical conversation that was a musical enbodiment (not just illustration) of Gogol's unchanged text. Prokofiev knew of *Marriage* before he wrote *The Gambler*, and may even have heard it performed at the Evenings of Contemporary Music in 1909. Both "The Ugly Duckling" and the Op. 23 songs had already shown a strong Mussorgskian influence in their treatment of a literary text; *The Gambler* took this idea much further.

Prokofiev's excitement about this new project led him to work even faster than usual: the piano score (for four acts in six scenes) was completed in only five and one-half months, between November 1915 and April 1916, and the orchestral score by late January 1917. During the summer of 1916, when he was orchestrating *The Gambler,* he wrote ten pages in full score each day, and sometimes as many as eighteen. Both he and his mother were evidently proud of his facility. Another reason that he worked so quickly was that the British conductor Albert Coates, then gradually taking over from the aging Edward Napravnik as principal conductor at the Mariinsky, was interested in revitalizing the conservative house; he thought that Prokofiev's avant-garde *Gambler* sounded intriguing, and promised Prokofiev a full-scale production as soon as the opera was completed.

All this sounded much easier than it turned out to be. Anticipating that the conservative members of the Mariinsky repertory committee— including the ubiquitous Glazunov and Cesar Cui, then eighty-one years old—would object to *The Gambler*'s dissonant, driving style (not to mention its psychotic subject), Coates waited until the regular committee session had ended to tell Telyakovsky, director of the Imperial Theaters, about Prokofiev's new opera. Another committee, composed of younger musicians and Ziloti, was assembled to evaluate it. Despite Telyakovsky's opposition, they approved it for production in the following 1916–17 season, and rehearsals with the singers began in October. But soon the cast members were claiming that Prokofiev's music was too difficult to sing; it certainly was radically different from the diet of Tchaikovsky, Rimsky-Korsakov, Glinka and Verdi to which they were accustomed.

Prokofiev's new opera found one influential defender at the Mariinsky—Vsevolod Meyerhold, one of the theatre's principal directors. During the preceding years, he had been earning a reputation for his controversial (and, to traditionalists, shocking) avant-garde Mariinsky productions of such operas as *Tristan and Isolde,* Strauss's *Elektra* and Gluck's *Orpheus and Eurydice.* Meyerhold heard *The Gambler* in an informal run-through at Coates's apartment in October 1916, where he met Prokofiev apparently for the first time; the director's response was unreservedly enthusiastic. Here was a composer who could put his new ideas about dramatically viable opera into immediate practice! Because he was so busy, however, Meyerhold entrusted *The Gambler* to another director, Nikolai Bogoliubov. The first orchestral rehearsal took place on January 28, 1917—although the singers were still complaining about the opera's strangeness and difficulty. There is no documentation of exactly what happened next, but *The Gambler* did not make it to the stage, most likely due to the chaos in all areas of cultural life that followed the first ("February") Russian Revolution that occurred less than one month later. Even Prokofiev's supporter Ziloti, who had replaced Telyakovsky at the Mariinsky, was unable to push the project through. By May, after a planned concert version failed to materialize, the Mariinsky omitted *The Gambler* from its repertory plans. There had also been talk of a possible production of the Bolshoi Theater in Moscow, but this, too, did not progress beyond the discussion phase.

Even though their first attempt at collaboration proved unsuccessful, Prokofiev and Meyerhold had laid the foundation for a long and important artistic relationship—one that would last for the next twenty-two years.

Composing *The Gambler* and arranging for its production took all of Prokofiev's energy in the spring of 1916. He was uncharacteristically stationary, remaining in Petrograd until summer and making no important appearances. One of his pastimes was gymnastics. He was a popular member of a gymnastics and social club called "Sokol" ("The Falcon"); occasionally the members put on theatrical programs in which Prokofiev participated, and, according to Nina Meshchersky, he once wrote a little march to be used as background for their calisthenics.

No one seems to have replaced Nina in his affections. The only evidence of a romantic attachment during this period comes from playful letters to Tatyana Ruzskaya, the daughter of the cellist Nikolai Ruzsky, but she was in Kiev and they did not see each other regularly. His notes to her sparkle with ostentatious wit and verbal play—archaic Slavonic vocabulary, ironically formal diction and polite French expressions rendered incongruously in the Cyrillic alphabet.

After spending June at a friend's home in the countryside near Petrograd, Prokofiev took a cruise down the Volga in July, on his way to the Caucasus. From Samara he wrote to Stravinsky. "Dear Igor Fyodorovich, In view of the distance and the difficulties in communication, it seems that corresponding with you is a rather hopeless undertaking. But in any case, I wanted to greet you from the Mother

Volga, where there is such quiet, such calm, such sweet repose." It was the last summer the Romanovs would rule Russia.

Autumn of 1916 was also the last Prokofiev would spend in Petrograd. Many years would go by before he would again see the birches turn gold in the Summer Gardens, or ice cover the Neva. Ironically, as the country hurtled toward revolution, Prokofiev's career was booming. His music was being performed more than ever before. He conducted the revised "Autumn" and "The Scythian Suite" in Petrograd, and made his first appearance in Kiev, playing the First Piano Concerto under the direction of his former tutor Glière, who had been appointed head of the Conservatory there. Curious about Prokofiev's evolution as a composer, Glière asked him which theory he believed in. "None at all," Prokofiev replied without hesitation.

In the audience in Kiev was a boy who would later, in America and France, become one of Prokofiev's close friends and a fellow composer: Vladimir Dukelsky. (In America he is better known under his Broadway-musical name, Vernon Duke.) Prokofiev's performance made a great impression on the future author of "Autumn in New York."

> He had white-blond hair, a small head with a large mouth and very thick lips . . . and very long, awkwardly dangling arms, terminating in a bruiser's powerful hands. Prokofiev wore dazzlingly elegant tails, a beautifully cut waistcoat, and flashing black pumps. The strangely gauche manner in which he traversed the stage was no indication of what was to follow; after sitting down and adjusting the piano stool with an abrupt jerk, Prokofiev let go with an unrelenting muscular exhibition of a completely novel kind of piano playing. . . . This young man's music and his performance of it reminded me of the onrushing forwards in my one unfortunate soccer experience; there was no sentiment, no sweetness there—nothing but unrelenting energy and athletic joy of living . . . there was frenetic applause and no less than six flower horseshoes were handed to Prokofiev, who was now greeted with astonished laughter. He bowed clumsily, dropping his head almost to his knees and recovering with a yank.

But the most famous of Prokofiev's concerts in the fall of 1916 was one that did not take place. Koussevitsky had scheduled a performance of "The Scythian Suite" in Moscow for December 12, but shortly before the concert, a number of his musicians were called up for military duty. The performance was canceled and another piece substituted. Even so, a review of "The Scythian Suite"—attacking it as barbaric and mechanical—appeared in a newspaper the following day. It was written by Leonid Sabaneev, an "educated musician and mediocre composer" who despised Prokofiev's music and used every possible opportunity to attack it. He had not attended the concert and had written a disparaging review of "The Scythian Suite" without even hearing the piece or seeing the score. The incident damaged Sabaneev's reputation, made Prokofiev's critics look ridiculous and provided more publicity for the suite—much to Prokofiev's delight. He wrote an open letter exposing Sabaneev's act that was published in two newspapers.

Even with all the performances and rehearsing, Prokofiev found time in November to compose what is perhaps his most successful song cycle—the "Five Poems of Anna Akhmatova" for voice and piano, Op. 27. In contrast to the sharp and satirical *Gambler*, they are soft and romantic: "After them, many people believed for the first time that I could also write lyrical music." They were written very quickly, in only five or six days. No doubt they provided a welcome relief from the enormous task of orchestrating the opera.

What is so attractive about the Akhmatova songs is how sensitively the vocal-piano settings illustrate and illuminate the fragile beauty of the poems. It does not appear that Prokofiev knew Akhmatova (1889–1966), one of the most gifted of the Acmeist poets. They were, however, almost the same age (she was two years older), and both lived in Petrograd. It is possible that her poetry was first brought to Prokofiev's attention by Sergei Gorodetsky, another Acmeist poet, who had written the scenario for *Ala and Lolly* a few years earlier. But more important than personal contact with Akhmatova was aesthetic contact. The tenets of Acmeism—clarity, brevity, restraint, transparency, rejection of clichés of imagery and language overused by the Symbolists and their imitators, a return to small and personal themes—to a certain extent reflected Prokofiev's own beliefs. Like Akhmatova, Prokofiev reacted against the overblown sentimentality and density of late Romanticism and Symbolism.

The Akhmatova poems that Prokofiev set to music were written at different times between 1910 and 1913, but they share a common image: the sun. Both the first and third songs are explicitly concerned with sunlight ("The Sun Filled the Room," and "Memory of the Sun"), while the others ("True Tenderness," "Greeting" and "The Gray-Eyed King") deal with the idea of light versus darkness, day and night, autumn and winter. Prokofiev may have borrowed his obsession with the sun from the Futurists, who often connected the sun with their idea of the coming Utopia, or from Konstantin Balmont, who had called one of his most famous collections of poetry *Let Us Be Like the Sun.* Or Prokofiev's fascination with the sun may simply have been a reflection of his own natural optimism and energy. Beginning in 1916, he maintained an album called "What do you think about the sun?," in which he requested his friends and acquaintances to write relevant comments. It was there that the pianist Arthur Rubinstein contributed his apt observation: *"Vous, mon cher Prokofiev, pourriez dire: 'Le Soleil c'est moi.' "*

The poems Prokofiev chose for the Akhmatova cycle are brief, and speak as much through silence, omission and ellipsis—like so many of Akhmatova's poems—as they do through words. The moods shift suddenly and subtly, like sunlight hiding and then reappearing among November clouds. The piano accompaniment is understated and wonderfully transparent, almost haiku-like. In order to react harmonically to the rapid changes in mood, Prokofiev does not use key signatures but writes in the many flats and sharps for the highly chromatic settings. Tonal centers shift constantly, and whole tone scales are used, giving the songs an open, hollow quality. The phrasing follows Akhmatova's lines almost exactly and the melodic line is through-composed, following the natural curves and intonations of the text after the example of Dargomyzhsky and Mussorgsky. Natural accentual and metrical patterns, which change frequently within each poem, are invariably and carefully maintained. The Akhmatova songs show the same scrupulous attention to the literary text as do *The Gambler* and "The Ugly Duckling," but they also possess a special warmth, roundness and emotional penetration that is unusual for Prokofiev. It is easy to understand why they are the most frequently performed of all his songs.

When they were performed for the first time by Zinadia Artemyeva, accompanied by the composer, on February 5, 1917, in Moscow, both Rachmaninoff and Medtner were in the audience. Also present was the critic Yury Engel, who commented on the unusual mixture of the old and new in Prokofiev's harmonic style that was to intrigue many subsequent listeners. "It is impossible to explain Prokofiev's harmony in terms of some concept of the new, or the refinement of the old—it is neither of these. Instead, the composer seems to be saying: 'This is the way I want it!' . . . Words like 'morbid' or 'fragile,' words so often applied to contemporary art, cannot be used to describe

Prokofiev. He is some sort of untamed and robust fellow, a mustang grazing in the meadow."

As 1917 began, Prokofiev had good reason to be optimistic. He and his music were being received with enthusiasm all over Russia. *The Gambler* was in rehearsal at the Mariinsky. He had found a congenial and lucrative new publishing arrangement with Koussevitsky at Gutheil. He was full of new projects. Prokofiev must have known, however, that the political and economic situation was rapidly deteriorating, that the Romanov monarchy was in a dangerously vulnerable position and, if only from Miaskovsky's depressed letters, that the War was going very badly for Russia—the number of Russian soldiers dead, wounded and taken prisoner were climbing into the millions. No doubt he was aware that unrest in the streets and factories was growing—it was impossible not to see the constant strikes and street demonstrations. The newspapers and the intellectuals talked in apocalyptic language, and even the Tsar's closest allies were worried. But preoccupied with his music, Prokofiev did not pay much attention to what was going on around him.

His growing fame was also bringing him into contact with other extraordinary people in the capital. At an exhibition of paintings at the chic Dobychina Gallery on the Field of Mars on February 13, 1917, he participated in a remarkable literary-musical evening. During the first part of the program, Maxim Gorky, not yet the father of Socialist Realism but already renowned for his plays, novels and stories, read from his autobiography *Childhood.* Just before intermission, violinist Jascha Heifetz made his last appearance before leaving Russia, playing a Chopin nocturne in B Major, and the Paganini Étude No. 24 as arranged by Leopold Auer. The entire second half of the program was devoted to Prokofiev and his music, including "The Ugly Duckling" and "Sarcasmes."

"The Ugly Duckling" was heard again in Petrograd only nine days later, in a chamber concert sponsored by the Russian Musical Society. The next day—February 23, 1917—rioting and demonstrations in the city intensified. Shortages of bread and coal were becoming unbearable. Soldiers returning from the front told tales of massive incompetence and official irresponsibility. Rasputin had been murdered a few months before, and the royal family was desperate and disoriented. On February 27, the Duma (the Russian Parliament) ignored the Tsar's warnings and established a provisional government. The Tsarist regime was by now so unpopular and so isolated even from its former political allies that Nicolas II had little choice but to abdicate. On March 2 he named his brother, Mikhail, as Tsar, and Mikhail in turn gave up his power to the Provisional Government. It had taken only a week to end more than three hundred years of Romanov rule.

CHAPTER 8

FUGITIVE VISIONS

Come, brothers, let us praise the twilight of freedom—
The great twilight year.
The heavy forest of snares has been
Lowered into the boiling nocturnal waters.
You are arising in dead years,
O sun, o judge, o people.

—OSIP MANDELSHTAM

"Both I and the circles in which I moved welcomed the February Revolution with joy," writes Prokofiev in his short autobiography. In 1941, when the autobiography was written, such statements were, however, an obligatory and empty convention for all Soviet recollections of the revolutionary era. In Prokofiev's case, it is particularly difficult to take these joyful sentiments at face value. He had never shown much interest in politics or ideology. His parents had always feared political change of any kind, and his mother's family was closely connected to the Tsar, both socially and professionally. Maria Grigorevna, who still exerted enormous influence over her son, was now a sixty-two-year-old widow; she was certainly not at a point in her life to feel enthusiastic about a social upheaval. Prokofiev, too, associated for the most part with the children of wealthy merchants, who were not anxious to see a radical transformation of the economic and social environment.

But had they been forced to choose, Prokofiev and his mother would certainly have preferred the Provisional Government, a bourgeois middle-class parliamentary democracy led for the most part by wealthy liberals, over the radical and anticapitalist Bolshevik regime which succeeded it after the second ("October") revolution only eight months later. The Provisional Government, led by the moderate socialist Alexander Kerensky, hoped Russia could develop a European-style system with complete civil liberties. Maria Grigorevna and her husband possessed a similar faith in the Western democratic tradition and passed it on to their son. Russia had no historical or social tradition on which to base such a system, however, and the loosely organized Kerensky government—overwhelmed by enormous economic and social problems and insisting upon continuing the extremely unpopular Russian war effort—was doomed almost from the start.

As he had during the Revolution of 1905, Prokofiev tried as much as possible to ignore the disturbing political events of 1917. Many artists of the younger generation were enthusiastic about the February Revolution. Its promises of greater social and artistic freedoms created a romantically dynamic atmosphere of change and optimism. Prokofiev shared this general and superficial enthusiasm. He did not, however, take any active political part in the revolutionary events of 1917; in fact, he avoided them, spending more than half of the time between the February Revolution and his eventual departure from Russia in May 1918 far away from Petrograd, the center of revolutionary activity. He probably knew little about Lenin and his small group of fanatically devoted followers; nor did Prokofiev identify himself with the Russian proletariat or peasantry who were at the center of Lenin's ideology. When, on October 25, 1917, Lenin and the Bolsheviks seized the Winter Palace, ousted the Provisional Government, declared Russia the world's first socialist state, and ended the short "October" Revolution, Prokofiev was far away in the Caucasus.

Strangely enough, 1917 was one of the most productive years in all of Prokofiev's career. It was during these earth-shaking months that he composed several of his most enduring compositions: the First Symphony ("Classical"), the First Violin Concerto, "Visions fugitives" for piano, the Sonatas Nos. 3 and 4 for piano, and the cantata *Seven, They Are Seven*. None of these works—with the possible exception of *Seven, They Are Seven* and a few of the "Visions fugitives"—reflects the political and social turmoil through which Russia was passing at the time. In fact, the symphony, the concerto and the sonatas are "pure" music in the strongest sense. Even as the world in which he grew up was collapsing all around him, Prokofiev took serene refuge in his craft.

In his autobiography, Prokofiev claims he wrote the nineteenth

(*Presto agitatissimo e molto accentuato*) of the twenty small pieces that make up the "Visions fugitives" at least in part as a musical response to the February Revolution. One of the shortest in the cycle, it lasts only thirty seconds. Nervous energy, frantic forward motion, athletic leaps, an insistently rising and raggedly chromatic line of eighth notes, a rumbling *fortissimo* climax in the low bass—these are the features which express Prokofiev's reaction to the political turbulence. Later, Prokofiev found it necessary to apologize for such a small and indirect response: "It was more a reflection of the crowd's excitement than of the inner essence of revolution."

The remaining nineteen "Visions fugitives" are similarly short, cryptic and atmospheric; the entire cycle lasts about twenty minutes. The pieces were written at different times between 1915 and 1917, but Prokofiev did not arrange them in simple chronological order, and none has a specific program. "Visions fugitives" is a French translation for the Russian title "Mimoletnosti," meaning fleeting and transient impressions or ideas; the root of the Russian word is "fly." The title comes from a poem, "I Do Not Know Wisdom," by Balmont, whom he met around this time:

> In every fugitive vision
> I see whole worlds:
> They change endlessly,
> Flashing in playful rainbow colors.

A sense of rapid, impressionistic change is what the evocative miniatures in this cycle convey; the mood is reminiscent of Debussy. There are several ironic, playful pieces—like the *Ridicolosamente* and the *Feroce*—but the overall spirit is reflective, not grotesque, more introspective than mocking. Prokofiev's usual fondness for velocity is also moderated here: of the twenty "Visions," nearly half have slow tempo markings, and even the faster ones are gentle—*Allegretto tranquillo, Con eleganza*. Harmonic development is more important to these haunting snapshots than the quirky rhythms that had predominated in much of Prokofiev's earlier piano music.

Not only the unusually "soft" "Visions fugitives" suggest that Prokofiev was in a reflective mood in the spring of 1917. After finishing the cycle and sketches for a new violin concerto, he wrote Miaskovsky that he had "fallen into a depression" and was spending his time looking at the stars through a telescope he had recently purchased. "I'm become very infatuated with this pastime." Several weeks later, he left on a steamboat trip along the Volga and Kama rivers, thousands of miles east of Moscow, traveling far from the mouth of the Kama—which flows into the Volga—into distant tributaries near the Ural Mountains. "The Kama is wild, virginally pure and incredibly beautiful here, with its red hilly shore covered with dark Siberian pine forest. I'm orchestrating my violin concerto and am planning to finish my symphony."

Both the "Classical" Symphony and the First Violin Concerto seem to reflect the virginal purity and clarity of the Siberian landscape. Simple in structure, harmony and rhythm, as well as witty, charming and remarkably "natural," they are two of Prokofiev's most successful works. Here, Prokofiev does not strive for effects and shock value as in "The Scythian Suite" or the Second Piano Concerto. This is seemingly effortless and remarkably direct music, transparent and light, and free of any sort of literary, visual or ideological baggage.

Of these two "neoclassical" works, the violin concerto was completed first. Its limpid and romantic main theme, announced at the very outset by the soloist against tremolo in the violas, had been written two years earlier, but other projects prevented Prokofiev from working on what he originally envisioned as a violin concertino. The concertino eventually grew into a full-scale, although small (about twenty minutes in length) three-movement concerto. Straightforwardly classical in form and harmony, and warmly lyrical in mood, the concerto exploits the singing quality of the violin, and boasts several of Prokofiev's most memorable melodies. In contrast to the first two piano concertos, it is ingratiating and restrained, but, like them, never descends into sentimentality or conventional rhetoric. The second movement *Scherzo* (*Vivacissimo*) is unmistakably "modern" and mischievous in its precipitous runs, wide intervals and insistent *spiccato*.

Prokofiev's first symphony, which he eventually called the "Classical," has much in common with the violin concerto, but is more ironic and joking. Interestingly, the best-known of his seven symphonies and one of the most frequently performed and recorded symphonies composed in the twentieth century was also the first significant composition that he wrote without using a piano.

Up to that time, I had usually composed at the piano, but I had noticed that thematic material composed without the piano was often better in quality. When transferred to the piano, it sounds strange for a moment, but after a few repetitions it seems that this is exactly the way it should have been written. I was intrigued with the idea of writing an entire symphonic piece without the piano. A composition written this way would probably have more transparent orchestral colors.

So this was how the project of writing a symphony in the style of Haydn came about—Haydn's technique had become particularly clear to me after working with Tcherepnin and it seemed it would be easier to dive into the deep waters of writing without the piano if I worked in a familiar setting. If Haydn had lived to our era, I thought, he would have retained his compositional style but would also have absorbed something from what was new. That's the kind of symphony I wanted to compose: a symphony in the classical style. Then, when it started to come together, I renamed it as the "Classical" Symphony. I called it that for several reasons: first of all, because it was easier that way; secondly, out of naughtiness and a desire to "tease the geese," secretly hoping that in the end I would have my way if the title "Classical" stuck.

Only fifteen minutes long, the "Classical" is the shortest of all of Prokofiev's symphonies. Like the First Violin Concerto, it is in the bright key of D Major. It is scored for a small (Mozartian) orchestra in four movements: *Allegro, Larghetto,* a tiny *Gavotta,* and *Molto vivace.* The *Gavotta,* a charmingly clumsy dance with grotesquely comic grace notes in the bassoon part and ungainly octave jumps in the melody, was written first, followed in 1916 by the first and second movements. Last came the fourth movement, which Prokofiev composed while "walking through the fields" in a small town outside Petrograd where he lived during June and July of 1917. Prokofiev devised a game for himself while finishing the last movement: eliminating all minor chords.

The "Classical" Symphony is the first of Prokofiev's compositions to show his fondness for the eighteenth century; it reappears in *Love for Three Oranges, Lt. Kizhe, Cinderella, Betrothal in a Monastery* and *War and Peace.* Classical symmetry, emotional restraint and courtly manners were more appealing to him (at least initially) than the more literal and overblown aesthetic of the nineteenth century. In the summer of 1917, perhaps, Haydn's harmonious eighteenth century also provided Prokofiev a welcome escape from ugly political realities.

According to his autobiography, Prokofiev spent the first part of the summer outside Petrograd "completely alone," reading Kant when he wasn't composing. Such intellectual concentration and isolation were hardly typical for him, however; it is tempting to see his mention of heavy German philosophy (Kant was very important in the formation of Russian Communist ideology) as an attempt to prove his seriousness at such a serious time. Philosophy had never interested him very much. In fact his old friend Morolev once said of Prokofiev, "You begin to talk with him about literature, and he shifts the conversation to music."

At some point during the summer, Prokofiev also met an American visiting Petrograd on business—Cyrus McCormick, the farm machinery magnate, who was a member of an official American delegation that had come to observe and encourage the newly formed democratic government in Russia. (The United States quickly recognized the Provisional Government, but withheld official recognition of the Bolshevik government until 1933.) Impressed with Prokofiev and his music, McCormick, interested in developments in new music, paid for a copy to be made of the still-unpublished "Scythian Suite." He also promised to help the composer if he ever decided to come to America. "Just send me a telegram." McCormick might have been surprised to know how soon Prokofiev would accept his offer.

In late July, Prokofiev traveled south to the Caucasus. He started work on a new cantata, *Seven, They Are Seven,* and performed his First Piano Concerto in a concert in Kislovodsk. He was back in Petrograd in September, but not for long. By now, Lenin's supporters had gained a majority in the Petrograd Soviet of Workers' and Soldiers' Deputies, and the future for the shaky Provisional Government appeared more uncertain than ever. News from the front warned of an impending attack on the city itself. Maria Grigorevna must have been frightened to return to the chaos of the capital for she decided to remain in the Caucasus, where she had spent the summer. Perhaps feeling it would be difficult to work in the city, Prokofiev returned south to join her. He was planning to come back north by early November, for he was scheduled to give piano recitals on November 9 in Moscow and on November 15 and 19 in Petrograd. Ziloti had also expressed interest in giving the premiere of the new violin concerto. On October 27, two days after the Bolsheviks had seized the Winter Palace, he wrote Miaskovsky that he was planning to leave Kislovodsk in a week.

But before he set off, hysterical and garbled reports of the overthrow of the Provisional Government began to reach the Caucasus. "A train arrived with its windows smashed; terrified passengers—members of the bourgeoisie—got off," he wrote years later in his official autobiography. Prokofiev asked them if it was possible to travel to Moscow and Petrograd.

"You've gone crazy!" they told me. "They're shooting people in Moscow and Petrograd. You won't get there at all." It seemed to me that even if it were possible to get there, no one would be very interested in concerts. Shortly afterwards, the front commanded by Kaledin [an anti-Bolshevik leader] formed near Rostov and cut off all news from Petrograd. I sat in Kislovodsk and wrote the orchestral score for *Seven, They Are Seven.*

Kislovodsk was peaceful, but surrounded by fighting. For the moment, there was little else for Prokofiev to do but sit and compose. Both *Seven, They Are Seven* and the Fourth Piano Sonata were written during these months of enforced isolation.

The Fourth Sonata formed a pair with the Third, which had been composed the preceding spring; both sonatas bear the subtitle "From Old Notebooks." The notebooks were from Prokofiev's Conservatory days; the mature Sonata No. 3 (Op. 28) is a reworking of the childhood Sonata No. 3, and the mature Sonata No. 4 (Op. 29) a reworking of the childhood Sonata No. 4. Despite their similar sources, however, the sonatas are quite different. The Third is brief—in one movement—and closely followed the childhood version, while the Fourth is more substantial—in three movements—and radically reworked its earlier source. Both sonatas show the composer in a reflective and less exhibitionistic mood; the Fourth is an impressionistic and surprisingly shapeless composition that recalls Schumann. Prokofiev played the new sonatas for the first time in two recitals in Petrograd, given only three weeks before he left for America in the spring of 1918.

If the two piano sonatas were compositions of "pure" music unrelated to the turbulent times, the cantata *Seven, They Are Seven,* which took most of Prokofiev's time in Kislovodsk, was a self-conscious attempt to write "something big and cosmic" reflecting the events of 1917. Prokofiev later claimed in his autobiography that what was happening in the country had permeated his subconscious and "demanded expression"; the result is one of his most bizarre and misguided compositions. Nor does it indicate that he comprehended what was going on around him.

The prevailing fashion for the "Primitive"—first embodied musically in Stravinsky's *Rite of Spring* and copied in "The Scythian Suite"—led Prokofiev to choose Konstantin Balmont's poetic reworking of Chaldean cuneiform writings as his text for *Seven, They Are Seven.* These writings had been recently uncovered by the German archaeologist Hugo Winckler on the walls of a Chaldean temple. Balmont used them as the basis for several poems; the one Prokofiev chose was called "Chaldean Incantation, Reading No. 2," addressed to the spirit of the earth to ward off the evil spirits (the "Seven, They Are Seven"). Apparently Prokofiev felt that the text's primitive imagery and rhythmic insistence reflected the elemental revolutionary forces being unleashed in Russia in 1917. "The fact that the ideas and feelings of that era had survived so many centuries stimulated my imagination."

Since it is an incantation, Balmont's poem is full of repetition, onomatopoeia and alliteration—devices for which he, like Poe, had a self-indulgent fondness in any case. In the original Russian, the word "Semero" (literally, "group of seven") is repeated over and over:

> *Semero ikh!*
> *Semero ikh!*
> *V glubine Okeana semero ikh!*
> *V vysotakh nebesnykh semero ikh!*

> Seven, they are seven!
> Seven, they are seven!
> In the ocean depths they are seven!
> In the heavens above they are seven!

Prokofiev chose to emphasize the incantatory quality of the text in his musical setting, which uses impressive forces: tenor soloist (*Tenore dramatico*), mixed chorus which divides into as many as eight different parts, and a huge orchestra with extra brass (four trumpets, eight horns, three tenor trombones, one bass trombone, tuba and contratuba) and percussion (two timpani, two bass drums, cymbals, tambourine, snare drum, tam-tam, chimes, xylophone, celesta and two harps). The part for the tenor soloist is not melodic but declamatory; he proclaims the text, with many repeated pitches, gradually rising— primarily by dissonant tritone jumps—far up in the tenor range. In almost every feature—its self-consciously "modern" idiom, the enormous size of the orchestra, the overblown proportions—*Seven, They Are Seven* represents a stark contrast to the understated "Classical" Symphony and the First Violin Concerto. It combines Prokofiev's infatuation with a huge, brassy and percussive orchestral sound—already obvious in "The Scythian Suite"—with his scrupulous attention to a text—as in "The Ugly Duckling" and *The Gambler*. Strangely enough, though, the piece lacks spontaneity and directness; it sounds overburdened, self-conscious and bombastic.

Seven, They Are Seven also requires huge performing forces, unavailable in Russia in 1917–18. So, Prokofiev's response to the Revolution would be performed for the first time only in 1924, in resolutely bourgeois Paris. The cantata's fate in Russia was further complicated because Balmont left the Soviet Union in 1920, and aligned himself soon after with the "White" Russian émigrés who despised and criticized the Soviet regime. Consequently, his poetry—and musical settings using it—remained for many years in official disfavor. Even today, *Seven, They Are Seven* remains one of Prokofiev's least-known works.

Provincial life, even in sunny Kislovodsk, was beginning to bore Prokofiev. He was eager to get back to Petrograd and Moscow—or to go somewhere else where he could compose in peace. "I did not have a clear understanding of the scope and significance of the October Revolution," Prokofiev apologized with hindsight in his short autobiography. "That I—like any other citizen—might be of use to it still had not occurred to me." In a letter to Derzhanovsky, written in early December, Prokofiev asked him, with remarkable obtuseness, to "drop me a few lines about Moscow musical life."

Only in March 1918, after the Kaledin front had collapsed, was Prokofiev finally able to leave Kislovodsk for Moscow and Petrograd. In that same month, Lenin moved the capital from Petrograd to Moscow, since it was farther from the front lines and easier to defend, and signed the ruinous Treaties of Brest-Litovsk with Germany, thereby giving up twenty-six percent of Russia's population and twenty-seven percent of her arable land.

As he set off from the Caucasus, Prokofiev was already thinking about trying his luck in America. His meeting with McCormick the preceding summer was only one of the factors that had led him to consider this alternative. It was becoming increasingly obvious to all Russian artists that it would be very difficult to work seriously in their country in the foreseeable future. Prokofiev, like many others, began to consider where he might go, at least until the situation improved. By now, traveling to Europe was dangerous because of the War, while he could travel to America across peaceful (for the moment) Siberia. Diaghilev and his company had recently been on tour in America so that he could probably count on some introductions and connections there through them. And of course everyone was saying that there was more money and more opportunity in the New World, which remained untouched by the ravages of combat that had leveled so much of Europe.

Still somewhat uncertain as to his ultimate destination, Prokofiev left his mother, who had devoted her entire life to his career and welfare, behind in the Caucasus, where she would stay until leaving Russia herself several years later. He convinced her—and himself—that he was going away for "only a few months."

To travel anywhere in Russia in 1918 was hazardous. The railroads were the main target in the vicious civil war that had begun between the Reds (supporters of Lenin and the Bolsheviks) and the Whites (assorted opponents of the Bolsheviks, including democrats and aristocrats). For protection, Prokofiev had obtained a certification from the Kislovodsk Soviet. It took eight days to get to Moscow, but there was no serious fighting along the way. Prokofiev spent several days in Moscow, taking care of passport and financial matters. Koussevitsky, who remained in Moscow for several years after the Revolution, paid Prokofiev an "advance" of six thousand rubles toward the publication of "The Scythian Suite," *The Gambler* and *The Buffoon*. The amount was not as large as it sounds: due to the unstable political and economic situation, the ruble had declined in value with such disastrous speed that it was almost worthless.

Despite the uncertainty and hardships, Moscow in early 1918 was an exciting place. History was being rewritten there. For many, particularly during these first heady months, the new socialist government represented the start of a wonderful new era of infinite possibilities, and the end of the oppressive and conservative old Russia. The Futurists, who had hoped for precisely such a radical transformation, were particularly enthusiastic. Vladimir Mayakovsky was ecstatic, declaiming his poetry for large and rowdy audiences, designing posters and reveling in the downfall of bourgeois culture. He called himself the "drummer of the Revolution." Mayakovsky had "made a great impression" on Prokofiev at a public reading in 1917 in Petrograd; it was then that the composer (already accused of "Mayakovskyism" in his music) and the poet had met for the first time.

During March 1918, Prokofiev got to know Mayakovsky better. They met several times in Moscow and performed for each other. Another Futurist poet, Kamensky, later described an evening at the Poets' Cafe—a Futurist cabaret—at which Prokofiev played some piano pieces: "Red and flickering, like a flame, he rushed out on to the stage, grasped our hands enthusiastically, announced that he was a devout Futurist and sat down at the piano." He played "Suggestion diabolique," which so pleased the audience that they demanded more. "It seemed that the cafe was on fire, and that the rafters and door frames—in flame, like the composer's hair—were crashing to the ground, and we stood, ready to be burned alive in the fire of this unprecedented music."

As a symbol of his respect for Prokofiev's art, Mayakovsky gave him a copy of his poem "The War and the World" with a signed inscription: "To the representative on the planet earth of the Department of Music, from the representative on the planet earth of the Department of Poetry. To Prokofiev from Mayakovsky." Mayakovsky also wrote some lines from his poem "The Cloud in Trousers" into Prokofiev's "sun" album and, according to Kamensky, drew a pencil sketch of Prokofiev. Underneath it he wrote: "Here is Sergei Sergeevich playing on Vladimir Vladimirovich's most tender nerves." The next time Prokofiev and Mayakovsky would see each other would be in Europe.

From Moscow, Prokofiev went on to Petrograd, which was still in the grip of revolutionary fervor. He spent only about a month there, but gave four world premieres: playing the Piano Sonatas Nos. 3 and 4 and the "Visions fugitives," and conducting the "Classical" Symphony. The symphony was performed by the former Court Orchestra, the same ensemble that had performed his student symphony ten years earlier, in a hall that only a year earlier still housed the Imperial Choir. In the midst of the creation of a new government and society, Prokofiev's delicate and whimsical First Symphony went almost unnoticed.

One of those in attendance for the premiere of the "Classical" Symphony was Anatoly Lunacharsky (1875–1933), newly appointed Soviet Minister of Culture. By now, Prokofiev had made up his mind to go to America, and wanted Lunacharsky's blessing. Maxim Gorky and Diaghilev's associate Alexander Bénois had agreed to introduce Prokofiev to Lunacharsky, a man of considerable refinement and intellectual discrimination. When Prokofiev told Lunacharsky of his intention to leave for the United States, he replied, "You are a revolutionary in music, as we are in life. We should work together. But if you want to go to America, I will not stand in your way." Prokofiev soon after received the necessary foreign passport and documentation "that I was traveling on artistic business and for reasons of my health." The decision had been made; as a result, he later confessed, "I had completely lost out on the opportunity to participate in the building of Soviet society." By the time Prokofiev would return to Russia in 1927, by then a husband and father, the country of his youth would be a very different place.

Prokofiev did not take much with him, for he continued to believe he would be returning soon. Some manuscripts had been left for safe-keeping with Koussevitsky in Moscow; others remained in his mother's Petrograd apartment, where they would perish from cold and neglect during the desperate years of the civil war. "The Scythian Suite," the "Classical" Symphony, the First Violin Concerto and a few piano pieces were Prokofiev's only companions on his voyage to the New World.

PART TWO

CHAPTER 9

AMERICA

Serge Prokofiev is very startling.

—*The New York Times*,
November 1918

It was a long way, in the difficult spring of 1918, from Petrograd to New York. By the time Prokofiev returned to the graceful city of his musical apprenticeship, nearly nine years would have passed, and it would bear yet another name: Leningrad. Its pastel palaces would be subdivided into apartments and administrative offices, its streets decorated with socialist slogans. The fashionable shops that lined Nevsky Prospect would be gone. Such sobering visions of the future were, however, far from Prokofiev's mind when, full of optimism and a sense of adventure, he boarded a train on May 7. Bound across Siberia, through Japan to California, he thought he would return to Russia after seeing a little more of the world beyond, and after the turmoil of the Revolution had died down. The War dragged on in Europe, but without the participation of Russian troops.

Like so many other Russians of his upbringing and education, Prokofiev at first failed to realize how completely the way of life in what had been the world's largest and most conservative empire would be changed by the world's first socialist revolution. Within a few months, Tsar Nicolas II and his family would be murdered in a cellar in the Urals. Along with them, an entire social and economic class would simply disappear. By nature uninterested in politics, Prokofiev failed to grasp the scope of the social and cultural transformation that was to come. Years later, he remembered the prophetic warning of an unidentified "wise man": "You're running away from great events, and the great events won't forgive you for it. When you return, you won't be understood."

As the "few months" of Prokofiev's time abroad turned into years, the news seeping out of Russia would become only more gloomy. Civil war between the Bolsheviks and their desperate opponents would ravage the countryside, dividing families and communities. Hundreds of thousands of Russians—including Prokofiev's mother—would flee to the West in terror before the fighting was over. Members of the aristocracy and bourgeoisie who didn't leave the country would starve along with the rest of the population. Bolshevik rule would become more oppressive, stern and ruthless.

Even by the time Prokofiev left Russia, material conditions made concentrating on artistic work extremely difficult. Food, firewood and paper were fast disappearing. Publishing houses operated with shrinking staffs and resources, while musicians and their audiences shivered in their overcoats in unheated halls. Assaulted on all sides and unable even to feed the population, the new Communist government could not place a high priority on culture. As a result, many creative artists— even those sympathetic to the Bolshevik cause—left Russia in the years immediately following the Revolution to seek a more comfortable environment. Emigrating was, in fact, almost more the rule than the exception for established artists in all fields. By the early 1920s, Russia had lost (to name only the most prominent) Nabokov and Bunin in literature; Kandinsky and Chagall in painting; Stravinsky, Rachmaninoff and Prokofiev in music. Among the composers, Stravinsky had left first, in 1914, and was living in Switzerland, while Rachmaninoff had taken advantage of concert dates in Sweden to take his family out in December 1917. He would arrive in New York shortly after Prokofiev the following autumn.

Many of these artists believed—like Prokofiev—that they were leaving Russia only temporarily. Some were confident that those Bolshevik hoodlums would soon be thrown out of power; others were simply waiting for the situation to "settle down."

Reaching Vladivostok, on the Pacific coast, took Prokofiev eighteen days. Had he waited much longer, he probably would not have made it there at all. Siberia was one of the primary theaters of the civil war: foreign interventionists and Russian armies were stumbling over one another in bloody chaos. Naturally, the trans-Siberian rail line along which Prokofiev was traveling was a major military objective and already the scene of fierce combat. All of this entertained Prokofiev more than it frightened him, at least judging from the account in his autobiography written from a comfortable distance twenty years later.

Reading about Babylonian culture, I only half paid attention to the dangers to which our train was subjected as it moved across wartorn Siberia. At the halfway point we stood for a long time, for trains with Czech troops [supporting the Whites] were blocking the track. Finally they let us pass somehow, and a Czech front formed quickly behind us. From that point on, the postcards I sent to my mother in Kislovodsk reached her only a year later. Around the city of Chita we halted again: Soviet troops were fighting with the Ataman Semyonov in front of us. Semyonov retreated along the line to Harbin [in China], and we pushed through to the left to Khabarovsk.

In spite of the dangers—or perhaps because of them—Prokofiev's mood was optimistic, even ebullient. The wild Siberian scenery inspired him; near the city of Irkutsk, the train passed along the shore of Lake Baikal, the world's deepest. "I'm writing you from Arkhara, which is remarkable in that it is the birthplace of all Arkhararites. (Where won't destiny land me on the way to this America!)," he wrote to Miaskovsky near the end of the trip. "Tomorrow we arrive in Khabarovsk, and thirty hours later, in Vladivostok. I embrace you tenderly and send you best wishes on your angel's day. I wish you success in your instrumentation, and in composing the orchestral *morçeaux*." This was the last contact Prokofiev had with his old friend and schoolmate for nearly six years.

From Vladivostok, Prokofiev took a steamer to Yokohama, arriving in Tokyo on June 1. Originally he had planned to head for South America, but, unable to make the necessary steamer connections, he decided to spend a little time in Japan before continuing on to North America. He gave piano recitals in Tokyo and Yokohama. "Books on contemporary music had already appeared in Japan in Japanese, and one of them included an article about me, so in Tokyo I played in the Imperial Theater. The Japanese didn't understand much about European music, but they listened attentively, sat incredibly quietly and applauded technique. The audience was small, and I earned few yen." From Yokohama he boarded a steamer bound for San Francisco, with a "wonderful stop" in Honolulu.

America did not welcome Prokofiev with open arms, however. He was not yet well-known in the West, and, even worse, he was a Soviet citizen. (Ironically, the Soviet government later disputed that fact, claiming Prokofiev had left the country before being properly registered.) In the fall of 1918 the American government—along with most Western governments—was hostile toward the new Bolshevik regime, which openly despised all capitalist countries. Customs officials therefore detained Prokofiev for three days on Treasure Island, in San Francisco Bay halfway toward Oakland. Even then, the irrepressible Prokofiev maintained a sense of humor. "They wouldn't let me on shore right away, since they knew that in Russia the 'Maximalists' (that's what Americans were calling the Bolsheviks then) were in power. These were incomprehensible—and probably dangerous—characters. After holding me for about three days on the island and interrogating me in detail ('Have you been in prison?'—'Yes, I have.'—'That's bad. Where?'—'Here on your island.'—'Oh, so you like to make jokes!'), they let me into the United States. I was already short of money, but a fellow traveler who took an interest in me gave me a three-hundred-dollar loan, and in early September of 1918 I arrived in New York." Prokofiev's ability to inspire interest and confidence in those he met was to serve him well in his American career.

Even after his long and difficult voyage, Prokofiev still believed he would soon return to Russia. Almost immediately upon arriving in New York, he wrote to Diaghilev in London. "I plan to spend several months here before returning to Russia, and would very much like to exchange a few pleasant letters with you." He also inquired after the fate of *The Buffoon*, "buried so traitorously in the recesses of your briefcase." Prokofiev was receiving news of Diaghilev and his company through Adolf Bolm, a Diaghilev dancer in whose apartment on 59th Street he stayed for a while.

A Russian in New York: Prokofiev soon became something of a curiosity, especially in a city stricken with a peculiarly naive American interest in the new, rigorously egalitarian (or so it was breathlessly reported by John Reed and others) Soviet society. Ironically, from the very beginning of his American career, which would sporadically flourish and decline for the next twenty years, Prokofiev was known as "that Bolshevik composer." Forgotten in the journalists' mad quest for a label was the indifference to the politics that led Prokofiev to leave Russia in the first place. But using the instinctive business sense that would become sharper over the years, Prokofiev would do little to destroy this popular image.

That Prokofiev's reputation as a pianist and composer had preceded him to New York is obvious in the speed with which he made his debut there. ("Report had set him down as a modern of moderns, a daring innovator in the piano and orchestral forms," remarked the *Musical Courier*.) Scheduled to perform on October 19, he had to cancel because of illness—the stress under which he had been living for the last few years was finally beginning to tell on his usually strong consitution. But he soon recovered, and ten days later, on October 29, Prokofiev made his American debut at the Brooklyn Museum. The performance celebrated the opening of an exhibition of work by another recent Russian arrival, the artist Boris Anisfeld. Anisfeld, who had worked as a designer at the Mariinsky Theater, would later do the scenery for the Chicago production of *Love for Three Oranges*. On this occasion, Prokofiev played the "Visions fugitives," as well as the Op. 12 pieces, which were choreographed and danced by Adolf Bolm.

But Prokofiev's first important performance—attended by the critics—took place on November 20, 1918, at Aeolian Hall. Assuming correctly that American audiences were not ready to hear an entire program of his own music, he chose works by Scriabin (two études and "Pages from an Album") and Rachmaninoff (three preludes) in addition to his own Op. 2 pieces and the Second Sonata. Rachmaninoff, recently arrived in New York, was in the audience.

Judging from the numerous and amusing reviews, the recital was a musical and social success. "His fingers are steel, his wrists steel, his biceps and triceps steel, his seapula steel," enthused *The New York Times*, reflecting the prevailing (and wrong-headed) American perception of the U.S.S.R. as the proletarian paradise. "He is a tonal steel trust. . . . He is blond, slender, modest as a musician, and his impassibility contrasted with the volcanic eruptions he produced on the keyboard. . . . A parterre of pianists greeted the newcomer with dynamic applause. Of his instant success there can be no doubt. Whether he will last—Ah! New music for new ears. Serge Prokofiev is very startling." *Theatre* described him as a "blond Russian giant" with the "size and build and strength of a football guard." Despite the misgivings of the American customs officials, the New York audience was fascinated, and "was not satisfied until Prokofiev had added number after number to the original programme." For encores, he played the "Prelude," "Scherzo" and "Gavotte" from Op. 12 and the inevitable "Suggestion diabolique." "The very character of the audience which filled Aeolian Hall to the last seat was indicative of the respect in which Prokofiev is held, for many of the city's prominent musicians were there," *The World* reported.

There were many new Russian émigrés in New York in 1918, not a few of them musicians. They helped to provide a solid and enthusiastic base of support on which Prokofiev could build a reputation. At age twenty-seven, barely six months out of Russia, Prokofiev was "the musical news of the season." He was a star, an "unusual but charming young man."

Only three weeks later, Prokofiev returned to the New York stage—this time with an orchestra, and in New York's most prestigious auditorium. Carnegie Hall had been opened in 1891, the year Prokofiev was born, by his childhood idol and countryman, Tchaikovsky. There, on December 10 and 11, 1918, Prokofiev played with the Russian Symphony Orchestra, a group of Russian émigré musicians conducted by Modest Altschuler. "A good musician, but a bad conductor," Altschuler had founded his orchestra in New York in 1903. The reviews for Prokofiev's performance of his First Piano Concerto were not as ecstatic as for the recital debut—perhaps because the orchestra was mediocre—but he was still in the musical headlines. Adjusting quickly to the world of American "beeznis," which he would always admire for its efficiency and technological sophistication, Prokofiev soon had an agent (Haensel, of Haensel & Jones) to represent him.

But Prokofiev's life was not only music and business. After one of his appearances in New York that season, he met a beautiful and temperamental young soprano who came backstage with her friends to meet this fiery and eccentric Russian virtuoso. Carolina Codina was twenty-one years old, six years younger than Prokofiev, and of an unusual and complicated background. Born in Madrid on October 21, 1897, she had a Spanish father; her mother was part Polish and part Huguenot (from Alsace). Her mother's family had been prominent in Poland, and her grandfather had held an important government post there. Since much of Poland belonged to Russia until World War I, he spoke both Russian and Polish fluently.

Both of Carolina's parents were singers. When she was still a little girl, her father brought the family from Spain to Cuba, and then, when she was about ten years old, to New York, where she remained through her high school years. The family lived in several different apartments in New York: on Central Park West near Columbus Circle, in Brooklyn, and on Riverside Drive. One of her uncles, a teacher of German and French, also lived in New York. As a teenager, Carolina (or Lina, as she was more often called) knew Spanish, English and some Russian; her linguistic gifts must have intrigued Prokofiev, for he had always been fascinated with languages and word games.

Lina's parents closely followed musical events in New York, so it is hardly surprising that she would have heard about Prokofiev. Her mother was especially knowledgeable about Russian music and musicians, and was already acquainted with Rachmaninoff. When Lina and her girlfriends went to hear Prokofiev play his exhilarating First Concerto at Carnegie Hall, her friends found his manner odd and his music distasteful, but she applauded loudly and enthusiastically. Prokofiev's stage bow—mechanical and stiff, "as though he would break in half"—amused her, and the wild energy of his music excited her.

Lina's friends suggested that she could meet him if he intrigued her so. But Lina was shy, and Prokofiev's fame intimidated her. Finally, after another New York recital, her friends went backstage to meet him, while she waited for them outside the Green Room. Looking to see if they were ready to leave, she poked her head in the half-open door. Prokofiev saw her and was immediately taken with her Mediterranean beauty. Small dark women like Lina—and photographs show that she was very attractive, with an animated face, flashing dark eyes and lustrous black hair—were always his favorite type. They were polar opposites: he was awkward and brutally frank, with the fair skin and white-blond hair of a Slav, while she was graceful and diplomatic, with an olive complexion and a southern disposition.

Not long after this first encounter, they saw each other again and Prokofiev began to court her, though Lina was at first reluctant. Lina's mother, who "adored" Prokofiev, encouraged the romance, however, even though she could see that her daughter was not spared the teasing and roughness that was second nature to her suitor. (Later, Prokofiev would become famous among his friends for his abrupt and rude manners toward his pretty wife.) On dates they sometimes went dancing at the Waldorf-Astoria, where he revealed the same clumsiness and eccentricity he had displayed at his teenage dancing lessons. Tall, blond, fair, slim, a brilliant talker and wit, Prokofiev was handsome in his own unique way, even if he was spoiled, stubborn and used to being the center of attention.

Despite its reputation as the most sophisticated American city, New York proved over the years to be less receptive to Prokofiev's music than its midwestern rival, Chicago. Two of his most popular works— the opera *Love for Three Oranges* and the Third Piano Concerto— would be first performed there. In the same month as his Carnegie Hall debut, Prokofiev made his Chicago debut with Frederick Stock and the Chicago Symphony, playing his First Piano Concerto. The orchestra also performed "The Scythian Suite," which one Chicago newspaper called "Bolshevik music," obviously unaware that it was originally written for Sergei Diaghilev, hardly an enthusiastic supporter of Bolshevik ideals or methods.

Prokofiev's first Chicago performances had been arranged by Cyrus McCormick, who had kept the promise he made to Prokofiev in Petrograd in the summer of 1917. McCormick also introduced Prokofiev to important Chicago cultural and musical figures. Among them was Cleofonte Campanini, director of the Chicago Opera, who—like everyone else—was intrigued by this brash young Russian and his music. Campanini asked Prokofiev if he had written any operas. No sooner had Prokofiev provided a description of *The Gambler* than Campanini wanted to stage it, but the score was back in Russia, at the Mariinsky Theater library. Obtaining it would be very difficult, if not impossible. So they discussed the possibility of a new commission, and Prokofiev remembered the strange little divertissement "Liubov' k trem apel'sinam"—"Love for Three Oranges"—that he and Meyerhold had been considering as a promising libretto source.

When Campanini discovered that "Love for Three Oranges" was a Russian adaptation of an eighteenth-century *commedia dell'arte* fairy tale by a fellow Italian, the playwright Carlo Gozzi (1720–1806), he was delighted. " 'Gozzi! Our lovely Gozzi! But that's wonderful!' " A contract was signed by January 1919; *Oranges* was to be presented the following fall. By March, citrus growers in Florida and California were competing vigorously for promotion rights. As was frequently the case with his most popular music—the "Classical" Symphony, *Peter and the Wolf*, the Fifth Symphony—Prokofiev wrote *Oranges* quickly. The score was finished in nine months, and was ready by October 1— even though in April, in the midst of composing it, Prokofiev was hospitalized with scarlet fever and diphtheria.

Prokofiev also wrote the libretto, basing it on the Russian adaptation of Gozzi's Italian tale ("L'amore delle tre melarance") that had appeared in Meyerhold's Petrograd literary-theatrical journal—

also called *Love for Three Oranges*. Meyerhold and two collaborators translated and adapted Gozzi's story, originally produced as a play in Venice in 1761, to inaugurate their journal, which examined *commedia dell'arte* theory and techniques. Before Prokofiev left Russia in 1918, Meyerhold reminded him of the Gozzi tale and, giving him a copy of the journal, encouraged him to write an opera based on it. Prokofiev replied that he would "read it on the ocean liner." Not only did he read it; he even made a first sketch for a libretto during those long hours of traveling across the Pacific.

Sarcastic, colorful, populated by acrobats, kindly monsters, silly princes and expiring maidens, Meyerhold's version of Gozzi's ironic fairy tale immediately appealed to Prokofiev's imagination and to his irreverent nature. It must have reminded him of the masks with which he and his playmates had created plays years before in Sontsovka. It is no coincidence that *Oranges*, Prokofiev's best-known and most frequently performed opera, is also the least realistic of the seven he wrote. His inability to understand and convey the feelings of realistic fictional characters would sometimes be a liability, as in *The Fiery Angel*, but for *Oranges* it was an asset. A strong sense of fantasy and the absurd—not realistic psychology—was needed to create a successful opera out of this aggressively stylized, antirealistic and artificial divertissement.

In writing the libretto, Prokofiev closely followed Meyerhold's adaptation. Leaving the basic plot and characters of Gozzi's version unchanged, Meyerhold added groups of characters—the Three Eccentrics, the Jesters in the Towers, the Extras in the Towers, the Everyday Comedians and the Pure Tragedians—who act as a sort of chorus, commenting on the action and emphasizing its pure theatricality.

The plot, although complicated, is little more than an excuse for a discussion of various theatrical techniques. The hero is the young Prince, the King's son. As the opera opens, he is suffering from a "chronic hypochondriacal illness"—an inability to laugh. The King sends for the jester, Truffaldino, to come and cure his difficult offspring with jokes. But none of Truffaldino's extravagant attempts to amuse the Prince produce the desired effect. Only when the evil Fata Morgana (one of the opera's several fairy tale villains) stumbles clumsily in her attempts to subvert Truffaldino's efforts does the Prince burst into healthy and prolonged laughter.

Insulted, Fata Morgana uses her magical powers to curse the

Prince, dooming him to a quest for three oranges guarded in a distant castle by a frightful lady giant (who sings in a *basso profundo*). Of course Truffaldino and the Prince, who becomes a stronger and more admirable character as the action progresses, eventually obtain the oranges. Thirsty, Truffaldino opens the oranges, only to find a beautiful maiden inside each one. The first two maidens die when the Prince is unable to fulfill their requests for water. (The first princess was named Linetta in honor of Lina Codina.) Just as it looks like the third princess, Ninetta, will also expire, the Eccentrics run in from offstage to supply a bucket of water. Ninetta is saved—and we are reminded that this is only a theatrical fairy tale. Instantly in love, the Prince promises to marry Ninetta, and goes off to bring his father and the court back to meet her. But once again, sinister magical forces intervene: Ninetta is transformed into a rat. All the complications are soon resolved, however, and the Prince marries Ninetta, restored to her virginal human beauty.

Oranges contains some of Prokofiev's most charming and playful music, in the tradition of his early, naughtily dissonant piano pieces. The quirky, ironically ceremonial March (also included in the orchestral Suite arranged from the opera and in a widely played piano version) is one of the most popular pieces Prokofiev ever wrote. Clumping along in a jerky rhythm punctuated by prominent eighth-note rests, leaping abruptly by wide dissonant intervals, displaying conflicting tonalities and mischievous intervals of seconds and tritones with wicked pleasure, it epitomizes the awkward and ironic "wrong note" style with which Prokofiev is most strongly identified. It even became "household music" in America, serving for fourteen years as the theme for the radio show "The FBI in Peace and War." The March is only one of several set-pieces in the opera—two others are the rich lyrical refrain of the princesses as they emerge from their oranges, and the orchestral interlude (*Scherzo*), after Scenes 1 and 2 of Act III. The *Scherzo* is also found in the orchestral suite and a piano transcription.

In their work on *The Gambler*, Meyerhold had encouraged Prokofiev to avoid traditional operatic forms—aria, ensemble, duets— that would hold up the narrative. In *Oranges*, however, despite the unconventional and theoretically more improvisational *commedia dell'arte* source, Prokofiev made considerably greater use of traditional operatic conventions. In this sense, the musical setting contradicts the pointedly antitraditional theoretical thrust of Meyerhold's adaptation.

One explanation lies in audience expectations. "Taking American taste into consideration, I chose a more simple musical language than I had used in *The Gambler*." For one thing, the words of the libretto are not nearly so important in *Oranges* as they were in *The Gambler*, where they determined the entire musical fabric and dramatic structure. (In composing *Oranges*, Prokofiev set the original Russian text, but the Chicago production was sung in a French translation.) Rather, the emphasis is on spectacle and broad theatrical gestures and not on the prose; the rigorously declamatory, even antioperatic, style of *The Gambler* acquires softer (but still far from romantic) contours in *Oranges*, becoming a mixture of *arioso* and declamation. Similarly, the symphonic texture is lighter and more transparent, representing a synthesis of the styles of the "Classical" Symphony and "The Scythian Suite."

While Meyerhold had a specific political reason—discrediting realism—for publishing his adaptation of Gozzi's *fiaba* in 1914, Prokofiev denied any such intentions. Many reviewers wondered what the target of the sarcasm was: "the audience, Gozzi, the operatic form or those who had no sense of humor. They found in *Oranges* mockery, challenge, grotesque, and what not; all I had been trying to do was write an amusing opera." Theories did not interest Prokofiev. A born pragmatist, he wanted to put on a good show.

But *Oranges* was only one part of Prokofiev's remarkably busy musical life in 1919. Still operating out of New York, he continued to attract attention with his piano recitals. The programs were usually mixed, but always included at least a few of his own compositions. During the winter, he gave two premieres of his own new music in New York: on January 7, the four piano pieces Op. 31 ("Tales of an Old Grandmother") and on March 30, the four piano pieces Op. 32. Except for the Fifth Sonata, these were the last piano pieces he would write for the next ten years.

"Tales of an Old Grandmother" show Prokofiev in an uncharacteristically reflective, soft and nostalgic mood; perhaps he was only beginning to feel the full force of his separation from Russia, and to realize how difficult it would be to return. The four short pieces bear an epigraph in Russian commenting on the cycle's title: "Some memories have been half-erased in her mind, but others will never disappear." It seems unlikely that there is a specific reference here; Prokofiev's paternal grandparents died long before he was born, and although his mother's mother lived with the family at Sontsovka during the first nine years of Prokofiev's life, in his autobiography he does not describe even her death as an important emotional event. Instead, the title for these quiet pieces seems to reflect a general yearning for an idyllic and uncomplicated childhood past. All four are markedly less dissonant, less chromatic and less rhythmic than most of his earlier piano music. The tempos are slow and the appealing melodies are wistful, simple and sustained.

Even for the apparently indestructible Prokofiev, fame exacted a price. Making a name for himself, and coping with being alone in a foreign country—now he was living in a hotel on Seventh Avenue—took enormous energy and stamina. In early spring he fell seriously ill with scarlet fever, diphtheria and a throat infection. "Serge Prokofiev, the interesting Russian composer-pianist, is now convalescing from a severe illness which necessitated the postponement of his Chicago recital and some Canadian concert dates. Mr. Prokofiev was taken ill two days after his third and last New York recital of this season," *Musical America* reported breathlessly. He was confined to bed at Mt. Sinai Hospital, where for a few weeks he was in fairly serious condition.

" 'I thought you would die—that's why I sent you such roses,' one American woman told me, a little sorry that they had gone for nothing. As I began to recuperate, I could hardly wait for the doctor's permission to continue work. Before the scarlet fever, work on *Oranges* was slowing down a bit, but the sickness refreshed me, as strange as that may sound." Having recovered, he spent the summer—the first and last summer he would spend in America—orchestrating *Oranges* for its scheduled fall staging. The full orchestral score was completed by early October, right on time.

In the fall, friends and acquaintances from Russia continued to arrive in New York. Among them was the Jewish musical ensemble (strings and clarinet and piano) named "Zimro." The members were Prokofiev's former fellow students at the Petersburg Conservatory. Giving him a notebook filled with Jewish musical themes, they asked him to write a piece for their sextet. At first he declined on the grounds that he composed only from his own musical material; especially in the early phase of his career, Prokofiev was reluctant to use existing themes, folk or otherwise. But after he looked closer at some of the themes, he grew interested, and quickly produced what came to be called the Overture on Hebrew Themes.

In this seductively "rustic" eight-minute composition, Prokofiev used the timbre and personality of the instruments with particular success, setting them against a foot-tapping but gentle eighth-note pulse (in 2/4 meter). The clarinet and cello dominate, by turns jocular and soulful. Despite its considerable popular success, Prokofiev considered the Overture an insignificant piece tossed off in "a day and a half and to which I didn't even want to assign an opus number. . . . From the musical point of view, the only worthwhile thing in it is the concluding part, and even that, in my opinion, is a result of my weakness for diatonicism." It was first performed in New York in early 1920.

Meanwhile, *Love for Three Oranges* had run into problems in Chicago. In December 1919, with the production already in preparation, and Boris Anisfeld already commissioned to design the sets, Campanini died, throwing the company and its season into confusion. *Oranges* was not put on that season after all, and would not reach the stage for two more years. This must have been keenly disappointing to Prokofiev, who had been counting on the production to build his reputation in America.

At loose ends, Prokofiev looked around for a new project and decided, unexpectedly, on another opera. In retrospect, he admitted that beginning a third opera before *Oranges* and *The Gambler* had reached the stage was perhaps ill-advised. "I had begun *Love for Three Oranges* with a commission in my pocket, and even so it ran into difficulties. To set to work on another big project now—without a prospective performance in mind—was silly. Perhaps I was being stubborn, unconsciously: one opera didn't work out, so I'll write another." Even worse, the new opera, *The Fiery Angel*, would prove very difficult to finish, and would fare no better with directors and producers than its two predecessors. In fact, aside from his sixth opera, *War and Peace*, which Prokofiev would write and rewrite throughout the 1940s and early 1950s, *The Fiery Angel* would take more years from conception to completion (eight, from 1919 to 1927) than anything else he would compose.

In 1919, most of Prokofiev's colleagues outside Russia did not share his fascination with opera. Convinced it was a moribund form, Diaghilev and Stravinsky had already warned Prokofiev not to spend too much time on it, for they believed the future lay elsewhere, particularly in dance. In Russia, however, opera remained the most important dramatic musical form; it was definitely more important and more respectable there than ballet. Soon after the Revolution it became an officially approved medium because the story it told could be exploited for propaganda value. Prokofiev's unwillingness to throw opera "overboard from the ship of modernity," and his insistence on the possibility of revitalizing operatic conventions, revealed his basic traditionalism—even conservatism, and his divergence from the trends of the European avant-garde. In his stubborn pursuit of operatic success, Prokofiev was actually closer to Soviet musical taste.

His unshakable faith in opera came from several sources: traditional Conservatory training at the hands of such fervent practitioners of the craft as Rimsky-Korsakov; love of the written word; inflexibility; and emotional isolation, which led him to pursue a course he set his mind upon without pausing for an objective reevaluation. In no other field of composition did Prokofiev spend so much time and effort with so little public or critical acceptance.

As he had for *Oranges*, Prokofiev wrote the libretto for *The Fiery Angel* (*Ognennyi angel*) himself. This was a formidable task, for the source was a long and complicated historical novel of the same title set in Germany and dealing with religious hysteria during the period of the Spanish Inquisition. Written between 1905 and 1908 by the Russian Symbolist Valery Bryusov (1873–1924), best known for his poetry and translations, it is an overwrought picaresque tale of a sadomasochistic *ménage à trois*. The participants are the beautiful and tormented Renata, the wandering virtuous knight Ruprecht, and Madiel, the "fiery angel" of the title, who may or may not be incarnated on earth as Heinrich. Madiel by turns seduces and abuses Renata, who stands at the center of the novel and the opera. Half-saint, half-whore, torn between the two extremes of sexual indulgence and religious self-denial, Renata is the third of the "fatal women" in Prokofiev's operas, after Maddalena and Polina (in *The Gambler*). The difference, however, is that Renata is motivated by less selfish concerns.

Like most of the Russian Symbolists, Bryusov was interested in various spiritual and mystical movements. In *The Fiery Angel*, Cornelius Agrippa and Doctor Faustus, renowned medieval practitioners of the occult, figure prominently. At least in part, the novel attempts to transfer to the Russian literary tradition the Faust legend which has inspired so many writers and composers.

Why would the "sunny," optimistic, sarcastic Prokofiev choose such a gloomy and symbol-laden subject for his third opera—and before his first two had even reached the stage? It sounds like something he would be more likely to parody. Bryusov had based the complicated sexual triangle on a relationship in his own life (another Symbolist poet, Andrei Bely, author of *Petersburg*, and the "second-rate writer" Nina Petrovskaya were the participants), but Prokofiev had no comparable autobiographical material on which to draw. The sort of kinky sexual activity implied in the novel was far outside his limited experience. This helps to account, perhaps, for the unconvincing, fragmentary and often static libretto, which tends to concentrate on external features (the demons who periodically assault Renata, for example) rather than on the more important psychological-sexual motivations. The first act of the opera was finished in piano score by March 1920, but the work would proceed slowly after that.

Prokofiev undertook *The Fiery Angel* mainly to prove that he could write "serious" dramatic music to a complicated subject—and not only the sassy piano pieces with which he was increasingly identified. Then, too, he was not in a positive frame of mind in late 1919; perhaps the gloominess of the novel suited his mood. *Oranges* had fallen through; he had little money; he was worried about his mother, who was still in the Caucasus; the news from Russia was ever more disturbing, and seemed to indicate that returning soon would be more difficult than he had first believed; he was having difficulty promoting his music with American publishers and managers. They were more interested in him as a pianist than as a composer, and were depressingly conservative in their taste. The endless repetitions of the eighteenth and nineteenth century classics that dominated concert programs disappointed him. He had not found reliable advocates for new music. Where were the American Derzhanovskys, Zilotis and Koussevitskys?

> Sometimes I would wander around enormous Central Park in the center of New York, looking at the skyscrapers that framed it, and I'd think with a cold fury of the wonderful American orchestras that were indifferent to my music; of the critics, who said what had already been said a hundred times—"Beethoven is a composer of genius"—crudely rejecting anything new; of the managers, who organized long tours for artists playing the same program of familiar numbers fifty times over. I arrived too early; this infant—America—still hadn't matured to an understanding of new music. Go back home? But how? Russia was surrounded on all sides by the forces of the Whites, and anyway, who wants to return home empty-handed?

The first two years after he left Russia were among the most difficult in Prokofiev's life. Although he had a group of Russian émigré friends in New York with whom he spent time and he did not lack for female companionship, he was forced to make many appearances as a pianist in order to make ends meet. The circumstances were sometimes humiliating. In early 1920 he gave concerts in Montreal and Quebec, and was cheated out of two-thirds of his fee. Even worse, many American music critics began to think of him more as a pianist than a composer. Under a photograph of Prokofiev and Stravinsky that appeared in *Musical America*, the caption reads: "The composer Stravinsky and the pianist Prokofiev." The remarkable rate at which he had been turning out new works in 1917–18 slowed as he tried to reorient himself and as an increasing amount of his time and energy went toward earning a living. After *Oranges*, he would complete no large new works for several years. Continuing to believe he would soon return to Russia, Prokofiev hesitated in signing long-term contracts with American publishers.

Meanwhile, in Russia, the Bolshevik victory over the Whites was nearing and thousands of Russians were fleeing from the Black Sea ports toward Turkey and Greece, anxious to avoid the bloodbath that followed the White retreat. Maria Grigorevna, now sixty-five years old, joined the desperate flood in early 1920, sailing to Constantinople. When they arrived there, the homeless Russians were placed in temporary settlements on the Prince Islands, where newly impoverished aristocrats slept on cots and wore identical drab uniforms. The conditions were extremely difficult, and Maria Grigorevna was so frightened and upset that she nearly lost her eyesight.

Even before he learned of his mother's departure from Russia— which severed another important link to his past and made a quick return to Petrograd even more unlikely—Prokofiev had been planning to travel to Europe. Now he decided to arrange to meet Maria Grigorevna in Italy or Marseilles and bring her to Paris. When he left New York for Europe in April 1920, Prokofiev had been in America for eighteen months. He was still not at all sure, however, if America was where he should be. His first visit to Europe since 1915—his first since the War and the Revolution—would help him decide.

C H A P T E R   10

A   S C Y T H I A N

I N   P A R I S

Even genius does not save one in Russia; in exile,
one is saved by genius alone.

—V L A D I M I R   N A B O K O V

A rriving from New York in the spring of 1920, Prokofiev soon discovered that the Russian Revolution was the big news in Europe.
London, Paris, Berlin and Rome were swarming with the recently
dispossessed victims of the new Russian diaspora. Most of them,
including members of families who had been prominent aristocrats for
centuries under the Romanovs, had landed in Europe with little more
than the clothes on their backs. The lucky ones had managed to salvage
a few jewels for capital.

Talent was the only capital the many writers, musicians and artists
among them possessed. Now more uncertain of his own future, Prokofiev showered them with questions. What they told him was not
reassuring. At London exhibitions of work by the Russian artists Nicolas Roerich (who designed *The Rite of Spring* for Diaghilev) and
Alexander Yakovlev, Prokofiev heard shocking tales from those who
"had turned into numb hungry stomachs on two legs" before fleeing
Petrograd. In their reports, they described a society in chaos, an
economy in ruins and a population too concerned with survival to pay
much attention to culture. Such stories must have made him wonder
if it would be advisable to return to Russia soon, as he had originally
intended.

In the five years that had passed since Prokofiev last visited
Europe, it had undergone great changes. The War had left a strong

mark—physically, spiritually, politically and culturally. A certain innocence and well-worn security had been lost forever. It took time for
Prokofiev to acquaint himself with this new world, and to reintroduce
himself to musicians and impresarios. In London, where Diaghilev had
been spending most of his time since late 1918, Prokofiev distributed
letters of recommendation and observed local customs. "The English
chomp on such disgusting things that after Paris I'm thinking about
staging a hunger strike." (Prokofiev always enjoyed good food and wine
and would, later in life, travel miles to try a recommended restaurant.)
"I haven't played bridge and miss it, although I've figured out that not
a single proper Englishman plays really vicious bridge. They have
heard of it, but smile condescendingly. . . . I like the lords here—
they have good faces, and the latest fashions in suits. The ladies are
stiff and tedious."

Prokofiev did not stay long in England, however. After succeeding
in bringing his mother from Constantinople to Paris, he settled her in
an apartment there, and spent most of the summer of 1920 composing,
in and near the French capital. He also renewed contact with Diaghilev
and Stravinsky, who were presenting a short spring season in Paris.
They were concentrating on regrouping the Ballets Russes in Europe,
as various dancers and designers straggled out of Russia. In May, they
collaborated on a very successful production of a new ballet at the
Paris Opera—Stravinsky's *Pulcinella*, with scenery by Picasso and
choreography by Leonid Massine. It was one of their most ambitious
premieres since the beginning of the War, and marked the return of
the Ballets Russes to the Parisian social and artistic limelight.

No longer considering it likely they would return to Russia, Diaghilev and Stravinsky no doubt told Prokofiev he was foolish to think
of going back now. Even before the 1917 Revolution, the royal family
and the official theatrical establishment in Russia had regarded the
bohemian style and flamboyant manners of Diaghilev and his company
with suspicion and indignation. The Bolsheviks—who were surprisingly humorless and puritanical—would prove to be even less enthusiastic about Diaghilev's elitist enterprise. The company's identification
with the monied classes and its rejection of the moral-political function
of art were anathema to Marxist-Leninist cultural ideology. Nor were
there funds in the struggling new Soviet Republic, where opera houses
were serving as hospitals and thousands of people were dying each
day, to support such "nonessential" activities.

It pleased Prokofiev enormously to find that Diaghilev had not forgotten him or the score of *The Buffoon* which he had sent to the impresario from Petrograd five years earlier. Their reunion was friendly; Diaghilev still wanted to stage *The Buffoon* and sat down with Prokofiev to talk over some changes he wanted. As in the past, Prokofiev did not object to Diaghilev's suggestions. In need of money, especially now that he was responsible for his ailing mother, and hoping to establish a reputation in Paris, Prokofiev retreated for much of the summer to Mantes-la-Jolie, a small town on the Seine northwest of Paris, to revise *The Buffoon* according to Diaghilev's instructions. Prokofiev was so engrossed in his work on the ballet, with which he hoped to make a well-publicized Paris debut, that he postponed his scheduled return to America until mid-October. (A big tour of eight American cities had also been put off until December.) Maria Grigorevna stayed with him in Mantes, resting, recuperating and describing what was happening back in Russia. Lina Codina, now following her parents' example in the pursuit of an operatic career, also came to visit occasionally.

Lina returned to New York before Prokofiev, and was there to greet him when he arrived from Europe in late October. During the Atlantic crossing, Prokofiev had some bad luck: his suitcase—containing a smoking jacket, warm clothing and valuable sketches by Mikhail Larionov and Natalia Goncharova for the upcoming production of *The Buffoon*—was stolen. It didn't help matters that he had no concerts lined up in New York.

Soon after arriving in America, Prokofiev also became embroiled in a nasty fight over the projected performance of *Oranges* at the Chicago Opera. He might have been poor and uncertain of the future, but he was determined to drive a hard bargain—sometimes just for the sake of being difficult. He knew his worth and demanded to be paid for it, viewing marketing and deals with the same fascination as an intricate chess problem. Campanini had been replaced by a new manager at the Chicago Opera, who was prepared to stage *Oranges* in the 1920–21 season. He refused, however, to compensate Prokofiev for the year's postponement, ignoring the composer's claim that his schedule had been disrupted. When the manager threatened to stage the opera without his permission, Prokofiev threatened legal action. "I decided that the opera could be canceled, but that I wouldn't let them make mincemeat of me. The manager decided that the $80,000 spent on the scenery could go to waste, but that I wouldn't get any money out of them. So the opera again failed to reach the stage, but to tell the truth, this time it was my fault."

From Chicago Prokofiev went on to California, where he made numerous piano appearances. Audiences in San Francisco and Los Angeles received him with considerably more warmth and friendship than the customs officials had shown upon his arrival in America in 1918. Like so many other artists, he fell in love with the dramatic landscape, which he found much more interesting than the routine concerts he was required to give. Seeing the ocean and lush vegetation helped him recover from his depression over the cancellation of *Oranges*. From the Hotel Clark in Los Angeles he wrote: "I'm as ecstatic about California as it is about me. I am smiling along with the California countryside, and I've gotten those Chicagoans out of my system. Idiots!"

His mellow mood is reflected in the serene and romantic "Five Songs Without Words" (Op. 35), most of which he composed in California. They are a good example of the "lyrical" Prokofiev. Melody— in soaring, long-breathing *legato* phrases—is more important in this cycle than in any of Prokofiev's previous works for voice. In the early phase of his career, Prokofiev had thought of the voice primarily as a medium through which to convey a text, and not as an instrument with its own unique sound and color. Here he explores these purely sonic possibilities against a piano accompaniment which is for the most part restrained, simple and subordinated to the melodic line. The highly rhythmic and harshly declamatory treatment of the voice characteristic of *Love for Three Oranges, The Gambler* and even "The Ugly Duckling" is replaced by a softer, more flowing style. So "instrumental" are these five songs that it was easy for Prokofiev to revise them slightly for violin and piano in 1925, in which version they are best known today.

Scrambling to support himself—and his mother, who had remained in France—on his piano appearances, Prokofiev must have been pleased when he finally received some good news: *Oranges* might be staged in Chicago after all. Mary Garden, an opera singer famous for her portrayal of Mélisande in Debussy's *Pelléas et Mélisande* and of Salome in Strauss's *Salome*, had been appointed to succeed Campanini as director of the Chicago Opera. Eager to put Chicago on the operatic map, perhaps more experienced in dealing with stubborn artistic temperaments than her predecessor, and certainly more knowledgeable about contemporary music, she signed a new contract with

Prokofiev to present *Oranges* in the 1921–22 season. "The curve of my American career again took an upswing." In fact, 1921 would turn out to be the best year for Prokofiev in some time—and not only in America. Three large works (*Love for Three Oranges, The Buffoon* and the Third Piano Concerto) would all receive well-publicized premieres.

In early spring of 1921, Prokofiev returned again to Europe, where, in Monte Carlo, he plunged into rehearsals with the Ballets Russes for *The Buffoon*. Diaghilev was anticipating that the ballet would introduce Prokofiev—a new and exciting discovery—to the Paris audience, but Koussevitsky, who also liked to showcase new talent, managed to upstage him by a few weeks. Exhausted by the terrible conditions in Russia, where he had been conducting musicians whose fingers were numb from the cold and whose energy was sapped by the desperate struggle for survival, Koussevitsky had finally left Moscow for Berlin in May 1920. In his baggage was a trunk full of the scores that Prokofiev had left behind in Russia. Soon after, Koussevitsky came to Paris, where he was very active until taking up the position of conductor of the Boston Symphony Orchestra in 1924. Koussevitsky continued to be an enthusiastic proponent of Prokofiev's music, which he regularly conducted in the concert series he organized in Paris. He also published Prokofiev's music at his two publishing concerns, the Russian Musical Publishing House and Gutheil, eventually transferred to Paris and renamed as the Éditions Russes.

And so, appropriately, it was his old Russian friend Koussevitsky who first presented Prokofiev to that ultimate arbiter of fashionable modern taste, the Paris audience, on April 29, 1921, at the Salle Gaveau. Prokofiev conducted an orchestra assembled by Koussevitsky in "The Scythian Suite." The mixture of outrage and delight that the Suite had provoked elsewhere also occurred in Paris, although the audience—accustomed to more adventurous fare—was less offended than intrigued by this barbaric composition and its startling creator. A few days later, Louis Schneider, critic for *Le Gaulois*, went to watch Prokofiev rehearsing the orchestra for *The Buffoon*.

"M. Prokofiev is a very young musician—slender, svelte—who carries himself like a student. As soon as the musicians are seated, M. Prokofiev sweeps on, like some elemental force. He molds them, he explains his ideas and his aesthetic, and they work with joy, for the musicians recognize that he is a real master. Yesterday morning at the end of the rehearsal, the musicians gave an ovation to the man who is going to direct them in *The Buffoon*." Prokofiev's reputation as a "bad boy" followed him to Paris, but only seemed to enhance his appeal in the eyes of the French.

From his very first appearance on the scene, however, Prokofiev was compared to another Russian émigré composer who had preceded him on the road to France. In fact, the newspapers and magazines obviously considered they were paying Prokofiev a big compliment by labeling him "the new Stravinsky" in the aftermath of the performance of "The Scythian Suite." (For his part, Diaghilev found them not at all alike: "The only resemblance between Prokofiev and Stravinsky is that both are Russian, and both are living in the same century.") By this time, Stravinsky was a respected and inevitable presence in Parisian cultural and musical life. Symbolically, when Prokofiev made his second appearance before the Paris public a few weeks after his debut with Koussevitsky, he shared billing with Stravinsky. The Ballets Russes program for May 17 featured the premiere of *The Buffoon* and a performance of Stravinsky's already popular *Firebird*. The premiere of Prokofiev's ballet "will be a date to remember in the history of Russian music," wrote Schneider in excited anticipation, "just as not so long ago was the appearance of *The Firebird*, which signaled the dawn of the young glory of M. Stravinsky. It will be interesting to compare the two works to be given on Tuesday."

When Tuesday came, the audience at the Théâtre Municipal de la Gaite on the Square des Arts-et-Métiers was treated to a brilliant visual and musical spectacle—even before the curtain rose. The exquisitely produced magazine program featured a full-page reproduction of a sketch of Prokofiev by Matisse, done in late April when the company was in rehearsal in Monte Carlo. (Sadly, the original of the sketch was later left behind in a hotel room and vanished.) Facing the Matisse sketch was one of Stravinsky by Picasso. A two-page centerfold in vivid color was devoted to the backdrops for *The Buffoon*, designed by Mikhail Larionov.

Unfortunately, the choreography for Prokofiev's ballet was not as interesting as the design or the score—which Prokofiev himself conducted. When *The Buffoon* finally reached the stage, the Ballets Russes was in a transitional phase. Leonid Massine, who had been the company's chief choreographer from 1917 to 1920, had left the troupe only a few months before. Otherwise, he would probably have choreographed *The Buffoon*, drawing on his considerable experience and talent. Instead, the production was assembled rather haphazardly by the set-designer Larionov; Fyodor Slavinsky, a dancer with no previous or subsequent experience as a choreographer, carried out Larionov's visual conceptions.

Attention focused on the brilliantly colorful sets and costumes, in a sort of folksy Cubist style. The costumes were so elaborate and heavy that they interfered with the dancers' movements. Serge Lifar, a company dancer and later a successful choreographer, condemned the result as "dilettante choreography" that was saved only by the excellence of the music. Nouvel agreed, calling *The Buffoon* a "magnificent failure" that might have turned out very differently with a strong choreographic conception. Significantly, *The Buffoon* dropped from the Ballets Russes repertoire after 1922, and has been done rarely since, although Diaghilev claimed to like it and immediately started searching for a subject for another Prokofiev ballet.

Musically, *The Buffoon* is full of startling inventiveness and abrupt changes in mood. More transparent in texture and more lightly orchestrated than *Ala and Lolly*, the score is bitingly sarcastic and ironic, like so many of Prokofiev's most successful works for the theatre—including *Love for Three Oranges*, composed just before he revised *The Buffoon*. Even tenderly lyrical melodies—like the elegiac theme to which the rich merchant attempts to woo the goat—occur at unlikely moments and are rich with irony. (The later score for *Lt. Kizhe* contains a nearly identical moment, when the nonexistent lieutenant is "married.") Working from a detailed, almost cinematic, scenario, and knowing exactly what the production would look like, helped Prokofiev to create concrete and definite musical equivalents for the action. The music follows the story closely; it is highly specific in its physical imagery, in contrast to most late nineteenth century ballet music. In 1922, Prokofiev reworked the full ballet score into a twelve-part orchestral suite.

Critical response to *The Buffoon* was overwhelmingly positive. "The point is simply this: Russian music is continuing. This formidable river of Mussorgskys and Borodins won't dry up after Stravinsky," Jean Bernier gushed in the program article. "What joy—Stravinsky is not alone!" *Bonsoir* predicted: "Yesterday barely known to a few musicians in France, here, all at once, fame's wing has touched him. Tomorrow this young man with the shaved head, myopic eyes and hesitant manner will be as well-known as Stravinsky." Roland Manuel of *Éclair* agreed.

"*The Buffoon* is, at least musically, the most important work that the Russians have shown us since the War."

On opening night, the company and its many hangers-on celebrated far into the morning in Montmartre.

Three weeks later, on June 9, *The Buffoon* opened in London at the Prince's Theatre, again with the composer conducting. This was Prokofiev's London debut, although "The Scythian Suite" had been performed the preceding autumn by the London Symphony Orchestra. At the premiere, the audience was noisily enthusiastic and created "as much controversy, praise and abuse" as at the London premiere of *Rite of Spring*. The English critics, however, were unimpressed. They seemed uncomfortable with the visual emphasis of the production and thought Prokofiev's score infantile. One English painter even dismissed the music as "Bolshevist propaganda." But Prokofiev always had trouble with the English critics, whom he found more conservative and resistant to innovation than the French, and almost as rude as the boorish Americans.

After the excitement of Paris and London debuts, Prokofiev retreated to St. Brevin-les-Pins, a village on the coast of Brittany. He spent most of the spring and summer there, with occasional trips to Paris. With him in St. Brevin were his mother and his old friend Boris Bashkirov, author (under his pseudonym of Boris Verin) of one of the peoms set in the song cycle Op. 23. He, too, had recently emigrated. Lina Codina also came for frequent visits; she had moved a few months earlier to Europe from America, having decided to continue her vocal studies in France and Italy. Their romance intensified.

While in St. Brevin, Prokofiev finished what would become his most popular piano concerto, the Third, composed a fine new group of songs, and continued work on *The Fiery Angel*. It was the happiest and calmest time of his life since leaving Russia; his first substantial foreign success had brought him new energy and confidence. Prospects for the future had improved, too: Diaghilev was planning to order another ballet score and *Oranges* was scheduled for the coming season in Chicago.

Even during the summer, Prokofiev followed a strict routine of work and exercise.

I get up at 8:30, put on a collarless shirt, white pants and rope-soled sandals," he wrote in a letter. "I knock on Boris Verin's door, who answers with an *"ooo"* or an *"eeee"* and gets up an hour and a half later. After drinking hot chocolate, I look to see if the garden is still where it's supposed to be. Then I sit down to work: I'm writing the Third Piano Concerto.

Lunch is at 12:30. One glass of St. Rafael, no more. At two, we have a game of chess. (We're having a tournament, and for the moment the results are five games for me, two for Boris Verin, and two draws.) At about 3:30, the game ends, we take our bathing suits, towels and thermometer, and Boris and I go for a swim. After we return, we have tea with jelly. The whiskered *facteur* (an important daily factor) arrives, always bringing four newspapers and two or three letters. Then it's time for reading and a leisurely tea. At six, I go off to work, usually to play the piano. Dinner is served at 7:30.

After dinner, Mama and Boris Nikolaevich go to the farm for milk—warm, straight from the cow—and I prepare for my lecture. I'm reading a chapter from the *Outline of History* by H. G. Wells, a most amazing book. At nine, the assistant professor—that's me—gives a lecture on the structure of the world for my audience, reclining on two sofas. Mama goes to bed at ten, Boris Nikolaevich to read, and I to write letters (as I am doing now), or to copy over music. At eleven, Boris Nikolaevich and I go to drop our letters in the mailbox, and then to the ocean, where we gaze at the stars. At 11:30, we eat some cottage cheese with milk, kiss goodnight and go off to bed. The daily schedule is strictly maintained.

Although not the most graceful or athletic individual, Prokofiev also engaged in various forms of physical exercise. On an outing in July, he fell off a bicycle and turned his face "into a cutlet."

Just a few miles away from the Prokofiev household, another Russian émigré artist—the poet Konstantin Balmont—was writing poems. Now suffering from profound depression over the enforced separation from his homeland, Balmont was pleased to discover that Prokofiev was his neighbor, and their casual acquaintance turned into a creative friendship. In a letter to his third wife, the Russian Princess Dagmar Shakovskaya, Balmont wrote, "Everything here is the same. The ocean, books, poems, Prokofiev. All the days are sunny." One day, Prokofiev played Balmont part of the Third Piano Concerto, which was nearing completion, and Balmont, inspired, responded with a sonnet. Its last lines are typical of the hyperbolic and "sing-song" musical style that characterizes most of Balmont's poetry—a style very different, in fact, from the spare, jagged line of Prokofiev's music:

Prokofiev! Music and youth in bloom,
In you, the orchestra yearns for forgotten summer sounds,
And the invincible Scythian beats on the tambourine of the sun.

Prokofiev eventually dedicated the Third Piano Concerto to Balmont, and during the same summer composed a new cycle of five songs (Op. 36) to his poems. As Prokofiev later observed, the strong natural musicality of Balmont's verses made it easy to set them to music. Three of the five new songs ("Voices of the Birds," "The Butterfly" and "Think of Me") used poems written during the summer of 1921 and never published separately: "He writes the poems one day, and I compose the song the next." The remaining two ("Incantation to Fire and Water" and "Columns") were published much earlier. All five poems make heavy use of images and symbols from nature; the cycle begins with one mysterious song about elemental natural forces—the hypnotic "Incantation to Fire and Water"—and ends with another—"Columns." A mood of dark and enigmatic shadows, irrational and almost sinister, predominates in the cycle, in marked contrast to the bright and rational clarity of the Akhmatova songs. Prokofiev's increasing romantic involvement with Lina—who had by now taken her paternal grandmother's surname, Llubera, as her stage name—may help to explain the unusual "warmth" and emotionality of the cycle, which was dedicated to her. Undoubtedly, Prokofiev was also hoping that she would perform the songs. Lina gave the premiere of the cycle in Milan in May 1922, and it was also heard soon after in Russia: in 1923 in Moscow, and in 1924 in Leningrad.

The underrated songs of Op. 36 grew out of a calm interlude in Prokofiev's frenetic life. Soviet writers and musicologists have always tried to downplay and distort the fruitful friendship between Prokofiev and Balmont that produced them, for during the 1920s Balmont became a harsh critic of life in the new Communist Russia. After this summer in Brittany, Prokofiev and Balmont continued to correspond and to see each other, but with decreasing frequency. Still intending to return to the U.S.S.R., Prokofiev became careful to dissociate himself from émigrés who were openly critical of the Communist regime. Later, in

his official Soviet autobiography, he took pains to clarify their relationship: "Soon after [1921], Balmont turned his pen against the 'suffering homeland' (as he called it), and we parted company."

Another product of that peaceful summer and another commem-
oration of their friendship is the magnificent Third Piano Concerto. By
the beginning of the summer, Prokofiev had already prepared most of
the musical material for the piece, destined to become his most famous
piano concerto and one of his most popular works. Ideas had been
gathering in Prokofiev's briefcase for ten years. The theme in parallel
thirds charging up the keyboard from the lower to upper registers,
heard at the end of the first movement, had been conceived first, in
1911. The charming dance-like theme of the second movement (An-
dantino), used as the basis for five sparkling variations, dates from
1913. In 1916–17, Prokofiev wrote two more themes for the first
movement, including the wonderfully simple "Russian" melody with
which the piece opens (in the clarinet). Two themes from an unfinished
string quartet "on the white keys"—absolutely diatonic—that he abandoned in 1921 found their way into the finale. All that remained to
be done was to compose the second theme of the first movement and
the third theme of the finale, and to put them all together.

Despite the piecemeal fashion in which its attractive themes were
assembled, the Third Concerto is remarkable precisely for its com-
pactness and neat structure. It wanders much less than the longer
Second Concerto, and adheres more closely to conventional concerto
and sonata-allegro form than the First. Like the Balmont songs, it
balances flashiness and introspection, irony and romanticism, yielding
a felicitous synthesis of Prokofiev's harmonic experiments, his rhythmic
genius and his instinctive understanding of the possibilities of the
piano. Mature and confident, the Third Concerto does not strive to
shock, like much of his early piano music. As Prokofiev later advised
Koussevitsky, "Let the maestro be calm. This is not a Stravinsky
symphony—there are no complicated meters, no dirty tricks. It can
be conducted without special preparation—it is difficult for the orchestra, but not for the conductor."

If the First Concerto succeeds in its use of the orchestral ensemble, and the Second in its treatment of the solo part, then the Third
does both. It is interesting for both virtuoso and orchestra. By turns
ethereal, majestic (even Brahmsian in the meno mosso of the third
movement) and playful, it is one of the most well-crafted (and yet

spontaneous) pieces written for piano and orchestra. Prokofiev never revised the Third Concerto; it had the same kind of "rightness" as the "Classical" Symphony.

Not long after finishing the Third Concerto, Prokofiev took Lina on a September tour along the French Atlantic coast, visiting Mont-Saint-Michel. Prokofiev went on to spend a few days in Paris, where, he complained, he pined for the countryside, feeling as harried as a "squirrel running inside a wheel." But there was no break in his busy schedule: in mid-October he left for America on the liner *Aquitania* and won first prize in a shipboard chess competition.

New York now struck him as "lively, rich and sunny—a fine city." He had good reason to be optimistic. By late autumn he was in Chicago, preparing for two important performances—the premiere of *Oranges* and the first performance of the Third Piano Concerto; both would take place in the space of two weeks. On December 16, 1921, Prokofiev himself premiered the concerto as piano soloist with the Chicago Symphony under Frederick Stock. "My Third Concerto has turned out to be devilishly difficult," he wrote a few days before the performance to Koussevitsky's wife and secretary, Natalia. "I'm nervous and I'm practicing hard three hours a day."

Chicago critics and audiences responded warmly if not ecstatically. Only after Russian and European audiences, more comfortable with new music, heard it in following years did the Third Concerto begin to achieve its present huge popularity.

But by far the most important event of Prokofiev's last full American season was the premiere of *Love for Three Oranges*—incredibly enough, his first opera to reach the stage. He took a very active part in the rehearsals, which went on for two months before the first performance on December 30. Although Mary Garden had arranged for the premiere, working on her own roles left her little time to deal with production problems. Apparently Prokofiev had been hoping the company would invite his friend Adolf Bolm to direct, but instead the assignment was given to an untalented man named Coini, who was, in Prokofiev's opinion, "as dense as a tree." Prokofiev took decisive action. "At first his lack of imagination upset me, but then I started explaining the roles to the singers myself, offstage, and showing the chorus what to do—right in plain view, onstage. Coini finally got mad and demanded, 'Speaking honestly, which of us is the master on stage—you or I?' I replied, 'You—so as to carry out my wishes.' "

Ever demanding and difficult in pursuit of perfection, Prokofiev developed a close relationship, however, with the designer Boris Anis-feld and with the musicians, many of whom were Russian-speaking Jews. He rehearsed with the orchestra sixteen times before the premiere, and at the dress rehearsal stopped the chorus four times in the Prologue until they sang it with greater precision.

After all this, the premiere enjoyed a respectable, if not tumultuous, success. Prokofiev joked that the Chicagoans "were both proud and confused" to have staged an expensive ($250,000) "modernistic" premiere, while the critic for *The Chicago Tribune* pronounced the music as being "too much for this generation." In New York, however, where the Chicago production received a single performance on February 14, 1922, the critics were openly hostile. Richard Aldrich's review in *The New York Times* was typical: "The audience was large, and after the first shock of surprise, evinced considerable amusement in the proceedings onstage. . . . There are a few, but only a very few, passages that bear recognizable kinship with what has hitherto been recognized as music. . . . What, in fine, is the underlying purpose of this work? Is it satire? Is it burlesque? Whose withers are wrung? If it is a joke it may be a good one, but it is a long and painful one."

Such vicious attacks on his music led Prokofiev to compare the New York critics to a "pack of dogs let out from behind the gate to bite my trousers to shreds. In Chicago, they did not understand everything, but still defended 'our' production. New York had nothing to defend; on the contrary, its competive feelings toward Chicago were aroused. 'You want to show us something that we didn't think of putting on ourselves? So take that!' " The negative reception which greeted the New York premiere of the Third Concerto (with Albert Coates conducting and Prokofiev as soloist) on January 26 only deepened Prokofiev's resentment. America seemed uninterested in new music—or in Prokofiev's, at any rate. "I had to look the facts in the face: the American season which had begun so brilliantly had in the end brought me nothing. In my pocket was a thousand dollars; in my head, noise from all the running around and a desire to go away somewhere quiet to work."

Ettal, a remote village in Bavaria near Oberammergau, would be that quiet place. With no reasonable prospects for financial or artistic success, Prokofiev had no compelling reason to remain any longer in the United States. No close personal or cultural ties bound him to the New World. If America was still a "child" in musical matters, he was unwilling to wait for it to grow up. There was greater promise in Europe:

his mother and Lina Llubera were there, not to mention Diaghilev, Stravinsky and Koussevitsky. Twenty years later, the situation would look rather different: Koussevitsky, Stravinsky, Schoenberg and Bartok would all be in America, making it the new center for contemporary music. In 1924, only two years after Prokofiev's decision to give up on America, Koussevitsky would accept the post as conductor of the Boston Symphony.

But as was often the case in his life, Prokofiev moved in a direction opposite to the prevailing flow. As many of his colleagues and friends moved farther away from Russia, leaving Europe for America, he moved ever closer. Prokofiev's decision to leave America in 1922 brought him one step nearer to Moscow.

E T T A L

My youth! My silly youth!
My shoe without a mate!
I watch with eyes inflamed with excitement
As a page is torn from the calendar.

— MARINA TSVETAEVA, "Youth"

Paris was Prokofiev's first stop after arriving in Europe in early March 1922, although he stayed there only briefly. Almost immediately, he traveled on to Berlin, then the home of many Russian émigré artists, including the novelist Vladimir Nabokov. But after the hectic pace of New York and Chicago, Prokofiev was tired of cities, and wanted to find a place where he could live cheaply with his mother, fully recover his health (which was still weak from the scarlet fever) and compose. So he rented a house in the southern German hamlet of Ettal—"two kilometers from the Oberammergau station, which is three hours from Munich on the Munich-Innsbruck line." One of the reasons he chose Germany rather than France was to absorb atmosphere for *The Fiery Angel*, his main project while living in Ettal. And both he and his mother had always loved the mountains. Originally they rented the modest house—the Villa Christophorus—for a year, but would stay for almost two, until December 1923.

Life in Bavaria was a welcome change from the frenetic vagabond virtuoso's life that Prokofiev had been leading since leaving Russia four years before. Glad for the rural isolation and quiet, he used it for reflection and consolidation. Maria Grigorevna, her health gradually worsening, lived at Ettal constantly. Prokofiev's friend Boris Bashkirov, who had spent the previous summer with him in Brittany, was often with them, and apparently provided some financial support during this transitional period before Prokofiev's European reputation was firmly established. Periodically Prokofiev would leave Ettal—usually for a month or two at a time—to make money from piano appearances in the European capitals. Strangely, he did not develop contacts in the German musical world, and displayed no interest in the music of Schoenberg, Berg, Webern or even Richard Strauss. Paris remained his musical center of reference.

In Ettal, domestic and romantic interests became more important: Lina Llubera (Codina), pursuing an operatic career in Italy, was an increasingly important presence at the Villa Christophorus and in Prokofiev's life. It was here that their romance intensified. Lina's reminiscences of this happy time, even accounting for the romantic veneer which tends to coat days of courtship in the distant past, provide a softer, more sentimental image of the egocentric *enfant terrible*.

All around it was quiet. There were picturesque mountain cliffs, and peasants dressed in Bavarian folk costumes. . . . We used to take trips to the surrounding areas, for example to Garmische-Partenkirchen, where Richard Strauss's house was. . . . During the walks that Sergei Sergeevich loved so much we made plans to take a walking tour through Switzerland. These plans never came to pass—it was hard to find an appropriate moment in our lives, so filled with creative work and concerts. Sergei Sergeevich had a thick book on botany, in which he was interested at the time—as he had been in childhood. We would gather flowers and plants during our walks, find out their names, and sort them by types; often we had to consult the book. When he would happen to find a wildflower that he had known in childhood, he would be very happy, as if he had met an old acquaintance. He would remember Sontsovka and its fields.

Sergei Sergeevich also taught me to play chess. At first I showed some talent for the game, and in fun he gave me the nickname of an outstanding young professional player. But the chess problems he gave me became more and more difficult, and I would end up in tears trying to solve them. Then he would say: "Forget it, Ptashka [his pet name for Lina, from the Russian word for "bird"], let's go sing instead," and we would play through his music, or pieces of Debussy, and we would study the role of Renata from *The Fiery Angel*.

Lina also spent hours in conversation with Maria Grigorevna, who, feeble and nearly blind, found comfort in telling an interested listener all about her only child's marvelous childhood in what now seemed like the fairy-tale pre-Revolutionary past. With Boris Bashkirov, Lina helped to write down Maria Grigorevna's memoirs of Prokofiev's childhood.

Most of Prokofiev's income came from his piano appearances. Reluctantly abandoning pristine mountain valleys, where "clouds lick my feet," for the "smoked hams of Londons and Parises," he played his Third Piano Concerto in Paris with Koussevitsky on April 20. A performance of the same work in London followed a few days later. Both cities received the concerto enthusiastically, in contrast to Chicago. After another peaceful month in Ettal, spent making a piano-vocal score out of *Oranges*, Prokofiev went back to Paris to preside over a revival of *The Buffoon* in the Diaghilev season at the Opera.

The important new ballet of the season was Stravinsky's *Renard*. Since Stravinsky's opinion obviously carried great weight with Diaghilev, one day Prokofiev played the piano score of *Oranges* for them, hoping that they would stage it. But they did not care for its obvious satire and heavy humor. "Stravinsky was sharply critical, and didn't even want to listen beyond Act I," Prokofiev wrote in his autobiography. "In a way he was right—Act I is the least successful. But I hotly defended my opera that day, and our conversation turned into a loud argument. Nor did I agree with Stravinsky's tendency to use Bach's devices in his music—'Bach with wrong notes.' More exactly, I didn't approve of taking over another composer's style as one's own. I, too, wrote a 'Classical' Symphony, but only in passing. For Stravinsky, though, this was the main thrust of his work. After this encounter, a certain coldness in our relationship set in, and Stravinsky assumed a not exactly hostile, but at least critical, attitude toward me for a number of years." After this falling-out, Vernon Duke later observed, becoming friendly with both Stravinsky and Prokofiev was "a miraculous feat."

That Prokofiev described this incident in such detail in his autobiography indicates—for he rarely admitted to other people's criticism—that it was of considerable significance in his subsequent career. But even more important than the understandably competitive relationship between Stravinsky and Prokofiev was the impact Stravinsky's critical attitude had on others, particularly on Diaghilev. Of all the composers with whom Diaghilev worked, none had closer access to or greater influence on the impresario than Stravinsky; they had been together from the very beginning, and had helped to make each other famous. Diaghilev listened to and respected Stravinsky's opinions.

In this case, Stravinsky's lack of enthusiasm for his rival's music contributed to Diaghilev's failure to commission another ballet score from Prokofiev right after the premiere of *The Buffoon*. Diaghilev had followed Stravinsky's first success, *The Firebird*, with *Petrushka* the very next season, and with *The Rite of Spring* shortly after. It would have been logical to do the same for Prokofiev, but instead Diaghilev waited for six years after *The Buffoon*, until 1927, before producing another Prokofiev ballet (*Le Pas d'acier*). That Diaghilev kept almost all of Stravinsky's ballets in the repertoire season after season, while *The Buffoon* disappeared after only two, is another sign of the preferential treatment given Stravinsky.

Two other factors also affected Prokofiev's relationship with Diaghilev and kept him from entering the inner circle of the Ballets Russes. One was his close relationship to Koussevitsky, whom Diaghilev viewed to some extent as a rival for the attention of the Paris public. The second—and more important—issue was Prokofiev's personality and upbringing. Diaghilev and Stravinsky operated easily in the aristocratic and sophisticated worlds of St. Petersburg, Paris and London. They were snobbish and condescending toward those with less impressive pedigrees and less brilliant manners. Although he was well-educated and far from a provincial, Prokofiev did not possess that same command of style and easy charm.

A musical elitist but not a social one, Prokofiev liked to think of himself as a democrat. He did not drop names or strive to be seen with the right people in the right places, like many members of the Ballets Russes crowd. To Nicolas Nabokov, another émigré Russian composer, Prokofiev used to complain about the snobbishness and superficiality of Paris audiences, but it was exactly because the Ballets Russes appealed to these sentiments—through lavishly printed programs and audiences sprinkled with royalty—that they were so successful. Despite his differences with Stravinsky and his failure to be socially ingratiating, however, Prokofiev impressed Diaghilev with his enormous and unique natural gifts. Even if, as Prokofiev once remarked venomously, Diaghilev had "better taste in boys than in music," he was an acute judge of talent. In his restless search for the new, Diaghilev could not ignore Prokofiev, and would periodically return to the composer he called his "second son."

The summer of 1922, spent back in Ettal, was quiet and productive. By now, Prokofiev was carrying on a lively correspondence with Koussevitsky, who had agreed to publish, through his Gutheil firm, a number of compositions—the piano version of *The Buffoon,* the "Tales of an Old Grandmother," the Op. 32 piano pieces, the Overture on Hebrew Themes, the "Songs Without Words," plus the piano-vocal score and new orchestral suite of *Love for Three Oranges.* Besides checking proofs of these and of a German translation of *Oranges,* and assembling the piano scores and suites, Prokofiev was working diligently on the burgeoning *Fiery Angel.*

For amusement, he and Bashkirov were engaged in a sonnet-writing competition. They each composed sonnets on three themes, and then sent them for numerical evaluation (on a scale of one to four) to Balmont and to another Russian émigré poet, Igor Severyanin. Prokofiev won easily, even though Bashkirov was the one who called himself a poet.

The "amazing serenity" of summer in Ettal—where "one can sit quietly and write huge opuses"—and the low cost of living there made Prokofiev more doubtful than ever that he would return to the United States. He wrote Nina Koshetz, who was in New York, that "it is somehow easier in Europe than with the Yankees, even though I have to travel outside of cozy Ettal." Then, too, Haensel, his agent in New York, had not managed to set up profitable appearances for him.

In October, Prokofiev went to Paris for an appearance with Koussevitsky, again in the Third Piano Concerto. Balmont was in the audience and described the concert in a colorful letter.

There is so much freshness in Prokofiev, and so many of those simple, completely unexpected charms—the kind we recognize and encounter with childlike joy in Nature when we see an unexpected little forest creature, a previously unknown flower, a butterfly that suddenly darts up into the air, when we hear, on an October day, a bumblebee's buzzing and the forest lark's crystalline song. During the intermission I dropped in at the Green Room. Koussevitsky's inflated self-satisfaction irritates and annoys me. He may be good, but he could be still better. When we are too enamored with ourselves, we don't move ahead.

Prokofiev produced an entirely different impression on me. Thin, pale, quick, he's just like a young boy. He was glad to see me, embraced me tightly and kissed me, and, embracing like that, we walked around backstage during the entire intermission, talking the way brothers do after a long separation. . . . Tomorrow I'll hear him again at his recital with [Vera] Janacopoulos. Unfortunately, he's completely overwhelmed with rehearsals and various business discussions with publishers. His life is rather difficult, although he is able to live in Bavaria with his family on twenty dollars a month.

For the two Paris appearances, Prokofiev—"harried, tired"—received about fifteen hundred francs. He told Balmont it would support him and his mother for the next three months, inspiring the poet to a diatribe against philistines.

How debased it all is, and what uncultured, heartless scum all these bourgeois are! . . . I'm sorry I didn't have the chance to really spend time with Prokofiev. His recent lack of success in business, and all the useless people around—from whom he's grown unaccustomed in his mountains—have left him completely wilted. His face was so sad and harried when we parted that I felt sorry for him.

Evidence supports Balmont's observation that Prokofiev was discouraged by how difficult it was to earn enough money from his music and performances. This disillusionment helps to explain the renewed interest Prokofiev showed around this same time in what was happening in the U.S.S.R. Whenever he left Ettal, Prokofiev tried to obtain as much information as possible about life in Russia. Later in the fall of 1922 Prokofiev met another Russian poet and friend, the larger-than-life Vladimir Mayakovsky, in Berlin, where they spent time talking with Diaghilev.

Prokofiev also revived his correspondence with old friends in the Moscow musical world—first with Boris Asafiev, and then, in early January of 1923, with Miaskovsky, who was now teaching at the Moscow Conservatory. For the next thirteen years, these two men supplied Prokofiev with information about what was happening in Soviet music (Asafiev in Leningrad and Miaskovsky in Moscow), and propagandized his music in Russia. In turn, he supplied them with information about European music, conductors and publishers, and arranged performances of works by Soviet composers, especially Miaskovsky.

Miaskovsky's steadfast support of Prokofiev, and his sense of his own insignificance when compared to his former classmate, fed Prokofiev's pride, wounded by the inconsistent treatment he had received at the hands of Diaghilev and, to some extent, from the American and European public. He knew what to expect of Miaskovsky and, by extension, thought he knew what to expect of Russia. Only later did

Prokofiev come to understand that behind Miaskovsky's stoic, stodgy reliability lay a peculiarly Russian fear of the West, which, mingled with his feelings of inadequacy, prevented him from telling Prokofiev the whole truth of what was happening in Russia. Nor, with his limited worldview—Miaskovsky traveled abroad only once, to Vienna, though Prokofiev would later invite him repeatedly to come to Paris—was Miaskovsky in a position to compare Soviet and European musical and cultural life.

In this way, they complemented each other: Prokofiev, susceptible to praise and yearning for a more simple, straightforward musical world than the unpredictable, flashy scene he discovered in America and Europe; and Miaskovsky, slow and inert, living vicariously through his friend's adventures in world capitals.

In early February of 1923, Prokofiev left Ettal for his first important European concert tour, using the Third Piano Concerto as his meal ticket. Before he left, he had managed to finish the piano score of *The Fiery Angel* ("I am indescribably happy, and have even forgotten that this whole mass of music still has to be orchestrated") and a twelve-part suite from *The Buffoon*. Prokofiev was right about how much work remained to be done on *The Fiery Angel;* constantly distracted by other projects and concert tours, he would finish the full score only in 1927. There were other disappointments as well, including Koussevitsky's postponement of the Paris premiere of the cantata *Seven, They Are Seven* from November 1923 to May 1924. It also annoyed Prokofiev that Koussevitsky was so slow in publishing his new compositions.

But Prokofiev was able to take consolation in his private life, which centered on his deepening romance with Lina Llubera. In May, Prokofiev made a joint appearance with Lina in Milan, where she made her debut as Gilda in *Rigoletto* the same season. They gave a recital together for the Societa delle Nouve Musiche, giving the premiere of the new Balmont songs. "The Italians turned out to be very nice," Prokofiev said later. "Since they are so wild about Verdi and Puccini, I thought they would turn their noses up at me, but they gave me a warm reception and much applause. (Although they underpaid me by one hundred lire.)"

Lina spent the summer in Ettal, and their romance matured into passion. After taking long walks along alpine trails, they would return home to amuse themselves with some chicks and an incubator they had purchased. "We're terribly proud of our one-hundred-percent cock, and, at a general assembly, granted him eternal life and a pound of alfafa," Prokofiev wrote to Koussevitsky. The romantic serenity of this summer is also reflected in the gentleness, spareness and emotional directness of the Fifth Piano Sonata (Op. 38), which Prokofiev composed at this time. Somewhat uncharacteristically for Prokofiev, the first movement (*Allegro tranquillo*) uses only two themes, although the first, in C Major, is a wonderfully simple and lyrical tune, one of his most ingratiating. While the harmonic style is chromatic, the piece possesses a refined and intimate classicism; it lacks the insolence and dissonant bite that first made Prokofiev's piano music famous. Even the ironic second movement, a sort of waltz in 3/8 time, smiles gently rather than mocks. When Miaskovsky saw the score, he was amazed by the slow tempos—"Nothing but restraint!" Prokofiev later blamed the sonata's restraint on his fragile health: the scarlet fever he had survived in America five years earlier had apparently weakened his heart, and he felt less energetic than usual.

As autumn approached, Prokofiev once again had to confront the issue of making a living. The money he had earned from his concert appearances did not last long. His mother's health was worsening, and there was an unexpected development: Lina was pregnant. Suddenly, Prokofiev found himself in the position of a man with two women to support—and soon, a baby. Maria Grigorevna was not a prude, but it is difficult to believe that she would have been happy about her son fathering a child out of wedlock. For this and other reasons, Prokofiev decided to marry Lina right away. They arranged a modest nonreligious civil ceremony in Ettal and became man and wife on September 29, 1923. There is every reason to believe in the genuine love between them; it was not a shotgun marriage. At the same time, Prokofiev's future was uncertain, and he seemed to be inclining toward returning to Russia. If not for the circumstances, he might well have waited until his situation was more definite before marrying.

Only a few weeks after his marriage, Prokofiev went to Paris for several appearances. On October 18, in the grand setting of the Opera, Koussevitsky conducted the world premiere of the First Violin Concerto. Composed on the eve of the Russian Revolution, it was being played for the first time six years later. The violinist was Marcel Darrieux. In the audience were numerous musical and cultural luminaries, including Picasso, Benois, the dancer Anna Pavlova, the Polish composer Karol Szymanowski, the pianist Arthur Rubinstein, and the violinist Joseph Szigeti, who would give the concerto its Leningrad premiere in 1924. But the Paris critics (including Nadia Boulanger), who considered themselves on the cutting edge of modern music, were less enthusiastic about the naive First Violin Concerto than about the chic *Buffoon* or the barbaric "Scythian Suite." They found it old-fashioned, insufficiently complex and even—horrors!— "Mendelssohnian." To most of them, traditional forms like symphonies, concertos and operas were *passé*—particularly when written in the resolutely tonal (although hardly hackneyed) language Prokofiev employed.

Moscow felt differently, however: only three days later, on October 21, the concerto was performed in a violin-piano version there by two brilliant emerging musicians: Nathan Milstein and Vladimir Horowitz. (Both left Russia permanently two years later.) Indeed, Miaskovsky joked that the popularity of Prokofiev's music in Moscow—where Derzhanovsky had arranged a whole series of performances of Prokofiev's music in the fall of 1923—was "simply indecent." The stark contrast in the reception of his music again showed Prokofiev that what succeeded in Moscow could bomb in Paris, and vice versa.

In his spare time, Prokofiev was reconstructing the Second Piano Concerto, for he had recently learned from Asafiev and Miaskovsky that its original manuscript score had perished in his apartment in Petrograd during the civil war. The apartment's new occupants had used it as fuel with which "to cook an omelet." But he had little time to wonder about what was going on in Russia. By now, he had decided to move permanently to Paris. One of the reasons was the sale of the house in Ettal, which they had been renting. Prokofiev's changed family situation and his need to be closer to sources of income were even more important factors, however; within a few months, Lina would give birth to their first child.

Paris would be their home for the next twelve years.

CHAPTER 12

A TALE
OF THREE SERGES

Have you noticed that every place has its characteristic smell? The smell of Paris is quite special
and I have always loved it.

—PYOTR ILYCH TCHAIKOVSKY

"Moving to Paris does not mean becoming a Parisian," observed
Prokofiev with sober hindsight in his autobiography. When he
and his new wife arrived in the City of Light in late 1923, it was
the artistic center of the world. Not only were Diaghilev and
Stravinsky regularly treating the Parisian public to lavish spectacles
combining the greatest talent available in music, art and dance, but
the group of French composers known as Les Six (Francis Poulenc,
Arthur Honegger and Darius Milhaud were the best-known) was in its
heyday. Chagall—who like Prokofiev had moved this same year from
Germany to Paris—and Picasso were painting. Literary Paris thrived
too, producing French writers like Jean Cocteau, and attracting expatriates, like the Americans Ernest Hemingway and Gertrude Stein.

For Prokofiev, Paris just after the Great War was more glamorous
and more inscrutable than any place he had known. Next to Paris,
New York (provincial and self-satisfied, content with repetitions of the
recognized classics) and pre-Revolutionary Petrograd (genteel and sentimentally conservative) must have seemed like villages. For a serious
artist, Paris of the 1920s was both Baghdad and Mecca. To make a
name there was to make a name once and for all.

In Paris, Sergei became Serge, joining two other Serges—Diaghilev and Koussevitsky. Along with Stravinsky (there is no French

equivalent for Igor), the three Serges would deeply influence musical life in Paris until the end of the decade. Prokofiev described this musical *troika* in a letter to Miaskovsky. "It's no secret to anyone that it's impossible to rely on Koussevitsky's taste, but neither can one deny that he knows which way the wind is blowing. He demonstrated that ability in Russia, and now, in Paris, he is excellently informed about what is going on in music. He doesn't try to take the lead in music, as Stravinsky wants to do at all costs, nor does he try to bring together and horsewhip all its prominent figures, as Diaghilev does, but he has a superb understanding of who is going where, and how various factions among the public and connoisseurs will react to various things. His attitudes . . . reflect the opinions of a rather important group."

Prokofiev's early years in Paris were not easy. Financially responsible for an ailing mother, a wife and soon a child, he had little money, and he was still in debt to his American agent. For the next seven years, he and his family would live in a bewildering succession of furnished apartments and hotels. Usually they would take an apartment in Paris in the fall and keep it until spring or early summer, when they would take up residence in another rented house in the countryside or at the seashore. Their first Paris apartment was on the top floor of a building on the rue Charles Dickens, in Passy, across the Seine from the Eiffel Tower. They settled there with their first child, a son born in late February 1924. They named him Sviatoslav.

In order to support his family—Lina's mother also came to live with them after the baby was born—Prokofiev had to make concert appearances, which meant he had to practice the piano. This displeased both the baby and the neighbors, who would call every day to complain about the noise. When Prokofiev continued playing, the tenants told the manager, and he appeared at their apartment one day to demand that he stop. Prokofiev refused to be intimidated, as Lina later recalled. " 'All right, you don't want to hear my music, but I have the right to do whatever I like in my own apartment. Instead of playing music I'll start hammering boxes together.' Placing a box on the floor, he started banging on it with a hammer. That's how it ended— apparently the neighbors threw up their hands and gave in."

Life in the apartment on the rue Charles Dickens was vividly sketched by another Russian composer recently arrived in Paris via Istanbul and New York. Vladimir Dukelsky (later Vernon Duke) had always been a great admirer of Prokofiev's music, even in his days as a student at the Kiev Conservatory just before the Russian Revolution, and he convinced their mutual acquaintance Pyotr Souvchinsky, a music critic, to introduce him. (Diaghilev had refused to introduce Dukelsky to Prokofiev, warning him that Prokofiev was "an utter imbecile" who "always can be counted on doing the wrong things.") Accordingly, Souvchinsky and Dukelsky made their way to the rue Charles Dickens, where Dukelsky at last met his idol. He was surprised to find that Prokofiev looked "like a cross between a Scandinavian minister and a soccer player. His lips were unusually thick, explaining to some degree the 'white Negro' sobriquet, and they gave his face an oddly naughty look, rather like that of a boy about to embark on some punishable and therefore tempting prank. His pretty wife . . . sang well, and was a good housekeeper and mother, which didn't prevent Serge from picking fights with her hourly and throwing her out of the room at the slightest provocation." Duke, Prokofiev and Lina soon developed a close friendship.

With the change in his domestic routine and the need to make money, Prokofiev had almost no time for composing in the winter of 1924. He gave concerts in London, Paris, Marseilles and Lyon; the Parisian public received his new Fifth Piano Sonata "with restrained approval." The need to expand his concert repertoire led him to devote hours to reconstructing and relearning the Second Piano Concerto. He introduced the revised version—it remained his Op. 16—to Paris with Koussevitsky on May 8. Prokofiev left the concerto's original thematic material intact, but made the contrapuntal development "slightly more complicated, the form more graceful—less square," and "worked to improve both the piano and orchestral parts." Only moderate enthusiasm greeted the premiere, however; the exciting storm of scandal which the Second Concerto had inspired in Pavlovsk in 1913 was not repeated. It was difficult to shock the Parisians.

Seven, They Are Seven, Prokofiev's bizarre "incantation" completed six years earlier as an emotional response to the Russian Revolution, was more to their liking. In this wild and noisy piece, performed for the first time on May 29 under Koussevitsky's direction, the French audience rediscovered the Prokofiev they loved—the brash and barbaric composer of "The Scythian Suite" and *The Buffoon.* The Balmont text was translated into French for the performance. In an attempt to make a dramatic point, Koussevitsky played the "incantation" two times in the same evening. Olin Downes described the concert—one of the high points of the Paris musical season and the final concert in

Koussevitsky's 1924 spring series—in unusual detail for *The New York Times*. Koussevitsky had already been selected as the new conductor of the Boston Symphony and would take up that post the following autumn, so American interest in what he was doing in Paris had grown. Koussevitsky, wrote Downes, "has the stamp of a leader" and, in Paris, "is the conductor of the hour, the storm center of friends and enemies, of the intrigues and rivalries of the various sections of the musical community.

"*Seven, They Are Seven*," he continued, "would have sent an audience accustomed to New York orchestral programs scurrying for the doors. For this Prokofiev is a bold and bad young man. How his music will sound ten years hence is an open question. How it would have sounded under a conductor less sympathetic to its nature than Koussevitsky it is hard to say. But on the evening in question and under the circumstances the work made a powerful impression. It is huge and rather horrible and primitive and the most effective composition by Prokofiev that we have heard." At its end, there was "enormous applause."

If Prokofiev's music impressed Downes, Prokofiev the man intrigued and even frightened him. "Prokofiev, the front of whose head is bald, whose face, nevertheless, seems incredibly young and very cerebral, like a being who has come from another age or planet, groomed and dressed in the style of today—come to examine a world upon which he may have sinister designs! A queer fellow, who seems to be delving, musically, in a certain hinterland of the human consciousness, listening to what he has discovered there, with as much calmness and detachment as if he had been a scientist discussing the theory of evolution." *Seven, They Are Seven* would not wear well, but it was Prokofiev's first important Paris success since *The Buffoon* three years earlier.

As a result of these performances, Prokofiev and his music had become much more familiar to Paris audiences by the end of the 1924 concert season. But almost all of the important performances—the First Violin Concerto, the Second Piano Concerto, *Seven, They Are Seven*—had featured old music. Only the Fifth Piano Sonata had been composed since Prokofiev left Russia, something the Parisian critics had not failed to notice. The time had come to write an important new work. Since a commission from Diaghilev was not forthcoming, Prokofiev decided to compose a new symphony for Koussevitsky, who gave him an advance to do so. Through the summer and early autumn of

1924, while living in the village of St.-Gilles-sur-Vie on the Atlantic coast in Brittany, he worked on what became his Second Symphony. Koussevitsky encouraged him to write a "hit," well aware that Prokofiev needed to establish himself as a European composer able to write for a European audience. Prokofiev's reputation was on the line.

Relieved to be away from Paris and surrounded by his family, Prokofiev quickly made the new symphony the centerpiece of his strict daily routine. As Lina recalled,

> Sergei Sergeevich would set out on a little walk in the morning to "air himself out," as he put it, and to think over projects. Then he would work almost until lunch, then take another walk, sometimes with me. More often, I would take advantage of his absence to practice my singing or to study a new piece at the piano. After lunch, Sergei Sergeevich would lie down to rest a bit (he called it "nestling down"). In the afternoon, he would work on orchestrating or on correcting scores. (I would help him do that.) He could orchestrate up to eighteen pages a day. He considered correcting proofs "rest," and never stopped doing it. Even during our many trips—on trains, boats and even airplanes—I was amazed that he would never forget the material in his briefcase that had to be proofread. To me fell the task of counting measures, checking dynamic markings and rests.

In addition to the Second Symphony, Prokofiev was composing a chamber work for a small dance company. He finished it quickly, by the end of August. It had been commissioned from him by Boris Romanov, a former Mariinsky dancer and ballet master who had also worked on the choreography for the ill-fated *Ala and Lolly*. After emigrating, Romanov founded his own traveling dance troupe, the Romantic Theater, for which he asked Prokofiev to write a new piece called *Trapeze*, in a circus setting.

Hoping to get maximum usage out of the commissioned score, Prokofiev produced a "quintet-ballet" in six sections that could also be performed as a concert piece. He chose an unusual ensemble: oboe, clarinet, violin, viola and double bass. Both the choice of instruments and the harmonic-rhythmic style reveal a strong influence of Stravinsky—particularly the Stravinsky of *L'Histoire du soldat* and the Octet for Wind Instruments. The third section is in a highly complex 5/4 meter that changes its configuration with nearly every bar. Harmonically, the quintet (Op. 39) is one of Prokofiev's most dissonant works, with a thick polyphonic texture. Echoes of some of the music Prokofiev had been hearing in Paris—particularly Ravel's—also emerge. What distinguishes it from Prokofiev's earlier ballet scores is its "abstract" quality; the music does not illustrate any specific dramatic action and is not evocative of a circus in mood, rhythm or timbre.

Romanov's company toured with *Trapeze* throughout Europe in the fall of 1925. At Romanov's request, Prokofiev added two short "numbers" to the quintet for the staged ballet which were not incorporated into Op. 39. Along with *Trapeze,* the Romantic Theater presented another dance piece using a Prokofiev score: a four-hand two-piano version of the Schubert waltzes which he had arranged (for two hands) in America several years earlier. The choreography called for the pianos to stand on stage as part of the scenery. "In the original version for one piano I had retained Schubert's scoring, but the large number of waltzes joined together sounded monotonous, so in arranging them for two pianos, I tried to liven up the music with harmonic and contrapuntal additions." Onstage pianos would be used in a similar fashion in numerous ballets choreographed by George Balanchine.

If the *Trapeze* Quintet was tossed off quickly, primarily for money, the Second Symphony was a huge and ambitious effort, which Prokofiev hoped would enhance his reputation as a serious symphonic composer. The advances he received from Koussevitsky were his main source of financial support in the autumn of 1924, allowing him to stay in St.-Gilles and compose rather than concertize. But the symphony did not come to him easily, perhaps because he was too aware of the importance of composing something "significant" and complicated, and because he knew how much was riding on its success. Even though he worked on it steadily during the summer and fall, he could only begin orchestrating in December. The Second Symphony was finally finished in late May of 1925, after nine months of "feverish work." Inspired by Beethoven's last sonata (Op. 111), Prokofiev chose an unusual two-part structure: an opening *Allegro ben articolato* followed by a "Theme and Variations" whose final variation reintroduces material from the first movement.

The Second Symphony could not be more different from the "Classical" Symphony (No. 1) which preceded it by seven years. Where the "Classical" Symphony is brief, restrained, symmetrical, transparent and scored for a small Haydnesque ensemble, the Second Symphony is long (more than twice as long as the First), remarkably aggressive in rhythm and dynamics, unwieldy, dense and scored for an oversized orchestra boasting a full percussion battery plus three trumpets, four horns, three trombones and a tuba—in stark contrast to the timpani, two horns and two trumpets of the "Classical" Symphony. Similarly, the main theme of the Second Symphony reflects Prokofiev's desire to write a work of "iron and steel": it leaps and falls by extravagantly energetic minor tenths, rising to a nearly unbearable level in pitch and volume. The orchestration is perversely complex and polyphonic; it took months just to write in all the parts. After the brassy turbulence of the first movement, the simple lyrical theme of the second, set against soothing arpeggios, is a welcome oasis, although soon submerged by excessively clever variations.

Generally speaking, the music Prokofiev had composed since leaving America had become increasingly complex, largely as a result of the more adventurous musical milieu in which he now found himself. It was a strange experience for Prokofiev, considered the most avant-garde composer of his generation as long as he lived in Russia, to be labeled "old-fashioned." But the Paris verdict on works like the First Violin Concerto and the Second Piano Concerto was that they were insufficiently "modern," so he sought a more difficult and unconventional musical language—in the Fifth Piano Sonata, the *Trapeze* Quintet, the Second Symphony—with sharply mixed results.

After Prokofiev and his entourage reluctantly left the seashore in mid-October and returned to Paris, they rented a pleasant house in suburban Bellevue. They were happy to be away from the crowded conditions and nosy neighbors on the rue Charles Dickens. The new house had a garden where Maria Grigorevna could sit, and where the baby, now seven months old, could play. The quiet atmosphere allowed Prokofiev to compose comfortably. On Sundays, guests would come from Paris to spend the day: among others, the French composers Georges Auric, Darius Milhaud, Francis Poulenc and Arthur Honegger; the Russian émigré painters Kuzma Petrov-Vodkin and Nicola Benois; the Russian pianist Alexander Borovsky; and Prokofiev's former teacher at the Petersburg Conservatory Nikolai Tcherepnin, who had also emigrated.

One sad event marred their domestic happiness that autumn: on December 13, 1924, Maria Grigorevna died from a heart attack, having reached the age of sixty-nine. Her health and spirit had never recovered from the shock and grief she felt over the great changes in Russia, or from the privations she experienced in the months before she fled to the West. Her love for her son, and her belief in his talent, had never wavered, and she had many times sacrificed her own comfort for his career, but she did not live to see his greatest triumphs. She was buried near their new house, in Bellevue. Oddly, Prokofiev hardly mentions his mother's death in his letters or autobiography, even though she had been a very important force in his life, and they had been almost unnaturally close throughout his childhood and adolescence. But Prokofiev seems to have demonstrated little more grief at her passing than he had at his father's death fourteen years earlier.

His regular routine of performances and composition continued uninterrupted. Perhaps the most gratifying performance of the 1924–25 season was the European premiere of *Love for Three Oranges* in Cologne on March 14. Directed by Hans Schtrobach and conducted by the Hungarian Eugene Szenkar, the production was "less luxurious, but more integrated" than in Chicago. It was also more successful, earning noisy ovations and the praise of German music critics, particularly those from Berlin. Their enthusiasm led other German opera houses, including the Staatsoper of Berlin, to investigate the possibilities of staging *The Gambler* and *The Fiery Angel*.

Returning only briefly to Paris in early spring, Prokofiev took his wife on a vacation to Monte Carlo. Diaghilev and the Ballets Russes entourage were also there, putting together new productions for the upcoming Paris season, including Dukelsky's *Zéphyre et Flore* and Georges Auric's *Les Matelots*. George Balanchine, a twenty-one-year-old Russian émigré dancer, was assuming an increasingly important role in the company; he choreographed his first two ballets (*Barabau* by Vittorio Rieti and a new production of Stravinsky's *Le Chant du rossignol*) that spring. Balanchine also directed a production of Ravel's new one-act opera, *L'Enfant et les sortilèges*, which Prokofiev saw. He wrote Koussevitsky: "The orchestration is heavenly, he has devised many charming tricks, but, as is often the case with Ravel, the music lacks substance." As Prokofiev many times remarked, however, the music of Ravel interested him more than that of any other contemporary French composer.

Prokofiev and Lina did not try their luck at the Monte Carlo gaming tables but amused themselves by watching the winners and losers stagger from the casinos. "The old ladies are especially good," he remarked voyeuristically. They must have reminded Prokofiev of the roulette scenes from his still unstaged *The Gambler*, and of Babulenka's sad departure from the tables. Prokofiev also played his Third Piano Concerto in the presence of the Prince of Monaco.

But Prokofiev had to get back to Paris, for the eagerly awaited premiere of the Second Symphony was looming on the horizon. Even though he had been working on it intensively for months, the dense orchestration was finished only two weeks before the concert. Dedicated to Koussevitsky, who also conducted the first performance, this "bulky and complicated thing" would, Prokofiev hoped, firmly establish him as a serious symphonic composer in Paris and silence the critics who claimed he was relying on his old music. The premiere took place on June 6, just as the orchestral season was ending for another year.

But when the dust had settled and the reviews were in, Prokofiev's (and Koussevitsky's) hopes for a "hit" were dashed. No one seemed to know what to make of this ungainly creation. For the French, the Second Symphony was too vulgar and aggressive, without the color and sarcastic wit that had saved "The Scythian Suite." Even worse, to a public hungry for *le dernier mot*, was its failure to say anything truly new about symphonic form. The critics damned with faint praise, looking in vain for the *bon ton*, refinement and intelligence which they respected as much as the raw talent with which Prokofiev had been so abundantly blessed. "A strange artist, splendidly gifted, Prokofiev is in urgent need of something that is not denied to much less important musicians: he has buckets of gold, but not two *sous* worth of reflection," wrote André George in *Nouvelles Littéraires*. "One rarely hears music so little composed—in the exact sense of that expression (*aussi peu composée*)." The symphony "continues indefinitely and stops, without any logic, even internal, to justify it. . . . It is everywhere insistent and tiresome, without restraint." Nor did Prokofiev hear many words of encouragement from the "horde" of Russian friends and associates—including Stravinsky, Souvchinsky, Nikolai Tcherepnin and Borovsky—who were in attendance.

The critical failure of the Second Symphony, his first important orchestral work conceived and composed entirely outside of Russia, was a serious blow to the optimistic and supremely confident composer. It was a turning point that sent him plunging to the nadir of his adult career. "This was probably the only time it occurred to me that I was fated to be second-rate," he wrote years later. Describing the premiere to Miaskovsky, he admitted he still could not figure out what had happened, and that he would not write another "complicated thing" for a long time to come. "The symphony has evoked nothing but uncertainty in every one else as well. . . . But somewhere in the depths of my soul is the hope that in a few years it will suddenly become obvious that the symphony is respectable after all, and even a graceful thing—for can it really be that with my maturity and high level of technical expertise that I have still somehow landed in the mud, and after nine months of furious effort?"

That moment of reevaluation never arrived, however, and even today, over sixty years after its premiere, the Second Symphony has remained one of Prokofiev's least-known compositions.

Prokofiev's fear of becoming second-rate haunted him throughout his years in Paris, where he was only one fish in a large and glamorous pool, competing for the attention of a sophisticated public and fickle promoters. Certainly it made him consider—often seriously—the alternative of returning to the U.S.S.R. Prokofiev had not been forgotten in Russia in his seven-year absence; in fact, his music was often being performed there to tumultuous ovations in packed halls. Miaskovsky told Prokofiev his music was "unrivaled in popularity" among the Moscow audience. His cantata *Seven, They Are Seven* had also been published (in a piano-vocal version) in the U.S.S.R. in 1922—the first work by Prokofiev to be published in Russia since the Revolution. That it was published is further proof of Prokofiev's continuing prestige in the Soviet musical world, for in the early 1920s terrible shortages of everything, including paper and trained personnel, made publication of anything—particularly music—extremely difficult. Even prominent Soviet composers rarely saw their works in print.

But predicting the course that Soviet cultural and musical life would take in the future had become more difficult since the death of Lenin in January 1924. (Petrograd was now called Leningrad.) Censorship had been increasing: Miaskovsky encountered obstacles in receiving Prokofiev's Balmont songs through the mail, and believed their "mystical-religious content" was probably the reason. "Something in them didn't please them [the censors]—you know a strict attitude has come into vogue here now." Around the time of its Paris performance in 1924, *Seven, They Are Seven* had also been banned in the U.S.S.R. (even though it had already been published there) "because of its mystical text," and no doubt, because it was authored by the anti-Communist Balmont.

Despite Miaskovsky's descriptions of the hardships of post-revolutionary musical life in Russia, Prokofiev was still interested in going there. He began mentioning the possibility in letters to his Soviet colleagues as early as spring 1924, a whole year before the disappointing Paris premiere of the Second Symphony. That several Soviet theatres, including the Mariinsky and the Bolshoi, were also discussing plans to stage *The Gambler* and *Love for Three Oranges* further intrigued him.

From Russia, too, came the most positive assessment of the Second Symphony. When Miaskovsky received the score in the mail, he called it an "excellent work" and blamed its failure to please the Paris audience on its "generally severe mood," which "would be understood completely differently" in Moscow. As far as Miaskovsky was concerned, music was in a sad state in Europe anyway, and audiences there had "lost all sense." New French and Italian music was "superficial and banal"; German music was "impossibly dry and crude"; Schoenberg, "obsessed with splitting hairs," wrote "amorphoprotoplasmically bloodless" music; while Stravinsky had "returned to childhood" and was composing "rubbish." Miaskovsky wrote that he had even lost all interest in traveling to Europe. His views were a reasonably accurate reflection of official Soviet attitudes toward European culture, which became increasingly critical and isolationist in the late 1920s.

Not that the situation in Russia was so wonderful, either. "I'm in deep despair, for if there is nothing happening in Europe, then where can we go?" asked the chronically depressed Miaskovsky. "The only reason we can compose whatever we want here is that there is nowhere to perform it."

But just when Prokofiev was most uncertain about his own future in Europe, Diaghilev reappeared on the horizon. Hoping to capitalize on the fascination in the West with the new socialist regime in Russia— at that time still regarded as an unknown but romantically exotic experiment—Diaghilev approached him to write the score for a new ballet on Soviet life. It has often been assumed that Diaghilev, an aristocrat and social snob, was hostile to the new Communist government from the very start. This was not entirely the case. He continued to see Soviet cultural figures when they visited Paris in the 1920s— particularly the directors Vsevolod Meyerhold and Alexander Tairov, the writer Ilya Ehrenburg and the artist-architect Georgii Yakoulov. As late as 1928, one year before his death, Diaghilev conferred with Meyerhold in Paris on the possibility of establishing an exchange between the Ballets Russes and the Moscow Art Theater. While he was surely no Communist (politically, socially or emotionally) and criticized many things about the new regime, Diaghilev continued to have faith in the power of the bold revolutionary art that Russia had produced since 1917. Some of Diaghilev's associates, including Benois and Nouvel, were, however, strongly opposed to his fraternization with Soviet cultural figures.

In 1923, Tairov's Chamber Theater came to Paris, and Diaghilev saw their productions. What he saw intrigued him, and he decided to stage a ballet about life in the new Soviet Russia. Several years went by, though, before he got around to ask Prokofiev—in the late spring of 1925—to write the score. By now, Prokofiev was more wary in his dealings with Diaghilev and told him frankly, "But I can't write in the style you favor," thinking of Stravinsky, Milhaud and Auric. "Write in your own style," replied Diaghilev to Prokofiev's satisfaction.

Diaghilev had hoped to convince Meyerhold or Tairov to direct the production, and Ilya Ehrenburg to write the scenario, but he was unable to resolve the political and logistical complications. In the end, he engaged Georgii Yakoulov. Yakoulov, who remained a Soviet citizen, had worked with Diaghilev in the early days, on the journal *The World of Art*. Later, his course changed toward such forthrightly socialist projects as the competition for the design of Lenin's tomb and the huge stadium on Moscow's Lenin Hills. Yakoulov had also recently won a diploma at the International Exhibition of Decorative Arts in Paris.

Sitting in a café on the Seine outside Paris, Prokofiev and Yakoulov worked out a scenario. The ballet eventually received the Russian title *Stal'noi skok*, but is referred to by its French title, *Le Pas d'acier*, which translates into English as something like *The Steel Trot* or *Steel Gallop*. The Russian word *skok*—"leap," "gallop," "jump," or "hop"— conveys a much stronger and more athletic image than the French *pas*, as in *pas de deux*. Since Yakoulov was an artist, not a writer, the ballet emerged from a visual, and not a narrative, conception—the source of its strengths and weaknesses.

Of primary importance to Yakoulov for a piece depicting Soviet proletarian society was the representation of building and tools—hammers, revolving transmissions, flywheels, flashing electric signals. The dancers would portray the joy of communal industrial labor, in choreography copying the movement of machinery and staged around scenery modeled on machines. The sketchy scenario has eleven short episodes divided into two scenes: the first portrays the breakdown of the old society ("Entrance of the Participants," "The Train with Peasants Carrying Supplies," "The Commissars," "Peddlars of Cigarettes and Chocolate," "The Orator" and "The Sailor in a Bracelet and the Female Worker") and the second the construction of the new ("The

Transformation of the Scenery," "The Sailor Becomes a Worker," "The Factory," "Hammers" and "Finale"). Yakoulov gave Prokofiev vague descriptions of the *tableaux* and action, which contained little psychological interest or conflict: the most important dramatic action involves the transformation of the male lead from a sailor into a proletarian. The story was both less complicated and less specific than for *The Buffoon.*

This "Futurist" project excited Prokofiev, and he completed the entire piano score (about thirty minutes of music) by the end of the summer, which he spent with his family at Bourron-Marlotte, Seine et Marne, "a quiet and colorful little place" about two hours outside Paris. In writing the ballet, Prokofiev was affected by the failure of the Second Symphony, and sought a simpler and more "Russian" idiom. He also turned consciously "from chromaticism to diatonicism" and used a number of themes "composed for the white keys alone." When he played the result for Diaghilev in early October, the impresario was pleased. *Le Pas d'acier* was originally scheduled for the 1926 spring season but finally reached the stage in 1927. The ballet would cause Prokofiev unforeseen and prickly ideological problems in his relationship with Soviet cultural bureaucrats, who objected to its "distorted view of Soviet reality."

Smarting from the failure of the Second Symphony and not quite sure where to invest his enormous creative energy, Prokofiev composed little else besides *Le Pas d'acier* during the summer of 1925. He spent most of his time writing arrangements of previously composed works, correcting proofs, and worrying about the fate of *The Fiery Angel,* on which he had already spent so many months and "which I just can't seem to finish orchestrating." When autumn came, Prokofiev and his wife left eighteen-month-old Sviatoslav with his grandmother and resumed their nomadic existence, traveling to perform in Sweden, Holland and Germany. Lina now began to take a more active role in her husband's recitals, singing his songs and those of other Russian composers as he accompanied her and played his own piano music.

But the most important event of the busy 1925–26 season was Prokofiev's first return to the United States in nearly four years. He and Lina sailed on the *DeGrasse* on December 23, bound for New York and a fourteen-concert tour of America. Koussevitsky and his wife, Natalia, who had adjusted quickly to American business and musical life, had been the moving force in arranging his American appearances: seven were with Koussevitsky and the Boston Symphony—in Boston (where they were guests in Koussevitsky's home), New York, Brooklyn, Cambridge and Providence. In addition, Haensel, Prokofiev's lethargic manager, succeeded in setting up five recitals in the West during January, under the auspices of the concert organization Pro-Musica. For appearances in St. Paul, Denver, Portland, San Francisco and Kansas City, Prokofiev received fifteen hundred dollars—"enough for poverty," he joked to Koussevitsky.

This time, America received Prokofiev and his wife with greater respect, as established musical personalities. That Prokofiev was sponsored by Koussevitsky, whose name was constantly in the musical headlines, helped him. Everywhere they went, they were lavishly entertained, as Lina recalled.

> They would meet us, show us the city and the surrounding area, then give a luncheon, usually at a private club. We would rest a little while, run through the program, and it would already be time to dress for the concert. Sometimes the schedule would be like this: after the concert a banquet, straight from the banquet to the train, then the next day another concert, and so on all over again.

American social customs, particularly the institution of the receiving line, amused Prokofiev. "In one of the provincial cities, the members of the organization that had organized the concert (there were about three hundred of them) wanted to shake our hands. The ritual was conducted in this way: a member of the society would go up to the secretary and say, 'I'm Mr. Smith.' The secretary would turn to me and say, 'I'd like you to meet Mr. Smith.' I would shake his hand and say, 'Very pleased to meet you, Mr. Smith.' Mr. Smith would say, 'I'm very pleased to meet you, Mr. Prokofiev!' and would go on to my wife. Meanwhile, Mr. Jones was approaching in the same way—and so on, three hundred times."

Prokofiev still felt that the American musical audience was conservative, superficial and fearful of the new. Later, he told Asafiev that the reviews of his American performances were too silly to bother sending, and that "no interesting American composers were visible." (Most of them, like Aaron Copland and Virgil Thomson, were in Paris.) When asked by one western reporter to give his opinion of the American musical scene, he replied bluntly, "You all ride in automobiles, and yet you lag behind in music. I would prefer you rode in horse-drawn carriages but were more up-to-date in music."

At the same time, he was impressed by the high level of performance and by the many talented European conductors working in America. In New York, after hearing Leopold Stokowski conduct the Philadelphia Orchestra ("unquestionably one of the greatest in the world") in Miaskovsky's Fifth Symphony, he wrote to its composer that the performance was "magnificent." Prokofiev also met some of the other podium luminaries then working in New York: Arturo Toscanini, Otto Klemperer, and even Alexander Ziloti, Prokofiev's old friend and sometime adversary from Conservatory days, who had also emigrated and turned up in America. As for Koussevitsky, he impressed Prokofiev with his ability to compete successfully with these formidable *maestros*, selling out the halls wherever he conducted.

Prokofiev's busy schedule in America left him little time for composing, but he did manage to orchestrate sixty pages of *Le Pas d'acier*, which was still scheduled for the spring Ballets Russes season. "We are roaming from city to city with our music," he wrote from Denver, "and in the intervals, in coffee shops and railroad stations, I'm orchestrating Diaghilev's ballet." Since carefully copying out the parts of a full score while bouncing on a train was nearly impossible, he devised a more efficient system: writing all the indications for instrumentation and dynamics into the piano score. The full orchestral score could be quickly written out from the piano score at a later point. As time went on, Prokofiev came to rely heavily on this system, so much so that some musicians have accused him (unfairly) of an inability to orchestrate. Like many composers, he often gave the tedious task of writing out the parts of the full score to a copyist.

Before leaving America after a very successful two-month stay, Prokofiev also made his first recordings—actually, piano rolls—on a Duo Art piano, whose mechanical workings fascinated him. Four of Miaskovsky's "Bizarreries" were among the pieces he chose to record. The 1926 American tour did a great deal to enhance Prokofiev's reputation and increase his popularity in the United States; henceforth, Koussevitsky, Stokowski and other important American conductors regularly included his works on their programs.

Hardly had the S.S. *France* docked in France in mid-March before Prokofiev, exhausted from the demands of the American tour, was off again, first to Frankfurt and then to Italy for a two-week tour that was "more a pretext for a pleasant trip than a serious musical demonstration." In Rome, Siena, Genoa, Florence and Naples, Prokofiev and Lina presented the same programs as in America, and then took in the sights: the sun, Mt. Vesuvius, the orange trees in bloom. They also paid two unusual visits: one to Pope Pius XI and the other to Maxim Gorky, the Russian writer then living on Capri supposedly for health reasons. The history and ritual of religion, if not its emotional appeal, had always fascinated Prokofiev; he found the elaborate Vatican ceremony of a papal reception intriguing. No doubt it supplied him with appropriate atmosphere for *The Fiery Angel.*

But Gorky interested him even more. It had been nearly ten years since the two men met in Petrograd in the turbulent atmosphere of 1917. Now, a decade later, Gorky (1868–1936) was in the strange position of being the most famous Soviet proletarian writer while living abroad, in the Italian town of Sorrento. (What Prokofiev and Gorky and a few other prominent Soviet cultural figures were allowed to do in the 1920s—to live in Europe while proclaiming themselves loyal Soviet citizens—would be impossible by the mid-1930s.) His voluntary exile, broken by regular triumphant return visits to the U.S.S.R., where he would make impassioned speeches before assembled cultural figures, was due to respiratory illness. He returned to Moscow permanently in 1931.

By the time Prokofiev saw him in Italy in 1926, Gorky had only one lung and less than ten years to live. Because of his early participation in the Bolshevik movement, and the publication of didactically political novels like *Mother* and his famous play *The Lower Depths*, Gorky would retain his saintly reputation even into the dangerous 1930s, when other cultural figures from the prerevolutionary period came under attack. His novels, stories and plays became the prototypes for Socialist Realism in literature, a doctrine he would help to formulate at the first Congress of Soviet Writers in 1932. This would signal the start of a general regimentation in Soviet culture that would eventually penetrate to the realm of music and profoundly affect Prokofiev's music and career.

But when Prokofiev met Gorky in April of 1926, all of this was still in the future. Eager to convey his interest in Soviet culture to the people who counted back in Moscow, Prokofiev was glad for the opportunity to hobnob with one of the figureheads of "proletarian" literature. After the Naples recital, Gorky came backstage and invited Prokofiev and his wife to his "rather large villa, a typical Italian *palazzo,* but damp and uncomfortable." If we are to believe Prokofiev's rather hagiographic account, Gorky talked of his concern with the education of orphans and discussed music.

Leaving Gorky and Italy behind, Prokofiev returned to Paris, where he maintained the same energetic pace. On May 6, the French conductor Walter Straram brought the Second Symphony before the Paris public once again, after intensive rehearsals. The critical response was more positive than a year earlier, but still guarded: "If they haven't learned to love it, then at least now they are afraid of it," Prokofiev told Miaskovsky. A bigger disappointment was Diaghilev's decision to postpone the premiere of *Le Pas d'acier* until 1927. Why he did so is not clear; perhaps the impresario had commissioned more scores than he could produce in one season. Among the new ballets Diaghilev did stage were Auric's *La Pastorale* and Constant Lambert's *Romeo and Juliet;* Prokofiev dismissed them as "weak" and accused Diaghilev of deception.

At the same time that his career in Paris appeared to be stalled, Prokofiev was hearing more encouraging tales of how popular his music was in Russia. *Love for Three Oranges* had been staged—in Russian— at the former Mariinsky Theater in Leningrad on February 18, 1926, receiving positive reviews and enthusiastic public support. Prokofiev was keenly disappointed that he didn't see the production. "Here I've been waiting for ten years for one of my operas to be produced on the Mariinsky stage, and when at last it happens, fate has put me on the opposite side of the globe!" he complained to Asafiev. A few months earlier, a popular conductorless ensemble, Persimfans (an acronym from the Russian "First Symphonic Ensemble"), had also performed "The Scythian Suite" in Moscow for the first time.

Prokofiev received firsthand descriptions of his musical successes in Russia from his old friend and collaborator Vsevolod Meyerhold, who visited Paris in the spring of 1926. They had not seen each other for eight years. In the meantime, Meyerhold had been aggressively defending Prokofiev—whom he called the "new Wagner"—and his music to Soviet cultural officials. Reunited in Paris, Prokofiev and Meyerhold talked about revising *The Gambler* for a production in the Soviet Union, and Meyerhold strongly encouraged him to come to Russia. By late May, Prokofiev was telling Miaskovsky and Asafiev that "I am very eager to come," and he was already thinking about making a trip to the U.S.S.R. the following winter. He was curious to see for himself what was happening there. One thing was sure: the loyalty and enthusiasm which Meyerhold, Miaskovsky, Asafiev and Russian audiences were demonstrating toward him and his music were not forthcoming in Paris.

After a long and tiring season of living in hotels, Prokofiev, Lina and Sviatoslav moved in mid-June to a small country house on the Seine in Samoreau, near Fontainebleau. They remained there until October. "We're living in a style befitting a monastery," Prokofiev wrote to Fatima Samoilenko. "We had wanted to make a trip to the ocean, but the house, business, and the boy—who, by the way, is two and a half years old today—have kept us here." The house belonged to an artist whose studio Prokofiev transformed into his working room, where he spent endless hours revising and orchestrating *The Fiery Angel* for a projected production in the following season at the Berlin Staatsoper, to be conducted by Bruno Walter.

When he grew tired of working on *The Fiery Angel*, Prokofiev would turn to composing a small piece commissioned from him by the American company for which he had made piano rolls. He chose a strange ensemble for the brief Overture for Seventeen Performers: flute, oboe, two clarinets, bassoon, two trumpets, trombone, percussion, celesta, two harps, two pianos, cello and two contrabasses. This is an odd and tinny-sounding piece in which Prokofiev reflected the hustle and bustle of life in New York in the Roaring Twenties. The overture was written quickly and was finished by September.

Homeless again in Paris, the Prokofievs perched in Koussevitsky's *pied à terre* until finding their own flat on rue Troyon near the Etoile, "a sort of funny mansard with a terrace on the roof." They had a view over the entire city, but Prokofiev was tired of moving. "All this looking around and vegetating in hotels has really interfered with my work," he complained to Koussevitsky. Making the complicated arrangements for his trip to Russia also took a lot of time away from composition. First of all, he had to clarify his passport situation: after leaving Russia in 1918, he was registered on a so-called Nansen passport, issued through the League of Nations to many Russian and other refugees left stateless in the aftermath of World War I. (Lina Codina was a Spanish citizen.) In order to go to the U.S.S.R., Prokofiev had to get a special visa valid for the period of his presence there.

Setting up his appearances in the Soviet Union was not easy, either. By the late 1920s, the situation in the musical world in Moscow and Leningrad was confused and highly fluid. Various organizations of composers, musicians and bureaucrats (whose power was rapidly increasing) competed with one another for control of repertoire and concert bookings. Political antagonisms between the factions were intense and volatile. Communications with the West, never easy, were worse than before the Revolution, and it was very difficult to formulate and negotiate agreements between Prokofiev—thousands of miles away in France—and local sponsors. As late as December 31, only days before their scheduled departure, it was still unclear what concerts Prokofiev would be giving in Russia and whether or not Lina would perform.

Characteristically, Prokofiev did insist on knowing the financial terms: he agreed to the respectable sum of five hundred rubles for each Moscow performance and four hundred for each "provincial" performance, plus transportation and hotel expenses. (As it turned out, however, it would be very difficult to change those rubles into foreign currency which Prokofiev could use in the West.) To pass the time before his departure date, Prokofiev took driving lessons "in the same school as Stravinsky," and Lina was preparing, after only two months at rue Troyon, to pack up all their belongings once again. They would move to yet another Paris apartment in the spring.

Although more than eight years had passed since Prokofiev left Petrograd, he had yet to put down deep roots in the West. He had not developed many close friends in Paris, and those who knew him there—including other Russian expatriates—found him emotionally distant and cold. Anna Ostroumova-Lebedeva, a Russian artist who painted Prokofiev's portrait (it shows him in an uncharacteristic pose, smoking from a cigarette holder), found him socially unpleasant and physically unattractive. "At that time, many who knew Prokofiev called him the 'white Negro,' because he was so ugly," she wrote later. "He had small bright eyes set in a large pale face, a squashed nose and a big mouth with wide lips. One of them was marked with a scar from some long-forgotten bicycle accident." (Most likely it was the one that befell him in St. Brevin-les-Pins in the summer of 1921.) Ostroumova-Lebedeva long held a grudge against Prokofiev for failing to keep his promise to return the original portrait to her after photographing it for publicity purposes. When it later turned up in a Moscow music store, she recalled what she had often heard said about him: "Rumor has it that Sergei Sergeevich is capable of dishonest actions."

Ostroumova-Lebedeva was not alone among Prokofiev's acquaintances in remaining wary of him. Alexander Borovsky (1889–1968), a brilliant Russian-born pianist who had known Prokofiev since Conservatory days and saw him frequently in Paris in the 1920s when they were both living there, later wrote, "I could not feel any warm feelings of friendship about him, for he did not allow anyone to develop sentimental feelings about him. I was never confident of relying on his friendship throughout life." (Stravinsky's evaluation of Prokofiev's character was strikingly similar: ". . . one could see Prokofiev a thousand times without establishing any profound connection with him.") If his friends made remarks that irritated him, Prokofiev would abruptly stop seeing them. In social situations he needed to dominate, and he took great pleasure in ridiculing others: "One could imagine that he was a real sadist." Added to his sadism, Borovsky wrote, were a steely arrogance and a "total absence of self-criticism"—qualities also reflected in his music.

But if Prokofiev had failed to find a real home in the West in the years since he left Petrograd, neither was it certain that his friends and associates back in Leningrad and Moscow still considered him Russian. In his letters, Miaskovsky tried timidly to prepare his cocky childhood friend for the enormous changes that had occurred in Russia in his nine-year absence, and for the stark contrast he would see between European and Soviet living standards: "I'm afraid you might not like it here." Miaskovsky also realized that many Soviet musicians and cultural bureaucrats by now identified Prokofiev—understandably—with Europe, and even resented him for his long absence. Where had he been during the difficult years of the Revolution, civil war and reconstruction? Soviet documents drawn up for Prokofiev's upcoming trip and concert appearances reflected his uncertain nationality: they referred to him explicitly as a "foreigner." The word surprised and even insulted Prokofiev, but it was a sign of things to come.

CHAPTER 13

THE PRODIGAL

ON TOUR

To realize his full potential, Prokofiev must return
to us, before the "evil spirits" of Americanization
overwhelm him.

— ANATOLY LUNACHARSKY

On the way to Moscow, Prokofiev and Lina stopped briefly in Riga,
the ancient Baltic port and capital of Latvia. Between the wars,
Latvia was for the first time in centuries an independent nation; in
1940 it would again become a Russian possession. On
January 17, 1927, in Riga's National Opera Theater—where Richard
Wagner spent two years as conductor in the 1830s—Prokofiev and
Lina combined in a typical program of piano music and songs,
featuring his own compositions and those of other Russian composers.
Riga received them warmly, but their thoughts were on Russia.

The following day, January 18, almost nine years after he left
revolutionary Petrograd for what he thought would be an absence of a
"few months," Prokofiev again set foot on Russian soil, at Bigosov.
The welcome he and Lina received when they arrived by train in
Moscow on January 19 was even more enthusiastic than they had
expected. They were met at the station by members of Persimfans, the
communal conductorless orchestra which had organized the Moscow
section of the tour. A frost-covered car drove them through Moscow's
frigid streets to the Metropol, one of the city's most elegant hotels,
built at the turn of the century and decorated with colorful mosaics by
the artist Mikhail Vrubel. Old friends and colleagues were waiting for

them there: Miaskovsky, Derzhanovsky, Asafiev. Photographers snapped reunion poses.

Prokofiev and Lina were shown to one of the hotel's finest rooms, where a piano waited. Their window looked out across the square (today called Sverdlov Square) toward the high columns of the Bolshoi Theater. A five-minute walk would bring them to Red Square, where inside the Kremlin the fierce struggle over who would succeed Lenin was entering its bitter final phase.

Later the same day, Lev Tseitlin, a violinist who was once Koussevitsky's concertmaster, took Prokofiev to a rehearsal of Persimfans, which he had founded in 1922. As they entered the hall, Prokofiev heard the *Love for Three Oranges* march. Thinking they were rehearsing, he advised them, in his usual frank manner, that the tempo was too slow. When he discovered they were playing the march in his honor, as a processional, he was only a little embarrassed. Overall, though, Prokofiev found that Persimfans performed remarkably well without a conductor, in the eighteenth-century tradition; their most difficult task was speeding up or slowing down together. Persimfans would remain active for a few more years, until the great changes in cultural and musical life of the early 1930s, and would introduce many of Prokofiev's compositions in Russia.

Prokofiev had never lived in Moscow for more than a few months at a time; Petersburg (Petrograd/Leningrad) was more familiar to him. Even so, seeing the hundreds of onion domes and the high brick walls of the Kremlin must have evoked powerful emotions. It was here that Taneev had looked at his first operas and rewarded him with chocolate; it was here that he had impressed the public with his fiery virtuosity.

And yet so much had changed. The Bolshoi Theater and the Moscow Conservatory now belonged to the Soviet government; many composers and musicians—Rachmaninoff, Chaliapin, Medtner—were in Europe. Musical life was controlled by conflicting ideological factions which often seemed more interested in polemics than in performances. On one side was the Association for Contemporary Music (ACM), founded in 1923. It was progressive, "modernist," and receptive to new developments in the West, including serialism. Not surprisingly, it was centered in Leningrad, Russia's "window on the West," although there were also a few Muscovites, including Miaskovsky and Pavel Lamm, among its supporters.

On the other side was the Russian Association of Proletarian

Musicians (RAPM), also founded in 1923. Centered in Moscow, the capital and holy city of Communist ideology, it advocated "proletarian" and purely "Russian" music, with minimal influence from the capitalist West. RAPM's language and tactics were intentionally crude, supposedly addressed to the "masses." The struggle between these two tendencies in Soviet music raged throughout the 1920s; in a sense, it was simply a reincarnation of the age-old rift between those Russian artists and intellectuals who believed Russian culture should follow the example of the more progressive West and those who believed Russian culture should reject that model and draw exclusively on native traditions. Both RAPM and ACM published journals in which they criticized each other endlessly and often viciously.

In 1927, when Prokofiev arrived, the groups enjoyed almost equal power, which led to a surprising diversity and energy in musical life. It was a period of confusion and sometimes wild experimentation. The young Dmitri Shostakovich (born in 1906) soared to fame during the 1920s with his First Symphony (first performed in 1926, when he was only nineteen) and the bizarre and innovatively dissonant opera *The Nose*. Alexander Mossolov (1900–1973) was composing futuristic works like *The Iron Foundry*, which imitated industrial noises, while Nikolai Roslavetz (1880–1944)—often called the "Russian Schoenberg"— devised his own atonal systems which he implemented in his music. Both Mossolov and Roslavetz disappeared from the musical scene as the atmosphere became increasingly conservative in the 1930s.

Foreign avant-garde composers made frequent visits to Leningrad and Moscow in the 1920s. Alban Berg came for the Leningrad premiere of his opera *Wozzeck* in 1927, only a few months after its world premiere in Berlin. At the same time, items from the classical operatic repertoire were subjected to strange political "updating." (A similar vogue swept through European and American opera houses in the 1970s and 1980s, but with less polemical intent.) Just as Petrograd became Leningrad, Puccini's *Tosca* was renamed and staged as *The Battle for the Commune;* Meyerbeer's *The Huguenots* as *The Decembrists* (depicting a group of progressive Russian artistocrats who rose in an abortive revolution against the Tsar in 1825); and Glinka's *A Life for the Tsar* as *Hammer and Sickle.* (In 1939 it was renamed yet again, as *Ivan Susanin.*)

Soviet society and culture were still in a transitional phase in 1927. In the early 1920s, Lenin and his advisers had been forced by the incredible devastation wrought by the civil war to renege temporarily on their Communist principles. They allowed free enterprise to rebuild the country under the New Economic Policy (NEP). By 1927, three-fourths of the retail trade was in private hands and the economy was expanding rapidly, although this ideological betrayal of socialism made Party officials very uneasy. After Lenin's death in early 1924, his advisers fought among themselves to assume his mantle, but only in late 1927 did Iosif Stalin, general secretary of the Party, emerge as the undisputed leader of the government. With his rise to power, the days of NEP were numbered and nationalization of all aspects of Soviet life—from agriculture to industry to literature and music— began in earnest. By the early 1930s, Soviet society would be vastly more centralized and less tolerant than it was when Prokofiev visited in 1927.

Moscow saw and heard the touring Prokofiev for the first time on January 24. The setting was the Great Hall of the Moscow Conservatory on Herzen Street; portraits of the great men of Russian and European music looked down from the ceiling. The program included the Suite from *The Buffoon* (Pierre Monteux had introduced it in Russia the year before), played by Persimfans, and the Third Piano Concerto with Prokofiev as soloist. A packed house greeted their grown-up Ser- yozha—whose music they already knew and loved—with enormous enthusiasm and thundering ovations.

"A trumpet flourish, followed by applause that was a long time dying down, announced Prokofiev's appearance," Asafiev recounted. "After the Third Piano Concerto, which he performed brilliantly, the joy already noticeable at the concert's start intensified, turning into unanimous enthusiasm. . . . The triumphant reception that Moscow has given him demonstrates the inextinguishable, spontaneously burn- ing creative energy of his homeland. It resounds in him and in his temperamental art." One would expect Asafiev, an old friend, to give Prokofiev a glowing review, but his enthusiasm was echoed even in so august a publication as the Party organ *Izvestiia,* which rarely deigns to comment on musical matters: "The composer's artistic health, op- timistic worldview and unshakeable creative initiative lead one to be- lieve that these qualities will turn out to be even more significant when they come into contact with contemporary life. . . . He is one of the most talented creators in music today."

For Prokofiev, such complimentary reviews, such unstinting en- thusiasm (numerous extra performances were added to his original schedule), and such immediate affection must have been seductive indeed. In Moscow, he was "our Seryozha," and received the respect and love lavished on a native son who has made good in the big world out there. In no place during the previous nine years—either in America or in Paris—had he received the kind of unqualified and serious attention that Soviet composers, critics and audiences were heaping on him. He was treated like a returning hero. These were the people who understood and appreciated him—never mind those crude Americans and faddish Parisians. Only a few days after he arrived, Prokofiev applied for renewal of his Soviet citizenship, which, according to a report in *Our Newspaper*, he had lost because of his long period of residence abroad. His request was granted.

From Moscow, Prokofiev took the express train to Leningrad, where he enjoyed an even warmer reception in the city where he had lived for nearly fourteen years. In his few free moments, he wandered along the streets and canal banks, lined with majestic, if now dingy and ill-maintained, palaces, "remembering with tenderness the city where I had spent so many years." Lina went shopping with the painter Anna Ostroumova-Lebedeva, who wrote in her diary that Prokofiev's foreign wife was "a beauty, but an unpleasant person." It must have been difficult for Lina, spoiled by years of shopping in Paris, to contain her amazement at how little there was to buy in Soviet stores.

Prokofiev talked late into the night with old friends from Petersburg/Petrograd days, like his former chess partner Sergei Radlov, now a theatrical director with whom he would collaborate extensively in the coming years, and his fellow student at the Petersburg Conservatory Vladimir Drashnikov, now a conductor. These two men honored Prokofiev in a special way, with a performance of their Mariinsky production of *Love for Three Oranges* on February 10—the first he had heard in Russian. The production had already been attracting large and enthusiastic audiences for a year.

Sitting next to Prokofiev at the performance was Anatoly Lunacharsky, who had given Prokofiev permission to leave Russia in 1918. *Oranges* delighted him—it was a "goblet of champagne." As the first People's Commissar for Enlightenment from 1917 to 1929, Lunacharsky controlled Soviet cultural policy, and acted as a force for restraint and diversity. Unfortunately for Prokofiev and for all Soviet artists, Lunacharsky's tolerant and innovative attitude toward the development of Soviet culture was not shared by Stalin and his advisers. They viewed literature and music above all else as media for propaganda and centralization of ideological control, and did not wait long to remove Lunacharsky from his influential position.

In both Leningrad and Moscow, Prokofiev heard the music of young Soviet composers. One of the most promising among them was the twenty-year-old Shostakovich, whose First Symphony was already on its way to achieving an international success. Prokofiev heard Shostakovich's First Piano Sonata, which, he later told Diaghilev, was composed "not without my influence." That Prokofievs' first visit to Russia since the Revolution coincided almost exactly with the beginning of Shostakovich's career is ironic. In 1927, Prokofiev was the celebrated virtuoso master, and his music was an important influence on the younger generation in Russia. By 1936, however, when Prokofiev would make his final commitment to a life in the Soviet Union, Shostakovich would be at least as famous and, as the years passed, would even eclipse Prokofiev as the premier "Soviet" composer.

Back in Moscow again after the Leningrad appearances, Prokofiev heard the world premiere of his *Trapeze* Quintet (Op. 39), which he praised as "lively and gloriously played." Many hours were also spent with old friends, especially Meyerhold. They continued the discussions they had begun in Paris about revising and producing *The Gambler*, whose original score Prokofiev had finally retrieved in Leningrad. Together, they spent an evening at Lunacharsky's flat. From this point on, Prokofiev and Meyerhold would correspond regularly, and would see each other whenever Meyerhold was in Paris or Prokofiev in Moscow. Despite many bureaucratic and political difficulties, Meyerhold was insistently following the path of theatrical innovation; only one year earlier, he had staged his seminal interpretation of Nikolai Gogol's play *The Inspector General* at his theatre in Moscow. This production would also have an impact on Prokofiev's revision of *The Gambler*, undertaken with Meyerhold's help over the next few years.

Toward the end of his two-month Soviet sojourn, in the course of which he gave twenty-three performances, Prokofiev toured the Ukraine. He played in Kharkov (not far from his childhood home of Sontsovka), Kiev and Odessa. Odessa has always had a thriving musical life and has produced a surprising number of world-class instrumentalists. Three young musicians destined to achieve world fame were in the audience to see Prokofiev play: one—David Oistrakh (1908–1974)—was a violinist, and two—Emil Gilels (1916–1985) and Sviatoslav Richter (b. 1915)—were pianists. All three of them would surely have been surprised to know how close they would later become to the object of their youthful adoration. Richter, whose father taught in the Odessa Conservatory, was twelve years old and already seriously studying

the piano. As the colorful account he later wrote makes clear, Prokofiev fascinated him.

> There were shadows in the hall. A long young man with long hands
> came out to the audience. He was dressed in a fashionable foreign
> suit, with short sleeves and short trousers—he seemed to have grown
> out of them. And they were checkered all over—like the cover for
> the score of *Three Oranges*. I remember his bow looked funny to
> me. He seemed to break in half—crack! But his eyes didn't change
> expression; they looked straight out, then for some reason stared at
> the ceiling as he straightened up. And his face—it didn't appear to
> express anything. . . . The audience was satisfied. Prokofiev too.
> He bowed in an orderly and satisfied way, like a circus magician or
> a character out of the *Tales of Hoffmann*.

On March 18, Prokofiev and Lina returned once again to Moscow
for two more concerts and several banquets in their honor. By this
point, he was (not surprisingly) "awfully tired out." Persimfans gave
a farewell concert and, having completed the elaborate Russian ritual
of leave-taking with countless kisses and hugs and promising to return
soon, Prokofiev and his wife boarded the train for Paris on the afternoon
of March 22.

Prokofiev took many impressions back with him to France: the
enthusiastic critical and public response, sentimental reunions with
old friends, hearing and seeing his native language on the streets,
enjoying a familiar landscape and habits. Russia refreshed and encouraged him, especially in view of the lukewarm response his music
had been generating in Paris, and the difficulties he had encountered
in finding loyal supporters, booking concerts and publishing there.
Legally, and to a large extent emotionally as well, Prokofiev came to
Moscow in 1927 as a Russian émigré, but departed a Soviet citizen.

Nearly all the composers, critics and cultural figures whom he
had seen in Russia did their best to make a good impression on him,
to present the new Soviet musical and artistic world in the most favorable light. Russian hospitality is, of course, legendary; Prokofiev
had not encountered such warmth in America or in Europe. Even more
important, the desire to present Russian reality to foreigners (and
Prokofiev was perceived as one when he arrived) as more attractive
than it is, to conceal the defects and emphasize the positive, is deeply
embedded in the Russian national character.

Both cultural officials and Prokofiev's old friends would have been reluctant to draw his attention to the shortcomings of their lives in 1927, even though many of them were well aware of the gulf which separated standards of living in Russia and Europe. One afternoon in Moscow, Miaskovsky took Prokofiev to the small apartment of Pavel Lamm, a Moscow Conservatory professor who would later become Prokofiev's meticulous copyist and loyal supporter. Pavel's daughter, Olga, was also there. Later, she recalled how ashamed they were of their own drab appearance when introduced to Prokofiev and his wife, both resplendent in chic Paris fashions.

> Prokofiev appeared in all the magnificence of a celebrated virtuoso— in an impeccable dark suit and a starched collar and cuffs (while we, in those years, dressed in whatever happened to come along). He had the free and easy manners of society and a purely Prokofievian way of talking—caustic and sharp, using short and very colorful retorts and replies, laconic and quick. One felt his desire to make a good impression on his friend's friends, but his habit of relating to those around him with a casual condescension asserted itself— as if against his will. . . . Many Moscow musicians and other artistic figures couldn't excuse Sergei Sergeevich for his cockiness and his mocking tone, his inability to spare the self-esteem of others.

In Moscow, where social behavior was less ostentatious than in Paris, Prokofiev's abrupt manner was out of place. Soviet etiquette called for modesty, communality and a certain measure of self-effacement. Even so, everyone agreed that Prokofiev was a genius: his playing "literally turned the heads of all of us in musical and artistic Moscow."

Prokofiev's old friend Miaskovsky also saw that clumsy Seryozha had acquired a new European polish—not to mention a stylish and pretty young wife. After Prokofiev had gone back to Paris, Miaskovsky wrote in a letter, "Extend a heartfelt greeting to Lina Ivanovna—I hope we didn't seem too barbaric to her!"

Russians have always tended to think of theirs as a less developed nation than the countries of the West. This was particularly true in the 1920s, when the U.S.S.R. was still recovering from years of ruinous famine and war, and only beginning to emerge from centuries of near-feudal conditions. Such feelings were intensified by resentment over the hostile attitudes of most Western governments toward the Bolshevik regime. These perceptions of Russia as underdeveloped and victimized have, at the same time, led to suspicion of foreign ways, to a kind of aggressive defensiveness that includes a strong sense of "us" and "them." Soviet Communist propaganda has not been above exploiting these sentiments.

As a conspicuous public figure of uncertain nationality, Prokofiev found himself the target of precisely such nationalistic and exclusive attacks. One came from an "anonymous reader" who wrote to the Leningrad journal *Artistic Life* during his tour.

> A strange bias has appeared in press accounts of Sergei Prokofiev's visit. The fact that this wonderful musician emigrated in the most vulgar and cowardly manner in 1918 from his own society—one that was becoming a worker-peasant society—has gone unmentioned, or has been obscured by very subtle and delicate turns of phrase. . . . But it is important to remember this fact, if only to mollify those artists who, although they didn't precisely understand what was happening in their revolutionary country, remained here, starving and freezing in self-sacrifice, and feeling, as if instinctively, that these torments were giving birth to a new truth.

It is safe to assume that the sentiments of the "anonymous reader" also reflected the views of at least one faction in the government, since the editorial content of all Soviet newspapers was controlled from above. Then, too, letters to the editor in Soviet publications have traditionally been used to introduce or discuss issues of ideological or political significance to the Party. The message—one that Prokofiev would hear more often, and more stridently expressed, in the years to come—was clear. His absence from Russia during the difficult decade of postrevolutionary reconstruction would never be completely forgotten—or completely forgiven.

C H A P T E R   1 4

C H O S E S   E N   S O I

While Stravinsky is much more tied to the Gods,
Prokofiev is friendly with the Devils.

—SERGEI DIAGHILEV, interviewed in
The Observer (London)

rokofiev had little time to reflect on his triumphant Russian tour.
Waiting for him back in France were Diaghilev and the belated
premiere of *Le Pas d'acier*. Prokofiev spent only a few days in Paris,
where he and Lina found Sviatoslav, who had celebrated his third
birthday while they were in Moscow, "thriving; his parents' absence
seems to have done him good." Then he was off to the usual spring
rehearsals of the Ballets Russes in Monte Carlo—where Diaghilev was
planning premieres of both *Le Pas d'acier*, with choreography by Leonid
Massine, and Henri Sauguet's *La Chatte*, with choreography by George
Balanchine. Monte Carlo's warm weather, tropical vegetation and casual atmosphere must have been startling after the cold and privations
of Communist Moscow.

Returning to Paris in mid-April, Prokofiev moved with his family
into yet another furnished flat. This one was in Passy, just around the
corner from their first Paris apartment on the rue Charles Dickens. He
spent his mornings writing out the dense orchestration of *The Fiery
Angel*; it was so complicated that he could complete no more than two
measures each day. In Moscow, *Love for Three Oranges* received its
premiere at the Bolshoi Theater on May 19. The critical and popular
response was generally positive, as it had been in Leningrad, but this
would turn out to be the first and last production of a Prokofiev opera

at the Bolshoi during the composer's lifetime. Buoyed by his warm Russian reception, Prokofiev was hoping (rather naively) that the Mariinsky *Oranges* would come to Paris, and even invited Asafiev to France to work out the arrangements. Neither the opera nor Asafiev would arrive that year, however.

But the big event of the 1927 spring season was the often delayed and highly publicized premiere of *Le Pas d'acier* at the Théâtre Sarah-Bernhardt on June 7. Because this was Prokofiev's most important Paris premiere since the much-maligned Second Symphony flopped so extravagantly in 1925, and his first score for Diaghilev since *The Buffoon*, he badly needed a hit. Ironically, the score was not really new; it had been written nearly two years earlier. Like all Ballets Russes premieres, opening night of *Le Pas d'acier* was as much a social as an artistic occasion, attended by *le tout Paris* and the artistic *crème de la crème*: Picasso, Stravinsky (whose new oratorio *Oedipus Rex* had been performed for the first time a week earlier), Jean Cocteau, Ravel, Aaron Copland, Nadia Boulanger, Villa-Lobos and Vladimir Horowitz were among them.

On the eve of the premiere, rumors were flying that anti-Bolshevik White Russian émigrés would disrupt the performance in protest over the ballet's glorification of life in Communist Russia. Some of Diaghilev's own collaborators, notably Benois and Nouvel, were also offended that he would choose such a political subject and refused to have anything to do with Yakoulov, the ballet's Soviet librettist-designer. But this was just the kind of publicity-generating scandal that Diaghilev adored and which had surrounded so many of his most successful creations in the past. In the end, there were no demonstrations, and Parisian critics and audiences liked *Le Pas d'acier* more than any of Prokofiev's music since *The Buffoon*.

Leonid Massine, who had returned to the company in 1925 after an absence of several years, choreographed the production and danced in it along with Serge Lifar. Massine later wrote that he used "strenuous character movements to suggest the Slav temperament and the conflict in the mind of a young man torn between his personal life and his national loyalty." The choreography required the dancers to move up and down ladders, and around machine-like constructions, with one foot booted and one bare. Yakoulov's scenery and costumes, in white and black, were inspired by Futurist and Constructivist ideas.

Stravinsky complained that the hammers on stage banged too

loudly, but André George of the *Nouvelles Littéraires*, who had assailed the Second Symphony, praised both the score and the choreography for *Le Pas d'acier* in rhapsodic prose. "In this vast mechanism, man is only one working part, only a little more detached. . . . The ensemble movements are innovative and unforgettable: the bodies resemble living cam-shafts, but something beautiful—like a human smile—is superimposed on their implacable metallurgical precision. . . . Perhaps this is no longer dance, but whatever you call it, it is a new and powerful form of art." This time, Prokofiev had satisfied the Parisian craving for *le dernier mot*. He shared the general enthusiasm over the "brilliantly mounted" production and the "large public success" that greeted his new ballet.

Although there were no demonstrations by White Russian émigrés, the premiere still caused a political scandal of healthy proportions. Jean Cocteau, a faithful Ballets Russes follower and frequent author of ballet scenarios, was offended by what he considered the frivolity of turning "something as great as the Russian Revolution into a cotillion-like spectacle within the intellectual grasp of ladies who pay six thousand francs for a box." He even got into a fight, and nearly into a duel, with Prokofiev's staunch defender Vladimir Dukelsky (Vernon Duke). The brouhaha delighted Diaghilev. In London, too, where it was staged in July, *Le Pas d'acier* received a "tempestuous reception" and, for the most part, highly complimentary reviews.

Nor did the ideological controversy over the new ballet end there. In their naivete and inability to understand the byzantine workings of Soviet cultural policy, Diaghilev and Prokofiev actually thought Soviet theatres might be interested in staging this "Soviet" ballet. On his second visit to the U.S.S.R. in the autumn of 1929, Prokofiev would propose it to the Bolshoi Theater. Not surprisingly, the cultural bureaucrats would attack him and his ballet with vicious hostility, barely able to conceal their pleasure at teaching him a lesson in Soviet reality. The official Soviet judgment on *Le Pas d'acier* would dismiss it as a superficial and distorted portrayal of the difficult construction of Soviet society. The cultural bureaucrats were also outraged that the ballet had been created by a group of selfish émigré artists who, by abandoning their homeland, had lost any right to depict such a glorious and painful era in human history. It was yet another example of the widening gap between French and Soviet taste.

Despite its enormous initial success in Paris, *Le Pas d'acier* disappeared from the stage rather quickly. Diaghilev revived it in the 1928 season, but after his death in 1929 the ballet would be homeless. Soviet theaters would not touch it, and no other Western ballet companies had the resources to revive it. Today it is one of Prokofiev's least-known ballet scores. Even the four-part suite ("Appearance of the Participants," "The Commissars, Orators and Citizens," "The Sailor and the Female Laborer," and "Factory") fashioned from the ballet's music in 1926 is much less often performed than his other ballet suites.

In Paris in June of 1927, however, *Le Pas d'acier* was the big news of the social and artistic season, and brought Prokofiev's name back into the headlines, if only briefly. Its flashy triumph set the tongues of Paris people-watchers wagging and made Prokofiev a sought-after dinner companion. *The New York Herald* reported this piece of important information one week after the premiere: "Miss Elsa Maxwell gave a dinner last evening at the Hotel Ritz and took her guests—M. and Mme. Prokofieff, Mme. Germaine Tailleferre, M. and Mme. Picasso, M. Stravinsky—afterwards to hear the Horowitz concert at the Théâtre-des-Champs-Elysées."

What the popular success of *Le Pas d'acier* reaffirms is just how much Prokofiev needed a father-figure patron, and just how essential Diaghilev's direction and support were for his career in Paris. It was surely no coincidence that the ballet, his first large orchestral score in six years to receive unanimous critical acclaim, was also commissioned, edited and produced by Diaghilev. As Diaghilev had once observed with his usual acuity, Prokofiev was always "very easily influenced." More than many artists, he needed a demanding editor and adviser to make suggestions and guide him; he did not have the artistic megalomania and broad cultural sense of a Richard Wagner or a Stravinsky. When left entirely to his own judgment, Prokofiev sometimes wandered, squandering his time and energy on unworthy and strangely impractical projects—the Second Symphony and *The Fiery Angel* are only two examples.

Like Haydn and Mozart, Prokofiev was a brilliant craftsman who felt most comfortable and worked most efficiently when he had a patron or collaborator to commission music from him and tell him exactly what was needed. It was this same impulse that contributed to Prokofiev's *rapprochement* with the Soviet Union, particularly after Diaghilev's death and Koussevitsky's increasingly demanding commitment to Boston: he wanted and needed another patron.

In a way, 1927 was a confusing year. Just as Prokofiev was beginning to consider returning to Russia after his triumphant return earlier in the winter, his fortunes in the West took an upturn. On the same evening as the premiere of *Le Pas d'acier*, the American conductor Vladimir Chavitch was conducting the Suite from *Oranges* in one of the Koussevitsky concerts in Paris. A few months earlier a performance of the *Trapeze* Quintet had earned the admiration of Poulenc. Ballets based on "The Scythian Suite" were running in Berlin and Buenos Aires. Koussevitsky would play a concert version of *Le Pas d'acier* in Boston in November. Bruno Walter was promising a production of *The Fiery Angel* in Berlin as soon as Prokofiev finished it.

Apparently Prokofiev's financial situation had also improved, perhaps as a result of the success of *Le Pas d'acier* and the numerous productions of *Oranges*, for he cut down the frequency of his piano appearances. He could now devote to composition some of the many hours he had been practicing and traveling. The money he was receiving from Koussevitsky for the publication and sale of his scores also helped, although he continued to complain that the firm was too slow in getting them out. The "Classical" Symphony, for example, which eventually became one of his most widely performed works, was published only in 1925, eight years after it was first performed.

Prokofiev's improved financial situation also permitted him to indulge in a few luxuries. One was renting a seaside villa in which to spend the summer of 1927, recuperating after the exhausting Russian tour and the noise surrounding *Le Pas d'acier*. Called "Les Phares," the villa was in St. Palais-sur-Mer, on the Atlantic Ocean near Royan; the veranda commanded a panoramic view of the sea. Nearby was a wild and deserted beach suitable for swimming. Another indulgence was Prokofiev's purchase of his first automobile, a used custom-made Ballot, with which he and his family would tour the surrounding countryside. Henceforth, Prokofiev was never without a car. Fascinated with his new toy, he loved to take his family and friends for long drives. He would buy unusual accessories, including a horn that played a tune, and spend hours studying road maps and calculating exactly when they would arrive at certain points along the route—just as he had spent hours studying train schedules as a boy.

Numerous visitors arrived from Paris, including Lina's parents and the pianist Boris Zakharov, Prokofiev's fellow student at the Petersburg Conservatory. Also living in the household that summer was

a young Russian composer named Popa-Gorchakov, who helped Pro-
kofiev in the tedious chore of writing out the full score of *The Fiery
Angel*. With his help, Prokofiev finally managed to finish the opera by
September—eight years after it was begun.

Like his operatic setting of *War and Peace*, another large historical
novel, *The Fiery Angel* is more a group of loosely connected scenes
than a coherent narrative. It was impossible for Prokofiev to include
all the complex action of Bryusov's novel, so he concentrated on separate *tableaux* that are widely disparate in location, time and dramatic
focus. Renata, the heroine, and Ruprecht, who loves and tries to protect
her from the demons that assault her periodically, appear and disappear
rather arbitrarily throughout the opera.

Many of the individual scenes—the wild concluding act in the
monastery where the Inquisitor and nuns try to exorcise the demons
from Renata, the austere setting of Ruprecht's visit to the laboratory
of the occult scholar Cornelius Agrippa, the vicious tricks played by
Faust and Mephistopheles—are evocative and cleverly set to music,
but they fail to tell a compelling story or to illuminate completely the
provocative main characters. What most fascinated Prokofiev in Bryusov's novel was the presence of so many "infernal" scenes involving
black magic, devils and wild episodes of exorcism—the same sort of
scenes on which he lavished the most attention in *Love for Three
Oranges*, although with ironic rather than serious intent. It is these
same devilish elements which predominate in *Angel*; too often, they
overwhelm the main story involving Renata and Ruprecht.

The criticism one reviewer made of the Second Symphony—that
it goes on for a while and suddenly stops—could also be made of *The
Fiery Angel*. When the opera ends, the important psychological-emotional
issues raised have been neither confronted nor resolved. We are not
given the dramatic satisfaction of seeing Renata die, or even of hearing
her response to her death sentence. Even more strange is Prokofiev's
failure to show us Ruprecht's reaction to Renata's tragic fate, even
though Ruprecht's changing involvement with the heroine has been
the focal point of the story. (In the final scene, he is seen standing on
a balcony above the action, but does not sing or participate.) The
opera's last words are given to the Inquisitor: "Torture her immediately,
burn the witch at the stake!" A mere six measures in the orchestra
follow, and the curtain falls, producing a strangely anticlimactic effect.
As soon as the colorful process of exorcism is ended, Prokofiev seems
to lose interest and moves immediately to an abrupt and unsatisfying

conclusion. The opera's huge weight and the intensely dramatic quality of what has preceded make the absence of a catharsis all the more keenly felt.

Then, too, at certain moments Prokofiev misses the opportunity for interesting dramatic effects: in Renata's long solo in Act I, when she explains her strange relationship to the Fiery Angel, he chooses an unimaginative stand-and-sing approach, rather than *showing* what happened. Even Prokofiev later admitted that there were "stagnant stretches" in the opera. It was his long-standing intention to break them into smaller and more dramatically viable sections, but unfortunately he never found the time to carry out that revision.

Musically, *The Fiery Angel* is ambitious, and represents a synthesis of many features of Prokofiev's earlier work in operatic and symphonic music. The orchestra plays a much more significant role than in *The Gambler* or *Oranges*, and the instrumentation is full of intriguing and beautiful moments. (There are two substantial orchestral interludes between the scenes of Act II and Act III.) Extensive use is also made of symphonic leitmotifs identified with the various characters. In *The Gambler*, too, characters have individual themes, but they tend to be intonational rather than orchestral, surface only when the characters are on stage and do not undergo lengthy development in the orchestral texture. In *The Gambler* and *Oranges*, the orchestra is there primarily to accompany the text; here, it participates aggressively as a dramatic force in its own right. It is no coincidence that the music of *The Fiery Angel* eventually became best known through its reworking as the Third Symphony.

Similarly, the vocal style in *Angel* is much less declamatory than in the preceding two operas, particularly for the positive characters in the main roles. Conventionally structured arias and operatic set-pieces are still absent, however. Some of the minor roles—Mephistopheles, Faust, the Inquisitor—are set in the same heavily declamatory and rhythmic style found in the music written for the negative characters (Fata Morgana, Celio) in *Oranges*. The chorus is used extensively and imaginatively, particularly in the concluding act.

It was a source of bitter regret to Prokofiev that he never saw the opera—on which he spent so many years—staged during his lifetime. Hardly had Prokofiev finally completed *Angel* when Bruno Walter reneged on his pledge to produce it at the Berlin Staatsoper in the 1927–28 season. Walter's explanation was that Prokofiev had been late in delivering the orchestra parts for the scheduled fall premiere. Prokofiev was understandably irritated and not entirely convinced, as he told Miaskovsky. "In my opinion, it is despicable on Bruno Walter's part: even if he didn't manage to do it in the fall, he could have done it in the spring." In the end, perhaps intimidated by the vocal and staging difficulties *Angel* posed and aware of its dramatic weaknesses, Walter never produced the opera at all.

Other European opera houses found *Angel* unwieldy and too demanding—the role of Renata requires an accomplished dramatic soprano with enormous stamina and vocal power. For decades, Soviet theaters were also unable to produce it, but primarily for ideological reasons: the mystical-religious subject of Bryusov's novel was simply too controversial, too closely connected to pernicious "decadent" trends in prerevolutionary Russian literature. When Prokofiev was in America in 1930, the Metropolitan Opera in New York expressed some interest in producing *Angel*, but the opera was finally judged too "subtle" for the large Met stage. Several incomplete concert versions were given in Europe during Prokofiev's lifetime (the first by Koussevitsky in the spring of 1928), but only in 1955, two years after his death, was *Angel* finally staged, at the Venice Festival. Performances in other European cities, and in America, followed, and, at long last, in a Soviet city, Perm, in 1983.

Barely was the ink dry on the full orchestral score of *Angel* in September 1927 when Prokofiev plunged into work on another opera, *The Gambler*. He had obtained its original orchestral score, left behind in 1918, the preceding spring in Leningrad. Ten years had passed since Prokofiev had finished his youthful "Dostoevsky opera," and, believing his greater command of musical technique would now produce a better result, he was eager to revise it. Meyerhold had promised to help him with the libretto. "The old version is very uneven—sections that are perfectly fine are stuck in with really bad ones," he told Miaskovsky as he started to work. There was a strong incentive to finish the revision quickly, since Meyerhold had managed to sign an agreement with the Mariinsky Opera in Leningrad for a production of *The Gambler* in the 1928–29 season. Much of Prokofiev's time during late 1927 and early 1928 was devoted to this project.

His trip to Russia in early 1927 had been so gratifying to Prokofiev that he had originally intended to return for another tour that same year, in December. The arrangements fell through, however, for vague "technical reasons," as he later wrote in his autobiography. At least part of the explanation lay in his reluctance to spend time practicing for piano appearances, for it took him away from composing, which he considered his first priority. Both the ensemble Persimfans and his faithful supporter Derzhanovsky had been setting up concerts for him in Russia, and were somewhat offended by his cancellation. Another trip to Russia, connected with the projected Mariinsky premiere of *The Gambler,* was also planned for the spring of 1928, but it, too, would be canceled when the premiere was postponed to the fall. Without a specific reason for making the long and tiring trip to the U.S.S.R., Prokofiev elected to remain in Paris for the entire 1927–28 season, "although," as he wrote to Miaskovsky, "I very much want to come."

Prokofiev and his family spent that year in the same Paris apartment on Avenue Fremiet where they had lived the preceding spring, although Prokofiev continued to make frequent trips around Europe, both for business and pleasure. In April, while driving through a heavy thunderstorm on the way to Monte Carlo, Prokofiev struck two bicyclists who darted out onto the road from a blind driveway. Fortunately, no one was injured. It was the first of several auto accidents in which Prokofiev, who loved driving fast in his new car, would be involved over the next few years.

The new ballets in rehearsal in Monte Carlo that spring of 1928—for what would be the penultimate Ballets Russes season—did not include any by Prokofiev. Stravinsky was represented by *Apollon Musagete* (with choreography by Balanchine) and Nicolas Nabokov by *Ode* (with choreography by Massine). Nabokov (born 1903) emigrated from Russia in 1919 and eventually came to the United States after spending a number of years in France; *Ode* was his first ballet for Diaghilev. Nabokov and Prokofiev became friendly around this time and saw each other frequently over the next few years.

"For four or five years in succession our relationship consisted in playing to one another our new music and that of others, and of bitterly criticizing and violently reacting to all the things we liked and disliked," Nabokov wrote later. "There were long telephone conversations about nothing and everything, about the most recent concerts, and Meyerhold's *Inspector-General* [which came on tour to Paris in 1930], about Stravinsky's *Apollon,* and about the best restaurants in Paris, and all this in the particular atmosphere of suspense and gaiety of which the Ballets Russes at that time was a symbol."

But Nabokov was not so impressed by Prokofiev's musical talent that he was blind to his flaws. "Prokofiev has always seemed a kind of big baby who must tell the truth on all occasions, and for whom to conceal his personal opinions is the most difficult thing in the world," Nabokov wrote in 1943. "Few composers have had so many quarrels and resulting lawsuits as Prokofiev, for, unlike many composers, he never lets himself be exploited."

> He could be just as boorish and disagreeable with his wife and with his friends. Normally jovial and friendly, Prokofiev was inflammable. He would blow up suddenly at the slightest provocation. His face would grow crimson and he would begin ranting and being abusive. Fortunately his outbursts would not last long, but after they had worn off he would sulk for a long while like a child, and during his sulking period he would have to be left alone, otherwise the rage might begin all over again.

For his part, Prokofiev at first dismissed Nabokov's music as "frivolous" and considered Diaghilev's interest in Nabokov as less than purely professional. As he came to know Nabokov better, he modified that judgment both personally and artistically, although he could never find a more complimentary word than "nice" to describe Nabokov's music.

While in Monte Carlo in the spring of 1928, Prokofiev also discussed possible subjects for a new ballet with the librettist Boris Kochno and other members of the Diaghilev entourage. Diaghilev encouraged them to select " 'something simple which would not need to have a long scenario printed on the programme, as had *Chout* and *Le Pas d'acier*, and something which would be familiar to everyone.' Boris thought of the Parable of the Prodigal from St. Luke's Gospel. The composer liked the idea at once." Prokofiev would begin composing what would be his most successful ballet for Diaghilev only during the following autumn, however.

For the remainder of the spring and early summer, Prokofiev stayed put in Paris. During the days, he would compose and correct proofs, and in the evenings attend concerts. One evening in late May, Dukelsky took Prokofiev and Diaghilev to hear a new piano concerto by a young American composer—George Gershwin. (Vladimir Golschmann played it at the Paris Opera.) Diaghilev disliked it, dismissing it as "good jazz and bad Liszt," but Prokofiev was intrigued enough to ask Dukelsky to bring Gershwin to his apartment for a visit. Gershwin "came and played his head off," impressing Prokofiev with his facility, although Gershwin's fondness for "dollars and dinners"—a fondness shared by Dukelsky—made him suspicious.

Dukelsky and Prokofiev shared billing in one of Koussevitsky's Paris concerts on June 14. The program included Dukelsky's First Symphony, the Suite from Rimsky-Korsakov's early opera *Pskovityanka* and the world premiere of excerpts (from Act II) of Prokofiev's *Fiery Angel*. (Koussevitsky presented the amazing number of thirty-two premieres during the 1927–28 season.) Confronted with Bruno Walter's decision not to stage *Angel* in Berlin, Prokofiev asked Koussevitsky to present at least a piece of his new opera to the Paris public. On Prokofiev's advice, Koussevitsky omitted the scenes with the bookseller Jacob Glok and the summoning of the evil spirits with which the first scene of Act II concludes, but included the long discussion between Renata and Ruprecht in which they discuss how to conjure up the Fiery Angel, and Ruprecht's meeting with Cornelius Agrippa. Prokofiev's friend Nina Koshetz sang the role of Renata.

In Prokofiev's view—and he was usually cautious in such assessments—the performance "did not go badly at all, and made an impression on the audience." Diaghilev's entourage turned thumbs down, however, and were joined by Prokofiev's friend Souvchinsky in dismissing the opera as *passé*. "Apparently they are obsessed with deciding what can be called modern, the latest thing and the very latest thing," Prokofiev wrote to Miaskovsky, "while *Angel* was conceived in 1920." Their lack of enthusiasm was surely a disappointment to Prokofiev, who continued—throughout his life—to consider *Angel* one of his most serious works. As has been the case with many other composers, Prokofiev's assessment of his own compositions often diverged from the public and critical response. Miaskovsky usually agreed with him, though; he praised *Angel* (Prokofiev had sent him the score), just as he had praised the outcast Second Symphony.

If the Diaghilev crowd found Prokofiev's music uninteresting, neither was he always charitable toward them. Of Stravinsky's *Apollon*, he remarked that the "material is absolutely pitiful, and, moreover, stolen from the most dishonorable pockets: Gounod and Délibes and Wagner and even Minkus. It is all assembled with great skill and mastery, which would be sufficient except that Stravinsky has overlooked the most important thing—horrible boredom." Stravinsky's pursuit of an intellectual and austere style was alien and even incomprehensible to Prokofiev, who relied on his natural rhythmic talent, a fondness for dramatic effects, and a preference for large orchestral forces. Prokofiev and Stravinsky continued to encounter each other socially and professionally, but their fates were diverging. Incomprehensible to Stravinsky was Prokofiev's intense desire to maintain contact with the Soviet musical world; he considered Prokofiev's grasp of politics underdeveloped and sadly naive.

Some bad news arrived from Moscow in June: Miaskovsky wrote that excerpts from the *Le Pas d'acier* Suite performed in Moscow on May 27 had encountered only "moderate success" with both the Soviet critics and audience. Just as the "Classical" Symphony and the First Violin Concerto, enthusiastically received in Russia, had not fared so well with the Paris audience, the unqualified success *Le Pas d'acier* enjoyed in Paris was not duplicated in Moscow. This self-consciously "modernist" Prokofiev was a different composer than the one Muscovites knew and loved in *Oranges* and the Third Piano Concerto. And if Paris taste ran toward the new and unexpected, the more conservative Moscow audience valued the familiar. If anything, the natural conservatism of the Russian musical public was intensifying in the late 1920s under increasing ideological pressure.

Then, too, specific political factors exercised a strong influence on the Moscow reception of the Suite from *Le Pas d'acier*. How could Prokofiev write music about the construction of Soviet society when he had been abroad since 1918, many Russians asked. "Unnerved and angered" by the negative reception, a stubborn Prokofiev nonetheless vowed to get the complete ballet staged in Moscow, believing it would succeed in reaching the Russian audience if presented in its original form.

When the Prokofievs left Paris for the countryside in mid-July, their domestic situation was about to change. Lina was pregnant for a second time. This summer, they had chosen to live in a château in the Haute Savoie which they had discovered earlier in the year on an auto trip. Visiting with them for part of the time were two of Prokofiev's old friends from Russia: Boris Asafiev, who had been in Salzburg with the Opera Studio of the Leningrad Conservatory of which he was artistic director; and Pavel Lamm, the Moscow Conservatory professor whom Prokofiev had met in 1927. Since the château (Le château de Vetraz) was near the Swiss border, they took drives together to Chamonix, Lausanne, Montreux, Bern, Zurich and Lugano. Lina later described their trips.

> Sometimes the road went through high mountain passes, for example the Furka Pass, where we met St. Bernards with little barrels attached to their collars. Sometimes we would descend into valleys as won-

derful as in a fairy tale, then rise up again to the glaciers of the Rhône. We would spend the night in the most diverse spots—once on a high summit in a little hut that opened onto a magnificent view.

Even on vacation, however, Prokofiev never stopped working, at least in his head; he always carried a little notebook in which he would jot down melodies and musical ideas as they came to him.

At their alpine château, Prokofiev completed a new symphony, among other things. Now that a production of *The Fiery Angel*, on which he had spent so many years, seemed highly unlikely, he decided to recycle some of its music in an orchestral form. Compulsive and organized, he could not bear to see good music go to waste. At first he considered assembling a suite from the opera, but Miaskovsky encouraged him to compose a full-fledged symphony on its themes.

Prokofiev was reluctant to call a composition using recycled themes a symphony—"People will stone me"—but he was so pleased with the result that he did so anyway. The possibility of "writing a new symphony for free" amused him, in the same way that getting away with something behind the teacher's back delights a naughty student. The ease with which Prokofiev could shuffle themes from one context to another was an important and unusual aspect of his working method and aesthetic: he tended to think in isolated themes, fragments and episodes, and could insert them in almost any setting to which they were emotionally, melodically or rhythmically appropriate (and sometimes inappropriate). He was not the sort of composer who could conceive of a given theme as a part of one and only one structure.

Despite its operatic origins, the Third Symphony is one of Prokofiev's more popular symphonies, after the First and Fifth. Powerful and loaded with interesting sonic and rhythmic effects, it makes up in energy what it lacks in structural grace. Its success seems to prove that *The Fiery Angel* was composed with themes—not characters or psychological development—in mind, and illustrates just how "symphonic" the opera is. (When he was writing a suite from *Love for Three Oranges*, on the other hand, Prokofiev complained that it lacked sufficient symphonic material.) Both *Oranges* and *The Gambler* were composed in immediate contact with the stage and the requirements of drama. *Angel*, however, was not; conceived and built more as an orchestral than as a dramatic work, it provided more malleable material for transformation into a purely symphonic form.

To Prokofiev, the Third Symphony was "one of my most significant compositions," and he was offended by criticism accusing him of re-cycling old themes. (He would compose his Fourth Symphony in much the same way, using material from the ballet *The Prodigal Son*.) Some-what unrealistically, he insisted that the audience should "listen to the Third Symphony just like any other symphony without a program." Prokofiev was not the only composer, of course, who reused operatic music in a symphony: only a few years later, Paul Hindemith would write a "Mathis der Maler" Symphony from his opera of the same name.

While composing the symphony, Prokofiev also worked on two other projects. One was a pair of piano pieces called "Choses en soi" ("Things in Themselves," a literal translation of the original Russian title "Veshchi v sebe") and the other, a new ballet for Diaghilev—*The Prodigal Son*. Five years had passed since Prokofiev had written any music for piano solo, and ten since he had composed any original incidental pieces. Perhaps this return to the piano now was an attempt to reaffirm the original sources of his music, which had been closely associated with the piano in the early years. Perhaps the piano would show him where he needed to go next, after the disappointing failure of *The Fiery Angel*. The enigmatically abstract title of the "Choses en soi," and their uncharacteristically introspective mood, also indicate a turn inward, in search of a new artistic direction. Prokofiev wrote the pieces "very slowly, because I don't want to toss them off without reflection," and viewed them as an opportunity to "penetrate deeply into music and into myself." Accordingly, "Choses en soi" lack both the tart rhythmic brilliance and the nostalgic lyricism of most of Pro-kofiev's incidental pieces for the piano. Highly contrapuntal, impres-sionistic and harmonically complex, they are reminiscent of some of the "Visions fugitives."

Of the three projects on which Prokofiev labored at the picturesque Château de Vetraz in the summer and early fall of 1928, it was the new commission from Diaghilev that was destined to achieve the great-est popular success. At first, however, Prokofiev responded to Dia-ghilev's request for a new ballet score with extreme caution. One of the reasons surely was the fickleness exhibited by Diaghilev, Stravinsky and their entourage toward Prokofiev's music; none of them, for ex-ample, had liked *The Fiery Angel*. Nor had Diaghilev always kept his promises to Prokofiev in the past: it had taken two years to get *Le Pas d'acier* on stage. But even more important were Prokofiev's plans to travel to Russia. As late as September 21, Prokofiev was still intending to spend six weeks in the U.S.S.R. in the fall, and another two months there in the winter. He was, therefore, reluctant to accept a commission for a big new ballet score. Instead, he urged Diaghilev to bring *The Buffon*, shelved since 1922, back into the repertoire, or to stage a ballet to his just-completed "Choses en soi."

Soon after his return to Paris in early October, however, Prokofiev's plans changed. Both trips to Russia fell through: the first in part because Soviet organizers were unable to guarantee Prokofiev that he would receive his fees for piano appearances in foreign currency, and the second because the often postponed Mariinsky production of *The Gambler* was put off yet again. This time, the postponement was permanent. That Lina was soon to give birth may also have been a factor in Prokofiev's decision to remain in Paris.

They were now living in a furnished apartment on the rue Obligado, which they had found only after considerable difficulty. Arriving in Paris from the Alps, they searched for hours for a hotel before finding one with a vacancy, and only after a few weeks—with Lina seven months pregnant—did they move in to their new residence.

Led by his wife's pregnancy and the change in his plans for Russia to reconsider Diaghilev's commission, Prokofiev decided to accept it after all. This time, Diaghilev assigned the job of writing the scenario to one of his closest advisers, Boris Kochno, who had first suggested the Prodigal Son story. An experienced and trusted librettist, Kochno was already the author of scenarios for the ballets *Zéphyre et Flore*, *Les Matelots*, *La Pastorale*, and *Ode*. George Balanchine, rapidly establishing himself as the company's most gifted choreographer, would stage it.

Kochno wrote a scenario in three scenes and ten episodes: "The Prodigal Leaves His Father and Sisters," "Meeting with His Comrades," "The Siren," "Men's Dance," "The Prodigal and the Siren," "Debauchery," "The Robbery," "Awakening and Remorse," "Dividing the Spoils" and "Return." Prokofiev's score is also divided into ten sections. In creating the scenario, Kochno added a large amount of material to the biblical account, which is sketchy and lacking in detail. The character of the Siren, who is very important in the ballet, is not found in the St. Luke version, which makes only a vague mention of "loose living" and "harlots" but does not provide an exact description of the Prodigal's debauchery.

The ballet also omits the character of the Prodigal Son's brother, and the contrast between them, which is an important part of the parable's message. In St. Luke, when the Prodigal returns home from his wanderings, he is greeted with rejoicing and gifts (including the killing of the fatted calf) by his father. This leads the Prodigal's brother, who has stayed at home like a loyal son, to protest. "Lo, these many years I have served you, and I never disobeyed your command; yet you never gave me a kid, that I might make merry with my friends." But the father defends his behavior: "It was fitting to make merry and be glad, for this your brother was dead, and is alive; he was lost, and is found." These are the concluding words of the parable, with which the narrator, Christ, meant to teach a lesson of absolute and unconditional forgiveness.

In their less "Christian" version, Kochno and Prokofiev emphasized the son's sins, which are, of course, more dramatically interesting than didactic messages. Scenes of the Prodigal with the Siren (representative of the temptations of the flesh) and his fellow carousers take up much of the ballet, although the essential concluding scene of the father's affectionate forgiveness also receives great musical and dramatic weight. The Prodigal's degradation at the hands of the drinking companions who befriend, then rob and abandon him is portrayed with graphic power. The emotional impact is so strong here, in fact, that it seems to reveal Prokofiev's strong identification with the gullible prodigal. Like the Prodigal, Prokofiev set off from his Russian home with a naive and trusting heart, eager to befriend and please those whom he encountered in the world beyond. But, also like the Prodigal, he found that his openness made him an easy target for those less scrupulous and more worldly wise than he; to some, he was a gawky hayseed easy to ridicule and take advantage of.

Working from Kochno's carefully crafted and detailed scenario, Prokofiev composed the music very quickly: the piano score was nearly finished by late November. Diaghilev was surprised at Prokofiev's speed but very pleased with the result.

Prokofiev's understanding of fatherhood, so important to *The Prodigal Son*, was certainly deepened when, on December 14, 1928, while he was writing the orchestration for the new ballet, his wife "created son Op. 2." They called their second child Oleg. Now that there were two children to raise, any thought of moving away from France—at least in the immediate future—became more problematic; Lina's mother was indispensable for childcare, and she would hardly be interested in moving from France to Moscow at this stage in her life. Nor, for that matter, would Lina herself. Three weeks after birth, Oleg was "flourishing, but his mama is only gradually getting back to normal."

As a father, Prokofiev was stern and unsentimental. His relationship with his sons was distant, even "military." Although he adored children in the abstract and remained fascinated with their games and imagination throughout his life, he was not interested in the details of child-rearing. Composing was his unchallenged first priority, and he was impatient when paternal duties interfered. Prokofiev's reluctance to express affection openly—a trait on which even his closest friends often commented—also governed his relationship with his sons. Like his own father, Prokofiev found it difficult to be demonstrative. He "wasn't at all like those sentimental fathers who take out a photo of their child at every step, or reproduce, breathlessly, their first sounds," Lina said. "He didn't have that sort of personality: in the first days after Sviatoslav's birth he was even jealous of him and called him 'the oyster.' Only when there was no one present would he look at him long and attentively."

Prokofiev's interest in his sons increased when they were older. Lina wrote,

> When little Sviatoslav started toddling, Sergei Sergeevich loved to walk around the garden with him and observe his reactions to his surroundings. He always laughed heartily when the child, stumbling, fell or plopped unexpectedly on the ground. When the children were older, he played and joked with them with even greater pleasure. He would take walks with them, help them build their stamp collections, sorting and gluing the stamps he brought them from different countries. He would send them postcards of locomotives, steamships, airplanes, write amusing letters.

Until the day he died, in fact, Prokofiev retained an uncanny understanding of how to capture the attention of children, and how to make them laugh. How much of this came from observing his own sons is difficult to say, but only an artist with an acute understanding of how a child's mind works could create *Peter and the Wolf*.

Twelve days after Oleg's birth, Prokofiev reported to Koussevitsky's wife that the full score for *Prodigal Son* was turning out well: "simple, clear, melodic—in a word, just right for Brooklyn." This time, his confident assessment coincided with critical and popular opinion. *Prodigal Son* is one of the most successful scores of Prokofiev's entire career, and a turning point in his development as a dramatic composer. Emotionally "round" but never sentimental, the music points the way to *Romeo and Juliet* in its careful balance of lyricism and satire, of romance and irony. Prokofiev's three earlier ballets—*Ala and Lolly, The Buffoon* and *Le Pas d'acier*—were emotionally one-dimensional, developing one idea or feeling to an absurd degree and giving the audience little opportunity for empathy with the characters. Although there are satirical and antiromantic moments in *Prodigal Son*—particularly in the characterization of the drinking companions and their carousing—the predominating mood is serious and psychological. Here irony plays a much less significant role; *Prodigal Son* is Prokofiev's first ballet populated by real flesh-and-blood human beings and not by cartoonish caricatures. At the same time, the harmonic and rhythmic freshness and variety, and the unmistakable personality of the music, are as strong in *Prodigal* as in the earlier ballets.

The younger Prokofiev might have laughed at the Prodigal Son, ridiculing his immaturity and gullibility, but the thirty-seven-year-old Prokofiev portrayed both him and his forgiving father in warmly sympathetic gestures. Sweet woodwind solos and sweeping romantic lines in the strings convey a new tenderness and emotional directness. The father's theme is the kind of long-breathing lyrical melody characteristic of Prokofiev's symphonies, operas and film scores of the 1930s and 1940s. If in much of his preceding music Prokofiev, like the poet Vladimir Mayakovsky, "stepped on the throat of my own song," in *Prodigal Son* he let that song free.

No doubt Prokofiev's own recent return to Russia, and his conflicting feelings about where he belonged, made him particularly sensitive to the parable's emotional issues. Indeed, nearly all the members of the Ballets Russes were in a sense prodigals; they had all left their homeland in search of artistic fortunes. Unlike the Prodigal, however, they would never experience the final scene of joyful reconciliation. As Prokofiev, the only one of them to return home, would discover, Russia was not a forgiving father.

Although Prokofiev did not travel to Russia that year, he kept in close contact with his friends there by mail and greeted Russian visitors in Paris. Among them were Vladimir Mayakovsky and Vsevolod Meyerhold. Since 1918, when he and Prokofiev exchanged revolutionary enthusiasms in Moscow, Mayakovsky had become the most visible and influential Soviet poet. His fame was legendary, nearly superhuman. But dealing with the bureaucratic aftermath of the Revolution, and restraining his irrepressibly iconoclastic personality, became increasingly difficult for Mayakovsky, particularly after Stalin came to power in the late 1920s. In the fall of 1928 Mayakovsky spent six weeks in Paris; he and Prokofiev would occasionally stroll through the city or play billiards. They would also meet at the apartments of mutual Russian friends, and Mayakovsky would recite his poems. Prokofiev would respond by playing selections from his music, and Mayakovsky "melted as he listened." One of Mayakovsky's favorite pieces was the March from *Oranges.*

Like Mayakovsky, Meyerhold saw the sinister power of the Soviet cultural bureaucrats growing. The pressure was especially intense on him and other outspoken members of the prerevolutionary avant-garde. But Meyerhold refused to be intimidated and proceeded with his usual energy and commitment, speaking his mind often and insistently. During the summer and fall of 1928, Meyerhold spent five months in Europe, where, in order to prepare himself to direct *The Gambler,* now scheduled to be produced at the Mariinsky Opera in early 1929, he visited casinos in Monte Carlo, Vichy and Nice, and researched Dostoevsky's European gambling career. In Paris, Meyerhold shared his experiences and advice with Prokofiev, and recommended appropriate reading on Dostoevsky. They also met with Diaghilev to consider arranging a joint season of Diaghilev and Meyerhold productions in Paris. Unfortunately, nothing came of it.

Meyerhold and Prokofiev continued to have trouble consummating their collaboration. Even after a special trip to Leningrad in January of 1929, Meyerhold was unable to convince the administration of the Mariinsky Theater to stage *The Gambler,* already extensively revised specifically for that purpose. The main obstacle was, once again, foreign currency. The score of *The Gambler* was now owned by Koussevitsky's firm, which demanded rental fees in dollars. There were even fewer dollars to spare for such purposes in the early years of the Soviet Union than there are today. Prokofiev, disappointed, canceled his planned trip to Leningrad for a third time.

Rehearsals for *The Prodigal Son* and the other new productions of what was to be the last Ballets Russes season began as usual in Monte Carlo in March. Prokofiev and Lina drove there—setting a record (for them) of seventy miles at one stretch—from Paris, arriving at the end of the month. Diaghilev participated in the rehearsals, as he had for more than twenty years, but his health was obviously deteriorating, and he tired easily.

All those who observed and participated in preparations for *Prod-*

igal Son noticed how unusually emotional Diaghilev was in his approach to this ballet, and what an active role he assumed in creating it. He encouraged both Balanchine and Lifar (who danced the role of the Prodigal) to stress the psychological aspects of the story, as the music did. Originally, Diaghilev had hoped that Henri Matisse would design the ballet, but when he declined, the job was given to Georges Rouault, who came to Monte Carlo to work out the designs with Prokofiev and Balanchine. Days passed without any sign of progress from Rouault, however, which made Diaghilev very uneasy. Annoyed, the impresario finally announced to the artist one evening that a train ticket had been booked for him to Paris the next day. By morning the sketches for the magnificent backdrops were finished, in a burst of inspiration, and presented to Diaghilev, who was pleased with the work.

The season promised to be a good one for Prokofiev; for the first time, two of his ballets would be running simultaneously—*Le Pas d'acier* (for the third season in a row) and *Prodigal Son*.

In these last months of his life, in fact, Diaghilev seemed to be taking a greater interest in Prokofiev and his music than ever before. According to Diaghilev's longtime adviser Nouvel, Diaghilev had "immense admiration" for Prokofiev and his art. Despite his failing health, he even traveled to Brussels to see *The Gambler*, which had its often delayed world premiere on April 29, 1929, at the Théâtre de la Monnaie. He praised it, especially the roulette scenes, although he confessed that he did not like the "declamatory operatic style."

For Prokofiev, it was gratifying to finally see his first serious opera on stage, although he was disappointed that it was given in Brussels, not in Leningrad, and in French, not in Russian. The revised version staged in Brussels had been completed with Meyerhold's help and became the standard performing version that is produced today. "Many dynamics of the soul which Dostoevsky illustrates would have been understood very differently in Russia," Prokofiev wrote of the Brussels production some years later. "In Brussels they were received with interest, but often as some incomprehensible mania peculiar to the Slavic soul." Overall, however, the Brussels production satisfied Prokofiev—particularly from a musical viewpoint—and the opera was sufficiently well-received to stay in the repertoire there for two years. After the final curtain on opening night, the entire audience responded with an enthusiastic ovation, turning around to face the loge where Prokofiev was sitting. The reviews were highly favorable as well.

Returning to Paris from Brussels in early May, Prokofiev threw himself into preparations for two more premieres in the space of four days. "I wandered from one premiere to another like a bee between three hives," he told Miaskovsky. The Third Symphony was introduced on May 17 by Pierre Monteux, whose interpretation struck Prokofiev as "conscientious, but earthbound." The reviews were respectful, if not ecstatic. One critic praised Prokofiev's independent spirit, pointing out that amid all the fads proliferating on the Paris musical scene, Prokofiev "thinks simply, in his own way, which is rare these days." Another decided that "the Scythian has descended to southern shores and become more human." Perhaps unexpectedly in view of their distaste for *The Fiery Angel*, Diaghilev and Stravinsky were among the symphony's admirers.

But the most well publicized of the premieres was, of course, *The Prodigal Son*, which opened the last Paris season of the Ballets Russes on May 21, 1929. In the last weeks before the opening, Prokofiev clashed frequently with Balanchine and Diaghilev over the staging. By the time Prokofiev returned from Brussels, the production was already assembled, and he was not at all pleased with what he saw. He had envisioned something more realistic and literal than Balanchine's spare, abstract and symbolic choreography, and complained that the dancing did "not fit the subject."

"He wanted a real garden and real wine and real mustaches and all that," Balanchine said many years later, with unconcealed disdain. "You know, Prokofiev was a great chess player, and that's how he thought—in straight mathematical lines. He wanted the *Prodigal* to look like *Rigoletto*. He complained so insistently that Diaghilev finally told him, 'Look, this is how we're doing it. If you don't like it, you can just get out of here.' " Diaghilev's will—and Balanchine's interpretation—naturally prevailed. In his autobiography, Prokofiev dismissed the disagreement as a result of his late arrival at rehearsals and claimed that Stravinsky, too, was arguing with Diaghilev at this time.

Appearing with *Prodigal Son* on the particularly rich opening program were Stravinsky's *Renard*, Auric's *Les Facheux*, and, appropriately for such an occasion, the dances from Borodin's *Prince Igor*, which had opened the first Ballets Russes Paris season in the same theatre twenty years earlier. Tickets had been sold out long before, and the papers were full of articles about the company and the composers, including Prokofiev. In several interviews, Diaghilev spoke highly of *Prodigal Son* and its creator, calling the score a "masterpiece" and a "great musical event. . . . At this moment when we are experiencing such a shortage of real feelings, it seems simply incredible that Prokofiev could have found such musical expressiveness."

Comparisons with Stravinsky were once again inevitable, however: "Stravinsky . . . is the living embodiment of genuine enthusiasm, of genuine love for art and of eternal searching—and therein lies the difference between him and Prokofiev," Diaghilev said. "Prokofiev does not stand still either, of course; he also evolves, but he proceeds along a path that is precisely laid out according to an immutable pattern established once and for all. Stravinsky is forever rushing about, searching, and, at each step, negating himself, negating, as it were, what he was in his preceding compositions."

The usual glitter surrounded the opening night at the Théâtre Sarah-Bernhardt. Prokofiev had little patience for the pretensions of *le tout Paris* and condemned the social "parade" in the lobby as "most dreadful." Rachmaninoff sat in the front row.

The evening began with *Renard,* conducted by Stravinsky. *Prodigal Son* followed. Prokofiev, who had not been seen on the podium for several years, conducted. Serge Lifar, fierce but vulnerable, achieved one of his greatest successes in the highly dramatic role of the Prodigal; dancing opposite him as the Siren, shrouded in white and black, was the statuesque Felia Dubrovska. At the final scene of reconciliation, when the chastened Prodigal returns to his father's embrace, accompanied by the wistful lyricism of one of Prokofiev's greatest themes, many in the jaded audience shed tears. Such open emotionalism had rarely been seen in the twenty-year history of the Ballets Russes, whose aesthetic had been founded on a hatred of sentimentality. But these tears were earned. As Balanchine explained, it was "Lifar, on his knees, that made the ballet."

Both the audience and critics responded with enormous affection and enthusiasm. "None of my works has been so unanimously well-received for a long time as this ballet," Prokofiev told Miaskovsky. In *Oeune,* Raoul Brunel even proclaimed that Prokofiev was more comprehensible to Europeans than Stravinsky, "whose gaiety appeals to infantile and monstrous impulses in the barbaric substratum of the Slavic soul." Many noted the new emotional quality of the score. "Together with the explosiveness and vibrant energy we have come to expect, he shows us gifts of feeling and simplicity that our public did not suspect in him."

After the performance, the cast, composers and crew celebrated lavishly at a happy gathering at the Restaurant des Capucines, attended by the usual socialites, including Coco Chanel and Misia Sert.

Despite Prokofiev's dissatisfaction with Balanchine's stylized choreography—he liked Rouault's sets—*Prodigal Son* was the first of his ballets to achieve an international reputation and become a standard repertory item. It enjoyed great success that same season in Berlin and London, and eventually, years after Diaghilev's death, Balanchine would re-create it with the New York City Ballet.

Prodigal Son did not create a friendship between Balanchine and Prokofiev, however. In fact, Prokofiev repeated his pattern of alienating those who could most help him by offending the choreographer, now clearly emerging as Diaghilev's heir apparent. In addition to their artistic differences over the staging, Prokofiev and Balanchine quarreled about money. In this era before elaborate contracts and unions, choreographers received no fixed percentage of the royalties and tended to rely on a gentleman's agreement. When they collaborated on *Apollon* the previous season, for example, Stravinsky had agreed to give a certain percentage of his royalties to Balanchine. According to Balanchine, when he approached Prokofiev with the same proposal Prokofiev refused to hear of it, and even became abusive. "Why should you get money? Who are you? You're nothing but a lousy ballet master. Get out!"

Not surprisingly, Balanchine and Prokofiev never worked together again. Like Diaghilev before him, Balanchine would turn to the less obstreperous Stravinsky.

As the Paris season of the Ballets Russes ended on June 12, 1929, and the company moved on to Berlin and London, Diaghilev's health was rapidly deteriorating. Diabetes—then an incurable disease—was sapping his strength, and his body was covered with abscesses. Even so, he was full of plans for the next season and pleased with how well the one just past had gone. In early August, Diaghilev went to Venice, where, becoming weaker by the day, he was nursed by Serge Lifar and Boris Kochno. They were by his side when he died on August 19, at the age of fifty-seven. With him an era in Russian culture came to a close; perhaps the strongest surviving link to the prerevolutionary past was severed.

For Prokofiev, who, absorbed with his own schedule and activities, seems to have been little aware of Diaghilev's delicate condition, the impresario's passing came as a shock. Despite the ups and downs in their relationship, Diaghilev had believed in Prokofiev's talent for fifteen years and had made him a name (with Koussevitsky's help) in Paris. Each of the scores Prokofiev composed for Diaghilev—*Ala and Lolly* ("The Scythian Suite"), *The Buffoon, Le Pas d'acier, The Prodigal Son*—had been highly successful in its own way. Each score attained its final form only with Diaghilev's help and guidance. If anything, Prokofiev had needed Diaghilev more than Diaghilev had needed Prokofiev. With Diaghilev's death and Koussevitsky's increasingly demanding commitment to the Boston Symphony, Prokofiev was suddenly deprived of his two most influential Paris sponsors. And unlike Stravinsky, Prokofiev had not developed strong independent relationships with other members of the Ballets Russes, many of whom did not share Diaghilev's admiration for Prokofiev as an artist and felt little personal affection for him.

"You can understand what a terrific impact the news about Diaghilev's death had on me," Prokofiev wrote to Asafiev in late August. "His death stunned me not so much musically, since it has seemed to me recently that *Prodigal Son* brought the cycle of our collaboration to an end, nor even personally, since his image is still so clear and vital that I can't picture him gone. Most of all, his death signals the disappearance of an enormous and unquestionably unique figure, whose stature increases as he recedes into history."

Even in his 1941 autobiography, written at a moment in Soviet cultural history when Diaghilev was reviled as a decadent escapist who had seduced Russian artists away from the difficult task of reconstructing the homeland, Prokofiev would defend him. "Diaghilev's artistic activities are still insufficiently valued in the Soviet Union," he would write, "and many are inclined to see him as nothing more than an impresario who sucked the brains out of artists. In fact, his influence on art and his services in the propaganda of Russian art were colossal in scope." If anything, Prokofiev's official defense of Diaghilev, delivered in the terrible aftermath of the purges which carried off many of their mutual friends, was over-eager and phrased to placate the cultural commissars. One hopes that Prokofiev did not really believe that Diaghilev, whose aesthetic and style of life were profoundly alien to the spirit of Socialist Realism, "would now be working in Russia if he were still alive." As Prokofiev should have known by then, Diaghilev would not have remained alive for long if he had returned to Russia.

But all of this was in the future. In the summer of 1929, this much was clear: the possibility of working with Diaghilev and the Ballets Russes—one of the possibilities that had led Prokofiev to leave Russia in the first place—had vanished. He had one less reason to stay abroad.

CHAPTER 15

OUR MUSICAL
ADVANCE POST

I work everywhere, always, and I have no need
for meditation or privacy.

—SERGEI PROKOFIEV, interviewed in *Candide*

The resounding success of *The Prodigal Son,* the premieres of *The Gambler* and the Third Symphony, and regular income from performances of popular published works like *Love for Three Oranges,* the "Classical" Symphony, "The Scythian Suite" and the Third Piano Concerto had significantly improved Prokofiev's financial position. Some of this money was spent on rental of a hilltop château near a lake in Culoz, in central France, where Prokofiev and his family spent the summer of 1929. Châteaux and castles had always fascinated him, perhaps because he could imagine their former inhabitants as characters in fairy tales. Discovered on one of their auto trips, the Château de la Flechère was a fourteenth-century structure rebuilt in the seventeenth and now owned by an impoverished aristocratic family. "Awkwardly laid out, not too comfortable, but with a marvelous view on all sides," it had "thick walls, towers and an enormous amount of space." It was so large that if its two pianos were placed at opposite ends of the château, they could be played simultaneously without either pianist hearing the other. At night, the huge cockroaches rustling in the kitchen inspired Prokofiev to invent stories of how they were really the château's former residents, now cast under a spell.

Prokofiev was now able to afford the luxury of a full-time personal secretary, who lived with them at the Château de la Flechère. His name was Mikhail Astrov. Grandson of a nineteenth-century Russian ballet composer, Astrov had been working at Koussevitsky's publishing house when Prokofiev hired him away to help with correspondence and to write out full orchestral scores from his annotated piano scores. Remarkably dedicated to Prokofiev, Astrov viewed him with unshakeable awe and admiration, and worked devotedly as his copyist until 1935. He spent several summers with the Prokofiev family and viewed these as the happiest years of his life.

Astrov paints a rosy and affluent picture of life in the Prokofiev household. There were governesses to help with the children, he recalls, and servants and cooks to take care of the meals and housework. Lina was elegant, beautiful and admired by society. Russian was the language most often spoken at home, although Prokofiev, Lina and the boys could all speak French quite well.

During the summer of 1929, Astrov helped Prokofiev complete two projects: a second revision of the youthful Sinfonietta and a new orchestral Divertissement. (Prokofiev was also in the early phases of work on his Fourth Symphony, some of whose themes came from *Prodigal Son*.) The Sinfonietta, of course, had first been composed twenty years earlier, when Prokofiev was a Conservatory student, but he kept tinkering with it. The piece had already been rewritten once, in 1914. Although no fresh material was added in 1929, Prokofiev considered the charmingly light and cheerful reworking extensive enough to give it the new double opus number 5/48.

Almost all of the material for the four-movement Divertissement had been composed originally for other purposes: the first and third movements had been written for the ballet *Trapeze* in 1925; the second was composed independently, in 1928; and the final movement came from music originally written for—but not used in—*The Prodigal Son*. In orchestrating the Divertissement, Prokofiev admitted that he was influenced by the "ascetic" ideas of Stravinsky, with whom he restored more cordial relations that summer. One of the reasons was that Stravinsky and his family were spending the summer nearby, at Lac d'Annecy. On their way there, Stravinsky and his sons Théodore and Soulima stopped to see the Prokofievs at Château de la Flechère. Later in the summer, the Prokofievs visited Stravinsky at Lac d'Annecy and, as Lina later wrote, "we saw all the family. I remember his mother, a small, rather severe little old lady, before whom Stravinsky seemed not at his usual ease." Stravinsky played them his new piece for piano and orchestra, which he eventually called a "Capriccio." Prokofiev pronounced it "less derivative" than Stravinsky's other music.

After Diaghilev's death and the collapse of the Ballets Russes, the relationship between Prokofiev and Stravinsky, never intimate, became more distant. As Prokofiev began developing a close relationship to the U.S.S.R. in the early 1930s, their paths diverged radically. Many observers, including Lina Prokofiev, have commented on how different the two composers were in personality and temperament. "They were both profoundly Russian, but in totally different ways," she said. "They both had their weaknesses. Prokofiev had this prankishness and Stravinsky had a sufficient touch of loftiness to react bitterly to every remark—unharmful as it might be." Or was the problem that they were too much *alike*—both being volatile, stubborn and domineering?

Prokofiev's relationship with the stoic and unexcitable Miaskovsky was much more stable. He had been hoping that Miaskovsky would finally shake off his paralyzing inertia and come for a visit from Moscow, as Asafiev and Lamm had done the previous summer. Making extraordinary efforts on Miaskovsky's behalf, he wrote an official letter of invitation to the Soviet Embassy in Paris promising to pay for his return trip, setting up official lectures for him, offering to lend him any money he might need and to provide food and lodging.

But Miaskovsky's fear of the new—he pleaded illness, family problems and financial complications with dogged persistence—got the better of him, and he stayed behind guiltily in Moscow. "I'm very much at fault," he wrote in August. "My behavior has been extremely boorish. . . . Don't be angry." No doubt political considerations— Soviet citizens were now discouraged from traveling to the West—also played a part in Miaskovsky's decision. Prokofiev forgave him, chiding gently: "The summer was nicely arranged to air you out in the hills and lakes, to dine you with various French delicacies and to wine you with a whole gamut of vintages, beginning with 1830."

In early October the summer idyll ended, and the Prokofiev entourage headed back to Paris in their car. On the way, the composer's career nearly came to an early end when he was involved in another auto accident. Before setting out, they had noticed something wrong with the rear left wheel, and had it repaired—or so they thought. Lina recalled,

Not far from Paris, I suddenly felt the car tilt sharply, and thought something had happened to Sergei Sergeevich. Then there was a horrible crash (in happened in a second). . . . I came around to the sound of the children crying. I could only open one eye—the other one seemed to have been knocked out. . . . There was wreckage and glass all around. . . . I rushed to Sergei Sergeevich. He was half-conscious. It turned out we had lost our rear wheel while traveling at full speed (about forty or fifty miles per hour). Sergei Sergeevich was at the wheel and could have been killed if the car had headed toward a nearby tree. Seeing that we were all alive, Sergei Sergeevich immediately asked, "Where are my manuscripts?"

In Paris, rumors spread that we were all in nearly hopeless condition after the accident. Articles about us appeared in the newspapers. Sympathetic telegrams arrived from nearly every country, asking us to clarify what had happened. We escaped with a few days of bed rest.

Miraculously, Prokofiev's injuries were confined to a lost tooth, "black and blue marks all over my body" and a pulled muscle in his left hand that prevented him from playing an octave spread on the piano. After this accident, Prokofiev drove much more cautiously—in fact almost overcautiously, as numerous of his subsequent passengers have recalled with chagrin. Indulging his fondness for velocity proved less dangerous to Prokofiev in his music than in his driving.

It was fortunate that Prokofiev's hand was only slightly injured, for he had an important American concert tour arranged for the coming winter season. He was also committed to a three-week trip to Russia scheduled for October 30, only a few weeks after the accident, but it did not include any piano performances. After the exhausting pace of his 1927 Russian tour—"I just didn't see any life for all the concerts"—Prokofiev had decided this time to refuse piano appearances. Instead, he wanted to concentrate on working out the details of proposed Soviet productions of his operas and ballets.

Before leaving for Moscow, Prokofiev settled his family into their last temporary home in Paris, on the rue Bassano near the Arc de Triomphe. They would stay there for only two months, and he for only a few weeks between trips. Even after nearly twelve years away from Russia, and six in Paris, Prokofiev still had no permanent home. He and his family had few possessions and rented furnished apartments. Clearly, Prokofiev still placed a premium on mobility and seemed reluctant to put down roots in the West.

On October 30, having traveled via Berlin and Warsaw, Prokofiev arrived by train in Moscow. This time, Lina had stayed home with the boys in Paris. It did not take long for Prokofiev to notice that the cultural climate in Russia in late 1929 had changed markedly from the time of his last visit almost three years before. Letters from Miaskovsky and Meyerhold had prepared him for the change to some extent; they had also been sending him clippings from Soviet newspapers and magazines, whose tone had become ever more strident, intolerant and self-righteous.

By late 1929, the chaotic pluralism that was characteristic of Soviet culture during the 1920s was fast yielding to regimentation. In the field of music, the "violently anti-modern, anti-Western, anti-jazz, often anti-classical" policies of the Russian Association of Proletarian Musicians (RAPM) now dominated. The pro-Western and "modernist" policies of their opponents, the Association for Contemporary Music, had been largely discredited and shouted down. After RAPM's victory, an extreme and dogmatic anti-Western attitude prevailed in the musical press, in the concert repertoire and in the conservatories. For nearly three years, until the radical reorganization of all cultural organizations in 1932, RAPM enjoyed a virtual monopoly, and engaged in gleeful and destructive polemics against its critics and opponents.

Being a "semi-European," Prokofiev came under sharp attack in RAPM's official organ, *Proletarian Musician*. In a long article in the first issue of 1929, a writer hiding behind the initials K.Sh. fumed,

> Prokofiev's works entered our daily musical life amazingly quickly, and became the most common sort of music for all of us. No longer did they astonish anyone, or create an impression of keen innovation or originality. At the same time, the aura surrounding Prokofiev was to a large extent disappearing as well. We had seen a genius in Prokofiev, and expected him to discover new horizons in music, but each one of his new works has only disappointed us in these hopes. More and more, disillusionment is replacing our former ecstasy and deference.

After reading the article, Prokofiev wrote Meyerhold, who had sent it to him in France, that it was a "sad specimen," full of "malicious stupidity and stupid malice," but he did not appear to take it too seriously.

But when he got to Moscow in the autumn, Prokofiev encountered even more direct criticism, particularly in connection with *Le Pas d'acier*. The Bolshoi Theater had long been considering staging the ballet; excerpts from its music had already been performed three times in concert in the capital. Now that Prokofiev was there in person, an official listening session was set up to present the ballet and its music to official representatives from the Bolshoi and RAPM. Held at the Bolshoi on November 14, the session was Prokofiev's first experience of a peculiarly Soviet ritual with which he could become only too familiar in subsequent years. Aware of the changing attitude toward Prokofiev, Meyerhold had already defended his friend against the charge of "émigré-ism" in a speech at the Bolshoi one month earlier. "Due to various circumstances," Meyerhold had said, "Prokofiev lives not in Moscow but in Paris. . . . This does not mean, however, that Prokofiev is not one of us. Though living in Paris, he can still maintain contact with us, he can build . . . because inside himself, he is with us."

Meyerhold added to his defense of Prokofiev and *Le Pas d'acier* at the listening session on November 14. The ballet should be staged, Meyerhold argued, because it could illustrate "the construction of the U.S.S.R. under the conditions of class welfare." Neither Meyerhold's loyal and eloquent arguments nor his offer to direct the ballet himself protected Prokofiev from the crude attacks of the RAPM members in attendance, however. For the most part, their criticisms applied not to the music but to the ballet's subject and setting.

An account of the strange question-and-answer session in which they and Prokofiev sparred appeared in *Proletarian Musician* not long after.

Prokofiev answered the workers' and members' questions about the ballet's content with the same irritability and rudeness found in his music. Sometimes he did not answer at all. Nor was there anything provocative in the questions: they were the sort familiar to any Soviet citizen. . . .

Question: "In the factory scene, is that a capitalist factory, where the worker is a slave, or a Soviet factory, where the worker is the master? If it is a Soviet factory, when and where did Prokofiev examine it, since from 1918 to the present he has been living abroad and came here for the first time in 1927 for two weeks?" (Answer: "That concerns politics, not music, and therefore I won't answer.")

Such arguments may have been an extreme example of the political rhetoric that had begun to afflict musical life in the late 1920s, but the trend they represented was clear and real. In the end, so heated and protracted was the controversy over *Le Pas d'acier* that the projected production was canceled. To this day, the ballet has never been staged in the U.S.S.R.

During his three-week stay in Russia, Prokofiev conducted a few pieces for a live radio broadcast of his music. Radio technology, and the ability to reach such an enormous audience all across the U.S.S.R. excited him. Once again, Meyerhold spoke up in support of his old friend, introducing Prokofiev to the radio audience in glowing terms: "Prokofiev is doing our work in the West. He is our musical advance post. . . . Prokofiev is in the full flowering of his abilities. We will rejoice in his life-affirming and brave music, which fills us with strength as we fight on the construction front, struggling against the class enemy."

Prokofiev also saw the Bolshoi Opera production of *Love for Three Oranges*, which had first been staged in 1927. The scenery by Isaac Rabinovich was so ornate and complicated that long intermissions were required to set it up—so long that the audience jokingly renamed the opera *Love for Three Intervals*.

Perhaps the most important accomplishment of Prokofiev's brief trip to Russia in 1929 was the strengthening of his relationships with his faithful correspondents Meyerhold, Miaskovsky and Asafiev. After his return to Paris, they would continue to press for more performances of his music and defend him against the attacks of the cultural bureaucrats. In Moscow he spent "many pleasant hours" in Meyerhold's apartment with the director and his wife, the actress Zinaida Raikh. He also traveled to Leningrad, where he saw Asafiev. But even warm reunions with well-meaning friends and colleagues could not conceal the unpredictable, dangerous and rapid transformation of the Soviet cultural environment. After returning to Paris in late November, Prokofiev wrote Koussevitsky that "life in Russia has become more difficult than during my previous trip, but there are still a lot of interesting things going on there. The attitude toward me was extremely cautious," he concluded with a strange logic, "so in the spring I'm planning to go again, and with Ptashka [Lina]."

It would take Prokofiev many years to understand the true nature of the Soviet Communist regime—if, indeed, he ever did come to understand it at all. Until the evidence was thrown in his face at the end of the 1930s, he was unable or unwilling to contemplate the sinister

1

1. Seryozha Prokofiev at age seven, 1898.
2. The building at 90 Sadovaya Street in
St. Petersburg (as it looks today), where
Prokofiev and his mother lived from 1904
to 1909.

2

3

3. Prokofiev, in the uniform of a Conservatory student, around 1909.
4. Prokofiev playing chess with his friend Vasily Moro-lev, 1909.

4

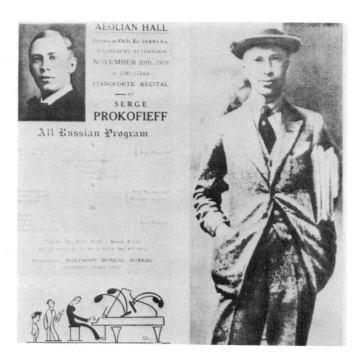

5

5. Prokofiev in America: the program for Prokofiev's official American debut in Aeolian Hall in New York, November 1918; Prokofiev on a New York street, undated.
6. Prokofiev aro nd 1920.

6

7

7. Prokofiev (far right) with (left to right) Ernest Ansermet, Sergei Diaghilev and Igor Stravinsky, London, 1921.
8. Portrait of Prokofiev by Henri Matisse, done in Nice in 1921 for reproduction in the Ballets Russes program for the premiere of *The Buffoon*.
9. Sketch of Diaghilev by Mikhail Larionov.
10. Sketch by Larionov for the curtain for *The Buffoon*,1915.(The ballet was not produced until 1921.)
11. Production of *The Buffoon*, with Larionov's curtain, 1921.

Serge Prokofieff
par Henri. Matisse

9

10

11

12. Prokofiev at work in Paris, around 1924. (The violinist is unidentified.)

13. Prokofiev with his wife Lina and their son Sviatoslav at Bellevue, outside Paris, in the spring of 1924.

14. Prokofiev with his wife Lina about to cross the English Channel by plane, 1927.

12

13

14

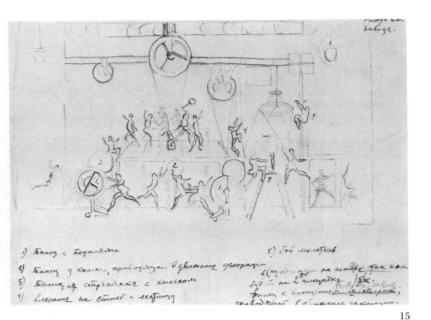

15

16

17

15. Sketch by Georgii Yakoulov for the final scene of *Le Pas d'acier*.

16. *Le Pas d'acier*: Leonid Massine and Alexandra Danilova, 1927.

17. *Le Pas d'acier*: Serge Lifar and Lyubov Tchernicheva, 1927.

18. Sketch of Boris Kochno by Pablo Picasso, undated.

19. Prokofiev in Monte Carlo, 1929.

18

19

20. Serge Lifar as the Prodigal
Son, 1929.
21. Serge Lifar as the Prodigal Son
and Felia Dubrovska as the Siren
in *Prodigal Son*, 1929.

20

21

23

22. Prokofiev in Paris, around 1932.
23. The building on rue Valentin Hauy in Paris (as it looks today), where Prokofiev and his family lived, 1930–36.
24. Prokofiev and Serge Lifar, around 1932.
25. Sketch of Prokofiev by Leonid Pasternak (father of Boris Pasternak), showing him playing at the Soviet Embassy in Berlin in 1937.

24

25

26. Prokofiev in the late 1930s.
27. The building on Chkalov Street in Moscow (as it looks today), where Prokofiev lived with his family, 1936–41.
28. Commemorative plaque near Prokofiev's Chkalov Street apartment.
29, 30, 31. Prokofiev at the Caucasus resort of Teberda in July, 1938: riding a cart; talking with one of the members of the staff; on the tennis court.

26

27

28

29

30

31

32

32. Prokofiev and Sergei Eisenstein working on the score for *Alexander Nevsky*,
1939.

33. Prokofiev (right), Sergei Eisenstein
(center) and Edward Tisse (left) dressed in
Russian costumes of the thirteenth century for a humorous photo taken during
the making of *Alexander Nevsky*.

34. Prokofiev and Mira Mendelson-
Prokofiev, during World War II.

33

34

35

37

35. The porch and dacha at Nikolina Gora (as it looks today), where Prokofiev and Mira lived, 1946–53.
36. The path to Prokofiev's dacha in Nikolina Gora.
37. The doorway of the building on Moscow Art Theater Lane in which Prokofiev and Mira lived, 1946–53.

36

38. Prokofiev reading at the dacha in Nikolina Gora.
39. Prokofiev's son Oleg, an artist, at his home in London, 1982.
40. Prokofiev's grave in Novodevichy Cemetery in Moscow. Mira Mendelson-Prokofiev was buried next to him when she died in 1968.

38

39

40

implications of the growing cultural regimentation. An optimistic, independent and organically apolitical personality, he did not believe boring bureaucrats could ever really affect his music or his life. From his earliest years, Prokofiev had become used to hearing criticism of his music—as too modern, too brash or too noisy. It was logical for him, therefore, to interpret the attacks leveled at him by RAPM as just another instance of the same sort of critical misunderstanding (or envy). Like the resistance of his professors at the Petersburg Conservatory, this criticism would also be proven incorrect with the passage of time, he thought.

What Prokofiev failed to understand was that in Soviet Russia, criticism of individual artists and their work was not merely the expression of a single critic's opinion but an ideological and political statement reflecting the views of the Party leadership. Since the Party leadership controlled the government and all cultural institutions, one review could affect every aspect of a composer's career. It is only fair to note, however, that Prokofiev was not alone among artists in failing to understand the dangers inherent in the Soviet cultural system. And in 1929, despite RAPM's strident rhetoric, the situation was still confused and Stalin was still consolidating his power.

That Prokofiev was viewed with considerable suspicion by a large segment of the musical and cultural establishment was by now very obvious. Even the honors he received reflected his ambiguous position. His appointment as permanent adviser to Soviet radio for foreign repertoire only emphasized his semiforeign status.

Hardly had Prokofiev set foot in Paris after his difficult sojourn in Russia before he and Lina left for a three-month tour of the United States, Canada and Cuba. They sailed to New York on the liner *Berengaria*, which was also carrying Rachmaninoff and the violinist Mischa Elman. Lina, who had known Rachmaninoff as a girl in New York, would stroll with him on the deck, or sit together with her husband in Rachmaninoff's cabin. Suffering from bitter nostalgia for his lost homeland, Rachmaninoff asked the Prokofievs many questions about what they had seen in Russia. Unlike Prokofiev, Rachmaninoff considered himself too old—he was Prokofiev's senior by eighteen years—and too inflexible to return to a socialist Russia.

The 1930 American tour was Prokofiev's most extensive yet and led him to revise his low opinion of American audiences and critics. It took him from New York to California and back for more than twenty major concerts and recitals (some with Lina) in nine different cities.

Nearly everywhere, he was received with enthusiasm and the seriousness he had previously found lacking. In Cleveland, where the *Cleveland News* gleefully called him "Russia's Naughty Boy," he described
the Cleveland Orchestra as "quite respectable and large—of course
there are Russians among the musicians. Cleveland is a most colossal
city, sown with skyscrapers: thirty-three kilometers along the shore of
Lake Erie! America is, after all, an incredible country."

While traveling between Cleveland, New York and Boston, Prokofiev became involved in another petty argument with Koussevitsky.
Although Koussevitsky had shown Prokofiev unfailing generosity over
the years and had set up many of Prokofiev's appearances for this
American tour, their relationship was periodically troubled by Prokofiev's childish temper tantrums. A few months earlier, they had
disagreed over the size of a commission Koussevitsky had offered to
pay for a new symphony—the Fourth—that Prokofiev was writing.
Koussevitsky had obtained a special commission for the piece from
the Boston Symphony, which had decided to celebrate its fiftieth anniversary by ordering a symphony apiece from Prokofiev and Stravinsky. (Stravinsky responded with the Symphony of Psalms.) "For one
thousand dollars you can order a symphony from Lazar or Tansman,"
Prokofiev complained to Koussevitsky, "but I find it awkward to accept
such a commission. Prokofiev is paid three to five thousand dollars for
a symphony, or even for the right to announce that 'we've commissioned
it from him.' "

Never one to underestimate his worth, Prokofiev told Koussevitsky
he would be willing to let the BSO buy the manuscript of the symphony
for its library for one thousand dollars, but not to commission it. He
also wanted Koussevitsky to help him obtain an endorsement fee from
the piano maker supplying the instruments for his American tour.

But Prokofiev was most offended by Koussevitsky's plan to invite
Prokofiev's former Petersburg professor—and sometime tormentor—
Glazunov to participate in a festival of Glazunov's music. (Glazunov
had finally emigrated from Russia shortly before.) It irritated Prokofiev
that Koussevitsky was unwilling to do the same for him: give a Prokofiev
festival in New York during his current tour. "It's especially important
pour me poser bien à New York, where fighting for a spot is so hard,"
he explained to Koussevitsky. "If you devote so much energy to Glazunov, couldn't you reserve a tiny bit for me, damn it all!"

Prokofiev's whining tone evidently annoyed Koussevitsky, for he
responded personally—and not through his wife, as he usually did—

only two days later. "I must tell you that in spite of all my propaganda during these past five years, your name is not so popular as that of Bach, Beethoven and Brahms, nor so popular that I can transport my orchestra to New York to give a Prokofiev festival," he scolded. "This doesn't mean that festivals should be given only to honor the dead— I hope that I will live to the time when a festival will be given in your honor—but we must be patient and not allow any silly little things, any pleasant nonentities, like your Sinfonietta, to be performed." Prokofiev made no further written comment on the matter.

Their quarrels notwithstanding, Prokofiev and Koussevitsky made five appearances together with the Boston Symphony, which included the American premiere of the Second Piano Concerto. The day after the second concert in New York, Olin Downes published a long interview with Prokofiev in *The New York Times*. "Why do they continue to speak of me only as a satirist or a sarcastic composer, or an *enfant terrible* of discord, etc.?" Prokofiev asked. "Perhaps this was true fifteen years ago, when that was my spirit, and somewhat my style. But I have left that period behind."

Stressing that he had rejected the complexity of such pieces as the Second Symphony, he said he was searching for a simpler style.

I have become simpler, and more melodic. We want a simpler and more melodic style for music, a simple, less complicated emotional state, and dissonance again relegated to its proper place as one element of music. . . . I think we have gone as far as we are likely to go in the direction of size, or dissonance, or complexity in music. Music, in other words, has definitely reached and passed the greatest degree of discord and complexity that can be attained in practice. I want nothing better, more flexible or more complete than the sonata form, which contains everything necessary for my structural purposes.

Prokofiev's steadfast defense of simplicity, melody, the sonata form and the classical tradition already put him strangely out of touch with new movements in music in the West in 1930. Few Western composers, obsessed as they were with rejecting tonality and the classical style, would follow his advice. Indeed, the full flowering of serialism and various atonal and highly dissonant systems was yet to come, and Prokofiev's assertion that music "has definitely reached and passed the greatest degree of discord and complexity that can be attained in practice" demonstrated a strange misreading of the contemporary musical scene in Europe and America. At the same time, his defense of tonality and classical forms brought him closer to what would soon be the enforced standard in the U.S.S.R. For the first time, Prokofiev was attempting to portray himself as a traditional force in music, turning away from the idol-smashing image he cultivated early in his career.

Similarly, if ten years earlier Prokofiev's music had struck American critics and audiences as difficult and "modernistic," now it was accessible and refreshingly direct. In *The New York Sun*, W. J. Henderson wrote, ". . . with the ripening of his years, this musician, whose individuality is marked, has gained in clearness of vision, in mastery of his material and mellowness of feeling." In Boston, the eminent Nicolas Slonimsky called Prokofiev a "celebrated figure, on his way to eminence. Beside Stravinsky, Prokofiev stands out as a healthy and virile composer. There is a heartening tendency nowadays toward sanity in music, and in this movement Prokofiev is one of the chief figures."

Prokofiev enjoyed his American fame and was not squeamish about cashing in on it. An advertisement he made for Steinway pianos shows impressive mastery of the vocabulary of public relations: "I have always found the Steinway piano a perfect instrument, combining remarkable brilliancy of tone in *forte*, with exquisite delicacy of tone in *piano*, and both based on a perfect action."

Everywhere they went, parties and receptions were held in their honor. Aaron Copland, whose music Koussevitsky also championed, encountered Prokofiev at a reception at Koussevitsky's house in Jamaica Plain. Copland and Prokofiev had met some years earlier in Paris, when Copland was studying there with Nadia Boulanger. "You never knew what to expect of Prokofiev," Copland recalled. "He was friendly, but not an easy guy to talk to. I don't remember ever talking with him about anything serious. He tended to play a light, bouncy game; he was boyish, easily bored, and even impolite at times. He enjoyed teasing people, and loved to make witty remarks and tell stories. He was very bright and outspoken, and I can't imagine that he would ever hide how he felt about anything." Lina, strikingly attractive, well-dressed and charming, always made a good impression at social gatherings, complementing her husband's abrupt manner.

From New York, Prokofiev and Lina took the Sunset Limited via New Orleans, Texas and the Southwest ("next to Mexico," Prokofiev informed Asafiev) to California. Near New Orleans, the train was ferried across the Mississippi, its banks lined with lazy alligators whose fantastic appearance delighted Prokofiev. Farther west, the train stopped briefly at an Indian reservation, where Prokofiev and Lina bought a small handmade rug with a primitive design of two cows woven into it. For many years afterward, the rug lay in the nursery between the beds of their two sons, and would eventually become an object of contention after Prokofiev's remarriage.

On the return trip to New York, they took the northern route, stopping in Chicago for three orchestral performances and in Detroit for a joint chamber recital. According to the critic from the *Detroit News*, Lina's performance was less than a complete success. "Unfortunately, the singer miscalculated the size of the hall and sang far too powerfully; and that may account for her lack of nuance, and the fact that she sang in the same style five songs differing widely in feeling." As for her husband, he "may be said to reflect the spirit of today—a spirit strong, vigorous, humorous, cynical, materialistic, somewhat lacking in poesy, but very refined in its mechanics."

During the many hours he spent on trains between performances, speeding across the western plains, Prokofiev worked on two new pieces: the Fourth Symphony and a string quartet (his first), which had been commissioned from him by the Library of Congress. On stationery of the Escondrijo Hotel in Santa Barbara, where he stayed en route from Los Angeles to San Francisco, Prokofiev had accepted the commission in a note to one of the Library's patrons, Mrs. Elizabeth Coolidge: "It will give me great pleasure to compose a quartet for the Washington Library." He would finish it by the end of the year.

Resting briefly in New York, the Prokofievs resumed their exhausting pace with a short trip to Havana. Lina, a Spaniard by birth, education and culture, loved Cuba; she had been there with her parents as a child. Prokofiev was less enthusiastic. Although intrigued by the lush tropical vegetation and the warm sea—he had never been this close to the equator—he confessed that he had "a northern soul, and I would not want to live there for long." His rigorous schedule—a recital on March 10 and another on March 13—left him little time to see the landscape anyway, but he did not seem to mind performing so frequently. "After twenty-five concerts, I'm in good form," he told Asafiev.

Back again in New York for a few days before leaving for more engagements in Montreal and Chicago, Prokofiev and Lina managed to see the great Toscanini rehearse. They watched, entranced, as the temperamental maestro would "break his batons and shout *vergogna!*

('shame!')." At one point, Lina recalled, he stopped and made each violinist play a phrase from the Mozart symphony they were rehearsing. Finally he lost his temper, "grabbed his head and started pointing his finger at one of the violinists (apparently the first violinist), shouted at him and called him a 'shoemaker,' making him repeat the passage several times. Then the violinists, who submitted without a murmur, played it together, and he calmed down."

Toscanini told Prokofiev he was planning to perform the Sinfonietta during the next season—the same piece that Koussevitsky had called a "pleasant nonentity." Prokofiev did not miss the opportunity to inform Koussevitsky of Toscanini's different opinion. "While the 'Symphony gets ready to play the Toscanetta,' you should definitely play it in Boston, as you promised," he wrote to Koussevitsky playfully. "The time has come to be convinced that it is in fact a good piece."

Prokofiev and his wife also met Leopold Stokowski, who invited them to his new New York apartment for breakfast. Like Koussevitsky in Boston, Stokowski would be a stalwart supporter of Prokofiev's music over the years of his long tenure with the Philadelphia Orchestra.

Indeed, in the three years since Prokofiev's previous visit to the United States in 1927, American musical life had become noticeably more lively, varied and sophisticated. This change had come about in part through the influx of European musicians (including many Russians) who were coming to America to live and work. Koussevitsky, for example, had adjusted to American life very quickly, and already enjoyed considerable popularity and influence.

For the most part, Prokofiev found that the American public and critical response in 1930, twelve years after his first appearance in the United States as the shocking Bolshevik pianist with steel muscles, was "completely serious: they had grown used to my name. Besides, in the twelve years that had passed since my first arrival, America had developed musically and even had some of its own innovative composers. My European reputation also played a role. Although the Americans like to make their own judgments ('We are the richest country in the world, we invite whom we like, and we have the right to decide'), out of caution they keep one eye on Europe. In any case, the tour went well in almost every way, without the petty irritations characteristic of my previous trips."

On March 28, satisfied but weary, the Prokofievs sailed from New York on the *Île de France*. But the concertizing would not end until

May 23, when Prokofiev finished the season in Warsaw, having also appeared in Brussels, Torino, Monte Carlo and Milan. During the 1929–30 season, one of his most active, he had given thirty-five performances on two continents. The life of a traveling virtuoso left him little time for serious composing, but his name and his music were better known than ever.

Originally, Prokofiev had also been planning to travel to the U.S.S.R. in May, but eventually decided against it. Despite his intense interest in Soviet musical life, European commitments and uncertainty over his position in Moscow would keep him from returning to the Soviet Union for another two and a half years. One of the reasons for the cancellation of the trip in the spring of 1930 was a seeming lack of interest on Asafiev's part in setting up concerts in Leningrad and Moscow. Another was a particularly depressed letter from Miaskovsky, who reported that musical life in Moscow was now in even greater turmoil than during Prokofiev's visit in the autumn. As RAPM gained in power and exerted pressure on its ideological opponents, various concert-giving organizations ceased to exist or drastically cut back their activities. Along with Prokofiev's own *Le Pas d'acier*, Shostakovich's avant-garde opera *The Nose*, first performed to critical and public acclaim in early 1930 in Leningrad, had also been condemned and withdrawn from the repertoire on political grounds. "It's hard to imagine what will happen next," said Miaskovsky. "In any case, good music— particularly contemporary music, and above all Russian—will have to be put aside for the time being. . . . Under the current circumstances, I do not think there is any need for you to come here."

The turbulent political-cultural situation affected not only composers but all Soviet artists, including writers. Prokofiev's friend Mayakovsky had come under intense ideological pressure and was finding it increasingly difficult to reconcile his fiery ego and artistic independence with the conformist demands of the growing cultural bureaucracy. Finally, in April 1930, he could bear the pressure no longer and committed suicide by shooting himself. His death must have come as a shock to Prokofiev, who had often been called the Mayakovsky of Russian music.

Even as Prokofiev was deciding not to visit Moscow, he was also making a move that strengthened his connection to Paris. After nearly seven years of a nomadic existence spent in trains, ocean liners and furnished apartments, in the spring of 1930 Prokofiev and Lina rented their first unfurnished flat in Paris—"henceforth our permanent apartment." No doubt the need to provide a stable environment for Sviatoslav, who had recently turned six, and for Oleg, who was now a year and a half old, strongly influenced their decision.

The apartment they chose was at 5 rue Valentin Hauy, in the fifteenth *arrondissement* near the Place de Breteuil. Surrounded by a serene residential neighborhood, the rue Valentin Hauy is short, quiet and tree-lined, bisected by a small square. Les Invalides, with Napoleon's tomb, is nearby; Prokofiev liked to walk down the Avenue de Breteuil toward the imposing structure. The building in which the Prokofievs lived had been constructed in 1905, in a graceful Art Nouveau style; they had a five-room apartment on the third floor, and Prokofiev's secretary Mikhail Astrov occupied a small *chambre de bonne* on the top floor. The apartment would be the Prokofiev family home for the next six years.

Contrary to their custom, Prokofiev and Lina stayed in Paris nearly the entire summer, until mid-August. Furniture had to be bought, and Prokofiev wanted to be sure they found the best bargains. What pleased him most about their new home was setting up a permanent working space. "Hurrah!" he wrote to Vladimir Dukelsky. "Now I have a real desk and a real bookcase and soon I'll have a real sofa." In choosing chairs, Prokofiev would sit in them quietly, testing to see if they were comfortable and conducive to reflection. On the threshold of forty, Prokofiev was finally beginning to appreciate the bourgeois comforts he had so far gone without.

Settling down had its headaches, too—one of the upstairs neighbors turned out to have a special fondness for Ravel's "Bolero," which he played over and over on his gramaphone. Despite his reputation for boisterous and loud music, Prokofiev, like Tchaikovsky, could not abide hearing noise at home where he composed. As he told Miaskovsky, who had also recently moved into a new apartment in Moscow, "The most important thing about any new apartment—much more important than furniture—is quiet."

Noisy neighbors notwithstanding, Prokofiev completed the Fourth Symphony, scheduled to be performed in Boston by Koussevitsky and the BSO in the fall, before retiring to the countryside in mid-August. When he learned that the symphony used themes from *Prodigal Son*, Koussevitsky—along with many others—harshly criticized Prokofiev for a poverty of imagination. (After all, the Third Symphony used recycled music, too, from *Fiery Angel*.) No doubt it annoyed Koussevitsky to present as a "new" symphony something that was actually based on old music.

Prokofiev defended himself by citing the example of Beethoven, who used music from the ballet *Creatures of Prometheus* in his Third Symphony. He also insisted that his Fourth Symphony treated the themes from *Prodigal Son* in a different way. A large amount of new material was also introduced, he explained, along with some music originally composed for *Prodigal Son* but not included in the ballet's final version.

In fact the relationship between *Prodigal Son* and the Fourth Symphony is less close than the one between *The Fiery Angel* and the Third Symphony. Owing to its smaller dimensions, dramatic structure and choreographic demands, *Prodigal Son* did not exhaustively treat the attractive themes that then reappeared in the symphony. The ballet was not "symphonic" in nature, but illustrative. *The Fiery Angel*, on the other hand, did include large symphonic interludes and more extensive orchestral development in its original form.

One of Prokofiev's largest symphonies, the Fourth has four extended movements in the Romantic tradition. As with the Third, the Fourth suffers from an overabundance of material; its seams show. What is "new" is a more reflective and quiet mood, a greater expansiveness, and a broadly epic quality (note the opening *Allegro eroico*)— a demonstration of Prokofiev's professed desire to find a new simplicity. All of these features would find fuller and more successful expression in Prokofiev's three "Soviet" symphonies (Nos. 5, 6 and 7). Notably muted here are the rambunctious dissonance, disarming rhythms and taunting sarcasm of the Second and Third Symphonies—and of so much of Prokofiev's earlier orchestral music.

Significantly, Prokofiev abandoned the form of the symphony for fourteen years after completing the Fourth. The tepid reception which it encountered in America and Europe must provide at least part of the explanation for this long hiatus. Koussevitsky conducted the world premiere on November 14, 1930, in Boston, and Monteux presented it to Paris on December 18. In neither city did it enjoy a notable success. *The Christian Science Monitor* damned with faint praise: "The symphony, if not calculated to rouse the public to frenzies of delight, is individual, and musically interesting."

Prokofiev explained the cool public response as an inability to appreciate his new and more subtle style: "Apparently, the public likes to be slapped in the face; when a composer probes more deeply, then they lose sight of where he is going." It vexed Prokofiev that his *enfant terrible* reputation continued to haunt him as a mature composer in the West: the critics and public treated him like a child star and didn't want him to grow up. In Europe, too, the form of the three- or four-movement symphony—which, like opera, continued to interest Prokofiev—was regarded in progressive circles as *passé* and uninteresting. (In the more conservative musical environment of the U.S.S.R., on the other hand, composers were encouraged and even expected to produce symphonies.) While disappointed by its lukewarm reception in Paris and Boston, Prokofiev continued to love the Fourth for its "wealth of material and absence of noise," although he did substantially revise it in 1947, after his great success with Symphonies Nos. 5 and 6.

The Fourth Symphony behind him, Prokofiev was ready to take a vacation. Apparently weary of traveling, he and Lina chose a spot about twenty miles outside Paris—La Naze, par Valmondois, on the Seine. They rented a house there for two months, until early October 1930. As usual, Prokofiev spent most of each day composing. He was working slowly on the string quartet for the Library of Congress, and on a new commission for a ballet to be staged at the Paris Opera by Serge Lifar (the original Prodigal Son), who was the newly appointed artistic director of the *corps de ballet* there.

During the summer, Lifar and Prokofiev collaborated on a "soft and lightly lyrical" original scenario for the new ballet, which was eventually entitled *On the Dnepr*. Set in the Ukraine, it was the sketchy story of a love triangle involving a Red Army soldier. The soldier falls in love with a peasant girl, but her father has promised her to another. Appearing at the engagement feast to claim his sweetheart, the soldier is overpowered by the guests and tied to a tree. In the final scene, he is freed by the girl, who reciprocates his love.

Lifar and Prokofiev intentionally left the dramatic action rather vague. "We proceeded from the choreographic and musical structure, considering that a ballet's scenario is of only secondary importance," Prokofiev told Asafiev. In this way, they thought—mistakenly—that the finished product would be "well-proportioned." Instead of giving the scenes specific titles related to the action of the story, as had been done in *The Prodigal Son*, *Le Pas d'acier* and *The Buffoon*, they chose generalized titles relating to the choreographic requirements, in the style of nineteenth-century ballet—"Men's Dance," or "Pas de deux."

This same trend toward greater abstraction profoundly affected the ballets created by Balanchine and Stravinsky.

This rejection of narrative specificity can also be explained as Prokofiev's attempt to avoid the sort of ideological scandal that had erupted over *Le Pas d'acier* in Moscow. Since the new ballet was also set in the present-day U.S.S.R., Prokofiev wanted to leave the story line as vague and flexible as possible, lest he again be accused of failing to understand Soviet reality. He hedged his bets in *On the Dnepr*, leaving room for the story line to be altered to suit the ideological requirements of Soviet theatres.

The music was written quickly. Prokofiev had finished eight of the ballet's twelve sections in piano score by late September, and all but one by early November. The original commission called for completion of the piano score in December and of the full score in January, with a production planned for February or March of 1931. As it turned out, however, *On the Dnepr* (*Sur le Borysthène* in French) would finally take the stage only several seasons later, in December of 1932.

Prokofiev ventured away from his work for a *tour gastronomique* of Alsace and the Vosges Mountains in September, joined by his wife and their friend Nicolas Nabokov, who did not find the excursion an entirely restful experience.

The tour had been long and tiring, partly because most of the day was spent in first ordering meals, then eating them and then attempting to digest them; but also because the Prokofiev *ménage* had hourly squabbles (often ending with tears) about what to do next. While Lina Ivanovna wanted to stop in every village, visit every cathedral, château and museum, her husband wanted to go from one three-star restaurant to the next one in the town he had scheduled as our next stop.

While his wife looked for "cozy" inns with "lovely" views, hidden in "green valleys" or on the slopes of a "charming" mountain, he wanted to stay in town in the best hotel advertised in the *Guide Michelin*. He was not a bit interested in museums and cathedrals, and when compelled to join us in what he called our "phony grave-digging ritual" he looked bored and gloomy. The only thing he could find to say looking at Chartres Cathedral was: "I wonder how they got those statues up so high without dropping them." But when he had a large, fancy menu in his hand his mien would change, he would brighten up and start ordering for each one of us the *plât du jour* or the *spécialité de la maison* with the concomitant *vin du pays*.

Returning from their travels, Prokofiev and Lina were visited at their rented summer house by Meyerhold and his wife, the actress Zinaida Raikh. They had come to Paris on tour with Meyerhold's theatre, which gave ten highly publicized performances in June at the Théâtre de Montparnasse, sweeping even the sophisticated Paris audience off its feet. After the troupe returned to Moscow, Meyerhold remained with his wife in France until September, and he and Prokofiev saw each other frequently.

Fascinated by a new medium to which he would later make important contributions, Prokofiev had purchased a movie camera that he and Meyerhold (one-time teacher to the filmmaker Sergei Eisenstein) used that summer to shoot home movies. One of them, which they called *The Baby Snatcher*, was inspired by the publicity surrounding the recent Lindbergh kidnapping. Meyerhold played the villain, grabbing the baby Oleg away from Lina and hiding him in a grotto at the end of the garden. The camera was then handed to Lina, who filmed Prokofiev as the hero, rescuing the child.

Meyerhold and Prokofiev also discussed the future of Prokofiev's music in Russia, and how to arrange for productions of his operas in Soviet theatres. Just before returning to Moscow, Meyerhold wrote an impassioned letter to Elena Malinovskaya, director of the Bolshoi Theater. He defended Prokofiev and encouraged her to stage his operas and ballets, bravely denouncing the anti-Prokofiev intrigues which had so many times prevented *The Gambler* from reaching the stage of the Mariinsky.

"I worked very hard on *The Gambler*," he wrote, "for such difficult things as *The Gambler* require a lot of thought, and then, on a whim of those in charge, through a lack of comprehension, they are tossed out the window. . . . And after all, Sergei Sergeevich is not an émigré. As is well known to our embassy in Paris, Sergei Sergeevich has nothing to do with émigré circles. And you yourself know how those who came to hear him on his recent visits to Russia responded to him." Tragically, Meyerhold's noble defense of his friend fell on deaf ears; indeed, only a few years later, Meyerhold himself would be in desperate need of defense.

By early October, Prokofiev and his family were back in Paris. A reporter from *Le Petit Marseillais* visited them and painted a cozy domestic picture. "There I was at his house, in the middle of suitcases and bags, surrounded by the turbulence of children, by movement— in a word, by life. Since the *salon* provided a small oasis, we sought refuge there, next to a piano covered with scores, manuscripts and proofs to be corrected. Let me describe him: he is large, blond, very Slavic, solid and full of health, with a very honest and appealing aura."

"Very Slavic"—Prokofiev's roots in Russia were still deep and strong. In the midst of this bourgeois domestic tranquillity, his thoughts still wandered persistently to his homeland. He had been planning to travel to the U.S.S.R. for three or four weeks in late October and early November, but was receiving little encouragement from Moscow. "I have a deep longing to come to the U.S.S.R.," he wrote to Miaskovsky, "but no official institutions are really inviting me." In the end, he decided not to go, partly because he wanted to finish the score for *On the Dnepr*, and perhaps because his future in Paris was beginning to look reasonably promising.

Now that they lived in an elegant apartment, Prokofiev and Lina more often entertained at home, and were frequently invited to dinner parties and receptions. Among the one hundred guests at their housewarming party that autumn were the artists Natalia Goncharova (who would design the costumes for *On the Dnepr*), Kuzma Petrov-Vodkin and Alexander Benois, who gave them paintings as gifts. According to Mikhail Astrov, Lina was "very much a society lady, and loved parties. This helped Sergei politically, for he was, as the French would say, *un peu sauvage*." Lina felt very much at home in Europe, and thoroughly enjoyed the Parisian social whirl to which her husband's fame gave them access. As Lina became known for her grace and charm, Prokofiev gained notoriety for his rudeness, acid wit and flashy, bright-colored clothing.

One of Prokofiev's friends during these years was the composer Francis Poulenc, a member of the group of French composers who called themselves Les Six. They had known each other since the early 1920s, through their involvement with the Ballets Russes. Bridge, not music, was their strongest bond, however: Poulenc and a few others gathered regularly for weekly games. They also occasionally spent weekends in the country together, sometimes joined by the composers Auric and Sauguet.

"Emotion was not Prokofiev's predominant trait," Poulenc wrote later. Nor, he said, agreeing with Souvchinsky and Stravinsky, was Prokofiev particularly interested in literature. "I believe what interested him most of all was the life and history of religions." As was the case with almost all who became acquainted with Prokofiev, Poulenc did not feel that the time they spent together led to emotional trust or closeness. After 1932, when Prokofiev was spending more and more time in Russia, they rarely saw each other.

A more intimate friend was the Russian composer Nicolas Nabokov, whom Prokofiev had also met in the Diaghilev entourage. Related to the writer Vladimir Nabokov, Nicolas's family, of old noble stock, had fled Russia soon after the Revolution. Twelve years younger than Prokofiev, who acted as a sort of mentor toward him, Nabokov was never as disciplined or methodical in his pursuit of a composer's career, which led Prokofiev to jokingly dismiss him (as he dismissed Vladimir Dukelsky) as a dilettante. Nabokov and Prokofiev both belonged to *La Sérénade,* a society of composers that gave regular concerts in the Salle Gaveau. They also shared an admiration for Ravel, who, Prokofiev once told Nabokov, was "the only one in France who knows what he's doing." What Prokofiev detested in French music of the twenties and thirties, he told Nabokov, were "formless and amorphous melodies."

Nabokov's suave, cosmopolitan manner also appealed to Lina, and they developed a joking friendship of their own. Nabokov often visited them at their summer villas, and would accompany them—as he did on the exhausting *tour gastronomique* in 1930—on motor trips through the French countryside, suffering the effects of Prokofiev's "abominable" driving. Nabokov later wrote:

> He drove slowly, overcautiously, and shook us up whenever he had to shift gears or stop. Consequently we crept along the roads of France in his tiny new four-seater at the rate of twenty miles per hour. He had computed every particle of our time at this average rate of speed and planned all our stops in advance. Everywhere we went we had to arrive on the dot of X o'clock and leave the same way.

This same passion for precision was evident in the rituals Prokofiev developed for their games of chess and bridge. He devised an elaborate system of graphs showing the relative position of each player at each phase of the game, very similar to the charts he had used to plot the grades each student received in composition class at the St. Petersburg Conservatory.

But what amazed Nabokov—and many others—most about Prokofiev was his incredible rudeness, sometimes bordering on sadistic cruelty. Once, after a concert where a well-known singer had performed some of his songs, he announced, in front of a large group, that "she did not understand anything about his music and had better stop singing it." When the singer burst into tears, Prokofiev was unmoved. "You see," he continued reprimanding her, "all of you women take refuge in tears instead of listening to what one has to say and learning how to correct your faults." Such outspoken, childishly honest behavior did little to win Prokofiev friends in Parisian musical circles, where frankness was to be avoided at all costs. As a result, "few composers had so many quarrels, feuds and lawsuits and made so many enemies as Prokofiev."

But even now that he had become a familiar (if not wildly acclaimed) figure on the Parisian musical scene, Prokofiev continued to miss Russia. It disturbed him that he was receiving less news of what was happening in Moscow—few Russians were coming to Paris these days, as Stalin made foreign travel almost impossible. Unable to set up any definite appearances and unsure of how he would be greeted in the Soviet Union, Prokofiev canceled his plans to travel there in the early winter of 1930–31.

What he failed to understand was that official Soviet musical and cultural policy, and attitudes toward "Westerners" like himself, were changing almost daily. Even composers living in the midst of it all, like Miaskovsky, found it difficult to keep up with all the necessary paperwork and ideological shifting. Miaskovsky described to Prokofiev how a colleague at the Moscow Conservatory—and his own former student—had denounced him to students for writing string quartets that "do not reach the wide masses."

If even loyal composers like Miaskovsky were coming under attack, then the official Soviet attitude toward Prokofiev—a strange mixture of suspicion, pride and envy—was much more negative. Miaskovsky warned him that his standing in Russia was precarious. "The Association of Proletarian Musicians does not want to forgive you for your careless treatment of them during the listening sessions for *Le Pas d'acier*, and, even more, considers *Le Pas d'acier* a mockery of our revolution," he wrote. "In good conscience, I have to agree with them that the titles of many of the ballet's numbers now appear tactless. It seems to me that Yakoulov did you a dirty trick."

Strangely deaf to the bleak tidings from Moscow, Prokofiev did not waver in his conviction that it was possible to maintain two careers, one in Paris and one in Russia, as so many Russian artists had done in the past. But by the early 1930s, such a balancing act was already becoming very difficult. Russia was plunging into dark isolation and xenophobia. Soviet citizens, including prominent artists, were no longer allowed to travel abroad at all, let alone live abroad for extended periods of time. In Stalin's view, Soviet composers, writers and artists should live in the Soviet Union. What need did they have to travel to the inferior and decadent West anyway, when they resided in a socialist paradise?

Prokofiev met the new year 1931 in Paris. Like previous winters, this one brought piano appearances throughout Europe, though the schedule was leisurely compared to the preceding season. Between appearances, he kept up with the musical season in Paris, which, to his ears at least, contained little of interest. A ballet to his "Classical" Symphony was produced in May, but quickly disappeared for lack of financial backing. Most of his time was spent at home, correcting the proofs for the soon-to-be-published orchestral score of the Divertissement and the piano score of *On the Dnepr*. He was also making sketches for a large new piece: a piano concerto (his first in ten years) commissioned by the Austrian pianist Paul Wittgenstein. Wittgenstein had lost his right hand at the front in World War I, and asked Prokofiev to write him a one-handed concerto. (Maurice Ravel also completed a left-handed concerto for Wittgenstein the same year.) The Fourth Piano Concerto would be finished by fall.

What with furnishing and maintaining an apartment, and feeding, clothing and educating two sons, Prokofiev's financial burdens were heavy. All his performances, commissions and royalties notwithstanding, he was still anxious about money. By mid-April the advance Wittgenstein paid for the new piano concerto—half of the total fee— had been spent, and Prokofiev wrote Miaskovsky that he "had to get moving."

Royalties were coming in from America, where Prokofiev's music was prominently featured in the spring of 1931. In April, Leopold Stokowski conducted the Philadelphia Orchestra in the American premiere of *Le Pas d'acier* at the Metropolitan Opera House in New York. Unaware of the political controversy it had spawned in Moscow, naive American audiences interpreted it as a true picture of the new Communist society. Natalia Goncharova designed the production, using "emblems of Soviet daily life" such as the hammer and sickle and red flags.

But more important for Prokofiev was the world premiere in Washington, D.C., of his First String Quartet on April 25, 1931—two days after his fortieth birthday. The piece was finished just after the new year and performed at the Library of Congress by the Brosa Quartet. The B Minor Quartet is a serious and introspective work, more substantial than earlier chamber pieces like the Overture on Hebrew Themes or the flashy and dissonant *Trapeze* Quintet. (Not strongly drawn to writing for small ensembles, Prokofiev wrote only two string quartets in his entire career.) Its "dark," intellectual, and complex polyphonic style surprised both Prokofiev's admirers and detractors. Here, opaqueness, complexity and reflectiveness replaced the transparency, brightness and eagerness to shock with which his music had long been identified. When Miaskovsky first heard it, he exclaimed, taken aback, "But it is very gloomy!"

One of the First Quartet's most unusual features—particularly for Prokofiev, who tended to like fast tempos and galloping rhythms—is that two of its three movements (including the finale) are slow. Only the first, *Allegro*, is fast. Unlike much of Prokofiev's music, which tends to stress exposition, the quartet introduces material sparingly, but develops it at considerable length. All the themes are memorable and have unusually smooth contours, particularly the main theme of the third movement, introduced in the viola. Moving in a gently circular pattern, it conveys a feeling of unusual (for Prokofiev) roundness and lyrical depth. In the First Quartet, as in the Fourth Symphony, Prokofiev was trying to shed the *enfant terrible* image and show his audience that he could write serious and reflective music, too.

When he was first writing down ideas for the quartet, crossing America by train during the early winter of 1930, he had studied Beethoven's quartets in a search for inspiration. "That is the source of the rather 'classical' language of the quartet's first section," he said later. Another interesting feature is the choice of B Minor as the tonic key; compositions for string quartets usually avoid it because B lies a half tone below the pitch of the lowest string (C) on both the cello and viola. Solving the resulting technical problems obviously intrigued the chess player in Prokofiev, and he overcame them with impressive skill.

Meanwhile, back in Paris, Prokofiev was taking advantage of an unusually quiet spring and early summer to work on a number of new projects. Among them were the left-handed piano concerto for Wittgenstein, which had been completely sketched out but required further shaping; a set of six pieces assembled from various works and arranged for piano as Op. 52; and a large orchestral suite based on material from *The Gambler*. Piecing together fragments of an opera whose text and music were so closely wedded was not an easy task. In the end, he decided to call the result "Four Portraits and the Dénouement from the Opera *The Gambler*, a Symphonic Suite for Large Orchestra."

"I invented the following method: after going through the piano score and selecting everything that pertained to a given character, I spread those pages out on the floor. Sitting on a chair, I spent a lot of time looking them over. Gradually the episodes would begin to adhere to each other, like raindrops." He arranged the piece in five sections: (1) Aleksei, (2) Babulenka, (3) The General, (4) Polina, and (5) a concluding "Dénouement," which used material from the opera's orchestral interludes. "Four Portraits" was first performed the following spring in Paris.

At the end of July, Prokofiev, Lina and the children piled in the car for their annual vacation. This year, they began by motoring southeast to Geneva, and then turned southwest through Savoie, traveling diagonally across the center of France toward Toulouse. Their final destination was the famous resort of Biarritz, near the Pyrenees and the Basque country on the Atlantic Coast. "We are spending the remainder of the summer at the Atlantic Ocean, seven kilometers from the Spanish border," Prokofiev wrote to Asafiev. "This is a remarkable place: the Pyrenees on one side, the warm ocean on the other. I have learned how to swim and dive."

They rented a villa in a village near Biarritz, one of Europe's most fashionable spas, frequented by numerous famous artists. Ravel's hometown of Ciboure was nearby, and they saw him there in passing. That summer the Prokofievs also counted among their companions the great Russian bass Chaliapin, with whom Prokofiev shared a mutual passion for bridge (Chaliapin had emigrated to the West in 1922), the violinist Mischa Elman and the film star Charlie Chaplin.

In the evenings they would all gather to watch Chaliapin and Chaplin improvise scenes in mime. Lina was entranced by their performances. "I remember how expressive and comical Chaliapin's huge, powerful figure was, when he would suddenly transform himself into a 'society lady' at her morning *toilette*, combing her hair and preening in front of the mirror, then sewing, threading a needle, and so on. He would depict these rather banal scenes with such energy and earnestness that I can't recall them without laughing. Much later, when Sergei Sergeevich and I would think back on those evenings, we remembered Chaliapin's acting more distinctly than Chaplin's. . . . Although Sergei Sergeevich was a great admirer of Chaplin as a film artist, we recognized that his brilliant improvisations were merely variations on his famous comic roles." Mischa Elman and the French violinist Jacques Thibaud would contribute to the domestic entertainment, playing Bach sonatas.

In the daytime Prokofiev would compose, and he and his family took swimming lessons. This summer was a particularly calm interlude in one of the most tranquil periods in his entire career—perhaps even too tranquil for the peripatetic Prokofiev. He spent more time with Lina and his sons during these years in the early 1930s than at any other time in their married life. Except for the squabbles that resulted from Prokofiev's insistence on having his own way and putting his music before all other considerations, they seemed happy together. The boys were growing up fast. Sviatoslav, now enrolled in a school run by a Russian émigré in Paris, won first prize in a contest for the most handsome child in a bathing suit.

Two important accomplishments had emerged from his vacation, Prokofiev announced ironically to Miaskovsky in mid-September: "I have learned to swim and I am done with the one-handed concerto."

When Wittgenstein received the Fourth Piano Concerto in the fall of 1931, he looked it over and sent the composer this cryptic note: "Thank you for the concerto, but I do not understand a single note in it and I will not play it." It is difficult to understand why he disliked this attractive and unfairly neglected piece. Perhaps his technique was not up to the level of Prokofiev's: some formidable, but not overwhelmingly difficult, virtuoso passages enliven the first and last movements. At the same time, its themes are lively and ingratiating, its style is not particularly dissonant or "modern," and, as a pianist himself, Prokofiev knew (better than Ravel or Strauss) how to write a piece for one hand that was playable but interesting. Prokofiev never performed the Fourth Concerto publicly himself, however, and was unsure how he felt about it: "Sometimes I like it, sometimes I don't."

He was also uncertain and anxious, even in the lush and soothing surroundings of Biarritz, about his status in Moscow. His frequent letters to Asafiev and Miaskovsky were full of concern for the fate of his music in Russia. Hoping to positively influence the official attitude (particularly among the members of RAPM) toward him, Prokofiev sent copies of his soon-to-be-published Six Pieces for Piano (Op. 52) to important Soviet pianists, including Lev Oborin, Heinrich Neuhaus and Vladimir Sofronitsky. "It would not be amiss, during this period when the attitude toward me has soured, to improve relations by means of these easily playable pieces," he told Miaskovsky.

The depth of Prokofiev's anxiety over his musical future in the U.S.S.R. is evident from another letter, to Asafiev, asking whether it would be wise to send the same pieces to the library of the Leningrad Conservatory, which had shown very little interest in Prokofiev or in his music on his most recent trip. He wondered if the situation had changed. "The real question is this," he wrote. "What's the policy there now, and do they want to have my compositions at all?" The prospect of being cut off from Russia forever, or treated as a musical pariah there, disturbed Prokofiev profoundly.

Soon after his return from Biarritz to Paris in early October, Prokofiev began yet another round of European concertizing. Playing the piano was still an important source of income, although as he grew older Prokofiev came to resent more and more the time that practice and touring took away from composing. In fact, one of the attractions of returning to the U.S.S.R. was the prospect of not having to concertize continually to feed himself and his family. Soviet composers might be subject to greater regimentation and political control than their European counterparts, but—as Prokofiev knew—the prominent ones also received ample financial support from the government. In addition, they received preferential housing that was virtually rent-free, and vacations in special summer colonies for artists. And like all Soviet citizens, they received free health care and free education for their children.

If by 1931 Prokofiev still found it hard to think of Paris as home, the fickle attitude of the French press and public toward his music did not help matters. He vented some of this frustration in a long interview published in *Candide* in mid-December. "In Paris, I started with success, but then, what trouble! Not always because the public didn't understand my music, but rather because at that moment there was too much modern music. As far as I'm concerned, my most recent works are the most successful: the Third and Fourth Symphonies, *Prodigal Son*, the First Quartet."

The interviewer, Nino Frank, also provided a description of the composer's laboratory: "A small studio, its walls covered in sombre blue and inundated with a very white light; a piano, a couch, that photograph of Diaghilev with his usual Pierrot eyes, and, on the work table, music paper, blue galley proofs, a chess set, a big glass of tea, a Larousse." But Prokofiev minimized the importance of domestic tranquillity: "I work everywhere, always, and I have no need for meditation or for privacy.

> Every morning I work on new pieces. If I do work rather quickly, that does not make me any less intolerant of work that is not completely thought out. In the afternoon I take care of other work, like reading proofs or writing transcriptions. My most important task consists in jotting down in small notebooks all my ideas and images— musical ones, obviously—as soon as I find them, even when I am occupied with composing something else. As a result I have at my disposal an abundant and essential supply of material, to weigh and ponder with *sang-froid*. By the time I return to it, I have already achieved a certain distance from it, but it has not become lifeless either. Such is my method—though it would be pretentious to call it that.

As for influences and favorite forms, he denied them. "I have no particular preference for one or another genre—I love everything. No single composer has especially affected my work." Curiously, Prokofiev spoke little in this interview of Russia or of plans to visit there.

Retaining a keen interest in Parisian musical life, if only to know what the competition was up to, Prokofiev tried to attend as many concerts as possible when he wasn't traveling. In December, he heard the premiere of Stravinsky's new Violin Concerto. As was usually the case with Stravinsky's music, it both fascinated and repelled him. "There's a lot that is interesting in it," he wrote to Miaskovsky, who shared Prokofiev's love-hate relationship with Stravinsky, "but at the same time the absence of material, or its lack of definition, left feelings of emptiness and disappointment in one's soul."

Prokofiev was also present that season at the acclaimed premiere of Ravel's new Piano Concerto in G, which he found wonderfully orchestrated but not very pianistic. "It was one of the few occasions in Paris I recall when the hall was so full that people had to be turned away," he told Miaskovsky. New works by Darius Milhaud and Arthur Honegger pleased him much less. Milhaud's opera *Maximilien* was a "punctured tire" and Honegger's First Symphony was marred by "boring pages." Prokofiev's sharp criticisms delighted Miaskovsky, who took them as proof of the decline of Western musical culture. "In the West they have forgotten how to write significant music, and only produce trinkets," he declared.

By the end of the 1931–32 season, Prokofiev's stature in the Paris musical world earned him invitations to serve on the jury for two different concert organizations, *Triton* and *Serenade*. *Triton* included several members of Les Six—Poulenc, Honegger and Milhaud—and presented performances of chamber music. Prokofiev used his influence to promote the music of Soviet composers (including Miaskovsky and Shostakovich), and would write one chamber piece of his own for *Triton*, the Sonata for Two Violins.

Despite his reduced activity as a pianist, Prokofiev composed (for him, at least) relatively little music that season. Besides a pair of piano sonatinas (Op. 54, Nos. 1 and 2), he was composing a large new work for piano and orchestra. Perhaps in a search for new inspiration, he had suddenly become interested in writing for the piano again. At first he was intending to avoid the concerto label and call it Music for Piano and Orchestra, but he finally agreed with Miaskovsky's objections that such a title was pretentious and, even worse, smacked of "Hinde-mithism." In the end, he called it the Fifth Piano Concerto. His last piano concerto, it was written quickly and completed in piano score by June.

At about this time, Prokofiev took a brief trip to London to make his first gramophone recording: the Third Piano Concerto, with Piero Coppola conducting the London Symphony Orchestra. As he was pre-paring, he joked in a note to Miaskovsky, "Just think—I can't sneeze or miss any notes!"

The slower pace of the 1931–32 season, and the strongly felt absences of Diaghilev and Koussevitsky, forced Prokofiev to think even more seriously about his future and his relationship with the U.S.S.R. His letters written in the spring of that year contain the first indications that he was seriously considering establishing a permanent residence in Moscow. Through his contacts in the Soviet embassy in Paris, Prokofiev began investigating the possibility of accepting a part-time teaching post at the Moscow Conservatory.

What he envisioned was coming from Paris to spend a few weeks there in the fall and a few in the spring, working with a small group of composition students. "It all depends on whether the people in charge will agree to my shuttling back and forth, but I think the students might be able to exert some influence on my behalf," he told Mias-kovsky. "I'm following all the changes occurring now on the musical front with interest."

And changes there were aplenty. By early 1932, Soviet culture was on the brink of a profound and irreversible transformation. Annoyed with constant ideological mudslinging among intransigent factions in literature, music and art, and eager to assert his absolute power over all areas of Soviet life, Stalin launched an ambitious program of cultural consolidation and regimentation. By decree of the Party Resolution of April 23, 1932—"On the Reconstruction of Literary and Artistic Organizations"—all "proletarian" arts associations were abolished. This meant the end of the Association of Proletarian Musicians (RAPM), which had monopolized (even terrorized) musical life for the last three years. In the place of the abolished organizations, unions were established in each field of the arts—a Union of Composers, a Union of Writers, a Union of Artists.

For composers, this initially seemed like a welcome change, since RAPM had reigned with crude, unpredictable and dogmatic fervor. Prokofiev was certainly among those who originally interpreted the abolition of RAPM as a positive development. Its members had been outspoken and insistent in their criticism of him and his music.

The change which took place in the Soviet musical-cultural environment in early 1932 led Prokofiev to consider returning to Moscow more seriously than he ever had before. (He learned about it from the Soviet Embassy in Paris, and through letters and newspapers sent from Russia.) Only a few years later would the negative aspects of the enforced unionization of Soviet composers become completely obvious to him and his colleagues.

Prokofiev's friends in Russia also encouraged him to come back, of course, particularly Miaskovsky and Meyerhold. They were uncertain, however, if he would be willing to confront the difficulties of Soviet life. "If a *pied-à-terre* could be found for you here, it would be just delightful to have you in the midst of Soviet composers," Miaskovsky wrote, "but I am afraid it is just a crazy idea." A natural pessimist worn down by a decade of privation and struggle against maddening bureaucratic and ideological obstacles, Miaskovsky was not at all sure that "any sort of decisions could be made" about arranging for Prokofiev to live and work in Moscow on a permanent part-time basis. Although he realized how much Prokofiev's presence could add to the prestige and professionalism of the Conservatory, Miaskovsky was also afraid he would find the level of the students unacceptably low. "It would really refresh and shake up our pedagogical and creative existence," Miaskovsky wrote to Prokofiev. "Soviet musical life needs fresh air—we have argued with each other too much and have forgotten about music." Whatever the bureaucrats finally decided, Prokofiev was intending to come to Russia for a few weeks in the late fall.

In the summer, he and Lina took a series of traveling holidays— first to the strange little island of Sark, in the English Channel, "a picturesque British protectorate with its own queen who reigns over six hundred inhabitants from a castle guarded by six cannons," and then to the French Riviera, where they stayed for two months. On the way south, they passed through Roc Amadour and the "marvelous" ancient fortified city of Carcassonne. "I'm very pleased with our trip," Prokofiev wrote to Fatima Samoilenko. "I get up at seven and set off with a serious mien, stopping in interesting places. The only problem is that there is no one to play bridge with in the evenings, although I do have cards in my suitcase."

In early August they settled in a remodeled farmhouse on the Mediterranean coast in Ste. Maxime, near St. Tropez. The house belonged to Jacques Sadoul, a well-known Communist and the French correspondent at the time for the Soviet newspaper *Izvestiia*. Sadoul himself lived in a smaller house next door. Called "Les Pins-Parasols" ("Umbrella Pines"), the main house sat on top of a hill and was surrounded by terraces that commanded views of a pine forest and the ocean. Even on the hottest days the house was cool and comfortable. As usual, the largest room, facing the Mediterranean, became Prokofiev's study. It was here that he completed the orchestration of the Fifth Piano Concerto. With considerable difficulty, he also started learning the piano part, in preparation for the Concerto's premiere with the formidable Wilhelm Furtwängler (1886–1954) and the Berlin Philharmonic at the end of October. In his spare time, he was correcting the proofs for the full score of "Four Portraits."

While in Ste. Maxime, Prokofiev also composed the Sonata for Two Violins in C Major (Op. 56). He had been moved to write it after hearing what he considered an unsuccessful sonata for two violins by another (unnamed) composer in Paris. "Sometimes hearing bad compositions gives birth to good ideas," he wrote later. "One begins to think: that's not how it should be done, what's needed is this or that."

In four austere movements, this restrained and spare sonata— about fifteen minutes long—seems to avoid intentionally the glitter and flash of the violin writing found in the exuberant First Violin Concerto. Prokofiev joked to Miaskovsky that he had written it "in order to irritate you once and for all with what you call my 'lenten vertical style.' " The sonata received its premiere the following December at the first *Triton* concert.

When not working, Prokofiev invented crossword puzzles, tried (without much success) to improve his swimming, walked in the pine forest and took car excursions with his family. Once, passing through Grenoble, the Prokofievs stopped in to visit the Stravinskys, who were living nearby in Voreppe, having recently moved there from Nice.

Provocative letters continued to arrive from Moscow. In one, Miaskovsky reported that even the former members of the Association of Proletarian Musicians—no doubt as a result of the resolution handed down in April—had adopted a more positive attitude toward Prokofiev and his music, and were anticipating beneficial results from his upcoming visit. This encouraging news even led Prokofiev to venture a political opinion. Although admitting that he lacked complete information, he told Miaskovsky that former RAPM members had "a right to exert influence, provided they straighten out their policy line somewhat."

The trend in Prokofiev's thinking was now clear—he wanted to become more involved in Soviet musical life. As early as October 5, almost two months before his scheduled trip to the U.S.S.R., he was already planning to return to Moscow a second time in the spring, since he was afraid that three weeks would not be enough time "to hear and see everything without rushing. As a matter of fact, the time has come to come more often and to stay longer."

By mid-October Prokofiev was back in Paris, but not for long. The 1932–33 season was much more busy than the previous one; it included two extended visits to the U.S.S.R., a tour to America, and numerous engagements in Paris and other European cities. (Prokofiev boasted that the only European capitals in which he had never performed were Oslo, Helsinki and Athens.) But he was concentrating on Berlin, where four days later he was the soloist in the world premiere of his Fifth Piano Concerto, with Wilhelm Furtwängler and the Berlin Philharmonic. Furtwängler was at the peak of his career, which would soon be complicated by Hitler's rise to power. Prokofiev breezed in just before the concert. "I have left one whole rehearsal for you," Furtwängler told him. "This is, of course, too little for such a difficult score, but each of us will try to work as hard as possible."

Although the Berlin audience—like those in Paris and America who would hear it in the following months—responded positively to the Fifth Concerto, Prokofiev in retrospect considered the work a failure. For him, it became an important example of his inability to find a style of his own in the faddish modernist environment of Paris, and an illustration of why he needed to return to Russia.

What he was groping toward was what he called a "new simplicity." In letters to Miaskovsky, and in other writings of the early 1930s, Prokofiev often spoke of his search, which led him to write the Fifth Piano Concerto, the Sonata for Two Violins, *On the Dnepr* and the Op. 54 Sonatinas. Significantly, these are among his least-known and least-performed compositions. Miaskovsky accurately observed that despite Prokofiev's professed goal of simplicity, these pieces represented "a more intellectual style. You no longer follow the creative stream, but try to direct it consciously into a foreordained and—at least this is how it sometimes strikes me on first glance—more narrow riverbed. . . . I do not think I am mistaken in believing that if formerly you tried to stun, then now you try to impress and intrigue, which does not possess the same spontaneity."

Prokofiev's difficulty in finding this new style came, at least in part, from his inability to reconcile his natural impulse toward simplicity and melody with the demands of the Paris musical scene, which valued complexity and intellectual games. Prokofiev would only succeed in creating the "new simplicity" which he was seeking in the Soviet musical environment. There, his natural impulse would find reinforcement; in Moscow, composers were encouraged to write music that was accessible, simple and melodic. The results would be some of his greatest compositions—*Lt. Kizhe, Romeo and Juliet*, the Second Violin Concerto.

Many critics have claimed that the "simplification" of Prokofiev's style so obvious in the music he wrote beginning in the mid-1930s for Soviet commissions was the result solely of his capitulation to the demands of the official Soviet aesthetic. In fact, however, this process of simplification had begun several years earlier (around the time of *Prodigal Son*) and was a natural stage in Prokofiev's artistic evolution. Ultimately, it was his desire to compose in a more simple style that led him to return to the U.S.S.R.

The coldness and stiffness which Miaskovsky observed in other compositions of the transitional period of the early 1930s are also present in the Fifth Concerto. In stark contrast to the earlier concertos, bursting with wonderful melodic ideas, its five short movements do not boast a single memorable theme. Here, contrary to the way he usually worked, Prokofiev proceeded from technical devices rather than from melodic ideas. The resulting cleverness does not compensate for the absence of substantial content. (Ironically, Prokofiev repeatedly accused contemporary French composers of exactly that vice—preferring technical display to thematic strength.) Most of the attempts to find interesting harmonic and pianistic devices sound contrived and self-conscious. That four of the five movements are fast and toccata-like contributes to the overall impression of emotional brittleness.

"The work turned out to be complicated, a fate that pursued me fatally in a number of opuses dating from this period," Prokofiev wrote in 1941. "True, I was searching for simplicity, but I was also afraid it would turn into refrains of old formulas, into an 'old simplicity,' which serves little purpose in a composer looking for the new. In my search for simplicity, I sought a 'new simplicity,' but then it turned out that this new simplicity, with its new techniques and—most of all—its new intonations, was not perceived as simplicity at all."

Prokofiev's dissatisfaction with the Fifth Concerto, and his belief that he had been unable to find anything "new" to say in it, led him to abandon the genre of the piano concerto for good. He had not yet pronounced his last word on the instrument that had first made him famous, however—there were several magnificent piano sonatas still to come.

A few weeks after the Berlin premiere, Prokofiev and Lina set off for Moscow, via Warsaw, where he repeated the Fifth Concerto and Lina sang "The Ugly Duckling" in a newly orchestrated version. They arrived in Moscow on November 21 for a brief but important two-week visit. Prokofiev made four appearances in Moscow (including one recital) and two (one a recital) in Leningrad. The programs introduced a number of pieces to the Soviet audience—"Four Portraits," the Fifth Piano Concerto, the second of the Op. 54 Sonatinas—and included one world premiere: the Sonata for Two Violins. On this visit Prokofiev also took the baton himself to conduct the suite from the often-reviled *Le Pas d'acier*, still determined to persuade Soviet musicians of its worth.

On this, his third visit to the U.S.S.R. in the last five years, Prokofiev was out to prove that, far from being a semi-émigré "fellow traveler," he could be a loyal Soviet composer. Accordingly, the response he received was more restrained. He was almost a familiar face by now, and there was none of the near-hysteria that greeted his whirlwind appearances in 1927. Then, too, after five years of Stalin's rule and the ruthless brutality of enforced agricultural collectivization,

Russia was less exuberant, demonstrative and trusting. It would take Prokofiev much longer than a few weeks to overcome the suspicion of many members of the Soviet musical establishment, who were coming to know fear as a fact of daily life and had already learned to view their colleagues as potential informers.

In his beautifully tailored clothes and bright leather shoes, with his curt manners and sharp wit, Prokofiev was immediately recognizable as alien and different. He stood apart from the gray mass of Soviet composers like a palm tree in the Arctic.

Before leaving Moscow to return to Paris, Prokofiev spoke out publicly for the first time on his desire to contribute to Soviet culture. In the same lengthy interview, published in *Evening Moscow* on December 6, 1932, he also mentioned his dissatisfaction with the musical environment in the West. It is probably safe to assume that his friends and the cultural bureaucrats encouraged him to make these comments, as proof of the seriousness of his intentions.

"I am not leaving the U.S.S.R. for very long," he said. "I plan to return in the spring, in April. In Paris, a production of my new ballet awaits me, and the Fifth Concerto will be performed there for the first time. Then I will make a tour of America. Such conditions—unceasing performances—are hardly conducive to intensive artistic work. I hope to begin such work after arriving in the U.S.S.R. and intend to use Soviet material almost exclusively. The dead end to which the search for subject matter has led in the West only intensifies my desire to find Soviet material. There, one has no feeling of necessity. One subject is as unnecessary as the next." Coming from an internationally famous Russian-born composer, such statements served as marvelous propaganda for the cause of Soviet culture.

In this same interview, Prokofiev also revealed that he had been conferring with a Soviet film studio on a project that would give him his first opportunity to work with "Soviet" material. This was the genesis of what would become one of his most popular scores, the music for the film *Lt. Kizhe.*

As this interview indicates, Prokofiev's visit to Russia in the fall of 1932 was a turning point both in his relationship with the Soviet Union and in his career as a composer. Henceforth, he would never be away from Russia for longer than three or four months at a time. When he returned to Paris in early December, Prokofiev was already committed to going back to Moscow for a longer stay in the spring, and had indicated a new willingness to spend a large amount of his time there in the future. For better or for worse, he had taken a decisive step toward identifying himself as a "Soviet" composer.

Lina also saw her husband's feelings changing. "During his trips to the Soviet Union in 1932–33, the thought that his residence abroad had dragged on too long began to bother Sergei Sergeevich," she wrote some years later.

> He was irresistibly drawn to his native country. . . . During our life abroad, I had always felt that Sergei Sergeevich was tied by unbreakable bonds to Russia. . . . After our numerous trips to the Soviet Union, after the warm ecstatic reception extended to us and our joyful reunions with friends, it became clear that Sergei Sergeevich must return to his homeland. Although the issue was much more complicated for me, since my parents, close friends and familiar surroundings all remained abroad, I supported Sergei Sergeevich wholeheartedly in this wish.

In fact, of course, the thought of moving to Moscow, a city she did not know and where she had no friends or relatives of her own, must have been profoundly disturbing to Lina—as it would have been for anyone in her position. The strange cheerfulness of the above passage is explained by the fact that it was published in the U.S.S.R. in 1963. If Lina had been truthful about her completely understandable misgivings, her memoirs would never have been published at all.

To think of uprooting herself and her sons from Paris, where they had lived for ten years, must have been difficult enough for Lina. But to confront a permanent move to an isolated and alien country thousands of miles away, with a living standard markedly lower than what they were used to, must have been nearly terrifying. Nor would her fears prove unfounded. No matter how unpleasant the prospect of moving to Moscow might have appeared to Lina in 1932, and no matter what difficulties she might have envisioned, the reality of her future in the Soviet Union would be many times worse than she could possibly have imagined.

For Prokofiev, the issue was more simple and straightforward— he wanted to go back to Russia for the sake of his music, and because he felt more comfortable there. Although it would take him a few more years to make the final and irrevocable decision, he had already started down the path that would bring him to it. By the time Prokofiev returned to the rue Valentin Hauy in early December, "our musical advance post" was preparing to rejoin the regiment.

CHAPTER 16

A NEW

SIMPLICITY

I would like to live and die in Paris, if not for
another land—Moscow.

—VLADIMIR MAYAKOVSKY, 1925

n their overeagerness to claim Prokofiev as "ours," Soviet musicologists have traditionally cited 1932 as the year of his "final return"
to the homeland. It is true that after 1932 nearly all the music he
wrote was composed for Soviet commissions and first performed in
Russia. And yet he came to the final decision to make Moscow his
permanent home only gradually, over the course of three years.

Several of Prokofiev's Paris friends have said that he originally
intended to divide his time between Europe and Moscow indefinitely,
following the example of the writer Maxim Gorky. As Stalin's power
was consolidated in the early 1930s, however, Soviet cultural figures
were discouraged even from traveling to the West, let alone maintaining
a part-time residence there. Gorky himself finally returned to the U.S.S.R.
in 1931, and lived there until his death in 1936.

After making the decision in late 1932 to align himself more
closely with Soviet music, Prokofiev would be subjected to increasing
pressure to make Moscow his primary residence, and to settle his
family there. The Paris apartment on the rue Valentin Hauy would,
however, remain the primary Prokofiev family residence until late
spring of 1936. Only then, after nearly four years of commuting the
long distance between France and Russia, would he and his family
finally move into a Moscow apartment and give up their Paris flat.
Even after 1936, Prokofiev would attempt for a while to retain a base

of operations in Paris, and would briefly retain a *pied-à-terre* there.

The years between 1932 and 1936 were transitional ones. Prokofiev made frequent trips to Russia and spent an increasingly large portion of his time there, usually staying for three or four months at a time. But he would return at regular intervals to Paris—where his children were in school and where Lina still maintained an active social life—to stay there for a few months. He continued to concertize in Europe; in fact he and Lina continued to give concert tours in the West even after 1936, at least for a few years.

Several important performances, including one world premiere and two Paris premieres, awaited Prokofiev almost immediately upon his return to France from Moscow in December of 1932. That none of them was especially successful (and one a resounding critical and popular failure) could only have reinforced his growing belief that his career would benefit from a move to the U.S.S.R.

On December 10, an all-Prokofiev symphonic concert conducted by Albert Wolff featured the Sinfonietta, the First Violin Concerto, the Suite from *The Buffoon,* the March from *Oranges* and also introduced the Fifth Piano Concerto to Paris. Six days later, Prokofiev presided over one Paris premiere—of the Sonata for Two Violins— and one world premiere—of the ballet *On the Dnepr*—on the same evening. The Sonata for Two Violins was heard first, in the inaugural concert of *Triton,* the chamber music society on whose jury Prokofiev now served. Performed by the accomplished duo of Robert Soetens and Samuel Dushkin, it was well-received by an audience composed primarily of musicians. Having heard the sonata, Prokofiev and an entourage of musicians and critics dashed over to the Paris Opera, where, after a delay of nearly two years, his ballet *On the Dnepr* was finally opening.

A great deal of publicity had preceded the Lifar-Prokofiev collaboration. Many observers in Paris were clearly hoping the choreographer and composer would be able to resurrect the imagination and style of the already legendary Ballets Russes.

On the day of the opening, the magazine *Comoedia* published an interview with Prokofiev in which he spoke of his recent trip to Russia. "One thing struck me above all else," he told Madeleine Portier, "the thirst, the enormous thirst, that Russians now have for music. For them, art has become a vital need. . . . In Moscow, the tickets for my first three concerts were sold out in a day."

The Parisians were apparently not so thirsty—at least not for

Prokofiev's music. Despite the big names involved with *On the Dnepr*—in addition to Prokofiev's music and Lifar's choreography, it featured costumes by Natalia Goncharova and sets by Mikhail Larionov, creator of the wonderful designs for *The Buffoon*—the production was greeted with almost universal disappointment. "Parisian composers warmly defended it, but it was removed after a few performances," Prokofiev admitted later. Among those "Parisian composers" who praised it were Stravinsky and Milhaud.

Many of the reviews were among the most damning Prokofiev had ever received. In *Le Figaro*, Robert Brussel wrote:

> Those who have admired the Russian musician will search in vain throughout the choreographic poem that the Opera has just presented for anything reminiscent of the verve and caricature of *The Buffoon*, of the vigorous scope of *Le Pas d'acier* or of the sentiment of *Prodigal Son*. What a shame! We love him so much. Here in Paris he is practically a citizen. . . . We hoped that the day he made his debut on the stage of our National Academy of Music and Dance would bring us a great deal. We were mistaken. M. Prokofiev has presented a score that the late Serge Diaghilev would probably not have wanted, and with which in any case he should not have been satisfied. Deep down, M. Prokofiev must be dissatisfied with it himself as well. . . . The music is some of the weakest M. Prokofiev has written.

And again there was the inevitable comparison with Stravinsky. "The action of a strong will appears in the successive self-denials of M. Stravinsky," wrote Dominique Sordet. "There is nothing of the sort in M. Prokofiev, who floats wherever the winds blow him."

Nor was the official Soviet view of this score any more complimentary. "*On the Dnepr* is the ballet which most fully exhibits the crisis of the 'foreign period' of Prokofiev's art," says the *Ballet Encyclopedia*. "Its music is weakly related to its subject, and characterized by abstractness." The ballet has never been staged in the U.S.S.R., and the music remained unknown in Russia for fifty years after its Paris premiere.

What went wrong? In his 1941 autobiography, Prokofiev blamed the ballet's failure on its overemphasis on musical content at the expense of musical invention, but if anything, the reverse seems to be true. The fatal flaw in the score, and the cause of the music's vague personality, is the absence of a clear dramatic backbone. As a theatrical composer, Prokofiev always worked more successfully (as in *The Buf-foon*, *The Gambler* and in his upcoming film scores, including *Lt. Kizhe*) when he had a very specific scenario with clearly detailed episodes and characters. *On the Dnepr* did not have this definite dramatic scheme.

In trying to write a ballet equally acceptable to Soviet and French taste, Prokofiev (and Lifar) ended up with a bland and tentative result in an international style. Also curious is the lack of folk elements and specific local color in a score supposedly reflecting a Soviet Ukrainian rural setting. It could as easily be set in Iowa.

On the Dnepr also embodies Prokofiev's conscious attempt to move away from his *enfant terrible* image. As he entered middle age in the early 1930s, he was frustrated to be known primarily as the creator of viciously satirical and wildly dissonant music. Accordingly, *On the Dnepr* contains almost none of the bitingly ironic rhythms and angular melodies found in his scores of the 1920s. Unfortunately, Prokofiev also fails to replace that style with something equally compelling. There are attractive themes in *On the Dnepr* (particularly the passionate love theme), but many of the numbers are perfunctory and melodically uninteresting, particularly when compared to the brilliantly colorful and "specific" melodies, and the imaginative orchestration, that make Prokofiev's early ballets so original.

On the Dnepr was the last project on which Prokofiev and Lifar would collaborate, and the last time that Prokofiev would work with a former member of the Ballets Russes. Perhaps if Diaghilev had been able to develop and guide *On the Dnepr*, the result would have been quite different. Lifar did not have Diaghilev's patience and insight, his abiding faith in Prokofiev's talent, or the ability to shape and direct every aspect of a production from the earliest phases through to opening night.

Nor did Lifar and Prokofiev develop anything more than a distant professional relationship. "My collaboration with him was always very amicable," Lifar observed more than twenty years later, a few days after Prokofiev's death. "He was an authoritative man—dry, brittle, hardly ever relaxed, a man with a great sense of duty. He raised his children in a slightly military manner, keeping all tenderness for his music alone."

The failure of *On the Dnepr* meant the end of an era for Prokofiev. His career as a composer of ballets for Western theatres and audiences had run its course. When he would turn to dance music again, it would be for a Soviet theatre and for a full-length, old-fashioned "story ballet"—*Romeo and Juliet*.

The day after the premiere of *On the Dnepr*—and before most of the uncomplimentary reviews had appeared—Prokofiev left on the liner *Europa* for America. (This time, Lina remained behind in Paris.) Three years had passed since his last tour of the United States. This one was not nearly so ambitious; it lasted only about six weeks and included only twelve appearances. After spending Christmas with the Koussevitskys in Boston, Prokofiev made appearances with Koussevitsky and the Boston Symphony, in Boston and in New York. The five concerts with the BSO earned him two thousand dollars, but they were a mixed success. Olin Downes of *The New York Times* liked the Fifth Piano Concerto. "And there at the piano sits the boy, playing like a whirlwind, and juggling rhythms, counterpoints, imitations and anything else you please as if he could toss three more balls in the air and still ride the orchestra. . . . Mr. Prokofiev has been blessed or cursed with a brain which travels very fast and with the nervous temperament of this era." A few weeks later, however, when Prokofiev performed his Third Piano Concerto with Bruno Walter and the New York Philharmonic on a program that also featured the American premiere of "Portraits," Downes expressed confusion over the composer's future.

> One still wonders what on earth Serge Prokofieff will evolve into. He is a born virtuoso. He appears to be a temperament and a mind very symptomatic of his age. He is also a very gifted composer, but of what category, and what future? . . . Perhaps, until recently the very abundance of his ideas and his eager temperament, by denying him a deep-breathing repose, have delayed the accomplishment of his deepest purposes as a composer.

"Four Portraits" baffled other members of the New York audience as well. To his great amusement, Prokofiev overheard one of them loudly complaining to his companion, "I'd like to meet the guy who wrote that music. I would tell him a thing or two!" Before leaving America in early February, Prokofiev also performed in Chicago with Frederick Stock and the Chicago Symphony.

Prokofiev's American tour of 1933—the year that the U.S. government finally granted official diplomatic recognition to the U.S.S.R.—

was not surrounded by the same curiosity and wild speculation that his first appearances in the United States had inspired. In America, as in Russia, he was no longer a glamorous and unknown figure; in a sense, he was taken more seriously now. After the many silly things journalists and critics had said about him, Prokofiev was glad to see this new maturity and sobriety in the American musical public.

"It seems that the Americans are beginning to take me the way they should—seriously," he wrote to Asafiev.

> You know they used to behave like savages who would giggle if you played Beethoven's Ninth Symphony for them on a gramophone. That's what the kind Yankees were like: if they didn't understand something, that meant that the author was doing it as a joke, or out of spite. But now they are gradually beginning to penetrate to the seriousness of my intentions.

Prokofiev was pleased with his reception in America, but disappointed when he returned to Paris and did not find the official invitations to teach at Soviet conservatories (especially the Moscow Conservatory) which he had been expecting. Nor did he receive the scores of new music which Soviet composers had been promising to send him. Now that he had announced an intention to become more involved in Soviet musical life, Prokofiev had become an energetic champion of the music of Soviet composers in Europe and America. Such activity was consistent with his promotion of the music of other composers in the past. Indeed, few composers have been more loyal, selfless and insistent in their efforts on behalf of other composers than Prokofiev was throughout his life—whether on behalf of Vladimir Dukelsky, Nicolas Nabokov, Miaskovsky or Shostakovich. But bureaucratic inertia in Moscow complicated his attempts to promote Soviet music.

On his most recent trip to the U.S.S.R., Prokofiev had discussed the establishment of an exchange of scores between Soviet and European publishers. He had apparently persuaded his publisher (Éditions Russes) to accept scores by Soviet composers as payment of the rental fee for his compositions performed in the U.S.S.R. This was also a favorable arrangement from the financial point of view, since the Soviet government was unwilling to pay the rental fees in foreign currency.

When no scores arrived, Prokofiev wondered if there had been some change in the official attitude toward him and his music. "If in one corner they have forgotten about the scores," he asked Miaskovsky, "then couldn't they have forgotten about me in all the other institutions as well?" But Miaskovsky reassured him that the delay was not intended as an affront. "Don't be offended," he wrote. "Our life is too hectic." Precise and efficient, Prokofiev would never fully adjust to the slow and inefficient pace at which the Soviet bureaucracy proceeded.

In early April, Prokofiev left Paris for his fourth visit since 1927 to the Soviet Union. This would be his longest: nearly two months, from mid-April to early June, with Lina joining him after the first few weeks.

As if to emphasize that he was not a touring virtuoso, but a semiresident Soviet artist, Prokofiev made few concert appearances in Russia in the spring of 1933. He gave two concerts (one recital and one symphonic concert) in Leningrad and two in Moscow. The recital programs ranged from his earliest to his most recent music, while the symphonic concerts included the first performances in the U.S.S.R. of his Third Symphony, plus "The Scythian Suite" and the Third Piano Concerto. Prokofiev was particularly pleased with the warm public response to the Third Symphony. "I wouldn't want the Soviet listener to appreciate me only for the March from *Three Oranges* and the Gavotte from the 'Classical' Symphony," he explained.

What excited him about being in Russia was the opportunity to introduce and explain his music to a huge new public hungry for culture. "When you arrive in the U.S.S.R. from abroad, you feel something completely different," he said. "Here, dramatic works are needed, and there is no doubt what subject they should address—the subject must be heroic and constructive (it must be creative, not destructive). This is what our era demands."

In Paris, Prokofiev had been only one of many talented composers competing for the attention of a sophisticated and satiated public; in Moscow, at least in 1933, he stood head and shoulders above the rest. His artistic influence and stature were much greater in the U.S.S.R. than in France. No doubt his special position in the Soviet musical world compensated to a large extent for the bureaucratic, political and material difficulties he encountered in Russia. Then, too, he was insulated from many of the frustrations of Soviet daily life, since he was living in the best hotels in Moscow and Leningrad.

His light concert schedule freed Prokofiev to take a closer look at the Soviet musical world that spring, and to investigate sources of commissions. His first important Soviet project was the score for the film *Lt. Kizhe*, first proposed to him the preceding autumn. In connection with the project, he spent some of his time in Leningrad, where the filming was taking place.

Interestingly, Prokofiev, who would become one of the most successful film composers in the history of cinema, had initially received the invitation to write the music for *Lt. Kizhe* with caution. When the film's producer had first approached him in the fall of 1932, asking him to collaborate on one of the first Soviet sound films, Prokofiev "categorically rejected my proposal. His time was scheduled far into the future, he had never written music for film, and he didn't know 'what kind of sauce to put on it.'"

What helped to change Prokofiev's mind was the wonderful literary source of the film, a story of the same title by Yury Tynianov (1894–1943), also a famous "formalist" critic and an important figure in the early history of the Soviet cinema. *Lt. Kizhe* is a charmingly dry and absurd tale that was perfectly suited to Prokofiev's own satirical sense of humor.

An office clerk of the era of the pompous Tsar Paul (Catherine the Great's son, he reigned from 1796 to 1801) makes a slip when copying over official military documents. Inadvertently repeating two letters (in Russian, "zh-e"), he adds a nonexistent lieutenant, Lt. Kizhe, to a list of soldiers presented for the Tsar's approval. The unusual name catches Paul's eye, and Kizhe is singled out for special treatment. So terrified are they of contradicting their sovereign that Paul's subordinates carry out his decree, promoting the nonexistent Kizhe to the Tsar's elite guard. As often happened to such soldiers, however, Kizhe eventually falls into disfavor and is sentenced to Siberia. Still unaware that Kizhe does not exist, and protected from the truth by his intimidated aides, the Tsar magnanimously pardons Kizhe and promotes him to general. Even his "wife" goes along with the scheme, concealing the truth that Kizhe is a creation of cowardly bureaucrats. When he "dies," Kizhe is buried in an empty coffin with imperial pomp and circumstance.

Underneath Tynianov's elegant, Pushkinian prose lies a witty attack on official stupidity and the profoundly Russian terror of displeasing one's superior. Kizhe is a direct descendant of Nikolai Gogol's disembodied civil servants, whose personalities are defined by their position on the table of ranks. It is to Prokofiev's credit that he understood Tynianov's deeper intentions, and told the filmmakers he interpreted the story (and the film) as basically tragic and would write the music accordingly.

Tynianov was also involved in the film version of his story and, perhaps acquainted with Prokofiev's affinity for the eighteenth century through the "Classical" Symphony, suggested to the film studio (Belgoskino) that Prokofiev write the music for it. At first, representatives of the studio objected, since they thought Prokofiev's frequent trips to Europe would hold up the project, but they were persuaded that he worked quickly and had an impeccable record of fulfilling his obligations.

When Prokofiev finally agreed to write the score, he specified from the very beginning that he wanted exact information about what was required of him. He wanted to know "the dimensions of the musical pieces, their character and length. . . . What is important to me is the era, the internal meaning of each event, the personality of each hero." He warned the filmmakers not to expect mere "illustrations."

Although at that time unfamiliar with the world of cinema, Prokofiev, who had loved machines and technology since childhood, had long been fascinated with cameras; the home movies he made with Meyerhold in the Prokofievs' garden are ample proof of that. Prokofiev's extensive work in the theatre had also made him very familiar with the demands (visual, dramatic, rhythmic, vocal) the stage made upon a composer, and these were helpful in understanding the requirements of film. His experience with dance was particularly useful, since film music required a similar kind of descriptive illustration of physical movement and pantomime.

In composing for *Kizhe*, which was directed by Alexander Faintsimmer, Prokofiev wrote the music only after the film had been completely planned out. (Later, in his work with Eisenstein, he would be involved at a much earlier stage in the process.) "Carefully watching the rehearsals, he would note down all the details, the mime of the actors, their movements, and it seemed that at that moment he already knew what kind of music he would write for this or that fragment." Prokofiev would then consult those notes while writing the score.

In his own account of the creation of *Kizhe*, Prokofiev agreed that he felt particularly confident about the music that came to him: "For some reason I never had any doubt about the musical language for the film." The score included several songs, which were modeled on eighteenth-century "urban songs." Two of them—"Troika" and "The Grey

Dove Is Sighing"—were subsequently rearranged for voice and piano.

In his music for *Kizhe,* as in almost all of his film scores, Prokofiev wrote in pieces and fragments, not in large symphonic movements. The original *Kizhe* score (which should not be confused with the very popular *Lt. Kizhe* Suite later arranged from it) has sixteen small "numbers," rather like a ballet score. For each separate dramatic episode or character Prokofiev sought a specific theme, timbre, rhythm and orchestration. He did not try to find one generalized symphonic "key" for the film. In this sense, Prokofiev's film music is influenced much more by his work in ballet and theatre than by symphonic forms.

Writing film scores appealed to Prokofiev in part because so many people would hear them. Like Lenin, who called film "the most important art," Prokofiev, along with many other Soviet composers, was intrigued by the enormous potential of cinema as a mass medium. In fact, "serious" composers have played an unusually important role in the Soviet film tradition, and have collaborated with filmmakers since the earliest days of the Soviet film industry. Prokofiev's colleague Shostakovich would eventually write music for more than thirty films (both silent and sound), and Aram Khachaturian for more than fifteen.

Soviet composers who have written for film have not been dismissed as "popular" or "commercial," as have their counterparts in America. One explanation for this difference is that the birth of "Soviet" (post-1917) culture, including music, happened to coincide almost exactly with the worldwide explosion of the film industry. Soviet music and Soviet film developed side by side, and it was natural that Soviet composers would work in this new "proletarian" medium with enormous potential for the dissemination of propaganda to the Soviet masses. Unlike American films, Soviet films, particularly in the early years, were not made primarily for purposes of light entertainment. They were intended to educate and enlighten.

The special role that music has played in the history of Soviet cinema also came about in part because a number of pioneer Soviet film directors—above all, Sergei Eisenstein—possessed a high degree of musical sophistication. They conceived of the role of music in film in new and highly theoretical terms. Their intellectual approach to the film score as an art in its own right, and their willingness to respect the composer as a collaborator on equal terms, led "serious" composers to view film music as a worthwhile and unique genre.

In his first attempt at writing a film score, Prokofiev was remarkably successful, demonstrating an instinctive understanding of the cinematic medium and its requirements. Writing film music exploited his greatest strength as a composer: illustration. In fact, Prokofiev's music for *Lt. Kizhe* achieved a much greater success than the film itself, which, according to him, was spoiled because the ending was too often changed.

In early 1934, Prokofiev fashioned a five-part suite (about twenty minutes long) from the *Kizhe* music: "The Birth of Kizhe," "Lyrical Song," "The Wedding of Kizhe," "Troika" and "The Funeral of Kizhe." It is in this form, which is quite different from the original film score, that it has become one of his "greatest hits." For Prokofiev, writing the *Lt. Kizhe* Suite (Op. 60) proved more difficult than the original film score; he had to create an appropriate form, reorchestrate many passages, redo some of the themes and link them all together.

What audiences have loved in this music are its many accessible—but strongly individual—melodies, its strong atmosphere of Pushkin's "classical" Russia, and its slightly ironic playfulness and charm. The scoring is transparent, highlighting the melodies in quirky instrumentation (especially the piccolos for the tongue-in-cheek military episodes and saxophones for the lyrical moments). The rhythms are pronounced, but only lightly sarcastic, not heavily grotesque as in *The Buffoon* or *Love for Three Oranges*.

Remarkably "physical" pictures of imperial Petersburg emerge from the film music and the suite: stiff military marches, snowy troika rides, simple lyrical laments (although with a touch of irony, particularly considering the dramatic situation described in the Tynianov story). That Woody Allen was later able to use pieces of the *Lt. Kizhe* Suite so successfully in his film parody of Russian literature, *Love and Death*, indicates just how well Prokofiev conveyed a sarcastic, ironic tone and an unmistakably "Russian" atmosphere. The musical style and forces are similar to those employed in the "Classical" Symphony and portions of *Love for Three Oranges*, which, like *Lt. Kizhe*, satirizes the stupidity of royalty. This was a world—half-fantastic, half-classical—in which Prokofiev had always felt comfortable. The *Kizhe* score, more lyrical, more homophonic, less complex in harmony and rhythm, and less aggressive than much of his earlier music, is the first truly successful example of his "new simplicity."

Prokofiev's unqualified critical and popular success (his biggest since *Prodigal Son*) with the music for *Lt. Kizhe* was very important for him in establishing a Soviet persona. It must also have reinforced his belief that he belonged in Russia. While working on the film, he had been very aware of how important it was for him to create something that proved his ability to convey Soviet reality and the Soviet aesthetic in his music. "The musical language necessary for writing about Soviet life had not yet been formed," he remarked later. "No one had a clear idea of it, and no one wanted to make a mistake." It was easier, of course, to begin with a subject like *Kizhe*, which, although written by a contemporary Soviet writer and filmed by a Soviet director, told an eighteenth-century story. It did not require Prokofiev to illustrate current Soviet reality, which was emotionally and visually much less familiar than the Petersburg of Tsar Paul. Over the next twelve years, Prokofiev would write seven more film scores, including the music for Eisenstein's *Alexander Nevsky* and *Ivan the Terrible*.

If in the spring of 1933 Prokofiev was attempting to become more familiar with Soviet musical life, he was also taking the time to become better acquainted with the Soviet Union. To become a Soviet composer, he needed to learn more about the nation. He began by taking a trip through Georgia and Armenia, visiting Erevan, Tiflis (now called Tbilisi) and Batumi.

Returning after twenty years to the Caucasus—where he had spent so many summers as a boy and a young man—must have brought back many happy memories. But in the postcards and letters Prokofiev was sending to friends in the West, a strange change was taking place: he was describing his impressions not in his usual Russian, but in French or English. Most likely, he did this to make it more difficult for the curious—and the Soviet censors, who closely watched all mail sent abroad—to keep track of his Russian émigré friends in the West. By the mid-1930s, those who had emigrated from Russia after the Revolution were, for the most part, considered as traitors with whom loyal Soviet subjects should have minimal contact. Prokofiev may also have wanted to make his comments more difficult to monitor, although his observations were positive and resolutely apolitical in any case.

Having spent nearly two months in the U.S.S.R., Prokofiev returned to Paris with Lina in early June. For the first time in many years, he stayed in Paris for almost the entire summer, making only brief trips away from the city. Part of the time he was alone, since Lina had gone for a vacation by herself to Geneva and the children were staying with her mother on the Riviera. At the end of the summer, Prokofiev and Lina went to the Mediterranean for several weeks together with the children before returning to Paris in mid-September. During the summer, he made sketches for a cello concerto, started work on three piano pieces called "Thoughts," and orchestrated a large new piece, the "Symphonic Song for Large Orchestra" (Op. 57).

The "Symphonic Song" would, he hoped, be an appropriate work with which to strengthen his position as a "Soviet" orchestral composer. Since many Soviet symphonies bore politically motivated programmatic titles (Shostakovich, for example, had called his Second Symphony "Dedication to October" and his Third "May First"), Prokofiev also assigned general "moods" to each of the three movements of the "Symphonic Song." *Andante assai, Allegro* and *Andante* corresponded to "darkness—struggle—achievement."

After seeing the piano score of the "Symphonic Song" the preceding spring, Miaskovsky had warned Prokofiev that it was "not entirely right for us. . . . it lacks what we would call monumentality—a familiar simplicity and breadth of contour." He advised Prokofiev to compose another ambitious piece specifically for a Soviet premiere, something "monumental, with definite personality and—don't be angry, o horrors—even cheerful."

Not long after completing the orchestration of the "Symphonic Song," Prokofiev headed back to Moscow. Most of his time was spent in composing and planning more projects. Done with the score for *Lt. Kizhe*, which was recorded onto the film's soundtrack under the direction of Isaac Dunayevsky in the autumn, he turned to other dramatic music. Alexander Tairov, one of the most innovative directors in twentieth-century theatre (and whom Diaghilev had wanted to direct *Le Pas d'acier*) had decided to stage a collage on the theme of Anthony and Cleopatra at his Moscow Chamber Theater. Tairov had founded the theatre in 1914, and since that time it had flourished as one of Russia's most important experimental theatres.

For this production, Tairov was planning to piece together Bernard Shaw's *Caesar and Cleopatra*, which focuses on Cleopatra's youth, and Shakespeare's *Anthony and Cleopatra*, which concentrates on her maturity. In between, Tairov placed a monologue from a dramatic fragment by Alexander Pushkin, "Egyptian Nights," which deals with the same characters. Pushkin's piece also provided the title for the production. The main character in Tairov's conception was Cleopatra, and the main theme the contrast between military, rational Rome and mysterious, sensual Egypt.

Although the combination of sources struck him as odd, Prokofiev had sufficient faith in Tairov's talent to agree to write the incidental music. In his first attempt at composing music for a dramatic production, Prokofiev tried to follow this principle: "If the presence of music in a given scene strengthens its dramatic force or lyricism, then the music is right. If when played without the music a given scene produces no less strong an impression, then the music is unsuccessful, or this scene needs no music."

According to Tairov, after he had described his basic concept to Prokofiev, the first piece of music he produced was Cleopatra's theme, "which he sketched out on a little piece of music paper—only a line and a half. We immediately found it unusually successful and it entered the production. When we had established Cleopatra's leitmotif, we proceeded from it to find the leitmotif for Rome." Prokofiev enjoyed working with Tairov, because the director was very specific in his instructions about what kind of music was needed at each moment in the action.

Because of the obvious difficulties involved in combining three dramatic sources, each from an entirely different literary-historical tradition and each with a strong personality, Tairov encountered many problems in putting the production together. "Despite Shaw's charming wit," Prokofiev said later, "old man Shakespeare turned out to be such a titan that one wanted to give him as much space as possible and as little as possible to Shaw. Thus edited, Bernard completely lost face and turned into an unnecessary appendage at the beginning of the production." Largely because of Tairov's close connection to the antirealistic theatrical avant-garde, which was coming under increasing pressure from the official cultural establishment, *Egyptian Nights* aroused intense interest in theatrical circles, although it would run into strong political opposition soon after its premiere.

As was his custom, Prokofiev subsequently turned the incidental music he wrote for *Egyptian Nights* into a suite (Op. 61) in seven parts. (He completed this in the late summer of 1934, even before the premiere of Tairov's production.) This suite contains some very interesting music, as well as many hints of the music composed soon after for two other dramatic projects: *Romeo and Juliet* and *Alexander Nevsky*. The opening chords of the suite are nearly identical to the opening chords of the first part of the *Alexander Nevsky* Cantata, in evocatively mysterious and "hollow" string tremolo. The military music for the Roman army prefigures the rhythmic and sinister martial music so important in many of Prokofiev's works to follow, from *Romeo* and

Nevsky to *War and Peace* and *Ivan the Terrible*. Also amusing is the section called "Alarum"; it lasts a mere minute and is scored for percussion alone.

Egyptian Nights and *Lt. Kizhe* mark the beginning of a period of about five years (1933–38) during which Prokofiev composed primarily program and dramatic music, turning away from classical sonata-based forms. These works include—besides *Egyptian Nights* and *Lt. Kizhe*— the ballet *Romeo and Juliet*, the symphonic fairy tale for children *Peter and the Wolf*, incidental music for several more theatrical productions (*Hamlet, Boris Godunov* and *Eugene Onegin*), music for the films *The Queen of Spades* and *Alexander Nevsky*, and a number of patriotic songs.

This shift toward programmatic music came as a response to the different demands of the Soviet musical market. A public and narrative style characterized Soviet music even in the early 1920s, and this trend intensified in the 1930s, when there was increasing pressure to produce music both edifying and accessible. At a point when he needed to publicly establish his "Soviet" credentials, Prokofiev eagerly accepted commissions for theatre and film music. Then, too, there was impressive talent working in Soviet theatre and film in the mid-1930s— Meyerhold, Tairov, Stanislavsky, Eisenstein.

Despite his superficial rebelliousness, Prokofiev had something of the "teacher's pet" in his personality and had always wanted to please the authority figures in his life. (Perhaps he was still pursuing the approval of his distant and silent father.) As an artist, he also enjoyed—even preferred—being given a specific assignment to fulfill. Now that Prokofiev was trying to develop closer ties with the Soviet public and cultural establishment, which was only too happy to tell its artists what and how to create, he wrote the sort of music that would be likely to please them. Once again, Prokofiev was writing to order.

Even the political gestures expected of Soviet cultural figures now began to come easier. On November 7, 1933, the sixteenth anniversary of the great October Revolution (which he did not witness), Prokofiev was in Red Square to observe the celebration. He wrote to Fatima Samoilenko that he found the parade of soldiers, workers and military equipment that passed by Lenin's tomb *"très impressionant!"* On the same postcard, which bore a group portrait of Stalin, Kalinin and Voroshilov, the leading figures of the Sixteenth Congress of the Communist Party, Prokofiev enthused, in French: "Everything is going well under the Moscow moon: concerts, friends, and even chess."

In his campaign to become more deeply involved in the Soviet musical establishment, Prokofiev also began to take a more active role in the life of the Moscow Conservatory during the fall of 1933. After extensive official negotiations, he had started working with a few composition students there. As Prokofiev had once admitted to Miaskovsky, he did not have the patience to be a good teacher. Prokofiev's highly individual, instinctual and anti-intellectual approach to music and the creative process made it difficult for him to formulate or communicate general methods of composition. Unlike Shostakovich and Miaskovsky, he did not cultivate a group of protégés and took little interest in the development of musical education.

One day, Prokofiev paid a visit to the young composers who were studying advanced composition at the Conservatory under Miaskovsky. One of those was Aram Khachaturian, already a promising artist at age thirty. That the great Prokofiev had come to critique their music terrified both Khachaturian and his classmates. "Fifteen years of living abroad had left a noticeable imprint on him," he later recalled. "He was dry, businesslike, at times even arrogant. With the exception of a few of his old friends, almost no one had access to him." Another student in that same class would later become a prominent official in the Composers' Union and would take a certain pleasure in chastening the arrogant and inaccessible master. His name was Tikhon Khrennikov.

Early in December, after several days in Leningrad, Prokofiev left Moscow—in time to avoid the dark and frigid days of midwinter—and traveled straight to Rome. There, he participated in a concert of "new Soviet music," which included his Fifth Piano Concerto (with Prokofiev as soloist) and Third Symphony, plus Miaskovsky's Sinfonietta for String Orchestra. The conductor, Bernardino Molinari, set aside five days of rehearsal—twice a day—in preparation for the program. "You never find such luxury anywhere anymore," he wrote to Miaskovsky. Even the climate in Italy seemed a pleasant change. "It's warm in Rome, and they're selling flowers on the street."

Numerous concert appearances were also scheduled for January, leaving Prokofiev only about three weeks free in December after his return to Paris from the south. He used them to finish the incidental music for *Egyptian Nights* and to catch up with the latest events on the Paris musical scene. What he heard—new pieces by Poulenc,

Milhaud and Sauguet—struck him as "totally nil." What Paris needed, he believed, was more music by Soviet composers, and he set about organizing a concert, to be underwritten by several French labor organizations, for the spring.

Prokofiev remained in Europe for four months. Before returning to Moscow in early April, he had a fairly active performing season in Europe. Everywhere he went, he pressed the cause of Soviet music, and tried to gather scores to bring to young composers in Russia. Prokofiev even wrote to the niece of Sergei Koussevitsky, with whom he now corresponded much less frequently than in the past, asking her to send some of the music her uncle did not need. "This isn't a personal request; it is a request for the young composers who must familiarize themselves with the techniques of foreign authors."

To a large extent, Miaskovsky had by now replaced Koussevitsky and Diaghilev as Prokofiev's primary mentor and adviser. To understand the strength of the relationship between the Conservatory classmates who had already known each other for nearly thirty years, one must remember how much Miaskovsky loved Prokofiev's music. At least he always said he did. After looking again at the score of Prokofiev's Second Symphony, he wrote, "You are now the only representative of a strict style in music. Even, I would add, irreconcilably strict. There is no weakness in you. Somehow, you manage to maintain a constant intensity of thought. You can sharpen the finest point— and that is true art of the very highest quality."

And yet it was dangerous for Prokofiev to rely so heavily on Miaskovsky's opinion. Because of their long friendship—the most intense friendship Prokofiev ever developed—Miaskovsky tended to indulge his younger and more talented friend. He rarely criticized his music with the same cold judgment exercised by Diaghilev and Koussevitsky, who had less tolerance for Prokofiev's emotional and artistic weaknesses (particularly his tendency to be easily influenced, and his erratic taste). Even more important, Miaskovsky was isolated from movements in European and American music. He had traveled abroad— and very briefly—only once in his life. Although he was to some extent familiar with Schoenberg and the other members of the "New Viennese School," Miaskovsky was uninterested in their techniques, which, by the early 1930s, were already becoming anathema in official Soviet musical aesthetics. (In their virulent anti-Westernism, the members of RAPM had sharply criticized Schoenberg, and his reputation in the

U.S.S.R. did not begin to recover until the 1950s.) In his own music, Miaskovsky was conservative, concentrating primarily on the symphony. Both Koussevitsky and Diaghilev had been much more adventurous, demanding and cosmopolitan mentors.

Occasionally, Prokofiev had to remind Miaskovsky that French taste and Soviet taste were not the same. Explaining why he considered it inadvisable to perform the music to Shostakovich's ballet *Bolt* in Paris, Prokofiev wrote, "Moscow requires a composer to be robust and cheerful above all. Paris has believed in Soviet robustness for a long time now, but often questions whether there is any depth of content behind it." Increasingly, Prokofiev was acting as a musical go-between, arguing for Soviet music in Paris and for European music in Moscow.

Prokofiev had always relied upon Miaskovsky's evaluations of his music, but now that he had thrown his lot in with Soviet music, Miaskovsky was also an important source of bureaucratic and political advice. During the winter of 1934, while Prokofiev was in Europe, Miaskovsky kept him abreast of developments affecting his music and his official position. At Miaskovsky's New Year's party, Prokofiev was "remembered very affectionately by a large group of friends, and they have asked me to send you their warmest greetings and New Year's wishes." With some surprise, Miaskovsky also reported that the magazine *Soviet Art* had reviewed the autumn performance of Prokofiev's Fourth Symphony and the Divertissement favorably. The critic had been relieved to discover that these works had nothing in common with the "screaming puppet-show quality of *The Buffoon* and the stridency of the finale of 'The Scythian Suite.' " Miaskovsky concluded, "In spite of my predictions, your new style seems to have a good chance of becoming understood and even appreciated."

Musical life in Moscow continued in Prokofiev's absence. Being in Europe in January, he missed an important premiere—almost simultaneously in Leningrad and Moscow—that solidified the claim of Prokofiev's only real competitor to the title of leading Soviet composer.

Even before it finally reached the stage that January, Dmitri Shostakovich's opera *Lady Macbeth of the Mtsensk District* had caused great excitement in the Soviet musical world. (After hearing it at a rehearsal the preceding June, Miaskovsky had written Prokofiev that it was "amazingly good.") The first reviews after the opening in early 1934 were rapturous, labeling *Lady Macbeth* "a work of genius" and "an opera that could only have been written by a Soviet composer brought up in the best traditions of Soviet culture." Over the next two years, it would be performed many more times in Moscow and Leningrad, and would also be seen in America.

Shostakovich, already well-known for his three symphonies, several ballets, and another opera, *The Nose*, became the musical celebrity of the moment. The bright new hope of Soviet music, he was so much in demand that Miaskovsky had been unable to talk with him about sending music to Prokofiev for performances in Paris. "He is at the peak of fame and therefore frivolous," Miaskovsky said.

Judging from his letters and comments through 1934, Prokofiev did not regard Shostakovich's music with particular enthusiasm. Their aesthetic views, temperaments, family backgrounds and educations were very different. Where Shostakovich was a child of the Revolution, Prokofiev was a child of the Tsarist *fin de siècle;* where Shostakovich, an introvert, viewed the world tragically and gave at times hysterical expression to his emotions in his music, Prokofiev was ironic, cheerfully extroverted and restrained; where Shostakovich was the son of parents with strong Communist sympathies, Prokofiev had been born into a middle-class bourgeois environment; where Prokofiev received his musical training in the prerevolutionary surroundings of the Petersburg Conservatory, Shostakovich had come of musical age during the chaotic years following the Revolution. Then, too, they had little opportunity to meet, since Shostakovich lived in Leningrad while Prokofiev spent most of his time in Moscow. Whatever their relationship, it was now obvious that Shostakovich—fifteen years Prokofiev's junior—would be a force to reckon with.

In late March, Prokofiev packed up again and left Paris for Moscow. This time, he stayed for nearly four months in Russia; apparently Lina came to spend a few weeks during the middle of his stay. The most significant musical event of his visit was the world premiere of his "Symphonic Song" on April 14 in Moscow. It was a complete failure with both the audience and the critics. According to Miaskovsky, "There were literally three claps in the hall." *Soviet Music* assailed it as "a symphonic monologue for the few, a sad tale of the decline of the fading culture of individualism."

After a concert tour of the Ukraine, Prokofiev was fortunate enough to spend a week in the countryside outside Moscow at the *dacha* of a new acquaintance, the artist Pyotr Konchalovsky (1876–1956). They had originally met in 1933, at one of Konchalovsky's exhibitions, and eventually decided that Prokofiev's portrait should be painted. It was with that end in mind that Prokofiev and Lina, who had recently arrived from Paris, went to stay with Konchalovsky for a week. "June was in full bloom," Konchalovsky's daughter, then in her twenties, later remembered. "The flowering jasmine was dropping its petals on the hot sand of the paths, the red caps of the peonies were swaying, the roses opening in the garden. Under a big pine tree, Sergei Sergeevich was having his portrait painted."

Prokofiev loved the Russian countryside in summer, its calm and muted beauty all the more eagerly awaited and treasured after the long winter. Strolling across the gently rolling landscape that surrounds Moscow, he must have remembered the fields of Sontsovka.

Sitting for Konchalovsky's portrait amused both Prokofiev and his hosts. They admired his fine European clothes, unavailable to them. "Sergei Sergeevich wore wide dark-blue trousers, a shirt of the same light material, a gray suede jacket with a zipper. . . . His long thin legs were crossed, relaxed, knee at an angle, an elbow at another angle on the back of the chair—like a chart of Prokofiev's character. His face was red, with a high bald forehead, his eyes alert and attentive under prickly yellow eyebrows. There was energy running through him—in the turn of his head, in the chin, the strange long upper lip, the thin nostrils, and the small ears pressed to the skull."

The days would begin with a long morning stoll. Returning to the house, Prokofiev would immediately write down the musical ideas that had occurred to him while walking through the fields. Then he would sit for Konchalovsky until breakfast, when the entire household, including Lina—"still young, lively and dark-eyed"—would assemble. Even while posing, Prokofiev frequently ran off to the piano in the house to bang out ideas for the *Lt. Kizhe* Suite, which he had nearly completed by then. In the afternoons, after resting, he would work more seriously on composition, and in the evenings, everyone would read, talk, or play a board game that Prokofiev had invented as a child—"Naval Battle." After fifteen sittings, the portrait, one of the best-known of Prokofiev, was finished. Prokofiev and Konchalovsky remained friends for the rest of their lives.

During that same June, another artist, Igor Grabar (1871–1960), also began painting Prokofiev's portrait. They had met many years before, in prerevolutionary Petersburg. One day in 1934, Prokofiev suddenly appeared in Grabar's Moscow studio. "He had the same glowing, youthful appearance he had always had, and was excited and eager to talk, to pour out his soul and share his future musical plans,"

Grabar said later. "He looked one-hundred-percent foreign, especially with his suede jacket, and its new foreign invention that we had never seen before—a zipper."

Prokofiev sat for Grabar a few times, but they were both so busy and distracted in Moscow that they decided to temporarily shelve the project. Seven years later, when they were both evacuated from beseiged Moscow to the Caucasus during World War II, Grabar would return to the portrait.

Sitting still for very long was never easy for Prokofiev. In early June, he set off from Moscow alone—Asafiev had decided not to join him as originally planned—on a boat trip down the Volga. Sailing hundreds of miles east along the Volga through the Tartar capital of Kazan to the extensive inland water route known as the "Five Rivers," Prokofiev was intending to travel on to the Altai, a remote mountainous region in southwestern Siberia near the Chinese border. Although Prokofiev gave no explanation for making such an extensive voyage on his own, it seems likely he was seeking a quiet atmosphere conducive to composition and inspiration. It was also a sentimental journey of sorts; he had taken a similar boat trip in 1917, when composing the "Classical" Symphony.

Prokofiev had his own small cabin. "You can lay out all your things, hang up what needs to be hung up on nails—in a word, settle in for the entire journey," he wrote to his childhood friend Vera Alpers. "Then you can calmly enjoy the riverbank, the views, the air and the bazaars at the stops along the way. As you travel farther east on the Kama and Belaya rivers, the bazaars become absolutely picturesque; they are full of Bashkirs, who don't speak a word of Russian." Ufa, the capital of the Bashkir Republic, on the western slope of the Urals, an exotic and primitive city of one-story buildings, delighted him, as did the entire voyage. But for some reason, Prokofiev returned mysteriously to Moscow before reaching the Altai, and then went on to Paris. His departure was so sudden that it stunned even Miaskovsky, who was accustomed to his sometimes impulsive behavior. Why he cut his trip short is not clear; perhaps Lina wanted him — understandably—to spend more time there with her and the boys that summer. By now, however, Prokofiev's growing emotional and professional attachment to Russia was irreversible. This summer of 1934 would be the last he would spend outside Russia.

For much of the summer, Prokofiev was alone in Paris, since Lina and the boys were in the south of France. This was the second consecutive summer during which Prokofiev and Lina had spent time apart. They had also spent a large part of the preceding year in different places—Prokofiev in Moscow, and Lina in Paris. In the winter, Prokofiev had toured the United States alone, and had often traveled without Lina on his briefer tours around Europe, even though the children were now older and could be more easily left at home. After ten years of marriage, Prokofiev and his wife seemed to be drifting apart, at least in part because of his decision to pursue his musical career in the Soviet Union. And yet this does not seem to be the only reason, for they were also choosing to spend time apart even when they were both in Europe, something they had not done in previous years.

Surely, Prokofiev's increasingly strong commitment to Soviet musical life, and his desire to spend more and more time in Russia, created some added tension in his relationship with his wife—which had been argumentative even in the best of times. Even before his decision to spend more time in Moscow, Prokofiev had earned a reputation among their friends for mistreating Lina when she interfered with his work. It is even possible that he welcomed the opportunity to spend more time alone, since it allowed him to concentrate on composing without dividing his attentions. For Prokofiev, his music had always been the first priority, ranking far above wife, children and friends. At the same time, Lina, never one to be timid about her feelings, was definitely ambivalent about moving to the U.S.S.R.

As he withdrew from his domestic life in Paris, Prokofiev was reestablishing and strengthening links with friends of his childhood and youth still living in the U.S.S.R. One of those was Vera Alpers, his Conservatory classmate, who had suffered from an acute crush on him when they were teenagers. She had remained since then in Petrograd/Leningrad, where she was now a piano teacher. Prokofiev had seen her on one of his trips to Leningrad, and they had begun to correspond regularly.

It must have been difficult for Lina to understand or share her husband's feelings completely as he became reacquainted with the people and places of his past. They meant a great deal to him but almost nothing to her. To some extent, all spouses have to deal with this problem, but the enormous cultural and political gap that separated Lina from Prokofiev's prerevolutionary life was more difficult to bridge than most.

Staying alone in Paris in August, the city deserted and oddly quiet, did not seem to depress Prokofiev. "Paris in August has its charms," he wrote to Vera Alpers. "It completely empties out, it isn't hot, there's a lot of greenery—in a word, it's an excellent place for work. I've taken advantage of it to compose quite a lot."

What he was completing were two small cycles of piano pieces: the Op. 62 "Thoughts" ("Pensées") and the Op. 59 Three Pieces. In composing both cycles—particularly the Three Pieces—Prokofiev was seeking a more "simple" pianistic language. The most obvious results are a less polyphonic texture and a somewhat less chromatic harmonic language. Sonatine Pastoral in C Major, the third of the Three Pieces (the others are "Promenade" and "Landscape"), provides the clearest example, particularly in comparison with the two Sonatinas Op. 54, which had been reviled as too "complicated" and self-conscious by Soviet critics only a few years before. A small and attractive one-movement piece with a strong singing melodic line, an uncluttered horizontal style and a surprisingly literal adherence to its tonic key of C Major, the Sonatine Pastorale succeeded, as Prokofiev had hoped, in turning out "more transparent and more sonatina-like" than the sonatinas of Op. 54.

As their title indicates, the three "Thoughts" are more intellectual and complex than the Three Pieces. They are, however, notably more simple, less polyphonic and less dense than "Choses en soi" or the "Visions fugitives," to which they bear a strong atmospheric and emotional resemblance. Prokofiev believed that the second of the three "Thoughts"—*Lento*—was "one of my greatest successes."

Along with the piano pieces, Prokofiev was working on a projected "Dance Suite" in four parts that had been commissioned by the Soviet All-Union Radio. He never completed the project as originally envisioned, however, and used the material only some years later in various other scores. Also in the works was another project that would take a long time to complete—the First Cello Concerto. Prokofiev had begun the concerto in early 1934, and Miaskovsky was urging him to finish it. But Prokofiev did not work on the piece that summer, and told Miaskovsky that "as before, it is still in a somnolent state." The Cello Concerto would give Prokofiev a great deal of trouble, even after its long-delayed completion and premiere in 1938.

In early September, he finally "closed up shop" in Paris and went to join his family on the Mediterranean. They spent a few tranquil weeks at "Les Pins-Parasols" in Ste. Maxime, where they had vacationed two summers earlier. Staying with them there was the Russian émigré music critic and writer Pyotr Souvchinsky, who had come with Prokofiev by car from Paris. (On the way, they stopped in to see Stravinsky, who was composing his Concerto for Two Solo Pianos.) In Ste. Maxime, Prokofiev and his entourage enjoyed a "peaceful life" and "fluttered about" in the warm Mediterranean. Prokofiev also managed to finish the orchestral Suite from the music for *Egyptian Nights*.

Life in Ste. Maxime must have been pleasant, for the Prokofievs stayed longer than originally anticipated. Only in early October did they return to Paris. Almost immediately, Prokofiev left again for a series of European concert appearances. He played with Bruno Walter and the Concertgebouw in Amsterdam, followed by an appearance in the Concerts Pasdeloup in Paris. Overcoming his misgivings ("I'm scared to death of it, afraid I'll get mixed up!"), he also took the baton to conduct his demanding Third Symphony in London on October 19.

After only a few days back in Paris, he once again left for Russia, where he would stay for nearly two months. For Prokofiev, at least, the apartment on the rue Valentin Hauy was becoming little more than a way station.

Arriving in Moscow in early November of 1934, Prokofiev assumed an even more public role in Soviet musical life. In his absence, Soviet culture had taken an important step toward greater regimentation. At the First Congress of Soviet Writers held in August, Stalin's cultural henchman Andrei Zhdanov (1896–1948), whose power and influence would increase enormously in the coming years and who would eventually interfere in Prokofiev's career, had set forth definite guidelines which all Soviet writers were expected to follow. Henceforth, all Soviet fiction should adhere to the "method" of Socialist Realism, in which "truthfulness and historical concreteness of artistic depiction must be combined with the task of ideological remolding and reeducation of the toiling people in the spirit of socialism." Heroes had to be "positive," providing a good example for the reading masses.

The message conveyed to the assembled writers was clear: Stalin and his men are watching you, and will regard deviation from the established literary party line as a serious infraction deserving of punishment. Soviet literature had no need of strongly individualistic nonconformist writers, they said. It was far more important to show that one shared the great communal spirit of the Soviet socialist aesthetic.

Fear of being called a literary maverick—and therefore a traitor—began to pit authors against one another.

The First Congress of Soviet Writers put Soviet artists in all fields—including music—on notice that all areas of culture were coming under increasingly close official scrutiny. The exciting days of chaotic pluralism were over.

In late 1934, the situation in music was still much less organized than in literature, always the first of the arts to catch the bureaucratic eye. The First Congress of Soviet Composers would be held only fourteen years later, in 1948. Literature tended to receive more official attention than music in part because no special technical training (except literacy) was required to read books. Reading scores, or attempting to analyze music after hearing it, posed more difficulties for most bureaucrats. They would, however, eventually overcome their hesitation, taking composers to task with no less gusto than they criticized writers.

As a result of this more tendentious atmosphere, and of his natural desire to please the paternalistic authority figures in his life at the time, Prokofiev seemed more eager than ever to reinforce his position as a loyal Soviet artist. Only ten days after arriving in Moscow, Prokofiev wrote an article for *Izvestiia* that discussed the problem of accessibility in music.

The issue of what kind of music we should write for the present era is one that disturbs many Soviet composers. I have studied this issue very carefully for the last two years, and I think the following is the best solution.

First of all, we must compose big music—that is, music whose conception and technical execution correspond to the breadth of our era. Such music should, above all, push us toward further development of musical forms; it will also show our real face abroad. Unfortunately, contemporary Soviet composers run a real risk of becoming provincial. Finding the right language for our music is not easy. It should first of all be melodic, but the melody, though simple and accessible, shouldn't become a refrain or a trivial turn of phrase. Many composers have difficulty composing melody in general—no matter what kind—and composing a melody for definitely stated goals is even more difficult. The same holds true for compositional technique and how it is set forth; it must be clear and simple, but not hackneyed. Its simplicity must not be an old-fashioned one; it must be a new simplicity.

A new simplicity—the concept Prokofiev had first set forth several years earlier in France was the same goal he was trying to pursue in his new career as a Soviet composer. Musically, this meant a more homophonic, transparent and emotionally lyrical style; less dissonance; an increased emphasis on melody; a preference for programmatic and "public" genres; an avoidance of the avant-garde extremism of the 1920s; and an emulation of the ideals, subject matter and techniques of the leading "classical" composers (particularly Mussorgsky and Tchaikovsky) of nineteenth-century Russian music.

To a surprisingly large extent, Prokofiev's idea of a "new simplicity" coincided with the tenets of Socialist Realism in music. His public statements on the role and creation of Soviet music were for the most part sincere, not just empty rhetoric designed to curry favor with the party ideologues. By nature, Prokofiev was not a hypocrite, and found it difficult to hide his true feelings or promote something or someone in which he did not believe. When he began to speak out in the mid-1930s on the future of Soviet music, he did so with real idealism and faith.

But Prokofiev did not just talk about music in the fall of 1934; he also made several appearances as a pianist and conductor in Leningrad, Moscow and Voronezh, on the Don River. It was in Voronezh in mid-December that he wrote down the theme that eventually became the first subject of the beautiful second movement of his Second Violin Concerto, which would be completed the following year.

And there were other demands on his time. "I am submerged in rehearsals for *Egyptian Nights*," he wrote in French to Fatima Samoilenko on December 7, "which is approaching its premiere, and a little frozen by the cold temperature of minus twenty [Centigrade]. I am hiding my nose and ears in the collar of my new overcoat made from a very warm animal—here they call it an 'ice beaver.' " When the premiere finally came, it was a brilliant occasion attended by "the entire theatrical-musical world of Moscow." The production was popular enough to enjoy a run of seventy-five performances during the 1935 season, although it disappeared from the repertoire and from Soviet theatrical history soon after, primarily for political reasons.

Alisa Koonen, a renowned Soviet actress, and co-founder with Tairov of the Moscow Chamber Theater, achieved one of the greatest triumphs of her career in the role of Cleopatra. Gordon Craig, a famous British actor and designer who had been involved with Russian theatre since before the Revolution, saw the production and praised it as courageously experimental. It was, in fact, too experimental for the cultural bureaucrats, who found it overly stylized, insufficiently "realistic" and politically irrelevant. By the mid-1930s, Soviet theatre was also under increasing pressure to conform to the doctrine of Socialist Realism. Members of the Russian theatrical avant-garde like Tairov and Meyerhold, who had built their careers on a rejection of realism, came under particularly heavy attack—no matter what they staged. Directors were now expected to put on more plays dealing with contemporary Soviet life, and to present them in a realistic (Stanislavsky) style.

The official suppression of information about *Egyptian Nights* also affected the fate of Prokofiev's score, which for many years remained little known. Even so, the music was successful enough to inspire several other theatrical directors, including Meyerhold, to commission more incidental music from Prokofiev in the future. Tairov and Prokofiev collaborated on a second project a few years later, an ill-fated dramatization of Pushkin's verse novel *Eugene Onegin*.

As the winter of 1935 approached, what Prokofiev had hoped and planned for was beginning to happen: he was becoming the most popular composer in the U.S.S.R. After some years of uncertain stagnation, his career was taking off again, and he was regaining his artistic confidence. While certain factions in the Soviet musical establishment still distrusted and criticized him, his reputation was growing. Interesting projects were coming his way, and he was collaborating with some of the most gifted theatre and film people in the world.

Before returning to Europe in late December of 1934, Prokofiev was approached with another intriguing proposal: to compose his first ballet for a Soviet theatre. It would become his first full-length "story ballet" and one of his greatest artistic successes—*Romeo and Juliet*.

The idea for the ballet originally came from the director Sergei Radlov, an important figure in the Russian theatrical avant-garde both before and after the 1917 Revolution. Radlov (1892–1958) was also very familiar with Prokofiev's music; he had staged the first Russian production of *Love for Three Oranges* in Leningrad in 1926. Like Prokofiev, Radlov was a close associate of Meyerhold, with whom he had studied—they had even collaborated on the journal *Love for Three Oranges* that had inspired Prokofiev's opera. It seems likely, therefore, that Radlov and Prokofiev had met before the Revolution. If not, they must certainly have become acquainted sometime during the late 1920s or early 1930s, when Prokofiev was spending a good deal of time with

Meyerhold and was often traveling to Leningrad. Radlov had also helped Meyerhold in his numerous and unsuccessful attempts to get *The Gambler* on stage in Leningrad in the late 1920s and early 1930s.

During the 1920s, Radlov had directed a number of adventurous productions at the former Mariinsky Opera, including the Russian premiere of Alban Berg's *Wozzeck* in 1927. From 1931 to 1934, he was artistic director of the theatre, then known as the Leningrad State Academic Theater of Opera and Ballet. In that capacity, he had also directed ballet, including two by Prokofiev's old friend and confidant, Asafiev—*The Flame of Paris* and *The Fountain of Bakhchisarai.* At the same time, Radlov was also running his own dramatic theatre in Leningrad, where he staged a number of plays by Shakespeare: *Othello* in 1932, and, in 1934, *Romeo and Juliet.* No doubt it was while working on this production that he came to the idea of creating a ballet based on the tragedy of the star-crossed lovers.

But soon after Radlov suggested the idea to Prokofiev in late 1934, anticipating a production of *Romeo and Juliet* at the State Academic Theater, the name of the theatre, along with its administration and artistic direction, underwent a sudden and drastic change. This time it became the Kirov State Academic Theater, in honor of the Leningrad Communist Party boss Sergei Kirov.

Kirov had been mysteriously assassinated in his office that same autumn—on December 1, 1934. Although the government claimed to deplore his murder, historians believe that it occurred on the orders of Stalin, who feared Kirov's power. Kirov's assassination signaled the start of the political, cultural and ideological purges which would grow in ferocity and scope over the next four years—just as Prokofiev was making his final permanent move to Russia. It was also the first blow in a long campaign to reduce the historical, political and cultural independence of Leningrad, a city resented by many members of the Kremlin elite, including Stalin. Kirov's place as head of the Communist Party organization in Leningrad was taken over by Andrei Zhdanov, Stalin's right-hand man and leading cultural adviser. He would achieve notoriety as chief architect of the purges of artists and intellectuals in the coming years.

Radlov did not work at the Kirov after the shakeup in late 1934, and the projects he had proposed—including Prokofiev's *Romeo and Juliet*—apparently fell into disfavor there. Like Tairov and Meyerhold, Radlov was strongly identified with the Petersburg antirealistic avant-garde, a favorite target for Zhdanov and his cultural bureaucrats. In his autobiography, Prokofiev did not (and could not) explain all this; he said only that the Kirov "went back on its word" and canceled the original commission for *Romeo*. In its place, the Bolshoi Theater would sign a new contract (also broken soon after) with Prokofiev in the spring of 1935. Radlov continued working with Prokofiev on the project even after the Bolshoi had taken it over; they would work out the scenario when Prokofiev returned to Russia in the spring of 1935.

Perhaps it was to visit Radlov that Prokofiev took a second brief trip to Leningrad in the last days of December 1934. He also saw Vera Alpers, who had promised to give him the second part of her childhood journal, which described their Conservatory days and her adolescent infatuation with Prokofiev. He had already read the first part, and told Alpers it was "like reading an interesting adolescent novel about a nice but clumsy girl." The second part, full of melodramatic emotions and descriptions of a vanished and gracious world, pleased him no less. Although he had by now seen ample evidence of the cultural repression practiced by Stalin and his advisers, and of the depressing homogeneity of the products of Socialist Realism, Prokofiev refused to part with his fond images of Russia. It was on Russia that he lavished the love, devotion and tenderness his friends and acquaintances found so oddly lacking in his relations with them. This love also provides the key to an understanding of why Prokofiev—in the face of so much resistance—did not waver in his conviction that he needed to come home.

Even after returning to Paris in late January—after a whirlwind tour of Vilnius, Poland, Budapest, Prague, Zagreb, Belgrade and Brussels—Prokofiev's mind remained on his homeland. He received some discouraging news about his relationship with the musical bureaucrats—or at least with those who controlled musical life in Leningrad. Asafiev, who had lived in Petersburg/Petrograd/Leningrad for many years, had endeavored to ascertain the official attitude toward Prokofiev, particularly at the Mariinsky-Kirov. Prokofiev continued to see that prestigious theatre as an appropriate house for his ballets and operas. He was still hopeful that it would finally produce *The Gambler*, and was anticipating *Romeo and Juliet*. Perhaps Prokofiev had heard something of the changes at the theatre following the assassination of Kirov, and wanted to find out how they would affect him and his music.

Asafiev reported his findings to Miaskovsky, who relayed the information to Prokofiev in Paris. "In the circles of the Leningrad

Composers' Union (and wherever it can exert influence—the Philharmonia, and, most of all, the theatres) they fear you terribly and will do everything they can to keep you out," Miaskovsky wrote. "Therefore [Asafiev] believes that your projects for productions at the Mariinsky Theater are built on sand." Not only the confusion following the change in administration at the Kirov and the shakeup in Leningrad cultural politics after Kirov's death, but also the fact that Prokofiev now worked in Moscow served to weaken his position in Leningrad. Although Prokofiev had grown up and received his education in Leningrad, his power base had shifted to Moscow, where he had been spending most of his time since 1932. Shostakovich had supplanted him in Leningrad.

Miaskovsky warned Prokofiev that the cultural situation was once again changing rapidly and unpredictably, and that it was difficult to know how Prokofiev's own official position would be affected. It seemed unlikely, though, that a planned brochure about Prokofiev would now be published. "Internal changes are occurring here now," Miaskovsky wrote. "Speaking in all good conscience, I don't think that anyone would commission a brochure about you, no matter who might write it."

Despite Prokofiev's energetic campaign to bolster his Soviet identity, then, and his frequent visits to the U.S.S.R., the political antagonism toward him and his music—first openly expressed in 1927—persisted in 1935. To some extent, the antagonism—fanned by the jealousy of less gifted but more "loyal" composers—grew even stronger and more dangerous as Prokofiev became more successful in the U.S.S.R. In the increasingly regimented political and cultural atmosphere, which became notably more tense after 1934, it was easy for personal feelings of rivalry or dislike to receive a political manifestation.

Just as Salieri used his official position to restrict the career of Mozart, whom he envied for his talent, so could Soviet Salieris punish Prokofiev for his greater genius. It did not help that Prokofiev, like Mozart, was a poor diplomat and a ruthlessly honest critic, who found it difficult to hide his disdain for mediocrity.

Prokofiev still failed to comprehend just how different were the rules governing musical life in Paris and in Moscow. In Paris in the 1930s, composers were individuals, not members of a political union. Although they might complain of public indifference and the difficulty they had in making a living from their music, they enjoyed various options for performances and publication. In Moscow and Leningrad, on the other hand, all composers were part of a single administrative body which ultimately controlled all access to performances, commissions and publications.

Not surprisingly, it was often the less gifted Soviet composers who occupied positions of greatest administrative power, from which they could control repertoire and careers. Their perhaps natural jealousy toward an extraordinarily talented, idiosyncratic, outspoken, half-Western and egocentric composer like Prokofiev would have very specific and far-reaching results. The rumblings from the Leningrad Union conveyed to Paris by Miaskovsky in early 1935 were only a prelude to the crude accusations that would later be hurled at Prokofiev and some of his colleagues. That he was too confident in his abilities, too disdainful of petty artistic bureaucrats—and too involved in writing music— to pay much attention to such harbingers speaks well of Prokofiev's complete dedication to his art but poorly of his political instincts. By the winter of 1934–35, he was also too committed to a Soviet career to reconsider his decision; he had already burned many of his bridges to the West.

In March 1935, after another of those recitals at the Soviet Embassy in Paris with which Prokofiev affirmed his Soviet identity, he departed Paris for Moscow. Once again, he went without Lina, who would remain in Paris until later in the spring, when she would join him in Russia. As on most of his previous visits, Prokofiev stayed at the elegant Hotel National, directly across from the Kremlin walls. In his first days in Moscow, he enthusiastically attended the Second International Chess Tournament as a "spectator and fan." His interest in chess was just as keen and active as ever, and he appreciated the great passion for the game which he found in his homeland, perhaps the greatest "chess country" in the world.

On March 21, Prokofiev left Moscow for a series of concerts in and around Sverdlovsk, a large industrial city just beyond the Urals. It is nearly as far to the east of Moscow as Paris is to the west. All around on the flat Siberian steppe, huge industrial complexes were rising with amazing speed. At the University of Musical Culture connected with the Chelyabinsk tractor factory at the enormous Uralmash (Ural Machine) complex, Prokofiev participated in a lecture-concert, playing his solo piano music. He repeated that program at several other cultural clubs, gave a recital in the Lunacharsky Theater in Sverdlovsk, and participated in a morning program for children sponsored by the newspaper *The New Shoots of Communism.*

The concerts were held in plain and drafty wooden buildings hastily erected near muddy construction sites. Most of those in the audience were dressed in drab work clothes and boots, and few had any musical education. The setting could not have been more different from the elegant and refined surroundings in which Prokofiev had been accustomed to play in Europe.

But the obvious thirst for music and culture, and the unaffected spontaneity and enthusiasm of the audience, invigorated him. He felt more needed here than he ever had in Paris. "I was simply amazed at the ecstatic attention with which the Chelyabinsk audience listened to my works," he said later in an article ("On Soviet Music and the Worker Audience") published in *Evening Moscow.* "I must say straight out that the Chelyabinsk worker-listener showed a great deal more interest in the program than a number of sophisticated audiences in Western European and American cities."

The spring, summer and early fall of 1935, which Prokofiev spent entirely in the U.S.S.R., was a period of remarkable productivity for him. His chief project was *Romeo and Juliet,* whose eventual enormous success is all the more striking in light of the persistent problems which plagued it from the very start. By the spring, when Prokofiev began serious work on the ballet, *Romeo* was intended for the Bolshoi, the Kirov having canceled its commission. Prokofiev went to Leningrad to consult further with Radlov on the scenario.

It was not an easy job, of course, to create a plot line appropriate for choreography that still retained the spirit, thematic richness, intelligence and passion of Shakespeare's complex tragedy. This was only one of many obstacles that would complicate the ballet's early history and prevent it from reaching the stage until several years after it was composed.

Radlov was not, perhaps, the ideal choice for a librettist, since he was a dramatic director and not a choreographer. His tendency was to retain as much as possible of Shakespeare's play—perhaps too much for a ballet. (Nor did it help that in his own work as a librettist, Prokofiev had always erred toward the literal, finding it difficult to pare a source down to its dramatic essentials.) Eventually, after *Romeo* ran into trouble with the Bolshoi administration and dancers, two more collaborators—the choreographer Leonid Lavrovsky and the critic and playwright Adrian Piotrovsky—would join Prokofiev and Radlov in creating the scenario.

It was this version, pieced together by four authors, which would finally take the stage at the Kirov Theater in Leningrad, where the ballet would eventually receive its Soviet premiere in early 1940. While preparing *Romeo* for the Kirov in 1938–39, Lavrovsky would also make numerous further changes in the original score and dramatic structure. Not surprisingly, the repeated revision of the scenario produced what dance critic Arlene Croce has called a "dramaturgical nightmare."

In the Radlov-Prokofiev scenario, the play's five acts and twenty-four scenes were divided into many short episodes, approximately equal in length. There were fifty-eight such episodes in the scenario's original version. Each episode bears a descriptive dramatic (not musical) title, like "The Street is Awakening," "The Nurse Delivers Juliet's Note to Romeo" or "Romeo Decides to Avenge Mercutio's Death." The episodes were arranged into nine scenes in four acts, preceded by an orchestral prologue: there are two scenes in Act I, three in Act II, three in Act III and one in Act IV. The number of episodes in each scene varies greatly. In many productions, the final scene—Act IV—of Juliet's funeral and death has been called "Epilogue," or even included as the fourth scene of Act III.

Prokofiev had worked from the same sort of episodic structure for most of his ballets, although the sections of his earlier ballets tended to be somewhat larger than the episodes of *Romeo*. Its more rapid, "montage-like" dramatic structure was no doubt influenced by Prokofiev's recent experience of writing the music for the film *Lt. Kizhe*, which required numerous small "numbers." Not surprisingly, the ballet's scenario expands greatly on the crowd scenes in Shakespeare, so as to accommodate the *corps de ballet*.

The original scenario (later altered) apparently changed the tragic ending of *Romeo and Juliet* to a happy one—just as nineteenth-century European stage directors had "improved" the play with a happy ending. Radlov and Prokofiev had Romeo arrive a minute earlier than in Shakespeare, finding Juliet still alive. "The reasons that led us to such a barbarism were purely choreographic," Prokofiev later explained. "Living people can dance, but the dead cannot dance lying down." As a lame justification for this violation of Shakespeare's intentions, Prokofiev and Radlov pointed to Shakespeare's own indecision about the ending to *King Lear,* and to the fact that the comedy *Two Gentlemen of Verona* is believed to have been written around the same time as the tragedy *Romeo and Juliet.*

Once the scenario was sketched out, Prokofiev began immediately to compose the ballet in piano score. Even for him, he worked with incredible speed, as he did when he was genuinely inspired by a project. Act II was completed on July 22, Act III on August 29, and the entire piano score was finished on September 8, 1935, after less than five months of work.

Romeo represents a giant step forward in Prokofiev's evolution as a dramatic and symphonic composer. It is a remarkable synthesis of different aspects of his musical personality. The aggressive "Scythianism" of Prokofiev's talent found fertile territory in the violent hostility between the Montagues and Capulets, and in the brutal darkness of the unenlightened medieval setting. His "classicism" found an outlet in the courtly dances required in an aristocratic setting. (He even used the eighteenth-century Gavotte from the "Classical" Symphony—rather anachronistically—during the ball scene in Act I.) Prokofiev's satirical style was entirely appropriate for some of the character roles, such as the Nurse, while his *scherzo* style worked well for volatile characters like Mercutio.

And finally, Prokofiev's lyricism, which had become an increasingly important part of his artistic personality since *Prodigal Son,* and which was encouraged by the Soviet musical environment, was both necessary and particularly successful in conveying the innocent passion that lies at the center of the action. Ten years earlier, his musical personality would have been too ironic, dry and one-sided to portray the great variety of emotions *Romeo and Juliet* required.

Diaghilev would never have staged a huge realistic ballet like *Romeo* and might well have ridiculed Prokofiev for writing it. Heavy story ballets that lasted an entire evening were one of the things Diaghilev disliked most about the Russian Imperial Ballet tradition. (The Ballets Russes had staged its own *Romeo and Juliet* in 1926, with music by the English composer Constant Lambert, but it was a small and sketchy piece that did not attempt to re-create the epic scope of Shakespeare's tragedy.) And yet Prokofiev would not have been able to confront the formidable theatrical demands of *Romeo* so confidently without the experience of dance and the stage that he had gained from Diaghilev. Another important influence was Prokofiev's recent work writing music for film and the theatre; this helped him to illustrate visual images more effectively, specifically and "physically"—as in the fight scenes.

Most of *Romeo* was composed amid the rural tranquillity of Polenovo, a country retreat for the staff of the Bolshoi Theater located in the town of Tarussa on the River Oka, where Prokofiev spent the summer and early fall of 1935. "The colony is very pleasant, the locale is picturesque, and all the inhabitants have some connection or other to the Bolshoi Theater," he wrote to Vera Alpers. "There are 150 people in five buildings, but I have a completely separate little cottage with a terrace on the bank of the Oka, and I am enjoying the peace and quiet. . . . I swim in the Oka, play tennis and chess, go for walks in the forest with our ballerinas, do some reading and work for about five hours a day. . . . I am not resting so much as writing *Romeo*."

Checking off the episodes of the ballet as he completed them one by one was the highlight of Prokofiev's day. "I can think of no greater pleasure than marking an 'x' next to a number that has been composed (a black 'x' if the music is conceived in principle; a red 'x' when the number is composed and copied down)." There was good reason to work quickly, since *Romeo* was now scheduled to be staged at the Bolshoi during the upcoming season.

Lina had come to spend some time with Prokofiev in Russia in the late spring, but then returned to Paris in early July. She came back about a month later with the children, and they all stayed with Prokofiev at Polenovo until October 1, when they moved to Moscow. In late October, Prokofiev took the boys back to Paris, and Lina remained behind by herself in Moscow.

At Polenovo, Oleg and Sviatoslav were "spoiled to pieces" by Prokofiev's colleagues and neighbors; an intense and indulgent love for children is a strong feature of the Russian national character upon which many observers have commented. Oleg was nearly seven years old that summer, and watching his father at work in this new environment was a great source of amusement.

> Father worked every day in a small secluded house on the bank of the Oka, converted from a bathhouse and consisting of one room with a terrace. The room had a writing desk, and the terrace a large table with sixteen chess boards that formed one huge board, four by four, lined with standing pieces. The pieces stood there all summer, intermingling as time went on; I do not know whom he played with

nor what happened in the game. Although I knew how to move the pieces and Father explained the complex rules for the transfer of every piece from one board to another, the only thing my memory retained was a feeling of something incredibly interesting by virtue of its very incomprehensibility.

Sometimes he permitted me to stay with him while he worked, provided I was absolutely silent. I accepted the condition because he allowed me to draw, sitting at the edge of his desk.

By October 1—with time off for a brief concert tour in the sweltering heat of the southern steppes—he had finished *Romeo* in piano score and begun orchestrating it. He worked at top speed, producing the equivalent of about twenty pages of full score each day, even while complaining to Miaskovsky how hard it was: "The most important thing is not to follow the line of least resistance."

Nor was *Romeo and Juliet* the only music Prokofiev composed during that remarkably productive Polenovo summer. He also completed the Second Violin Concerto and "Music for Children: Twelve Easy Pieces for Piano" (Op. 65).

The Second Violin Concerto was Prokofiev's last non-Soviet commission. It had been requested earlier in the year in France by a group of admirers of the French violinist Robert Soetens, on the condition that Soetens have sole right to perform the concerto for one year. In composing it, Prokofiev used some themes he had already been collecting with a violin piece in mind. "Reflecting my nomadic concertizing existence, the concerto was written in the most diverse countries: the main subject of the first movement was written in Paris, the first theme of the second movement—in Voronezh, the instrumentation was completed in Baku, and the premiere took place in December of 1935 in Madrid."

Just as Prokofiev had hoped, the Second Violin Concerto is "completely different" from the equally brilliant First Violin Concerto written nearly twenty years earlier. Although both pieces have three movements, the first two of the Second Concerto—each about ten minutes in length—are relatively slow. The First Concerto has faster tempos (including a precipitous *Vivacissimo*) than the Second, and puts greater emphasis on velocity and flashy technical dexterity in the solo part. But what is most different about the Second Concerto is its predominantly *cantilena* character: its melodies are some of the most beautiful, flowing and lyrical that Prokofiev ever wrote. Nor does he cut them short, impatient with emotional display, as he did in many of his earlier compositions—including, to some extent, the First Violin Concerto.

The Second Concerto never descends to the sentimental "Glazunovism" which Prokofiev always detested, however. Its characteristically "Prokofievian" rhythmic drive and strategically placed dissonances provide a bracing contrast to the prevailing lyrical mood. Particularly witty and original is the use of percussion—including castanets, triangle, bass drum and snare drum—in the concluding movement. In combination with the staccato double stops in the solo part, it creates a slightly ironic "Spanish" atmosphere. Perhaps to break the lyrical spell of the opening movements, the concerto comes to an abrupt end with an ascending run in eighth notes—*tumultuoso*—in the solo part. The First Concerto does precisely the opposite, ending with an ethereal return to its fragile opening theme to counterbalance the predominating speed and aggressiveness of what has come before.

The Second Concerto achieved an immediate and lasting success both with critics and the public. Even Prokofiev was pleased, and told Miaskovsky, after the premiere in Madrid on December 1, "It seems as though the concerto is a success. . . . somehow the music immediately reached the audience. But now I still want to look it over again and add a few details here and there." It would be published in full score by Gutheil in Europe in 1937, and in a piano-violin version in the U.S.S.R. in 1938, and has been many times recorded by leading violin virtuosi.

Perhaps it was as a respite from composing two large orchestral works—the Second Violin Concerto and *Romeo and Juliet*—that Prokofiev wrote the twelve small pieces for piano that he called "Music for Children." This was the first of many compositions aimed at an audience of children that Prokofiev would write in the coming years. According to Soviet cultural ideology, children were almost the most important audience for the arts. They were the hope of the Communist future. As a result, writers, filmmakers, directors and composers were strongly urged to create works that addressed them, for art could be used to educate children in the ideals necessary for the creation of a strong Soviet state.

For Prokofiev, writing music for children came very naturally anyway. His love of fairy tales and his unique understanding of the way children viewed the world made him an unusually gifted creator of art for the younger generation. He responded to the official Soviet demand for such music with enthusiasm. One wonders, in fact, if

Prokofiev, who always wrote for the market, would have composed so many wonderful compositions for children (including *Peter and the Wolf*) if he had remained in Paris.

"Music for Children" was very successful. The twelve small pieces are reminiscent of mischievous early piano works like "Suggestion diabolique" or the four pieces of Op. 3, although they are more transparent in texture, less dissonant and harmonically simpler. A few of the twelve pieces are as accomplished and original as any of Prokofiev's incidental music for the piano, like the oddly galloping "Tarantella" or the impressionistic "The Rain and the Rainbow," in which dissonant clusters of major seconds alternate with scales and chords in "bright" C Major. What made Prokofiev such a master at writing music for children was his instinctive realization that it had to be simple, unexpected and pictorial. A few years later, in 1941, Prokofiev recycled seven of these twelve piano pieces in a "children's suite for small orchestra" entitled *A Summer Day*.

If the main reason behind Prokofiev's decision to return to Russia had been his belief that he would have more time to compose there, without the necessity of making so many distracting concert tours, and that the familiar surroundings would give him inspiration, then his productivity in the spring and summer of 1935 must have made him feel he had been right. It had been many years since he had completed three major works—all of them eventually successful with the public and critics—in such a short space of time.

And yet there were many adjustments to be made to the realities of Soviet musical and cultural life. Toward the end of his stay at Polenovo that summer, Prokofiev wrote a revealing letter to his old Paris friend Vladimir Dukelsky, who had moved to New York. In his letter to Duke, with whom he had always enjoyed exchanging witty and sometimes cutting observations on other musicians, Prokofiev shared his opinions of his new Soviet colleagues.

"Shostakovich is talented, but somehow unprincipled, and, like some of our other friends, has no gift for melody," Prokofiev wrote. "By the way, they make too much of him here. Kabalevsky and Zhelobinsky are *zéro-virgule-zéro*." But his barbs were aimed not only at Soviet composers: "The rumors about my friendship with Poulenc and Stravinsky are greatly exaggerated, while Markevich [a composer and former companion of Diaghilev] I can barely tolerate."

This letter to Duke (oddly, it is written in Russian) shows—somewhat refreshingly—that Prokofiev had not lost the brutally frank and nasty edge to his personality for which he had been so famous in his early years. In Soviet society, however, such openly discourteous behavior was frowned upon as frivolous, antisocial and condescending, so he tended to restrain it somewhat. Like his music, Prokofiev the man was mellowing.

On October 4, a few days after Prokofiev returned to Moscow from Polenovo, *Romeo and Juliet* received a first informal hearing in front of the Bolshoi Theater staff. It must have been fairly well received, for he wrote Vera Alpers a few weeks later that a production was planned for spring. But many problems arose when rehearsals began. Accustomed to the predictable square rhythms and familiar musical conventions of ballets by Tchaikovsky, Glazunov and Minkus, the Bolshoi dancers declared Prokofiev's highly syncopated rhythms and episodic music "undanceable." Objections were also voiced over the scenario's happy ending, which struck many as an unacceptable affront to Shakespeare.

In the end, Prokofiev agreed to restore the original tragic ending, but for musical and not dramatic reasons. He had decided that the music he had written for the happy ending was insufficiently joyful and dramatically unconvincing. After being assured by choreographers that it was possible to stage the deaths of Juliet and Romeo after all, he agreed to retain the original ending and rewrote the music accordingly.

Whatever the precise reasons, which have remained obscure in accounts of the ballet's history, the planned Bolshoi production of *Romeo* was canceled sometime during late 1935 or early 1936. The Bolshoi's agreement with Prokofiev was scrapped, and no other theatre came forth to take on the project. Three years would pass before the ballet would at last reach the stage, and five before it would be produced in the Soviet Union. Soviet audiences would hear the music from *Romeo* in the form of orchestral suites long before they would see the ballet on stage. Although—characteristically—Prokofiev left no description of his reaction to this serious setback, he must have been sorely disappointed to see his first Soviet ballet, and an ambitious work to which he had devoted months of intensive labor, treated with such disrespect. Even so, he never abandoned hope that *Romeo* would eventually be staged in the U.S.S.R.

On October 25, Prokofiev took his sons back to Paris. This time, Lina stayed behind in Moscow, making preparations for their final move, which was now only six months away. She also gave several performances in Moscow, apparently in an attempt to establish a singing career in the Soviet Union. Significantly, Miaskovsky did not hear her, but he wrote Prokofiev that those who did found that "her intonation had suffered somewhat." These performances did not lead Lina to develop a serious career as a singer in Russia, and she performed there only rarely in subsequent years. If she had been able to establish an independent artistic identity in the U.S.S.R., it would certainly have helped her make the difficult adjustments that their new life in Moscow demanded more easily.

Back in Europe, Prokofiev was so busy with preparations for the impending move that he had little time for composition. He spent only a few weeks in Paris that autumn, before and after an extended tour of Spain, Portugal and north Africa with the violinist Robert Soetens. The highlight of the trip was Soeten's world premiere performance of the Second Violin Concerto in Madrid. By mid-December, after a month of traveling, Prokofiev was weary of "playing the same thing over and over. As a matter of fact, I want to get back to Moscow—the time has come to take my hat out of the trunk."

Returning to Paris for only a few days around Christmas, Prokofiev then left to join Lina in Moscow in time to greet the New Year 1936. This was the first New Year's they had ever spent together in Russia, and marked the start of what would be the first year of their permanent residence in the U.S.S.R. They were beginning a new and very different stage in their life together, one that would bring enormous and terrible changes.

Since the 1917 Revolution and the official de-Christianization of Russia, New Year's Eve and Day have replaced (and incorporated) Christmas as the most important nonpolitical holiday in the Soviet calendar. In Moscow and other Soviet cities, New Year's *(Novy god)* is an occasion of extravagant feasting, drinking and gift-giving. In accordance with tradition, friends gather a few hours before midnight and make merry until dawn, when they finally straggle home through the frigid streets.

Prokofiev and Lina celebrated with friends and acquaintances at an elegant party at the Moscow Art Theater that went on until five A.M. Perhaps the Meyerholds, and Tairov, were there. The festivities included "quite a lot of imbibing and several Christmas trees, according to *la dernière mode moscovite*." Countless toasts were made and happy drunken kisses were exchanged.

Surrounded by the members of the Soviet artistic elite, on the threshold of a new career that despite some setbacks appeared to be more promising than the one he was leaving behind in Paris, Prokofiev had good reason to feel confident and optimistic about the future on New Year's Eve 1936. Famous in all the great cities of Europe and America, he had come a long way from Sontsovka and Petrograd. In their excitement and good cheer, he and Lina had little reason to suspect that the new year which they were celebrating would be one of the most difficult that they had ever faced, or that the ones to follow would be yet more trying.

But even if Prokofiev and Lina had been able that evening to foresee the hardships and sadness that awaited them, it was already too late to change the course they had chosen. The process was complete: Prokofiev had come back home.

PART THREE

CHAPTER 1 7

FROM MACY'S
TO MOSCOW

A stone that strikes the surface of the water sends
out a widening circle of ripples, and then sinks
down into the depths where it finally disappears.
I have gone down into the deeper realms of music.

—SERGEI PROKOFIEV, 1936

January is rarely a cheerful month in Moscow. The holidays have
passed, and the long winter stretches ahead endlessly. The faint
sun shines—when the skies are not a leaden gray—for only seven
hours a day, the temperature plunges to numbing depths, snow and
ice blanket the streets and squares, life moves indoors. In previous
Januaries, Prokofiev had usually been on tour in the more temperate
climate of Europe, but in 1936 he and Lina spent most of this gloomy
month in Moscow, still living in a hotel. They would receive their own
apartment only in the early summer.

Neither winter nor living out of a suitcase caused any reduction
in Prokofiev's rate of productivity, however. Some of the dark winter
hours were devoted to his first piece of explicitly political music—a
group of six popular songs (Op. 66). Four were submitted to a song
contest sponsored by *Pravda*, and two were propagandistic "Mass Songs,"
a form admired and encouraged by Stalin himself. The texts of all the
songs are highly tendentious and simplistic, dealing with such uplifting
subjects as Ukrainian partisans during the civil war; the new opportunities for formerly oppressed peasants (this one is named Anyutka)
to obtain an education; Marshal Clement Voroshilov, a military hero
of the civil war and a close associate of Stalin; and the ongoing col-

lectivization of agriculture. "Beyond the Hills" reduces one of the most brutal, bitterly resisted and controversial acts in Soviet history to a painless fairy-tale transformation: "I became a person when I joined the kolkhoz."

It is difficult to believe that Prokofiev—who had always hated sentimental rhymed verses and berated Vernon Duke for writing popular "tra-la-la"—did not realize how cheap these texts were or how undistinguished his music was. ("Anyutka" was awarded second prize in the *Pravda* song competition.) But writing songs like these was important to his career in the U.S.S.R. They would help to convince his colleagues and the bureaucrats that he was serious about joining the ranks and contributing to the general cause of Soviet culture. Perhaps they would make it easier for his large serious compositions to be accepted for performance—just as Soviet poets were sure to include a paean to Lenin or Stalin in a book of poems to assure its publication.

In late January, Prokofiev left Moscow—"without particular enthusiasm," he claimed—to make a number of concert appearances in Europe. By now, it was highly unusual for Soviet artists of any kind to be allowed to travel abroad; Prokofiev's situation was a conspicuous exception, and indicates that he had been given special assurances before he made his final move to Moscow that he would be allowed to continue touring in the West. He was already far away from Russia when, on January 28, an event of far-reaching importance for the future of all Soviet composers erupted in the Soviet capital. The controversy centered on Prokofiev's colleague Dmitri Shostakovich, who had been enjoying tremendous popularity and official favor during the preceding few years, and his opera *Lady Macbeth of the Mtsensk District*.

Based on a Russian short story of the same title by Nikolai Leskov (1831–1895), *Lady Macbeth* describes the boredom and frustration of Russian provincial life as so excruciating that the heroine, Katerina Izmailova, a merchant's wife, murders her father-in-law, her mealy-mouthed husband, and even her defenseless cousin for the sake of an insatiably passionate love for her manipulative peasant lover, Sergei. Shostakovich's music is extraordinarily gloomy and powerful, nearly savage in its intensity and sarcasm. Passages of intense lyricism emphasize the fierce sexual attraction around which the action revolves, while the rising tension and starkly dramatic climax reveal the composer's instinctive theatrical sense. *Lady Macbeth* had made an instant celebrity of Shostakovich when it was first performed in Leningrad and Moscow in January 1934, and had already received almost two hundred performances by early 1936. Only twenty-nine years old, Shostakovich was an internationally acclaimed composer with a future of infinite promise.

Until January 28, 1936, that is. That day, an unsigned article entitled "Muddle Instead of Music," appeared—from out of nowhere—in *Pravda*. It contained a vicious attack—obviously emanating from the very highest official levels—on *Lady Macbeth*. That the article appeared in *Pravda*, organ of the latest Party line and rarely the forum for comment on music, only indicated how important Stalin and his cultural commissars considered the issue.

> From the first moment, the listener is shocked by a deliberately dissonant, confused stream of sound. Fragments of melody and embryonic phrases appear, only to disappear again in the din, the grinding and the screaming. . . . This music is constructed as a rejection of opera. . . . The danger of this trend to Soviet music is clear. . . . And "love" is smeared all over the opera in the most vulgar manner. . . . *Lady Macbeth* enjoys great success with audiences abroad. Is it not because the opera is absolutely apolitical and confusing that they praise it? Is it not explained by the fact that it tickled the perverted tastes of the bourgeoisie with its fidgety, screaming, neurotic music?

The denunciation, which, as Shostakovich later wrote, "changed my entire existence," was apparently the result of Stalin's own visit to the opera sometime in late December or early January, when the Great Leader saw a performance of *Lady Macbeth*. Some have suggested that the explicit sexuality of the opera, which includes a rape onstage, and the insinuating musical style which one writer has called "pornophony," genuinely offended Stalin's puritanical sensibilities. It is also possible that he found the depressing story unsuitable fare for Soviet audiences, who in his view needed to be inspired to greater feats of construction and sacrifice for the cause of Communism. They did not need to see a violent drama of exaggerated lust and jealousy.

But the most important motivation behind the attack on Shostakovich was Stalin's desire to demonstrate his absolute and unlimited power over Soviet culture and its creators. By 1936, Stalin's foes in the Party and government—those with more moderate and tolerant views—had been eliminated one by one, through various violent and nonviolent means. The total control that the Great Leader would wield until his death in 1953 was nearly in place.

Confident of his hegemony over such primary concerns as the economy and education, Stalin began to pay more attention to cultural matters. The time had come to formulate a more definite policy on the arts, and to proclaim it publicly. Socialist Realism was already established in literature, and rapidly expanding into film and theatre as well.

With the *Pravda* attack on Shostakovich—chosen as the first target because he was so well-known and visible—composers now joined writers as fair game for the cultural bureaucrats. It is logical that an opera provoked the first organized assault on Soviet music, since opera, of all musical genres, is the easiest for a person without technical training to "understand"—it has a story and words. Based on literature, opera is more amenable to the doctrine of Socialist Realism, and has always (along with ballet) received more attention from the guardians of Soviet culture than symphonies or concertos or chamber music.

The article in *Pravda* had a profound affect on Shostakovich's career. *Lady Macbeth* was instantly withdrawn from the Soviet stage and reappeared only after Stalin's death. After being so roughly handled, Shostakovich abandoned opera forever, despite his obvious fondness and talent for the genre. *Lady Macbeth* was originally intended as the first opera in a trilogy about Soviet women, but the composer never dared to write the next two. Shostakovich also withdrew his nearly completed Fourth Symphony from a planned public performance, afraid that it, too, would be considered too "confused" and "complicated." Nor did the official campaign against Shostakovich end here: only ten days after the first article, *Pravda* published another attack, this time criticizing his ballet *The Clear Stream*, a description of life on a mythical collective farm in the Caucasus. For months afterward, Shostakovich was referred to in the press as an "enemy of the people." Many of his colleagues shunned him, and he feared—with good reason—even for his life.

Just as Stalin had intended, the assault on Shostakovich shook the Soviet musical world to its foundations, sending a chill through every Soviet composer, and strongly influencing the subsequent evolution of Soviet music and musical life. The message was this: if the world-famous Shostakovich, only recently the object of lavish official praise, could so suddenly fall into disgrace and humiliation, then so could anyone. What Prokofiev had said in 1932—that no one wanted to make a mistake in seeking the musical language appropriate for Soviet life—was more true than ever in the winter of 1936. The fate of those who made "mistakes" had now been graphically illustrated.

Touring in Europe during the immediate aftermath of the *Lady Macbeth* scandal, Prokofiev did not witness the first brutal assertion of government control over Soviet music. If he had, perhaps he would have been better prepared for the many other such incidents that would follow. By a sad coincidence, the attack on Shostakovich, which signaled the beginning of an intensified ideological campaign against all artists, came at exactly the moment when Prokofiev had irretrievably committed himself to living and working in Russia. This irony was not lost on Shostakovich.

> Prokofiev was an inveterate gambler and, in the long run, he had always won. Prokofiev thought he had calculated perfectly and that he would be a winner this time, too. For some fifteen years Prokofiev sat between two stools—in the West he was considered a Soviet and in Russia they welcomed him as a Western guest. But then the situation changed and the bureaucrats in charge of cultural affairs started squinting at Prokofiev, meaning, Who's this Parisian fellow? And Prokofiev decided that it would be more profitable for him to move to the U.S.S.R. Such a step would only raise his stock in the West, because things Soviet were becoming fashionable just then, they would stop considering him a foreigner in the U.S.S.R., and therefore he would win all around. . . .
>
> And this was where Prokofiev landed like a chicken in soup. He came to Moscow to teach them, and they started teaching him.

Prokofiev's European tour took him to Strasbourg, Antwerp, Brussels, Poitiers, Prague, Budapest, Sofia, Warsaw and Paris. Some of the concerts were joint recitals with Robert Soetens; others featured him as soloist or conductor for his own compositions. He was received as an established and important artist wherever he went, though he was disturbed that the French public still insisted on regarding him as the rambunctious barbarian who had thrilled and shocked them fifteen years earlier when he first blew in from America.

His schedule was so full that it left Prokofiev little time to regret that he would never again stay in the elegant apartment on the rue Valentin Hauy, his home with Lina for the last six years. Nor did he spend much time with his Paris friends, many of whom found his decision to return to Russia incomprehensible and foolish.

Some of them, including Stravinsky, thought that financial considerations were the main reason behind Prokofiev's decision to give up his Paris base. "Prokofiev was always very Russian-minded and always primitively anticlerical," Stravinsky said later. "But in my opinion these dispositions had little to do with his return to Russia. The latter was a sacrifice to the bitch goddess, and nothing else. He had had no success in the United States or Europe for several seasons, while his visit to Russia had been a triumph. . . . he was despondent about his material and artistic fate in France. He was politically naive, however, and learned nothing from the example of his good friend Miaskovsky. He returned to Russia, and when finally he understood his situation there, it was too late."

In fact, however, Prokofiev's "Russian-mindedness"—not money—was the most important motivating force behind his momentous move. Even during the few years—since 1932—that he had been spending a large amount of time in the U.S.S.R., Prokofiev had found the cultural and musical atmosphere there more congenial, and more supportive of his natural orientation toward a simpler style, than the Paris musical world had been. He also occupied a more influential position in Moscow and enjoyed the feeling of being needed there. Financial considerations—he was receiving numerous attractive commissions from Soviet sources, while he no longer had many European sponsors—certainly contributed to his difficult decision, but they were not the only ones.

If we are to believe Nicolas Nabokov, who was closer to Prokofiev than Stravinsky was, Prokofiev did not hide the fact that he was encountering problems in adjusting to the Soviet musical world, and that he had numerous enemies there. By the late 1930s, Nabokov said later, he began to see in his old friend "a feeling totally contradictory to the very nature of Prokofiev's character: the feeling of profound and terrible insecurity." Perhaps this insecurity was a response to the news of the attack on Shostakovich, which may have made Prokofiev wonder—if only momentarily—about the wisdom of the irrevocable step he had just taken. But then Nabokov, like Prokofiev's other émigré Russian colleagues, wanted to portray Soviet society as negatively as possible in order to justify their own decisions to remain in exile.

Prokofiev returned to Moscow alone, arriving there (after a concert in Warsaw) in early March 1936. He left Lina and the boys behind in Paris, where they would remain for a few more months, until the end of the school year. Then the flat on the rue Valentin Hauy would be permanently vacated and the furniture, books and clothing sent on to Moscow. After his tour in early 1936, Prokofiev did not travel abroad again for nearly nine months—the longest period of time he had spent in Russia since the Revolution. His timing was unfortunate; this was one of the saddest years for Russian artists since 1917.

And yet Prokofiev proceeded—almost blindly—with his usual energy and cold discipline. His natural optimism and naivete led him to interpret what had happened to Shostakovich as a temporary aberration, and to ignore—with a certain arrogance born of a sense of his "specialness"—the frightened voices of his friends and associates. During the next two years, however, as scores of writers, directors, critics and journalists—including some of Prokofiev's oldest friends— fell victim to the purges, it would become more and more difficult to view each new disaster as an isolated instance. The scandal over *Lady Macbeth* proved to be only one of the first incidents in a horribly systematic series of similar events, a vortex into which Prokofiev and his powerless colleagues would be drawn irrevocably even before they completely understood what was happening. Only a few years later, the punishment meted out to Shostakovich over *Lady Macbeth* would seem mild.

Living alone in the Metropol Hotel across from the Bolshoi Theater—the same hotel where he and Lina had been so warmly greeted on their first visit in 1927—Prokofiev buried himself in new projects in the late winter of 1936. One of them would become his most famous and most often recorded work: *Peter and the Wolf*. Perhaps the grim atmosphere of winter 1936—unusually frigid both politically and meteorologically—led Prokofiev to seek escape in a bright and carefree world of childhood summer and crafty animals. If so, this was a remarkably imaginative form of avoidance behavior.

Peter and the Wolf, a Symphonic Fairy Tale for Children (Op. 67), came out of a collaboration with Natalia Satz, the thirty-three-year-old director of the Moscow Children's Musical Theater. Prokofiev had become acquainted with the theatre the previous summer, when he took Sviatoslav, Oleg and Lina to see one of Satz's productions, an opera for children. On that occasion, Satz later recalled, Prokofiev intimidated her and the performers nearly to paralysis. "In his foreign suit he seemed stiff and arrogant. He answered questions unwillingly, in one syllable."

Satz was convinced he would dislike the performance, but a week later he brought the family back to see another show and to meet Satz and the actors. Prokofiev responded "more spontaneously than his sons. . . . If he liked something, he liked it a lot—if he didn't like it, he didn't like it at all. He spoke curtly, directly, enthusiastically, even sharply. One had to get used to his unusual answers, which were short—like stumps."

In February 1936, about six months after Prokofiev first came to the theatre, Satz and her company had moved into a new home. It was the former Nezlobin Theater in the city center, diagonally across from the Bolshoi. In this famous old concert hall Koussevitsky and Rachmaninoff, among others, had performed before the Revolution. Shortly after returning from Europe in March, Prokofiev paid another visit to Satz and saw another performance, this time in the company's new home. Fond as he was of children's stories, Prokofiev was fascinated—he had never seen children's theatres like this in Europe or America. The excited audience of youngsters and the funny fairy tales on stage must have reminded him of the productions he had created with Stenya and Ustinya in Sontsovka forty years before. Seeing his enthusiasm, Satz suggested to Prokofiev that he compose something for them. He called with some ideas only a few days later.

"We must start with something specific, something full of con-trasts, something that makes a strong impression. The most important thing is to find a common language with the kids," he told her. They agreed to create a story involving animals and at least one human character; each animal would be personified by a different instrument of the orchestra, and the human character by the more complex string ensemble. "The distinct characters will be reflected in the distinct quality of the various musical timbres; each character will have its own leitmotif." As for his fee, which worried Satz, Prokofiev said he wanted to write the music no matter what and would accept whatever they could afford—an unusual act of *largesse* on his part.

Originally, the text for the scenario, which they had decided would be read by a narrator, was to be written by Nina Saksonskaya, a young poet whom Satz had hired. Satz told her in general terms what was required, and she set to work.

One day she appeared at Prokofiev's hotel room with the completed text. When Satz arrived a few minutes later, she found the timid Saksonskaya "huddled against the door, or rather clinging to it. Sparks were flying from the composer's eyes. Prokofiev gave me a real dressing-down for the poet's uninvited visit." The abundance of rhymed words and clichéd language in Saksonskaya's version also failed to satisfy Prokofiev, so he decided to write the text himself, in prose. Only a few days later, on April 15, he had completed both the text and the entire piano score for *Peter and the Wolf*. The orchestration was finished on April 24, one day after Prokofiev's forty-fifth birthday.

When he played it through for Satz, she was amazed: the text laconic but evocative, the music successful both as an illustration of the words and as a composition in its own right.

Peter, the hero of the tale, is a Pioneer. Pioneers are members of a Soviet organization for children of grammar-school age—a sort of politicized Cub Scouts. The most upstanding members of the Pioneers later join the Komsomol (the Young Communist League), whose most energetic members often become members of the Communist Party. There is, however, no explicit political message in *Peter and the Wolf*. Peter goes walking in the meadow one day and sees various animals going about their business. A bird is flying and singing, a duck is swimming and quacking, a cat is stalking the bird and duck as he creeps through the grass. But Peter's grandfather spoils the fun by insisting that he come back inside the gate. "If a wolf should come out of the forest, then what would you do?" he asks.

No sooner has Peter retired behind the gate, of course, than a wolf (announced by a lyrical brass fanfare) appears out of the forest. The cat and bird escape up a tree, but the duck, flustered and frightened, jumps out of the pond. She tries to run away, but the wolf overtakes her and swallows her down in one gulp. Now circling the tree, the wolf tries to figure out how to catch the bird and cat. But meanwhile, clever Peter, who has been watching from behind the fence, has come up with a plan. Climbing over the wall to a branch on the tree, he tells the bird to fly around the wolf's head, confusing him. When the wolf is distracted, Peter lowers a lasso over his tail, pulling it tight. The wolf's struggles only tighten the noose.

Hunters now appear from the woods, to the accompaniment of a march, and Peter persuades them to spare the wolf and take him away to a zoo. In the grand finale, they all proceed toward the zoo, the march music continuing in the background. Peter is at the head of the procession, followed by the hunters carrying the wolf, the cat, Grandfather (still complaining, "Well, and if Peter hadn't caught the wolf? What then?") and the bird. "And if you listened very carefully, you could hear the duck quacking inside the wolf, for, in his hurry, the wolf had swallowed her alive," the narrator concludes drily.

If the story has a moral, it seems to be this: don't be afraid to challenge established beliefs (Grandfather's caution) or to take risks. It is Peter's independence, shrewdness and courage that save the day; if he hadn't disobeyed his grandfather by climbing over the wall, the wolf would never have been caught. Seen in this light, *Peter and the Wolf* is a subtly subversive tract, encouraging children to rely on their wits and not on the greater experience (and inertia) of their elders.

Musically, *Peter and the Wolf* is one of the most successful examples of Prokofiev's remarkable ability to "see" personalities in timbre, rhythm and melody. The choice of instruments to represent each character—the string quintet for Peter, the flute for the bird, the oboe for the duck, the clarinet for the cat, the bassoon for Grandfather, the brass for the wolf and the full orchestral march for the hunters—is not surprising, but exactly right. Each brief portrait is distinct in gait, appearance and mood.

Peter, for example, has confident square rhythms and predominantly major intervals in the strings; the bird has brilliant trills and runs in the flute; the duck has mournfully sliding half steps in the oboe; the cat has sly staccato jumps *(con eleganza)* in the clarinet; Grandfather has grotesquely clumsy and irritable octave leaps in the bassoon; the wolf receives a dashingly "masculine" brass fanfare; and the hunters proceed to a cheerfully quirky (and, in its strutting conceit, more than slightly ironic) march.

The same "visual" quality so important to *Peter and the Wolf* had already been obvious in many of Prokofiev's earlier scores, from *The Gambler* to *Love for Three Oranges* to *Prodigal Son* to *Lt. Kizhe* to *Romeo and Juliet,* and would continue to be important in many to follow—particularly the later film scores. In few other works, however, is this special visual talent—a key to understanding Prokofiev's music— more appropriate to the setting and requirements of the piece, or more skillfully used.

Children enjoy *Peter* not only for the exciting and funny story it tells, but also for what it teaches them about the various instruments of a symphony orchestra. It has often been used as a teaching tool in music education, alongside Benjamin Britten's *Young People's Guide to the Orchestra.*

At its first impromptu performance for a group of children at the theater, with Prokofiev at the piano, *Peter and the Wolf* was an immediate success. The children demanded to hear the concluding march of the hunters three times. Satz was scheduled to read the narration at the official premiere of *Peter and the Wolf* at her theatre on May 2, 1936, but she fell ill at the last minute. Another reader, less prepared and less familiar with the spirit of the piece, substituted for her, and, even with Prokofiev conducting, *Peter* was received with only moderate enthusiasm. A few weeks later, however, Satz read the text when the tale was repeated at the Central Pioneer Palace in Moscow, and it was a smash hit. Lina and the boys, recently arrived from Paris, were also in the audience, and loved *Peter and the Wolf* as much as anyone. Soon after, it was performed abroad, where it became equally popular, translated into a variety of languages.

Peter and the Wolf has become especially popular in the years since Prokofiev's death, and has been recorded endlessly in many different languages by an amazingly diverse selection of narrators. Among the more notable have been Sir Ralph Richardson, Mia Farrow, Sean Connery, David Bowie, Hermione Gingold, William F. Buckley, Jr., Leonard Bernstein and even former Mets pitcher Tom Seaver. Today, *Peter and the Wolf* is still in the repertoire of the Moscow Children's Musical Theater, in its new modern home opposite Moscow State University. Natalia Satz, now in her eighties, still reads the text.

Analysis and dissection alone fail to explain why *Peter and the Wolf* has earned the lasting affection of such a large audience. Perhaps, as Lina Prokofiev has remarked, it is because Prokofiev—even more than most artists—always remained a child in spirit, and had an uncanny insight into how children think and what amuses them. "Above all, the piece is spontaneous, sincere and truthful," she said. Or perhaps it is because *Peter* appeals to the child in all of us, and provides, in Peter, a spunky and clever hero who, like Mickey Mouse, resists the ravages of time and the boring caution of maturity. When we listen, we escape them, too.

Whatever the reasons for its enormous and enduring popularity, it must have irked Prokofiev that this little children's tale, dashed off quickly and possessing (in his opinion) little musical significance, achieved such success while his "serious" dramatic works like *The Fiery Angel, The Gambler* and *War and Peace* would reach the stage only after years of disappointments, and even then to lukewarm receptions.

About two weeks after the first public performance of *Peter and the Wolf,* on May 15, Lina arrived in Moscow with Sviatoslav and Oleg. They had made the long-awaited final move from Paris, and Moscow was now their home.

During May, Prokofiev amused himself by going to the Third International Chess Tournament. "Even his creative work began to take second place," Lina wrote later.

> He went to the Hall of Columns every day through the service entrance (otherwise it was impossible to get in). I often went along. We met many chess players, including our old friend Capablanca, as well as Botvinnik, Alatortsev, Kan, Flohr and Lilienthal. At the conclusion of the tournament a banquet was held and we were invited. Sergei Sergeevich even gave a little speech. Capablanca spoke in Spanish, and they asked me to translate. Later, some of these chess players would take part in tournaments in our apartment, and our neighbor, David Oistrakh, a first-class chess player, would join them.

Prokofiev supplied an article about the tournament to *Izvestiia*, praising the "collective" of Soviet chess players as the best in the world.

The apartment into which Prokofiev and his family finally moved at the end of June 1936 was at 16/14 Zemlyanoy Val, on the eastern side of Moscow near the Kursk Station. It is a wide and busy section of the road that encircles the city. Later, the street was renamed, like so many in Moscow, and given a more "Soviet" name—Chkalov Street, in honor of the heroic air force pilot Valery Chkalov who once lived in the building.

Called a "House of Specialists," the building is solid, square and imposing, if architecturally undistinguished in the extreme. It has, however, housed many famous artists, including the pianists Heinrich Neuhaus and Emil Gilels, in addition to the violinist David Oistrakh. Residence there was a reward given to those who had performed special cultural or other services to the Soviet state. Prokofiev and his family received Apartment 14, four comfortable but far from luxurious (at least by Parisian standards) rooms on the third floor, with a balcony overlooking the noisy boulevard. It was here that they received the "eleven boxes of furniture and household goods that had arrived from Paris, as well as a new piano, sent to me free of charge from Czechoslovakia."

When they moved in, the Prokofievs must have thought they would all be there together in this apartment for many years to come. Once you had an apartment like this in Moscow—where many people were still crammed into communal apartments or lived five and six to one room—you did not give it up. By Moscow standards of 1936, this was a dream apartment, but it would not prove to be a happy home for them.

The family's belongings were hardly out of boxes before Prokofiev fled the stuffy capital, retreating for the second consecutive summer to the tranquil artists' colony at Polenovo on the banks of the Oka River. To his disappointment, it was unusually hot and dry there. "The fields have all burned, and the smell of smoke is rising from the peat bogs." Prokofiev preferred cool weather. They lived in the main building, but Prokofiev worked in the little cottage where he had lived the summer before when composing *Romeo*. Besides composing, Prokofiev passed the time playing tennis and chess, swimming and reading stories by Alexander Kuprin, whose fiction deals mainly with Russian rural themes.

At Polenovo, Prokofiev was writing music for several large projects commissioned in connection with the upcoming celebration of the hundredth anniversary of the death of the poet Alexander Pushkin, often called "Russia's Shakespeare." One project was a score for a film version of the famous Pushkin short story, "The Queen of Spades," directed by Mikhail Romm. Also in the works was incidental music for two theatrical productions: the tragedy *Boris Godunov*, to be directed by Meyerhold, and a dramatization of the long novel in verse, *Eugene Onegin*, to be staged by Tairov at his Moscow Chamber Theater. Originally, Prokofiev had also planned to write incidental music for a production of the "little tragedy" in verse, "Mozart and Salieri," but never did.

All three of Prokofiev's Pushkin scores—on which he spent a substantial amount of time—were ill-fated. Mainly as the result of political complications, none of the three productions for which they were written was ever completed or shown to the public.

The setting for *The Queen of Spades*, like the setting for *Lt. Kizhe*, was "classical" St. Petersburg around 1800. Mikhail Romm (1901–1971), best known for his numerous films about World War II and fascism, had long wanted to make a film of Pushkin's cold, gothic story of ghosts, gambling and chance. " 'The Queen of Spades' seduced me first of all because there are very few words in it, because it is, in fact, a silent film and pantomime, with an enormous amount of expressive material," he said. Romm also saw the story—in appropriately Socialist Realist terms—as a social commentary on the impoverished and dying aristocracy. "I tried to make the film in the style of that time—as realistic as possible, and psychologically motivated."

When Romm asked Prokofiev to write the music, he responded enthusiastically, for Pushkin had always been one of his favorite writers. Precision, balance and a combination of romantic themes with classical control were characteristic both of Pushkin's prose and of Prokofiev's music. As an avid card player and the author of his own opera on gambling *(The Gambler)*, Prokofiev took a special interest in *The Queen of Spades*.

Prokofiev worked quickly; by late July 1936, the music for the film—twenty-four separate "numbers"—was completed in piano score. Apparently (and, if so, uncharacteristically) he composed from descriptions of the scenes supplied by Romm, since filming had not yet begun. "With his characteristic precision and accuracy, he composed music that was not at all dramatic or lyrical," Romm later wrote of their collaboration. "He used an obsessive idea as his motif; therefore, all the musical phrases were repeated many times, in the most simple form, like piano exercises, like one *idée fixe:* three notes and seven notes were repeated endlessly, endlessly, giving the film an essential 'dryness.' Sergei Sergeevich felt that Tchaikovsky's opera *The Queen of Spades* was in very bad taste. At least that is what he told me."

The obsessively repeated three notes and seven notes were an exact numerical "illustration" of the first two cards the phantom Countess tells Hermann, the story's doomed hero, to play—a three and a seven.

Work on the film was disrupted, however, by a personal conflict between Romm and the manager of the studio where he was filming, and was resumed only a year later. By the spring of 1938, nearly two years later, after a number of scenes had already been completed, Romm was once again forced to stop shooting, this time because of a new official policy that required directors to make films based on "contemporary themes." *The Queen of Spades* remained unfinished, although twenty of the twenty-four musical "numbers" had been orchestrated by the time filming ended.

Romm was understandably despondent over the film's fate, and discarded all materials connected with it: the scenario, historical research, sketches for scenery, photographs. As usual, Prokofiev was more prudent. Eight years later, he used Liza's lyrical theme in the slow movement of his Fifth Symphony.

While working on *The Queen of Spades*, Prokofiev was also writing incidental music for Tairov's planned dramatization of *Eugene Onegin*. Of all the Pushkin projects, this one most interested him, for *Eugene*

Onegin was one of his favorite works in all world literature, and one "from which he could never be parted." At the same time, both he and Tairov were well aware that they were working under the long shadow thrown by Tchaikovsky's popular opera on the same subject. Tairov was therefore planning to emphasize scenes Tchaikovsky omitted, such as the long chapter in which Tatyana, rejected by the callous Onegin, wanders through the country house where he had lived, examining his library and attempting to understand his behavior. Prokofiev worked hard on the project, producing forty-four separate musical "numbers" in piano score.

But soon after Tairov and his company heard what Prokofiev had composed, the production was canceled and never reached the stage. Prokofiev later used some of the *Eugene Onegin* music in *War and Peace*, where it worked well: the era—the first quarter of the nineteenth century—and the aristocratic milieu were nearly identical in both works.

Like *Eugene Onegin, Boris Godunov*—Pushkin's great historical tragedy set in the early seventeenth century—had already received a definitive operatic treatment, but at the hands of Mussorgsky, not Tchaikovsky. Unintimidated, Meyerhold had been preparing to stage *Boris* for several years and had approached Prokofiev about writing incidental music for it as early as 1934.

From the very start, Prokofiev stressed that he needed to "see it," to know what Meyerhold's *Boris* would "look like." This, in fact, was the guiding principle for Prokofiev's work in theatre and film throughout his career, as he said in a 1936 interview.

When I am asked to write music for a dramatic production or for a film, I almost never agree right away, even if I know the text of the play. I take five to ten days so that I can "see" the production—so I can picture the personalities of the characters, their emotions and the action. As I think these things over, the main themes usually come to me. By the time I finally agree to write the music, I usually have the main thematic material ready in my head, and, therefore, the starting point for the work.

I am happiest when the playwright or the director has specific requests. It helps me when he says, "Here I need a minute and a quarter of sad and tender music." Then I know what a person without special musical training expects from a given situation, or, more exactly (since many of our playwrights and directors understand music very well), what the creator of the production wants from the music—what he thinks appropriate for a given moment in the production.

Meyerhold worked in very much the same way; specific, exact, even mathematical, he was the perfect collaborator for Prokofiev. He even called his production notebooks, which contained exact descriptions of the physical movement on stage for each moment in the text, "scores." Although they had already worked together extensively on operatic projects, Prokofiev and Meyerhold had never before collaborated on a dramatic production. Sadly, *Boris* would be no less ill-fated than their previous attempts at collaboration.

Thorough and painstaking in his research, Meyerhold spent years preparing *Boris Godunov*. His staff began working on it in 1934, more than two years before its projected premiere. Prokofiev wrote most of the music in the early fall of 1936, following detailed instructions that Meyerhold had given him in a letter written the preceding summer. For Meyerhold, the many lavishly "realistic" productions of Mussorgsky's opera had perverted the true spirit of Pushkin's historical tragedy, presenting the character of Boris as too calm, and the era—around 1600—as too civilized.

"Boris is of Tartar origin," Meyerhold told the members of his troupe. "He is a warrior. He has to be 'Tartarized' and made capable of violent outbursts." Similarly, Meyerhold wanted Prokofiev's music to reflect the violence and brutality of the era ("The Time of Troubles"), one of the most bloody in all of Russian history. Meyerhold told Prokofiev to take his "Scythian Suite" as the "starting point" for the score. "Only a 'Scythian' orchestra can provide the *couleur locale,* and the appropriate atmosphere for this time and place."

In the music, as in all aspects of the production, Meyerhold strove to return to authentic historical sources, to dig beneath the layers of romantic clichés that had been piled onto Pushkin, and particularly onto the story of Boris Godunov, over the years. His instructions to Prokofiev included detailed descriptions of the music he wanted for each scene—how many minutes, what kind of rhythm, the volume level, and occasionally the instrumentation. Meyerhold encouraged Prokofiev to use musical instruments of the era—alarum bells, drums and hunting horns—in order to create a more authentic atmosphere. Prokofiev pasted Meyerhold's descriptions into a copy of the play from which he worked while composing the twenty-four numbers.

As it turned out, Prokofiev was the only participant in the production who managed to complete his contribution. "On November 16, 1936, Prokofiev played through all the musical numbers that the director had asked him to write. Before playing each number, he spoke, concisely and in his own words, about Meyerhold's specifications for the scene. All those in attendance responded ecstatically to the music. At the end of the run-through, Meyerhold warmly embraced Prokofiev and they kissed." But this was as far as it went.

Why *Boris Godunov* was abandoned in early January 1937, when it was nearly ready for the premiere and after more than two years had been devoted to preparing it, is not entirely clear, but the causes seem to have been primarily political. There is some evidence that Meyerhold was hoping to stage *Boris* in his new, much larger theatre currently under construction, and therefore stopped rehearsals until they could resume there. Also, in 1937—the twentieth anniversary of the Bolshevik Revolution—all theatrical directors were under intense pressure to stage "topical" plays about Soviet life by loyal contemporary playwrights. *Boris* was supposedly too old-fashioned and irrelevant for a Soviet audience.

But in fact part of the problem with *Boris*, a damning examination of the roots of tyranny and the abuse of absolute power, was that it was *too* topical. The thorny issues it raised might well prove embarrassing to the autocrat Stalin, or even stir up popular unrest. (Just how topical *Boris Godunov* is for a twentieth-century Russian audience was confirmed in 1982, when censors refused to allow Yury Lyubimov's new production of the play to open at the Taganka Theater, for similar reasons.)

Meyerhold's own increasingly precarious position, and the worsening cultural environment, played the key role in the cancellation of *Boris*. During the following year, Meyerhold and his theatre would come under unrelenting attack. One year after the last rehearsal of *Boris Godunov*, his theatre would be closed down permanently, and one of the greatest artists of the modern theatre would be an outcast.

The enormous body of music Prokofiev wrote for the Pushkin centennial was another casualty of the reactionary turn Soviet culture was taking by the late 1930s. Only his least interesting composition—the three songs (Op. 73) to Pushkin poems—ever became known to the public in its original form. Here Prokofiev was paying homage to the classical and accessible Tchaikovsky-Rachmaninoff vocal tradition of *romansy*—art songs. Conventional in structure and sentimental in their melodies, the songs are much less interesting than his early "prosaic," Mussorgskian songs to poems by Akhmatova and Balmont. (In fact, Prokofiev had called those earlier songs "poems," not *romansy*.) Where the early songs were spare, angular and stark, the Pushkin songs, first performed by Lina on Soviet radio in April 1937, were surprisingly sweet and cloying.

Around the same time, Prokofiev also wrote three songs for children (Op. 68). One, "Sweet Song," was written at the suggestion of Natalia Satz to words by Nina Saksonskaya, whose text for *Peter and the Wolf* Prokofiev had so brusquely rejected. It was an advertisement for chocolate:

> My life is always sweet,
> For children I'm a treat.
> My name is very simple—
> They call me chocolate!

When Prokofiev and his family returned from Polenovo to Moscow in the fall of 1936, Sviatoslav, now twelve, and Oleg, nearly eight, began attending Soviet schools. "During the pre-War years," Oleg said, "my brother and I changed schools several times. The last one, which we attended until the War, was undoubtedly the best. I was not teased there quite so much." It was a special school for the children of Soviet citizens who had been living abroad—mostly the children of diplomats. The instruction was in German and English as well as in Russian.

"Because of the changes I went through, or perhaps because my true interests were at home, I was a rather careless student, though I understood the lessons with no difficulty," said Oleg.

Then my father decided that school interests needed stimulation. My brother and I were guaranteed monetary compensation for good grades brought home. The higher the grade, the more money he paid. He established a schedule of fines for bad grades as well.

All of this was announced by my father with considerable mystery, as if he were involving us in a conspiracy. We showed no emotion, realizing, perhaps even condescendingly, that grownups should be left alone not only at work, but at play, since the wind was always liable to change.

We were right. Our new, rather affluent, student life did not continue too long. Father called us into his study and said, this time without a trace of the conspiratorial tone, seriously, that our contract was up: people in the know had explained to him that his method was wrong and unpedagogical. In all probability, someone with whom he had shared his secret told him that capitalist incentive was in contradiction with the Soviet system of education and ultimately presented him in a bad light politically.

Now that Moscow was their home, Prokofiev insisted that the boys speak French within the family, lest they forget the language; in Paris, he had insisted they speak Russian. Sviatoslav and Oleg were easily distinguished among their schoolmates in their first years in Moscow not only by their foreign clothing and manners, but by their slightly accented and unsure Russian. Both boys studied music, but Prokofiev never encouraged them to become professional musicians. "Between myself and my wife there is already too much music in the house," he said later.

There was also a lot of Prokofiev music in the concert halls: three world premieres in Moscow that fall. One was the new Russian Overture, a small and attractive piece composed the preceding summer, using folk techniques in a manner rather reminiscent of *The Buffoon*. Another was "Thoughts" (Op. 62), the cycle of three piano pieces composed several years earlier, performed by Prokofiev on November 13. The last was the First Symphonic Suite from *Romeo and Juliet*. Frustrated that he was still unable to get the ballet on stage, Prokofiev put together two suites from the score in late 1936—one of the few instances in dance history when a ballet's music was heard in concert form before being staged. The suites, which eventually became very popular, served to promote the cause of the ballet, convincing audiences and directors that it deserved a production.

Only a few days after the premiere of the First Suite from *Romeo*, Prokofiev left Moscow for a three-month concert tour of Europe and the United States. For the moment, Soviet officials were keeping the promise they made to Prokofiev before he moved permanently to Russia: he would be able to continue touring abroad. Prokofiev's prestige as an international composer was still great enough to preserve this special privilege. By late 1936, very few Soviet citizens—no matter how prominent or talented—were allowed to travel to Europe, let alone to evil capitalist America.

For the first few weeks, Prokofiev was alone on the road; Lina would come to join him in Paris in mid-December. The first stop was Brussels, where, only hours after arriving, he conducted an all-Prokofiev radio concert including "The Scythian Suite" and a rare revival of

Seven, They Are Seven. "During the afternoon we had two rehearsals, so somehow we managed to pull it together. As a result, however, I was dead tired," he wrote to Miaskovsky.

Appearances followed in Bordeaux, Paris, Lausanne and Prague. A program conducted by Albert Wolff in Paris on December 19 must have tested the endurance of both audience and performers: the First Suite from *Romeo and Juliet,* the *Love for Three Oranges* and *Le Pas d'acier* suites, as well as the symphonic version of the Overture on Hebrew Themes (conducted by Prokofiev) and the Third Piano Concerto with Prokofiev as soloist. The Parisian opinion on *Romeo* was divided; some praised it, but others "heaved sighs of regret over the simplification of my style."

While Sviatoslav and Oleg stayed behind in Moscow, Lina arrived in Paris to join her husband just before Christmas, after "passport troubles." (Like her husband, she was now a Soviet citizen and was treated like one by the border police.) In Paris, they let a furnished flat for two months in the fifteenth *arrondissement*—the last apartment they would rent in the city where they had spent so many years together.

Judging from his letters, Prokofiev took great pleasure in renewing his contract with European composers and musical life after nine months of nearly complete isolation. He heard Stravinsky play his Concerto for Two Solo Pianos, and examined several pages of Stravinsky's new ballet "In Three Deals" *(Jeu de cartes)* pronouncing it a "splendid piece of work." He also attended a concert performance of Darius Milhaud's early opera *Christophe Colomb,* which he preferred to its sequel, *Maximilien.*

Musical life in Paris continued to flourish, but by December 1936, the political situation in Europe was more tense than at any time since the First World War. The civil war raging in Spain was upsetting the balance of power, pitting the European powers against each other and attracting the intense interest of the Soviet government. Germany and Japan had signed the Anti-Comintern Pact, aimed against the U.S.S.R., in November. Hitler's power in Germany, and his imperialistic aspirations, continued to grow at an alarming pace. All over Europe, artists were searching for a place of refuge; many (including Stravinsky) would choose America. Characteristically, Prokofiev has left no record of his reaction to the pre-War political climate; even after his difficult experience with the Russian Revolution, he rarely seemed to notice such things.

On January 6, 1937, Prokofiev sailed for New York. This time, he stayed for less than a month in America and gave many fewer concerts than in the past. By now, Prokofiev's relationship with Koussevitsky, his strongest advocate in America, was considerably more distant; they had even stopped corresponding regularly. Now that Prokofiev had officially embraced the identity of a Soviet composer, it became more difficult for him to fraternize with émigrés like Koussevitsky or Stravinsky, damned by the Soviet cultural bureaucracy as traitors.

After performances in New York, he went on to Chicago to play the Third Piano Concerto with the Chicago Symphony under Hans Lange. To Vernon Duke, Prokofiev wrote sarcastically that "the orchestra was attentive and played well, and even during an afternoon concert the old ladies clapped conscientiously, risking their white gloves." Next came St. Louis, where, as the program noted, Prokofiev played on a Steinway, "the instrument of the immortals." The tour ended with a stop in Boston for two appearances with Koussevitsky and his thriving Boston Symphony (the program was limited to old works), and the inevitable recital at the Soviet Embassy in Washington.

The most important result of Prokofiev's 1937 American tour, however, was not musical but automotive. Before leaving the United States, he made an extravagant purchase that he immediately shipped back to Moscow: a 1937 Ford. "Blue and streamlined," the car would become the envy of Prokofiev's friends and colleagues in Russia; private cars were an unheard-of luxury in Moscow in 1937, and would be for many years to come. That Prokofiev could possess one only emphasized his different and privileged status in what was, at least theoretically, a socialist society. It would also serve to feed the jealousy and resentment many of his colleagues already felt toward him. But Prokofiev was used to enjoying the material rewards of fame, and was not about to give them up, even in Stalin's Moscow.

Prokofiev's first trip to America in four years—and his first since moving to Moscow—apparently pleased him, for he returned a year later, for what would be the last time.

By mid-February, Prokofiev was back in Paris, staying again at the rented flat on the rue Dr. Roux—just long enough to play his Third Concerto under Albert Wolff. Before starting on the long train trip that would once again cut him off from the Western world, Prokofiev wrote another playful note to Vernon Duke that demonstrates a new understanding of what he could and could not do in Moscow. Promising to help Duke publish his symphonies, Prokofiev asked for American books for his sons, and warned his old pal not to mention "$$" in letters sent to the U.S.S.R.

So even the brutally frank Prokofiev, always so proud of his honesty and his insistence on saying what he thought, had come to realize there were certain things—many things—it was better not to say in correspondence to Stalin's Russia. Merely receiving letters from abroad was now viewed by the Soviet authorities as highly suspect. As Stalin's xenophobia intensified, the flow of information between the U.S.S.R. and the rest of the world, severely restricted since 1917, dried to a trickle. Only a few years later, all contact would be lost. As Nicolas Nabokov observed, fear was for the first time in his life beginning to affect Prokofiev's behavior.

Even so, in Moscow he and his family still displayed—at times ostentatiously—their special and privileged position, and their unwillingness (or inability) to blend in with the gray and homogenous background of Soviet society. Sviatoslav Richter, then a budding twenty-two-year-old pianist, encountered Prokofiev and his family one day that spring on the street near their apartment building. They created quite a spectacle. "His clothes were checkered all over, with bright yellow shoes and a reddish-orange tie," Richter recalled some years later. Oleg and Sviatoslav were "charming," while Lina stood by "with an impatient expression on her face."

After moving to Moscow—particularly for the first few years, when he was still touring abroad—Prokofiev continued to dress extravagantly in clothes he had purchased abroad. Lina also retained her fondness for Parisian *haute couture* and expensive perfumes. This fact was more important than it might appear on the surface: in the grim and spartan surroundings of Stalinist Russia, such luxury and extravagance were shocking to behold. They bespoke both arrogance and a strange insensitivity to one's surroundings. For most Muscovites (including many musicians and composers), the struggle to scavenge for daily bread left little energy—or money—to devote to one's wardrobe. Attractive clothes were next to impossible to find in the stores in any case. When Prokofiev's new blue Ford arrived in late spring, the sharp material contrast between him and his colleagues became only more striking and awkward.

But even with their special privileges and their ability to travel abroad (at least initially), Prokofiev and Lina did not find the adjustment to Soviet reality of the late 1930s an easy one. Now that they had their own apartment and two boys to feed, Lina had to confront the ordeal of shopping in Moscow (although she did have domestic help). Shortages of the most common necessities of day-to-day life were chronic. Finding the selection of fresh produce and meat that had been readily available in Paris was impossible—and Prokofiev had always enjoyed eating well. Dealing with the overregulation and massive inefficiency of Soviet retail and service establishments must also have been frustrating to people accustomed to European efficiency.

For Lina, all these difficulties and adjustments were even more traumatic than for her husband, since she had never lived in Russia before and had left her friends and relatives behind in Europe. Being so far away from her mother, who had so often taken care of Sviatoslav and Oleg when she and Prokofiev were traveling or busy, must have made her feel lonely. One of Prokofiev's relatives who lived in Moscow, Veronika Burtseva, did provide some help in taking care of the boys, but Lina missed her own family.

Russian society has never absorbed foreigners easily. They have been traditionally isolated and segregated, for fear they will ideologically contaminate or spiritually corrupt the general population. Such deeply ingrained xenophobic attitudes, which had existed in Russia at least since the time of Ivan the Terrible, intensified under Stalin, who was acutely suspicious and at the same time defensive in all his dealings with foreigners and foreign governments. Foreigners could be out to subvert the cause of Soviet Communism, he warned.

Lina's situation was somewhat different in that she spoke Russian well, but Prokofiev's Russian friends were still very much aware of her "foreignness." They treated her with courtesy and consideration, but found her distant, formal and distinctly different—as they had when she first came to visit in 1927. Her elegance and beauty only made many of them ashamed of their drab clothes and lack of sophistication. Nor, judging from most accounts, did Lina make a great effort to break down the barrier that separated them. Understandably, she spent much of her time with other foreigners, particularly with European diplomatic personnel stationed in Moscow. In her experience (and in her husband's), there was no reason to think this dangerous or inappropriate.

If, as seems fair to suggest, Lina was unhappy over the move to Moscow, her unhappiness must have affected her relationship with Prokofiev. It was for the sake of his music and career, after all, that she had made this radical change in her life; otherwise she would never have found herself living in Russia. Seeing her unhappiness must have also—if only subconsciously—made Prokofiev feel guilty, since he was solely responsible for bringing her there. Lina had made an enormous sacrifice, one that not every wife would make, for the sake of his art.

Despite the adjustments and the new demands placed on him by Soviet cultural politics, Prokofiev remained basically content to be back in Russia. He felt that the move had been essential for his muse and his spirit, and he was beginning to find the new inspiration and gifted collaborators (Meyerhold, Tairov) he had lacked in Paris. To be confronted daily with Lina, who did not share his enthusiasm and even had good reason to dislike their new home, must have presented him with an uncomfortable dilemma.

That the music he wrote over the next few years was for the most part critically unsuccessful could not have made it any easier for Prokofiev to deal with the stress at home. After his early Soviet successes, Prokofiev encountered a number of obstacles. Between *Peter and the Wolf,* composed in April 1936, and the music for the film *Alexander Nevsky,* composed in late 1938, an unusually large number of his new compositions went unperformed and unpublished. Of all the music written for the Pushkin centenary, only the three songs were played in their original form during his lifetime. *Romeo and Juliet* was still homeless. A big new work composed in 1937 for the twentieth anniversary of the Bolshevik Revolution—*Cantata for the Twentieth Anniversary of October*—was judged undeserving of a performance.

The explanation for these failures lies mainly in the volatile political-cultural situation at the time. As the Great Purges intensified in 1937–38, it became nearly impossible to predict what would be acceptable to Stalin and his cultural henchmen. Two of the Pushkin projects—*The Queen of Spades* and *Boris Godunov*—were canceled because they did not conform to the prevailing official view of what was "appropriate" for a Soviet audience. *Romeo and Juliet,* at least initially, became entangled in the political upheaval in Leningrad following Kirov's assassination and the rise of Zhdanov.

Nor was Prokofiev's experience unique: many prominent cultural figures came under attack, finding their books banned or productions shut down. Some, like Shostakovich, simply retreated for a while: his output declined drastically during the uncertain period that followed the attack on *Lady Macbeth* in 1936. Another victim of Stalin's wrath, the poet Osip Mandelshtam, returned briefly to Moscow in 1937 after spending several years in exile for writing an anti-Stalin epigram, only to be rearrested as a "counterrevolutionary" and sentenced to five more years in a remote Siberian labor camp. He died on the way there.

Under the circumstances, one could even consider Prokofiev lucky.

In the spring of 1937, Prokofiev conducted the world premiere of the Second Suite from *Romeo and Juliet* in Leningrad, and accompanied Lina in the premiere of the Pushkin songs at a Moscow concert broadcast on radio and television. Television technology was then in its infancy, and special preparations had to be made.

> Before the program they asked us to make ourselves up and color our lips green. I remember how much this amused Sergei Sergeevich and how he laughed when he looked at himself in the mirror. The lighting was very bright, and it was hard for him to play because his eyes kept filling with tears. At that time no one yet had television sets, so no one could tell us what it looked like.

After a rigorous season during which he had traveled thousands of miles, Prokofiev left Moscow with his family to spend a few months in the countryside at Nikolina Gora. This small settlement about thirty miles west of the capital was a place that would figure importantly in his life from that point on. Spread along the flat land on the fertile banks of the Moscow River, clear and slow-flowing before its entrance into the metropolis, Nikolina Gora (literally, Nicolas's Hill) has long been a vacation spot for high-ranking military, political and cultural figures. Driving out to Nikolina Gora—a chauffeur had been hired, since driving in Moscow "required special effort"—Prokofiev and his family would pass through the city outskirts, the horizon cluttered with huge apartment complexes under construction, into a rural and timeless world that must have recalled his childhood in Sontsovka. Peasant women, their heads wrapped in kerchiefs, stooped to pick potatoes from the rich black earth. Thick groves of birches and pines stretched beyond the fields. Long, luxuriant grass covered the forest paths.

The special section of Nikolina Gora in which Prokofiev and his family lived that summer, and where he would spend many summers to come, was known by its acronym RANIS (for Scientific and Artistic Workers). The country's finest surgeons, chemists, musicians and directors spent their leisure time in rustic wooden *dachas* hidden among the trees. That first summer, Prokofiev and his family lived on the second floor of a *dacha* they rented from Roza Ginzburg, a surgeon and professor. Their wide windows faced trees on all sides, and provided a fine view of the Moscow River in the distance. At the back of the house, a balcony extended from the single large room that Prokofiev and Lina shared with the boys.

Many of Prokofiev's musical associates also summered at Nikolina Gora, including Miaskovsky, Pavel Lamm and Vissarion Shebalin, one of the rising young stars on the Soviet musical scene. During part of the summer, Lina left Prokofiev alone with the children in Nikolina Gora, and, unused to the responsibility of caring for them, he would run over to the Lamms' house to ask for advice on how to feed and clothe them.

On the balcony of their rented *dacha*, Prokofiev worked on a huge piece commemorating the twentieth anniversary of the Bolshevik Revolution, to be celebrated with all the pomp and circumstance that Stalin and his entourage could muster.

The *Cantata for the Twentieth Anniversary of October* (Op. 74) was also Prokofiev's first attempt to write a large-scale work in the explicitly political style expected of good Soviet composers. He undertook the task with the same total commitment he made to anything he wrote. But for Prokofiev to compose music commemorating a revolution he did not witness, for which he had little sympathy when it occurred, and whose significance he admitted he had failed to grasp was not easy. Perhaps this helps to explain the cantata's resounding critical failure.

In ten parts, the cantata was conceived on a scale as enormous as Russia and as ambitious as Communism. It required "no less than five hundred" singers and instrumentalists. The huge dimensions were dictated at least in part by Stalin's fondness for the grandiose and monumental, as immortalized in the ubiquitous Stalinist "birthday cake" skyscrapers that dominate the Moscow skyline even today. Scored for two mixed choruses (one professional and one amateur) and four orchestras (symphonic, brass, percussion and *bayan*, a Russian-style concertina often used in folk music), the cantata uses texts by the saints of Soviet Communist ideology—Marx and Engels, Lenin and Stalin. The words are sung by the choruses and, in one episode, spoken by a narrator.

The dramatic narrative follows the spread of Communism from Europe ("A spectre is crossing Europe, the spectre of Communism," from the *Communist Manifesto*); to the struggle for recognition in Russia before the Revolution ("We are marching in close ranks," from Lenin's

What Is to Be Done); to the October Revolution (an extended montage of excerpts from Lenin's speeches and writings during 1917); to victory (also from an address delivered by Lenin in the spring of 1918); to Stalin's pledge to industrialize the nation; to the formulation of Stalin's new 1936 Soviet constitution, based on the principle "From each according to his ability, to each according to his needs."

The longest and most important of the ten sections, which include several orchestral interludes, is "Revolution." Here, Prokofiev employs all his choral and orchestral resources in painting a wild cinematic picture of combat, complete with percussion gunfire, joyful folk dances on the *bayan*, clanging alarum bells and screaming sirens. Gradually increasing in intensity as more forces join in, growing in volume and excitement, "Revolution" is a kind of politicized version of the frenetic concluding act of *The Fiery Angel*. The vocal style in the cantata is a strange mixture of abrupt incantation reminiscent of some episodes in *Love for Three Oranges*, and the more lyrical, epic line (particularly for the female voices) that finds fuller expression in *Alexander Nevsky* and *War and Peace*.

The 250 pages of the cantata's orchestral score were completed on August 16. But when Prokofiev showed the piece to his colleagues, they were more confused than complimentary. "I sat for two months at Nikolina Gora . . . scribbling a cantata for the twentieth anniversary, and it has already provoked more indignation than rapture," he wrote to Vera Alpers in late August. "What will happen when it is performed?"

What happened was that the powers-that-be, who controlled publication and performance, wanted to have nothing to do with the cantata. The bureaucrats objected most, apparently, to the insufficiently heroic setting of the words of the "brilliant and graphic leaders of the Revolution." The odd *Cantata for the Twentieth Anniversary of October* was shelved, remaining unpublished and, until 1966, unperformed.

This enormous piece behind him, Prokofiev "gave up on the north" and went south to his favorite resort of Kislovodsk in the Caucasus. He had hoped to rest there, but found "a pile of things to be attended to: correcting proofs, chess, etc."

More work awaited him in Moscow in the autumn. Apparently undaunted by the failure of the *Cantata*, Prokofiev devoted his days to another large political work, *Songs of Our Days*, and spent the long evenings with new and old friends. Among the old friends were the critic Vladimir Derzhanovsky, who had promoted Prokofiev's music even before the Revolution; the conductor Konstantin Saradzhev; Miaskovsky; Meyerhold; and, of course, Pavel Lamm, whose service in accurately copying over so many of Prokofiev's compositions from piano score (with detailed indications for instrumentation) was simply heroic. Among the newer friends were the composer Vissarion Shebalin and the pianist Heinrich Neuhaus.

Prokofiev frequently participated in musical evenings held in the apartments of Lamm or Derzhanovsky. The composers in attendance—who often included Miaskovsky, Khachaturian and Khrennikov—would perform their new works in the hope of hearing constructive advice and criticism. Prokofiev's colleagues noted, though, that he seemed uninterested in playing or listening to the eight-hand piano arrangements that were one of their favorite pastimes. They also observed that Prokofiev seemed reluctant to reciprocate with invitations to his own apartment on Chkalov Street.

That same autumn, Prokofiev conducted a concert devoted exclusively to his works (including the Fourth Symphony) in the prestigious Great Hall of the Moscow Conservatory. And yet the very next day—November 21, 1937—Prokofiev found himself again upstaged by Dmitri Shostakovich. When Evgeny Mravinsky conducted his Leningrad Philharmonic in the world premiere of Shostakovich's Fifth Symphony, Shostakovich was suddenly once again the toast of the Soviet musical world. The critics raved: just as abruptly and arbitrarily as it had been ruined, his reputation was restored. With this epic and solemn symphony, Shostakovich became the leading Soviet symphonic composer, a position he would hold firmly until his death. The Fifth Symphony was so popular with Soviet conductors, orchestras and cultural commissars that it at least temporarily overshadowed the performance and publication of music by all other Soviet composers—including Prokofiev. Like *Lady Macbeth*, the Fifth Symphony was soon after played by orchestras all over the world, and became one of the most often performed symphonies written in the twentieth century.

Prokofiev could hardly ignore Shostakovich's talent and stature, but he remained ambivalent about his music, finding it overly emotional and thick. After hearing his Fifth Symphony, Prokofiev wrote Shostakovich a note, complaining that it had been praised for the wrong reasons, but calling it "a truly fresh thing. . . . Could I reproach you for one detail, however? Why is there so much tremolo in the strings? Just like *Aida*. But that could be easily corrected if your viewpoint coincides with mine." Needless to say, the tremolo remained.

At this point in their careers, Shostakovich and Prokofiev were moving in opposite directions. In contrast to Prokofiev, who spent most of his time during the difficult years 1936–37 composing political cantatas and songs, Shostakovich instead chose to concentrate on symphonies. He had completed his Fourth in May 1936, although he had decided to cancel its upcoming premiere after a few rehearsals. One year later, in 1937, he composed the Fifth. As Prokofiev's music was becoming more "public," Shostakovich's was becoming more "private." While Prokofiev would write the explicitly nationalistic music for *Alexander Nevsky* in 1938, Shostakovich would write his First String Quartet.

Another example of Prokofiev's more overtly civic persona during this period was the piece on which he was working during the late fall and early winter of 1937: *Songs of Our Days,* a cycle of eight songs preceded by an orchestral march. The forces are large, though not so gargantuan as for *Cantata to October:* orchestra, mixed chorus, and soloists. For the texts—most of them intensely nationalistic, and even embarrassing in their simplistic optimism—Prokofiev turned to popular Soviet poets, including the children's writer Samuil Marshak. The longest song, "A Twenty-Year-Old," sets his dramatic and edifying verses about a young passerby who crawls up a drainpipe to save a little girl from a burning building. "The Golden Ukraine," a jingoistic verse that appeared originally in *Pravda,* glorifies the (enforced) modernization of farm life: "And now my spacious land is clothed in flowers, I have been plowing up the earth in the wide fields with tractors."

Although he claimed to have sought a melodic, simple and straightforward musical language, using "folk-style" melodies of his own invention, Prokofiev again failed to achieve a definite critical success with *Songs of Our Days.* As one critic expressed it, the prevailing opinion was that "to be simple and at the same time remain himself proved too difficult for the composer."

In his works of the later 1930s (*Cantata to October, Songs of Our Days, Alexander Nevsky, Zdravitsa* and the opera *Semyon Kotko*), Prokofiev shifted radically away from the international style, genres and subjects characteristic of his music of the 1920s and early 1930s, and toward the nationalistic and topical. A few years earlier, Prokofiev had warned that in their isolation, Soviet composers ran the risk of becoming "provincial"; his own music was—at least to a certain extent—now proving that prediction correct. Works like *Cantata to October, Songs of Our Days* and *Zdravitsa* are at best of limited interest to a non-

Soviet listener. Of all of them, only *Alexander Nevsky* would gain an international audience.

In early 1938, Prokofiev and Lina left Moscow for an extended tour of Europe and the United States. It would be—though they might not have realized it at the time—their final tour together, and Prokofiev's last trip abroad. Their full and demanding schedule took them across Europe and the United States, and they returned to Moscow only in mid-April, staying abroad longer than they had originally planned.

In Paris, Prokofiev arrived just in time for the last rehearsal of his First Piano Concerto. It began at 8:30 on the morning of the concert and continued until two in the afternoon. "I lay down from two to four," he told Miaskovsky, "and the concert took place at 4:30—a Saturday matinee. After the concert I had dinner with Stravinsky, who told dirty jokes."

The Paris critics paid few compliments to Prokofiev's "Soviet" music, which they considered a sadly simplistic shadow of his former vigor and complexity. Such attitudes irritated him. In an interview with Lola Bassan of *Page Musicale*, he complained that his views and comments had been distorted in the press, and insisted, "I'm not trying to defend any one single trend, and—most of all—I seek to make no concessions, but simply to follow my inspiration." He also denied that he had ever been "guilty of 'committing' any atonal harmonies."

In America, too, Prokofiev had attempted to define his new image as a Soviet composer. He told William G. King of the *New York Sun* that the problem of writing music in the U.S.S.R. was "an inspiring one," and more invigorating than in Europe, where serious music was "of interest only to a small circle." He seemed anxious to shed the "bad boy" image that clung to him in America even twenty years after his New York debut. "In my youth my music was purposely 'smart' and, on account of its new language, seemed provoking," he said. "They began to think of me as a kind of *enfant terrible*. While twenty or more years have passed they have never changed their views of me—although I have changed my ideas and intentions very much as a result of constant work to develop myself."

Despite his desire to prove that he had changed as an artist, Prokofiev concentrated on his own warhorses during this extensive tour of nine American cities. He played the First Piano Concerto and conducted the "Classical" Symphony, composed more than twenty years earlier.

In Colorado, where he was performing for the first time, Prokofiev
was a guest at the home of a Mr. Cranmer, one of the founders of the
then-fledgling Denver Symphony. Many years later, in an interview in
the *Denver Post,* Mrs. Cranmer recalled that Prokofiev was a terrible
"grouch" during the ten days he spent at her home in February 1938.
"He hardly spoke to anyone, even though he did know English," Mrs.
Cranmer said. "He'd sit through a meal just not saying a word. Nobody
could get anything out of him."

Prokofiev's appearance with the Denver Symphony was, in her
opinion, "unfortunate. The music did not arrive until the same day he
did, and the orchestra had insufficient time to rehearse. And this
terrible Russian paper it was printed on had been refingered and erased
and refingered again. Half the men in the orchestra didn't know what
notes they were playing, and they had a terrible time." Trying to cheer
him up, Mrs. Cranmer threw a party. After it was over, he announced
he had not liked any of the guests. But one of her ideas did please
him immensely: she took him to see the recently released Walt Disney
film, *Snow White and the Seven Dwarfs.* Predictably, "he was enrap-
tured. He wanted to see it again the next day."

Prokofiev would have the opportunity to meet Walt Disney, the
man behind *Snow White,* soon afterward in Hollywood, where he spent
several weeks in late February and early March. Disney, the wizard
of animation, and Prokofiev had some important traits in common: a
fascination with technology and the possibilities of recorded sound,
plus a fondness and unusual talent for entertaining children through
their art. One can only regret that they never had the opportunity to
work together, especially considering Disney's later work with "serious" music, as in *Fantasia,* which set Stravinsky's *Rite of Spring* (along
with other scores) to animation.

Hollywood, then in its heyday, fascinated Prokofiev. "It is very
warm here—I've forgotten what an overcoat is, and the trees are covered with oranges and pineapples," he wrote to his sons.

Most American films are made in Hollywood, and they build whole
houses, castles and even cities of cardboard for them. Today I went
to a filming session. A big tall warehouse had been turned into the
square of an old town and people galloped through it on horses. I
have also been to the house of Mickey Mouse's papa, that is, the
man who first thought up the idea of sketching him.

He signed the letter "Papa"—which means the same thing in Russian as in English—but with a characteristic comic twist: both *a*'s written upside down.

Only a few months before Prokofiev had arrived in the United States, his *Lt. Kizhe* Suite had been performed in Boston and New York by Koussevitsky and the Boston Symphony. Such clear evidence that Prokofiev could compose interesting music for film intrigued American film moguls, some of whom courted Prokofiev during his stay in Hollywood. Director Rouben Mamoulian even held a banquet in Prokofiev's honor after Lina arrived from New York. A number of Hollywood stars attended, including Mary Pickford, Marlene Dietrich, Gloria Swanson, Edward G. Robinson, and Douglas Fairbanks, Jr.

Also invited was Arnold Schoenberg, the grand old man of the New Viennese School, who had been living in the United States since 1933. (He had briefly considered moving to the U.S.S.R., but wisely decided against it.) Although Prokofiev was curious to meet Schoenberg—whose music he had been the first to play in Russia in 1911—in the flesh, he remained unmoved by Schoenberg's complex twelve-tone system. The more glamorous film people, who were working in such a modern and exciting medium, made a much greater impression on him.

Hollywood was so fascinating, and Prokofiev so flattered by the attention he was receiving, that he stayed considerably longer than he had first planned. He must have been tempted to remain there forever. But like so many things in his life, Prokofiev's encounter with Hollywood came at the wrong moment. He had made his decision to live in Moscow, and his sons were there. Prokofiev's chance to live in America had already passed him by. Hollywood would always remain alluring but impossible.

Returning briefly to the East Coast, Prokofiev made two appearances in Boston with Koussevitsky and the BSO. One of the programs featured the American premiere of *Peter and the Wolf*.

During this and previous tours of the United States, Prokofiev listened to American music of all kinds. In his extensive record collection, he had "at least a hundred recordings" of jazz, which he "liked a great deal and played very often." In a long article on American music for a Soviet magazine, Prokofiev devoted considerable space to jazz, arguing that some of its aspects deserved to be considered on the same level as "serious" music. He cited the example of George Gershwin, who had successfully included native American jazz and folk elements in his classical pieces—though Prokofiev believed Gershwin's serious style had been undermined by all the "light" music he had written.

Perhaps this fear of becoming facile explains why Prokofiev did not make much use of jazz techniques in his own music. Stravinsky, on the other hand, who was less concerned about the "purity" of his serious music, turned to jazz for inspiration on numerous occasions.

After Gershwin, Prokofiev saw a blank page in American music. "At the present time in the U.S.A. there is a great thirst to create American music—I would even call it a longing for a native composer." Prokofiev did not yet seem to know much about Aaron Copland, who would to some extent fill that gap; his reputation was only beginning to grow.

Quality of performance in the United States, however, was something else again. Like many other Europeans, Prokofiev was impressed by the excellent orchestras and the great number of impeccable soloists. "I've noticed that many artists who arrive from Europe have to buck up, lest their defects become immediately obvious." He was less impressed by the repertoire they played. "I have heard little interesting music here, since I've been moving around and playing all the time," he wrote Miaskovsky in March. "I slept through Sibelius's Second Symphony. . . . I heard Toscanini, who played trash, but how he played it!"

In general, Prokofiev thought much more positively of American musical life by 1938 than he had in 1921, and even preferred it in many ways to musical life in Europe. He was sufficiently pleased with the 1938 tour to plan another one for the following winter, but it would not take place, even after a number of concerts were scheduled and some tickets had been sold. Prokofiev's American friends (particularly Ephraim Gottlieb, a Chicago insurance agent and music-lover) and associates would continue to write to him until the mid-1940s, although their letters would frequently go unanswered—something that had never happened in the past.

Not long before he was scheduled to leave for Europe in the last days of March, Prokofiev received an intriguing message from Vernon Duke, who was flourishing in Manhattan. Through Duke's Hollywood agent, a movie studio had made a handsome offer to Prokofiev, at a salary of $2500 a week.

I showed Serge the telegram exultantly; there was a flicker of interest for a mere instant, then, his face set, his oversize lips petulant, he said gruffly: "That's nice bait, but I won't swallow it. I've got to go back to Moscow, to my music and my children. And now that that's settled, will you come to Macy's with me? I've got to buy a whole roomful of things you can't get in Russia—just look at Lina's list."

The list was imposing, and we went to Macy's department store, another sample of capitalistic bait designed by the lackeys of Wall Street to be swallowed by oppressed workers. Although he wouldn't admit it, Serge enjoyed himself hugely in the store—he loved gadgets and trinkets of every description. Suddenly he turned to me, his eyes peculiarly moist, his voice even gruffer than usual: "You know, Dima, it occurred to me that I may not be back for quite some time. . . . I don't suppose it would be wise for you to come to Russia, would it?" "No, I don't suppose it would," I answered, smiling bravely, my happiness abruptly gone. I never saw Prokofiev again.

Perhaps it was the Nazi takeover of Austria in March 1938 and the worsening political situation throughout Europe that made Prokofiev think he might not be returning soon to America. Or perhaps it was his knowledge that foreign travel was becoming very difficult for Soviet citizens, even for those with privileged status like himself. Prokofiev and Lina sailed on March 30 for France; they stopped in Paris for a few days and he gave a recital at the Soviet Embassy. Then they continued on to Moscow, arriving there on April 16.

Prokofiev's performance at the Embassy in Paris was his last appearance abroad. He would never again see America, Europe or Paris—the city where he had spent so many years and where he had composed so much music. Lina would see Paris only many years later, in what would seem like another century.

CHAPTER 18

LESSONS IN
SOVIET REALITY

If a wolf should come out of the forest, then what
would you do?

—*Peter and the Wolf*

The excitement and intense activity of his tour to Europe and America
had left Prokofiev little time for composing in the first few months
of 1938. As soon as he was back in Moscow, perhaps in an attempt
to distract himself from the personal responsibilities and political
pressures that awaited him there, he plunged into new projects. Over
the next eight months, Prokofiev would preside over three world premieres in Russia; a fourth would occur abroad.

Before going on tour, he had nearly completed incidental music
for a production of *Hamlet* to be directed by Sergei Radlov, his collaborator on the original scenario of *Romeo and Juliet*. Unlike so many
of his recent theatrical projects, *Hamlet* actually reached the stage
soon after Prokofiev's return to the U.S.S.R.—on May 15, 1938, at
the Radlov Theater-Studio in Leningrad. Prokofiev was in attendance.
Radlov was a veteran director of Shakespeare, having already staged
Romeo and Juliet, *Othello* (twice) and *King Lear*.

For *Hamlet*, Prokofiev followed the same procedure he and Meyerhold had used for *Boris Godunov*. He began composing only after
Radlov had supplied him with an exact description of how much and
what kind of music was needed for each scene.

Less music was needed for *Hamlet* than for *Boris Godunov* or
Eugene Onegin: only ten small "numbers." Five were "little songs"
(pesenky), four for Ophelia and one for the grave-digger, all using folk-

style material from the Shakespearean era. The remaining five numbers were "The Ghost of Hamlet's Father," which Prokofiev interpreted not as a "mystical" moment, but one that emphasizes the father's demand for revenge; "The March of Claudius," an "exhibitionistic and 'chic' march conveying the brilliance with which the usurper-king attempted to surround himself"; several similarly pompous fanfares; music for the "mousetrap," the mimed play within a play that implicates Claudius in the murder of Hamlet's father—Prokofiev uses a gavotte to convey the necessary mixture of irony and theatricality; and a concluding "Fortinbras' March" stressing the optimistic subtext of Shakespeare's ending.

Prokofiev also began another collaboration in the spring of 1938, one that would be an important source of inspiration, encouragement and emotional support during the difficult decade to come. He was already acquainted with the film director Sergei Eisenstein (1898–1948); they had met in Paris in the late 1920s (or perhaps earlier), when Eisenstein was still making frequent trips abroad. They did not come to know each other well, however, until they worked together in 1938 on *Alexander Nevsky*.

The director and the composer—both regarded as among the most important figures in their respective fields of Soviet culture—had a great deal in common. Seven years apart in age, they both came from educated prerevolutionary middle-class backgrounds; both had come of age during the turbulent years of the Revolution; and both were regarded with suspicion in the 1930s because of their extensive international connections, travel abroad and supposed "cosmopolitanism." Both had worked with and been profoundly influenced by Vsevolod Meyerhold; Eisenstein had studied in Meyerhold's famous "directors' workshop" in the early 1920s.

Like Prokofiev, Eisenstein had lived briefly in America. He had even worked—unsuccessfully—for a time in Hollywood in the early 1930s. By the mid-1930s, both artists were searching in their respective media for an appropriately "popular" and "Soviet" style that would satisfy the demands of the official cultural establishment but still retain artistic integrity. Both were precise and demanding, and thrived on intense activity.

One important difference between Prokofiev and Eisenstein (especially in Stalin's Russia) was that Eisenstein, like Meyerhold, was a Jew. Another was Eisenstein's much stronger and more consistent connection to Soviet postrevolutionary culture. Eisenstein had remained in Russia after 1917 and throughout the 1920s, when he became a leading figure in the creation of Soviet—and world—cinema. Films like *Strike, The Battleship Potemkin,* and *October (Ten Days That Shook the World)* immediately became classics of revolutionary cinema both in the U.S.S.R. and abroad.

With such successful films behind him, Eisenstein went to Hollywood in the early 1930s to work on a mammoth project with the American novelist Upton Sinclair, *Que Viva Mexico.* It was a financial and artistic fiasco. Returning to the U.S.S.R. in 1932, around the same time that Prokofiev was binding his future more closely to Russia, Eisenstein found the situation there greatly changed and his own position in the film establishment tenuous. It disturbed him to see the increasing regimentation of the once lively Soviet film industry and the enforced homogenization of style and subjects, which amounted to a betrayal of revolutionary artistic ideals for which he and Meyerhold had struggled.

Eisenstein's position in the rapidly changing Soviet cultural environment was now so uncertain that in spite of his enormous international fame he had great difficulty making new films during the 1930s. Sixty percent of his ambitious and very expensive 1937 project *Bezhin Meadow,* a film version of a Turgenev short story, had been shot when it was canceled due to the same sort of political and bureaucratic complications that had killed the Romm-Prokofiev *Queen of Spades.*

At this difficult point in his career, just after the *Bezhin Meadow* debacle, Eisenstein reencountered Prokofiev. As early as autumn of 1937, Eisenstein had been considering making a new film on the life of the thirteenth-century Prince of Novgorod, Alexander Nevsky (1220–63). The subject of a medieval hagiographic biography, Nevsky had achieved heroic stature in Russian history as a fair, god-fearing and brave statesman, and as leader of the Russian forces in their victory over the invading Catholic Teutonic Knights. After the failure of *Bezhin Meadow,* Eisenstein realized how important it was for him to choose a project that would please the cultural bureaucrats; *Nevsky* seemed appropriate. Soviet film directors have always been highly dependent upon official approval in the pursuit of their art. Their predicament was brutally simple: if they were not granted access to the equipment—all of it owned by the state—they could not make films.

It is possible that Prokofiev and Eisenstein had discussed the project before Prokofiev's tour of Europe and America in early 1938.

Prokofiev's visit to Hollywood, where he took a firsthand look at the latest advances in filmmaking technology, no doubt made the prospect of working with one of the world's great film directors even more attractive. In May 1938, soon after Prokofiev returned, Eisenstein made him an official proposal to compose the music for the new film, already in the early stages of production.

Nevsky would open an important new stage in the careers of both director and composer. It would be Eisenstein's first well-received film in almost ten years, and inspire Prokofiev's first unambiguously successful "nationalistic" music.

Eisenstein's choice of Alexander Nevsky as the focus of a historical film epic was a shrewd one. The subject was nationalistic and sufficiently large in scale to satisfy Stalin's megalomaniacal craving for the pompous and grandiose. The story also had topical significance, since Nevsky's greatest achievement had been to crush the imperialistic aspirations of the invading Germanic forces. As Hitler gained power in Germany, the relevance of this history lesson grew.

The film encouraged audiences to draw a parallel between the heroic Nevsky and Stalin, who always thought of himself as the latest and most glorious in the long line of strong leaders in Russian history. In an essay on the film, Eisenstein enthused, "If the might of the people's spirit could avenge itself so successfully on an enemy even when the country was still exhausted from the fetters of the Tartar yoke, then what force could be strong enough to destroy this country today, now that it has thrown off all chains of oppression? For today our country has become a socialist Motherland, and is led to unprecedented victories by the greatest strategist in world history—STALIN!"

What Eisenstein was unable to foresee, however, was Stalin's changing relationship with Hitler, which veered from apparent friendship after the signing of the nonaggression pact in August 1939 to hatred after the Nazi attack in June 1941. These shifts for a while complicated the fate of Eisenstein's rabidly anti-German film.

To assure that Eisenstein did not repeat the "mistakes" of *Bezhin Meadow*, which lost two million rubles, the giant Mosfilm Studio surrounded him with new advisers "whose task was to see to it that he did not lose his way again." Eisenstein was instructed that *Nevsky* should be direct, patriotic, less intellectual than his earlier films, and aimed at the widest possible audience. The tense international situation was to be reflected in *Nevsky* in order "to prepare . . . every Russian man, woman and child to meet any war which came with a sense of optimism." Party watchdogs were assigned to the project to guide Eisenstein; the actor chosen to play Nevsky, Nikolai Cherkasov, was a prominent Communist Party member and sat on the Supreme Soviet of the U.S.S.R.

Nevsky was also Eisenstein's first completed sound film, and one of the first Soviet sound-film epics. Prokofiev accepted the commission to write the score with pleasure and enthusiasm, for he was more interested than ever in the possibilities of music in cinema, and regarded Eisenstein as "unquestionably our best film director." From the very beginning of their collaboration, Eisenstein and Prokofiev worked exceptionally well and closely together. Like his teacher Meyerhold, Eisenstein knew a great deal about music, and had enormous respect for Prokofiev's talent and rigor. He involved Prokofiev in all aspects of the production. Generally, Prokofiev would see preliminary rushes and then go home to write the music, which he would deliver the next day. Even the highly disciplined Eisenstein was amazed at Prokofiev's rate of creativity and punctuality, as he later described in a colorful article.

". . . At twelve noon you'll have the music." We are coming out of the small projection room. And although it's now midnight, I'm completely calm. At exactly 11:55 A.M., a small dark blue car will drive through the studio gates.

Sergei Prokofiev will get out of it. In his hands will be the next musical number for *Alexander Nevsky*.

We look at a new piece of film at night. In the morning a new piece of music will be ready for it.

Prokofiev works like a clock. This clock isn't fast and it isn't slow.

As the filming progressed, Prokofiev would, for the first time in his work in cinema, sometimes write music for sections before they were shot. Eisenstein would then tailor the rhythm and imagery of his shooting to the score. Prokofiev also helped write the texts for the vocal sections (several for chorus and one for mezzo-soprano solo). Their work went so well that the entire film was finished by November 1938, in the incredibly short span of five months, five months ahead of schedule.

During June, Prokofiev frequently visited shooting sessions. The central episode of the Battle on the Ice, which takes up nearly half of the film, was shot during the summer heat, using crushed asphalt, glass and white sand for snow. "Only the horses failed to behave themselves," Prokofiev joked, "and the 'ice' had to be continuously cleaned off."

In his score—containing twenty-one separate "numbers" — Prokofiev avoided direct citation of music of the era of the action (the thirteenth century), just as he had avoided direct citation in Lt. Kizhe. "Original musical material from the thirteenth century has become so alien to us in an emotional sense that it cannot supply sufficient food for the spectator's imagination," Prokofiev explained.

What he did instead was to use this material as a model, "recomposing" the original themes rhythmically and harmonically, and using the instrumental possibilities of a twentieth-century orchestra. This was, in fact, his guiding principle in using folk music or other "alien" musical material in all of his compositions. One of the best examples from Nevsky is the liturgical chanting, in Latin ("Peregrinus expectavi/Pedes meos in cymbalis"), of the Catholic Teutonic Knights. It remains obviously "Catholic" in its intervals, monotony and rhythm, but these features are grotesquely exaggerated to make a dramatic point and to convey a negative image of the invaders. Catholic Latin chant is used in a very similar manner and for similar purposes in the final act of The Fiery Angel.

In the same way, the songs sung by the Novgorodians—"Arise, Ye Russian People," "Song About Alexander Nevsky," and "On the Field of the Dead"—use phrasing and rhythms familiar in Russian folksong, but, as in Songs of Our Days, these are refracted through Prokofiev's own "modern" style. Great emphasis is placed on a flowing, epically legato line in the music associated with Nevsky and the Russians, which lends their characterization an air of serene nobility and lyrical power.

While working on Nevsky, Prokofiev also discovered the enormous potential of recorded sound. Mixing, distortion and altering the balance offered fascinating new possibilities. He discovered, for example, that changing the usual position of instruments could yield startling dramatic effects. If the bassoons were placed very close to the microphone, and the trombones farther away, their conventional sound relationship was obviously changed. Prokofiev also played with enhanced volume. To make the horns of the Teutonic Crusaders sound even more sinister, he had the brass blow directly into the microphone. "The sounds of their horns would have certainly been unpleasant to the Russian ear," he explained. The possibilities of amplification were also used, to convey the emotional content and rhythm of the action.

What allowed Prokofiev and Eisenstein to work together so successfully was their similar understanding of the active (not just accompanying) role that music could play in film. Eisenstein believed that a film was musical "not when an accordion player comes out onto the screen one minute, and another minute some popular song is sung, and then the rest is only film with conversation," but "where the absence of music on screen feels like a pause or a caesura. Even if that pause sometimes lasts for a whole reel, it should be no less strictly maintained than a calculated rhythmic break in sound, no less strictly counted than measures of rests."

Eisenstein also believed that the rhythm and emotional impact of the music should often work in counterpoint against the rhythm and emotional impact of the visual image, depending on the desired effect. He avoided obvious and literal sound-image connections. Naturalistic sounds emanating from the visual image—for example, the sound of women crying—are not always reproduced; instead, music is heard in the background to express the emotion of sorrow.

As Prokofiev was viewing the newly completed pieces of *Nevsky* in the screening room—before he had written the music—he would tap his fingers, finding the rhythm of the scenes. These rhythms (rhythm and meter were always a central structural principle in his music anyway, often more important than harmony or counterpoint) would provide the basis for the musical texture. In setting music to a text (particularly in *Betrothal in a Monastery* and *War and Peace*) he often worked in a similar manner, "fitting" the music over the rhythmic skeleton formed by the accentual patterns of the words and lines.

Prokofiev's uncanny ability to understand and interpret musically the rhythm of a given scene, and to delineate the rhythmic/emotional contrast between shots and scenes (montage) amazed Eisenstein. "Prokofiev's music is incredibly plastic; it never becomes mere illustration," he said. In Prokofiev, he and his cinematographer Edward Tisse "found the third companion in our crusade for the kind of sound cinema we had been dreaming about."

Working on *Nevsky* took virtually all of Prokofiev's time during the late spring, summer and early fall of 1938. To finish it on schedule, he had to abandon temporarily another project, the often delayed and nearly completed First Cello Concerto (Op. 58). Until early summer, Prokofiev remained in Moscow, then left the city to spend time in the countryside at Beryozovye Roshcha ("Birch Groves"), near Nikolina Gora, where, as in the preceding summer, he let part of a summer *dacha*. Early in July, he went south to the Caucasus, staying first at a House of Rest high in the mountains in Teberda, "the roof of the world," and then in his beloved resort of Kislovodsk. Even after returning to Moscow in the fall, Prokofiev was "up to my ears" in *Nevsky,* and twice postponed a planned trip to Leningrad so he could finish it.

In his few spare moments, Prokofiev was sketching out another big project—his first "Soviet" opera. By the time he arrived in Teberda, he had already conferred at length with the novelist Valentin Kataev, who was preparing a libretto from his novel *I Am a Son of the Working People.*

A prominent member of the Soviet literary establishment and a very popular novelist, Kataev was a "safe" choice. His most famous work, *Time, Forward,* a "Five-Year Plan novel," described the frenetic construction of a huge coke-chemical industrial complex in Siberia. *I Am a Son of the Working People,* published in 1937, was both less interesting and less innovative. This conventionally narrated and heavily didactic novel dealt with the chaotic political situation in the Ukraine in the years immediately after the 1917 Revolution—when German forces in temporary occupation there fought against the newly created Red Army—and contained most of the ingredients Soviet composers were encouraged to insert into their operas, including a folksy setting, a positive hero and nasty enemies of Communism.

Kataev and Prokofiev had very little in common, either in background or in personality, and never became close friends. They were slightly acquainted before their collaboration, mainly through occasional conversations at the Writers' Club. To Kataev, a former journalist from Odessa, Prokofiev was rather unapproachable—"very decisive, exact, abrupt and unsentimental." Nor did Kataev's limited knowledge of music and opera help. When they first discussed the project, Kataev told the horrified Prokofiev he wanted their opera to be "in the style of *Carmen,* or Verdi, something that could be performed everywhere." Prokofiev, whose career as an operatic composer—at least so far— had been devoted to a rejection of that tradition, responded with disdain. "I don't want that," he said. "I don't recognize that kind of opera.

There will be no arias, there will be no verses—your prose text as it stands will be entirely satisfactory."

At the same time, Prokofiev was aware of the danger of working with a topical subject. He wrote Vera Alpers that "I want something different than he has in the novel—without propaganda, which quickly goes out of style." He also changed the tendentious title, calling the opera *Semyon Kotko* after its peasant hero.

Beginning *Semyon Kotko* and finishing *Nevsky* were not the only projects that occupied Prokofiev during the busy autumn of 1938. He also completed the First Cello Concerto, and started conferring with the choreographer Leonid Lavrovsky about staging *Romeo and Juliet* at the Kirov in Leningrad.

Although Prokofiev was happy at the prospect of finally seeing a production of *Romeo* in Russia, he was annoyed by the many changes in the score and scenario which Lavrovsky was requesting. As usual, he did not hide his feelings. After listening to Lavrovsky explain why the music for a certain section had to be rewritten,

> Prokofiev was silent. Wrinkling up his nose, he made a rather sour face, expressing his obvious displeasure. How familiar this gesture became to me later on—but then I was seeing it for the first time. I must say that Sergei Sergeevich responded to my suggestions— necessitated by dramatic considerations—with great difficulty and extreme unwillingness.

Even after all the problems he had already encountered over *Romeo*, Prokofiev remained firm in the defense of his music, and fought tenaciously against what he considered unnecessary changes in the score. From the start of their collaboration in the fall of 1938 until the Kirov premiere on January 11, 1940, Prokofiev and Lavrovsky had an argumentative, lively and far from easy relationship.

In early November, Prokofiev took a few days off from his routine and traveled to the Arctic port city of Arkhangelsk for a joint recital with Lina, who sang some songs and "The Ugly Duckling." They admired the brilliant northern sunsets and the city's wooden sidewalks, built to withstand the yearly onslaught of snow, ice and polar cold.

As busy as he was, Prokofiev did find some time for his children. Around this time, he was invited to perform at Oleg's school in connection with one of the many Soviet political holidays.

> To a ten-year-old schoolboy, the idea seemed impertinent, and so the invitation was conveyed with trepidation. To my surprise, Father

readily agreed. I was more nervous that evening than I would have been if I had to perform myself, since I did not realize that, for him, the whole thing was amusing. But to play that awful piano — completely out of tune—for a noisy, undisciplined crowd that knew nothing about music ("Dad's music"). . . . I was worried that something would go wrong.

I cannot remember what he played; probably some early, easily accessible gavotte, perhaps the march from *Three Oranges*. Every note must have been so familiar that, in my state, I couldn't possibly tell what was what. My classmates enjoyed themselves, sticking out their tongues and pointing fingers at me, while I suffered and blushed because of squeaky chairs, whispering people, untuned strings— but I think everyone was actually quite attentive. But my suffering was to continue. Having taken his bow, my father apparently decided that this was insufficiently festive, and on his way offstage, without turning around, playfully waved his hand at the audience; this drove the audience into a frenzy of joy, as if that gesture was the high point of his appearance.

Preoccupied with performances and composing, Prokofiev probably paid little attention to the disturbing news that was coming from Europe as 1938 ended. Hitler was poised to occupy Czechoslovakia, having received the Sudetenland from Great Britain and France under the agreement signed by Chamberlain in Munich in September. Soon after, his armies would invade Poland.

For Prokofiev, though, 1938 ended well—with three world premieres in the space of five weeks. On November 26, the cellist Beryozovsky performed the First Cello Concerto with the State Symphony Orchestra in Moscow. On December 1, *Alexander Nevsky* had its official opening, also in Moscow. And on December 30, far away in Brno, Czechoslovakia, *Romeo and Juliet* finally reached the stage.

Prokofiev had been working on his First Cello Concerto since 1934, although he had repeatedly laid it aside to complete other projects. No sooner had Beryozovsky given its highly anticipated premiere, however, than the critics attacked it with a rare and unfortunate unanimity. According to Sviatoslav Richter, who worked with Beryozovsky as he was rehearsing, the premiere was a "complete failure." So devastating were the reviews and the remarks he heard from his colleagues that Prokofiev (uncharacteristically) withdrew the concerto from circulation soon after.

Alexander Nevsky was as wildly successful as the Cello Concerto was disappointing. *Nevsky* was an immediate hit with Stalin, whose alleged response after seeing it was to slap Eisenstein on the back and declare: "Sergei Mikhailovich, you are a good Bolshevik after all!" Both Eisenstein and Cherkasov (Nevsky) were awarded the prestigious Order of Lenin, and Prokofiev's heroic music received lavish praise. This was Prokofiev's first large-scale popular success for his new Soviet audience, and earned him a great deal of money. Soviet schoolchildren at play sang the choruses, and the film was screened all over the U.S.S.R.

Nevsky came at a crucial moment for Prokofiev, when Soviet artists were literally under the gun to produce work that pleased Stalin and promoted the appropriate ideological line. Its success helps to explain why he and Eisenstein would be spared in the purges that were already engulfing so many others around them. Eisenstein was so happy with the result and with Prokofiev's music that he tried to persuade him to collaborate on another film the following summer, but Prokofiev was overloaded with other projects. They would not work together again until 1942, on *Ivan the Terrible*.

After *Nevsky* was released, Prokofiev set to work fashioning a concert cantata from its score. This was a challenging task, since he had to rethink the effects created by recorded sound and find an appropriate form. In the end, he scored the cantata for a mezzo-soprano soloist (who appears in only one section, "On the Field of the Dead"), mixed chorus and orchestra, and divided it into seven large sections corresponding to the broad outline of the film's narrative: "Russia Under the Mongol Yoke," "A Song About Alexander Nevsky," "The Crusaders in Pskov," "Arise, Ye Russian People," "The Battle on the Ice," "On the Field of the Dead" and "Alexander's Entry into Pskov."

Like the film, the *Alexander Nevsky* Cantata has enjoyed unflagging popularity (except for the brief period of Stalin's "friendship" with Hitler, when its anti-German sentiments became an embarrassment) since its first performance the following spring in Moscow. One of its few detractors was Dmitri Shostakovich, who after hearing it for the first time wrote to Prokofiev: "Despite a number of amazing moments, I did not like this composition as a whole. It seems to me that it breaks some aesthetic norms. There is too much physically loud illustrative music." Even so, Shostakovich told Prokofiev he hoped *Nevsky* would receive a Stalin Prize, since "it is worth as much as many of the other candidates." But Prokofiev would have to wait a few more years for his first Stalin Prize.

In December, the same month when *Alexander Nevsky* was released, *Romeo and Juliet* also took the stage at last—but in Czechoslovakia, not Russia. Prokofiev was not there to see it. Always insistent on giving premieres where they would receive the most attention, he would not have been satisfied with the first *Romeo*, produced in unimposing fashion in the Czech provincial capital of Brno on December 30, danced by the Yugoslav National Ballet of Zagreb and choreographed by Vania Psota. (Psota also took the role of Romeo.) Little has been written about this production, which was overshadowed by the ambitious Soviet *Romeo* at the Kirov one year later, featuring Galina Ulanova's definitive Juliet.

The winter that followed these three premieres was as uneventful for Prokofiev as the autumn had been hectic. A planned concert tour to America was mysteriously canceled—it seems fair to assume that the tense political situation in Europe, the uncertain domestic atmosphere under the purges (at their height in late 1938 and early 1939) and the Soviet crackdown on foreign travel were the reasons.

In late October 1938, Prokofiev had received a letter from Ephraim Gottlieb, the Chicago insurance agent who had taken a great interest in him after his visit to Chicago earlier in the year, inquiring about his plans. "The Chicago music lovers are looking forward with great anticipation to your appearance at Orchestra Hall on February 7," he wrote. "The manager of the concert tells me that the house is already sold out for that night. . . . I am at a loss to understand why you never answered my letters regarding appearances next summer at the Hollywood Bowl, Lewisohn Stadium and Ravinia Park." It is difficult to believe that Prokofiev, a compulsive and meticulous correspondent, would have failed to inform Gottlieb of any change in his schedule if he had been able to, or that he did not want to travel to the United States.

Prokofiev's formerly thriving correspondence with various friends and business associates in Europe and America dropped off drastically after 1938. No doubt he was advised that it was wiser, under the prevailing xenophobic atmosphere, to curtail his exchange of letters, which might be read by the mail censors and held against him in some way, as had happened to numerous victims of the purges. Whatever all the reasons, his horizons were clearly shrinking.

Semyon Kotko was by now Prokofiev's main new project. A production at the Opera Studio in Moscow (renamed the Stanislavsky-Nemirovich-Danchenko Musical Theater) was planned for the end of the spring season. Until recently, the theatre had been run by Stanislavsky himself. In early 1938, he had magnanimously appointed his former student Meyerhold as his assistant, several months after Meyerhold's own theatre had been closed down. Stanislavsky died only a few months after appointing Meyerhold, who then took over his job—briefly, as it turned out—as artistic director of the Opera Studio. Now that he had a new forum, Meyerhold invited Prokofiev to give the premiere of *Semyon Kotko* at the Opera Studio.

By the time Meyerhold began working with Prokofiev on *Semyon Kotko*, however, his political position was dangerously precarious, which helps to explain why he had so much less influence on the composition of *Semyon Kotko* than on *The Gambler* or *Love for Three Oranges*. His nonrealistic techniques, and his fondness for sarcasm and irony, were considered heretical by the high priests of Socialist Realism—so heretical that his theatre had been closed down and he was under constant attack in the press. Prokofiev must have been aware of this as they were collaborating on *Semyon Kotko*.

The project was further complicated by Kataev's participation as co-librettist. Kataev and Meyerhold represented diametrically opposed artistic views, and held very different opinions on how *Semyon Kotko* should be written and staged. Kataev envisioned something realistic, accessible and tuneful; Meyerhold's operatic productions had ridiculed realism, sentimentality and the standard conventions of the genre. Thus there was a three-way tug-of-war between Prokofiev, Kataev and Meyerhold in creating the opera, which helps to explain *Semyon*'s oddly half-hearted musical and dramatic personality, and the difficult future that awaited it.

In his own statements, Prokofiev was unusually cautious.

To write an opera on a Soviet theme is by no means a simple task. One is dealing with new people, new emotions, a new way of life. Many forms applicable to classical opera might be unsuitable. An aria sung by the chairman of a village Soviet could, with the slightest awkwardness on the composer's part, be extremely puzzling to the listener. One could also easily misinterpret the recitative of a Commissar making a telephone call.

I had long wanted to write a Soviet opera, but hesitated to undertake the job until I had a clear idea of how to approach it. Nor was it easy to find a plot. I did not want a commonplace, static, trivial plot—or a plot that pointed too obvious a moral. I wanted live flesh-and-blood human beings with human passions, love, hatred,

joy and sorrow arising naturally out of our new conditions of life. . . .
This is what attracted me to Valentin Kataev's novel.

From March until June, as Europe rushed toward war, Prokofiev
would meet with Kataev at his *dacha* on the River Klyazma to work
on the libretto.

> The work went at an intense pace. Prokofiev was terribly pedantic
> in his work. He was constantly driving me. If some act or scene had
> to be written, he would demand persistently: "Hand it over, what
> are you doing, anyway? You're irritating me."
>
> He would take it, grab it, and go off to Moscow. . . . When
> we were deciding how to construct a scene, Prokofiev would often
> play through musical fragments. . . . I remember well how he would
> arrive at our house and then play the piano with his long, powerful
> hands. He was very excited by the idea, by the opera.

The libretto was written almost entirely in prose (like *The Gambler* and
The Fiery Angel), although Kataev kept trying to persuade Prokofiev
to include some "folksy" verses.

What literary charm Kataev's novel does possess resides largely
in its language—which makes extensive use of "quaint" Ukrainian
turns of phrase—and in the elaborate description of peasant village
rituals, particularly those surrounding courtship, engagement and marriage. Emphasis is placed on external events and behavior, not on
psychological development or analysis. As in most works of Socialist
Realism, there is little change in the characters from the beginning of
the story to the end: for the most part, they are "types."

The "positive hero," Semyon Kotko, is a virtuous peasant called
up to serve as a gunner—first in the Tsarist army, then in the army
of the Provisional Government, and finally in the Red Army. He is
unambiguously enthusiastic about the advent of Soviet power in his
village, finally liberated from the oppressive control of the greedy
landowners. He is good to his aging mother and protects his younger
sister, Frosya. His sweetheart, Sofya, is the daughter of a rich peasant
opposed to the Communists and to Semyon; this conflict is the basis
of the plot.

In the course of the story, which takes place before World War
I has ended but after Soviet Russia has withdrawn from the fighting,
German forces invade and occupy the village. (In the years immediately
following the 1917 Revolution, the Ukraine changed hands several

times. It was ruled in turn by an independent local government, the Germans, the Bolsheviks and the anti-Communist Whites before finally becoming a part of the U.S.S.R. in late 1919.) Semyon flees to the forest, where he joins the anti-German partisan forces already gathered there. Failing in his attempt to rescue Sofya from a forced marriage to the one remaining heir of the former landowning family, Semyon is taken prisoner.

But soon after, the partisans retake the village, freeing Semyon and sentencing Sofya's evil father to death. The novel ends with an epilogue twenty years later: Semyon has become the exemplary manager of an aluminum plant and his son is a Red Army soldier. Frosya has become the director of a model pig farm "that is famous throughout the Soviet Union."

In *Semyon Kotko*, Prokofiev attempted to satisfy the demands placed on Soviet operatic composers to depict Soviet reality and the supposedly idealistic aspirations of the Magnificent Soviet People. Composers who did not address such issues were likely to be reprimanded (or even worse), as the case of Shostakovich's *Lady Macbeth* had made abundantly clear. What most pleased Stalin was a form that came to be known as "song opera," a light, tuneful and highly politicized genre actually closer to operetta or musical comedy. This form exercised an obvious influence on *Semyon Kotko*.

And yet Prokofiev also tried to compose a serious opera that was consistent with his own aesthetic beliefs and experience. As in *The Gambler* and *The Fiery Angel*, he strove to avoid static moments in the action. Hoping to achieve a sense of continuous dramatic movement, he introduced the same montage-like structure used in his film scores and in *Romeo and Juliet*. The five acts and seven scenes of *Semyon Kotko* are divided into forty-eight short cinematic episodes *(stseny)*, most lasting only a few minutes and often occupying no more than three of four pages of the score. Meyerhold no doubt approved of this fragmentary structure, although Kataev did not.

The grotesque exaggeration found in the vocal parts and rhythms associated with the negative characters—such as the German military villains and the wealthy anti-Communist peasants—may also have been suggested by Meyerhold. Such caricature is reminiscent of *The Gambler* and *Love for Three Oranges*, but here it serves an explicitly political function.

But Meyerhold's influence on *Semyon Kotko* was incomplete and diluted. The opera is a transitional work, perched between Prokofiev's earlier operatic style—which rejected realism, "libretto verse," set pieces and conventional dramatic structure—and his later operatic style. In these later "Soviet" operas—*War and Peace, Story of a Real Man* and to some extent *Betrothal in a Monastery*—he would return to nineteenth-century operatic traditions, include rhymed verse and "set pieces," and focus on "real" characters in real historical situations.

Despite its hybrid personality, *Semyon* does have numerous interesting musical and dramatic moments. Among them are the choruses sung by the village women as part of the matchmaking procedure; the raucous concluding episode of Act III, in which a fire set by the Germans engulfs the village, building to an enormous ostinato-based climax similar to the one at the end of *The Fiery Angel;* and the pure lyrical melodies sung by Semyon and Sofya. Melody was, in fact, of utmost importance to Prokofiev as he composed *Semyon*.

As work on the opera continued intensively throughout the spring, Meyerhold's political situation deteriorated even further. On June 13, the national Conference of Stage Directors, an important forum for official cultural policy, opened in Moscow. Meyerhold was invited to give a speech to the assembled delegates. The proceedings remained secret, and Meyerhold's exact words are still a matter of debate, but it is clear he refused to "apologize" for his former "mistakes." Instead, defiant and unbowed, he insisted on the right of Soviet stage directors— along with all other Soviet artists—to experiment, to express themselves freely without fear of punishment, and to seek new techniques. He was also critical of the increasing regimentation in the dramatic repertoire and in production style, which he rejected as harmful to the pluralistic atmosphere necessary for the creation of true art.

Meyerhold's speech shocked the assembly and proved to be the last straw for Stalin and his cultural commissars. Such openly heretical artists could not be allowed to remain in responsible and prominent positions from which they could spread their subversive ideas.

A few days after his speech, on June 20, 1939, Vsevolod Meyerhold, one of Prokofiev's oldest friends and most talented collaborators, and one of the most original thinkers in the history of the modern theatre, was arrested—only a week before Prokofiev finished the piano score of *Semyon Kotko*. Prokofiev and Meyerhold had tried for twenty years, but they had not succeeded in bringing a single production to the stage.

Soon after Meyerhold's arrest, his wife, the actress Zinaida Raikh, was found murdered in their apartment. Her body was mutilated, covered with stab wounds. According to official Soviet reports, her death was the work of unknown "thugs." Less than one year later, Meyerhold was executed in prison.

There is no evidence that Prokofiev came to Meyerhold's defense after his arrest, although Meyerhold had often defended Prokofiev from the charge of "émigré-ism" during the 1920s. It is possible Prokofiev was not sure what had happened to Meyerhold or where he was. It is even more possible that he was afraid for himself and his family.

While he failed to register his response publicly, Prokofiev must have felt Meyerhold's disappearance as a traumatic and sobering blow. The terrible reality of the society in which he had chosen to live out his life was suddenly exposed in all its brutality. One of his most trusted advisers, one of the great artists of the twentieth century and a friend who had shared his eccentric sense of absurd humor had simply disappeared. His name would be erased from Soviet theatrical history for decades to come. In the huge volume of material published on Prokofiev in the U.S.S.R. in 1961, Meyerhold's name merited only one mention, in an obscure footnote in tiny print buried in the appendix.

In that same collection, Serafima Birman, the director who would eventually replace Meyerhold in staging *Semyon Kotko*, wrote cryptically, "The theatre named after the People's Artist of the Soviet Union K. S. Stanislavsky assigned me to finish the work on the opera begun— but left unfinished—by another director."

As a result of Meyerhold's arrest, the fate of *Semyon Kotko* was greatly complicated. For Prokofiev, the opera must have forever after evoked uncomfortable associations with his old friend. The production would be staged the following season, but problems would continue to haunt it.

With Meyerhold's death, Prokofiev's eyes were opened to evil and a certain innocence was lost forever. Even worse, he and Lina could no longer escape by traveling abroad—they were in a real sense prisoners in the U.S.S.R. It must have now become even more difficult to confront Lina's understandable dissatisfaction with their life in Moscow, since he was more powerless than ever to change it. He must also have realized that he and Lina could themselves become targets of Stalin's displeasure. Already vulnerable as a foreigner and an outsider, Lina had good reason to feel especially uneasy; in the hysterically paranoid atmosphere, Prokofiev's colleagues may well have regarded his non-Russian wife with increased suspicion and uncertainty. If Prokofiev had previously felt guilty about her fate, he must have felt that guilt much more intensely now. These extraordinary pessures could only have exacerbated any difficulties that existed in their marital life.

Threatened and confused, Prokofiev was ready to take support and affection where he could find them.

CHAPTER 19

MIRA

All ages submit to love.

—ALEXANDER PUSHKIN,
Eugene Onegin

igh among the snowy peaks of the Caucasus, its dry alpine air warmed by the southern sun, Kislovodsk was one of Prokofiev's favorite places. It was there he had spent so many happy summers with his mother as a boy and later as a precocious Conservatory student; that he first heard about the Bolshevik Revolution; that he composed *Seven, They Are Seven,* and the Second and Fourth Piano Sonatas. For Prokofiev, Kislovodsk held many happy memories.

He spent part of the summer of 1939 in Kislovodsk, resting and composing—alone. For the first time in several years he did not spend any time in Nikolina Gora. Lina was vacationing separately, and the children had been sent to summer camp.

Sources on Prokofiev's activities that summer in Kislovodsk are scarce—as they are for the next few years—but all available ones agree that it was then and there he met a young woman who would play a very important part in his life from that point on: Maria-Cecilia Abramovna Mendelson. Everyone called her Mira. Prokofiev was exactly twice as old as she; when they met, he was forty-eight and she was twenty-four. Born in 1915 in Kiev, Mira was an only child whose father, Abram, was a respected professor and economist. He also happened to be a Jew. At the time Prokofiev met her, Mira was an aspiring writer and a student at a prestigious literary institute in Moscow, today known as the Gorky Literary Institute.

Photographs show that Mira was not an especially beautiful woman—slim, almost skinny, with a thin face and strong features. Awkward, shy and even clumsy, she did not shine in social situations. Unlike Lina, she dressed without special care or style, although in 1939 Soviet women could hardly do otherwise. In almost every way, she was Lina's opposite—plain while Lina was glamorous; intellectual while Lina was a socialite; retiring while Lina was gregarious; introverted while Lina was extroverted; unsophisticated while Lina was at home in nearly all the world capitals. Mira had never traveled to the West—so familiar to Prokofiev—and knew of the world beyond the Soviet Union only through books, which she adored.

In her several brief articles on life with Prokofiev, Mira avoided the personal, concentrating instead on music and literature. One of her strongest memories of the summer of 1939 in Kislovodsk was hearing Prokofiev talk about reading Romain Rolland's book on Beethoven, which she claims influenced him in his work on the Sixth, Seventh and Eighth Piano Sonatas, all first conceived in Kislovodsk. Mira's emotional reticence is hardly surprising, given the very awkward and difficult circumstances of the early years of her relationship with Prokofiev. It also conforms with the Soviet practice of biography, which, particularly in the case of cultural icons like Prokofiev, has always downplayed an artist's personal life and psychology, instead emphasizing the influence of social and economic issues.

Some accounts of Prokofiev's life that have appeared in the West have claimed that Mira was a Communist Party member, and even a niece of Stalin's favorite, Lazar Kaganovich. Others have said that she was a member of the KGB sent on a mission to "get" Prokofiev and remove him from the supposedly malignant influence of the non-Russian Lina. There is, however, absolutely no factual basis to these allegations, and they have been denied even by Lina herself. It is true that Mira's father was for many years a prominent Marxist, but he was an academic and did not move in high government circles. Judging from the modest life Mira later led with Prokofiev, it seems highly unlikely she had access to any special influence or harbored any political ambitions. One reliable Soviet source, a friend to Mira for many years, has asserted that she never even joined the Communist Party. (Neither did Prokofiev.)

What all these stories do prove is just how polarized, politicized and mysterious the atmosphere around Prokofiev became after he met

Mira. Since communication between the Soviet Union and the West—where Prokofiev and Lina still had many friends—would be so difficult in the coming years, it was easy for wild rumors to arise, distorting and politicizing what was in fact a fairly simple case of a new romance and a broken marriage.

Accounts of Prokofiev's life written by anti-Soviet Russian émigrés (notably Victor Seroff), who attempted to prove that Prokofiev's decision to return to Communist Russia was exclusively harmful to him both personally and musically, and that there was something suspicious about his relationship with Mira, are in their own way no less biased than those written by Soviet authors (notably Nestyev), who have tried to prove exactly the opposite. The truth of the matter—at least for Prokofiev—lies somewhere in between: he gave up a great deal by leaving Paris, but he also found a new inspiration and strength in Russia. For Lina, who would suffer terribly as the result of her husband's decision to return to the U.S.S.R., the issue is more clear-cut. Sympathy among émigré Russians over her difficult situation also helps to explain the origin of some of the accusations made against Mira.

What was it about this young and unremarkable woman that led Prokofiev to break up a sixteen-year-old marriage?

Strangely enough, one attraction may well have been her very Soviet provinciality. Although she had never traveled abroad, Mira was much more familiar with Soviet reality than Lina, who, not being Russian, relied on Prokofiev to guide her. But Prokofiev had spent so much time outside the U.S.S.R. that he, too, was unsure of the social, cultural and political rules. Mira, a native Soviet who was only two years old at the time of the 1917 Revolution, could help him. And encountering a young girl awed by his reputation and talent, prepared to sacrifice herself for him and his art, must have been seductive to Prokofiev after dealing with the difficulties and strains that had developed in his relationship with Lina since their move to Moscow in 1936.

Another important source of Prokofiev's attraction for Mira was her literary training and aspirations. Alhough her literary talent was modest, she read a great deal and would soon begin to collaborate with him on song texts and operas. Perhaps Prokofiev also felt that she would be able to help him select literary sources that would find favor with the cultural bureaucrats. Soon after they met, they began discussing possible sources for operas, ballets and songs; within a year she was helping him write the first of several libretti. She would also help him with his nonfictional writing, and patiently record and preserve his autobiographical memories for posterity.

Prokofiev's attraction to Mira was not primarily sexual, but intellectual; she offered him creative companionship and complete devotion. Dazzled by his great talent, she was willing to sacrifice any artistic ambitions of her own to help him. After the many difficulties of the preceding few years, and particularly after the disturbing Meyerhold affair, the quiet, simple and uncomplicated support Mira seemed to be offering him must have been very appealing. Sometime later, after he had been living with Mira for a few years, Prokofiev told a colleague that compared to her, Lina was "a beautiful desert." In the letters he wrote to Miaskovsky in coming years, Prokofiev made frequent and obvious mention of Mira, often calling her by an affectionate nickname, Mirochka. Both he and Miaskovsky had always referred to Lina in their correspondence as Lina Ivanovna, the formal term of address.

A role as Prokofiev's secretary, companion and source of encouragement apparently satisfied Mira. Unlike Lina, she was not a musician, and did not attempt to compete with him in that arena.

The relationship between Prokofiev and Mira developed slowly, intensifying over the course of several years. Little information is available on the exact circumstances of their first and subsequent meetings during the summer of 1939 in Kislovodsk. One of the most detailed accounts of Prokofiev's life there comes from Serafima Birman, who, recently assigned to replace Meyerhold as director of *Semyon Kotko*, happened to be vacationing at the same time in Kislovodsk, a resort popular with artists, intellectuals and prominent politicians. Even before Birman had received a letter from Moscow asking her to take over *Semyon*, she had seen Prokofiev playing tennis.

"It didn't seem to me that Sergei Sergeevich was a good tennis player, but his inexhaustible passion for the game was obvious," Birman said later. "Each volley that he failed to return caused him torments, and he would argue with his open-mouthed partner. He took defeat hard and was delighted with victory. I remember a green visor that protected Sergei Sergeevich from the blinding sun, his hot excited face under the visor, and the quick changes in his expression depending on how the game was going."

When she began meeting with the composer to plan the production of *Semyon*, she found him arrogant and distant—as most people did upon his first acquaintance. It must also have been difficult for Prokofiev to entrust to a young and unknown director the opera he had dreamed of staging with Meyerhold. (Birman was better known as an actress, and would later appear in the Eisenstein-Prokofiev film *Ivan the Terrible* as Ivan's conniving relative.) One day, Prokofiev came over from the sanatorium where he was staying and appeared in Birman's hotel room to acquaint her with the story and music.

> My room was furnished extremely simply: a table, two chairs, a bed and wardrobe, a bookshelf on the wall. A piano was out of the question. All the same, Sergei Sergeevich played! and sang!! *Semyon Kotko* from a to z!!!, all without leaving this confining sanatorium cell. The bed became his piano. He put two chairs in front of it, sat down in the one on the left and ordered me to take the one on the right—"Sit down!" He sat on the edge of the chair, like a pianist on the concert stage, then lowered his hands to the bed, covered with a white blanket. But it was clear that he didn't see a blanket— in front of him was the keyboard of a precious piano. He began playing the overture.

Prokofiev continued this way for two hours, until he had "played" her the entire opera. They would begin rehearsals of *Semyon* the following winter.

When Prokofiev left Kislovodsk to return to Moscow, he and Mira resumed their separate lives. He went back to his apartment and family, and it became difficult for them to see each other. But they did continue meeting: sometimes Prokofiev would give the chauffeur time off and he would sit with Mira in his little blue Ford and talk. Prokofiev's friends and colleagues started seeing them together around the city. Outwardly, however, there was no change in Prokofiev's routine. He continued to perform regularly—although a planned joint recital with Lina in Leningrad in early October was canceled "due to illness."

Prokofiev's relationship with Mira made its first public apearance in a cycle of Seven Songs (Op. 79) that he completed that autumn. Mira supplied the verse text for the fifth song, "Bravely Forward." Like most of the songs in this cycle, it is resolutely nationalistic, and indistinguishable from thousands of other patriotic verses set constantly by Soviet composers. "Bravely forward! Red Army, bulwark of peace, into combat! You will meet the hostile regiments with bayonets ready, you will stand firm, like a wall of green." The remaining two verses sing the praises of the Soviet system that the fighting of the civil war protected.

That same autumn, Prokofiev composed another tendentious "Soviet" work, a cantata for chorus and orchestra called *Zdravitsa* (Op. 85). The title is the Russian word for a congratulatory toast. An English subtitle—"Hail to Stalin"—has sometimes been added; the cantata was intended as a sixtieth-birthday tribute to the Great Leader. The text is an eclectic collage using various Russian, Ukrainian, Belorussian, Mordovian, Kumyk (one of the nationalities of the Republic of Daghestan), Kurd and Mari folk sources, and glorifies the development of the U.S.S.R. under Stalin. Though scored for large orchestra, *Zdravitsa* is rather restrained in mood; the prevailing musical image, arising in part from the prominent role given to the strings and harp, is of happy pastoral serenity, under a firm but benevolent *pater familias*.

Since Stalin liked to hear himself and Soviet life portrayed in precisely such imagery, *Zdravitsa* was one of Prokofiev's most officially successful attempts in the genre of the political cantata. First performed in Moscow on December 21, 1939, it was judged edifying and accessible enough to be broadcast on loudspeakers "in all the squares and streets of Moscow. Incredibly lonely it seemed as it resounded throughout deserted Chkalov Street, where we lived then," Oleg Prokofiev has recalled. "Winter, the wind whirling snowflakes over the dark, gloomy asphalt, and the national choir booming out these strange harmonies. I was used to them, though, and that reassured me. I ran home to tell the big news: 'Daddy! They're playing you outside . . .' But he already knew; and, as usual, the matter was never discussed again."

If Prokofiev did hold Stalin in any way responsible for Meyerhold's death, he was forced to praise him anyway—like many others.

At the same time that he was writing this extravagantly extroverted paean to Communism, however, Prokofiev was working on some equally introverted music—three new piano sonatas. According to Mira, Prokofiev began working on his Sixth, Seventh and Eighth Piano Sonatas simultaneously during the second half of 1939, after being away from this form for sixteen years. One is tempted to make a connection between his rekindled interest in the piano sonata and his new romantic feelings for Mira, which, perhaps, created a store of "intimate" energy that found natural expression in a small and personal medium. (That he wrote the Fifth Piano Sonata in 1923, during another "romantic period" in his life, just before marrying Lina, seems to support that theory.) For Prokofiev the tranquil surroundings of Kislovodsk, where he and Mira met, had always been conducive to piano sonatas.

Prokofiev's relationship to the piano, the instrument that first made him famous and for which he had written some of his greatest music, had always been strong and close. Acutely aware of the piano's possibilities and special musical personality, he thought as a performer when he wrote for it. Perhaps his return to piano music in 1939, during a turbulent period in his life, was an attempt to reaffirm and draw strength from the original pure sources of his music. In any case, the Sixth, Seventh and Eighth Sonatas, written at the height of Prokofiev's artistic maturity and command, contain some of his most magnificent, intense and profound music—in any genre.

Initially, Prokofiev worked on all ten movements of the three sonatas at the same time, flitting from one to another as his interest flagged. This was not unusual in the context of his working method; he had always tended to think in terms of themes and separate pieces, rarely in entire compositions. (That same approach had allowed him to transfer chunks and themes from one work to another so easily— from *Ivan the Terrible* to *War and Peace*, or from the "Classical" Symphony to *Romeo and Juliet*.) After this preliminary phase, however, Prokofiev did begin to concentrate on one sonata, which became the Sixth. It would be completed by the early spring of 1940.

What remained of Prokofiev's creative energy was going to the upcoming Kirov production of *Romeo and Juliet*. He was present in Leningrad for many of the rehearsals, which did not go smoothly. Galina Ulanova, who would become famous in the role of Juliet, used to notice Prokofiev in the auditorium. "From the day of the first read-through a rather sullen, tall man sat in the hall almost every time. He looked around with hostility and anger—especially at our dancers."

But what irritated and offended Prokofiev more than the dancers were the many changes Lavrovsky was making in the score—often without consulting him beforehand. Hardly a stranger to ballet and choreography, Prokofiev had never been unwilling to make changes in his music during the years of his association with Diaghilev and the Ballets Russes. But Diaghilev would always point out to him why it should be changed and they would exchange opinions; the impresario had never altered the music without Prokofiev's knowledge or permission.

At the Kirov, Prokofiev found that Lavrovsky and others involved with the production were cutting and adding to his score at will. Lavrovsky insisted, for example, that the first scene of Act I needed another dance number, but Prokofiev disagreed, replying testily, "Make do with what music there is." Undaunted, Lavrovsky persevered, and, selecting the *Scherzo* from Prokofiev's Second Piano Sonata, called it "Morning Dance" and inserted it into the ballet.

> "You have no right to do that. I won't orchestrate this number," Prokofiev shouted indignantly when he saw the insertion on the rehearsal stage.
>
> "What's to be done," Lavorovsky replied. "We'll play it on two pianos, and that would be awkward for you."
>
> Prokofiev got up and left the rehearsal. For several days we didn't see each other and didn't telephone.

Although Lavrovsky has claimed that he and Prokofiev eventually developed a congenial working relationship, Prokofiev never forgot or forgave the choreographer's insolence in tampering with a score over which he had worked so hard and which had been conceived as an artistic and dramatic whole. Each piece had its function and place; the ballet was not a collection of interchangeable numbers in the style of Minkus. The Ballets Russes had always operated in a spirit of true collaboration, but the experience with Lavrovsky and the Kirov showed Prokofiev that dealing with Soviet theatres was a very difficult proposition. Here, his rights and desires as the composer counted for much less. By the time he came to write his 1941 autobiography, Prokofiev's anger had cooled somewhat (or was edited), for he said merely that the Kirov production had "deviated somewhat from the authoritative version."

His quarrels with Lavrovsky and his feelings of impotence made Prokofiev even more grouchy than usual during the rehearsals. He frightened Ulanova and the other dancers, who found him unreasonably demanding, condescending and stiff. Ulanova and her partner complained that Prokofiev's orchestration was inaudible on stage, as in the scene of the lovers' parting at the beginning of Act III. "I know what you need—you need drums, not music," Prokofiev shouted. On this occasion, however, at least according to Ulanova, Prokofiev eventually yielded, agreeing to bolster the orchestration after he was persuaded to sit on stage on the spot from which they needed to hear the music.

As the rehearsals progressed, both dancers and musicians became more comfortable both with the "un-balletic" (at least to them) score and with Prokofiev's jagged personality. Lavrovsky later admitted that *Romeo* earned the "understanding and sympathy" of the Kirov troupe "far from immediately. Sergei Sergeevich failed to understand that his music in a ballet production was something unusual and demanded a certain period of adjustment."

What was difficult for the Kirov dancers, including Ulanova, was the unconventional structure of the ballet. Divided into episodes emanating from the dramatic action or from a character's feelings, it did not follow the familiar structural conventions of the nineteenth-century ballet. The dancers had to act, and not only rely on their technique. *Romeo*'s rhythms, highly syncopated and rarely square, were also very different from anything they had danced to before.

The troupe was so discouraged and baffled that in late December, several weeks before the scheduled premiere, they threatened to boycott the production, fearing they would make fools of themselves. Some of them were so sure that the ballet would fail that they came up with an anecdote playing on a line from Shakespeare's tragedy: "For never was a story of more woe / Than Prokofiev's music for *Romeo*." But somehow their faint-heartedness was overcome, and the premiere took place as scheduled on January 11, 1940.

Lina was at Prokofiev's side that night. Because of the war between the Soviet Union and Finland, the Leningrad streets were blacked out. Joined by Sergei Radlov, who had first encouraged Prokofiev to write *Romeo and Juliet* five years before, they had to grope their way along the canals from the Astoria Hotel to the Kirov, arriving barely in time for the opening curtain.

To the relief and surprise of the cast, *Romeo* was a great success. Prokofiev remained dissatisfied with many aspects of the production, and was still angry over the changes Lavrovsky had made in the score. He felt sufficiently pleased, however, to join the cast, after "countless curtain-calls," for a supper celebration, where Ulanova made impertinent jokes at his expense.

The official response to *Romeo* was also positive. Ten days after the premiere, *Soviet Art* proclaimed, blithely ignoring the years of difficulties that had preceded the first performance, "The success of *Romeo and Juliet*, a production of rare beauty, content and interest,

374 ▾ SERGEI PROKOFIEV

is not just an ordinary success for Leningrad ballet, it is a success for all of Soviet choreography, and a testament to its colossal creative and ideological growth." That *Romeo* was based on a non-Russian source set in Italy in the Middle Ages perhaps helped to protect the ballet from political criticism, since it had no topical subtext on which to seize. This did not prevent Lavrovsky, however, from portraying Romeo and Juliet as virtuous and idealistic victims of the class struggle in his notes to the Kirov program: "In Shakespeare's tragedy, the conflict between the outmoded beliefs of the Middle Ages and those newly born ideals introduced to Italy by the epoch of the Renaissance appears in sharp outline."

In the spring of 1940, the Kirov production of *Romeo* was taken to Moscow, where it also enjoyed a warm reception. After the first performance, Ulanova returned to her hotel, tired but satisfied. Suddenly there was a knock at the door. "I was very surprised when I saw Prokofiev standing there. In a tone not admitting to objections, he said, 'Let's go now to the Writers' Club. They're waiting for us there.' " Reluctantly, Ulanova agreed to go. At the club they were met with applause, and "to this accompaniment we proceeded to the head table." She continued:

> I was very embarrassed when Prokofiev asked me to dance. It was a very ordinary foxtrot, but Sergei Sergeevich seemed always to be hearing some rhythm of his own, somehow stepping "out of the rhythm of the music," somehow lagging behind. I got confused, fell out of step and was afraid I wouldn't be able to find the rhythm, that I would step on my partner's toes, lose the beat—in a word, reveal that I couldn't dance at all. But the dance gradually gathered momentum, and I started to feel confident and free. At last, I caught my partner's unusual and utterly marvelous rhythm. The evening passed in a very friendly manner.

Later, in 1946, the Bolshoi Theater mounted its own production of *Romeo and Juliet*—again with Lavrovsky and Ulanova. It has also been staged by many other Soviet companies, from Tartu to Novosibirsk.

Leaving the noise and frustration of the Leningrad *Romeo* behind, Prokofiev returned to Moscow, retreating to the quiet world of the Sixth Piano Sonata, which was finished by late winter.

He had more time to devote to composition than he originally anticipated, since plans for a winter tour of the United States had been scrapped. Ephraim Gottlieb wrote from Chicago on February 13, "This week you were to have conducted the Chicago Symphony Orchestra in a full evening of your compositions, but, unfortunately, due to the European conditions you were unable to come to the U.S. . . . We all hope that next year will bring you to our shores." Stravinsky was also scheduled to come to Chicago, Gottlieb added, and was bringing "a lecturer to boost him. This is his new scheme to make himself popular—and I am sure it won't help him. All this made me think how different your actions are from his, as you are so modest and he is so aggressive."

But by now, America and Stravinsky must have seemed as far away to Prokofiev as the moon. Thousands of miles, Stalin's xenophobia and Hitler's armies separated him from Chicago. More than ever, Prokofiev's present and future were in Russia.

One evening toward early spring, soon after completing the Sixth Piano Sonata, Prokofiev played it for his closest colleagues at Pavel Lamm's apartment. Among the guests was the promising young pianist Sviatoslav Richter. By now, Richter was living in the same building as Prokofiev, in the apartment of his mentor, pianist Heinrich Neuhaus, who brought Richter along that evening to hear Prokofiev's new sonata.

"Serious musical people would gather at the Lamms', in a dark old Moscow apartment furnished mostly with piles of music," Richter wrote later in his colorful memoirs.

Muscovite composers—important musicians of the older generation—made up the nucleus of the group. Miaskovsky was always there. Silent, infinitely tactful. If someone asked for his opinion, he would offer it as an expert, but quietly, as if he weren't needed. Invited guests also came—pianists, conductors. . . . One evening something special was in store—Prokofiev was supposed to come.

Prokofiev arrived. He came not like a regular visitor, but like a guest—one felt that strongly. He looked like a birthday boy, but a bit condescending. He brought his Sonata and said, "Well, let's get to it!" and immediately, "I will play." . . . Speed and attack! He was younger than most of those present, but one felt a strong undercurrent—everyone felt it—"I might be younger, but I'm worth all of you!" His rather haughty attitude to those who surrounded him did not, however, extend to Miaskovsky, toward whom he was pointedly attentive. Prokofiev behaved in a businesslike manner, professionally. . . . It seems he played the sonata twice and left. He played from the manuscript copy, and I turned pages for him. . . . Even before Prokofiev had finished playing, I had decided—I will play that!

Richter would play the Sixth Sonata the following autumn, to great popular and critical acclaim. Even Prokofiev—one of the great pianists of the century and a man notoriously stingy with compliments—would be impressed with his interpretation. But it was Prokofiev himself who gave the premiere, on April 8, 1940, at the Composers' Union, in a performance broadcast on the radio. This was the sixth and last time that Prokofiev would himself introduce a new piano sonata that he had composed. Henceforth, he would entrust this honor to other pianists, saving his own energy for composing.

One of these pianists was Richter, whose virtuosity made a great impression on Prokofiev. After Richter's performance of the Sixth Sonata six months later, on November 26, he would in fact become Prokofiev's favorite pianist, and was subsequently entrusted with the premiere of the Seventh Sonata. The relationship between Richter and Prokofiev remained purely musical, however. "I was never especially close to Prokofiev the man," Richter wrote. "I was intimidated, and for me, he was wholly contained in his music—both then and now. I met Prokofiev in his music."

The piece that marked the beginning of Richter's long relationship with Prokofiev—the Sixth Piano Sonata—is serious and forceful. Some Soviet critics have interpreted its dark, even fierce, mood as an angry response to fascism, but the true explanation for the music's grim determination seems rather to lie in the difficult circumstances of Prokofiev's personal life at the moment—and perhaps in his grief over the death of Meyerhold. Dense and packed with ideas, it is the longest of all his sonatas, twice as long as the preceding Fifth. In four movements, it represents a return to the highly chromatic and rhythmically eccentric piano music that Prokofiev was writing around the time of the Russian Revolution. The muscular and strongly punctuated main theme of the opening *Allegro moderato* is structured around a hammering juxtaposition between the tonic A Major and parallel A Minor—and between sixteenths and eighths—in an obsessively repeated figure of descending thirds. The movement ends on an aggressively dissonant minor second.

Also imaginative in its use of traditional forms is the third movement, *Tempo di valzer lentissimo,* a tantalizingly slow and thickly harmonized waltz in 9/8 time. The final movement, *Vivace,* starts out like another one of Prokofiev's naughty, toccata-like exhibitionistic displays, but takes an unexpectedly serious turn in the middle, bringing back the main theme of the first movement. Masterfully interwoven among the lightly ironic sixteenth-note runs, it produces an eerie and ominous play of light and dark, a sort of *danse macabre.* In the Sixth Sonata, Prokofiev is again the *enfant terrible,* but he has lost his optimistic naivete and gained maturity and passion.

The Sixth Sonata made a great impression on Prokofiev's colleague and competitor Shostakovich. "The Sixth Sonata is magnificent," he wrote to Prokofiev from Leningrad. "From beginning to end. I am very happy that I had the opportunity to hear it two times, and regret that it was only two times."

One other important Prokofiev premiere took place during the spring season of 1940. Almost a year to the day after Meyerhold's arrest halted work on the production of *Semyon Kotko,* it was finally staged at the Stanislavsky Opera Theater on June 23, directed by Serafima Birman. Rehearsals had gone on all winter. Anxious over the fate of his opera in the aftermath of Meyerhold's arrest, Prokofiev often attended, providing suggestions. During this period, Prokofiev was "in a permanently excited state"—not surprising, considering the enormous personal and political pressure he was experiencing.

The rapid changes in the international situation had dictated some bizarre alterations in the strongly anti-German *Semyon Kotko.* Since Stalin had signed a nonaggression pact with Hitler in August 1939, the negative portrayal of the German soldiers had to be modified. It was suddenly inappropriate to ridicule Germans on stage or on film. (It was at this time, too, that *Alexander Nevsky* was temporarily shelved for the same reasons.) "We had to tone down the setting," Kataev said. "The Germans were recostumed as Austrians, but even so there was some kind of diplomatic unpleasantness."

All this led to endless discussion and worry, even at home. "I don't think that any of my father's compositions was so much discussed at home as *Semyon Kotko,*" Oleg Prokofiev has written. "My brother and I took turns playing Germans and the Austrian *haidamaks* who later replaced them on stage so unnaturally." Ironically, the Germans would again become suitable villains only one year later.

Prokofiev was still hopeful that *Semyon* would be the breakthrough he had so long sought in the Soviet operatic world, but when the dust had cleared and the reviews were in, he was again disappointed. While *Semyon* was not found to be ideologically heretical, most important official critics judged it too complicated, unmelodic and an opera that "will not be comprehensible to the masses." *Semyon* did have its defenders, including Sviatoslav Richter, who said, "The evening that I heard *Semyon Kotko* for the first time, I understood that Prokofiev was a great composer." Unfortunately, these voices had little influence over repertoire.

Semyon fell out of the repertoire soon after its initial run, to reappear only long after Prokofiev's death. It entered the repertoire of the Bolshoi Theater in 1970, and has been performed regularly there since then.

The failure of *Semyon* must have been intensely frustrating to Prokofiev. He had tried very hard to write a "Soviet" opera that would please the cultural bureaucrats, and they still rejected it. The problem was that he was still Prokofiev, a genius. He couldn't transform himself into a mediocre hack whose music had no individuality and pleased everyone. He had taken Diaghilev's advice too much to heart: "In art, you must learn to hate, or else your own music will lose its personality."

After the demanding winter and spring season, Prokofiev needed some rest. He spent the summer with Lina and the boys—their last summer together—at Nikolina Gora, where they rented the upper story of a *dacha* owned by an artist they knew. But Prokofiev was still spending a great deal of time with Mira. During the spring, he had begun working on a new opera—*Betrothal in a Monastery* (also known as *The Duenna*)—and Mira was helping him with the libretto. Their collaboration provided a pretext for their meetings.

One day that spring, a family friend of the Prokofievs was riding on a bus down a Moscow street when she suddenly saw Prokofiev walking along with a young woman she didn't recognize. But what impressed her most was not the presence of the unknown woman (Mira), but the unfamiliar expression on Prokofiev's face—happy, relaxed, light-hearted. "He had always been rather grim and serious, but after he met Mira he became more affectionate and friendly," she said. "The change in him was very noticeable."

Prokofiev's choice of subject for the opera on which he began working that spring seems in fact to reflect a more light-hearted and romantic mood. *Betrothal in a Monastery* is based on an eighteenth-century English comic opera, *The Duenna*, by Richard Brinsley Sheridan (1751–1816). (Prokofiev changed the original title because it sounded strange in Russian.) This resolutely apolitical, frothy and mischievous entertainment is centuries and worlds away from the heavy military tendentiousness of *Semyon Kotko*, *Zdravitsa*, and *Alexander Nevsky*. In choosing Sheridan's play, Prokofiev was returning to his beloved eighteenth century, and to the self-consciously theatrical world of *Love for Three Oranges*.

According to Mira, the idea to write *Betrothal in a Monastery* first came from her. In early 1940, she and a friend had been collaborating on a translation of Sheridan's comic opera into Russian; Mira was translating the verse sections, and her friend, the prose. As was already their custom, Mira one day "began to retell (or, to use Sergei Sergeevich's expression, 'shake down') the story of *The Duenna* to Sergei Sergeevich. At first he listened distractedly, but I saw that gradually he was becoming more interested, and when I stopped he said, 'But that's champagne—it could make an opera in the style of Mozart, Rossini!' After reading *The Duenna*, Sergei Sergeevich immediately decided to write an opera and set to work right away."

So convinced was Prokofiev that *The Duenna* would make an amusing and successful opera that he abandoned another project—a planned opera based on "The Wastrel," a story by Nikolai Leskov, for which he had already sketched out a detailed libretto plan in five acts. He had also been considering other libretto sources during the preceding winter: *King Lear*, *The Merchant of Venice*, and a play by the Russian playwright Nikolai Ostrovsky, *The Fiancée Without a Dowry*.

That the satirical and ironic spirit of *Betrothal* suited Prokofiev's temperament and mood seems clear from the speed with which he completed the opera: it took him only about two months, from July to September, to write it.

Sheridan's original *Duenna*, first staged in London in 1775, is an example of "ballad opera," which used familiar ballad melodies (set to verses included in the play's text) inserted between sections of prose dialogue. An instrumental ensemble provided accompaniment, but instrumental scores for *The Duenna* and most other examples of ballad opera have not been found. During Sheridan's lifetime, *The Duenna* was more popular than any of his other works, including *The School for Scandal* and *The Rivals*.

The fast and silly plot is dense with exchanged and mistaken

identities, local Spanish color, and innocent and debauched love. Set
in Seville, the action occurs in the course of twenty-four hours. Don
Jerome, a nobleman of Seville, has two children, Ferdinand and Louisa.
The dashing young Antonio loves Louisa, and she him. But Don Jerome
has other plans for his daughter; he wants her to marry his friend, the
rich Jew Isaac Mendoza. But the Duenna, Don Jerome's bawdy and
corrupt housekeeper, also wants to marry Mendoza, to which end she
arranges to be expelled from Don Jerome's employ and then exchange
roles with Louisa. Louisa adopts a second disguise as her friend Clara,
who is being pursued by Ferdinand. Disguised as Clara, Louisa begs
Mendoza to help her in her supposed love for Antonio. Thinking he
will be removing a rival to Louisa's hand, Mendoza agrees.

After many further complications, disguises and misunderstand-
ings, the action is resolved at a concluding masquerade ball at the
house of Don Jerome. The characters end up with their deserved
partners: Louisa with Antonio, Clara with Ferdinand, and the Duenna
with Mendoza. At first angry that he has failed to marry his daughter
off to the rich Mendoza, Don Jerome quickly resigns himself to his
fate with the good humor expected of a noble patriarch. The greedy
Mendoza is properly humiliated.

Since Sheridan's play had never been translated into Russian,
Prokofiev translated it himself, with Mira's help. From their translation,
they then fashioned a libretto—which diverges significantly from the
Sheridan original—in four acts and nine scenes. These were further
subdivided into smaller episodes. Mira's contribution to this, the first
of their three operatic collaborations (the other two would be *War and
Peace* and *Story of a Real Man*), consisted primarily in producing the
rhymed verses. Of the twenty-seven verse texts in the Sheridan original,
Prokofiev decided to include only six in his opera, supplementing them
with original verses written by Mira. Prokofiev produced the libretto's
prose text.

The style and level of language of their Russian adaptation are
more folksy and crude than Sheridan's; together with the often satirical
musical setting, the earthy language introduces a grotesque element
not found in the original ballad opera. Prokofiev did not overdo the
grotesque in *Betrothal*, however, and made a conscious decision to
emphasize the romantic nature of the subject.

In undertaking to write an opera based on *The Duenna*, I had first
to decide which element to stress in the music: the comic or the

romantic. I chose the second. I do not think I was mistaken in emphasizing the lyrical side: the love of the two young, spirited, imaginative couples—Louisa and Antonio, and Clara and Ferdinand, the obstacles to their love, the happy betrothal, the poetic background of Seville where the action takes place, the tranquil evening landscape spreading before the lovers' eyes, the nighttime carnival, the old abandoned nunnery.

At the same time, I was careful not to overlook any of the comic elements, for here Sheridan excels—old Don Jerome, so blinded by rage that he drives his own daughter out of his house instead of the maid whose clothes she is wearing, thus unwittingly helping her to elope with her lover; the greedy Mendoza, so blinded by ducats that he allows himself to be duped and marries the old nursemaid instead of the young enchantress Louisa; the impetuous Ferdinand who, maddened by jealousy, sees his Clara in every girl he meets in the company of a young man. These characters and the comic situations in which they are placed are offset by the lyrical scenes, especially if the comic *quid pro quo* is played with the appearance of seriousness.

When performed by singers who are also talented comic actors, *Betrothal* can be one of Prokofiev's most theatrically and musically satisfying operas. Wisely, he controlled his natural tendency toward brittle cardboard caricature (as in *Love for Three Oranges* and *The Buffoon*) and humanized the roles. In the same way, Prokofiev made use of a number of operatic conventions—arias clearly set off in the musical texture, ensembles, rhymed verses—which he had previously rejected. If *Three Oranges*, the opera which *Betrothal* most closely resembles in spirit and subject, intentionally turned away from established operatic traditions, then *Betrothal* makes at least a partial return to them, particularly to the conventions of Mozart and Rossini. This rediscovery of the possibility of renewing operatic formulae would continue in Prokofiev's next opera, *War and Peace*.

And yet there is much in *Betrothal* that does come from Prokofiev's earlier experimental work in opera. His distaste for dramatically stagnant scenes, his fondness for portraying "physical" images (in this case, drunkeness) in musical terms, and his close attention to the rhythm and intonation of language are only a few examples.

Scene 6, the "music-making" scene, is one of the most lively and imaginative pieces of musical business that Prokofiev ever devised. Against the background of a constantly interrupted domestic trio (clar-

inet, trumpet, bass drum) played with humorous lack of polish by Don
Jerome and two friends, Don Jerome reads two letters and unwittingly
agrees to give his daughter in marriage to Antonio (thinking he is
Mendoza). The interruptions in the music-making become comically
repetitive, the humor heightened by the trumpeter's reluctance, and
then the drummer's, to stop playing when Don Jerome does.

Although Prokofiev completed *Betrothal in a Monastery* very quickly
during the autumn of 1940, he would have to wait six years to see it
on stage. Originally, it was scheduled for a production at the Stanislavsky Musical Theater in the summer of 1941. Several closed performances were held during May and June, but momentous international
events would force the premiere's cancellation.

Working on *Betrothal in a Monastery* apparently rekindled Prokofiev's interest in light subjects set in the eighteenth century, for he
turned to another one—the fairy tale *Cinderella*—soon after completing the opera.

Prokofiev met the New Year 1941, which would be one of the most
difficult in his own life and in the life of his country, in Leningrad,
giving a holiday recital in the glittering hall named after his former
professor, Glazunov. (It was later renamed in honor of Shostakovich.)
One of the pieces on the program was his new Sixth Piano Sonata. A
few weeks later, also in Leningrad, *Alexander Nevsky* was included in
a concert commemorating the seventeenth anniversary of Lenin's death—
an indication that Prokofiev was still enjoying a strong measure of
official favor despite his difficulties with *Semyon Kotko*.

In Moscow, Prokofiev made his last concert appearance in the
Soviet capital for nearly three years on March 9. It was a particularly
gratifying appearance, for he conducted Sviatoslav Richter in a performance of his long-forgotten Fifth Piano Concerto, composed in Paris
ten years before. Richter's performance of his Sixth Sonata a few months
earlier had made such a great impression on Prokofiev that he had
persuaded the twenty-five-year-old pianist to tackle his last and least-
known concerto. After studying it, Richter had played it for Prokofiev one day in the neighboring apartment of Heinrich Neuhaus.
This was also one of the last times—it was in late February or the
first few days of March 1940—that Prokofiev appeared with Lina in
public.

Prokofiev arrived with his wife, and the room filled with a strong fragrance of Parisian perfumes. Seated, he started telling some incredible stories, at full speed, about gangster life in America. He related all this in his uniquely "Prokofievian" style—with humor and directness. We were sitting around a little table that didn't leave enough room for our legs, and we were drinking tea with the same kind of ham that Neuhaus always served. Then we played. Prokofiev was satisfied: standing in front of us, behind the two pianos where he had been conducting, he pulled two chocolates out of two pockets simultaneously, presenting them to us with a stylish gesture. We started making plans for rehearsals right then and there.

At the first rehearsal he sat me down at the piano so the orchestra could get used to me. Prokofiev's style as a conductor couldn't have been more suited to his compositions. Although the orchestra members understood little in this music, they played well anyway. Prokofiev didn't mince words and would say, straightforwardly, "Try to do this or that. . . . And you—try to do it this way. . . ." Of course he was demanding. We had only three rehearsals, which were extremely productive.

To Prokofiev's bemused surprise, and to Richter's relief, the performance on March 9 in the massive Tchaikovsky Concert Hall on Mayakovsky Square was very successful. True, it was cold in the big auditorium, and there were numerous empty seats, but those present demanded many curtain calls.

As the snow began to melt and Russian winter yielded slowly to spring, the international atmosphere was more tense and complicated than ever. By the spring of 1941, German forces occupied most of Europe, and the U.S.S.R., by the terms of Stalin's agreement with Hitler, had taken possession of the eastern part of Poland and the previously independent states of Lithuania, Latvia and Estonia. The brief war with Finland had ended inevitably in a Soviet victory and territorial concessions from the Finnish government. The U.S.S.R. had also received territory from Rumania and created from it the new Moldavian Soviet Socialist Republic. Stalin was confident, despite warnings from many of his military advisers, that Hitler would abide by their nonagression pact.

As a result of all these changes, the thriving Europe in which Prokofiev had lived in the 1920s and early 1930s was no longer there to go back to. Many of his colleagues had fled Europe for America.

Stravinsky settled in California in early 1940, moving even farther away from Russia in a move reminiscent of his flight to Europe on the eve of World War I. Schoenberg and Bartok had also gone to the United States.

Being so isolated from Europe—the world in which they had grown up—was difficult for Prokofiev's wife and sons. "Memories of our Paris life, which had been ours only a few years before, seemed so very distant," Oleg remembered later.

> I adapted to the new life, no better and no worse than any other child of my age, although even then I had an acute sense of the profound difference between the two worlds. I loved to look at the Mickey Mouse magazines that we had brought from France; they reminded me of that sweet other life.
>
> Once I returned from school with torn trousers. They started out new, and so I expected a scandal. Instead, I had a severe educational lecture read to me by my father; its moral was that "in Paris, the difficulty lay in finding money, not things, while here it is hard to get things, even though there is plenty of money." I understood how this applied to the torn trousers, but on the whole the lecture seemed a trifle too academic (I had a hard time with generalizations). Memorable about the incident was the unpleasant seriousness of the talk.

But such father-son talks stopped not long after. In late March of 1941—just before his fiftieth birthday—Prokofiev made the final break that had been coming for almost two years. After eighteen years of marriage, he left Lina, Oleg, Sviatoslav and the household on Chkalov Street for a new life with Mira. Neighbors told of hearing loud disputes through the walls and doors of the Prokofievs' apartment, but the exact details of the rupture remain mysterious. What is clear is that Prokofiev never went back, at least not as Lina's mate. Some Soviet sources claim Prokofiev tried to persuade Lina, either then or later, to grant him a divorce so he could marry Mira, but Lina refused. She maintained this position insistently until his death. In fact, there is no evidence that Prokofiev and Lina were ever officially divorced. She also refused to live with him for the sake of appearances—as he suggested—in an "open marriage" that would have allowed him to continue his relationship with Mira.

Lina and the boys remained in the apartment on Chkalov Street for the time being, and Prokofiev provided money for their support. For the next seven years, Prokofiev lived with Mira without being married to her; his lawful wife was still Lina. In articles and correspondence written after early 1941, however, Prokofiev often referred to Mira as "my wife," which has created considerable confusion among critics, historians and biographers. This ambiguous legal situation prevailed until early 1948, when a strange turn of events would further complicate the relationship between Prokofiev and his two women.

Before Prokofiev moved out to be with her, Mira had been living with her parents in a small apartment in a nineteenth-century building in the center of Moscow, on what is now called Moscow Art Theater Lane (Proyezd khudozhestvennogo teatra), between the Bolshoi Theater and Gorky Street. It was not a luxurious apartment—in fact, it was communal, its kitchen and bathroom shared by several neighboring apartments. Housing in Moscow is in short supply even today, but in 1941 the situation was much more desperate. Single people almost never received their own apartments, and young married couples frequently lived with their parents—and then with their children—in one room. Flimsy curtains divided the room into sections, and privacy was nonexistent.

By comparison, Prokofiev and Mira were fortunate: at least they had their own room when they moved in with her parents that spring. (They would live there sporadically until Prokofiev's death.) They had Mira's former room, which served them as bedroom, living room, dining room and Prokofiev's study. Mira's parents lived and slept in the room next door. Although the apartment was crowded and much less luxurious than the one on Chkalov Street, it was very conveniently located, within walking distance of the Bolshoi Theater, the Composers' Union and the Conservatory.

If, as seems likely, their first home together was with Mira's parents on Moscow Art Theater Lane, they stayed there only briefly in early 1941. Prokofiev spent some time in Sochi, a resort on the Black Sea coast, in late winter, and it seems likely that Mira was with him there. Later in the spring, they moved to a rented *dacha* outside Moscow, in Kratovo. Not far from Nikolina Gora, Kratovo was where Mira's parents usually vacationed. Apparently Mira's parents did not disapprove of her relationship with Prokofiev, a married man, and developed a congenial relationship with him. Prokofiev got along particularly well with Mira's father, Abram, whom he treated "partly with irony and partly with respect." After Mira's mother died during the War, Prokofiev and Mira would remain close to her father, continuing to share the Moscow apartment with him.

Given the guilt, uncertainty, difficult material conditions and new responsibilities which Prokofiev assumed by leaving Lina for Mira, it seems safe to say that his relationship with Lina—for whatever reasons—had reached an intolerable level of incompatibility. Numerous friends, acquaintances and neighbors support that view, recalling frequent arguments and open hostility in the Prokofiev household during the years preceding the breakup. Living with the demanding and frequently selfish Prokofiev had never been easy for Lina, a strong-willed woman of great charm, energy and independence, but under the extreme stress of adjusting to a radically different life in Stalinist Moscow, it became nearly impossible. To expect Lina to start all over again, after years of a comfortable European existence, was perhaps too much to ask. The cultural, linguistic and political barrier that separated her from Prokofiev's past and present rose ever higher between them, exaggerating the tension that had always existed in their volatile relationship.

In Paris, Lina had been a great help to Prokofiev, lending him the social grace and tact which he lacked and that was so important for success in that arena. But Moscow of the Stalinist era demanded very different qualities for success—grace and tact ranked far below prominently displayed nationalistic loyalty and the ability to foresee changes in the ideological line. It was certainly no fault of Lina's that she, a non-Russian, could not help Prokofiev in these areas, and could even be viewed as an obstacle to the successful development of his Soviet career.

Under the threat of attack himself, vulnerable and unsophisticated in Stalinist power games, neither can Prokofiev be blamed for seeking out an unquestioning source of support. He sought unconditional encouragement and guidance in negotiating the political minefield on which he now found himself. Mira offered those things. Placing himself in a domestic and personal environment that was as conducive as possible to composing was Prokofiev's primary concern, and it seemed that Mira could create that environment for him.

If one can reproach Prokofiev for anything, it is for his failure to get Lina out of the U.S.S.R., where a terrible ordeal awaited her. It is impossible to know, however, if he tried to arrange for her return to Europe, or whether Lina was receptive to the idea of leaving Moscow at the time. And only a few months after Prokofiev left his family, the possibility of sending them anywhere disappeared. The reason was entirely beyond his control—Hitler's attack on the U.S.S.R.

In the end, Prokofiev left Lina less for personal considerations than for the sake of his art, which meant more to him than anything or anyone. Throughout his life, he had always placed his music first, following where it led him. His music had brought him back to Russia; now it had led him to Mira.

CHAPTER 20

BEHIND THE LINES

The fear that furrowed their faces
Will never be forgotten.
The enemy will have to pay for this
One hundred times over.

—BORIS PASTERNAK,
"A Terrible Tale"

I n that spring of important changes in his life, Prokofiev escaped—
as he had escaped difficult times in the past—into a fairy tale. He
was working on a new ballet that told the story of *Cinderella* (in
Russian, *Zolushka*), the modest downtrodden maiden whose virtue
and simplicity win the love of the handsome prince. Parallels between
the fairy tale and recent events in their lives (Prokofiev, the world-
famous composer, as the Prince, and Mira, only recently an obscure
literature student, as Cinderella) may well have occurred to both of
them—even if Prokofiev was handsome in his art, and not in his profile.

Living quietly with Mira in the country at Kratovo, not far from
Moscow, Prokofiev was making extensive revisions in a *Cinderella*
scenario prepared earlier in the year by Nikolai Volkov, the author of
scenarios for ballets by Asafiev (*The Flame of Paris* and *The Fountain
of Bakhchisarai*) and Khachaturian *(Spartak)*. The *Cinderella* project
had been commissioned the preceding winter by the Kirov Theater in
Leningrad, in the wake of the great success of *Romeo and Juliet*.
Working quickly, Prokofiev had composed the first two acts of *Cinderella* in piano score by June.

But once again, momentous historical events upset Prokofiev's plans. "On June 22, a warm sunny morning, I was sitting at my desk. Suddenly the watchman's wife appeared and asked me, with an anxious expression, if it was true that 'The Germans have attacked us and they are saying that they're bombing the cities.' The news astonished us. We went over to see Sergei Eisenstein, who lived not far from us. Yes, it turned out to be true. . . . Everyone immediately wanted to make his contribution to the struggle. The first response from composers was, naturally, heroic songs and marches—music that could resound directly at the front. I wrote two songs and a march." The songs went into the Seven Mass Songs (Op. 89) completed the following year.

"It was during these days that my idea of writing an opera on Tolstoy's novel *War and Peace* assumed a definite outline. The pages that told of the struggle of the Russian people against Napoleon's hordes in 1812, and of the expulsion of Napoleon's army from Russian soil, became somehow particularly relevant."

The less heroic *Cinderella* was now put aside, and would only be completed three years later. *War and Peace* became Prokofiev's major project for the remaining years of the War.

> Soon afterward, the fascist air raids on Moscow began. We were living about fifty minutes by car from the city. Although that vacation spot was not a target of attack, at night, enemy planes appeared overhead with a roar, illuminating the area with blinding orientational flares. Then Soviet fighters would appear. Occasionally a German bomber would crash, and, still loaded with its undropped bombs, would explode with a huge thundering. The white beams of spotlights filled the sky. The spotlights, the green trails following the fighter planes, the yellow flares launched by the Germans—they all created a picture horrible in its beauty.

So the first summer Prokofiev and Mira spent together turned out to be far from peaceful. Sadly, the beginning of what Prokofiev had hoped would be a more tranquil new life coincided almost exactly with the beginning of a gruesome and exhausting era in Soviet history. For the next few years, Prokofiev—like all Soviet artists—would live a nomadic existence, moving farther and farther east to flee the rapid German advance.

The Soviet Union was disastrously unprepared for Hitler's attack, and the German forces swept across the Ukraine toward Moscow with incredible speed. Leningrad was surrounded in the early days of the War, and would be isolated from the rest of the country by an impenetrable blockade for nearly three horrible years. The Germans would come within twenty miles of Moscow itself by the fall of 1941. Only the coming of winter, and the belated Soviet mobilization, would begin to slow the *Blitzkrieg*.

Life became extremely difficult for all Soviet citizens, including artists and intellectuals. Many in Leningrad would starve or freeze to death. By the end of the War, twenty million Soviet citizens would be dead, and millions of others wounded.

Despite the hardships (or perhaps even because of them), the war years were a time of exceptional productivity for Prokofiev. In less than four years—between the summer of 1941 and the last months of 1944—he would complete the first version of his opera *War and Peace*, *Cinderella*, one of his greatest symphonies (the Fifth), a string quartet, two piano sonatas, a flute sonata (also transcribed for violin), five film scores (including one for Eisenstein's *Ivan the Terrible*) and several large orchestral compositions, not to mention numerous songs and piano pieces.

Prokofiev's output during the War is remarkable not only for its quantity but also for its quality; the music he wrote includes some of his most profound and enduring compositions. Having reached the age of fifty, beginning a new life with Mira and eager to contribute to the war effort in his own way, Prokofiev entered a new phase in his protean career. So intense was the pace of these years that they would leave him—like many Russians of his generation—weakened and spent. These were the last years in which Prokofiev would command the full strength of his talent, energy and health.

With Moscow under nearly constant bombardment, and the city in imminent danger of falling to the Germans, the Soviet Committee on Artistic Affairs decided to evacuate Moscow's leading artistic figures far to the south, to Nalchik in the Caucasus. On August 8, 1941, Prokofiev and Mira joined a group of Moscow Conservatory professors (including Miaskovsky and Lamm), actors from the Moscow Art Theater (including Chekhov's elderly widow, the actress Olga Knipper-Chekhov) and other "artistic laborers" on a special train. They pulled out of the capital, already seriously damaged by German bombs, on an overcast and solemn evening. "We all shared one thought," Olga Lamm, the daughter of Prokofiev's loyal copyist, said later. "Will we ever again see those we are leaving behind—and when?"

For Prokofiev, the evacuation was a turning point. He was leaving behind another life—Lina, Oleg and Sviatoslav would remain in Moscow in the apartment on Chkalov Street throughout the War. Prokofiev would not see them again for nearly two years. If there had been any question whether Prokofiev's relationship with Mira was merely a passing infatuation, it was answered the day that he and Mira departed together—callously, it might seem—for Nalchik. Although even the self-centered Prokofiev must have felt guilt over abandoning his wife and sons to the uncertainty of bombing and war, he and Mira may well have felt a certain relief—they now had the opportunity to make a clean break with Prokofiev's life before Mira. Suddenly, fate had given them the opportunity to start over, in an environment new to both of them.

On the three-day train trip to the Caucasus, most of Prokofiev's friends and colleagues had their first opportunity to meet and talk with Mira. Judging by the memoirs of Olga Lamm, she made a positive impression.

> Sergei Sergeevich appeared in our compartment, where Miaskovsky and his sister were sitting, holding a rather small young woman who was clinging to him shyly by the hand. She had very thick black hair that came down to her shoulders, and a charming, very alert expression in her dark eyes. The affectionate greeting she received from Nikolai Yakovlevich [Miaskovsky] and the tender maternal kiss of Valentina Yakovlenva [Miaskovsky's sister] immediately reassured her, and she started to deal with us all confidently and simply, which quickly won general sympathy.

The train brought Prokofiev and his colleagues to Nalchik, the capital of the Kabarda-Balkar Autonomous Republic in the foothills of the Caucasus. Prokofiev was happy to find that this small but pleasant town had a park (destroyed by the Nazis only a few months later) and fresh clean air. When he was not composing in the small room he shared with Mira in the Hotel Nalchik—which was most of the time—Prokofiev socialized with his interesting companions. Olga Knipper-Chekhov, "who retained all of her great artistic aura despite her advanced age," taught Prokofiev to play a new card game, a kind of Patience that Chekhov had taught her. Hereafter, Prokofiev called it "Chekhov's Patience." The musicians and actors gave concerts in Nalchik's small theater, and visited hospitals to entertain the troops wounded in battle. And Prokofiev and Miaskovsky would walk and talk in the hills.

Another one of Prokofiev's fellow evacuees was the artist Igor

Grabar. He used their sojourn in Nalchik as an opportunity to complete the portrait of Prokofiev begun but left unfinished seven years earlier. As Prokofiev sat working on *War and Peace*, Grabar painted him.

> A notebook of music paper stood in front of him on the piano music stand. He was holding a pencil in his hand, and would take a long look into the distance, as though listening to sounds audible to him alone. Then, suddenly turning his head to the music paper, he would raise the pencil, beginning to race across it, filling it with notes. He would continue like that for a quarter of an hour—and sometimes a half hour or longer—until he would again return to his former position of immovable concentration.

Even though the circumstances were difficult, Prokofiev was apparently content—and definitely productive—in Nalchik. In three months, he wrote nearly half of *War and Peace*, his Second String Quartet, a large orchestral piece (*The Year 1941* Suite) and several songs. Prokofiev's happiness was obvious to the old friends who surrounded him. They claimed to have noticed a marked "softening" in his character, a new openness and kindness. Mira would invite the Lamms and Miaskovsky to their cramped hotel room for tea; when Prokofiev had been living with Lina in their spacious Moscow apartment, such invitations had not been extended.

"All of us immediately noticed the significant change that had taken place in Prokofiev," Olga Lamm wrote.

> Despite the depressed mood of those who surrounded him, and despite a life that was far from easy for him materially (he tried to help his family that had stayed behind in Moscow—his sons and his first wife—as much as he could, even though he himself often lacked basic things), he was happy, and this happiness was written on his face: it was always beaming. He was composing a great deal and with enormous inspiration, and, like all happy people, was filled with a sort of amazingly affectionate and kind attitude toward all those around him, with robust optimism.
>
> We were astonished: what had happened to the carelessly condescending attitude toward others? He was simple and kind with everyone, received guests in his room with the greatest pleasure—sharing everything that he had on his table—and was concerned and welcoming. If at times a mischievous spark did flare up in his eyes, it would end with a good-natured joke aimed at the person

who had provoked his joking mood, and not with the sharp and even crude attacks characteristic of him in the past.

Mira revealed great tact in dealing with people, and a marvelous ability to manage Sergei Sergeevich's relationships with his colleagues, smoothing over, in a very kind and pleasant manner, the rough moments that sometimes occurred. She behaved with great simplicity. As for Sergei Sergeevich, she could not hide her admiration for him, or her joy and pride in his love. When they wandered, hand-in-hand, through the Nalchik marketplace in search of tomatoes or something else to eat, they were so busy with each other that they didn't notice anything or anybody. One could only wonder how they would manage to buy anything!

Most of Prokofiev's time and energy in Nalchik went into *War and Peace*. Mira was deeply involved in every stage of its composition and numerous revisions, which would stretch over the next twelve years, until Prokofiev's death. Although it was the Nazi invasion that inspired Prokofiev to finally begin the project, he had been "nursing" the idea of writing an opera on *War and Peace* for some time. In 1935, an opera singer friend had given him a copy of Tolstoy's mammoth novel in an English translation. Five years later, in 1940, Mira began to read *War and Peace* aloud to Prokofiev (in Russian). Another Tolstoy novel, *Resurrection*, written after Tolstoy's religious conversion, had also briefly attracted Prokofiev's attention as a possible libretto source.

Like all literate Russians, Prokofiev had grown up with *War and Peace*. (Written between 1863 and 1869, Tolstoy's semi-fictional chronicle follows the lives of several aristocratic Russian families from 1805 to 1820—just before, during and after the Napoleonic Wars.) Prokofiev first read the novel in autumn 1905, when he was fourteen; it was one of a number of Russian classics that had been suggested as appropriate reading material by his father. In keeping with his childhood habit of assigning a "grade" to the music he heard and the books he read, Prokofiev had then given *War and Peace* the unusually high mark of five on a scale of five. He was not so awed by Tolstoy's classic, however, that he could not offer the author a few suggestions, which he later recalled in that part of his autobiography written in the late 1940s while he was completing work on his opera.

I read *War and Peace* with enthusiasm, although, of course, I got bored during the endless reflections at the novel's end. But even if these reflections were to be discarded, it was still clear to me that if Tolstoy had been able to condense his novel twice over, making two volumes from four, then the whole thing would have benefitted. This impression was only strengthened when I returned to *War and Peace* on subsequent occasions.

Interestingly, it was not the leading character of Natasha Rostova, the effervescent young countess, who had elicited the greatest sympathy from the teenaged Prokofiev, but her less fortunate and less glamorous companion Sonya, "whose fate greatly disturbed me."

In choosing *War and Peace* as the source for an opera, Prokofiev was turning to a novel that was regarded as a cornerstone of Russian realism—and an appropriate model for Soviet literature. Throughout the 1930s, as the doctrine of Socialist Realism was being formulated, Tolstoy was held up as a good example to Soviet writers for a number of reasons: he took his material from important historical events; he described them in an accessible, edifying and epic style; and he glorified the *narod* (the simple Russian people), emphasizing their central role in historical and political processes. Numerous Soviet writers— Mikhail Sholokhov in *Quiet Flows the Don* and Alexander Fadeyev in *The Rout* are only two examples—consciously copied Tolstoy.

After Hitler's incursion into holy Russian soil, the special nationalistic significance of *War and Peace* became even more relevant. The parallels between Tolstoy's account of Napoleon's march on Russia in 1812 and the Soviet reality of 1941 were obvious and inescapable. (The war with France was called "The First Fatherland War," and World War II "The Second Fatherland War.") Hitler had now assumed Napoleon's role, and Stalin that of Tsar Alexander I. The Russian moral and military victory with which Tolstoy's novel ends also provided an appropriate source of inspiration in the struggle against the Third Reich.

Despite the apparent political "rightness" of his libretto choice, Prokofiev would encounter endless problems getting his Tolstoy opera on stage. Only *The Fiery Angel* would face more obstacles. For setting a literary source as well-known and prestigious as *War and Peace* contained an inherent danger: all Russians, especially the cultural bureaucrats, had very strong preconceptions about it. They would later reproach Prokofiev for being insufficiently faithful to the novel, and even for perverting its heroic spirit.

Prokofiev would spend more years and energy on *War and Peace* than on any other single composition in his entire career, but his conscientious efforts would be frustrated and sabotaged at nearly every step in the composition and production process. What the critic R. F. Christian wrote of Tolstoy's novel—that "the numerous draft versions and plans for *War and Peace* are considerably longer than the finished novel itself"—is also true of Prokofiev's opera; it exists in a bewildering variety of versions.

Fashioning a thirty-page libretto from more than one thousand pages of prose was a daunting task on which Mira and Prokofiev collaborated closely. Their successful work on *Betrothal in a Monastery* helped them. As early as April 1941, before the German attack, they had already worked out a sketchy libretto plan. While living at Kratovo in July, they had refined the outline and begun to put scenes together. From the very beginning, they envisioned the opera in two sections— the first devoted primarily to scenes of peace and the second to scenes of war.

The libretto did not attempt to condense and retell the entire plot of *War and Peace,* or to include the hundreds of characters. Representative scenes were selected on the assumption that the audience— the Russian audience, at least—would already be intimately familiar with Tolstoy's novel. (Tchaikovsky operated on the same assumption in composing his Pushkin opera, *Eugene Onegin.*) In the opera's original (1941–43) version, there were eleven scenes, six of peace and five of war. All of these eleven scenes survived in the opera's final performing version, established only after Prokofiev's death. Several were repeatedly revised, however, both musically and dramatically, and two more scenes would eventually be added.

The original eleven scenes were: (1) at the Rostov estate, where Prince Andrei Bolkonsky first meets Natasha Rostova; (2) Natasha's visit to Andrei's misanthropic father, the old Prince Bolkonsky, who disapproves of his son's intention to marry the young and flighty Natasha; (3) a *soirée* at the home of the debauched and scheming Helene, Pierre Bezukhov's wife, whose equally depraved brother Anatole decides to pursue the delectably innocent Natasha; (4) Anatole carousing on the eve of carrying out his plan to abduct Natasha and elope with her; (5) Anatole's unsuccessful attempt to abduct Natasha, her disgrace, and Pierre Bezukhov's attempt to comfort her; (6) Pierre's upbraiding of Anatole, and the announcement of Napoleon's attack; (7) among the Russian commanders and troops on the eve of the decisive Battle of Borodino; (8) Napoleon and his suite during the Battle of Borodino; (9) Moscow occupied by the French, and Pierre's meeting with the wise peasant *raissoneur* Karataev; (10) Natasha's visit to Prince Andrei in a roadside hut, where he is dying from a wound received in battle and she begs his forgiveness for betraying him; (11) the disastrous retreat of the French along the Smolensk Highway, the arrival of the victorious Russian commander-in-chief Kutuzov, and celebration of the Russian victory.

In 1945–47, in connection with a planned production at the Maly Theater in Leningrad, two more scenes would be added to these eleven. One, placed after the opening scene at the Rostov estate, is a magnificent ball (filled with dance numbers) held at a nobleman's palace, attended by the important characters. The other, "A Hut at Fili," comes after the scene with Napoleon during the Battle of Borodino, and shows the members of the Russian high military command, led by Kutuzov, deciding upon strategy. It is this thirteen-scene version of *War and Peace* that is included in the Soviet edition of Prokofiev's collected works, and the one which is usually staged today.

Both chronologically and dramatically, *War and Peace* is a collection of loosely connected "scenes." The action of Prokofiev's opera covers three years, from 1809 to 1812, and is set in many different locales. This same sprawling, "historical" structure is found in several other Russian operas which obviously influenced Prokofiev: Tchaikovsky's *Eugene Onegin*, and Mussorgsky's *Khovanshchina* and *Boris Godunov*. Tchaikovsky called *Onegin* "lyric scenes in three acts," while Mussorgsky called both his operas "musical folk-dramas." Prokofiev finally called *War and Peace* "lyric-dramatic scenes."

None of these Russian operatic classics conforms to the classical dramatic unities of action, time and place. The unusual form of *War and Peace* has inspired critics to devise an arsenal of labels for it: dramatic chronicle, lyrico-psychological drama, heroic-epic narrative, historical opera-novel.

But then Tolstoy himself was reproached for breaking the rules of form in his huge and unwieldy novel. He addressed such accusations in an 1868 article. "What is *War and Peace?*" he asked. "It is not a novel, even less is it an epic poem, and still less a historical chronicle. *War and Peace* is what the author wished and was able to express in the form in which it is expressed. . . . The history of Russian literature since the time of Pushkin not merely affords many examples of such deviation from European forms, but does not offer a single example to the contrary."

The same can also be said of Russian opera. Mussorgsky's *Boris*

Godunov, Borodin's *Prince Igor* and Glinka's *Ivan Susanin (A Life for the Tsar)* all break dramatic and narrative "rules." They cover a long time span, they lack a central romantic interest, the dramatic action is loose and follows the vagaries of history, the "people" is treated as a protagonist almost equal in importance to the main characters. In this sense, Prokofiev's *War and Peace* continues a long tradition of untidy form in Russian music. It is, in fact, the most self-consciously "Russian" of Prokofiev's operas in its literary source, dramatic structure and musical language.

In writing the libretto for *War and Peace,* Mira would assemble appropriate episodes from various parts of the novel, usually centering a scene around one chapter and one major event. As much as possible, she would retain Tolstoy's words, although Prokofiev was not obsessed with retaining every nuance of the language, as he had been while composing *The Gambler* twenty-five years earlier.

"First, we would usually look over the text that I had prepared for the next scene, and Sergei Sergeevich would then write the music. If necessary, he would later introduce changes and additions into the text himself, or ask me to do it." Sometimes Prokofiev would give Mira a rhythmic outline of the music he had already written for a part of a scene, indicating the precise accents and meter for each measure. She would then produce verse or prose to "fit" the music.

Just how seriously Mira and Prokofiev took the task of confronting *War and Peace* is obvious from the research they undertook. Prokofiev originally intended to examine Tolstoy's numerous drafts for the novel, stored at the Tolstoy Museum in Moscow, but the evacuation to Nalchik made that impossible. He and Mira did, however, consult many historical sources on the Napoleonic era, including those which Tolstoy himself had used. To be sure his treatment of the Battle of Borodino was accurate, Prokofiev studied the battlefield's topography in *A Guide to the Sites of the Battle of Borodino.* Given his fascination with military games and strategy, this was a task he probably enjoyed.

Prokofiev was so excited by his work that—despite working conditions far from ideal—he managed to complete the first six scenes ("Peace") in piano score in only three months, between August 15 and November 12.

This was not the only music Prokofiev completed while living in one room with Mira in a Nalchik hotel. He also composed a large symphonic suite *(The Year 1941)* and some mass songs to political verses written by Mira, and began his Second String Quartet, which was directly inspired and influenced by the unique locale and traditions of Nalchik. Flattered by the presence of so many artistic luminaries in their midst, the local cultural bureaucrats had encouraged them to investigate the folk customs of the region. The composers were introduced to Kabardinian folk music, which had interested other Russian composers in the past, including Prokofiev's early patron Taneev, who had assembled a collection of Kabardinian folk songs.

Perhaps as a respite from *War and Peace*, the idea of using this material appealed to Prokofiev, and he decided to incorporate some Kabardinian themes in a string quartet. "It seemed to me that bringing new and untouched Eastern folklore together with one of the most classical of all classical forms—the string quartet—could yield interesting and unexpected results." After he had begun composing the quartet, however, Prokofiev began to worry that such a sophisticated form would be inaccessible to Nalchik's musically uneducated audience. But the reigning cultural bureaucrat (the chairman of the Committee on Artistic Affairs) reassured him.

Write what you feel," he told Prokofiev. "If we don't understand your quartet right away, we will come to appreciate it later."

More than ten years had passed since Prokofiev had written his First String Quartet for the Library of Congress. The string quartet was not a form for which he felt a strong natural affinity, and his Second Quartet would also be his last.

In three movements (*Allegro sostenuto*, *Adagio* and *Allegro*), the Second Quartet is less polyphonic than the First, harsher in sonority, and more ambiguous harmonically. In his treatment of the folk material, Prokofiev rejected the "oriental" salon style characteristic of late nineteenth-century Russian chamber music, and attempted to reproduce as faithfully as possible the "non-Western" intervals, rhythms and phrasing of Kabardinian music. He did retain, however, the stable framework of Western tonality and sonata form.

The Second Quartet includes a few passages which imitate the sound of Caucasian stringed instruments. Open intervals (particularly fifths) abound, with a general avoidance of consonant intervals, lending the music a strangely primitive and ragged character strengthened by insistent rhythms (staccato *marcato* in the second subject of the first movement) and repetition.

Perhaps the most haunting and inventive section is the middle slow movement. Here, an "ametrical" accompaniment combining simultaneous motion by major second (in the first violin) and major fifth (in the second violin), rising from the original pitch and then returning to it—eighth note to quarter note, eighth to quarter—provides a stark background for the simple lyrical melody in E Minor, announced by the cello in its high register. The effect is eerie, somehow distant and melancholy, but "tart" and hollow.

When first performed a year later in Moscow by the Beethoven Quartet, the Second Quartet enjoyed a considerable success, although some orthodox critics decided Prokofiev had sinned by distorting unduly the sacrosanct folk material. To Miaskovsky, however, it was "simply monstrously, even 'nightmarishly' interesting." In the West, the Second Quartet has enjoyed somewhat greater popularity than the First, perhaps because of its more exotic personality.

In the midst of composing the Second Quartet, Prokofiev was suddenly informed that he and his colleagues had to pick up and leave Nalchik. Rostov-on-Don had already been taken, and the town was in danger of imminent German attack. One night in late November they were loaded into railroad cars, overcrowded and uncomfortable, and transported through Baku to Tbilisi, the capital of the Georgian Republic. The next morning, they awoke to a dramatically different landscape of sandy hills traversed by camel caravans. Arriving in Tbilisi, a large city with about one million inhabitants, Prokofiev and his colleagues dispersed to live in various houses and hotels. Prokofiev and Mira were assigned to a hotel near Erevan Square.

Life in Tbilisi, where they stayed for about six months, was not unpleasant. Georgian culture is an intriguing mixture of Turkish, Russian and European influences, the product of a long and proud intellectual, religious (Christian) and artistic history. A cosmopolitan city with a mild, sunny climate and wide tree-shaded boulevards, Tbilisi has a spectacular view of the mountains, and delicious and abundant food. The conservatory, opera house and dramatic theatre are known throughout the U.S.S.R.

While staying in Tbilisi during the winter and spring of 1941–42, Prokofiev saw Shakespeare, Balzac and Sheridan (The School for Scandal), heard both European and Georgian opera, and attended symphonic concerts of music by Beethoven, Tchaikovsky, Scriabin and Shostakovich. He also performed himself, giving several piano recitals and conducting a program of his symphonic music, including the two Romeo and Juliet Suites. In early February, he made a brief trip to Baku, the oil-rich capital of the Republic of Azerbaidzhan, for several more piano appearances.

Work on the second half of *War and Peace*—the war scenes—kept Prokofiev and Mira very busy in Tbilisi. They spent hours in the city's library, researching sources on Napoleon's campaign, and searching for folk and military songs (and instruments) characteristic of the Napoleonic era. Prokofiev would dash off musical phrases on scraps of paper, envelopes—even the hotel bill. The work so completely absorbed and satisfied him that he told Mira he wanted to stop performing as a conductor and pianist, since such appearances distracted him and took too much time away from composing. In fact, Prokofiev did perform publicly much less frequently after early 1942, although the nomadic conditions of his life during the War, and his subsequent illness, were also important factors.

By April, Prokofiev had completed the first version of *War and Peace* in piano score. Hoping for a production in the near future, he sent it off to the Committee on Artistic Affairs in Moscow for an official evaluation. By the time he would receive an answer three months later, Prokofiev would no longer be in Tbilisi; nor would the official reaction be as positive as he had hoped. He did, however, receive a speedy and very encouraging response to *War and Peace* from Shostakovich, who had the opportunity to examine Prokofiev's score briefly in Moscow. In a letter, Shostakovich wrote that the opera made an "enormous impression on me," particularly the first four scenes.

While completing the first version of *War and Peace*, Prokofiev was also finishing another big project: his Seventh Piano Sonata, whose themes had been conceived at the same time as those of the Sixth.

Like the Sixth, the Seventh Sonata is dark and ominous in mood, even though it is written (like the Sixth) in a major key—B flat. In scale and length it is smaller than the Sixth, with only three movements (*Allegro inquieto, Andante caloroso* and *Precipitato*) instead of four. It is also highly chromatic. Prokofiev gives the key as B flat Major, but the first (and longest) movement, in sonata-allegro form, has no key signature. Its two main themes (both notably brief) are highly contrasting: a mocking and strongly rhythmic phrase in 6/8, and a languid one *(espressivo e dolente)* in 9/8. Particularly in the first theme, dissonant intervals are prominently, almost grotesquely, displayed, in the manner of "Suggestion diabolique."

The second movement, lush and warm, brings us into a different rhythmic and harmonic world, almost Schumanesque in its rich and elaborately accompanied *cantabile* melody. (Like the third movement of the Sixth Sonata, it is in waltz time.) Formidable obstacles are presented to the performer, who must negotiate sixty-fourth note runs in the right hand against thirty-second note runs in the left.

But the sonata's shortest movement—the concluding *Precipitato*, just over three minutes long—is the show-stopper. Impossibly dissonant chords proliferate; open minor sevenths alternate forte *marcato* between the right and left hand, in a "clumsy" but relentless 7/8 meter. The movement is built around a simple, insistently repeated and strongly syncopated three-note figure in the bass, played in octaves, rising and falling from B flat to C sharp to B flat, eighth note to quarter to eighth. Aggressively pointing to the major resolution in the tonic key, Prokofiev withholds it with satanic mischief, flaunting the parallel minor.

In its compelling interplay of tension and balance between the negative ("images of formlessness, disharmony and chaos") and the positive ("images of harmony, order and beauty"), the sonata emerges as one of Prokofiev's most accomplished compositions written since his return to the U.S.S.R. It is a dramatic embodiment of the strength and driving intensity of Prokofiev's (and Russia's) existence during the war years.

By now, Prokofiev no longer felt obliged to present his new piano music to the public. He entrusted the premiere of the Seventh Sonata to Sviatoslav Richter, who would first play it—with enormous success—in January 1943 in Moscow.

Having completed the sonata and the first version of *War and Peace*, Prokofiev was in the market for another big project. Since their successful collaboration on *Alexander Nevsky*, Eisenstein had several times asked Prokofiev to write music for films, but he had been too busy to accept. Now that he was free, he enthusiastically accepted a new proposal from Eisenstein: to write the score for a film biography of Tsar Ivan IV ("The Terrible"). Eisenstein invited Prokofiev to come to Alma-Ata, far out in Central Asia, where most of the Soviet film studios had been operating since the German attack in 1941. In late May, Prokofiev and Mira left Tbilisi and their friends for the long and tiring journey to Kazakhstan.

Prokofiev's colleagues were sorry to see them go. "We were all orphaned—and not only musically—by their departure," wrote Olga Lamm. "In his creative inspiration, Prokofiev had exerted a joyful influence on all of us, and forced others—through his wonderful music and robust, energetic presence—to face the trials of the time more courageously." Only a few months after Prokofiev and Mira left, Miaskovsky and the Lamms were forced to evacuate threatened Tbilisi.

They were sent to Frunze, another Central Asian city near the border between Kazakhstan and the Kirghiz Republic, where they encountered living conditions "a hundred times worse" than in Tbilisi or Alma-Ata.

To reach Alma-Ata, the capital of Kazakhstan, several thousand miles from Moscow and not far from the Chinese border, Prokofiev and Mira had to travel by ship across the Caspian Sea, then by train across desert wasteland. Because of the water shortage, they had to bring a keg of drinking water from Tbilisi. They finally reached their destination only toward the end of June.

"In Krasnovodsk it rained," Prokofiev wrote to Miaskovsky,

> although it stopped before we reached Alma-Ata. It wasn't too hot in the train, and sometimes at night we even wanted our overcoats. Alma-Ata (its name means "father of apples" or "apple father") has turned out to be a pleasant place with straight, wide streets drowning in greenery—poplars in rows. It would be like a summer resort if not for the asphalt, so we are not pining away for a *dacha*. The hotel is like the one in Nalchik, and the room is similar. . . . They've brought me an upright piano, made of lemon wood. Although it doesn't have a trademark, it has a pleasant sound.

Within weeks of moving in, Prokofiev had filled their small room with music. It was piled everywhere—"on the piano, on the floor, the chairs, the window sills."

The climate in Alma-Ata was warm and sunny, but food was rationed. Even so, life there was comfortable compared to the near-starvation many Soviet cities endured during the War. By now, Leningrad had been under siege for nearly a year, and thousands of people were dying of hunger and disease each month. After hearing of the hardships that Miaskovsky and the Lamms were confronting in Frunze, Prokofiev tried to arrange for them to come to Alma-Ata, but was unable to secure the necessary living space or ration cards.

Almost immediately, Prokofiev and Eisenstein plunged into work on *Ivan the Terrible*. Inviting Prokofiev to write the score, Eisenstein had promised him "great freedom in all areas." Since their collaboration on *Alexander Nevsky*, Eisenstein had deepened his knowledge and experience of music—he had even directed a controversial production of Wagner's *Die Walküre* at the Bolshoi Opera in November

1940. After the catastrophe with Meyerhold, Prokofiev had hoped to get Eisenstein to direct his opera *Semyon Kotko*, but other commitments prevented him from accepting.

Prokofiev had written no music for film in nearly four years—since *Alexander Nevsky*—but he had remained intensely interested in the artistic potential of the cinema. In 1939, turning down an offer from Eisenstein for another film score, Prokofiev had reassured him, "I continue to regard the cinema as the most contemporary art. Precisely because of that newness, though, we still haven't learned to appreciate its various components. Most people still consider the music as a little ditty off to the side, undeserving of special attention."

Like *Alexander Nevsky*, *Ivan the Terrible* was an ambitious project with strong political overtones. The film's subject, the enigmatic Tsar Ivan IV, ruled medieval Muscovy from 1533 to 1584—one of the longest reigns in Russian history. Renowned for his ferocity, piety, mercurial temperament and fanatical suspicion, Ivan was eventually given the descriptive title *Grozny*. The usual English translation of this word—"Terrible"—fails to convey the sense of awe and splendor contained in the Russian adjective, a reflection of the strange mixture of reverence and terror with which Ivan IV was viewed both by contemporaries and later generations.

Ivan IV's achievements included a notable expansion in Russian territory and military strength; an increase in state power at the expense of the fractious, scheming and wealthy land-owning aristocrats (the *boyars*); and the creation of a secret police force, the *oprichniki*, who, loyal to Ivan alone, meted out notoriously brutal punishment (often torture) to his real and imagined domestic enemies. The *oprichina* was the first of many purges to be carried out by Russian leaders against their own subjects in the centuries to come.

One of these, Stalin, had great respect and affection for Ivan. In Stalin's eyes, Ivan was a model ruler, despotic but respected by the masses. He once called Ivan "a great and wise ruler, who guarded the country from the penetration of foreign influence and strove to unify Russia." Pleased with Eisenstein's film biography of Nevsky—another of his favorite Russian military heroes—Stalin approved of his intention to make a film on the life of Ivan IV.

But Eisenstein would discover that Ivan's character and legacy presented many more contradictions and moral dilemmas than the rather one-dimensional *vita* of the saintly Alexander Nevsky. Ivan's legendary brutality and his oppressive rule made it difficult to idealize him in the same fairy-tale style. If Nevsky was a man at war only with the Teutonic invaders, Ivan was a man simultaneously at war with evil foreigners, his countrymen and his own psychotic personality. Making a film about such a complex and morally ambiguous figure—one of the most bloodthirsty leaders in world history—would have been a daunting undertaking even under the most favorable circumstances, but given Stalin's special emotional and political relationship to Ivan, it was fraught with danger. To his credit, Eisenstein was not intimidated, and refused to whitewash the troubling issues.

Originally, Eisenstein planned to cover Ivan's life in three full-length films. Only two were made, however, and only the first was released in Eisenstein's lifetime.

By the time Eisenstein and Prokofiev set to work on *Ivan* in the early summer of 1942, they were so familiar with each other's work and habits that they and the crew "understood each other almost without speaking." Since Eisenstein was so confident of Prokofiev's ability to compose the appropriate music, he instructed him to write a large portion of it before the shooting had even begun, using precise descriptions and pencil sketches of the various scenes. Prokofiev relied heavily on these visual images. Once he wrote a number—"The Pledge of the *Oprichniki*"—solely on the basis of Eisenstein's oral description, and it had to be redone, leading him to swear that he would never again compose without sketches. Without a visual reference point he said, he "could never catch all the nuances of Eisenstein's conception."

Even when Prokofiev would write music to completed sections of film, Eisenstein provided supplementary oral description, often in strong imagery. "Here it should sound like a child is being torn out of his mother's arms," or "Give me something that sounds like a corkscrew scraping on glass," Eisenstein would say after they had watched the scenes together.

After the music had been composed, Prokofiev would record it on the piano so it could be played with the film running. "If the image corresponded well to the music and there was no need for changes, I would set to work orchestrating the fragment."

It never seemed to bother Prokofiev that Eisenstein always had the last word. If anything, he enjoyed working for a strong-willed master with a clear artistic vision who knew exactly what he wanted—as his collaborations with Diaghilev and Meyerhold had already shown.

Prokofiev wrote a large amount of music for the two parts of *Ivan*—twenty-nine "numbers." Spanning a wider musical and dramatic range than those for *Alexander Nevsky*, they include epic patriotic choral episodes, extended sections drawing on the Russian Orthodox liturgy, grotesque music for the portrayal of Russia's enemies (particularly the Tartars), numerous folk-inspired songs connected with marriage and other rituals, a triumphant brass theme associated with Ivan's royal power, and a pathetic one played by the strings associated with his doubts and depression.

Part I of the film emphasizes Ivan's rise to power and his important military victories, while Part II concentrates on the change in his character toward increasing violence after the death of his beloved wife Anastasia. (In the film, she is poisoned by the conniving Yefrosinia Staritskaya, played by Serafima Birman, although historians have never definitely proven that Anastasia was in fact poisoned.) Some of the most interesting music is found in the "Scythian" numbers for the ruthless and coarse *oprichniki*.

Ivan the Terrible took several years to complete. Eisenstein agonized over the correct portrayal of Stalin's favorite Tsar, anxious not to make a mistake but intent on preserving his artistic integrity. Part I would be completed and released several years later, in late 1944, and Part II would be completed only in 1946. Although most of the music for the film was written in Alma-Ata in 1942, Prokofiev continued working sporadically on *Ivan* until 1946.

When not busy with *Ivan*, Prokofiev was spending his time in Alma-Ata gradually orchestrating *War and Peace*. (Since Pavel Lamm was in Frunze, Prokofiev had to begin the tedious job of writing out the full score himself.) He was working to incorporate suggestions made in a long-awaited letter he had recently received from Moscow; it contained the official response to his opera. After hearing *War and Peace* in a four-hand piano version played by Sviatoslav Richter and Alexander Vedernikov, the members of the Committee on Artistic Affairs had suggested certain changes, primarily in the military scenes. They advised him to "strengthen the dramatic and heroic aspect" and shorten the "genre" episodes. "They also wondered if it was best to begin *War and Peace* with a lyrical scene."

Setting to work on the revisions, Prokofiev conferred with Eisenstein, who helped him replace some of the "genre" scenes—particularly the French soldiers in Moscow—with more dynamic patriotic episodes. A bland epigraph, set for a large chorus in the style of a Soviet mass-song, was also added before the first scene. Its words make an explicit link between the opera's action and Soviet reality at the moment: "But our country has not yet risen to all her awesome, monstrous height, and woe betide the enemy in the hour when she does. A cruel end awaits him. Huge is this Russia of ours, our own Russian land."

Drawn from some of the most glorious pages of Russian history, both *War and Peace* and *Ivan the Terrible* were intended to portray the struggle against Hitler as a continuation of the ongoing defense of the Motherland over the centuries. Ironically, however, neither the opera nor the film would find unqualified official favor until long after the war was over.

Living in Alma-Ata, Prokofiev found his talents as an experienced and efficient composer of movie music in great demand. The several different film studios from Moscow and Leningrad temporarily located there had been combined into the Central United Studio for feature films. Since he was on the spot working with Eisenstein, other directors and producers were soon offering him projects. Times were hard, and Soviet artists—like all Soviet citizens—were doing work they might have avoided in peacetime. Like everyone else, Prokofiev felt he should make his contribution to the war effort, even if it meant collaborating on some clearly second-rate projects. He had less patriotic reasons, too, judging from a letter he wrote to Miaskovsky in early October. "Film work is interesting, profitable, and does not require strenuous creative energy. Alma-Ata is a pleasant city, and full of money."

In addition to *Ivan the Terrible*, he wrote scores for four other films. Three were "war films" (*Tonya, Kotovsky* and *Partisans in the Ukranian Steppe*) and one, *Lermontov*, was a biography of the Russian romantic poet Mikhail Lermontov (1814–41).

Lermontov had actually been in the works since before the War. The film's director, Albert Gendelstein (born 1906), had first approached Prokofiev in the spring of 1941, the hundredth anniversary of Lermontov's death, and they had met in Leningrad for preliminary discussions. The studio where the film was scheduled to be made, Soyuzdetfilm (Union Children's Film), was evacuated to Stalinabad after the War began, and Gendelstein continued working on *Lermontov* there.

Further delays followed when the censors demanded changes in the screenplay "strengthening the film's patriotic resonance." The author of the screenplay was Konstantin Paustovsky, a prominent Soviet prose writer. After the necessary changes had been made, by early

1942, Prokofiev and Gendelstein began corresponding about finishing the project.

Eight musical numbers for *Lermontov* had already been composed by then: a scene at the opera using music from Auber's opera *Fenella;* several waltzes; a polonaise; a quadrille; and one song. Preoccupied with his work on *War and Peace,* Prokofiev had inserted one of those waltzes (subtitled "Youth") and the polonaise into the opera, since it is set in the same historical era as *Lermontov.*

This led to an odd disagreement between Prokofiev and Gendelstein. The director still wanted to use the "Youth" waltz in *Lermontov,* but Prokofiev—uncharacteristically—refused, declaring, "It has moved once and for all into another world." Such reluctance to recycle a theme was highly unusual for Prokofiev, and seems to indicate that he had developed a strong emotional attachment to *War and Peace,* and particularly to Natasha Rostova, with whom the waltz is identified.

Just how difficult it was for Prokofiev to write a film score when he was not on the spot, involved in the actual shooting, is obvious from the problems he and Gendelstein encountered working together by correspondence. Prokofiev repeatedly complained that he needed more specific descriptions of what kind of music was required. Exactly how many "pieces" were needed, and exactly how many minutes should each one last? Unable to compose "in general," Prokofiev wanted precise specifications.

Another disagreement arose over Prokofiev's refusal to write all the music for *Lermontov* in one large block—as Gendelstein had suggested—and even inspired Prokofiev to deliver a stern lecture on how to construct a film score. Since the shots and montage would be edited and changed until the very last minute, it was much more efficient to compose small "separate fragments" that could be easily rearranged, Prokofiev told Gendelstein impatiently. A large block composed in one piece, on the other hand, would have to be entirely rewritten for every small change.

"My method is more convenient, more portable, and, in the final analysis, should yield better results. Your method would be fine if your montage were chiseled into stone once and for all—but that doesn't happen in the film business."

Prokofiev also complained that Gendelstein wanted too many different themes. "The spectator will leave without remembering a single theme," he wrote. "If one theme is repeated insistently, it will stick in the memory and become popular." Since the themes would occur each time in altered form, depending on the development of the narrative and characterizations with which they are associated, repeating them would not bore the audience.

Their disagreements (and Prokofiev's refusal to travel to Stalinabad) eventually led Prokofiev to abandon *Lermontov*. Its score was completed by another composer. Characteristically, Prokofiev later used the pieces he had already written in other compositions.

The remaining three films on which Prokofiev worked in Alma-Ata in 1942 reveal a little-known aspect of his Soviet career: Prokofiev the propaganda composer. All three films were made hastily. Two (*Tonya* and *Partisans in the Ukrainian Steppe*) were immediately topical stories of Soviet heroism against the Nazis. *Tonya*, directed by Abram Room, is the story of a simple telephone operator who sacrifices her life by secretly summoning Soviet artillery fire onto German weapons collected in front of her office. *Partisans in the Ukrainian Steppe* describes the heroic efforts of Ukrainian guerrilla fighters in 1941. *Kotovsky* deals with an earlier Soviet struggle against the Germans, in the Ukraine in 1918—the same setting used in *Semyon Kotko*.

On all these "war films," Prokofiev worked very differently than he had on films in the past. Here, he did not try (or, more precisely, he did not have enough time) to illustrate visually and "physically" each scene and episode. Instead, he worked from a generalized musical plan, using one musical idea (usually a song) as the emotional-psychological "key" that conveyed a general mood. Mira contributed the texts for the patriotic songs used in *Tonya* ("A Soldier's Love") and in *Kotovsky* ("Bessarabian Song").

Nor did Prokofiev hold the music he wrote for these three "war films" in particularly high regard. He never attempted to turn them into suites, and made few public comments on their composition or genesis. His other large projects—*Ivan the Terrible, War and Peace, Cinderella*—left him little energy to devote to them, and he must have known that they were more valuable as inspirational material than as art. They were also useful to him as a source of income. He was now providing not only for himself and Mira, but also for Lina and his sons in Moscow.

By autumn of 1942, the momentum of the War was beginning to shift in Russia's favor. The second great German offensive launched during the summer had bogged down in Stalingrad (now called Volgograd), an industrial city on the Volga. Hitler would suffer a decisive defeat there after one of the most destructive battles in world history. The incredible speed of the German advance across the U.S.S.R. was slowing. Supplies arriving from Russia's allies were helping the Soviet army and people to stiffen their resistance.

By early winter of 1942, it was even safe to return to Moscow. Having completed the first revision of *War and Peace*, and done for the moment with his work on *Ivan the Terrible*, Prokofiev traveled to the capital, arriving there in late December. During their six-week stay, he and Mira lived in Prokofiev's favorite hotel, the National.

One of the main goals of his trip was to arrange for a performance of *War and Peace*. Soon after he arrived, the opera was given an official hearing at the Composers' Union, where it provoked widely divergent reactions. Many critics and musicians, finding it difficult to accept the idea of Tolstoy's novel as an opera, judged the whole project "untheatrical" and doomed to failure on the stage.

But *War and Peace* gained one ardent defender—Samuil Samosud (1884–1964), a conductor then working at the Bolshoi Theater. He and Prokofiev immediately began discussing how to revise and produce the opera, and Samosud arranged a special private hearing for the staff of the Bolshoi Theater in mid-January. Prokofiev played *War and Peace* through on the piano, singing the arias in his weedy voice, but he failed to remove his critics' doubts. "The opera provoked obvious interest, but it was clear that many of the theatre's staff considered the difficulties it posed insurmountable."

Samosud persisted in his efforts on behalf of *War and Peace*, even initiating negotiations the following spring with Sergei Eisenstein, hoping he might direct it at the Bolshoi.

Prokofiev's comic opera *Betrothal in a Monastery*, shelved when the War broke out, had also attracted Samosud's attention. When it was heard in a special run-through at the Bolshoi in January, the official and critical reaction was so positive that a production at the Bolshoi Annex was tentatively scheduled for the coming season. Most of the cast and crew of the Bolshoi was still scattered all over Russia as a result of the War, however, and would return to Moscow only in the summer of 1943. This made it virtually impossible to draw up a definite production schedule. As a result of these and other problems, Samosud's ambitious plans for Prokofiev's operas at the Bolshoi would unfortunately come to nothing.

Prokofiev had much better luck with the new Seventh Sonata, which he had shown to Sviatoslav Richter in early January. "It was intensely fascinating, and I learned it in four days," Richter said later. He was also quick to formulate a very personal view of the violent sonata.

> Disorder and uncertainty reign. Man observes the raging of death-dealing forces, but what he lived for doesn't cease to exist. He feels, he loves. The fullness of what he is feeling reaches out toward others. He is together with the rest of mankind, protesting and suffering deeply with them in their common grief. Full of a will for victory, he makes a headlong running attack, clearing away all obstacles. He will become strong through struggle, expanding into a gigantic and life-affirming force.

Pleased with Richter's poetic enthusiasm, and hoping that he would agree to give the sonata's premiere, Prokofiev invited Richter to his hotel room to play it through.

> He was alone. There was a piano in the room, but it turned out that the pedal was broken, so Prokofiev said, "Well, let's fix it then. . . ." We crawled under the piano, repaired something, then suddenly knocked our foreheads together so hard that we saw stars. As Sergei Sergeevich used to recall later on, "But we did fix the pedal!" It was a businesslike meeting; we were both busy with the sonata. We spoke little. I have to say that I never had any serious conversations with Prokofiev. They were limited to a few explanations. Actually, besides this meeting over the Seventh Sonata, we were never alone together. And when there was a third person present, that third person would do all the talking.

Richter's premiere of Prokofiev's Seventh Sonata on January 18, 1943, in the Hall of Columns near the Bolshoi Theater, was one of the most memorable musical events of the War years. Prokofiev and Mira attended together, in one of their first public appearances in Moscow as a couple. Most of the city's important musical figures were there, too, and when Richter had finished playing, the hall exploded into tumultuous applause. Richter was called back again and again. Prokofiev also appeared on stage to acknowledge the ovation. After most of the audience had filed out, a few musicians who had remained behind, including David Oistrakh, asked Richter to repeat the sonata for them. They wanted to listen more carefully and calmly, savoring its energy and power. It was a gratifying moment for Prokofiev, a reward after months of intense and difficult work.

If Prokofiev took time away from his music to see Lina and his sons in the apartment of Chkalov Street while he was in Moscow in early 1943, he (understandably) left no record of what must have been a difficult visit. It seems likely that he met with Lina, perhaps alone; Sviatoslav and Oleg do not remember seeing their father during the War years. Despite the obvious love for and understanding of children found in so much of Prokofiev's music, his relationship with his own children was strangely distant, and even exhibits a certain selfishness and indifference to their plight. His sudden disappearance from their lives had confused and saddened his sons; Oleg would spend hours looking through the many books that Prokofiev had left behind, searching for an explanation. Prokofiev continued to provide for them financially, and Lina also supplemented the family income by doing translating and interpreting work in some of the many languages (Spanish, English, French, German, Italian) she knew. She spent many evenings socializing with European and American diplomatic and military personnel stationed in Moscow.

It seemed more unlikely than ever that she and Prokofiev would reconcile; Prokofiev's relationship with Mira—strengthened by their professional collaboration—was stable and apparently happy. In early February, buoyed by the success of the Seventh Sonata, and by Samosud's pledge to produce both *War and Peace* and *Betrothal in a Monastery* at the Bolshoi, Mira and Prokofiev set off on the long trip back to Alma-Ata.

There, as Prokofiev continued to work with Eisenstein on *Ivan the Terrible,* he received news of an important official honor that signified a solidification of his position in the musical hierarchy. On March 19, the recipients of the Stalin Prize were announced, and Prokofiev for the first time was among them. And yet the prize he received for the Seventh Piano Sonata was not "first class," but "second," indicating that the cultural bureaucrats still had some reservations about him. Awarded for particular compositions in various genre categories, the Stalin Prizes were also intended to honor a composer's contributions to Soviet music over the course of his career.

When the Stalin Prizes had been given out for the first time in 1940–41, Prokofiev had been conspicuously overlooked as many of his less famous colleagues, including Miaskovsky, received them. Shostakovich had also received one that year, for his Piano Quintet

(Op. 57). That Prokofiev had lived so long abroad and had only recently become a full-fledged Soviet composer was certainly one reason that he was passed over the first few times around, since the Stalin Prizes were awarded for loyalty to Soviet culture as well as for musical talent and craftmanship. In addition to the prestige, the Stalin Prizes carried a large cash award: 100,000 rubles for first class, 50,000 rubles for second class and 25,000 rubles for third class.

It may have been embarrassing for Prokofiev to receive a second-class prize for the Seventh Sonata, especially since first prize went to a younger composer, Shebalin. But Miaskovsky consoled his old friend, telling Prokofiev that Shebalin's winning quartet was "rather simple and worth much less than your sonata," a judgment that has proven true in terms of the international repertoire. Miaskovsky also advised Prokofiev to view the prize at least as a step in the right direction. "The important thing was to break the ice, and, it seems, it has now been broken," he wrote. Miaskovsky was right: over the next few years Prokofiev would receive a pile of official honors. Only a few months after his first Stalin Prize (he would receive five more), he was awarded the Order of the Red Banner of Labor and the label of Honored Artist of the Russian Soviet Socialist Republic.

Receiving these official honors must have pleased Prokofiev—he was always very aware of receiving his just recognition from those in authority—but they contained a hidden danger. Once a composer was decorated by the cultural bureaucracy, he also became more eligible for official punishment: the government giveth, and the government taketh away.

During the late winter and spring of 1943 in Alma-Ata, Prokofiev worked on a variety of projects, both old and new. Further revisions were made in *War and Peace* and in *Betrothal in a Monastery* for the anticipated Bolshoi productions. Other projects included writing more music for *Ivan the Terrible*; orchestrating a piece sketched out the preceding summer, *Ballad of an Unknown Boy*, an intensely patriotic cantata for dramatic soprano, dramatic tenor, chorus and orchestra set to a journalistic text by the popular Soviet poet Pavel Antokolsky; and gathering material for a new opera on Kazakh folk themes. Prokofiev's productivity was all the more impressive considering the difficult conditions under which he and Mira were living. Food was not the only rationed commodity; because it had to be conserved for military purposes, the electricity was turned off in the evenings, shortening the work day.

By far the most intriguing of Prokofiev's new projects was the "lyric-comic Kazakh opera" *Khan Buzai*. Prokofiev had intended to begin this opera for many years, and had collected a number of Kazakh folk melodies for it even before coming to Alma-Ata. While living there in 1942–43, he and Mira researched and compiled local folk material, attended concerts of Kazakh music and saw plays in the local theatres, and Mira began work on a libretto. Unfortunately, however, *Khan Buzai*—which promised to be a very interesting work—was left unfinished. Prokofiev's archives contain a nearly complete libretto, with many sections sketched out in musical detail. But Prokofiev's failing health, and other commitments, never allowed him to complete the opera.

For *Khan Buzai*, Prokofiev was planning to use a new compositional method, inspired by his work with film. The libretto was divided into very brief episodes—"like shots in a film"—and the musical material was to be similarly divided into small fragments corresponding to each episode. (*Semyon Kotko* and *Romeo and Juliet* had also been influenced strongly by cinematic techniques, but less completely and systematically.) In its musical and dramatic personality—a mixture of the lyric and comic—*Khan Buzai* would have been similar to *Betrothal in a Monastery*.

While Prokofiev was hard at work composing, his music was receiving performances back in Moscow that spring. His Second Quartet was played again by the Beethoven Quartet, and enjoyed an "extremely turbulent success." Sviatoslav Richter gave several recitals featuring the piano sonatas. David Oistrakh played his Second Violin Concerto, and Maria Yudina the Second Piano Concerto. On April 19, Natan Rakhlin conducted the belated Moscow premiere of the orchestral suite *The Year 1941* to a mixed critical reception. Even the faithful Miaskovsky admitted that "the composition seemed rather boring."

But on the whole, the official Soviet attitude toward Prokofiev and his music was definitely improving during the War years. His constant presence in Russia, his more collegial manner, and his willingness to write whatever sort of music was required, were finally convincing the bureaucrats that he was sincere in his commitment to Soviet culture. He was paying his dues. Leading Soviet instrumentalists and conductors were performing his works, and he was lauded in the press.

In part, this change in attitude toward Prokofiev reflected a general cultural relaxation during the War years. Now that Stalin had a real enemy—Hitler—his campaign against the bogeyman of the Russian artistic intelligentsia had eased. Writers, composers and artists were finding that they could speak out more freely in wartime than in peacetime. All of Russia was united in the noble fight for survival, leaving the government little energy for a second war against its own people. Despite the hardships, it was an oddly optimistic time. The relaxation also led many to believe—mistakenly—that the Soviet cultural environment would be much freer when the War was over.

America, now an ally of the U.S.S.R., was also taking a renewed interest in the work of Russian writers and composers, including Prokofiev. Magazines and newspapers featured inspiring articles on the difficult lives of the brave Soviet artists. In May, the conductor Leopold Stokowski wrote to Prokofiev from Beverly Hills. "I am often thinking of you and your family in these difficult times," he said. "After the War is over I am going to Russia and look forward to meeting you all again then." Like most of Prokofiev's former colleagues in America, Stokowski did not yet know that the composer had left Lina and his sons for Mira.

"Last winter I conducted your *Alexander Nevsky* with the NBC Orchestra and the Westminster Choir," Stokowski continued. "I was deeply impressed by this Russian epic that you have created and feel it is one of your greatest works. I have heard that you have finished your new opera *War and Peace*. I would like very much to conduct this in America, if you are willing." Stokowski continued to negotiate with Prokofiev and the Soviet Embassy in Washington over the next few years in an attempt to produce the opera.

During the War years, as America and Russia joined forces against fascism, Americans wanted to think the best of Stalin and his government. Trusting, naive and unfamiliar with the Soviet system, they tended to believe that once the War was over, the two countries would develop a closer cultural and political relationship. To a certain extent, Soviet citizens shared this belief, for during the War America received more positive coverage in the Soviet press than at any other time in Soviet history. But both Americans and Soviets—including Stokowski and Prokofiev—would discover that the apparent bonhomie of their wartime alliance was superficial and ephemeral.

By early summer of 1943, the tide of the War was turning in favor of the Allies. The disastrous German defeat at Stalingrad in the winter had dealt a death blow to the Nazi campaign to conquer Russia. The Soviet army began slowly to win back its territory, confidence and strength. In Moscow, life was returning to a semblance of normality; symphonic concerts began again.

Restless in isolated Alma-Ata, and eager to tackle new projects, Prokofiev was glad when the Kirov Theater invited him to come to the city of Molotov, on the European side of the Urals, its temporary home during the War. The Kirov wanted him to complete *Cinderella*, put aside two years earlier. With *War and Peace* behind him (he thought), Prokofiev was anxious to complete the interrupted ballet.

In mid-June, after saying goodbye to Eisenstein, Prokofiev and Mira left exotic Alma-Ata for the last time, bound for Molotov and, a few months later, Moscow.

CHAPTER 21

SWAN

How could he have dreamt of such happiness when
he was an ugly duckling?

—SERGEI PROKOFIEV, "The Ugly Duckling"

Traveling from Alma-Ata to Molotov, a distance of nearly two thousand miles across desolate Kazakhstan, was complicated and arduous even in peacetime. In June of 1943, as the German army prepared for its last major offensive in Russia, it was exhausting, slow and dangerous. Prokofiev and Mira followed a route through Kuibyshev, a city on the Volga upstream from Stalingrad. Formerly known as Samara, Kuibyshev had served temporarily as the Soviet capital at the beginning of the War, when it appeared that Moscow might fall. By the early summer of 1943, the government had long since returned to Moscow, and Kuibyshev's most prestigious visitors were the members of the Bolshoi Theater, evacuated there in 1941, at the same time that Prokofiev and his colleagues had fled to Nalchik.

In Kuibyshev, the Bolshoi Theater administration found room for Prokofiev and Mira on a steamboat sailing north up the Volga, then up the Kama to Molotov.

Today, Molotov is known by its original ancient name, Perm. Located on the western slope of the Urals at a strategic bend of the Kama, one of the chief tributaries of the Volga, Perm has belonged to Russia since the fifteenth century. Under Stalin, it briefly bore the name Molotov to honor Viacheslav Molotov, one of Stalin's closest and most resilient advisers, and Commissar for Foreign Affairs during World War II. After Stalin and Molotov were reviled by Khrushchev at the

Twentieth Party Congress in 1956, however, the city that bore his name again became Perm, just as Stalingrad's name was changed to Volgograd.

Thousands of miles to the east of Moscow, Perm has always been an important regional center, with a university, an opera house and a long cultural tradition. Even so, it was far from easy for the members of Leningrad's Kirov Theater, used to their large and luxuriously appointed home in a cosmopolitan European city, to adjust to Perm's small theatre and provincial atmosphere. Prokofiev later wrote:

> I found the enormous collective of the Kirov squeezed into the modest facilities of the local opera house. It was difficult for the artists to alter the scale of the scenery to fit the small dimensions of the stage. It was even more difficult for the dancers, accustomed to the stage of the Leningrad theater, to "dance on a dime." But the interest— even adoration—that the inhabitants of Perm lavished upon every performance, upon every performer, provided compensation for all these difficulties. The auditorium was full to overflowing, and every evening a large group of people would gather around the entrance, their faces full of disappointment because they had been unable to get tickets.

Despite the cramped conditions, the Kirov Theater continued to create new productions in Perm. In December of 1942, a new ballet by Aram Khachaturian, *Gayane,* had received its premiere there, and went on to enjoy great success both in the U.S.S.R. and abroad.

Prokofiev had come to Perm, where he would stay for four months, to finish work on *Cinderella* (Op. 87). Two of its three acts had been sketched out "for better or for worse" two years earlier, in early 1941, before Prokofiev abandoned the ballet to write *War and Peace.* Since relatively little work remained, the Kirov was intending to begin staging *Cinderella* in Perm by August of 1943, and to give the public premiere before the new year. "It seems I'll be able to kill the beauty off in the time the theatre has allotted," Prokofiev had written to Miaskovsky on the eve of his departure from Alma-Ata.

Like *Romeo and Juliet,* however, *Cinderella* would take longer to reach the stage than either Prokofiev or the theatre administration anticipated. In fact, the premiere would take place two years later, after the War had ended, and at the Bolshoi Theater in Moscow, not the Kirov in Leningrad.

From the very start of his work on *Cinderella* in early 1941,

Prokofiev had concentrated on writing a ballet that was "as danceable as possible." He wanted to create dances "that would emerge naturally from the story line, that would be varied, that would allow the dancers to do enough dancing and to exhibit their technique." No doubt Prokofiev wanted to avoid the arguments and humiliation he had encountered at the Kirov in 1940, when the supposedly "difficult" and "undanceable" score of *Romeo and Juliet* was disfigured and simplified against his wishes.

Cinderella makes much greater use than *Romeo* of the forms and conventions of nineteenth-century Russian ballet music. Soviet dancers and choreographers were trained in that tradition, and felt more comfortable in it. Not surprisingly, Prokofiev's most obvious model for *Cinderella*—a fairy-tale ballet with strong thematic similarities to *Swan Lake*, *The Nutcracker* and *Sleeping Beauty*—were the ballets of Tchaikovsky.

Cinderella's score is filled with static conventional ballet "numbers" that would have disappointed Diaghilev: several *pas de deux*, an *adagio*, a gavotte, many waltzes, a pavanne, a passepied, a bourrée, a mazurka, galops. Many of them have no direct connection to the psychological or dramatic action. "Each character has his (or her) own variation," Prokofiev wrote, apparently proudly, forgetting or ignoring his former disdain for static "numbers" intended to show off a ballerina's technique. If Diaghilev had commissioned a *Cinderella* from Prokofiev, it would surely have been a much shorter one-act opera in the style of *Prodigal Son*.

Both musically and dramatically, *Cinderella* was the most traditional ballet Prokofiev had ever written. It contains hardly a hint of Prokofiev the theatrical reformer, the fierce young defender of dramatic truth and movement.

The ballet's scenario was written by Nikolai Volkov, an experienced if conventional librettist. His retelling of the universal Cinderella story closely follows the most famous version of the tale, written by Charles Perrault in 1697 and later reworked by the Brothers Grimm. Volkov and Prokofiev considered, but eventually decided against, using the Russian folk version of the Cinderella tale recorded by the Russian folklorist Alexander Afanasiev.

In that colorful Russian version, Cinderella is called "Chernushka"—"Blackie." (The more Europeanized "Zolushka" is a literal translation of the name "Cinderella" or "Cendrillon," using the Russian word for cinders.) She also has a given name, Masha. Other details of the Russian tale—which is strikingly violent and primitive—are also different. Cinderella's magic helpers are two doves, not a fairy godmother. The scene at the ball takes place not only once, but three evenings in a row, and Cinderella finally loses her slipper because the Prince has coated the staircase with tar to prevent her from escaping. When the prince comes searching for the owner of the slipper, Cinderella's evil stepmother orders her two daughters to cut off their toes so the slipper will fit. After Cinderella tries on the slipper and is once again transformed into a beautiful princess, the Prince marries her. She also has her revenge: as they leave the church, the two magic doves attack each stepsister, pecking out an eye.

The folksy storyteller who narrates the tale concludes, "The wedding was merry, and I was there. I drank mead and beer and it ran down my whiskers, and wouldn't go in my mouth."

But Volkov and Prokofiev did not—unfortunately—use this variant of the Cinderella tale, adhering instead to the more popular and conventional Western one. Their libretto sets the action in the eighteenth century, Prokofiev's favorite era, and one which he had already illustrated in *Betrothal in a Monastery, Love for Three Oranges, Lt. Kizhe* and the "Classical" Symphony. The setting also gave him the opportunity to include numerous courtly dances, both affectionate and ironic.

Although Volkov wrote the original scenario, Prokofiev made many changes and additions. Most important, Prokofiev strengthened the humorous and grotesque elements, demonstrating once again his lifelong fondness for caricature, the ironic and the silly. Not surprisingly, it is Cinderella's wicked stepsisters—Khudyshka and Kubyshka (Skinny and Fatty)—who are the prime targets of the satire. The satire is, however, much less persuasive and vicious than in *Love for Three Oranges* or *The Buffoon,* which provided similar thematic material. *Cinderella*'s spirit is more gentle.

In revising the libretto, Prokofiev added the nasty argument between the two stepsisters over the shawl *(Pas de Shawl)* in Act I and the incident with the three oranges in Act II; made the "Dancing Lesson" scene in Act I more specific and comic; and emphasized the meanness of the stepsisters, turning the scene of their elaborate preparations for the ball into a "comic episode." From Prokofiev also came the wonderfully succinct characterization of the Prince, who is close in spirit to the spoiled Prince of *Three Oranges:* "The Prince mounts his throne like a saddle." Like the Prince in *Oranges,* this one also achieves maturity only after experiencing and pursuing love for a non-royal heroine, who becomes his Princess.

The positive characters (Cinderella, her father, the Prince, the Fairy Godmother) are treated with sympathetic lyricism. Prokofiev toned down the heavily romantic and sentimental atmosphere of Volkov's original scenario but did not eliminate it entirely, as he might have done in earlier years.

Each of the three acts (there are no scenes) of *Cinderella* is divided into short episodes. But unlike the episodes of *Romeo and Juliet*, many of them bear the names of dance forms—"Gavotte," "Variation of the Fairy of Winter," "Duet of the Prince and Cinderella," "Grand Waltz"—rather than titles descriptive of the dramatic action. This structure is strongly reminiscent of the musical-dramatic organization of the ballet scores of Tchaikovsky or Glazunov, whom Prokofiev was consciously imitating. Similarly, the music for *Cinderella* is less "specific" than in many of Prokofiev's scores for the stage and screen; the close visual connection between music and physical gesture that makes *Romeo and Juliet* and *Alexander Nevsky* so unique is much weaker here.

One possible explanation for this difference is the limited amount of dramatic action in *Cinderella*. A short and slight story already very familiar to the audience, it needed padding—and therefore extraneous material—to fill three acts.

In the music, Prokofiev said he wanted to stress the lyrical quality of the tale. "I wanted to convey the poetic love between Cinderella and the Prince—the birth and flowering of that feeling, the obstacles thrown in its path, the realization of the dream." Perhaps his own relationship with Mira influenced Prokofiev's interpretation; he had begun working on *Cinderella* immediately after leaving Lina for Mira. In any case, Cinderella receives three broadly lyrical themes. The first is associated with her humiliation at the hands of her stepmother and stepsisters, the second with her purity and longing for a more beautiful existence, and the third with her happy love for the Prince.

Some of the ballet's most interesting musical moments, however, are given to the fantastic characters, including the four fairies representing the four seasons (perhaps directly inspired by Glazunov's 1899 ballet *The Seasons*) and the Fairy Godmother. Another fantastic scene, one of the most famous in all of Prokofiev's ballets, comes when the clock strikes midnight: the mischievous gnomes (representing the hours of the clock) scamper about the stage in a wild tap dance, a wooden pendulum strikes threateningly, and the entire orchestra shudders in dissonant dismay.

Prokofiev completed most of *Cinderella* in piano score while living in Perm during the summer and early fall of 1943, but the scheduled production failed to take place there as planned. This time, the postponement was not caused by political objections. It was simply too difficult to design an ambitious production in the small confines of the Perm theatre, and some of the necessary dancers were unavailable. Prokofiev would complete the orchestration of *Cinderella* in 1944, and it would be produced at the Bolshoi in Moscow only in late 1945. Even before the score was finished, though, Prokofiev was using pieces of it in other compositions.

Cinderella was not the only work Prokofiev composed during his Perm sojourn. He also completed the Sonata for Flute and Piano. Commissioned by the Committee on Artistic Affairs, the Flute Sonata (Op. 94) had been begun in Alma-Ata in late 1942. Prokofiev had sought the commission himself, after becoming intrigued with the idea of writing a piece for flute, an instrument "insufficiently represented in musical literature." This was his only sonata—and one of his very few compositions—written for a wind or brass instrument. When he began it, the sonata provided a welcome diversion from feverish work on two big projects, *War and Peace* and *Ivan the Terrible*. Creating a purely abstract and apolitical work was "perhaps inappropriate at the moment, but pleasant," he told Miaskovsky almost apologetically.

One of the most popular pieces in the flute repertoire today, the sonata was originally intended "to sound in bright and transparent classical tones." Prokofiev achieved that goal with complete success. The resolute optimism, emotional directness and nearly total absence of irony are almost startling in the context of his music.

An extensive piece in four movements *(Moderato, Scherzo, Andante, Allegro con brio)*, the Flute Sonata is unambiguously diatonic and closely follows classical sonata-allegro form. It shares its "sunny" key of D Major with the equally bright and transparent "Classical" Symphony and First Violin Concerto. Both of the main themes in the long first movement are marvelously simple and singing, and notably (for Prokofiev) free of accidentals. The first theme, firmly rooted on dominant and tonic, is in longer note values, while the second moves more quickly in a dotted, but still square, rhythm. The form is almost self-consciously classical, even down to the repeat of the exposition.

The second movement *Scherzo* is relatively restrained, with an uncharacteristic and highly lyrical slow section in the middle. The piano accompaniment here is minimal, allowing the flutist to show off his technique in extended eighth and sixteenth note runs. Occasional flashes of mischievous dissonance—minor seconds and ninths—do occur, however, in the piano part.

The shortest movement is the *Andante,* in disarmingly distant F Major, followed by the rather martial finale, firmly planted, like the first movement, on the dominant and tonic of D Major. Here, the piano accompaniment becomes more aggressive, in slightly humorous octaves imitating a diligent student's exercises.

Oddly enough, flutists "did not rush" to perform the Flute Sonata, even after its first performance by the flutist N. Kharkovsky and Sviatoslav Richter in Moscow in late December 1943. Violinists, including David Oistrakh, took an immediate interest in the piece, however, believing correctly that it would "enjoy a more full-blooded life on the stage" if rearranged as a sonata for violin and piano.

Although he had been able to make productive use of his months in Perm, Prokofiev was now eager to get back to Moscow, where—he hoped—*War and Peace* and/or *Betrothal in a Monastery* would soon be staged. The Bolshoi administration had already paid him an advance of five thousand rubles for *Betrothal,* but there was still no definite word on when it would be produced. Eventually, this proposed Bolshoi *Betrothal* fell through, and the Kirov took over the project.

With *Cinderella* nearly finished, Prokofiev left Perm for Moscow in early autumn of 1943. At the time, he thought he would be returning to Perm in January for planned Kirov productions of the ballet and perhaps of *Betrothal in a Monastery,* but both would be postponed.

Prokofiev and Mira remained in and near Moscow for the next ten years—the remainder of their life together. After nearly thirty years of almost constant traveling, Prokofiev's days of wandering were over. The last phase of his life would be more sedentary.

As the momentum of the War continued to build against Germany, most of the artists evacuated from Moscow at the beginning of the War were now happily returning to their homes. But Prokofiev and Mira did not have a Moscow home to return to—they had been evacuated only a few months after he had left Lina and the apartment on Chkalov Street. For most of the next year, Prokofiev and Mira would have to live in hotels crowded with soldiers and officers in transit, never knowing how long they could stay in one room or hotel. Through the winter and early spring of 1943–44, they lived in the Hotel Moscow, a grimly imposing concrete fortress between the foot of Gorky Street and Red Square, a newly constructed example of the monumental architecture favored by Stalin. Only in late 1944 would Prokofiev and Mira finally receive a small apartment of their own.

By the last years of the War, Moscow was chaotic and overrun, teeming with thousands of dispossessed peasants seeking food, shelter and lost relatives. The Soviet economy, never noted for its efficiency, had been shattered and plundered. Severe even in peacetime, the housing shortage was terrible: ten or fifteen people frequently lived together in one room. Privacy was nonexistent. Even for famous artists and intellectuals, the basics were very hard to come by. Prokofiev and Mira must have felt lucky even to have a room of their own.

Glad to be back in Moscow, surrounded by old friends and stimulated by the reviving cultural life, Prokofiev plunged with his usual energy and enthusiasm into the musical scene. Despite the material inconveniences, the next year would be one of the happiest and most productive of his entire career. Peace was coming, his music was played and praised, he was receiving official recognition, he was financially secure, he had found personal contentment with Mira. For the moment, his health was good.

After he was settled, Prokofiev's first priority was *War and Peace.* Samosud, the Bolshoi conductor, had agreed to give a concert performance, sung by members of the Bolshoi company, in December—the first step, Prokofiev hoped, in getting the opera to the Bolshoi stage.

In the meantime, Prokofiev's music was flooding the concert halls. In late November, his compositions were included in an evening of music by "the older generation of Soviet composers" at the Central Workers' House. (Other members of this generation were Miaskovsky and Yury Shaporin, but not Shostakovich, considered to belong to the "younger" generation.) On December 7, Kharkovsky and Richter gave the world premiere of the Flute Sonata. On Christmas Day, Prokofiev made one of his increasingly rare piano appearances at the Great Hall of the Moscow Conservatory with the Beethoven Quartet, celebrating its twentieth anniversary; they performed his Overture on Hebrew Themes. Two days later, another Prokofiev world premiere was given in Moscow—the eight-part orchestral suite he had constructed from *Semyon Kotko.*

But the premiere that was most important to Prokofiev—*War and Peace*—again ran into trouble. In late December, just before the opera was to have been performed in concert, Samosud, its most vocal and energetic defender, was "unexpectedly released" from his job at the Bolshoi Theater. The concert performance was canceled, and *War and Peace*, which still had many critics at the Bolshoi, was dropped from the theatre's repertoire plans, its future fate again uncertain. A few years later, in his new position at the Maly Opera Theater in Leningrad, Samosud would try again to put *War and Peace* on stage.

In a letter to Eisenstein in Alma-Ata, Prokofiev explained that the new Bolshoi administration was under pressure to present "a couple of classical operas," so *War and Peace* had been "a little bit delayed." The Bolshoi tried to "pacify" him by promising a production of *Cinderella* in the upcoming fall season. None of this would come to pass as Prokofiev hoped, however.

Despite the improvement in the official attitude toward Prokofiev and his music during the War, his operas and ballets continued to encounter stubborn resistance. In part, these difficulties were a natural result of the wartime atmosphere, which made long-range planning difficult and forced theatres to work with a troupe whose size and composition were in constant flux. But this was not the only reason. During the same period, composers like Kabalevsky and Dzerzhinsky guided their much less interesting operas and ballets to the stage without such problems. The difference between them and Prokofiev, of course, was their unblemished political backgrounds.

Even his nearly eight years of full-time residence in the U.S.S.R. had failed to erase completely the traces of Prokofiev's "decadent" capitalist past, of his close relationships with suspicious figures like Meyerhold and Diaghilev, or of his foreign family connections. Many of the ranking Soviet cultural bureaucrats, as well as many composers, still resented and mistrusted Prokofiev, and were unwilling to forgive his years abroad. They used this issue as an excuse to vent their envy and frustration at his superior talent and discipline. Although by 1944 he was much more integrated into the Soviet musical establishment than when he had first moved back to the U.S.S.R. in 1936, Prokofiev was still regarded as something of an outsider. Assimilation was still incomplete—and always would be.

Not that Prokofiev wasn't making a concerted effort to become an accepted member of the cultural establishment, as a note he wrote to his old friend and mentor Koussevitsky in late 1943 shows. Aware that all mail sent to the United States would be scrutinized for political rectitude, Prokofiev adopted a stiff and formal tone, in stark contrast to the racy and even nasty letters he used to send to Koussevitsky during his Paris years.

"I'm taking advantage of this opportunity to send you greetings and to express my joy at discovering that you are—as in the past— robust, active and productive in your work," he wrote. "We were all very happy to learn that you have become head of the musical commission of the National Council on American-Soviet Friendship, and we expect lively artistic communication with this organization." Unfortunately, this "communication" never really materialized, either for Prokofiev or for other Soviet composers.

The War and his new "official" role as a Soviet composer had led to a nearly complete break in Prokofiev's formerly close contact with friends and colleagues in Europe and America. Most of them were unaware of the important changes in his personal life and could not imagine the terrible hardships Soviet citizens were enduring.

Mira was always at Prokofiev's side now, even for his public appearances in Moscow. Although in fact they had not yet been married nor had he ever been divorced from Lina, he referred to Mira in conversation and writing as his "wife": in a letter to his old friend Vera Alpers, who had remained in Leningrad throughout the nine hundred days of the Nazi blockade, Prokofiev explained, "Big changes have also taken place in my life: I divorced Lina Ivanovna, married a second time, and am happy in my second marriage."

Why did Prokofiev insist on speaking of Mira as his wife? Religious or moral reservations about living publicly with a woman out of wedlock were not the cause. Prokofiev had always been a stubborn atheist; his first marriage to Lina was not performed in a church. But he was concerned about his official public image. In the early 1940s, Soviet attitudes toward marriage were changing, becoming more respectable and bourgeois.

After the 1917 Revolution, marriage had for several decades been regarded as a politically reactionary institution—primarily because of its close association with the Russian Orthodox Church. With the destruction and discrediting of the Church, marriage temporarily lost its meaning. Couples frequently lived together for long periods without marrying, encountering no social ostracism. Record-keeping during the early years of the Soviet regime was so chaotic, and the law changed so often, that people weren't always sure how to register their marriages in any case.

By the late 1930s, however, this free-for-all situation had changed. As Stalin's power grew, the unconventional social and moral attitudes of the postrevolutionary era were replaced by more conventional—even puritanical—values. Increasingly, couples were expected to receive official sanctification for their marriages, which were performed in the solemn pseudo-religious atmosphere of Marriage Palaces, under the inspiring gaze of Lenin. The chaos of World War II led to an easing of this requirement, but only partially and temporarily. In fact, toward the end of the War, in July 1944, a sweeping reform of Soviet marriage and divorce laws was carried out. Henceforth, only marriages that were officially registered with the Census Bureau would be regarded as binding. Divorces, formerly granted almost automatically, now had to be considered by a court.

The increasing regimentation of marriage laws helps to explain why Prokofiev chose to distort the truth about his legal relationship with Mira, whom he was as yet unable to marry. To his close friends, it made no difference. Few of them were aware that he was still married to Lina, and even if they were, they chose to overlook it. As far as they were concerned, Mira was his wife—especially since he seemed so happy with her, and she with him.

Now that he was back in Moscow, Prokofiev still had little contact with Lina and his sons, although he did provide for them financially. They continued to live in the apartment on Chkalov Street. Lina refused to give her husband a divorce, in part because she was apprehensive—and rightly so—about what might happen to her in the U.S.S.R. without the legal protection of being Prokofiev's wife. Sviatoslav, who had recently turned twenty, and Oleg, going on sixteen, saw their father only rarely if at all. They would meet Mira only after the War. Not surprisingly, they would never develop a close relationship with their father's second partner, even after their own mother disappeared from the scene.

Most of those who had known Prokofiev with both Lina and Mira found that he seemed happier and calmer now. To the soprano Nina Dorliak, wife of Sviatoslav Richter, Prokofiev in the war years was still "abrupt, but with a great sense of humor, tall, striding widely, always extravagantly dressed—a little bit in the American style." She found

Mira a "very generous woman" who enjoyed inviting her husband's musical colleagues for tea and conversation.

Even Mira could not smooth over all of Prokofiev's legendary rough edges, however. One day, Dorliak recalled, she and her mother arrived a little late for an appointment with him. "He got terribly angry—he couldn't stand it when people were late, even by a minute. He was really furious!"

As he established a new Moscow life with Mira during that hopeful winter and spring of 1944, an unusually cheerful Prokofiev presided over numerous performances of his music, including the premiere of the *Ballad of an Unknown Boy*. He also continued to produce occasional political pieces, like his March for Band (Op. 99) in honor of May Day (May 1, International Workers' Day), the most important political holiday in the Soviet calendar after the anniversary of the October Revolution. It was broadcast on the radio as part of the festivities.

But most of his time went to more "private" compositions. One was the rearrangement of the Flute Sonata for violin and piano which David Oistrakh had been encouraging him to undertake. The composer proceeded in his usual organized fashion, impressing Oistrakh. "Everything happened very quickly," Oistrakh said later. "As Sergei Sergeevich suggested, I provided two or three variants for each place in the Sonata that required editing. Then I numbered them and gave them to him to look over. With a pencil, he marked what he found suitable and made a few corrections. That is how—with a minimum of discussion—the violin version of the Sonata was completed." The number of changes made in the flute part were "minimal," mostly for bowing. No changes were made in the piano accompaniment.

Oistrakh introduced the Sonata for Violin and Piano No. 2 (Op. 94-bis) to the world in Moscow on June 17, 1944, accompanied by Lev Oborin. (In fact this was Prokofiev's first completed violin-piano sonata, but the name Sonata No. 1 for Violin and Piano had already been given to the still-unfinished Op. 80.) In this violin-piano form— more aggressive and biting than the original flute version, and loaded with technical difficulties for the violinist—the sonata has enjoyed great popularity with audiences and performers.

Prokofiev was not in the audience for the premiere, however. A week earlier, he and Mira had happily abandoned the noise and confusion of the capital for the countryside, where they would remain through the summer and early fall. They took up residence in a House of Creative Work belonging to the Composers' Union, on the grounds of a collective poultry farm near the town of Ivanovo. Many composers had lived and worked in quiet and isolated Ivanovo throughout the war years. Here, their material needs were taken care of, and they could concentrate more fully on writing music.

Despite the wartime shortages—as Prokofiev told Miaskovsky, attempting to persuade him to join them—the food in Ivanovo was "wonderful—fresh, tasty, abundant. The forest is no worse than the one at Nikolina Gora, and now, with the young foliage, simply beautiful. I don't understand why in the devil you must hang around in the city!"

The main house at Ivanovo, a one-story structure that had once served as a landowner's manor house not unlike the one in which Prokofiev spent his childhood, sat on the bank of a small stream. The windows looked over fields, birch groves, and, far in the distance, a deep forest. Some of the composers lived in the main house and worked in special rooms set aside as studios in the neighboring village. Others lived and worked in separate cottages near the main house.

Among Prokofiev's companions at Ivanovo in 1944 were the greats of Soviet music. Prokofiev's first teacher, Glière, now seventy years old, was there, along with Shostakovich, Khachaturian and Yury Shaporin. Also spending the summer in Ivanovo was Dmitri Kabalevsky (born 1905), whose bureaucratic power in the Composers' Union was rapidly growing. For many composers resting and working at Ivanovo, this was their first opportunity to spend time with the world-famous Prokofiev in a relaxed and informal atmosphere.

Prokofiev's treatment of his Soviet colleagues had mellowed somewhat since 1935, when, on the eve of his final return to the U.S.S.R., he had dismissed Kabalevsky and his ilk as "zeros." By the summer of 1944, he had become almost sociable. Instead of taking one of the separate cottages, he and Mira lived in a room in the main house. In their free time, they participated in the social life of the community; the near-sighted, awkward and "completely helpless" Prokofiev even tried to play volleyball with his younger and more athletic associates. But some observers insist that Prokofiev still retained his arrogance and wit; he did not suddenly turn into the generous, kind and unfailingly cheerful icon official Soviet spokesmen (particularly Kabalevsky) like to paint.

As usual, Prokofiev worked regularly and methodically at Ivanovo, so much so that he amazed and even intimidated his fellow composers. He was also unable to refrain from teasing those who failed to produce new music—just as he had kept track of the grades each student received at the Conservatory forty years earlier. Such an overbearing and self-confident attitude did not endear him to those less prolific or self-confident than he.

Never late for breakfast, Prokofiev would head straight from the dining room at nine and, his thick briefcase under his arm, walk across the fields to the nearby village where he had a studio, furnished with a piano. Kabalevsky, who has tended to sentimentalize his descriptions of the famous colleagues he would later discredit, used to accompany him across the meadow.

On the edge of the village was a nursery school, where the children of the workers from one of the Ivanovo factories lived in the summertime. As we were on our way to the village, they would usually be walking with their teacher through the birch grove that lay on our route. Sergei Sergeevich was the first to establish friendly relations with them. He won over their hearts first with some bright cigarette packages [the children were fascinated with the bright shiny paper], then with lollipops, but most of all with his warm and affectionate manner.

Even accounting for Kabalevsky's tendency to sugar-coat his memoirs of Prokofiev, giving him the qualities required of a Great Soviet Socialist Artist, it does appear that Prokofiev's mood in the summer of 1944 was unusually relaxed.

After his morning constitutional, part of his daily routine throughout his career, Prokofiev would work on new music for a few hours, until lunchtime. In the afternoon he rarely composed; he would look over what he had completed, plan his work schedule, and prepare works to be written out in full score. This daily schedule almost never varied. Prokofiev rarely composed for more than a few hours at a time, but he worked every day. In his approach to composing, Prokofiev was methodical and calculating, working with control and regularity rather than in great bursts of frenetic inspiration followed by fallow periods.

For relaxation, Prokofiev would walk in the woods around the main house, where he once encountered a stray white scraggly dog that became his constant companion. He also took a strange fascination in the activity of ants, stopping to stare intently at ant hills along the forest paths. Perhaps what attracted him was their ceaseless movement, their directed activity, their organization and their unending passion for work—much like his own. And of course there was his favorite game, chess. He still took great pleasure—even too much pleasure— in beating his colleagues.

The comfortable and peaceful conditions at Ivanovo in the summer of 1944 allowed Prokofiev to devote all his energy to composition. Content and invigorated, at the peak of his musical and emotional power, he produced two of his greatest works—the Fifth Symphony and the Eighth Piano Sonata. Although they reflect two very different aspects—the epic and the lyrical—of Prokofiev's musical personality, they share a new maturity, seriousness and depth of expression. They also share a common key: solid but dark B flat Major. But most importantly, both compositions synthesize and summarize the many different artistic stages through which Prokofiev had passed, surveyed from a new height of experience and wisdom.

The Eighth Piano Sonata was the last of the three "Kislovodsk" Sonatas, all originally conceived during the summer of 1939 in Kislovodsk, when Prokofiev and Mira first met. Dedicated to Mira, the Eighth Sonata is, both musically and emotionally, a gentle and romantic tribute to the love that had helped him survive and create during the difficult years of the War. Their first meeting in Kislovodsk had, in fact, occurred almost exactly five years before the completion of the Eighth Sonata. On the last page of the score Prokofiev recorded the date: "Ivanovo-Sortirov, June 29, 1944."

Among Prokofiev's nine piano sonatas, the Eighth yields in length (nearly thirty minutes) only to the Sixth—and by less than a minute in most performances. Composed in three movements, the Eighth also has both the longest first movement (about fourteen minutes!) and the most thoroughly lyrical and reflective temperament of the nine. For Prokofiev, whose original reputation was built on a nearly perverse fondness for velocity, the predominance of slow tempos is striking: both the first movement *(Andante dolce)* and the second *(Andante sognando)* are slow, followed by a concluding *Vivace*.

"Sweet" and "dreamy" are words rarely associated with Prokofiev or his music, but they occur with surprising frequency in the Eighth Sonata. Not only does the first movement begin *Andante dolce*, but instructions to the performer at the beginning of the second movement—*Andante sognando* ("dreamy andante")—and elsewhere throughout the piece advise *dolce* ("sweetly"). Prokofiev's observation in a press release of May 1944, that his new piano sonata would be "primarily lyrical in character" was, if anything, an understatement.

Both main themes of the extended first movement are in long, flowing lines. The first is a wandering, thickly harmonized and mellow "Schubertian" theme, contrasting in texture with the shorter and more transparent second theme, which, announced in a high register, is fragile and brittle, like the tune from a music box. An episode *(Allegro moderato)* in ascending chromatic explosions of sixteenth notes briefly punctuates the prevailing lyrical mood, and later returns to conclude the movement.

The second movement is short and slow, another of the many slow-motion dances found in Prokofiev's piano music. This one is in D flat Major. The final fast movement, in 12/8 meter, moves primarily in triplets, set off by a middle section in square 3/4 time where Prokofiev the lover of awkward and obvious dissonant intervals makes an obligatory, if abbreviated, appearance. Here—and throughout the sonata—the intervals of the tritone and second play an important harmonic role, although they are used with somewhat less irony and aggressiveness than in Prokofiev's earlier piano music.

After some initial doubts, Sviatoslav Richter, who knows Prokofiev's sonatas more intimately than any other pianist, came to consider the Eighth—perhaps unexpectedly—"the richest" of them all. "It has a difficult inner life, with profound contradictions," he would write later. "The sonata is rather difficult to grasp, but difficult because of an abundance of riches—like a tree loaded down with fruit." For Richter, only the Fourth and Ninth Sonatas rank with the Eighth.

But Richter would not give the premiere. That honor fell to another brilliant Russian pianist—Emil Gilels—who introduced it in late December 1944 in Moscow.

Having completed the Eighth Piano Sonata, Prokofiev turned all his attention to a big new symphony, his Fifth. For Prokofiev, as for Beethoven and Shostakovich, Five would prove to be an important number: as for them, his Fifth would be an artistic breakthrough. After the "Classical," it has become his best-known and most frequently performed symphony.

Later, Prokofiev would say that he considered his work on the Fifth Symphony "very important not only for the musical material that went into it, but also because I was returning to the symphonic form after a break of sixteen years. The Fifth Symphony is the culmination of an entire period in my work. I conceived of it as a symphony on the greatness of the human soul."

Approximately forty-five minutes long, the Fifth is the largest of Prokofiev's seven symphonies, and nearly three times as long as the terse First ("Classical"). Where the "Classical" Symphony took its inspiration from Haydn and the eighteenth century, the Fifth turns to the late Romantic tradition (Brahms, Tchaikovsky, Sibelius) and to the tradition of the Soviet symphonic masters—especially Shostakovich. It provides a graphic illustration of the sea change that had occurred in Prokofiev's thinking about symphonic form and language since the time of the Russian Revolution.

What is most striking about the Fifth Symphony—appropriately, it was designated Op. 100—is its epic scale and character. Here, for the first time, Prokofiev used the massive patriotic style that had proven so successful in his vocal and dramatic music of the late 1930s and early 1940s (*Alexander Nevsky, Zdravitsa, War and Peace, Ivan the Terrible*) in a purely symphonic context. The themes, the orchestration and the mood are broad and strong; irony and the grotesque play a greatly reduced, though still essential, role. Even more important, the Fifth Symphony is Prokofiev's first non-pragmatic work to achieve a convincing sense of tragedy.

Critics had often complained that the fragmentary "montage" style of Prokofiev's symphonic music failed to develop ideas to their full potential, and that his large compositions—including the Third and Fourth Symphonies—consisted merely of a succession of unrelated episodes. This criticism cannot be leveled at the Fifth, however. Its individual movements and the symphony as a whole proceed with a strong sense of continuity and drama, building to a satisfying musical and emotional climax. One cannot charge that the Fifth Symphony "goes on for a while and then stops," as one critic said of the Second. It creates the impression of beginning and ending exactly where it should.

Like the Eighth Piano Sonata, the Fifth Symphony demonstrates an unusual preference for slow tempos. Both the first *(Andante)* and third *(Adagio)* movements—which together make up more than half of the symphony—are predominantly slow. These two movements also represent the symphony's most important achievement: finding an abstract (without the aid of a specific text or program) orchestral language that is somehow "Soviet" but still retains Prokofiev's personality. The long first movement begins with a heroic but supple theme, free of chromatic alteration and ironic leaps, in the tonic key of B flat Major. Few themes in Prokofiev's entire *oeuvre* can match it for power and expansiveness. The second theme, announced by oboes and flutes *(dolce)*, is more chromatic, but in the optimistic "classical" idiom of the recently completed Flute Sonata.

The slow third movement reveals Prokofiev's debt to Shostakovich, particularly to his Fifth Symphony, the "model" for the Soviet symphony since its premiere in 1937. This influence appears not so much in the contour of Prokofiev's melody as in the nearly expressionistic orchestration, thick with strings in the upper register—very reminiscent of the *Largo* of Shostakovich's Fifth. And yet the juxtaposition of triplets in the accompaniment against eighth notes in the melody is unmistakably "Prokofievian," as is the use of the rich 3/4 (9/8) meter.

Like Shostakovich, Prokofiev balances the gloomy power of the third movement with the high spirits of the two movements which precede and follow it. The second movement *(Allegro marcato)* contrasts a gently tongue-in-cheek martial theme with a free-falling one hinting at modality, while the concluding *Allegro giocoso* is playful and jaunty, with the quirky off-beat rhythms and sour dissonances that are the composer's trademarks. Here, Prokofiev combined the marvelous orchestral color of *The Buffoon,* the driving rhythm of *The Gambler* and the heroic stature of *Alexander Nevsky* into a stirring and completely original finale.

In the Fifth Symphony, Prokofiev finally succeeded—after a decade of searching—in finding a language sufficiently accessible and optimistic, one appropriate to "Soviet reality," and yet highly individual. It accomplished in the realm of the symphony what *Romeo and Juliet* had in ballet. Even as most twentieth-century composers were turning away from the symphony, dismissing it as an exhausted form, Prokofiev was exploring its undiscovered possibilities. Emotionally, too, the fifth was a milestone for Prokofiev—an affirmation of his faith in the human spirit, and a celebration of his ability to endure, learn, grow and prevail, even in tragic circumstances. According to Richter and Kabalevsky, Prokofiev considered the Fifth Symphony his finest creation.

At Ivanovo, Prokofiev worked on the Fifth with the white heat of inspiration. No doubts about the symphony's value, or how it should be written, assailed him. When Eisenstein wrote in late July, begging him to come to Moscow to work out some final problems on the first part of *Ivan the Terrible*, Prokofiev refused categorically. "I'm busy now with work on my Fifth Symphony. Its composition is proceeding at full speed, and I can't possibly break it off to switch over to *Ivan the Terrible*. I'm sure that you'll understand." By the end of Prokofiev's stay at Ivanovo, most of the work was completed. The orchestration was finished by late November, and the symphony would be performed in January.

But before conducting its premiere, Prokofiev had to attend to the other performances that awaited him in Moscow after his return from Ivanovo in early autumn. First came a private performance of the new Eighth Piano Sonata, given by Prokofiev for his colleagues at the Composers' Union in early October. He played it through twice, and Sviatoslav Richter noticed that Prokofiev's piano technique, formerly so impeccable and forceful, had lost its assurance. "His hands dragged somehow." While most praised the sonata, some expressed surprise at how "old-fashioned" it was.

On October 16, *War and Peace* also received its first public hearing. The performance was much less than Prokofiev had hoped for: a modest concert presentation of eight of the opera's eleven scenes, performed by members of the Ensemble of Soviet Opera of the All-Union Theatrical Society, conducted by Konstantin Popov with piano accompaniment. The soloists were not well-known.

Although well-received, and repeated in Moscow at least twice that same autumn, the concert performance still provided only an approximate sense of what *War and Peace* could sound and look like. Even after hearing this first performance, representatives of the prestigious Soviet opera houses continued to have doubts over whether the opera was stageable. Samosud never lost his faith in *War and Peace*, but at the moment he was not affiliated with a theatre capable of tackling such an ambitious project. The stage production Prokofiev wanted so desperately still seemed no closer to reality. Adding to Prokofiev's disappointment was the postponement of Kirov and Bolshoi productions—planned for the fall of 1944—of *Cinderella* and *Betrothal in a Monastery*.

But 1944 ended optimistically, with two important successes on the same day—December 30. After studying and preparing under Prokofiev's guidance, Emil Gilels (then twenty-eight years old) gave the public premiere of the Eighth Piano Sonata in a solo concert at the Great Hall of the Conservatory. Meanwhile, Part I of Eisenstein's *Ivan the Terrible*, with Prokofiev's music, was receiving its first public screening. Both the sonata and the film were greeted with great critical and popular enthusiasm. So much did *Ivan the Terrible* please Stalin and his cultural bureaucrats that the film later earned both Eisenstein and Prokofiev Stalin Prizes—and this time, first class. Prokofiev's close association with the project considerably enhanced his prestige and improved his official position.

By now, Prokofiev and Mira were living in their own small apartment, which they had finally received in late autumn. Simple and modestly furnished—Prokofiev often said that the only things that mattered to him about an apartment were a piano, a desk and a comfortable chair—it was located on the Mozhaisk Highway, today named Kutuzov Prospekt, near the Kiev Station in southwest Moscow. After nearly four years of living in cramped hotel rooms all over the Soviet Union, Prokofiev and Mira had a place of their own, with a telephone and working gas.

It was in their new apartment that they celebrated the New Year 1945 with a few close friends. Not since New Year's 1936, the first one Prokofiev and Lina had celebrated together in Russia, had the future looked so bright for him and his music. But once again, the happiness which appeared so close would be snatched away. The year 1945 would bring joy to his country but misfortune to Prokofiev.

It began well. Only a few weeks into the new year, on January 13, Prokofiev made a rare conducting appearance, introducing the Fifth Symphony with the State Symphonic Orchestra of the U.S.S.R. in the appropriately historic setting of the Great Hall of the Moscow Conservatory. Preceding the Fifth on the all-Prokofiev program were the "Classical" Symphony and *Peter and the Wolf*. Anticipation was running high over Prokofiev's new symphony, his first in sixteen years, and his first "Soviet" symphony.

All the prominent figures in Moscow musical life were present. Among them was Sviatoslav Richter, sitting in the third row. "The Great Hall was illuminated, no doubt, the same way it always was, but when Prokofiev stood up, the light seemed to pour straight down on him from somewhere up above," he wrote later. "He stood like a monument on a pedestal. And then, when Prokofiev had taken his place on the podium and silence reigned in the hall, artillery salvos suddenly thundered forth. His baton was raised. He waited, and began only after the cannons had stopped. There was something very significant in this, something symbolic. It was as if all of us—including Prokofiev—had reached some kind of shared turning point."

The salvos that delayed the performance came from Soviet cannons, paying tribute to the Red Army soldiers who were finally crossing the Vistula on their victory march into Nazi Germany. The end of the War was now clearly in sight.

When the orchestra began to play, it seemed to continue the music begun by the cannons. As the final measures of the *Allegro giocoso* passed into silence forty-five minutes later, the audience, inspired and moved, exploded into applause and cheers.

The dramatic setting in which the Fifth Symphony received its premiere only enhanced its aura and immediate, enormous success— it became a part of the work's legend. Nothing else Prokofiev had composed since returning to the U.S.S.R. more brilliantly captured the spirit of a moment—even of an entire era—or generated more unanimous and genuine critical, political and popular enthusiasm than his Fifth Symphony. Its heroic tone and large scale conformed to what was expected of Soviet composers at the moment, but also emerged spontaneously and naturally, as though Prokofiev was writing for himself alone. The unqualified success of the Fifth also restored Prokofiev's confidence in his ability to write symphonies—over the next eight years he would create two more, and revise his Fourth.

At last, Prokofiev seemed to have earned the respect and admiration of the Soviet audience and the cultural establishment. He had finally found the "new simplicity" that he had been seeking for more than a decade. The future promised peace and prosperity, and, perhaps, a freer environment for artists. There was so much for Prokofiev to look forward to as 1945 began: the difficult times appeared finally to be over.

But the incredible tension and strain under which Prokofiev— now nearly fifty-four years old—had been living for the last ten years had taken a severe toll on his health. Since 1936, he had lived through one crisis after another—adjusting to life in Soviet Russia, seeing his friends arrested and murdered, leaving Lina for Mira, facing the privations of the War. He was tired and depleted: the weakness that Richter had noticed in his piano playing was only one symptom of a greater exhaustion. So much energy had been expended in the struggle for survival and recognition that little remained for celebration.

Only a few days after his triumph on the podium at the Conservatory, at the very pinnacle of his career, Prokofiev's body failed him. The good health he had enjoyed his entire life was lost, irretrievably, sacrificed—like so much else in Prokofiev's life—to the pursuit of his art.

CHAPTER 22

BEFORE THE STORM

You don't die from happiness.

—ALEXANDER OSTROVSKY

Soon after the triumphant premiere of the Fifth Symphony, Prokofiev and Mira invited friends to their new apartment on Mozhaisk Highway for a housewarming. Miaskovsky, Kabalevsky and a few others spent an evening in typical Russian style—talking, joking and eating. They had no reason to suspect this would be the last time they would see their host and colleague—whose new symphony was the talk of the capital—in the energetic good health he had always enjoyed.

A few days later (strangely, even Mira never noted the exact date), overcome by a spell of dizziness, Prokofiev took a bad fall and suffered a brain concussion. His dizziness had been caused by a sudden flow of blood to the brain due to hypertension—high blood pressure. Prokofiev's friends and colleagues disagree over where his fall took place. Some claim he fell down a staircase, either while visiting or at home, while others maintain he fell while shopping with Mira at an open-air market near their apartment. Wherever it happened, the fall and concussion marked the beginning of a long period of ill health. Until his death eight years later, Prokofiev would never again be entirely free of medical problems.

Apparently, Prokofiev's high blood pressure had gone undetected before this incident. At least accounts of the composer's life before 1945 make no mention of it.

It is difficult to avoid the conclusion that the extraordinary personal and political pressure under which Prokofiev had been living since 1936 was at least a contributing, if not determining, cause in his illness. High blood pressure is a condition associated with and aggravated by tension. Nor, unfortunately, would subsequent events in Prokofiev's professional and personal life provide the peace and quiet that his fragile health required. In the past, he had always been remarkably resilient, bouncing back from seemingly irreversible setbacks with amazing ease and speed. But age and struggle had undermined his energy. Despite a formidable will and an intense desire to recover, Prokofiev would never find the strength to completely overcome this reversal.

Many other Soviet artists belonging to Prokofiev's generation were physically affected by the high stress of their lives. Sergei Eisenstein, seven years younger than Prokofiev, and subject to many of the same pressures, would suffer a heart attack one year after the onset of Prokofiev's illness. He, too, would never fully recover, and would die before his friend and collaborator.

In the struggle to regain his strength, Prokofiev could not have asked for a more solicitous nurse than Mira. Most likely, he would not have lived as long as he did without her constant support, care and devotion. In the first days after his fall, Prokofiev lay gravely ill in a hospital, and Mira and their friends thought he might die. Returning from a trip to Finland, Kabalevsky paid Prokofiev a visit.

"He lay completely motionless," Kabalevsky later recalled. "From time to time he could not recognize the people he was talking with, and would lose consciousness. In a weak voice he asked a few questions about my visit with Jean Sibelius, complaining bitterly about the enforced break in his own working routine. I went away from him with sad thoughts. It seemed this was the end."

Mira stayed by his bedside constantly, trying to raise his spirits.

One day, an ironic little note arrived from Eisenstein. "I am aware of and in complete agreement with your 'Molièreian' attitude toward doctors, but I do think you still have to put on a good show," he wrote. Wondering what would happen to the unfinished score for the second part of *Ivan the Terrible*, Eisenstein also advised Prokofiev to come to a sanatorium where he was then staying, at Barkhiva, in the countryside outside Moscow. When Prokofiev's condition had improved somewhat and the severe winter cold had passed, he took Eisenstein's advice and moved to Barkhiva (the sanatorium was called "Podlipki"—"Under the Lindens"), staying there through the spring.

The weather was cool and spring came late that year, but the mood in the country was joyful. By April, Soviet armies had entered the ruins of Berlin, and on May 8, 1945, the German command surrendered.

This happy news aided Prokofiev's slow convalescence, but his condition remained serious and even precarious. What depressed the formerly hyperactive Prokofiev more than anything were the strict rules set down by his doctors: lots of rest, no work of any kind, no excitement, no reading, no wine, no cigarettes. No composing was allowed. To be forbidden to write music was sheer torture for Prokofiev; he had never been able to bear sitting (or lying) idle. Amused by the game of outsmarting his doctors, Prokofiev composed in his head, working out ideas for a large piece celebrating the end of the War *(Ode to the End of the War)*.

Visitors from Moscow arrived frequently. Prokofiev would pump them for information about the rehearsals for the upcoming concert performance of *War and Peace*, to be conducted by Samosud in June. Somehow he even managed to compose a new aria for General Kutuzov, to be inserted into the "Before the Battle of Borodino" scene. He was also intensely curious about preparations for the premiere of *Cinderella*, planned for the fall at the Bolshoi Theater.

Despite his weakness and fatigue, Prokofiev was full of optimism and music. Mira would read aloud to him, especially from the prose of Nikolai Leskov (author of the story "Lady Macbeth of the Mtsensk District)." When he was feeling stronger, Prokofiev loved to walk through the woods around the sanatorium, examining the small unfolding leaves.

By early June, his condition had improved sufficiently to allow him to go visiting in Moscow. Prokofiev and Miaskovsky spent an evening at Kabalevsky's apartment, engaged in "animated conversation."

On the following day, June 7, most of *War and Peace*, the opera on which he pinned such great hopes, was performed by the Moscow Philharmonic in the Great Hall of the Conservatory. Samosud conducted, presenting nine of the eleven scenes (all except Scenes 6 and 8) of the first version. Prokofiev and Mira attended all three performances, on June 7, 9 and 11.

Samosud wrote later,

An unusual holiday atmosphere reigned in the hall. It was already summer, but the performance attracted literally the entire cultural elite of the capital—writers, musicians, scholars, military men. They gave Prokofiev a genuine ovation, and he was very moved. Observing the conflicting feelings of his doctor, an important Moscow professor, was amusing. A sincere music lover, the doctor was unable to conceal her interest in Prokofiev's opera. At the same time, she was saying to us, with unfeigned anxiety, "What is he doing! He should be at home in bed, not here getting excited for nothing."

In reply, someone recalled the line from Ostrovsky, "You don't die from happiness."

Seeing his opera done so well, and the warm reception it received, gave Prokofiev even greater motivation to recover. Now encouraged, he was determined to guide it to the stage, with Samosud's help. The official and critical response to the concert performance was positive, urging a full staged production as soon as possible. When Samosud received an important new appointment as artistic director of Leningrad's Maly Opera and Ballet Theater shortly after the concert performance, he began almost immediately to make preparations for staging *War and Peace* there.

After his fall, Prokofiev and Mira spent little time in their new apartment on Mozhaisk Highway. Perhaps they connected that place with his illness, and no longer felt comfortable there. Soon after the performance of *War and Peace*, they again left Moscow to spend a second summer at the Composers' Union resort in Ivanovo. Prokofiev would spend much less time in the city in the coming years, preferring to remain close to nature. The trees and fields calmed him. "I'm not an agronomist's son for nothing," he once joked to Mira.

Almost every day they would take walks through the woods, dressed in comfortable, loose-fitting clothes, and often, as photographs show, hand in hand. To Mira, Prokofiev's love for nature was "one of the manifestations of the rare purity of his soul. While he was strolling he would often write down musical themes, and talk about music, his plans for the future, and possible subjects for new compositions. He would discuss details connected with composing various works, and think up titles. If he didn't have his little notebook with him, he would write the themes down on a scrap of paper, on a cigarette package, a medicine box, or a used envelope. Later, he would try out on the piano what he had written down, and then include it in his organized music notebook." These themes were later used in new compositions.

His health was still fragile, but Prokofiev spent a relatively productive summer at Ivanovo in 1945. Working considerably less than in previous years—only an hour or an hour and a half a day—he nonetheless was able to boast of his achievements in a letter to Miaskovsky written in late August. "The air is marvelous, the food is tasty, and my health has significantly improved—at least my head aches only rarely." He had managed to sketch out the *Ode to the End of the War,* and had completed nearly two sections of his new Sixth Symphony in piano score.

To facilitate his recovery, Prokofiev was forced to turn down many projects. Eisenstein was begging him to complete some music ("The Dance of the *Oprichniki*") necessary for the continuation of the filming of the second part of *Ivan the Terrible,* but Prokofiev—in part at Mira's insistence—refused. Mira explained that he "could not possibly" write the music as he had promised. "He tried to work, but recently he has had several nosebleeds, which disturbed the Moscow professor treating him. . . . She strictly prohibited any work for the moment. Sergei Sergeevich very much wants to do the dance for you, but it is unlikely he will get to it soon, especially since it would demand intense concentration. He, too, is eager to work and is enduring this enforced inactivity with great difficulty."

During the coming autumn, Prokofiev's health improved sufficiently to allow him to compose the dance, along with the rest of the music for the second part of *Ivan.* Eisenstein finished editing the film by early February of 1946.

Aware of Prokofiev's fiercely competitive nature, his doctors also forbade him to engage in his favorite nonmusical pastime—chess. But he was incapable of surviving without games, so he invented a new one that summer. Inspired by the military situation at the end of the War, it was called "Captured German Generals" and unfolded strategically on pieces of graph paper.

In the early autumn, Prokofiev and Mira returned to Moscow, and exchanged the apartment on Mozhaisk Highway for rooms adjoining the apartment belonging to Mira's father on Moscow Art Theater Lane. (By now, Mira's father was living there alone, her mother having died during the War.) Within short walking distance of Red Square, the Bolshoi Theater and the Conservatory, this small apartment was much more convenient for Prokofiev. It would be their Moscow residence until he died.

Whenever they moved into a new residence, Mira took care of all the domestic arrangements. Prokofiev's total lack of interest in furniture, decorating and houses amazed and amused her. "One would try in vain to get any information from him about the new apartments of friends or acquaintances—the only thing he would remember would be the bookshelves," she said. "If I would rush around to put our room in order when someone was coming to visit, Sergei Sergeevich would tell me not to tire myself out, assuring me that 'people don't pay attention to such trivial things.'"

When they invited people into their home—which was often— Prokofiev and Mira entertained informally, in the Russian style. Their Moscow social life was nearly rustic compared to the glittering round of parties he and Lina used to attend in Paris.

By autumn of 1945, World War II had ended on all fronts—Japan signed a statement of capitulation on September 2. Across the Soviet Union, the resulting celebration was nearly delirious, the sense of relief overwhelming. Even with the massive rebuilding that now confronted them, Soviet citizens looked forward to the future with optimism and a new confidence in their country's strength. After decades of being treated as a second-class nation, the U.S.S.R. had, if only by default, become a world power.

Composers, writers and artists shared in the optimism. The more relaxed artistic-intellectual atmosphere of the war years, and a renewed sense of cultural solidarity, led them to believe—mistakenly—that the fearful nights of the pre–War purges were behind them, that the security of victory would allow Stalin and his commissars to ease their control over art and artists. There was reason to believe, too, that the country's cultural isolation from the rest of the world would now end, in the afterglow of the allied victory.

Relations with the United States seemed the most likely to improve. At the War's end, Prokofiev suddenly received many telegrams from old friends and associates in America, who were even more naive than the Russians about the possibilities for future cooperation between their countries. Ephraim Gottlieb wrote from Chicago, "No one has hastened to shorten the war as the valorous Russian armies with its great leader Marshal Stalin. I wish some day when I visit the U.S.S.R. perhaps through your assistance I will have the privilege of shaking hands with that great and wise man."

Cecil M. Smith, Chairman of the Music Department at the University of Chicago, invited Prokofiev to come and lecture. Leopold

Stokowski sent greetings, admiration for Prokofiev's "creative fertility of the years during the War," and a request for a new score of the *Alexander Nevsky* Cantata. Prokofiev also heard from Vernon Duke for the first time in five years. "There is so much I could and should tell you that I don't know where to begin," Duke wrote.

Prominent Soviet cultural figures were often featured in the American press. *Time* magazine even devoted the cover of its issue of November 19, 1945, to Prokofiev. Inside, an article enthused that recordings of his music had outsold Mozart during the preceding year. Ten days earlier, on November 9, Koussevitsky had given the American premiere of the Fifth Symphony with the Boston Symphony. Prokofiev sent a telegram: "Happy you conducting American premiere my Fifth Symphony. Work very close to my heart. Sending sincere friendly greetings you and all members your magnificent orchestra."

Meanwhile, back in Moscow, artists of all kinds were expected to respond to the coming of peace. Prokofiev's contribution to the celebration was his recently completed *Ode to the End of the War* (Op. 105). One of his more eccentric and raucous creations, in the tradition of "The Scythian Suite" and the *Cantata for the Twentieth Anniversary of October*, it is scored for a huge orchestra shorn of violins, violas, and cellos but including four pianos and eight harps. An expanded brass section (three trumpets, six horns, three trombones, three tubas and three saxophones) join a large group of woodwinds and percussion in this one-movement work. The timpani and chimes receive solo passages.

"The *Ode* begins severely and solemnly," Prokofiev told a Soviet radio audience. "Then comes an energetic section—these are the themes of rebirth and creation. Next, the theme of awakening joy gradually rises from the surrounding silence, growing more and more toward the finale, which I would call 'Beat the chimes and timpani.' "

Samosud conducted the State Symphony Orchestra in the premiere of the *Ode* on November 12 in Moscow. It received an uncertain response, failed to enter the repertoire and was published only in 1969. One of the reasons the piece did not become popular was the extraordinary demands it placed upon orchestras that might have wanted to perform it. Eight harps and four pianos?

But as his health continued to improve that autumn, Prokofiev also enjoyed important artistic successes. One, in early October, was the first complete concert performance of all eleven scenes of the first revision of *War and Peace*, by the State Symphony Orchestra under

Samosud. By now, Samosud was already planning to stage the opera at the Maly Theater in Leningrad in the near future. Boris Pokrovsky, a young director who would exert an enormous influence on the development of Soviet opera for the next forty years, was working with him on the staging.

Samosud, Prokofiev and Mira had now decided to split the long opera into two separate halves—"Peace" and "War"—and to present each half on a separate evening. They had also decided to add another scene to the first half. Filled with grand dance numbers in the style of Tchaikovsky's *Eugene Onegin*, it became Scene 2—"A Ball at the Home of a Nobleman in the Style of Catherine the Great." They collaborated on this revision through the fall, winter and spring of 1945–46, preparing for the production of Part I ("Peace") in early June.

Another success that fall was the long-awaited premiere of *Cinderella*, on November 21 at the Bolshoi Theater. Amazingly, this was the first Bolshoi production of a Prokofiev ballet. The choreographer was Rostislav Zakharov, who had been trained in Leningrad, where he had studied with Sergei Radlov and served as the ballet master at the Kirov Theater. His most famous Kirov production was Asafiev's *The Fountain of Bakhchisarai* in 1934. From 1936 until 1956, Zakharov was ballet master and an opera director at the Bolshoi. The scenery for *Cinderella* was designed by Pyotr Vilyams, designer of the original Kirov *Romeo and Juliet*.

Prokofiev had written the role of Cinderella with Galina Ulanova in mind. Much as Ulanova admired the character and the ballet, she realized, like everyone else involved in *Cinderella*, that it did not have the remarkable power and originality of *Romeo and Juliet*. By now, she had forgotten how bitterly she and her fellow dancers at first resisted *Romeo*, complaining that it was undanceable and inaudible. The more conventional structure and music of *Cinderella* disappointed her.

Although his poor health prevented him from taking an active role in the rehearsals for *Cinderella*, Prokofiev still asserted his control over the score. Ulanova tried to persuade him to give the Fairy Godmother's ethereal theme to Cinderella, but he of course refused. "If he saw or heard a given theme as the Fairy Godmother's theme," Ulanova wrote later, "then there was no force on earth capable of compelling or persuading him to give it to Cinderella or anyone else, no matter who."

The Bolshoi company had little difficulty learning to dance the Tchaikovsky-like *Cinderella*, and the rehearsals went much more smoothly than for *Romeo*. At the premiere, Ulanova did not dance the role of Cinderella; it was taken by another Bolshoi ballerina, Olga Lepesh-inskaya. Ulanova danced the role, which would become her most famous after Juliet, in subsequent performances. Mikhail Gabovich was the Prince, and an up-and-coming twenty-year-old, Maya Pliset-skaya, danced the Fairy of Autumn. Trying to conserve his energy and excitement for composition, Prokofiev saw the production of *Cinderella* one act at a time, over three evenings.

The popular and critical response was very positive. In *Pravda*, Shostakovich praised it as "worthy of the glorious traditions of Russian ballet," and a "step forward" in the art. When staged at the Kirov in Leningrad the following spring (with Natalia Dudinskaya as Cinderella, and choreography by Konstantin Sergeev, who also danced the role of the Prince), *Cinderella* was similarly well-received. The ballet has remained ever since in the repertoire at the Kirov and the Bolshoi, and has been staged in many other Soviet, European and American cities. After *Romeo*, it is Prokofiev's most frequently produced ballet.

Cinderella's resounding success also signaled a change—at least for a few years—in Prokofiev's remarkably bad luck with dramatic music. Not only *Cinderella* (in Moscow and Leningrad), but *Betrothal in a Monastery*, the first part of *War and Peace* and a new production of *Romeo and Juliet* (at the Bolshoi) would all reach the stage by late 1946.

That Prokofiev's position in the Soviet musical hierarchy had improved since the beginning of the War became even more obvious when the winners of the Stalin Prizes were announced in late January of 1946. Prokofiev had won two, first class: one for the Fifth Symphony and the Eighth Piano Sonata, and another for the score to Part I of *Ivan the Terrible*. In July, Prokofiev received yet another Stalin Prize first class for *Cinderella*—for a total of three in one year. Already exhausted by the great material sacrifices he had made in order to come home to Russia, Prokofiev was at last—if only briefly—receiving the unambiguous official (and financial) recognition he deserved.

But prizes and premieres could not restore Prokofiev's health. As his nosebleeds, headaches and fatigue persisted, he continued to spend many hours in hospitals and clinics. In early February, he received an emotional blow when his trusted friend and collaborator Eisenstein collapsed, the victim of a heart attack, at a party celebrating the awarding of the Stalin Prize for Part I of *Ivan the Terrible* and the completion of Part II. In the following months, Prokofiev often visited

Eisenstein in the Kremlin Hospital, depressed by his lack of energy and enthusiasm. Eisenstein would never fully recover, although he lived for two more years.

Not only Prokofiev's own illness but the illness and deaths of his old friends and associates now began to speak to him of his own mortality.

On April 23, 1946, Prokofiev reached the age of fifty-five, an event observed by his friends and colleagues for nearly a month. On May 9, Sviatoslav Richter played the Sixth, Seventh and Eighth Piano Sonatas at the Hall of Unions. A few days later, Richter joined Nina Dorliak, performing Prokofiev pieces at a concert honoring the recipients of the Stalin Prize. (Miaskovsky was also among them.) On May 19, Richter and Dorliak again honored Prokofiev with a performance of his Akhmatova songs, as part of a birthday gala in the Small Hall of the Conservatory. Other "old" and rarely heard pieces were also played that evening: the First String Quartet, the Seventh Piano Sonata (performed by Yakov Zak), the "Ballade" for Cello and Piano, Op. 15, and the Overture on Hebrew Themes.

An orchestral concert on May 28, conducted by the young Kiril Kondrashin, concluded the birthday festivities. Yakov Zak achieved the marathon feat of performing three Prokofiev piano concertos—the First, Second and Third—in a single evening.

In recent memory, no other Soviet composer—not even Shostakovich—had been so extravagantly and affectionately honored. Prokofiev had reached the highwater mark of his Soviet career.

In June, Prokofiev was healthy enough to travel with Mira to Leningrad for the stage premiere of the first half (with the new added Scene 2) of *War and Peace*. It opened on June 12 in the gracefully columned Maly Theater, during what Leningraders call the "white nights," a period around the summer solstice when the sun—because of the city's extreme northern location—never sets. The canal embankments, churches and palaces, many still in ruins after the brutal blockade, were illuminated with an eerie golden glow that must have reminded Prokofiev of his days at the Petersburg Conservatory.

That he was finally about to see at least one-half of *War and Peace* onstage, exactly five years after it was begun, was a source of great pleasure and inspiration to him. He continued—insistently—to consider it one of his most important works. Too weak to help with the preparation of the production, he was nevertheless very happy with what Samosud and Pokrovsky had done. At the dress rehearsal, attended by "the cream of the Leningrad artistic intelligentsia," the company gave Prokofiev a very warm reception. It "turned into a real celebration both for the theater and for the composer, who was called to the stage many times."

Audiences flocked to the new production, and the reviews were highly complimentary. By March of 1947, less than a year later, Part I of *War and Peace* had been performed at the Maly Theater fifty times—a nearly unprecedented number for a new opera. When Prokofiev left Leningrad after attending the first few performances, he had every reason to believe, as Samosud and Pokrovsky were promising, that Part II of the opera ("War") would be produced at the Maly the following season.

While in Leningrad, Prokofiev also saw his childhood friend Vera Alpers for the first time in many years, and introduced her to Mira. Judging from Alpers's letters, she, too, like most of Prokofiev's friends, was very favorably impressed by his companion. Later, Alpers wrote to them in Moscow that it had become "fashionable to praise and enjoy" *War and Peace* in Leningrad, and that the opera's success had led to a resurgence of interest in his music, which was often broadcast on the radio.

Prokofiev's recent successes had increased his income, and he was now able to purchase a *dacha* in Nikolina Gora, where he had spent many happy vacations before the War. He and Mira settled in there upon their return from Leningrad. Several of his friends, including Miaskovsky, also maintained small country houses nearby.

The small cottage that Prokofiev bought from an opera singer was in shabby condition, but the location was very appealing. Hidden behind trees and thick underbrush, at the end of a long grassy lane lined with high birches that turn brilliant gold in autumn, the *dacha* was simple and rustic. A porch at the back looked over a large yard and garden, and a short walk led to the Moscow River. The silence was total and the air pristine. For his studio, Prokofiev chose the small room at the corner of the house, its windows looking out onto thick forest green.

This small house, furnished without luxury or pretensions to style, soon became Prokofiev's favorite place. Besides Sontsovka, it was the only real home he ever had. Mira's father helped them fix up the *dacha* and often lived with them there. As time went on, Prokofiev could not bear to be away from it for long. So content were he and Mira at Nikolina Gora that they even stayed there through the winter as long as Prokofiev's health allowed, traveling the thirty miles to Moscow only for concert appearances or appointments. Guests frequently came, sometimes staying for weeks at a time in the extra room. Eventually, Prokofiev enclosed the porch in glass, so he could sit there talking with his colleagues even in cooler weather, admiring the flowers and trees.

"Sergei Sergeevich loved the *dacha*," Mira said. "He took part happily in all the details—even the most prosaic ones—of our country household. He would make many household purchases, believing that it wasn't the price, but the pleasure to be gained by obtaining the item, that mattered." As always, technical gadgets intrigued him. "The round electric lamps on both sides of the porch gave him special pleasure— he would turn them on himself when greeting guests or seeing them off."

Life at Nikolina Gora was simple, peaceful and slow. After many years of endless and exhausting travel all over the world, Prokofiev had finally found a place to rest.

Most of his waking day at the *dacha* was spent at the desk in his studio, in front of the window. There, he spent his time composing, "reading, looking over notes on chess games that he had played, playing Patience. On Sergei Sergeevich's desk, in addition to literature about music, lay Pushkin's *Eugene Onegin*, books about the origin of the earth, a geographic atlas, the latest issue of a contemporary literary-artistic journal, and books on the history and theory of chess.

"Sergei Sergeevich loved to think over new music when he was sitting in his easy chair. Before the doctors forbade it, he would always smoke while he thought. He loved to smoke so much that if he didn't have any cigarettes, he was prepared to walk several miles in any kind of weather to buy them." (He had begun smoking more heavily after returning to the U.S.S.R.) To refresh himself from work, he would putter in the garden, lavishing special attention on his favorite flowers, lilies.

During his first summer in his new home, Prokofiev also finished his fierce and dark Sonata No. 1 for Violin and Piano (Op. 80), begun eight years earlier. He had told Mira that he was first inspired to write the sonata after hearing some music by Handel in the summer of 1938, while staying at the Caucasus resort of Teberda. It was then that he assigned the project an opus number and called it the First Violin

Sonata. Other projects had long kept him from completing the piece, however. Perhaps it was his new friendship with the virtuoso David Oistrakh that inspired him to return to the sonata in 1946. Although labeled as his First Violin Sonata, this was in fact his second. The Second Sonata (Op. 94-bis) had been finished earlier, in 1944, with Oistrakh's help.

Oistrakh was one of the first to hear the new piece; Prokofiev invited him to Nikolina Gora as soon as it was finished. It was a pleasant summer day. Also present was Miaskovsky, who, like Oistrakh, was hearing Prokofiev's new composition for the first time. As was his custom when introducing something new to his colleagues, Prokofiev briefly described its sections and then played it through on the piano.

"It seemed to me that on this occasion he played somehow with great restraint, even timidly," Oistrakh later recalled. "Even so, the music itself made an enormous impression—one had the feeling of being present at a very great and significant event. Nothing written for the violin in many decades—anywhere in the world—could equal this piece in beauty and depth. I can make that statement without the slightest exaggeration."

After Prokofiev had finished, Miaskovsky remarked, with his usual laconism, that it was "a thing of genius," and asked his friend of forty years, " 'Don't you really understand what you've written?' "

In fact, there is nothing like the gloomy First Sonata for Violin and Piano in Prokofiev's entire *oeuvre*. Dense, intellectual and tragic, it stands in a class by itself. Some years later, Oistrakh would play its first and third movements at Prokofiev's funeral; the sonata was the only piece he could find, amidst Prokofiev's overwhelmingly optimistic music, that conveyed an understanding of grief.

In general mood, it is reminiscent of the reflective First String Quartet; these two compositions also share an emotional and musical kinship with Beethoven. But the sonata is more intense and fragmentary, a troubled and probing look through the eyes of a mature and seasoned genius. Only two years separate the first Violin Sonata from the Second, but the First, whose virile themes erupt in violent fits and starts, could not be more different from the Second, a sunny and transparent piece filled with long, singing lines.

Nearly thirty minutes long, the First Violin Sonata (in F Minor) has four movements—*Andante assai, Allegro brusco, Andante, Allegrissimo*—which are, strangely for Prokofiev, nearly identical in length. The themes are magnificent enough, but the atmosphere is the more remarkable achievement, created by subtle sonic and impressionistic effects, such as the chilling runs in the solo part *(freddo)* in the first movement. Prokofiev likened them to "wind in a graveyard." In the third movement, the dialogue between trembling *pianissimo* sixteenth-note triplets in the accompaniment and a mellow theme in the violin's lower register produces a similarly mysterious effect. Metrical oddities abound, such as the alternating 3/4–4/4 time in the first movement, and the complicated 5/8–7/8–8/8 in the last. Significantly, the sonata goes out with a whimper, a fragmentary reminiscence of one of the first movement themes, marked *piano*.

In this masterpiece, the mischief and high spirits so typical of Prokofiev's music have been distilled, refined and transcended. Wisdom replaces wisecracks.

For the remainder of the summer and early fall, Oistrakh and his accompanist Lev Oborin—they had also given the premiere of the Second Sonata for Violin and Piano in 1944—made frequent trips to Nikolina Gora to consult with Prokofiev, preparing for the premiere of the First Sonata in late October. "I never worked with such passion on any other work," said Oistrakh. "Until the sonata's first public performance, I couldn't play or think about anything else."

Absorbed in his work on the First Sonata and the Sixth Symphony, happily out of touch with what was happening in Moscow, Prokofiev probably paid little attention to the ominous change that was occurring that summer in government policy toward art and artists. The brief cultural honeymoon that followed the War was abruptly ending. Uncertainty and fear were replacing feelings of relief and freedom as artists saw the unmistakable signs of a new campaign of official repression.

As early as February 1946, Stalin had implied in a speech that there would be no relaxation in cultural policy after the exhausting war effort. But it was only when Andrei Zhdanov, Stalin's loyal *oprichnik* for culture, began to pointedly assail artists who were straying too far from the hallowed canons of Socialist Realism that the seriousness of the new assault emerged in its terrifying clarity. By now, Stalin had given his longtime aide Zhdanov, who had played an instrumental role in regimenting Soviet artists into unions, *carte blanche* to formulate and execute—the double meaning is, unfortunately, relevant—Soviet cultural policy.

Zhdanov, a master at exploiting professional envy and human frailty, wasted little time, justifying all his actions as a noble attempt to protect Russo-Socialist culture from ideological defilement. In August 1946, what came to be known as the "Zhdanovshchina" ("Zhdanovism") began in ugly earnest, with three resolutions from the Party Central Committee—one on literature, one on theatre and one on film. For the moment, music was spared.

The official "Resolution on the Journals *Star* and *Leningrad*" viciously attacked wayward (i.e., apolitical) literature, and personally smeared two of the most distinguished living Russian writers. Anna Akhmatova, whose poetry Prokofiev had set to music, was slandered as "half-nun, half-whore." Also attacked as a "scum of literature" was the brilliant satirist and short-story writer, Mikhail Zoshchenko.

The official attacks on theatre and cinema were similarly crude and insulting. Included among the film directors who had strayed from the straight and narrow was Eisenstein, only recently released from the hospital. Part II of *Ivan the Terrible,* which had been seen privately by the cultural bureaucrats, was severely criticized for its ambiguous portrayal of the Tsar's later years.

Eisenstein, according to the statement, had "betrayed his ignorance of historical fact by showing the progressive bodyguards of Ivan the Terrible—the *oprichniki*—as a degenerate band rather like the Ku Klux Klan, and Ivan the Terrible himself, who was a man of strong will and character, as weak and indecisive, somewhat like Hamlet." The film also showed traces of that terrible disease of "formalism"— an excessive interest in structural techniques at the expense of all-important and immediately accessible content.

Weak, ill and exhausted from years of defending his art from political interference, Eisenstein eventually published what amounted to an apology. "We committed a misrepresentation of historical facts that made the film worthless and vicious in an ideological sense," he said. "We . . . must fulfill our duty before the Soviet people, state and party by creating highly ideological fictional films."

For the moment, the attack on Eisenstein and *Ivan* did not spread to Prokofiev. It was not a hopeful sign, however, that another one of his closest and most trusted collaborators had come under official attack—like Meyerhold before him. Because of the negative evaluation of Part II of *Ivan,* it was not released publicly for more than ten years. Only in 1958—after Eisenstein, Prokofiev and Stalin were dead— would it be screened publicly.

Music and composers were conspicuously spared in the first wave of the "Zhdanovshchina," just as they had been the last to be regimented in the past. Perhaps the abstract language of music still eluded and confused the bureaucrats, although such considerations had not prevented them from meddling in philosophy, language and linguistics. Whatever the reasons, Zhadanov chose to wait one more season before intruding into the world of composers.

Out at Nikolina Gora, where the birches were turning from green to gold, Prokofiev tried to conserve his energy for his music. He continued to make progress on the Sixth Symphony, and was putting together three orchestral suites from the music to *Cinderella*. Encouraged by the great success of Part I of *War and Peace* at the Maly Theater, Prokofiev and Samosud were preparing Part II for a spring production. They had decided to add another nationalistic scene, which became Scene 10—"A Hut in Fili." Here, Kutuzov confers with his generals on how best to defend Moscow from Napoleon's army. The scene includes a stirring aria about Moscow sung by Kutuzov, based on a melody used in *Ivan the Terrible*.

In his weakened physical state, Prokofiev relied more than ever on Mira to help him in his work. Her role in the revisions of *War and Peace* was decisive. Although she was not a trained musician, Mira's literary training and "good poetic sense" allowed her to give Prokofiev solid professional help. She also wrote his letters and took care of his business dealings, acting almost as his agent, protecting him from unnecessary decisions and anxieties so what little energy he did possess could be devoted exclusively to composition. Colleagues and friends claim she performed these duties willingly, without presenting herself as a martyr. She seemed content to serve as his collaborator-secretary-companion in what was by then primarily a platonic relationship.

Prokofiev's health periodically improved and deteriorated. Adjusting to such a drastic reduction in the number of hours he could compose was very difficult for him, and even when he was gravely ill—when his head ached, his nose bled and he had to take to bed—he continued creating, at least in his head. "Don't they understand," he would say, "that I write anyway (in my mind), that I compose? It's much better for me to write down a thought as it comes to me, write it down and be finished with it, than to keep it in my memory, where it disturbs me because it will disappear, be forgotten, and never come back."

The delicacy of Prokofiev's condition even prevented him from traveling to Leningrad for the often postponed Soviet premiere of *Betrothal in a Monastery* at the Kirov Theater on November 3, 1946.

Like *Cinderella* and Part I of *War and Peace*, it enjoyed a strong popular and critical success. Shostakovich called *Betrothal* "one of Prokofiev's most radiant and buoyant works," and compared it to Verdi's *Falstaff*. *Betrothal* has remained in the repertoire at the Kirov, and has been staged at many other theatres both in the Soviet Union and abroad. After *Love for Three Oranges*, it is Prokofiev's most frequently performed opera today.

Other significant performances that season included the world premiere of the First Sonata for Violin and Piano, given to great critical acclaim by Oistrakh and Oborin on October 23, and a new Bolshoi production (the theatre's first) of *Romeo and Juliet* in late December. It was this production that would first introduce *Romeo* to a wide audience in the West when taken on tour by the Bolshoi in 1956. The same production later served as the basis for a lavish film version. Ulanova again danced the role of Juliet, opposite Mikhail Gabovich. (They had also danced the leading roles in the Bolshoi's *Cinderella* one year earlier.) Lavrovsky choreographed and Vilyams designed; they had also worked on the original Kirov *Romeo*. This time, though, there were no fiery arguments, the dancers did not complain about the "undanceable" music, and Prokofiev was too ill to participate in the rehearsals.

Now that Prokofiev's life was more tranquil and sedentary, he had reestablished closer contact with Lina and his children. He had been providing for their financial support since 1941—a considerable drain on his income. His sons began to come from the apartment on Chkalov Street for extended visits at Nikolina Gora, and they were developing a civil, if far from intimate, relationship with Mira. Sviatoslav, twenty-two, was studying in an architectural institute, and Oleg, eighteen, having decided to become a painter, was studying at the Moscow Art School. Painting had always been Prokofiev's favorite art after music, and he suddenly took a great interest in Oleg's future.

Prokofiev talked it over with Robert Falk, an important Russian Post-Impressionist with whom Oleg had been studying privately. It also happened that Falk was acquainted with N. E. Dobychina, at whose Petrograd gallery Prokofiev had made a celebrated appearance just before the February Revolution in 1917.

Because of its prestige, Prokofiev was insisting that Oleg should study at the Institute of Art. Falk did not agree, arguing that the professors at the Institute were undistinguished. "They stood next to each other, a striking and picturesque contrast," Oleg wrote. "My father, self-confident and smiling, wearing an elegant suit with a bright orange tie, his face very pink, slapping one of his hands with a glove he held in the other while talking. And Falk, dressed in a gray-green sweater stained with paint, his face pale, almost gray, speaking quietly and with sad conviction."

Eventually, Oleg took the entrance exam for the Institute but failed it and continued to study with Falk.

Due to their "foreignness," and to the fact that Prokofiev had not been living with them for more than five years, Lina and her sons were in a rather ambiguous social and official position. According to numerous sources, after the War Lina attempted several times to travel abroad with her sons to visit friends and relatives in France, but her requests were denied. In the late 1940s, requests for foreign travel—no matter who made them—aroused great official suspicion and displeasure. Oleg and Sviatoslav had even been called in for questioning. Why did they want to travel to France when they lived in the most perfect society in the world and had access to everything they could possibly want, they were asked.

By early 1947, the Stalinist xenophobia of the late 1930s had returned in force, after easing slightly—if only toward the Allies—during the War. Soviet soldiers captured by the Germans were sent to labor camps as spies for "fraternization with the enemy." A new law was passed making it a punishable offense for Soviet citizens to give foreigners *any* sort of information. Soviet women who dated foreigners were arrested and often sent to the camps as "Socially Dangerous Elements." Even knowing foreigners was tantamount to treason; wanting to travel abroad was a yet more heinous crime.

As Soviet citizens, Lina and her sons were subject to all the whims of Stalinist law. They received no special treatment, and, like almost all Soviets, they were prisoners in the U.S.S.R. Even worse, they were viewed with intense suspicion by the government and their fellow citizens because of their foreign background.

But Prokofiev had his own problems, and by now his ability to help them—other than financially—was very limited.

Enjoying the peace of country life, Prokofiev and Mira decided to remain in Nikolina Gora for the winter of 1946–47. They heated the drafty *dacha* with a wood stove, and hired a peasant woman from a nearby village to cook, clean and shop for them. Life was not easy;

just keeping warm through the months of subfreezing weather took a lot of energy. They had no telephone. Mira managed the household, carefully watching Prokofiev's precarious health.

One day, Mira ran to tell a neighbor—Alissa Shebalin, wife of composer Vissarion Shebalin—that Prokofiev was hemorrhaging from his nose. They ran to get Roza Ginsburg, the doctor in whose house Prokofiev once spent a summer with Lina and their sons. If Ginsburg had not quickly applied bandages, Prokofiev might have died. There were days when he felt much better, though, and he would walk along the forest paths in an old winter overcoat. Shebalin used to say Prokofiev was so regular in his daily walks that "you could set your watch by him."

The long winter days were devoted to work on the Sixth Symphony, which was finished in piano score by late February, and to the new "Fili" scene for Part II of *War and Peace*.

Samosud made frequent visits to Nikolina Gora that winter to confer with Prokofiev and Mira on the revisions in *War and Peace*, scheduled for a premiere in May or June at the Maly Theater. Like so many others, Samosud was amazed at Prokofiev's ability to work under any conditions, consistently and systematically. "His secret wasn't only a brilliant command of technique, a knowledge of the most subtle tricks of the trade. The important thing was his unceasing creative 'exercise'—his inexhaustible readiness for work, his constant 'advance work,' which went on somewhere in his subconscious."

As they walked together in the woods near the *dacha*, Prokofiev would seem to be concentrating intently on the snowy scene around them. "And then suddenly he would whip his little notebook out of his pocket, noting something down as we walked. Obviously he would figure things out in his subconscious before he would finally 'spit out' a thought, a theme, a musical turn of phrase."

To his acute disappointment, Prokofiev was—at least according to his doctors—too frail to travel to Leningrad for the dress rehearsal of Part II of *War and Peace* in July. Samosud, Pokrovsky, and the musicians and crew at the Maly Theater had prepared Part II with scrupulous attention to detail and to Prokofiev's intentions. The huge crowd scenes on the battlefield at Borodino, and in the streets of burning Moscow, were demanding and innovative, incorporating cinematic techniques, especially montage, to portray the acceleration and speed of events.

One of the most memorable scenes of Part II—and of *War and*

Peace—portrays Prince Andrei's death in a roadside hut, where he has a final and cathartic reconciliation with Natasha. It brings us back full circle to the lyrical "Peace" scenes with which the opera began, providing an emotional and historical sense of closure. In fact, it was this scene in Tolstoy's novel—whose words are virtually unchanged in the libretto—that first inspired Prokofiev to write his opera.

To convey Andrei's confusion and delirium, Prokofiev has an offstage chorus of altos intone soft nonsense syllables—"pi-ti, pi-ti, pi-ti"—against Andrei's stream-of-consciousness solo. The lilting incantation comes and goes, illustrating musically the flashes of lucidity and unbearable pain passing alternately through Andrei's brain. Although composed before Prokofiev fell ill, this deathbed scene (Scene 12, the penultimate one) now possessed an even greater resonance for the performers, audience, and for Prokofiev himself.

One morning in July, Part II of *War and Peace* was shown in dress rehearsal to prominent musicians and cultural authorities. It appeared to be well-received. Enthusiastic—at times even "tumultuous"—applause greeted each scene. Samosud was exuberant; *War and Peace* was at last receiving the praise it deserved.

But almost overnight, the whole picture changed. Even though it was completely ready, Part II of *War and Peace* was not allowed to open publicly. Party officials had suddenly discovered significant political flaws in the "historical concept" of the military scenes, finding them insufficiently heroic and nationalistic. "As a result, the theatre's management was instructed—'unofficially,' but in a manner that made discussion impossible—to remove many of the very most important scenes." Among the offending scenes were the rather sarcastic portrayal of Napoleon during the battle of Borodino, and the colorful tableau of Moscow on fire.

Prokofiev and Samosud refused to cut the scenes, insisting that the opera would be "incomprehensible" without them. The bureaucrats also refused to budge, and Part II was "stashed away in the desk drawer." Despite the months of work that Prokofiev, Samosud and Pokrovsky had devoted to it, this evening-long version of Part II would never reach the stage. For the moment, *War and Peace* was again shelved.

The cancellation must have been a crushing blow to Prokofiev, who regarded *War and Peace* as one of his most important works. He was more obsessed with its fate than with almost anything else he had written, and continued to press for its performance over the coming years, telling Kabalevsky, "I am prepared to accept the failure of any one of my works, but if you only knew how much I want *War and Peace* to see the light of day!" Sadly, the entire opera would reach the general public—in yet another revised one-evening version in thirteen scenes—only after Prokofiev's death.

The sudden and—in light of the enormous official favor he had recently been enjoying—unexpected official attack on *War and Peace* was more than a personal assault on Prokofiev. It also had little to do with the supposed "historical inaccuracies" of the military scenes. First and foremost, it was a warning to all Soviet composers that Stalin and Zhdanov were watching them, and were all too happy to demonstrate their absolute control. The situation recalled the 1936 scandal over Shostakovich's opera *Lady Macbeth of Mtsensk,* although the *War and Peace* case received less publicity.

The incident also indicated that Soviet artists—including the most established, such as Prokofiev—were in for another rough period. Despite all his recent successes, and the receipt (in June 1947) of his fifth Stalin Prize for the First Sonata for Violin and Piano, Prokofiev was not exempt from official censure. If anything, his fame made him an especially attractive target in the ongoing campaign to keep Soviet artists in line. The sudden cancellation of Part II of *War and Peace* was only the first strike in a long and bitter assault on Prokofiev and Soviet music.

During what would be the last peaceful and productive summer of his life, Prokofiev remained at Nikolina Gora. He must have been feeling somewhat better, for he managed to complete five new compositions—and revise his Fourth Symphony—by fall. Besides the orchestration of the Sixth Symphony, scheduled to be performed in Leningrad in the autumn, he was writing, perhaps in response to the more conservative cultural climate and the official criticism of *War and Peace,* two blatantly political works in celebration of the upcoming thirtieth anniversary of the 1917 Bolshevik Revolution.

One was for symphony orchestra—*Festive Poem* (subtitled "Thirty Years")—and the other, a cantata for mixed chorus and orchestra, to a text by the staunchly "official" poet Evgeny Dolmatovsky—*Flourish, O Mighty Land.* Dolmatovsky, a former war correspondent, had written many popular song lyrics. Both of these compositions were performed in Moscow in the fall, as part of extravagant and protracted festivities.

At the same time, though, Prokofiev was writing two "private" pieces—his Ninth (and last) Piano Sonata, and a Sonata for Solo Violin.

The Ninth Piano Sonata (Op. 103) had been in the works for the last two years, and was completed by early autumn of 1947. Prokofiev dedicated it to Sviatoslav Richter, now the leading interpreter of his piano music. When he first heard the Ninth Sonata, Richter was surprised—and even disappointed—at its remarkable "simplicity," but he later came to regard it as one of his favorite Prokofiev sonatas.

Like the much shorter Fifth Piano Sonata, the Ninth is in C Major. What key could be more simple, and, seemingly, less interesting? Yet Prokofiev makes marvelous discoveries in this most familiar of keys, and without resorting to excessive chromaticism. The main subject of the first movement (*Allegretto*), a leisurely theme in 3/2 meter, is absolutely diatonic. The second theme, too, is restrained and highly lyrical—as is the mood of the entire sonata. In the second movement, *Allegro strepitoso*, Prokofiev gives us the racing triplets and crashing dissonant intervals he always found hard to resist, but even here the effect is muted by an extended slow section.

The third movement, *Andante tranquillo*, in A flat Major, is another reflective narrative in a Schubertian style, followed by a lively concluding *Allegro con brio, ma non troppo presto*. Filled with dotted rhythms, it contains one of Prokofiev's trademark marches, in the style of *Love for Three Oranges*, with quirky open intervals and a clumping bass line. But the movement, and the sonata, come to a gentle close with a return to the first movement's softly lyrical main theme, set high above fluttering seconds in the left hand, creating a shimmering, impressionistic effect. The final measures—to be played *da lontano*, "as if from a distance"—sound like bells ringing far away in the mountains, serene and pure.

Strangely, the first performance of the Ninth Sonata—by Richter—only took place three and a half years later, in April 1951. It had been delayed by the political and personal problems which overtook Prokofiev in early 1948, soon after the sonata was finished.

A similar fate awaited another piece written around the same time—the Sonata for Violin Solo (Op. 115). Apparently Prokofiev had conceived of this brief three-movement composition (in D Major) as a sort of practice piece—an extended étude—that could be played by groups of student violinists. Considerably less challenging technically than his other music for the violin, it was performed for the first time after Prokofiev's death, in 1960.

As his continuing productivity indicates, although Prokofiev was still smarting from the official attack on *War and Peace*, he was nonetheless in a positive frame of mind during that summer of 1947. One of the ways he coped with stress was by having Mira read aloud to him. Vasily Kachalov, a well-known actor and reciter of poetry, would also come to visit and, as they gathered on the porch in the evening, would read Chekhov plays and verses by Pushkin, Lermontov, Bunin, Mayakovsky, Blok, Esenin and even Boris Pasternak. Pasternak and his poetry were especially close to Prokofiev; only one year apart in age, both Pasternak and Prokofiev had chosen to remain in the U.S.S.R. through very difficult years, even though they had many connections abroad and could easily have emigrated. (Pasternak's father, Leonid, was a well-known artist and once drew a sketch of Prokofiev playing at the Soviet Embassy in Berlin.) By late 1947, Pasternak, too, was under intense official pressure, and he and Prokofiev had developed a casual friendship.

"What united them was mutual admiration and a sense of their importance," Oleg Prokofiev has said. Both had struggled with the problem of creating art that was accessible and useful to a mass audience but still retained originality and integrity. Pasternak had started out as a composer before turning to poetry and was always interested in Prokofiev's music. He once remarked that the "thin and simple line, like in the drawings of Picasso or Matisse, by which Prokofiev conveys musical form" was "especially dear to him." The poet and the composer also shared a similar understanding and appreciation of nature; like Prokofiev, Pasternak lived outside Moscow, at his *dacha* in Peredelkino.

In 1946, when it became obvious to Pasternak that a new wave of cultural repression was coming, he had decided he must create a document recording the tragedy of the Russian artistic intelligentsia since the Russian Revolution. The result was *Doctor Zhivago*, one of the great novels of twentieth-century Russian literature, written slowly over the coming years. Prokofiev would not live to read it, though it is likely he would have strongly identified with Zhivago's difficulties in coming to terms with Soviet society, and his abiding love for Russia.

Judging by his friendships with writers of radically different political and aesthetic views (Balmont and Mayakovsky, for example) and his ability to create operas out of novels as different as *The Fiery Angel* and *I am a Son of the Working People*, Prokofiev's taste in literature—like his taste in music—was catholic. In rummaging through the library his father had temporarily abandoned at Chkalov Street, Oleg found H. G. Wells's *Outline of History*, D. H. Lawrence's *Lady*

Chatterley's Lover, and the early Russian novels of Vladimir Nabokov, whom Prokofiev had always admired. Nabokov and Prokofiev shared a similar artistic restraint, a distaste for emotional display, an admiration for Pushkin, a dry wit, and a love of chess. Not surprisingly, Prokofiev's favorite Nabokov novel was his "chess novel," *The Defense.*

The autumn of 1947 that followed the quiet summer at Nikolina Gora was the most active for Prokofiev since his accident nearly three years earlier. It was also his last successful season, and the last one—for reasons of health and politics—during which he would make frequent public appearances.

During October and November, as the U.S.S.R. celebrated the thirtieth anniversary of the October Revolution, there were two world premieres in Moscow of "official music" by Prokofiev: *A Festive Poem* and *Flourish, O Mighty Land. Ode to the End of the War* was also resurrected, on the same program with Shostakovich's enormously popular Seventh Symphony ("Leningrad"). In late December, a slim 20-year old cellist revived another neglected Prokofiev piece—the First Cello Concerto—in the Small Hall of the Conservatory. Prokofiev came backstage to praise the young man's playing, and promised to rewrite the concerto for him. The skinny cellist's name was Mstislav Rostropovich.

But the most important event for Prokofiev had taken place earlier in the fall in Leningrad. On October 11, the world-famous Leningrad Symphony, under Evgeny Mravinsky, gave the premiere of the Sixth Symphony (Op. 111) in the Great Hall of the Leningrad Philharmonic. The doctors had even allowed Prokofiev to travel to Leningrad for the performance. After the enormous success of the Fifth Symphony, public anticipation was running high.

Like the Fifth Symphony, the Sixth—in E flat Major—is large and ambitious, if somewhat more personal and stark in mood. Only a few minutes shorter than the robust Fifth, it has three movements, nearly identical in length—*Allegro moderato, Largo,* and *Vivace.* After a brief and sarcastic introduction—a descending scale in the brass, in strongly accented eighth notes—the symphony's most important theme appears. Rather melancholy, it rolls in easy 6/8 meter; the second theme, in 9/8 and 6/8, is similar in character.

The thickly scored second movement, in A flat Major, begins with extended passages for the winds and brass in the upper register, producing an intense, shrill, almost hysterical sound. Several themes of deep lyricism follow, similar to the love themes of *Romeo and Juliet* or *Cinderella*. In the concluding *Vivace*, Prokofiev returns to the more sunny world of E flat Major, creating a cheerfully martial atmosphere that brings us back to the concrete world of *Peter and the Wolf*. (The treatment of the clarinet is particularly reminiscent of *Peter*.) The symphony comes to an imposing finish with the return of the second theme from the first movement, which climaxes in huge modulations before a brief but decisive return of the *Vivace* material.

At first, the critics received the Sixth Symphony with gushing enthusiasm. In his program notes, the musicologist Grigori Shneerson wrote, "It is one of the most beautiful, most exalted of his works, imbued with the creative spirit of Soviet humanism. . . . It is a great landmark not only in the art of Prokofiev, but in the whole history of the Soviet symphony. . . . This great work shows once again how immeasurably superior Soviet music is to the music of the capitalist West, where symphonism has long ceased to be an art of lofty ideas and high emotionalism, and is now in a state of profound decadence and degeneration."

Soon afterward, however, in connection with the coming assault on the leading Soviet composers, official attitudes toward the Sixth Symphony were sharply revised primarily for political reasons. In late December, when Mravinsky conducted it in Moscow for the first time, the critical response was restrained and cool, and within a month, the Sixth was singled out for particular criticism by Zhdanov and his fellow bureaucrats. It suddenly disappeared from the repertoire, not to be heard again in the Soviet Union for many years.

Even in 1957, four years after Prokofiev's death, Nestyev still found it necessary to "apologize" for the Sixth. "It seems as though the two Prokofievs, the old and the new, were engaged in a struggle, revealing in the course of this struggle both powerful, genuine lyricism and sudden outbursts of unrestrained expressionism utterly incomprehensible to the listener," he proclaimed.

As was the case with Part II of *War and Peace*, the official attack on the Sixth Symphony had much less to do with its musical language—which is resolutely tonal and highly accessible—than with the government's (or at least Stalin's) obsession to exert control over all Soviet artists, no matter how famous or respected. For the second time in less than six months, Prokofiev had come in for harsh official criticism. The state could award attractive prizes (in fact, Prokofiev had received another official honor in November—the title of People's Artist of the Russian Republic), but it also reserved the right to censure and punish.

Ironically, in his own public statements on the Sixth Symphony, Prokofiev had stressed that he was producing a work particularly responsive to the country's demands at the moment. "In working on [the Sixth Symphony], I strove to express in music my admiration for the strength of the human spirit, manifested so clearly in our era and in our country."

As part of the elaborate observation of the thirtieth anniversary of the Bolshevik Revolution, a scholarly conference was held in Moscow in early December to discuss the current state of Soviet music. Sponsored by the Gnesin Institute, the presentations included a musicologist's report on Prokofiev's "creative path." Perhaps as a result of the worsening cultural climate, Prokofiev took great interest in this report, underlining it in ink several times in the conference program. Even now that his international fame and importance seemed undisputed, he remained surprisingly sensitive to what scholars and critics said about him and his music.

Prokofiev's colleagues also noticed his strong desire for public and official recognition. In his alleged memoirs, Shostakovich said, "Prokofiev was always afraid that he was being overlooked—cheated out of his prizes, orders, and titles. He set great store by them and was overjoyed when he received his first Stalin Prize. This naturally did not further our relationship, or improve the friendly atmosphere, so to speak. . . . Prokofiev had the soul of a goose; he always had a chip on his shoulder." Prokofiev wore his official medals proudly, like a decorated general.

Another example of Prokofiev's continuing desire to please the cultural authorities is the new opera he began in the fall of 1947. This unfortunate project (his seventh, and last, opera) grew out of the difficult political position in which he found himself in late 1947, as it became apparent to all Soviet artists that the vise was tightening once again. Understandably frustrated over the cancellation of *War and Peace*, he was also eager to compose an opera that could find its way to the Soviet stage.

As he approached the end of his life, Prokofiev was more disturbed than ever that his operas—with the single exception of *Love for Three Oranges*—had still failed to win wide critical or popular acceptance. Although numerous productions had been promised, *The Gambler* had never yet been staged in Russia, and would not be until 1974. The controversial religious theme of *The Fiery Angel* made it an unthinkable addition to the Soviet repertoire. After its troubled 1940 premiere, *Semyon Kotko* had quickly dropped out of the repertoire, and would return only in 1970. The future for *War and Peace* did not look bright, and even *Love for Three Oranges* was now considered too sarcastic and frivolous for Soviet audiences. Only *Betrothal in a Monastery*, finally produced in 1946, looked like it might stay around for a while.

Amazingly—even stupidly—Prokofiev continued to believe, however, that he could compose a successful "Soviet" opera if only he could find the appropriate subject. During the fall of 1947, Prokofiev and Mira looked through a "huge number of books" in their search for the right one. Among the novels they considered were such overwhelmingly tendentious "classics" of Soviet literature as *How the Steel Was Tempered*, by Nikolai Ostrovsky, and *The Young Guard*, by Alexander Fadeyev.

Their choice was facilitated by the Kirov Theater. Also fearing for its artistic life, and eager to present a new and sufficiently orthodox "Soviet" opera, the Kirov proposed to Prokofiev that he compose an opera on an enormously popular novel published the year before— *Story of a Real Man*, by Boris Polevoy, one of the most ideologically "safe" writers available. Thinking such an opera would surely be censor-proof, Prokofiev and Mira agreed to the Kirov proposal, and set to work on the libretto.

The very model of Socialist Realist respectability, Polevoy, born in 1908, had been active in official Soviet literary organizations since the 1920s. He worked as a journalist through the 1930s, and reported from the front for *Pravda* during World War II. His fiction—including *Story of a Real Man*, his most famous book and the cornerstone of his literary reputation—drew heavily on his war experiences. So dearly does the official Soviet cultural establishment love Polevoy that more than twenty-three million copies of his books were published in fifty-two languages between 1927 and 1975.

Today, Polevoy is Secretary of the Union of Writers, and one of the most "official" and honored Soviet writers living—a creation of Soviet publishing policy, a very minor talent made famous for his compliance with official demands.

It is hard to imagine that any real communication could have existed between Prokofiev, a privileged child of the prerevolutionary middle class, and Polevoy, who grew up working in a textile plant. Neither left any record of their brief collaboration.

Story of a Real Man, awarded a Stalin Prize in 1947, is based on a true story that began with Polevoy's meeting during the War with a Soviet fighter pilot, Aleksei Maresyev. Maresyev had been shot down by the Germans earlier in the War, and both his legs were amputated. Determined to return to combat as a pilot, he overcame enormous physical and bureaucratic obstacles (in the novel, he crawls through snow and subfreezing temperatures from the crash site to the nearest village) to realize his dream. Just before Polevoy met him, Maresyev had made his first successful flight after retraining with artificial limbs. He remained in combat for the duration of the War, and even distinguished himself in battle.

The stridently nationalistic tone of *Real Man* corresponded to an enormous resurgence of Soviet pride after World War II. Even today, forty years after the German defeat, the War remains a favorite subject for novels, plays and films. Maresyev's nearly superhuman determination and endurance became an immediately recognizable symbol of the patience and strength of the Soviet people in their struggle against Hitler, and help to explain the novel's popularity in the U.S.S.R.

Transforming this blatantly propagandistic novel (what a distance Prokofiev had traveled from *The Gambler* and *The Fiery Angel!*) into an opera was not easy. Like so many works of Socialist Realism, *Real Man* has no dramatic conflict; Maresyev (renamed Meresyev in the novel and opera) is in conflict only with his own initial self-pity. Even worse, the novel's real-life hero was still very much alive as the opera was being written; the War had ended barely two years before. One Soviet critic even had to admit that "not a single composer" had ever attempted to write an opera about a living person, or about an event still so fresh in public memory. Prokofiev's first "Soviet" opera, *Semyon Kotko,* was also very topical, but even it had been composed twenty years after the events it described.

How Prokofiev could have forgotten the hard lesson of *Semyon Kotko,* and all the tragic complications to which an explicitly political subject could lead, is puzzling. In choosing a subject like *Story of a Real Man,* which was bound to attract the intense interest of the cultural authorities, Prokofiev showed a strange lapse in artistic and political judgment, and a serious misreading of the highly volatile situation on the eve of the decisive First Congress of Soviet Composers. And yet he was only trying to write music that could be performed.

Unlike Shostakovich, Prokofiev had never before been the target of a full-scale ideological attack; his fame and foreign reputation had always protected him. This may help to explain why he found it difficult to negotiate the perilous waters of Soviet artistic politics. Even after all he had seen—including the catastrophe with Meyerhold—he refused to believe his career could be seriously harmed by the bureaucrats. He did not suspect that within a few months, the fragile peace he had been enjoying since the War would be shattered forever. Hadn't he received a fistful of honors from the Soviet government?

Surely encouraged by Mira, who had more influence over him than ever, Prokofiev may well have reasoned that *Story of a Real Man* could protect his privileged position. He may also have thought that if he produced an edifying and accessible opera depicting "Soviet reality," the bureaucrats would reconsider their criticisms of *War and Peace*. And perhaps he felt a real emotional affinity for the stubborn character of Maresyev, who, like him, had been struck down by physical infirmity. The story provided hope that he, too, could ultimately overcome his body's limitations and return to full-scale musical battle.

In late October, a small article appeared under Prokofiev's name in *Evening Moscow*, describing the opera-in-progress in the stentorian and hyperbolic tones of Soviet officialese. One searches in vain beneath the platitudes for the wonderfully biting and idiosyncratic literary style of Prokofiev's younger years. "I am dedicating my new opera to Soviet man, to his limitless courage," he wrote woodenly.

Prokofiev would need courage himself to face what the next few months would bring.

CHAPTER   2 3

UNDER   FIRE

Worship the night,
Lest you wake up to be famous.

—ANNA AKHMATOVA

etween mid-January and late February 1948, not long before his
fifty-seventh birthday, three momentous events abruptly changed
the course of Prokofiev's personal and professional life. The first
was his marriage to Mira Mendelson. The second was the most
intense and damaging ideological attack ever launched against Soviet
composers. The third was the arrest in Moscow of his first wife, Lina.

Only one of these events was happy—his marriage, on January
13, 1948. The civil ceremony, performed in the marriage bureau of
the Sverdlovsk district where their Moscow apartment was located, was
simple and stark. By now, they had been living together as man and
wife for nearly seven years. Because of Prokofiev's frail health and the
awkward circumstances of their relationship, they celebrated their
marriage quietly, even furtively, without the usual extravagant eating,
drinking and toasting that typically accompany a Russian wedding.

For many years, in fact, it was unclear if and when the marriage
had taken place at all. Soviet musicologists and writers have never
specifically mentioned this important event in any of their countless
books on Prokofiev and his music. Neither Prokofiev nor Mira refer to
it in their respective memoirs. When interviewed, even close friends
and colleagues expressed confusion and uncertainty about the date
and circumstances of the wedding. None of them has provided any

written or oral account of what must have been a bittersweet occasion on a dark and cold mid-January day.

But proof that it occurred is found on a dated official document—"Witness of Marriage" *("Svidetel'stvo o brake")*—issued by the State Records Office of the Sverdlovsk district. After Prokofiev's death, Mira gave this document, along with many other papers, to the Central State Archive of Literature and Art in Moscow. Only recently has it been shown to foreign scholars—perhaps to counteract wild rumors in the West about the relationship between Mira and Prokofiev, particularly the charge that Mira was an agent for the Soviet secret police. The general appearance, condition and printing of the document provide no reason to doubt its authenticity.

If Soviet Prokofiev specialists have been allowed to see this document (which is unlikely), they have chosen, or have been instructed, not to mention it in print. None acknowledged its existence when questioned about it. At the same time, their books and articles universally refer to Prokofiev and Mendelson as "husband and wife"—without explaining how that came about. Most of Prokofiev's friends and associates still living in Moscow with whom I spoke said they had always assumed he and Mira were married, although they offered different versions of when and how this marriage took place.

Why, then, did Prokofiev and Mira choose this moment to finally officialize their long-standing liaison? Why were they so secretive about it?

In the spring of 1941, after leaving Lina to live with Mira, Prokofiev had apparently asked Lina to grant him a divorce, most likely so he could remarry. But Lina refused, and never changed that position. It is impossible to know all the reasons behind Lina's refusal, but she must have realized by then that to be left divorced and "foreign" (although Lina was a Soviet citizen) in Stalin's xenophobic Moscow was to be vulnerable to harassment and isolation. Lina's legendary stubbornness, and a desire to assert her strong will by making things difficult for Prokofiev, may also have played a role.

Lina had been financially dependent on Prokofiev—he had even encouraged that dependence—for many years. He had continued to provide money for her and their sons after he left the household. There is, therefore, no reason to believe that he would not have continued to provide financial support if granted an official divorce. Lina's objections to the divorce were not so much financial, then, as personal and legal. For one thing, if she did grant Prokofiev a divorce, she would be thrown at the unreliable mercy of the Soviet government, and would sacrifice what little leverage she had as the wife of a world-famous composer. Lina had come to Moscow in 1936 as the wife of Sergei Prokofiev; having little else to protect her there, she was hesitant to give up that identity. Perhaps if she had been able to leave Moscow and return to Paris easily, or even to travel back and forth between Russia and Europe, Lina might have felt more willing to grant the divorce, but her applications to go abroad had been rejected by Soviet officials.

Surely aware of her difficult position, and guilty for his role in putting her there, Prokofiev could not force Lina to grant him a divorce. Nor does it appear that Mira exerted much pressure on him to marry her; she seemed more than willing to live with Prokofiev out of wedlock.

We will never know all the reasons that led Prokofiev to alter this seven-year-old status quo by marrying Mira in January 1948, but the worsening cultural climate must have played a role. One explanation is that officials of the Composers' Union, or even the Party leadership—who had access to the most private information about every single Soviet citizen—pressured Prokofiev to legalize his union with Mira. To be simultaneously "married" to two different women—one of them foreign-born—was highly unorthodox under the strict and puritanical Stalinist mores of 1948 even for a normal citizen. But for a decorated national figure of Prokofiev's stature and reputation to be a bigamist was potentially scandalous and politically dangerous—as the cultural bureaucrats may well have pointed out to him. And even if political pressure was not brought to bear on Prokofiev to clarify his marital situation, it is entirely possible that he and Mira themselves began to feel uneasy about continuing to live in a legally vulnerable relationship at a time when all aspects of the personal lives of Soviet citizens were coming under intense official scrutiny.

Another explanation is much more sinister: that Party officials (perhaps in collaboration with representatives of the secret police) encouraged Prokofiev to marry Mira without revealing their real motive—to deprive Lina of her legal protection as his wife, thereby clearing the way to arrest her. There is absolutely no evidence (nor does it conform at all to his character) that Prokofiev had any knowledge of what was about to happen to Lina. He must have realized, though, that she would now be placed in greater danger—which may explain why he hadn't married Mira sooner. In failing health, concerned about the intensifying attacks on his music, torn between his love for Mira and his feelings of responsibility for Lina and their sons, Prokofiev found himself in an impossible situation. He was finally forced—after thirty years of trying to have it both ways—to make a terribly clear-cut decision between Russia and the West, as personified in the two women in his life. Russia won—again.

But one obvious question remains: how could Prokofiev have legally married Mira if he had never been officially divorced from Lina?

Under the reform of Soviet marriage law carried out near the end of World War II, in 1944, all marriages—both new and old—had to be registered with the Census Bureau to be regarded as valid. Only registered marriages would henceforth be considered binding. By 1944, Prokofiev had been living with Mira for three years. It seems highly unlikely that he would have officially registered his existing marriage to Lina. The situation was further complicated because Prokofiev and Lina had not been married in Russia, but in Ettal, Germany, in September 1923, when Soviet marriage law was in chaos. At that time, too, Prokofiev was still registered on a temporary "Nansen" passport (he did not become a Soviet citizen until 1927) and Lina was a Spanish citizen. All these factors only made it easier for the validity of Prokofiev's first marriage to be brought into question, providing additional support for the position that he was legally free—under Soviet law, which was all that mattered—to marry another woman.

Nor was Prokofiev's case an isolated one. In her autobiography, Soviet opera singer Galina Vishnevskaya describes a similar situation. Vishnevskaya and her first husband—a Soviet citizen—had also failed to officially register their marriage, which eventually broke up. This meant that she did not need to obtain an official divorce when she married a second time, to cellist Mstislav Rostropovich, after Stalin's death. "We had been married during the war," she wrote of her first marriage, "when no one worried about paperwork, and after the war we never did anything about it."

Prokofiev had never abandoned Lina and his sons. Because he had been providing for them financially ever since leaving the household, they still lived a privileged existence by Soviet standards. His sons had become young men with increasingly independent lives. Perhaps he felt that now, with his own health so uncertain, he had earned the right to normalize his relationship with Mira. These were lonely and mistrustful times, when, it was said, a man could say what was on his mind only to his wife, late at night underneath the covers.

Even if the legal and emotional background to his second marriage had not been so complicated, the ominous atmosphere of early 1948 was hardly conducive to celebration. No sooner had Prokofiev and Mira been married than the community of Soviet composers was rocked by the opening salvos in an ideological attack led by Comrade Zhdanov. Already firmly in control of literature, Zhdanov now turned his attention to music. The "decadence" and "formalism" he discovered there profoundly disturbed him.

As had happened in 1936 with Shostakovich's *Lady Macbeth*, the guns were aimed first at one erring composition—*The Great Friendship*, an opera by the otherwise forgotten Georgian composer Vano Muradeli. This time, though, the criticism of Muradeli quickly expanded, drawing nearly every Soviet composer, including the "Big Five"—Prokofiev, Shostakovich, Khachaturian, Miaskovsky and Kabalevsky—into a riot of denunciation and slander.

Ironically, *The Great Friendship* was originally conceived as a tribute to Stalin's native land of Georgia. But when Stalin saw the opera in late 1947, the libretto's "historical inaccuracies" (the same defect bureaucrats found in Part II of *War and Peace*) angered him. Most likely, it was the opera's favorable portrayal of his political rival, Grigo Ordzhonikidze, that disturbed him. As usual, Zhdanov happily translated Stalin's displeasure into immediate action, upbraiding Muradeli and the director of the Bolshoi Theater (where the premiere had taken place), and perhaps contributing to the director's fatal heart attack shortly afterward. Like the much greater *Lady Macbeth* before it, *The Great Friendship* was instantly withdrawn from all opera houses.

Unfortunately for Prokofiev and his colleagues, the criticism did not stop here. Stalin and Zhdanov seized upon the Muradeli affair as an example of the rampant laxity of discipline and political rigor among composers. In his alleged memoirs, Shostakovich claims that when criticized, the terrified Muradeli apologized, claiming he had been prevented from writing a simple melodic opera by the "formalist conspiracy" in conservatories and publishing houses. "This version from Muradeli interested Stalin, who was always interested in conspiracies. . . ." The evil "formalism" had to be rooted out of Soviet music, Stalin decided.

In mid-January, Zhdanov summoned Moscow's composers to a secret three-day meeting, supposedly held to air opinions on the current state of Soviet music. But none who attended failed to perceive the crude and incriminating tone of the proceedings, so unpleasantly reminiscent of the recent slanderous attacks on writers and filmmakers. It is unknown who attended, but it seems unlikely, in view of his delicate health, that Prokofiev was there. He tried to avoid such meetings, and would not be present even at the much more important conference in February.

Prokofiev's name was frequently mentioned at that first gathering in January, however, as we know from an eyewitness account recorded by the British journalist Alexander Werth. For the first time since Prokofiev had returned to the U.S.S.R. in 1936, some composers joined the cultural bureaucrats in a gloves-off attack on him and his music. Many in the younger generation of Soviet composers—who had never been allowed to travel or study in the West—resented Prokofiev for his international past and connections, his foreign manners, his arrogance and, most of all, his special privileges. At last, they saw an opportunity to vent their spite. The partial immunity from official criticism that Prokofiev had so long taken for granted had vanished.

Serebryakov, the director of the Leningrad Conservatory, used the opportunity to berate *War and Peace,* calling it an opera that "cannot appeal to the people," and a work composed for "a narrow circle of connoisseurs." A fellow composer, Viktor Bely, accused Prokofiev of "artistic snobbishness, a false fear of being commonplace and ordinary." Zhdanov, whose musical training was primitive at best, gleefully joined in the accusations thrown at the ailing composer who had sacrificed more than any of them to devote his art to Russia. "Any listener will realize the vast difference between classical Russian music and the false, ugly, idealistic music of the formalists," he said. "Not all that is accessible is a work of genius, but a real work of genius is one that is accessible. . . . Bad, disharmonious music undoubtedly has a bad effect on man's psycho-physiological activity."

Prokofiev was branded a "formalist," a term that struck terror into the hearts of all Soviet artists during the last five years of Stalin's reign. Originally, "formalism" applied to art that was excessively concerned with technique and insufficiently concerned with uplifting ideological content. As time went on, however, "formalism" came to mean simply "anti-Soviet," or unpatriotic. In music, "formalism" tended to mean any hint of atonality or prominent dissonance, or an absence of immediately recognizable melody.

Once the accusations against Prokofiev (and against Miaskovsky,

Shostakovich, Khachaturian and many others) had begun, composers turned upon one another in a desperate attempt to escape denunciation. The stakes were high—prominent figures in the other arts had been sent to prison and exile for "formalism." In his alleged memoirs, Shostakovich wrote that his name was "number one" on the list of offenders, and Prokofiev's number two. "Meeting upon meeting, conference upon conference. The whole country was in a fever, the composers more than anyone. It was like a dam breaking and a flood of murky dirty water rushing in. Everyone seemed to go mad and anyone who felt like it expressed an opinion on music."

Those attacked at the January meetings suddenly found their well-established careers foundering. Concerts and commissions were abruptly canceled, and most performers feared to play the music of the leprous "formalists." Prokofiev's music, heard with great frequency during the autumn, was suddenly regarded as seditious and harmful, and would be performed much less often for the next several years.

There were a few brave souls. Long before the January meetings, Sviatoslav Richter and Nina Dorliak had been planning to give a concert of music by Prokofiev and Rimsky-Korsakov on January 28. The concert manager advised them to cancel it, but they refused, and even performed Prokofiev's settings of poems by Balmont—by now considered a sworn enemy of the Soviet state. Prokofiev attended the concert, which was, despite the ongoing official attacks, warmly received. As Richter said later with characteristic understatement and unusual candor, "The attitude toward Prokofiev's music at that time was personally incomprehensible to me."

In early February, the private discussions of the January meetings were made public in an official resolution—"On the Opera *The Great Friendship* by Muradeli"—released by the Party Central Committee. It appeared in the newspapers on February 10, immortalizing and sanctifying the vicious criticisms leveled at Prokofiev's music. A week of meetings—from February 17 to 26—followed, called by the anxious leadership of the Composers' Union. Demoralized and frightened, the composers endorsed the Resolution and praised Stalin. A new spokesman for the government's position also arose from within the composers' own ranks—Tikhon Khrennikov, a young man of thirty-five. Originally representing the disgruntled younger generation, he would control the Composers' Union, faithfully executing the wishes of the Party leadership, for many years to come. He had no special affection for Prokofiev.

At the official meetings during February, many of those criticized—including Shostakovich—were pressured into reading official apologies. Prokofiev's poor health gave him an excuse to stay away: the persistent rumors that he attended, and even behaved truculently by sitting on a piano stool with his back to Zhdanov, are colorful, but have no basis in fact. He did send a letter to the assembly, however. It is neither a complete apology nor a statement of indignant rebellion. He explained that after his return to the U.S.S.R. in 1936, he had made a conscious attempt to find an accessible but artistically viable style, and that he believed he had succeeded in *Alexander Nevsky, Romeo and Juliet,* and the Fifth Symphony, among other works.

Unlike Meyerhold's audacious—and suicidal—remarks to the 1939 directors' conference, Prokofiev's letter did not question the right of Zhdanov or any Party officials to pass judgment on culture in general or music in particular. "The Resolution is valuable precisely in that it pointed out how alien the formalistic movement is to the Soviet people," his statement declared loyally. "This movement leads to the impoverishment and decline of music. At the same time, the Resolution has shown us the goals toward which we need to strive to better serve the Soviet people."

Responding to the original attack on Muradeli's *The Great Friendship,* Prokofiev also focused on the more narrow issues of operatic style and form, describing his work on *Story of a Real Man.* He was using "clear melodies and a harmonic language that is as simple as possible," he said. Unfortunately, the cultural bureaucrats would not share Prokofiev's view of *Story of a Real Man,* and he may even have created more problems for himself by raising official expectations.

As if the relentless official attacks on his music were not gloomy enough, Prokofiev also received some shocking news in the midst of the February conference. One day his sons came to tell him (Prokofiev was living in Moscow that winter) that Lina had been taken away by the police. They were not even sure where she was, and she had not been allowed to call them. Shortly after she disappeared, they told their dumbfounded father, agents armed with search warrants had arrived and ransacked the apartment on Chkalov Street.

Lina's arrest—"on suspicion of spying"—was tragically typical of thousands (perhaps even millions) of others that occurred during 1948. On February 20, as she was lying in bed with a cold, Lina received a telephone call from a friend in Leningrad. The friend told Lina she had sent her a package via another friend who was arriving that day in Moscow by train. She asked if Lina could meet this person at the railroad station not far from Lina's apartment. When Lina explained that she was sick, and asked if the person couldn't come to the apartment with the package, her friend insisted that Lina needed to go herself. Reluctantly, Lina agreed. Since she thought she would return in a few minutes, she didn't even bother to dress very warmly.

As she was waiting in front of the station, a dark-colored car suddenly drove up right in front of her. Someone got out and asked Lina whom she was waiting for.

"What business is that of yours?" she replied indignantly.

"Do you know that you're waiting for a criminal?" the man asked her.

"You must have made a mistake," Lina replied, beginning to feel uneasy. "You have the wrong person."

The men in the car were very insistent that she was the person they wanted, however. Finally they instructed her to get into the car.

"Come with us and we'll explain everything," they said. "If we've made a mistake, you can go—we'll even bring you back home."

They forced Lina into the car and drove off. As they passed the apartment building on Chkalov Street, Lina was hoping desperately that Oleg or Sviatoslav would appear. She asked where they were taking her.

"We'll explain everything in a minute," they said.

But there was no need to explain when the car passed through the gates of the Lubyanka, Moscow's most infamous prison, on Dzherzhinsky Square across the street from the Children's World Department Store. When they were inside, Lina immediately recognized a man sitting there as someone she had seen in the subway and on the streets. He had been following her. There had been a few other subtle signs that she was being watched, but Lina had failed—or refused—to take serious notice.

The manufactured crime with which Lina was charged was passing information to foreign powers. This same charge was also used to imprison thousands of Soviet prisoners of war after they returned from Germany. Just as these prisoners were innocent, there is absolutely no evidence that Lina ever did any spying. Nor did she have access to any important classified information. Lina was a European by birth, however, and she was often in and out of the European and American embassies, attending parties and receptions. She was also fluent in several European languages, and did occasional interpreting and translating work for diplomats. This was enough to arouse official concern. Even today, in a much more liberal atmosphere, most Soviet citizens are terrified of entering foreign embassies in Moscow; since the early 1930s, these places have been considered strictly off-limits. They are heavily guarded by Soviet police. To go inside the embassies of Western powers is tantamount to treason.

Lina's connection to the American Embassy was particularly close; she knew the ambassador and many members of the staff, and was a regular guest at social functions. Given the increasingly hostile atmosphere developing in 1948 between the United States and the U.S.S.R., her frequent and regular contact with the American Embassy was bound to create suspicion. That Lina still had numerous relatives and friends in Europe and the United States, and that she had expressed a desire to travel abroad with her sons, were other factors leading to her arrest. Soviet officials may also have feared that she would create an international scandal by appealing to foreign diplomats for help in going abroad, or by taking some other drastic action.

In the hysterically xenophobic atmosphere of Stalinist Moscow in 1948, such open, even flamboyant, fraternization with the capitalist enemy was sufficient evidence to accuse a person of spying. At the mockery of a trial which followed, Lina persistently denied any wrongdoing, but she was sentenced to a long term in Siberia. She would spend eight years in the labor camps and would be released only in 1956, three years after Prokofiev's death.

Even in the camps, where she was eventually offered an early termination of her sentence if she would admit to having engaged in espionage, Lina refused to "confess." She was finally released as part of the general clemency extended by Khrushchev to most of the similarly innocent victims of the Stalinist purges.

Within hours of Lina's arrest, police agents arrived at the apartment on Chkalov Street to search through Lina's belongings. Sviatoslav and Oleg huddled in the next room, wondering when their mother would reappear. Lina was not allowed to call them to explain what had happened to her, and would not see her sons again until after Stalin's death in 1953. Prokofiev was never even officially notified that his first wife had been arrested.

When Oleg and Sviatoslav brought him this terrible news, Prokofiev must have felt tremendous guilt. He was responsible for bringing

Lina to the U.S.S.R., and she had been reluctant to come. He must also have realized that his recent marriage to Mira—which implied that he no longer wanted to be held accountable for Lina's welfare— could have been a factor in Lina's arrest.

For obvious reasons, there is no record of Prokofiev's reaction, or of his attempts to help Lina. His colleagues and friends claim that he did try—although not especially persistently—to aid her, but without obtaining results. Clearly, the arrest was timed to coincide almost exactly with the official attacks on Prokofiev; his own vulnerable and precarious position made it nearly impossible for him to protest. If anything, Lina's arrest was intended as a demonstration of just how powerless all Soviet composers—even the most famous and prestigious—were. It provided an excellent opportunity for Zhdanov and Stalin to back up their verbal attacks on musical "formalism" with a graphic demonstration of their ability to intrude brutally into private lives.

Stripped of his influence, under rising suspicion for his own "foreign connections," in frail health, Prokofiev was advised by his friends and colleagues not to push too hard for Lina's release. Otherwise, he ran the real risk of being arrested himself. Considering all the circumstances, his behavior was understandable, if not courageous. Prokofiev never saw Lina again.

By the end of February 1948, the worst month of his life, Prokofiev must have been drained as never before. Misfortune, guilt and grief surrounded him. Those who had provided support in the past were under attack themselves, or had left this world behind. On February 11, only a week before Lina's arrest, Prokofiev had lost another old friend. The seemingly immortal Sergei Eisenstein—a trusted adviser, inexhaustible source of inspiration and an irreplaceable link to the past—died after a long illness. Prokofiev stood proud watch next to the coffin as Eisenstein lay in state. He was buried in Novodevichy.

C H A P T E R   2 4

" M Y   S O U L   H U R T S "

Sergei Prokofiev's fate and art arose from a tragic
source.
                                        —ILYA EHRENBURG

After the painful professional and personal setbacks he suffered in
early 1948, life was never again the same for Prokofiev. Reper-
cussions of those events would haunt him and his music throughout
the five difficult years that remained to him. Now, the aura of
privilege and distinction that had formerly set him apart from the
common herd of Soviet composers had been brutally smashed; he had
to struggle even harder for his music to be accepted and performed.

His last years were filled with rejections, disappointments and
the deaths of his closest friends; his income was drastically reduced.
His health deteriorated even more rapidly. But Prokofiev never gave
up, continuing until his very last minutes to compose, create and devote
as much energy as possible to his art.

Soon after the February meetings, Prokofiev returned to Nikolina
Gora, where he and Mira continued working on *Story of a Real Man*.
Its first six scenes (Acts I and II) had been composed in piano score
before the fatal Resolution; the remaining scenes of the original version
were finished in piano score by mid-May, and the orchestration by
mid-August. Responding to the official call for more accessible opera,
Prokofiev was making extensive use of folk music (from northern Russia) and set-pieces. The musical model he was following was Tchaikovsky—specifically, the *arioso* style (midway between aria and recitative)
of Tatyana's famous letter-writing scene in Act I of *Eugene Onegin*.

Prokofiev remained hopeful that *Real Man* would restore him to favor and open the way to performances of his other works, especially *War and Peace*.

In creating the libretto, Prokofiev and Mira condensed Polevoy's novel into four acts in ten scenes, which were further subdivided into small cinematic-style episodes, following the same structural principle used in *Semyon Kotko*. Act I is set in the forest where Aleksei was shot down by the Germans; Act II in the hospital where he convalesces from the amputation; Act III in the sanatorium where he learns to walk again and proves to the doctors that he can fly by dancing (an unintentionally grotesque waltz and rumba) on his artificial legs; and Act IV at an airstrip, where Aleksei makes a triumphant return to combat, shooting down several German planes. In 1960, seven years after Prokofiev's death, Mira significantly revised the original libretto for a production at the Bolshoi Theater, condensing it into three acts, omitting a number of scenes and rearranging others.

Both dramatically and musically, *Real Man* is almost more appropriately described as a cantata or an oratorio than an opera. It is heavily influenced both by the tradition of Soviet "song opera" and by Prokofiev's own work with Soviet mass forms, like *Zdravitsa* or *Ballad of an Unknown Boy*. Due to the intense political pressure under which he was operating, Prokofiev was extremely sensitive as he was writing *Real Man*—particularly in the opera's second half, composed after the February disaster—to the impact his chosen musical style would have on the "average" Soviet listener.

Whenever he had used folk sources in large dramatic works before, Prokofiev had always radically reinterpreted them in his own musical style—as in *Alexander Nevsky*, *Ivan the Terrible* and *Semyon Kotko*. He had always regarded direct citation of folk tunes as cheap and easy. But the score of *Real Man* is filled with nearly unchanged quotations of folk tunes; they are not reworked through Prokofiev's contemporary aesthetic, or altered to conform to the opera's own musical style. *Real Man* is stylistically eclectic, a series of "numbers" strung together without the internal dramatic or musical logic Prokofiev had formerly regarded as essential in a successful stage work.

Heavy use of folk-style and mass songs is not the only thing that makes *Real Man* the most musically simple and unchallenging of Prokofiev's operas. Gone is the unending flow and drive of the vocal line that propels *The Gambler*, *Love for Three Oranges* and even *Semyon Kotko* in their pursuit of dramatic "truthfulness." Instead, Prokofiev employed an inoffensive and bland *arioso* style that does little more than link the numbers.

With *Real Man*, Prokofiev's evolution as an operatic composer came to a sad end. The exciting and extravagantly stylized ideas with which he had begun thirty years earlier—in *The Gambler, Love for Three Oranges* and *The Fiery Angel*—were by now so diluted by contact with Soviet conventionality that they had disappeared, buried under a pile of Socialist Realist bombast and political caution. The path Prokofiev took as a serious Soviet operatic composer, from the experimental *Semyon Kotko* to the more careful *War and Peace*, to the reactionary *Real Man*, is a sad testament to how completely Soviet culture had betrayed the revolutionary principles for which it originally stood. It is also a striking—and not entirely flattering—example of how much Prokofiev craved and pursued the approval of those in authority. If Meyerhold had survived to hear the uninspired pages of *Real Man*, he might have been ashamed to have once called Prokofiev "the new Wagner."

The opera's failure to win the official favor Prokofiev sought, then, is all the more depressing. On December 3, 1948, *Story of a Real Man* was heard for the first time, in a closed concert performance at the Kirov Theater conducted by Boris Khaikin. The inevitable band of cultural bureaucrats attended. His health somewhat improved, Prokofiev had come to Leningrad for the performance and was sitting anxiously in the audience. The doctors had allowed him to attend the performance on the condition that he not stay for the official discussion.

It is fortunate that he didn't. Attending as his representative, Mira was forced to listen as *Real Man* came under unanimous and vicious attacks. It was as if Prokofiev's international reputation and years of experience now counted for nothing. Despite his conscientious efforts to create an accessible and realistic opera, Prokofiev was accused of a whole assortment of sins, expressed in the abstract and meaningless language of the cultural commissars: "failing to convey a real sense of the people's life during the War" and "overshadowing the great heroic theme" with an excess of "naturalistic details" and a "conventional portrayal of everyday life."

The cultural bureaucrats were so eager to flex their muscles that they would have criticized any opera Prokofiev might have written at the time, but the poor quality of the Kirov performance only intensified Prokofiev's despair. "As I was listening, I couldn't even recognize my own music!" he later told Samosud angrily. "They weren't playing my music!"

In his unnaturally cheerful memoirs of Prokofiev, Kabalevsky claims that the failure of *Real Man* ran off like water from a duck's back. After the nasty official discussion at the Kirov, Kabalevsky went to console Prokofiev in his hotel room nearby at the Astoria. He found him huddled in a warm blanket, working on a new ballet (*The Stone Flower*) and unwilling to talk about what had happened. To Kabalevsky, this meant that Prokofiev had already put the failure behind him and was intently focused on the future. But Prokofiev must have been demoralized; even when he made a good-faith attempt to respond to the petty and envious criticism of his colleagues, his music remained unperformed.

Later in December, at a plenary session of the Composers' Union held to evaluate new works composed during the preceding year, *Real Man* came in for even stronger criticism at the highest level. "Formalism still lives in the music of Soviet composers," Khrennikov warned. "This is demonstrated by Prokofiev's new opera." So negative was the official response to *Real Man* that all plans for a production at the Kirov—or anywhere else—were dropped. It would finally reach the stage only twelve years later, long after Prokofiev's death.

Another acute disappointment awaited Prokofiev the day after the Kirov debacle with *Real Man*. Samosud had managed to convince the administration of the Maly Theater to put on a concert version (without scenery, makeup or costumes) of Part II of *War and Peace*, shelved since the summer of 1947 because of official criticism. Prokofiev attended, full of anticipation, now more anxious than ever. Following doctors' orders, he did not attend the official discussion which followed. There, the actors passionately defended *War and Peace*, but their voices "had no decision-making power." Those who did have power repeated their earlier reservations, and Part II of the opera stayed on the shelf.

A new suggestion was also made—that Prokofiev condense the unwieldy two-part *War and Peace* into a one-evening presentation. Prokofiev's determination to get the opera on stage was so strong that he immediately drew up a plan for the cuts and revisions a one-evening version would require. This new plan was the embryo of the final one-evening, thirteen-scene *War and Peace* that would be staged in 1955. But Prokofiev would never see that revised one-evening version, today the accepted performing version. The closed run-through of Part II at the Maly Theater in December of 1948 was the last performance of *War and Peace* he would ever see.

Two more crushing defeats. Prokofiev had spent nearly a year writing *Real Man*, and already more than seven years on *War and Peace*, and still had nothing to show for his labor.

That he was upset seems clear from a letter he received a few days later in Moscow, from Vera Alpers. "Don't despair after these failures," she said, "I am telling you this even though I know, perhaps, that it will not convince you at the moment."

As he had so many times in the past, Prokofiev sublimated his disappointment into composition. As Kabalevsky had noticed, Prokofiev was already working on a big new dramatic project, his seventh—and last—ballet. Responding to Alpers's note of consolation, he told her he had already completed the second act. But *The Stone Flower* would fare no better with Soviet producers and bureaucrats than *War and Peace* or *Story of a Real Man*. Like *War and Peace*, it would be many times revised—under intense official pressure—and even then would reach the stage only after Prokofiev's death.

There is some confusion over when and how Prokofiev began working on *The Stone Flower*. In his account of their collaboration, the choreographer Leonid Lavrovsky claims the ballet was begun as the result of a conversation at Nikolina Gora in the summer of 1949, but according to dates on the manuscript score, Prokofiev had begun composing it much earlier, in September of 1948, and had completed its first version in piano score by March of 1949. It seems likely that the conversation between Prokofiev and Lavrovsky, who was co-author with Mira of the ballet's scenario, actually took place in the summer of 1948.

The Stone Flower (sometimes called *The Tale of the Stone Flower—Skaz o kamennom tsvetke*) was based on folktales of the Urals, as collected and reworked by the Soviet writer Pavel Bazhov in *The Malachite Box*. The tales are primarily concerned with the renowned Ural stonecutters, who work with malachite, a copper ore abundant in that region. Russian craftsmen have been creating intricate ornamental objects from this hard, dark-green stone for centuries.

For their scenario, in four acts and nine scenes, Mira and Lavrovsky concentrated on two tales dealing with Danilo, a talented young stonecutter, and his sweetheart, Katerina. Danilo is so obsessed with his work—making the most perfect and natural objects from malachite—that he pays little attention to anything else, including Katerina. His curiosity eventually leads him to the fantastic underground realm of the Mistress of Copper Mountain, who reveals the secret of absolute beauty—the Stone Flower—for which he is searching. Katerina finally finds her way there, too, where she wanders in the malachite forest. The strength and purity of her love for Danilo melts the hard heart of the Mistress of Copper Mountain, and she allows them to return to their village to live happily ever after.

Lost in the ballet's scenario, unfortunately, is the central message expressed in Danilo's quest for the stone flower: art requires great sacrifices. Some critics have claimed that it was precisely this message that first attracted Prokofiev—no stranger to sacrifice himself. But episodic and stuffed with dance numbers unrelated to the story line, the ballet obscures this theme. The development of the relationship between Katerina and Danilo is also strangely thin and unconvincing. Perhaps too concerned with producing a ballet that could please the bureaucrats and theatre administrators, Prokofiev was sure to include many conventional and easily danceable numbers.

Like *Story of a Real Man, The Stone Flower* retreats from the sharp characterizations and dramatic probing of Prokofiev's earlier music for the theatre. The relentless forward thrust of *Romeo and Juliet,* whose every scene contributes directly to the unfolding of the tragedy, is not to be found here. *The Stone Flower* is the most static and conventional of all of Prokofiev's ballets, just as *Story of a Real Man* is the most static and conventional of his operas.

In its subject and setting, *The Stone Flower* bears a strong resemblance to *The Buffoon,* written more than thirty years earlier for Diaghilev. The two ballets could not be more different in tone, however. Where *The Buffoon* is sarcastic, witty and highly stylized, *The Stone Flower* is placidly romantic, slow-moving and literal. Diaghilev would have hated it.

And yet there are interesting moments in *The Stone Flower,* and it is certainly more sophisticated than *Real Man.* The portrayal of the Mistress of Copper Mountain—who receives the most memorable music, particularly her main theme, shining with cold brilliance in the brass— is particularly successful. The numerous set-pieces are also attractive, if unsurprising. Among them are a Russian dance, a gypsy dance and the well-known Ural Rhapsody, set at a country fair. As in *Cinderella,*

Tchaikovsky is an important influence, notably in the music for the fantastic scenes, such as the "Waltz of the Diamonds" and the "Dance of the Russian Semi-Precious Stones."

From the very beginning of their collaboration on *The Stone Flower*, Prokofiev and Lavrovsky disagreed over many places in the score. Both the choreographer and representatives of the Bolshoi Theater, where the ballet was scheduled to be produced, demanded frequent and significant revisions. The campaign to humiliate Prokofiev continued. When portions of the score were performed for the theatre staff and the bureaucrats in late 1949, there was yet another repetition of the familiar scene.

Lavrovsky wrote later,

> Voices were raised sharply criticizing the music. It was thought that the music poorly corresponded to the artistic imagery of Bazhov's tales, that it was somber, heavy, undanceable. Many thoughtless, careless (and even sometimes tactless) things were said. Sergei Sergeevich took the postponement of the theatre's work very hard, and became offended. Around this time, his health began to noticeably deteriorate. There were long periods when he was categorically forbidden to work. Unfortunately, I could do nothing to cheer him up—in fact, I had to hide a great deal from Sergei Sergeevich, protecting his health and well-being. It was especially difficult then for Mira Alexandrovna, who, aware of everything that was going on, tried to calm Sergei Sergeevich, using her characteristic sensitivity and caution.

The squabbling over the music and staging dragged on for several years after the score had been finished; Prokofiev seemed to have less control over his own creations than ever. When Lavrovsky tried to interest Prokofiev in writing a ballet based on Shakespeare's *Othello*, he replied, "Why write ballets only to put them on the shelf?"

If success in ballet and opera was stubbornly elusive, Prokofiev did find some consolation in a purely musical collaboration. In late 1947, just before Zhdanov's assault, Prokofiev had heard the young cellist Mstislav Rostropovich, then beginning to make a name for himself, play his long-forgotten First Cello Concerto. Rostropovich's brilliant resurrection of the concerto had inspired Prokofiev to tell the cellist backstage that he would rewrite it for him, and Rostropovich, then twenty years old, reminded Prokofiev of that promise on every possible subsequent occasion.

But before rewriting the concerto, Prokofiev composed a cello sonata. After completing it in 1949, Prokofiev sent the sonata to Rostropovich, then invited him to Nikolina Gora to play it through and talk it over. When he arrived at Prokofiev's *dacha* with their mutual acquaintance the musicologist Levon Avtomyan, to whom the sonata was dedicated, Rostropovich was surprised to find Prokofiev in a robe, a towel wrapped around his head like a turban. The chickens and roosters he had just finished feeding were chasing after him.

" 'Good day, sir,' Sergei Sergeevich said jokingly, and, seeing my confusion, added, 'Excuse me for my rustic appearance.' "

Their meeting that day was the beginning of an intense, but unfortunately brief, collaboration. Prokofiev's respect for Rostropovich's talent and technique, and Rostropovich's love for Prokofiev's music, led to the creation not only of the Cello Sonata, but also of the Sinfonia Concertante for Cello and Orchestra (the rewriting of the Cello Concerto) and several cello pieces that remained unfinished at the time of Prokofiev's death. Rostropovich's wife, Galina Vishnevskaya, has written that her husband saw "his ideal" in Prokofiev, and "tried to be like him in everything, even in trifles. Prokofiev liked perfumes— Slava developed that same fondness. His penchant for neckties also came from Sergei Sergeevich."

Their friendship eventually became so close that Rostropovich spent several summers living with Prokofiev and Mira at Nikolina Gora, helping to rewrite the First Cello Concerto.

As for the Cello Sonata (Op. 119), composed during 1949, it has become one of the most popular pieces in the cello repertoire. Prokofiev very rarely placed epigraphs on his compositions, but the first page of the original manuscript score bears this famous line by Maxim Gorky: "Man—that has a proud sound." The sentiments expressed in the epigraph correspond well to the broad, sweeping and warm spirit of the piece.

In three movements (*Andante grave*, *Moderato* and *Allegro, ma non troppo*), the sonata exploits the deep singing tone of the cello, but also provides ample opportunity for technical display. (Rostropovich guided Prokofiev toward this happy medium.) The harmonic and rhythmic style are relatively simple—the key is C Major, as in the recently completed Ninth Piano Sonata—and the piano accompaniment spare and uncluttered. Reflective, even somber, in mood, it bears a certain kinship to the First Violin Sonata, although it is not nearly so dissonant or rhythmically aggressive.

Rostropovich gave the first performance of the Cello Sonata, with Sviatoslav Richter at the piano, at a closed plenum of the Composers' Union on December 6, 1949. They also gave the first public performance, on March 1, 1950, in the Small Hall of the Moscow Conservatory. Both performances were well-received, even by the official critics.

Prokofiev was unable to attend the March premiere at the Conservatory, for his health had taken a sharp turn for the worse. Although he had written Vera Alpers in November that "my health is almost completely in order," he suffered a reversal not long after, and lay in the Kremlin Hospital for six weeks during the winter of 1950. Sviatoslav Richter visited him not long after he was taken there, and was depressed to see Prokofiev so "soft." His voice was "as insulted as it could possibly be." He complained that the doctors wouldn't let him compose—they even took away all his paper. But Prokofiev refused to give in, scribbling down musical ideas on little paper napkins that he hid under his pillow.

"All this didn't fit at all with the picture of a giant of Russian music. It was hard to believe: a man who had always created energy was now a helpless creature."

A month later, though, Prokofiev's condition had dramatically improved. When Richter came back for another visit, Prokofiev saw him to the stairway, and, with his usual mischievous energy, waved good-bye with his foot. By spring, Prokofiev was well enough to go to the sanatorium at Barkhiva and returned to Nikolina Gora for the summer.

After this illness, the doctors further restricted the number of hours Prokofiev could work each day to a maximum of an hour or an hour and a half. Even so, he maintained the same strict schedule he had observed throughout his life, never giving in to depression or self-pity. Rising early at the *dacha*, he would take his favorite chair out to the porch and quietly survey the natural surroundings. Returning to his study, he would shave with an electric razor, then put on a jacket and tie for breakfast. After breakfast, he would work for a little while, walk on his favorite forest paths, feed the chickens and roosters, play with his dog (named Mendoza after the ugly fish merchant in *Betrothal in a Monastery*) and cat, and listen as Mira read to him. Life was quiet and uneventful, but no time was wasted.

Prokofiev often strolled over to chat with Miaskovsky, whose *dacha* was nearby. But on August 8, 1950, Miaskovsky died after a brief illness, at the age of sixty-nine. Prokofiev had lost his oldest and closest friend in the world, a man he had known for forty-five years and whose advice he had taken more seriously than anyone's. Boris Asafiev, their classmate from the Petersburg Conservatory, had died the year before. There was almost no one left of Prokofiev's friends and colleagues: Mayakovsky, Balmont, Diaghilev, Meyerhold, Eisenstein and now Miaskovsky were all gone. Prokofiev was too sick—perhaps emotionally as well as physically—to attend "Kolechka's" funeral.

What little time he was allowed to devote to composition that summer Prokofiev gave to a new "official" work, an oratorio called *On Guard for Peace*. The text was provided by Samuil Marshak, a popular Soviet children's writer. Marshak had also written the spoken text for Prokofiev's orchestral suite *Winter Bonfire*, composed in the fall of 1949. Both pieces are for children. *Winter Bonfire* (Op. 122) is scored for an orchestra, a chorus of boys and a narrator, and tells the story of a group of boys from Moscow who travel by train for a winter outing in the deep forest. Prokofiev's music is simplistic in the extreme, but has a certain illustrative charm, particularly in the first and last sections, where the orchestra re-creates the sound and rhythm of a speeding locomotive.

There is no irony in Prokofiev's approach to this saccharine material. If Peter from *Peter and the Wolf* had disobeyed his grandfather in this setting, the other boys might have turned him in to the Party officials for punishment.

On Guard for Peace is more ambitious. It is scored for a very large ensemble—narrator, contralto, boy alto, chorus of boys, mixed chorus of adults and full orchestra with large percussion section—and uses texts dealing with the War and the need for future peace. Perhaps the most affecting is a section sung by the boys' chorus that provides a view of war through the eyes of children. Musically, *On Guard for Peace* is remarkably bland, homogenous and considerably less interesting than the official music Prokofiev wrote in the 1930s. Nevertheless, its political merits were sufficient to earn Prokofiev a Stalin Prize (second class) in 1951, awarded jointly for *On Guard for Peace* and *Winter Bonfire*.

The premiere of these two works in the Hall of Columns in Moscow—on the same program on December 19, 1950—was the first concert prominently featuring Prokofiev's music since Zhdanov's attacks on him in early 1948—nearly three years before. (Zhdanov had died in the meantime.) Over the next two years, Prokofiev's orchestral and chamber music would gradually reenter the concert repertoire, although the complete rehabilitation of his *oeuvre* in the U.S.S.R. would be a long and painful process that began in earnest only after his death.

On April 23, 1951, Prokofiev celebrated his sixtieth birthday. His health continued to fluctuate. A few days before his birthday, he wrote wistfully to Vera Alpers, "My health is behaving itself nicely, but I have to live quietly and modestly. I can work, but only a little bit at a time." On April 21, some of Prokofiev's friends, including Sviatoslav Richter, organized a concert in his honor at the Composers' Union, but Prokofiev's health had again taken a turn for the worse and he was unable to attend. He listened by telephone from his Moscow apartment.

Richter used the special occasion to give Prokofiev a birthday present: the world premiere of the Ninth Piano Sonata. "It's a bright, simple, even intimate sonata," said Richter. "To me, it even seems like a kind of *sonata-domestica*. The more you hear it, the more you come to love it and yield to its attraction—the more complete it comes to seem. I love it very much."

During 1951, Prokofiev felt well enough to work steadily, although at a snail's pace compared with his frenetic activity of the past. *The Stone Flower* was still enmired in difficulties at the Bolshoi, so Prokofiev arranged some of its music into separate orchestral pieces: the "Wedding Suite" (Op. 126), the "Gypsy Fantasy" (Op. 127) and the "Ural Rhapsody" (Op. 128). Both the "Wedding Suite" and the "Gypsy Fantasy" were performed publicly in late 1951, more than two years before the ballet itself was staged—just as the *Romeo and Juliet* Suites had been heard before *Romeo and Juliet* was produced.

Encouraged by Samosud, Prokofiev also continued to make revisions in *War and Peace*, cutting it to one-evening size and attempting to make the vocal style more melodic. He would continue to revise the opera almost until the day of his death.

But the most important projects of Prokofiev's last two years were the transformation of his First Cello Concerto into what amounted to a new work, the Sinfonia Concertante for Cello and Orchestra, and a new symphony—his Seventh.

The history of the Sinfonia Concertante is an unusually long and complicated one that demonstrates Prokofiev's passion for revision. After the highly successful premiere of the Sonata for Cello and Piano in early 1950, Rostropovich finally convinced Prokofiev to rework his 1938 First Cello Concerto, which Rostropovich had also premiered, in 1947. They collaborated on this new project from early 1950 until early 1952, and produced what they at first called the Second Cello Concerto (Op. 125). But Prokofiev remained dissatisfied with the reworking, made further (less significant) changes in the Second Concerto during 1952, and changed the name again, to Sinfonia Concertante for Cello and Orchestra (also Op. 125). It is in this final form that the piece is best-known today, although Prokofiev never heard it in performance.

The Sinfonia Concertante is an enormously appealing and powerful composition, and one of Prokofiev's crowning achievements in the concerto form. As the title indicates, the orchestra and soloist play equally important roles. After all the bland and oddly lethargic orchestral music he had written since the Sixth Symphony, the Sinfonia Concertante reaffirms, on the eve of his death, Prokofiev's forceful and unique artistic personality, and demonstrates once again how important it was for him to collaborate with artists as talented as he was. It brings back the wonderfully bold rhythmic experimentation, ironic lightness and transparent lyricism of the works for which he is best known— *Lt. Kizhe, Romeo and Juliet,* the Third Piano Concerto.

There are only three movements in the Sinfonia Concertante, but it lasts nearly forty minutes. The largest is the middle *Allegro giusto,* preceded by an *Andante* and followed by an *Andante con moto— Allegro.* Each of the movements flashes with marvelous contrasts: the "motor" rhythms so familiar from Prokofiev's piano music clash with serene and flowing melodic lines. As in the best of Prokofiev's music, the Sinfonia Concertante is almost overloaded with interesting ideas and material. And Rostropovich was sure to see that the cellist received ample opportunity to show off; extended, and formidably difficult cadenza passages abound, particularly in the second and third movements. The balance between soloist and orchestra is unusually subtle and surprising. The Sinfonia Concertante represents the same remarkable synthesis of the "old" and "new" Prokofiev as do *Romeo and Juliet* and the Fifth Symphony. In the capable hands of Rostropovich, the piece has become very familiar throughout the world.

Prokofiev's last symphony, the Seventh, composed in 1951–52, does not possess the energy and richness of the Sinfonia Concertante. Perhaps because his most recent attempt to write a symphony, the Sixth, had been reviled as too full of jarring contrast and dense, expressionistic harmonies, Prokofiev retreated to an oddly flat and placid style in the Seventh. Its simple form, square rhythms and unusually thin scoring—only rarely does the entire orchestra play—were also chosen so that the Seventh would be accessible to the audience at which Prokofiev said he was aiming: children.

Prokofiev himself had some doubts about the symphony. After a closed performance at the Composers' Union in late December 1951, he insistently asked his colleagues. "But isn't the music too simple?"

The first movement, *Moderato,* is unadorned, straightforward and uncharacteristically timid. Built around ingratiating *Cinderella*-style waltzes, the second movement, *Allegretto,* says nothing Prokofiev has not said better before. The concluding *Vivace* contains little hint of the fiery brilliance for which the fast movements of his earlier concerti and symphonies were justly famous. It is difficult not to agree with the assessment of Olin Downes, who wrote that the work represents "a retrogression and not a step forward." The Seventh is an old man's symphony, beyond strife and conflict.

But the Soviet cultural bureaucrats praised art that avoided conflict—how could conflict exist in a Socialist society, where all people were happy? It was entirely logical, then, that Prokofiev's Seventh Symphony should have been awarded a Lenin Prize (so renamed after Stalin's death) in 1957, while the much greater Sixth Symphony went unplayed and unknown.

In addition to the Seventh Symphony and the Sinfonia Concertante, Prokofiev also worked on an "official" piece for symphony orchestra—his last—in 1951. Composed to celebrate the building of the canal linking the Volga and Don rivers, it was called *Festive Poem— The Meeting of the Volga and the Don.* Prokofiev (or Mira) wrote, in the mindless optimism of Stalinist publicity, "As I work, I remember the endless expanse of our great rivers, I remember the songs which our people have sung about them, and the lines by Russian classical and contemporary poets devoted to them. I am striving in this poem to write music that is melodious, reflecting the joy of construction that now seizes our entire people."

Samosud conducted the premiere for a radio broadcast on February 22, 1952, four days after Rostropovich had given the first performance of the Second Cello Concerto (soon to be revised as the Sinfonia Concertante).

Another important performance for Prokofiev during 1952 was a "viewing" of fragments from *War and Peace* (it was actually advertised as *Natasha Rostova,* although this name change never stuck) at the Composers' Union on October 10. The prospects for the opera were at last looking brighter. Prokofiev would be thrilled to hear one of the scenes, "The Council at Fili," broadcast on the radio in early February 1953, just a month before he died. But he would miss the first full-scale concert performance of the revised one-evening version by only three months; it took place in June.

Prokofiev made his last public appearance at a concert featuring his music on October 11, 1952, in the Hall of Columns. The Seventh Symphony received its world premiere on an all-Prokofiev program including *On Guard for Peace.* Samosud, one of Prokofiev's most loyal supporters for nearly a decade, conducted.

Not long after this concert, the beginning of the 1952–53 season—one that would bring great changes to the Soviet Union—Prokofiev's health began to deteriorate more rapidly. The medicines, massages and a daily regimen "strict to the point of severity" failed to improve his condition. The doctors advised Mira and Prokofiev to stay in their Moscow apartment that winter, since it was difficult to maintain a constant temperature at the *dacha,* and Prokofiev needed to be close to medical help at all times. He missed Nikolina Gora, and found it difficult to be confined in their small city apartment. Once or twice, Mira took him out to the *dacha* to spend a few hours walking through the snow.

Summoning what little strength the nearly constant headaches and dizziness left him, Prokofiev still continued to work. He managed to complete a new version of the Fifth Piano Sonata (Op. 135), originally composed thirty years before in Ettal in the days of his first happiness with Lina, and to begin two new pieces—his Sixth Concerto (for two pianos and string orchestra) and his Tenth Piano Sonata.

As his health worsened, he was more troubled than ever that so many of his compositions remained unperformed and unpublished in the U.S.S.R. And yet he continued to refuse numerous offers from foreign publishers who wanted to publish his collected works abroad. "I don't think it is acceptable that they should appear somewhere abroad and not here," he said with almost insane loyalty in light of the abuse his country's government had heaped upon him.

New Year's Eve 1953 was the twelfth New Year's Prokofiev and Mira had spent together. They celebrated quietly at home, joined by Mira's father. "At midnight we raised our glasses, and then read aloud some letters written by Chekhov, who had recently become very important—even necessary—to Sergei Sergeevich." In an unusually sentimental mood, remembering the many new years they had greeted with Miaskovsky, Prokofiev recited these lines by the Russian Romantic poet Zhukovsky:

> Of our dear companions, who gave
> Life to our world with their friendship,
> Let us not say sadly—*they are no longer,*
> But thankfully—*they were.*

By early February, Prokofiev was weaker. The doctors told him to spend a few days in bed, and to apply leeches. No sooner had he recovered some strength than he fell ill with a serious case of the flu. About to depart for a foreign tour, Rostropovich came to see him, finding him listless, with a high temperature. It was the last time he saw Prokofiev.

Some good news cheered him at the end of the month: the Bolshoi Theater was at last beginning rehearsals for *The Stone Flower*. Galina Ulanova was preparing the main role of Katerina. Prokofiev was irritated, however, that the Bolshoi and Lavrovsky kept demanding changes in his score—they wanted him to tone down the orchestration. According to Mira, these demands "deeply disappointed him. He said how difficult it was for him to undertake a 'coarsening' of the instrumentation."

To make these changes in *The Stone Flower*, Prokofiev laid aside a project he and Mira had been working on for many years now—writing his childhood autobiography. Since the end of the War, Prokofiev had been dictating his memoirs to Mira, who copied them down and organized the volume. Vera Alpers had helped by providing Prokofiev with her teenage journals and letters, full of colorful descriptions of life at the St. Petersburg Conservatory on the eve of the Russian Revolution.

When rehearsals of *The Stone Flower* began at the Bolshoi on March 1, Prokofiev's condition was no better. Mira did her best to cheer him up. "When I would ask him—as I did every morning—how he felt, and if he had any pain anywhere, I would sometimes hear a very uncharacteristic response from him now—'My soul hurts.' " He also told Mira she had to "put my affairs in order," and said helplessly, "But I could have—I should have—composed so much more!"

On March 5, Mira and Prokofiev talked about going out to Nikolina Gora—perhaps the country air would improve his spirits and renew his depleted energy. After a visit from the doctor, he went for a short walk, then returned to work on one of the problem spots in *The Stone Flower*—Katerina's scene at the end of Act II, when she comes to believe that Danilo is alive and will return to her. Lavrovsky dropped by for a minute to see how the scene was coming; it was only a five-minute walk to the Bolshoi. Later, the Bolshoi concertmaster, Stuchevsky, came to work out a few more details.

Stuchevsky and Lavrovsky might have mentioned the persistent rumors that had been circulating through Moscow for the last few days—that Stalin was ill, or even dying. The atmosphere in the capital was strangely uncertain.

In the evening, around 8 P.M., Mira was sitting in the parlor giving instructions to a woman who was going to Nikolina Gora to open up the *dacha*. Mira's father had gone out. Suddenly, the door to Prokofiev's study opened. He came out, staggering from side to side. Mira jumped up.

"Forgetting myself, I instinctively took hold of his shoulders so that he wouldn't fall, and helped him back into his room so he could lie down on the divan." He was dizzy, nauseous and feverish, and his head was aching.

Prokofiev apologized to Mira for frightening her in the middle of her conversation; his concern for her at such a moment only increased her pain. The doctor was summoned and arrived with orders to send for medicine and leeches.

But by 9 P.M. it was over. "Sergei Sergeevich was still conscious. Only in the very last seconds did his breathing become hoarse and heavy. One after another, our friends began arriving."

Sergei Sergeevich Prokofiev died on a raw Moscow evening. Spring was not far away.

NOTES, APPENDICES, BIBLIOGRAPHY AND INDEX

NOTES

TO THE TEXT

Notes are cited by page number and by the first few words of the passage (either in direct quotation or in paraphrase) to which they pertain. Informational notes follow the same system. Sources used fall into the following main categories:

1. Primary published sources in Russian including collections of articles written by Prokofiev's relatives, friends and colleagues, and Prokofiev's own autobiographical writings.
2. Published correspondence (primarily in Russian).
3. Unpublished correspondence, collected in various archival holdings (primarily in Russian, but some in French and English) as specified.
4. Other materials collected in various archival holdings as specified.
5. Secondary sources (published articles and books, in Russian, French and English).
6. Interviews, cited individually.

Sources used repeatedly will be cited according to the following key. (Russian titles in the notes follow the Library of Congress transliteration system, but Russian names used in the body of the text will be cited the same way in the notes.) All translations from the Russian and French are mine unless indicated.

AB: Sergei Prokofiev, *Avtobiografiia (Autobiography)*.
Edited by M. G. Kozlova. Moscow, 1973. This autobiography (Prokofiev wrote the first part between 1937 and 1939, and the second part between 1945 and 1950) covers only Prokofiev's childhood and youth, up until 1909. Another edition was published in 1982, which includes a small amount of new material on the years 1909–10.

Buckle: Richard Buckle, *Diaghilev*. London, 1979.

CSA: Central State Archives of Literature and Art (Tsentral'nyi gosudarstvennyi arkhiv literatury i iskusstva), Moscow. Items are cited by the number of the general fund and by their individual catalogue numbers.

Delson: Viktor Del'son, *Fortepiannoe tvorchestvo i pianizm Prokof'eva (Prokofiev as Pianist and Composer for the Piano)*. Moscow, 1973.

SD: *Sergei Diagilev i russkoe iskusstvo (Sergei Diaghilev and Russian Art)*. Edited by I. S. Zil'bershtein and V. A. Samkov. Moscow, 1982. Two volumes, including articles, correspondence, interviews and the memoirs of Diaghilev's contemporaries.

Duke: Vernon Duke, *Passport to Paris*. Boston, 1955.

Karatygin: Viacheslav Karatygin, *Izbrannye stat'i (Selected Articles)*. Moscow, 1965. Articles and reviews by Karatygin from other sources will be cited in full.

Krivosheina: N. A. Krivosheina, "Sergei Prokof'ev," in *Chetyre treti nashei zhizni (Three Quarters of Our Life)*. Paris, 1984, pp.53–64.

Lamm (1): Ol'ga Lamm, "Druz'ia Pavla Aleksandrovicha Lamma i uchastniki muzykal'nykh vecherov v ego dome (20-e gody XX veka)" ("The Friends of Pavel Alexandrovich Lamm and the Participants in the Musical Evenings in His Home in the 1920s"). Edited by T. N. Livanova. In *Iz proshlogo sovetskoi muzykal'noi kul'tury (From the Past of Soviet Musical Culture)*, Vol. I. Moscow, 1975, pp. 72–103.

Lamm (2): Ol'ga Lamm, "Druz'ia Pavla Aleksandrovicha Lamma. V evakuatsii (1941–1943)" ("The Friends of Pavel Alexandrovich Lamm. In Evacuation"), in *Iz proshlogo sovetskoi muzykal'noi kul'tury*, Moscow, 1976. Vol. II, pp. 99–109.

Letter of KB: Konstantin Balmont, Letters. (Originals in Russian.) Unpublished, courtesy of Beinecke Rare Book and Manuscript Library, Yale University, and Svetlana Shales Balmont.

Letter to M: Sergei Prokofiev, "Pis'ma k V. E. Meierkhol'du" ("Letters to V. E. Meyerhold"), in *Muzykal'noe nasledstvo*, Vol. II, Part 2. Moscow, 1968, pp.214-31.

Letter to FS: Sergei Prokofiev, Letters to Fatima Samoilenko. (Originals in Russian and French.) Unpublished, by permission of the Houghton Library, Harvard University.

Letter to VD: Sergei Prokofiev, Letters to Vernon Duke (a.k.a. Vladimir Dukelsky). (Originals in Russian and French.) Unpublished, courtesy of Music Division Archives, Library of Congress. Also reprinted as "Ob odnoi prervannoi druzhbe" ("About One Broken Friendship") in *Istoriia i sovremennost': Sbornik statei*. Leningrad, 1981. Pp. 239–60.

Macdonald: Nesta Macdonald, *Diaghilev Observed*. London, 1975.

MDV: *S. S. Prokof'ev: Materialy, dokumenty, vospominaniia (Materials, Documents, Memoirs)*. Edited by S. I. Shlifshtein. Second edition. Moscow, 1961. Articles, reviews and letters from this collection will be cited individually.

Meyerhold: V. E. Meyerhold, *Stat'i, pis'ma, rechi, besedy (Articles, Letters, Speeches, Conversations)*. Vols. I and II. Moscow, 1968.

Meyerhold-P: Meyerhold, *Perepiska V. E. Meierkhol'da 1896–1939 (The Correspondence of V. E. Meyerhold 1896–1939)*. Edited by Korshunova and Sitkovetskaia. Moscow, 1976.

Nabokov: Nicolas Nabokov, *Old Friends and New Music*. Boston, 1951.

Nestyev: Israel Nestyev, *Prokofiev*. Stanford, 1960. Translated into English by Florence Jonas from the 1953 Soviet edition. A revised version of this biography was published in 1973 (*Zhizn' Sergeia Prokof'eva*, Moscow).

NYT: *The New York Times*

LP: Lina Prokofiev, "Iz vospominanii" ("From My Memoirs"), in SM, pp. 160–209.

MP: Mira Mendelson-Prokofiev. "O Sergee Sergeeviche Prokof'eve" ("About Sergei Sergeevich Prokofiev"), in MDV, pp. 370–97.

OP: Oleg Prokofiev, "Papers from the Attic: My Father, His Music, and I." *The Yale Literary Magazine*, Vol. 148, No. 2 (Sept. 1979), pp. 17–29.

P-Alpers: S. S. Prokofiev and V. V. Alpers, "Perepiska" ("Correspondence"). Edited by L. M. Kutaleladze. In *Muzykal'noe nasledstvo*, Vol. I. Moscow, 1962, pp. 422–44.

P-Asafiev: S. S. Prokofiev, "Pis'ma S. S. Prokof'eva—B. V. Asaf'evu" ("The Letters of S. S. Prokofiev to B. V. Asafiev"). Edited by M. Kozlova. In *Iz proshlogo sovetskoi muzykal'noi kul'tury*, Vol. II. Moscow, 1976, pp. 4–54.

PD: S. S. Prokofiev, "Pis'ma S. S. Prokof'eva k V. V. Derzhanovskomu" ("The Letters of S. S. Prokofiev to V. V. Derzhanovsky"). Edited by A. I. Volkov. In *Iz arkhivov russkikh muzykantov*. Moscow, 1962, pp. 93–118.

PE: S. S. Prokofiev and S. M. Eisenstein, "Iz perepiski S. Prokof'eva i S. Eizenshteina" ("From the Correspondence of S. Prokofiev and S. Eisenstein"), in SM, pp. 277–89.

PK: Correspondence between S. S. Prokofiev, Sergei Koussevitsky and Natalia Koussevitsky. (Originals in Russian and French.) Unpublished, courtesy of Music Division Archives, Library of Congress.

PM: *S. S. Prokof'ev i N. Ia. Miaskovskii: Perepiska (S. S. Prokofiev and*

N. Ya. Miaskovsky: Correspondence). Edited by Dmitri Kabalevsky and M. G. Kozlova. Moscow, 1977.

SS: Archives of the Saltykov-Shchedrin Public Library, Leningrad. Items are cited individually by catalogue numbers.

SAB: Prokofiev's short autobiography (written between 1939 and 1941), covering his career from birth until 1936. In MDV, pp. 15–196.

Schwarz: Boris Schwarz, *Music and Musical Life in Soviet Russia* (Enlarged edition, 1917–81). Bloomington, 1983.

Seton: Marie Seton, *Sergei Eisenstein*. London, 1952.

Shostakovich: *Testimony: The Memoirs of Dmitri Shostakovich* (as related to and edited by Solomon Volkov). New York, 1979.

Shostakovich-P: S. S. Prokofiev and D. D. Shostakovich, "Vsegda dorozhu vashim mneniem: Perepiska" ("I Always Value Your Opinion: Correspondence"). Edited by M. Kozlova. In *Vstrechi s proshlym*, Vol. III. Moscow, 1978, pp. 253-59.

Skorino: Liudmila Skorino, *Pisatel' i ego vremia: Zhizn' i tvorchestvo V. P. Kataeva (A Writer and His Era: The Life and Work of V. P. Kataev)*. Moscow, 1965.

SM: *Sergei Prokof'ev 1953–1963: Stat'i i materialy (Articles and Materials)*. Edited by I. V. Nestyev and G. Ia. Edel'man. Moscow, 1962. Another slightly different edition of this collection appeared in 1965, and will be cited as SM (1965). Articles, reviews, interviews and letters from each collection will be cited individually.

Swallow: Norman Swallow, *Eisenstein: A Documentary Portrait*. New York, 1977.

PROLOGUE

Information used in the description of the events of March 5–7, 1953, comes from interviews with Soviet eyewitnesses, from "The Days of Stalin's Death" by Harrison E. Salisbury (*The New York Times Magazine*, April 17, 1983) and from "Poslednie dni" ("Final Days") by Mira Mendelson-Prokofiev, SM (1965), 281–92.

Page 2 " 'Only a few hours before' . . . "—"Final Days," 290. **2** " 'the greatest Russian composer of today—*après* moi' . . . "—cited in "The Unknown Prokofiev" by Edward Lockspeiser (*The Listener*, Oct. 22, 1953). **3** " 'wind in a graveyard' . . . "—"Iz vospominaniia o S. S. Prokof'eve" ("Remembering S. S. Prokofiev") by David Oistrakh, MDV, 453.

PART I

CHAPTER 1

Primary sources for Chapter 1 are Prokofiev's *Avtobiografiia* and Maria Grigorevna Prokofiev's "Vospominaniia o detstve i iunosti Sergeia Prokof'eva" ("Remembering the Childhood and Youth of Sergei Prokofiev") MDV, 331–40.

8 There is some question about the exact date of Prokofiev's birth. Although he gives it as April 11, his official birth certificate gives it as April 15. **11** " 'She had little musical talent' . . . "—AB, 33. **14** " 'They started playing the overture' . . . "— AB, 58. **16** " 'In a little while I had some ideas . . . ' "—AB, 188. **18** "Taneev and Prokofiev's parents chose a young composer . . . "—Taneev's first candidate was Alexander Goldenveizer, a brilliant composer and pianist, but Prokofiev's parents feared that such a dazzling celebrity would feel restless and out of place in rustic and isolated Sontsovka. **18** " 'Very soft and affectionate, tenderly attached to his parents' . . . " and " 'perfect pitch, a good memory' . . . "—R. M. Glière, "Vospominaniia o S. S. Prokof'eve" ("Remembering S. S. Prokofiev"), MDV, 351–52. **20** " 'Not only because I grew stronger in harmony . . . ' "—AB, 112. **21** " 'a terribly boring opera' . . . "—AB, 127. **21** " 'I was indifferent' . . . "—AB, 130. **22** " 'sharp and ringing, like the dripping of snow in spring' . . . "—Galina Vishnevskaya, *Galina, A Russian Story* (New York, 1984), 158. **22** " 'Let me offer you a free seat' . . . "—Glière, 358. **23** " 'big head on a little torso' . . . "—AB, 135. **23** " 'August 3, Sunday' . . . "—AB, 143–44. **24** *La quarantaine* apparently refers to a one-act vaudeville comedy in French by Eugène Scribe. **24** "Many features characteristic of Prokofiev's nine mature sonatas . . . " It was only with his Sonata No. 1, Op. 1, completed in 1909, that Prokofiev started officially numbering his sonatas. **24** " 'who advised me to penetrate' . . . "—AB, 151. **26** " 'If a child like yours' . . . "—AB, 169–70. **27** " 'It was very good, but too long' . . . "—AB, 161. **27** " 'I was sick of all the harmonies' . . . "—AB, 178. **28** " 'I wasn't strong' . . . "— AB, 175. **29** " 'I left Sontsovka without special regret' . . . "—AB, 189.

CHAPTER 2

30 " 'a dream come true' . . . "—AB, 93. **33** " 'Seryozha was always interested in painting' . . . "—Vera Alpers, "Iz proshlogo" ("From the Past"), SM, 225. **33** " 'Our apartment on the Sadovaya' . . . "—AB, 196–97. **33** "It was a handy location . . . "—Today, no plaque marks the building to testify to the fact the Prokofievs once lived there. **34** " 'I think that Glazunov' . . . "—AB, 208. **34** " 'He was very indifferent' . . . "—AB, 195. **35** " 'tall lively boy' . . . "—Alpers, "From the Past," 211. **35** " 'I responded with indifference' . . . "—AB, 209. **36** " 'So who is it you're striking up' . . . "—AB, 215. **37** "Anatoly Lyadov, his composition instructor . . . "—Lyadov was almost more famous for his slothfulness than for his music.

When he was too slow in fulfilling Diaghilev's commission of a ballet score to the "Firebird" tale in 1909, the project was handed over to the unknown Stravinsky. **37** " 'I saw the lessons' . . . "—AB, 217. **39** " 'Generally speaking' . . . " and " 'My fainting spell' . . . "—AB, 224. **40** " 'not finding in him' . . . "—AB, 257. **40** " 'Operas which I have attended' . . . "—CSA: 1929, 1, 306. **41** " 'a profoundly provincial lady' . . . "—AB, 246. **41** " 'this stupid incident' . . . "—Prokofiev may also have included this incident in his autobiography as an example for his Soviet readers of the unpleasant snobbishness of prerevolutionary society. **42** " 'when there are such disturbances' . . . "—AB, 244. **42** " 'My mother's point of view' . . . "— AB, 252. **43** " 'This is such an unprecedented time' . . . "—AB, 268. **43** " 'What a nice thing' . . . "AB, 426.

CHAPTER 3

46 " 'roosters laid bigger eggs' . . . "—AB, 320. **47** " 'one measure would come out well' . . . "—CSA: 1929, 1, 397. **47** " 'barely passed' . . . "—S. Prokofiev, "Iunye gody" ("Youthful Years"). *Leningradskaia konservatoriia v vospominaniiakh 1862–1962*. Leningrad, 1962, 63. **48** " 'Capable, but immature' . . . "—*Ibid.*, 63. **48** " 'as though an electric current' . . . "—AB, 337. **48** "By liking Scriabin . . . "—When Lyadov and other Conservatory professors looked over the pieces that Prokofiev submitted for his final exams in 1909, Lyadov exclaimed in disgust, "They are all determined to make themselves into Scriabins!" **48** " 'one of his best' . . . "—AB, 310. **49** " 'The first two are fine' . . . " and " 'out of snobbism' . . . " and " 'I didn't like all those' . . . "—AB, 333–35. **50** " 'with a biblical appearance' . . . "—AB, 230. **51** " 'squat down on the sidewalk' . . . "—Alpers, "From the Past," 216. **51** " 'greatest Soviet symphonist' . . . "—Stanley Krebs, *Soviet Composers and the Development of Soviet Music*. London, 1970, 96. **52** " 'with admiration, gratitude' . . . "—*Ibid.*, 105. **52** " 'juxtaposed distant tonalities' . . . "—AB, 365. **53** " 'were rather bad little dogs' . . . "—AB, 395. **53** "without adornments . . . "—AB, 396. **53** " 'Intellectual pursuits led' . . . "—AB, 421. **54** " 'He talked about innovation' . . . " and " 'and that's where' . . . "—S. Prokof'ev, "Youthful Years," *Leningradskaia konservatoriia*, 67. **54** " 'put together, but not composed' . . . "—AB, 456. **54** " 'boring and nothing new' . . . "—AB, 519. **55** " 'saying that this was the very most modern' . . . "—AB, 458. **55** "who responded in kind . . . "—Alpers, "From the Past," 215 and 224. **55** "Two girls particularly intrigued him . . . "—AB, 431. **56** " 'no matrimonial tendencies' . . . "—AB, 361. **56** " 'Listen, I dressed you up' . . . "—AB, 555. **56** " 'unable to hear two right notes' . . . "—AB, 458. **57** " 'daring and irreverent' . . . "— AB, 458. **57** " 'antithesis to Scriabin' . . . "—AB, 482. **58** " 'the instant imprint of personality' . . . "—Igor Stravinsky, *Memories and Commentaries*. New York, 1960, 66. **58** " 'The walls were hung' . . . "—AB, 484. **58** "A surprising amount of space . . . "—AB, 524–25. **59** " 'I'm very disturbed' . . . "—AB, 505. **60** " 'He just didn't pay attention' . . . "—AB, 517. **60** " 'at breakneck speed' . . . "—AB, 566. **61** " 'But that's some sort of incantation!' . . . "—AB, 513. **61** Reviews cited in AB, 538–39. **62** "the label 'Decadent' . . . "—Stravinsky has written on this misuse of the term at the time: " 'Decadent' and 'modern' were interchangeable then, whereas 'decadent' now very often means 'not modern enough.' " *Memories and Commentaries*, 32. **62** " 'not used to denying himself anything' . . . "—AB, 552. **62** " 'terribly upset' . . . "—AB, 551. **62** " 'wild and teeth-gnashing' . . . " and " 'foaming at the mouth' . . . "—AB, 575. **63** " 'when you have a goal in sight' . . . "— AB, 571. **63** " 'What a night!' . . . "—AB, 583.

CHAPTER 4

66 " 'her dark, lustrous beauty' . . . " and " 'apple-green, rose-pink' . . . "—Buckle, 139–41. **66** " 'I've heard something' . . . "—CSA, 1929, 1, 418. **66** "But he did use a good deal of material from these early pieces . . . "—The second childhood sonata became the Piano Sonata No. 1, Op. 1; the third childhood sonata became the Piano Sonata No. 3, Op. 28; the fourth childhood sonata was used in part in the Piano Sonata No. 4, Op. 29, "From Old Notebooks"; the piano pieces he had played at the Evenings of Contemporary Music were grouped with others in the piano pieces Op. 3 and Op. 4. **67** " 'bear's lair' . . . " and " 'for whom I don't always feel' . . . "— Alpers, "From the Past," 269–71. **67** " 'very pleasant, soft' . . . "—AB, 586. **68** " 'fiery temperament' . . . "—AB, 592. **68,69** " 'both hands play' . . . " and " 'and even my chess set' . . . " and " 'a gaggle of aunts' . . . "—Alpers, "From the Past," 273–75. **70** " 'everything that contained' . . . "—SAB, 146. **70** " 'barbaric, impudently innovative' . . . "—A. V. Astrov, *S. A. Kusevitskii*. Leningrad, 1981, 153. **70** "Koussevitsky circumvented Rachmaninoff's intransigence . . . "—In 1920, after he emigrated, Koussevitsky transferred his publishing operations to Paris, where they were renamed the Éditions Russes. Later they were taken over by Boosey & Hawkes and moved to London. **71** " 'I strongly insist' . . . "—"From Early Letters," 232. **71** " 'obvious talent and a completely serious attitude' . . . "—PM, 488. **71** operas cited in MDV, 638. Over the next four years, Prokofiev also conducted music by Glazunov, Anton Rubinstein (the musical tableau "Ivan the Terrible"), Haydn, Dargomyzhsky, Beethoven, Weber, Liszt, Saint-Saëns, Tchaikovsky and Brahms. **71** " 'Only after I graduated' . . . "—SAB, 143. **72** " 'wanted to fit all' . . . "—SAB, 142. **73** " 'has assimilated my method' . . . "—Delson, 242. **73** " 'too unusual' . . . "—Nestyev, 42. **73** "Prokofiev would turn repeatedly to Balmont . . . "— Besides the two songs of Op. 7, one of the songs of Op. 11, one of the songs of Op. 23, the cantata *Seven, They Are Seven* and all five songs of Op. 36 use Balmont texts. The title of the cycle "Visions fugitives" ("Mimoletnosti") also comes from a line of Balmont poetry. Balmont wrote several poems about Prokofiev, including "To the Child of the Gods, Prokofiev," of 1917, and Prokofiev later dedicated his Third Piano Concerto to Balmont. **74** "which he had shown to the composer . . . "—Alpers, "From the Past," 220. **74** "the choice of the title was inspired . . . " and " 'reveals little influence' . . . "—SAB, 143. **74** " 'Papa's health' . . . "—"From Early Letters," 233. **75** " 'You know that I love you' . . . "—PM, 84. **75** " 'I don't know if you'll like it' . . . "—PM, 85. **75** "In his autobiography . . . "—SAB, 144. **76** " 'The critics wrote about' . . . "—PM, 145.

CHAPTER 5

77 " 'lazily scribbled' . . . "—PM, 89. **77** " 'bicycle and a photograph' . . . "—PM, 88. **78** " 'The sonata was especially successful' . . . "—"From Early Letters," 235. **78** " 'after each étude' . . . "—Alpers, "From the Past," 217. **78** "Prokofiev was the first to perform Schoenberg . . . "—Schoenberg (1874–1951) soon became a hero in Russian avant-garde musical circles, and his music provoked strong feelings. In 1912, Schoenberg came to Russia himself to conduct his *Pelleas und Melisande*. By the late 1930s, however, Schoenberg, his system and disciples were being reviled in the Soviet press as evidence of the "rotting musical culture of the West." **79** " 'subordinated his art' . . . "—Nestyev, 49. **79** " 'there was no music' . . . "—SAB, 151. **80** " 'something like the cover' . . . "—CSA, 1929, 1, 424. **80** " 'The reception for "Dreams" ' . . . "—"From Early Letters," 236. **81** " 'Derzhanovsky was a sincere' . . . "—Nestyev, 53. **81** " 'fiercely' . . . "—"From Early Letters," 235. **81** " 'society lady more charming' . . . "—SAB, 144. **82** " 'I finished this' . . . "—from the manuscript score, of *Maddalena*, courtesy of Oleg Prokofiev. **83** " 'One can feel' . . . "—MDV, 639. **83** " 'It's not a full score' . . . "—PM, 101. **83** "Subsequent attempts to produce *Maddalena* . . . "—Prokofiev left the score of *Maddalena* behind when he left Russia in 1918, and reclaimed it there only in 1927. When Prokofiev returned permanently to Russia in 1936, *Maddalena* remained behind in Paris, where it lay in the basement of the Éditions Russes until discovered in a trunk in 1953. In 1979, the British conductor Edward Downes completed the orchestration, and *Maddalena* has been performed several times since in that version. **84** " 'wonderfully charming' . . . "—"From Early Letters," 242. **85** " 'by the way, is not at all easy' . . . " and " 'otherwise I won't be able' . . . " and " 'Saradzhev knew all the tempos' . . . "—*Ibid.*, 241–44. **86** " 'the three whales' . . . "—PD, 111. **86** " 'hit on the head' . . . "—Duke, 24. **86** " 'didn't go too badly' . . . "—CSA, 1929, 1, 405. **86** " . . . critics and audiences now knew who he was . . . "—Given his passion for revision, it is significant that Prokofiev never returned to revise this work: he considered it successful and complete in its first incarnation. Jurgenson published the First Piano Concerto in 1913. **86** " 'Every morning I go to the drug-store' . . . "—PM, 103. **88** " 'a two-part sonata' . . . "—SAB, 145. **88** " 'a very nice person' . . . "—AB, 547. **88** " 'At that time I was not always myself' . . . " and " 'Dear Seryozha' . . . " and " 'I was very close to him' . . . "—S. Prokofiev, "Pis'ma k E. A. Shmidtgof-Lavrovoi" ("Letters to E. A. Shmitgoff–Lavrova"), MDV, 275. **89** " 'This is how it happened' . . . "—*Ibid.*, 277.

CHAPTER 6

92 " 'Dear Kolechka' . . . "—PM, 106–107. **92** " 'The liveliness' . . . "—"From Early Letters," 245. **93** " 'People shouted insults' . . . "—Buckle, 252–53. **93** " . . . in a letter to Tcherepnin . . . " and " 'As a rule' . . . "—"From Early Letters," 245. **93** " 'aromatic and evocative' . . . "—*Ibid.*, 245. **93** " '*Petrushka* is highly entertaining' . . . "—PM, 107. **94** " 'The material in these ballets' . . . "—SAB, 150. **94** " 'suffered from not knowing' . . . "—CSA, 1929, 1, 414. (Letter to N. Tcherepnin.) **94** " 'has turned out to be' . . . "—"From Early Letters," 246. **94** " 'Exhausted after my back-breaking work' . . . "—PM, 109. **95** " 'The Martian' . . . "—Krivosheina, 54. **95** " 'very satisfied with my idleness' . . . "—PM, 111. **95** " 'In a word' . . . "—Krivosheina, 56. **96** " 'A youth with the face' . . . "—SAB, 147. **96** " 'Ten years from now' . . . "—Karatygin, "O Prokof'eve" ("About Prokofiev"), MDV, 302. **97** " 'It will be very interesting' . . . "—Alexander Ziloti, "Perepiska A. I. Ziloti s S. S. Prokof'evym" ("Correspondence of A. I. Ziloti and S. S. Prokofiev"). In *Aleksandr Il'ich Ziloti. Vospominaniia i pis'ma.* Leningrad, 1963. 265. **97** " 'Can it really be' . . . "—PM, 144. **97** " 'nightmarishness' . . . "—Karatygin, 82. **99** " 'would have resounded' . . . " and " 'When I came out on stage' . . . "—SAB, 148.

CHAPTER 7

101 " 'my benefactor and father' . . . "—"From Early Letters," 250. **102** " 'But he is some sort of *fauve*' . . . "—SAB, 150. **102** " 'some sort of mimed scenes' . . . "—"From Early Letters," 250. **103** " 'insolence' . . . "—SD, II, 124. **103** " 'the end of *la belle époque*' . . . "—Buckle, 274. **103** " 'Let it be said' . . . "—PM, 119. **103** " 'very amusing and ingenious' . . . "—"From Early Letters," 250. **104** " 'a triumph of staging' . . . "—Macdonald, 118. **104** " 'a lot of gratuitous' . . . "—PM, 118–19. **105** " 'It would come out marvelously' . . . "—Krivosheina, 58. **105** " 'finishing off the despicable' . . . "—PM, 132. **105** " 'All misfortunes' . . . "—"Letters to E. A. Shmitgoff-Lavrova," 280. **106** " 'The main thing, of course' . . . "—Krivosheina, 202. **106** " 'not just a song . . . ' "—CSA, 1929, 1, 424. (Letter to Boris Jurgenson.) **107** " 'White Negro' . . . "—Duke, 24. **107** "Reviewing the first performance of 'Ugly Duckling' . . . "—The first performance was given on January 17, 1915, in the Small Hall of the Petrograd Conservatory. Prokofiev's friend Anna Zherebtsova-Andreeva sang, and he accompanied. **107** " 'The deficiency in "Ugly Duckling" ' . . . "—Igor Glebov (Boris Asafiev), "O 'Gadkom Utenke' " ("About 'The Ugly Duckling' "), MDV, 318. **107** "something 'intricate' . . . "—PM, 119. **107** " 'the ninth century' . . . "—*Ibid.*, 124. **108** "Many years later, in his autobiography . . . "—SAB, 151. **108** "Nina and Prokofiev saw each other again . . . "—Krivosheina, 60–61. **109** " 'dinners and lunches' . . . "—"From Early Letters," 253. **109** " 'The ballet needs major changes' . . . "—*Ibid.*, 254. **109** " 'Petersburg trifle' . . . "—SD, II, 124–25. **110** " 'very good friends' . . . "—PM, 210. **110** " 'wandered between the old and the new' . . . "—Nestyev, 99. **110** "a series of tales about a buffoon . . . "—The ballet eventually received the Russian title *Shut* (the Russian word for "buffoon"), which was later transformed into a French phonetic version, *Chout*. **111** " 'Write Russian music' . . . "—SAB, 151. **111** " 'abuse Petrograd' . . . "—PM, 132. **111** " 'In art' . . . "—SAB, 152. **111** " 'not at all pleased' . . . "—PM, 135. **111** " 'pathos, inspiration and internationalism' . . . "—PM, 133. **112** "In a letter to Stravinsky . . . "—CSA, 1929, 1, 408. **112** " 'Diaghilev and I had agreed' . . . "—SAB, 152. **113** " 'I am for the moment putting off' . . . "—PM, 136. **114** "only an 'apprentice' . . . "—Karatygin, 179. **114** " 'At the end' . . . "—SAB, 153. **115** "Karatygin wrote . . . "—Karatygin, "O Skifskoi siuite 'Ala i Lolii' " ("About the Scythian Suite 'Ala and Lolly' "), MDV, 303. **115** " 'sumptuous, significant, vivid' . . . "—PM, 141. **115** " 'search for a new' . . . "—SAB, 149. **115** " 'Sometimes we laugh maliciously' . . . "—SAB, 155. **116** "for he paid Prokofiev five hundred rubles . . . "—CSA, 1929, 1, 424. (Letter to Boris Jurgenson.) **116** "poems by five different writers . . . "—Boris Verin was the pseudonym of Prokofiev's friend Boris Bashkirov. The cycle was performed for the first time on November 27, 1916, by the soprano Evgenia Popova and the tenor Ivan Alchevsky. **117** "After Prokofiev played his Second Piano Sonata . . . "— CSA, 1929, 1, 903. **117** " 'When Scriabin played this sonata' . . . "—SAB, 153. **118** " '*The Gambler* is the least Dostoevskian' . . . "—SAB, 183. **118** " 'The subject of the story' . . . "—quoted in Konstantin Mochulsky, *Dostoyevsky: His Life and Work*. Princeton, 1967, 278. **119** " 'lost his last penny' . . . "—*Ibid*., 238. **119** " 'The orchestration will be transparent' . . . "—S. Prokofiev, "Dva zabytykh inter- v'iu" ("Two Forgotten Interviews"), SM, 297. **119** " 'Encouraged by the interest' . . . "—SAB, 154. **119** "Prokofiev knew of *Marriage* . . . "—See Harlow Robinson, "Dostoevsky and Opera." *Musical Quarterly*, Winter, 1984, 96–106. **121** "*The Gambler* did not make it to the stage . . . "—In 1927–28, Prokofiev and Meyerhold worked on a revised (and now the standard performing version) of *The Gambler* that was first performed in Brussels in 1929. See Chapter 14. **121** "according to Nina Meshchersky . . . "—Krivosheina, 54. **121** " 'Dear Igor Fyodorov- ich' . . . "—CSA, 1929, 2, 277. **122** "Prokofiev's career was booming . . . "—On November 27 in Petrograd, Ziloti presented the first all-Prokofiev chamber music concert, which included three premieres: "Sarcasmes" (with Prokofiev as pianist), four of the five Op. 23 songs (with Prokofiev as accompanist) and the "Humorous Scherzo," a rescoring of the Op. 12 piano scherzo for the odd ensemble of four bassoons. **122** " 'None at all,' he replied . . . "—Glière, 369. **122** " 'He had white- blond hair' . . . "—Duke, 25. **123** " 'educated musician and mediocre com- poser' . . . "—SAB, 156. **123** " 'After them, many people believed' . . . "—SAB, 155. **124** " 'Vous, mon cher Prokofiev' . . . "—*S. S. Prokof'ev: Al'bom*. Moscow, 1981, 53. **124** "When they were performed for the first time . . . "—With the Akhmatova songs, Prokofiev changed publishers from Jurgenson to Gutheil, the Aus- trian firm recently purchased by Koussevitsky. In 1917, Gutheil published three sets of Prokofiev songs—Op. 9, 23, and 27—and the "Visions fugitives." Gutheil was Prokofiev's main publisher for the next ten years. **124** " 'It is impossible to ex- plain' . . . "—Iurii Engel', "Na vechere 'muzykal'nogo sovremennika" ("At the Eve- ning of the 'Musical Contemporary' "), SM, 343.

CHAPTER 8

127 " 'Both I and the circles' . . . "—SAB, 158. **129** " 'It was more a reflection' . . . "—SAB, 158. **129,130** " 'fallen into a depression' . . . " and " 'The Kama is wild' . . . "—PM, 147. **130** "the violin concerto was completed first . . . "—Ziloti had expressed interest in organizing the concerto's premiere for the 1917–18 season, but the Revolution altered those plans. It was heard for the first time only six years later, in 1923, under Koussevitsky in Paris. **130** " 'Up to that time' . . . "—SAB, 158–59. **131** " 'walking through the fields' . . . " and " 'completely alone' . . . "—SAB, 158–59. **132** " 'You begin to talk with him about literature . . . "—Nestyev, 81. **132** " 'Just send me a telegram' . . . " and " 'A train arrived' . . . "—SAB, 160–61. **133** "The Fourth Sonata formed a pair with the Third . . . "—The Third Sonata was dedicated to Prokofiev's friend Boris Bashkirov (Boris Verin). Both sonatas were published by Gutheil in 1918. **133,134** " 'something big and cosmic' . . . " and " 'The fact that the ideas and feelings of that era' . . . "—SAB, 159. **135** "*Seven, They Are Seven* remains one of Prokofiev's least-known works . . . "—Prokofiev also wrote a revised version of the cantata in 1933. **135** " 'I did not have a clear understanding' . . . "—SAB, 160. **135** " 'drop me a few lines' . . . "—PD, 107. **136** " 'only a few months' . . . "—SAB, 162. **136** " 'made a great impression' . . . "—SAB, 161. **136** " 'Red and flickering' . . . "—MDV, 647–48. **137** " 'To the representative on the planet earth' . . . "—SAB, 161. **137** " 'Here is Sergei Sergeevich' . . . "—MDV, 648. **137** " 'You are a revolutionary' . . . "—SAB, 161–62.

PART II

CHAPTER 9

142 " 'You're running away' . . . "—SAB, 162. **143** " 'Reading about Babylonian culture' . . . "—SAB, 162. **143** " 'I'm writing you from Arkhara' . . . "—PM, 148. **143** " 'Books on contemporary music' . . . " and " 'They wouldn't let me on shore' . . . "—SAB, 162. **144** " 'I plan to spend several months' . . . "—SD, II, 129. **145** "*Theatre* described him . . . "—*Theatre*, January 1919. **145** " 'was not satisfied until Prokofiev had added' . . . "—*Boston Transcript*, November 21, 1918. **145** " 'The very character of the audience' . . . "—*The World* (undated clipping), November 1918. **146** " 'the musical news of the season' . . . "—*Boston Transcript*, December 21, 1919. **146** " 'unusual but charming young man' . . . "—*The Musical Courier*, December 16, 1918. **146** " 'a good musician, but a bad conductor' . . . "—SAB, 164. **146** "Born in Madrid . . . "—Mme. Prokofiev did not spend her childhood in Russia, as numerous biographers have erroneously claimed. **147** "as though he would break in half . . . "—Sviatoslav Richter, "O Prokof'eve" ("On Prokofiev"), MDV, 456. **147** "Prokofiev was handsome . . . "—Prokofiev's characteristic reticence about personal matters—some have called it prudishness—led him to omit any mention of his early courtship of Lina in his short autobiography. Another reason for his silence was that the autobiography was completed in 1941, when he was in the process of leaving Lina for another woman. **148** " 'Bolshevik music' . . . " and " 'Gozzi! Our lovely Gozzi!' . . . "—SAB, 164. **149** " 'read it on the ocean liner' . . . "—Meyerhold-P, 388. **150** " 'Taking American taste' . . . "—SAB, 164. **151** " 'the audience, Gozzi, the operatic form' . . . "—SAB, 177. **151** "he wanted to put on a good show . . . "—Despite his great influence on *Oranges*, Meyerhold did not see it on stage until 1926 in Leningrad. **152** " 'Serge Prokofiev, the interesting Russian composer-pianist' . . . "—*Musical America*, April 26, 1919. **152** " 'I thought you would die' . . . "—SAB, 165. **153** "tossed off in 'a day and a half' . . . "—PM, 158. In 1934, Prokofiev arranged the Overture on Hebrew Themes for symphony orchestra, but it has remained more popular in its original version. **153** " 'I had begun *Love for Three Oranges*' . . . "—SAB, 165–66. **154** "Bryusov had based the complicated sexual triangle . . . "—See Harlow Robinson, *The Operas of Sergei Prokofiev and Their Russian Literary Sources*, p. 167. (Unpublished dissertation, University of California, Berkeley, 1980.) **155** " 'Sometimes I would wander' . . . "—SAB, 166. **156** " 'The composer Stravinsky and the pianist Prokofiev' . . . "—Delson, 250.

CHAPTER 10

157 " 'had turned into numb hungry' . . . "—Letter to FS, May 29, 1920. **158** " 'The English chomp on such disgusting things' . . . "—Letter to FS, June 8, 1920. **159** " 'I decided that the opera could be canceled' . . . "—SAB, 167. **160** " 'I'm as ecstatic about California' . . . "—Letter to FS, December 29, 1920. **161** " 'The curve of my American career' . . . "—SAB, 168. **161** " 'M. Prokofiev is a very young musician' . . . "—*Le Gaulois*, May 14, 1921. **163** " 'dilettante choreography' . . . "—Boris Kochno, *Diaghilev and the Ballets Russes*. New York, 1970, 223. **163** " 'magnificent failure' . . . "—Arnold Haskell, *Diaghilev: His Artistic and Private Life*. London, 1935, 315. **163** " 'Yesterday barely known' . . . "—Pierre Scize in *Bonsoir*, May 20, 1921. **164** " '*The Buffoon* is, at least musically' . . . "—Roland Manuel in *Éclair*, May 23, 1921. **164** " 'as much controversy, praise and abuse' . . . " and " 'Bolshevist propaganda' . . . "—Macdonald, 263. **165** " 'I get up at 8:30' . . . "—Letter to FS, June 23, 1921. **165** " 'into a cutlet' . . . "—PK: to NK, July 21, 1921. **165** " 'Everything here is the same' . . . "—Letter of KB, September 9, 1921. **166** " 'He writes the poems one day' . . . "—Letter to FS, August 12, 1921. **167** " 'Soon after, Balmont turned his pen' . . . "—SAB, 169. **167** " 'Let the maestro be calm' . . . "—PK: to NK, March 21, 1922. **168** " 'squirrel running inside a wheel' . . . "—Letter to FS, October 15, 1921. **168** " 'lively, rich and sunny' . . . "—Letter to FS, October 21, 1921. **168** " 'My Third Concerto has turned out to be' . . . "—PK: to NK, December 6, 1921. **168** " 'as dense as a tree' . . . "—Letter to FS, January 9, 1922. **168,169** " 'At first his lack of imag-

ination' . . . " and " 'Chicagoans were both proud and confused' . . . "—SAB, 170.
169 " 'pack of dogs' . . . " and " 'I had to look the facts' . . . "—SAB, 170–71.

CHAPTER 11

169 " 'two kilometers from the Oberammergau station' . . . "—SD, II, 135. **172**
" 'All around it was quiet' . . . "—LP, 164–65. **173** " 'clouds lick my feet' . . . "—
Letter to FS, April 8, 1922. **173** " 'Stravinsky was sharply critical' . . . "—SAB,
171. **173** " 'a miraculous feat' . . . "—Duke, 184. **174** " 'better taste in boys' . . . "—
Ibid., 208. **175** " 'one can sit quietly and write huge opuses' . . . "—Letter to Nina
Koshetz, July 11, 1922 (Music Division Archives, Library of Congress). **175** " 'there
is so much freshness' . . . "—Letter of KB, October 27, 1922. **176** " 'harried,
tired . . . How debased it all is' . . . "—Letter of KB, October 29, 1922. **177** " 'I
am indescribably happy' . . . "—Letter to FS, January 27, 1923. **177** " 'The Italians
turned out to be very nice' . . . "—Letter to FS, May 30, 1923. **177** "Lina spent
the summer in Ettal . . . "—Specific mention of Lina is curiously absent in letters
Prokofiev wrote at this time to Sergei and Natalia Koussevitsky, and to Fatima Samoilenko. Neither does she figure in his letters to Miaskovsky and Asafiev, although
in this case it is possible that references to Lina have been cut by the Soviet editors
of the correspondence, who have tended to deemphasize Prokofiev's relationship with
Lina in particular and his personal life in general. **178** " 'We're terribly proud' . . . "—
PK: to NK, July 8, 1923. **178** Fifth Piano Sonata—the sonata was dedicated to
Pyotr Souvchinsky (born 1892), a Russian critic and writer whom Prokofiev knew
before the Revolution and who eventually emigrated to France, where he became a
close associate of Stravinsky's. Prokofiev revised the Fifth Sonata in 1952–53, and
considered the reworking substantial enough to give it a different opus number (Op.
135). **178** " 'Nothing but restraint!' . . . "—PM, 189. **178** "he felt less energetic . . . "—PM, 200. **179** " 'Mendelssohnian' . . . "—SAB, 173. **179** " 'simply
indecent' . . . "—PM, 176. **179** " 'to cook an omelet' . . . "—P-Asafiev, 6.

CHAPTER 12

180 " 'Have you noticed that every place' . . . "—Pyotr Ilyich Tchaikovsky, *Letters
to His Family: An Autobiography*. Translated by Galina von Meck. London, 1981,
189. **180** " 'Moving to Paris' . . . "—SAB, 173. **181** " 'It's no secret to anyone' . . . "—PM, 181. **181** " 'All right, you don't want to hear my music' . . . "—
LP, 67. **182** " 'an utter imbecile' . . . " and " 'like a cross between a Scandinavian
minister' . . . "—Duke, 120–21. Duke was associated with the Diaghilev entourage
in the early 1920s, and wrote several ballets for the Ballets Russes, including the
successful *Zéphyre et Flore*. **182** " 'with restrained approval' . . . "—PM, 187. **182**
" 'slightly more complicated' . . . "—PM, 200. **183** " 'has the stamp of a
leader' . . . "—NYT, June 15, 1924. **184** "Koussevitsky encouraged him to write
a 'hit' . . . "—PK: to SK, August 26, 1924. **184** " 'Sergei Sergeevich would set

out' . . . "—LP, 168. **185** " 'In the original version for one piano' . . . "—SAB, 173. **185** " 'feverish work' . . . "—PM, 216. **187** " 'less luxurious, but more integrated' . . . "—SAB, 174. **187** " 'The orchestration is heavenly' . . . "—PK: to NK, March 25, 1925. **187** " 'The old ladies are especially good' . . . "—Letter to FS, March 24, 1925. **188** " 'bulky and complicated thing' . . . "—P-Asafiev, 13. **188** " 'A strange artist' . . . "—André George, *Nouvelles Littéraires*, June 13, 1925. **188** " 'horde' . . . "—PM, 223. **188** " 'This was probably the only time it occurred to me' . . . "—SAB, 174. **188** " 'complicated thing' . . . " and " 'The symphony has evoked nothing but uncertainty' . . . "—PM, 216. **189** " 'unrivaled in popularity' . . . "—PM, 235. **189** " 'Something in them didn't please them' . . . "— PM, 197. **189** " 'because of its mystical text' . . . "—PM, 202. **190** " 'generally severe mood' . . . " and " 'lost all sense' . . . " and " 'superficial and banal' . . . " and " 'I'm in deep despair' . . . "—PM, 219–28. **191** " 'But I can't write in the style you favor' . . . "—SAB, 175. **192** " 'a quiet and colorful little place' . . . "— PM, 218. **192** " 'from chromaticism to diatonicism' . . . "—SAB, 175. **192** " 'distorted view of Soviet reality' . . . "—MDV, 651. **192** "writing arrangements . . . "—Prokofiev arranged the Op. 35 "Songs Without Words" for violin and piano, and a suite of Schubert waltzes for two pianos. He also added two numbers to *Trapeze* for Romanov's dance troupe. **192** " 'which I just can't seem to finish orchestrating' . . . "—PM, 218. **192** "first return to the United States in nearly four years . . . "—Prokofiev performed in St. Paul on January 8, in Denver on January 12, in Portland on January 15, in San Francisco on January 17, in Kansas City on January 22, in Boston on January 29 and 30, in New York on February 4 and 6, in Brooklyn on February 5, in Cambridge on February 11, and in Providence on February 16. **193** " 'enough for poverty' . . . "—PK: to NK, October 10, 1925. **193** " 'They would meet us, show us the city' . . . "—LP, 175. **193** " 'In one of the provincial cities' . . . "—SAB, 176. **193** " 'no interesting American composers were visible' . . . "—P-Asafiev, 18. **194** " 'magnificent' . . . "—PM, 231. **194** "but he did manage to orchestrate . . . "—PM, 238. **194** " 'We are roaming from city to city' . . . "—Letter to FS, January 13, 1926. **194** " 'more a pretext for a pleasant trip' . . . "—PM, 239. **195** " 'rather large villa' . . . "—SAB, 217. **196** " 'If they haven't learned to love it' . . . "—PM, 242. **196** " 'weak' . . . "—PM, 244. **196** " 'Here I have been waiting' . . . "—P-Asafiev, 17. **196** " 'new Wagner' . . . "— Meyerhold, II, 70–71. **196** " 'I am very eager to come' . . . "—PM, 242. **197** " 'We're living in a style' . . . "—Letter to FS, August 27, 1926. **197** Overture for Seventeen Performers: The "American" Overture was performed for the first time not in New York but in Moscow, by the conductorless Persimfans ensemble during Prokofiev's 1927 tour of the U.S.S.R. A year later, he rewrote it for full orchestra, after realizing its impracticality: the overture was too large for chamber groups, but too small for symphony orchestras. **197** " 'a sort of funny mansard' . . . "—PK: to SK, November 18, 1926. **198** " 'in the same school as Stravinsky' . . . "—PK: to NK, December 31, 1926. **198** " 'At that time, many who knew Prokofiev' . . . " and " 'Rumor has it' . . . "—Anna Ostroumova-Lebedeva, "Iz moikh vospominanii" ("From My Memoirs"). SS, 1015,174. **199** " 'I could not feel any warm feelings of friendship about him' . . . " and " 'One could imagine that he was a real sadist' . . . "—Memoirs of Prokofiev by Alexander Borovsky (unpublished), courtesy of William Jones. **199** " 'one could see Prokofiev a thousand times' . . . "—Stravinsky, *Memories and Commentaries*, 66. **199** " 'I'm afraid you might not like it here' . . . " and " 'foreigner' . . . "—PM, 251–55.

CHAPTER 13

200 " 'To realize his full potential' . . . "—Anatoly Lunacharsky, *V mire muzyki: Stat'i i rechi (In the World of Music: Articles and Speeches)*. Moscow, 1971, 514. **203** "The program included the Suite . . . "—Prokofiev and Asafiev differ in their accounts of what else was played: Prokofiev claims Persimfans performed the Suite from *Oranges* and that he honored Miaskovsky with a performance of his "Bizarreries" as an encore. According to Asafiev, Prokofiev played the piano arrangement of the Gavotte from the "Classical" Symphony and his Toccata (Op. 11). **203** " 'A trumpet flourish' . . . "—Igor Glebov, "Pervoe vystuplenie Sergeia Prokof'eva" ("Sergei Prokofiev's First Performance"). MDV, 324–25. **203** " 'The composer's artistic health' . . . "—Anton Uglov, *Izvestiia*, January 28, 1927. **204** "according to a report . . . "—*Nasha gazeta (Our Newspaper)*, January 29, 1927. **204** " 'remembering with tenderness' . . . "—SAB, 180. **204** " 'a beauty, but an unpleasant person' . . . "—Ostroumova-Lebedeva. **204** " 'goblet of champagne . . . "—SAB, 180. **205** " 'not without my influence' . . . "—SD, II, 143. **205** " 'lively and gloriously played' . . . "—P-Asafiev, 22. **206** " 'There were shadows in the hall' . . . "— Richter, 456. **206** " 'awfully tired out' . . . "—P-Asafiev, 22. **207** " 'Prokofiev appeared in all the magnificence' . . . "—Lamm (1), 84. **207** " 'Extend a heartfelt greeting' . . . "—PM, 257. **208** " 'A strange bias has appeared' . . . "—*Zhizn' iskusstva (Artistic Life)*, March 1, 1927.

CHAPTER 14

209 " 'While Stravinsky is much more tied to the Gods' . . . "—Diaghilev in the *Observer*, July 3, 1927. **209** " 'thriving' . . . "—PK: to NK, March 29, 1927. **210** " 'strenuous character movements' . . ."—Buckle, 486. **211** " 'In this vast mechanism' . . . "—André George, *Nouvelles Littéraires*, June 21, 1927. **211** " 'brilliantly mounted' . . . "—SAB, 180. **211** " 'something as great as the Russian Revolution' . . . "—Buckle, 490. **211** " 'tempestuous reception' . . . "—Macdonald, 348. **212** "Miss Elsa Maxwell . . . "—*The New York Herald*, June 14, 1927. **213** "Numerous visitors arrived . . . "—LP, 183. **215** " 'stagnant stretches' . . . "— SAB, 86. **216** " 'In my opinion, it is despicable' . . . "—PM, 268. **216** " 'was finally judged too "subtle" ' . . . "—SAB, 186. **216** " 'The old version is very uneven' . . . "—PM, 265. **216** " 'technical reasons' . . . "—SAB, 181. **217** " 'although . . . I very much want to come' . . . "—PM, 270. **217** " 'For four or five years in succession' . . . "—Nabokov, 151. **217** " 'Prokofiev has always seemed a kind of big baby' . . . "—Nicolas Nabokov, "Sergei Prokofiev," *Atlantic Monthly*,

July 1943. **218** " 'He could be just as boorish' . . . "—Nabokov, 156. **218** "he could never find a more complimentary word . . . "—MP, 356. **218** " 'something simple which would not need' . . . "—Buckle, 498. **218** " 'good jazz and bad Liszt' . . . 'Came and played his head off' . . . "—Duke, 209. **219** " 'did not go badly at all' . . . "—PM, 284. **219** " 'Apparently they are obsessed' . . . " and " 'material is absolutely pitiful' . . . "—PM, 281. **220** " 'moderate success' . . . " and " 'Unnerved and angered' . . . "—PM, 279–81. **220** " 'Sometimes the road went through' . . . "—LP, 184. **221** " 'one of my most significant compositions' . . . "— SAB, 182. **222** "also indicate a turn inward, in search of a new artistic direction . . . "—Soviet critics for a long time dismissed these intriguingly reflective studies as unnecessarily difficult and cerebral. Nestyev wrote: "The coldly intellectual piano style which he had developed in Paris was far removed from the healthy, virile style which had delighted listeners in his youthful works." (Nestyev, 231). **222** " 'very slowly, because I don't want to' . . . "—PM, 284. **222** " 'penetrate deeply into music' . . . "—SAB, 182. **223** "Instead, he urged Diaghilev . . . "—SD, II, 142–43. **223** "because Soviet organizers were unable to guarantee . . . "—PK: to NK, December 26, 1928. **224** " 'created son Op. 2' . . . "—PM, 291. **225** " 'flourishing, but his mama' . . . "—letter to M, 219. **225** " 'military' . . . "—Interview with Pyotr Souvchinsky, Paris, June 1982. **225** " 'wasn't at all like those sentimental fathers' . . . "—LP, 185–86. **225** "simple, clear melodic . . . "—PK: to NK, December 26, 1928. **227** " 'melted as he listened' . . . "—LP, 186. **227** "Meyerhold and Prokofiev continued to have trouble consummating . . . "—In early January 1929, after Meyerhold had returned to Moscow, he wrote to Prokofiev inviting him to compose incidental music for the premiere of Mayakovsky's new play *The Bedbug*. Occupied with *Prodigal Son*, Prokofiev reluctantly declined, and Shostakovich accepted the commission in his place. **228** " 'immense admiration' . . . "—Haskell, 315. **228** " 'declamatory operatic style' . . . "—letter to M, 221. **228** " 'Many dynamics of the soul' . . . "—SAB, 183. Despite extensive negotiations with Soviet theatres, *The Gambler* would not be heard in the U.S.S.R. until 1963, and was staged for the first time there only in 1974. **229** " 'I wandered from one premiere to another' . . . " and " 'conscientious, but earthbound' . . . " and "did 'not fit the subject' . . . "—PM, 311–13. **229** "The reviews were respectful . . . "—reviews cited in MDV, 183. **229** " 'He wanted a real garden' . . . "—from a filmed interview with George Balanchine, for the television special "Sergei Pavlovich Diaghilev 1872– 1929: A Portrait." (Co-produced by RM Productions and BBC Television; written and produced by Tamara Geva; 1980.) **230** "In several interviews . . . "—SD, I, 253–55. **230** " 'Stravinsky . . . is the living embodiment' . . . "—SD, I, 259. **230** " 'most dreadful'—letter to M, 221. **230** " 'Lifar, on his knees' . . . "—Buckle, 523. **230** " 'None of my works' . . . "—PM, 313. **230** " 'whose gaiety appeals' . . . "—Raoul Brunel, *Oeune*, May 23, 1929. **230** " 'Together with the explosiveness' . . . "—Émile Vuillermoz, *Excelsior*, May 23, 1929. **231** " 'Why should you get money?' . . . "—Bernard Taper, *Balanchine*. New York, 1984. 112. **232** " 'You can understand what a terrific impact' . . . "—P-Asafiev, 24. **232** " 'Diaghilev's artistic activities are still insufficiently valued' . . . "—SAB, 184.

CHAPTER 15

234 " 'I work everywhere' . . . "—Interview with Nino Frank, *Candide*, December 17, 1931. **234** " 'Awkwardly laid out' . . . "—PM, 316. **235** "Astrov paints a rosy picture . . . "—interview with Mikhail Astrov, Paris, June 1982. **235** " 'ascetic' ideas . . . "—SAB, 184. **235** " 'less derivative' . . . "—P-Asafiev, 26. **236** " 'They were both profoundly Russian' . . . "—Lina Prokofiev, "My Recollection of the Relationship Between Prokofiev and Stravinsky." Edited by Malcolm Brown. In *Slavonic and Western Music: Essays for Gerald Abraham*. Ann Arbor, 1985. pp. 280–81. **236** " 'I'm very much at fault' . . . " and " 'The summer was nicely arranged' . . . "— PM, 318–19. **236** " 'Not far from Paris' . . . "—LP, 188–89. **237** " 'black and blue marks' . . . "—PM, 323. **237** " 'I just didn't see any life' . . . "—SAB, 185. **238** " 'violently anti-modern, anti-Western' . . . "—Schwarz, 58. **238** " 'Prokofiev's works entered our daily musical life' . . . "—*Proletarskii muzykant (Proletarian Musician)*, No. 1, 1929. **238** " 'malicious stupidity' . . . "—letter to M, 221. **239** " 'Due to various circumstances' . . . "—Meyerhold, II, 187. **239** " 'the construction of the U.S.S.R.' . . . "—Meyerhold, II, 496. **239** " 'Prokofiev answered the workers' and members' questions' . . . "—*Proletarskii muzykant*, No. 6, 1929. **240** "a live radio broadcast . . . "—The broadcast featured a performance of the newly revised Sinfonietta. **240** " 'Prokofiev is doing our work in the West' . . . "—Meyerhold, I, 496. **240** " 'many pleasant hours' . . . "—letter to M, 22. **240** " 'Life in Russia has become more difficult' . . . "—PK: to SK, November 25, 1929. **241** "It took him from New York to California . . . "—Prokofiev gave the world premiere of his "Choses en soi" in a recital at Town Hall in New York on January 6. **242** " 'quite respectable and large' . . . "—P-Asafiev, 28. **242** " 'For one thousand dollars you can order' . . . "—PK: to SK, November 25, 1929. **242** " 'It's especially important' . . . "—PK: to NK, January 15, 1930. **243** " 'I must tell you that in spite' . . . "—PK: from SK to SP, January 17, 1930. **243** Olin Downes interview in NYT, February 2, 1930. **244** " 'with the ripening of his years' . . . "—*The New York Sun*, January 7, 1930. **244** " 'celebrated figure, on his way to eminence' . . . "—*The Boston Transcript*, January 30, 1930. **244** " 'I have always found the Steinway' . . . "—CSA, 1929, 1, 927. **244** " 'You never knew what to expect of Prokofiev' . . . "—phone interview with Aaron Copland, July 1982. **244** " 'next to Mexico' . . . "—P-Asafiev, 29. **245** "Prokofiev and Lina bought a small handmade rug . . . "—LP, 191. **245** " 'Unfortunately, the singer miscalculated' . . . "—W. K. Kelsey, *The Detroit News*, March 3, 1930. **245** " 'It will give me a great pleasure to compose' . . . "—Letter to Elizabeth Coolidge, February 16, 1930. (Music Division Archives, Library of Congress.) **245** " 'a northern soul' . . . " and " 'After twenty-five concerts' . . . "—P-Asafiev, 29. **245,246** " 'break his batons' . . . " and " 'While the "Symphony gets ready to play" ' . . . "—PK: to SK, March 18, 1930. **246** " 'grabbed his head and started pointing' . . . "—LP, 191. **246** " 'completely serious: they had grown used to my name' . . . "—SAB, 186. **247** " 'It's hard to imagine what will happen next' . . . " and " 'henceforth our permanent apartment' . . . "—PM, 330. **248** " 'Hurrah!' . . . "—letter to VD, November 9, 1930. **248** " 'The most important thing about any new apartment' . . . "—PM, 341. **249**

" 'The symphony, if not calculated to rouse the public' . . . "—*Christian Science Monitor*, November 14, 1930. **249** " 'Apparently, the public likes to be slapped' . . . "—PM, 439. **250** " 'wealth of material' . . . "—SAB, 185. **250** " 'soft and lightly lyrical' . . . "—PM, 343. **250** " 'We proceeded from the choreographic' . . . "—P-Asafiev, 32. **251** " 'had finished eight of the ballet's twelve sections' . . . "—PM, 343. **251** " 'The tour had been long and tiring' . . . "—Nabokov, 157. **252** " *'The Baby Snatcher'* . . . "—LP, 192. **252** " 'I worked very hard on *The Gambler'* . . . "—Meyerhold-P, 311–12. **252** " 'There I was at his house' . . . "—Hector Fraggi, *Le Petit Marseillais*, September 22, 1930. **253** " 'I have a deep longing to come' . . . "—PM, 344. **253** " 'very much a society lady' . . . "—Astrov interview. **253** " 'Emotion was not Prokofiev's predominant trait' . . . "—Francis Poulenc, *Moi et mes amis*. Paris, 1963, 161. **254** " 'the only one in France' . . . " and " 'formless and amorphous melodies' . . . " and " 'He drove slowly' . . . "—Nabokov, 141, 168, 157–58. **255** " 'she did not understand anything' . . . "—*Ibid.*, 156. **255** " 'Few composers had so many quarrels' . . . "—Nabokov, *Atlantic Monthly*. **255** " 'do not reach the wide masses' . . . " and " 'The Association of Proletarian Musicians' . . . "—PM, 350–53. **256** " 'had to get moving' . . . "—PM, 354. **256** " 'emblems of Soviet daily life' . . . "—PM, 359. Accompanying *Le Pas d'acier* on the program, sponsored by the New York League of Composers, was the American premiere of Stravinsky's *Oedipus Rex*. **257** " 'But it is very gloomy!' . . . "—PM, 365. Prokofiev later arranged the third movement of the First Quartet for full string ochestra, but preferred the original version. **257** " 'That is the source' . . . "—SAB, 186–87. **257** "a set of six pieces assembled from various works . . . "—Three came from *Prodigal Son*, one from "Songs Without Words," one from the First Quartet (the *Andante*) and one from the Sinfonietta. **258** " 'I invented the following method' . . . "—SAB, 187. **258** " 'We are spending the remainder of the summer' . . . "—P-Asafiev, 31. **258** " 'I remember how expressive and comical' . . . "—LP, 193. **259** " 'I have learned to swim' . . . "—PM, 361. **259** " 'Thank you for the concerto' . . . " and " 'Sometimes I like it' . . . "—SAB, 189. The Fourth Piano Concerto was performed for the first time only after Prokofiev's death, by Siegfried Rapp in Berlin in 1956. **259** " 'It would not be amiss' . . . "—PM, 358. **260** " 'The real question is this' . . . "—P-Asafiev, 32. **260** " 'In Paris, I started with success' . . . "—Nino Frank, *Candide*, December 17, 1931. **261** " 'There's a lot that is interesting in it' . . . "—PM, 369. **261** " 'It was one of the few occasions in Paris I recall' . . . "—PM, 373. **261** " 'In the 'West' they have forgotten' . . . "—PM, 378. **262** " 'Just think—I can't sneeze' . . . "—PM, 384. **262, 263** " 'It all depends on whether the people in charge' . . . " and " 'If a *pied-à-terre* could be found' . . . "—PM, 380–81. **263** " 'any sort of decisions could be made' . . . " and " 'It would really refresh and shake up' . . . "—PM, 382. **263– 264** " 'Soviet musical life needs fresh air' . . . " and " 'a picturesque British protectorate' . . . "—PM, 386–87. **264** " 'I'm very pleased with our trip' . . . "—letter to FS, August 3, 1932. **264** " 'Sometimes hearing bad compositions' . . . "—SAB, 191. **264** " 'in order to irritate you once and for all' . . . "—PM, 392. **265** " 'a right to exert influence' . . . "—PM, 390. **265** " 'to hear and see everything without rushing' . . . "—PM, 393. **265** " 'I have left one whole rehearsal' . . . "—SAB,

190. **266** " 'a more intellectual style' . . . "—PM, 391. **267** " 'The work turned out to be complicated' . . . "—SAB, 190. **267** "and included one world premiere . . . "—The Sonata for Two Violins was first heard in a closed performance in Moscow on November 27, followed by a public performance six days later in Leningrad. **268** " 'I am not leaving the U.S.S.R. for very long' . . . "—S. Prokofiev, "Zametki" ("Notes"), *Sovetskaia muzyka*, No. 3, 1933, 99. (MDV, 212). **269** " 'During his trips to the Soviet Union' . . . "—LP, 196–97.

CHAPTER 16

271 " 'One thing struck me above all else' . . . "—interview with Madeleine Portier, *Comoedia*, December 16, 1932. **272** " 'Parisian composers warmly defended it' . . . "— SAB, 188. **272** "Among those 'Parisian composers' . . . "—PM, 396. **272** " 'Those who have admired the Russian musician' . . . "—Robert Brussel, *Le Figaro*, December 20, 1932. **272** " 'The action of a strong will' . . . "—Dominique Sordet, *Action Française*, December 24, 1932. **272** " 'On the Dnepr is the ballet' . . . "— *Balet: Entsiklopediia (Ballet Encyclopedia)*. Moscow, 1981, 416. **273** " 'My collaboration with him was always very amicable' . . . "—Serge Lifar, March 22, 1953. (Untitled newspaper clipping, in the Prokofiev clipping files of the Library of the Paris Opera.) **273** "The failure of *On the Dnepr* . . . "—A few months later, Prokofiev wrote a six-part orchestral suite (Op. 51-bis) from the music for *On the Dnepr*. **274** "earned him two thousand dollars . . . "—PK: to SK, December 6, 1932. **274** " 'And there at the piano sits the boy' . . . "—Olin Downes, NYT, January 6, 1933. **274** " 'One still wonders what on earth' . . . "—NYT, January 20, 1933. **274** " 'I'd like to meet the guy' . . . "—SAB, 191. **275** " 'It seems that the Americans' . . . "— P-Asafiev, 41. **275** " 'If in one corner they have forgotten' . . . "—PM, 395. **276** " 'Don't be offended' . . . "—PM, 371. **276** " 'I wouldn't want the Soviet listener' . . . " and " 'When you arrive in the U.S.S.R.' . . . "—S. Prokofiev, "Notes," MDV, 213. **277** " 'categorically rejected my proposal' . . . "—I. Rummel, "Iz istorii *Poruchika Kizhe*" ("From the History of *Lt. Kizhe*"), *Sovetskaia muzyka*, No. 11, 1964, 69. Also see Harlow Robinson, " 'The Most Contemporary Art': Sergei Prokofiev and Soviet Film," *Studies in Comparative Communism*, Vol. XVII, Nos. 3 & 4, Fall/ Winter 1984, 203–18. **278** "told the filmmakers he interpreted . . . " and " 'the dimensions of the musical pieces' . . . " and " 'Carefully watching the rehearsals' . . . "—Rummel, 69–70. **278** " 'For some reason I never had any doubt' . . . "— SAB, 191. **281** " 'No one had a clear idea of it' . . . "—SAB, 190. **281** "Part of the time he was alone . . . "—letter to VD, August 14, 1933. **282** " 'darkness-struggle—achievement' . . . "—SAB, 193. **282** " 'not entirely right for us' . . . "— PM, 400. **283** " 'If the presence of music' . . . "—SAB, 214. **283** " 'which he sketched out on a little piece of music paper' . . . "—Iu. Golovashenko, *Rezhisserskoe iskusstvo Tairova (The Director's Art of Tairov)*. Moscow, 1970, 218. **283** " 'Despite Shaw's charming wit' . . . "—SAB, 192. **285** " 'Everything is going well' . . . "— letter to FS, November 10, 1933. **285** "Prokofiev had once admitted to Miaskovsky . . . "—PM, 381. **285** " 'Fifteen years of living abroad' . . . "—Aram Khachaturian, "Neskol'ko myslei o Prokof'eve" ("A Few Thoughts About Prokofiev"), MDV, 404. **285** " 'You never find such luxury' . . . " and " 'It's warm in Rome' . . . " and " 'totally nil' . . . "—PM, 407–408. **286** " 'This isn't a personal request' . . . "—PK: to Olga K, February 5, 1934. **286, 287** " 'You are now the only representative' . . . " and " 'Moscow requires a composer' . . . "—PM, 415. **287** "arguing for Soviet music in Paris . . . "—Prokofiev was particularly energetic as an advocate of Miaskovsky's music, which he persuaded many European and American conductors to perform. **287** " 'remembered very affectionately by a large group' . . ."—PM, 412. **287** " 'screaming puppet-show quality' . . . "—*Sovetskoe iskusstvo*, December 26, No. 59, 1933. **287** " 'In spite of my predictions' . . . "— PM, 410. **287** " 'amazingly good' . . . "—PM, 403. **288** " 'He is at the peak of fame' . . . "—PM, 422. **288** "According to Miaskovsky" and " 'a symphonic monologue for the few' . . . "—quoted in Nestyev, 255. **289** description of the sitting from Natal'ia Konchalovskaia, "Prazdnik v budni" ("A Holiday on Workdays"), *Moskva*, No. 11, 1969, 183. **289** " 'He had the same glowing' . . . "—Igor' Grabar', "Sergei Sergeevich Prokof'ev. Vstrechi i vospominaniia" ("S. S. Prokofiev: Meetings and Memories"), MDV, 495. **290** " 'You can lay out all your things' . . . "—P-Alpers, 425. **292** " 'Paris in August has its charms' . . . "—*Ibid.* **292** " 'more transparent and more sonatina-like' . . . " and " 'one of my greatest successes' . . . "—SAB, 193. **292** " 'as before, it is still in a somnolent state' . . . "—PM, 426. **292** " 'closed up shop' . . . "—P-Alpers, 425. **293** " 'enjoyed a "peaceful life" ' . . . "—letter to FS, September 14, 1934. **293** " 'I'm scared to death of it' . . . "—PM, 431. **293** " 'truthfulness and historical concreteness' . . . "—Gleb Struve, *Russian Literature Under Lenin and Stalin 1917–1953*. Norman, 1971, 262. **294** " 'The issue of what kind of music we should write' . . . "—S. Prokofiev, "Put' sovetskoi muzyki" ("The Course of Soviet Music"), MDV, 214–15. **295** "It was in Voronezh . . . "—SAB, 193. In Moscow on November 30, Alexander Gauk conducted an all-Prokofiev concert in the Hall of Columns, featuring the Moscow premieres of the Second Symphony and of the orchestral version of the Overture on Hebrew Themes. **295** " 'I am submerged in rehearsals' . . . "—letter to FS, December 7, 1934. **295** " 'the entire theatrical-musical world of Moscow' . . . "—LP, 198. **295** "a run of seventy-five performances . . . "—CSA, 1929, 1, 353. **298** " 'went back on its word' . . . "— SAB, 193. **298** " 'like reading an interesting adolescent novel' . . . "—P-Alpers, 425. **298** " 'In the circles of the Leningrad Composers' Union' . . . "—PM, 434. **299** " 'Internal changes are occurring here now' . . . "—PM, 437. **300** "In March 1935 . . . he departed from Paris for Moscow . . . "—During the less than two months that Prokofiev spent in Paris, he devoted much of his time to practicing for recording sessions. Between 1935 and 1937, he recorded—among other piano pieces— "Suggestion diabolique," "Landscape," Sonatine Pastorale, "Tales of an Old Grandmother" and some of the "Visions fugitives." He was also reading the novel *1919* by John Dos Passos, considering it as a possible libretto source, although he eventually rejected the idea. **300** " 'spectator and fan' . . . "—P-Asafiev, 54. **301** " 'I was simply amazed at the ecstatic attention' . . ."—SAB, 215. **302** " 'dramaturgical nightmare' . . . "—Arlene Croce, *The New Yorker*, May 13, 1985, 132. **302** " 'There were fifty-eight such episodes' . . . "—P-Alpers, 427. **302** " 'Living people can dance' . . . "—SAB, 194. **303** "the entire piano score was finished . . . "—PM, 546. **304** " 'The colony is very pleasant' . . . " and " 'I can think of no greater pleasure' . . . "—P-Alpers, 427. **304** " 'spoiled to pieces' . . . "—letter to VD, September 29, 1935. **304** " 'Father worked every day' . . . "—OP, 23–24. **305** " 'The most important thing is not to follow' . . . "—PM, 440. **305** " 'Reflecting my nomadic concertizing existence' . . . " and " 'completely different' . . . "—SAB, 193. **306** " 'It seems as though the concerto is a success' . . . "—PM, 443. **307** " 'Shostakovich is talented' . . . "—letter to VD, September 29, 1935. **308** "for he wrote Vera Alpers . . . "—P-Alpers, 427. **308** " 'undanceable' . . . "—SAB, 194. **309** " 'her intonation had suffered somewhat' . . . " and " 'playing the same thing over and over' . . . "—PM, 445. **310** " 'quite a lot of imbibing' . . . "—letter to FS, January 3, 1936.

PART III

CHAPTER 17

313 " 'A stone that strikes the surface' . . . "—S. Prokofiev, "I Shall Be Classical in the Next Generation," *Europe: An American Monthly*, Vol. II, No. 4 (April 1936), 20. **314** " 'without particular enthusiasm' . . . "—P-Alpers, 428. **315** " 'From the first moment' . . . "—in Schwarz, 123–24. **315** " 'changed my entire existence' . . . "—Shostakovich, 113. **317** " 'Prokofiev was an inveterate gambler' . . . "— Shostakovich, 35–36. **318** " 'Prokofiev was always very Russian-minded' . . . " —Stravinsky, *Memories and Commentaries*, 65. **318** " 'a feeling totally contradictory' . . . "—Nabokov, 180. **319** "a remarkably imaginative form of avoidance behavior . . . " Interestingly, Prokofiev composed "The Ugly Duckling," another fairy-tale setting, at a similar moment of historical gravity—in the first months of World War I. **319** " 'In his foreign suit he seemed stiff' . . . " and " 'more spontaneously than his sons' . . . "—Natalia Satz, "Kak sozdavalas' *Petia i volk*" ("How *Peter and the Wolf* Was Created"), MDV, 506. **320** " 'We must start with something specific' . . . " and " 'huddled against the door' . . . "—*Ibid.*, 509–10. **323** " 'Above all, the piece is spontaneous' . . . "—in Harlow Robinson, "Prokofiev's 'Peter and the Wolf' Is Fifty Years Old," NYT, November 10, 1985. II, 21. **324** " 'Even his creative work' . . . "—LP, 201. **324** "praising the 'collective' . . . "—S. Prokofiev, "Zametki zritelia" ("Notes of a Spectator"), MDV, 217. **324, 325** " 'eleven boxes of furniture' . . . " and " 'The fields have all burned' . . . "—P-Alpers, 428. **325** " 'The Queen of Spades' seduced me first of all' . . . "—Mikhail Romm, *Izbrannye proizvedeniia v 3-kh tomakh (Selected Works in Three Volumes)*. Moscow, 1981. II, 156. **325, 326** " 'I tried to make the film in the style' . . . " and " 'With his characteristic precision' . . . "—*Ibid.*, 159. **326** "films based on 'contemporary

themes' . . . "—Ibid. 161. **327** " 'from which he could never be parted' . . . "—
MP, 387. **327** "he needed to 'see it' . . . "—letter to M, 225. **327** " 'When I am
asked to write music' . . . "—S. Prokofiev, "Kompozitor v dramaticheskom teatre"
("The Composer in the Dramatic Theatre"), MDV, 219–20. **328** " 'Boris is of Tartar
origin' . . . " and " 'Only a "Scythian" orchestra' . . . "—V. Gromov, "Zamysel
postanovki" ("The Conception of a Production"), *Tvorcheskoe nasledie V. E. Meierkhol'da*. Moscow, 1978, 374–75. **329** " 'On November 16, 1936' . . . "—*Ibid*.,
392. Prokofiev had orchestrated more than half of the twenty-four "numbers" composed for *Boris* before the production was canceled. Some of this music was later
used in other projects, including *Semyon Kotko* and (twenty-five years after Prokofiev's
death) a ballet on the life of Boris Godunov staged at the Maly Theater in Leningrad
in 1978. **330** " 'My life is always sweet' . . . "—Satz, 513. **330** " 'During the
prewar years' . . . " and " 'Because of the changes' . . . "—OP, 21–23. **331** " 'Between myself and my wife' . . . "—from a questionnaire, "Heredity and Musical
Talent," filled out by Prokofiev on February 8, 1938. (Music Division Archives,
Library of Congress). **332** " 'During the afternoon we had two rehearsals' . . . " and
" 'heaved sighs of regret' . . . " and " 'passport troubles' . . . " and " 'splendid piece
of work' . . . "—PM, 449–50. **333** " 'the orchestra was attentive' . . . "—letters
to VD, January 24 and January 24, 1937. **333** " 'the instrument of the immortals' . . . "—CSA, 1929, 1, 909. **333** " 'Blue and streamlined' . . . "—LP, 205.
333 "warning him not to mention '$$' . . . "—letter to VD, February 28, 1937.
334 " 'His clothes were checkered all over' . . . "—Richter, 457. **337** " 'Before
the program they asked us' . . . " and " 'required special effort' . . . "—LP, 204–
206. **338** " 'no less than five hundred' . . . "—S. Prokofiev, "Rastsvet iskusstva"
("The Flowering of Art"), MDV, 224. **339** " 'I sat for two months' . . . "—P-Alpers,
430. **339** " 'brilliant and graphic leaders' . . . "—Nestyev, 290. **339** " 'gave up
on the north' . . . "—P-Alpers, 430. **340** "They also observed that Prokofiev seemed
reluctant . . . "—interview with Olga Lamm, Moscow, October, 1982. **340** " 'a truly
fresh thing' . . . " —Shostakovich-P, 255. In his own appraisal of Shostakovich's
Fifth, Miaskovsky discovered a strong Prokofievian influence in the raucously martial
finale. **341** " 'to be simple and at the same time' . . . "—Nestyev, 292. **342** " 'I
lay down from two to four' . . . "—PM, 454. **342** " 'I'm not trying to defend' . . . "—
Lola Bassan, *Page Musicale*, February 2, 1938. **342** " 'an inspiring one' . . . "—
William G. King, *The New York Sun*, February 9, 1938. **342** " 'In my youth my
music' . . . "—Prokofiev, "I Will Be Classical in the Next Generation," 20. **343**
" 'He hardly spoke to anyone' . . . "—Arlynn Nellhaus, "Jean Cranmer Hosted Early
DSO Artists," *The Denver Post*, February 26, 1978. **343** " 'It is very warm here' . . . "—
SM (1965), 222–23. **344** "a number of Hollywood stars attended . . . "—LP, 203.
344 " 'at least a hundred recordings' . . . "—OP, 19. **344** "Prokofiev devoted
considerable space to jazz . . . "—S. Prokofiev, "Muzykal'naia Amerika" ("Musical
America"), MDV, 232–35. **345** " 'I have heard little interesting music' . . . "—
PM, 457. **346** " 'I showed Serge the telegram exultantly' . . . "—Duke, 367.

CHAPTER 18

347 description of the *Hamlet* music in S. Prokofiev, "O muzyke k 'Gamletu' V. Shekspira" ("About the Music for Shakespeare's *Hamlet*")—MDV, 227–28. Only two years after Radlov's production, Boris Pasternak completed his new translation of *Hamlet*, which was used later in the Soviet film version directed by Grigori Kozintsev and with a score by Shostakovich. **350** " 'If the might of the people's spirit' . . . "— Sergei Eisenstein, "Aleksandr Nevskii," in *Sovetskii istoricheskii fil'm: Sbornik statei (Soviet Historical Film: A Collection of Articles)*. Moscow, 1939, 19. **350** " 'whose task was to see to it' . . . " and " 'to prepare . . . every Russian man' . . . "—Seton, 379–80. **351** " 'unquestionably our best film director' . . . "—P-Alpers, 431. **351** " . . . 'At twelve noon you'll have the music' . . . "—Eisenstein, "Zametki o S. S. Prokof'eve" ("Notes on S. S. Prokofiev"), MDV, 481. **352** " 'Only the horses' . . . "— P-Alpers, 431. **352** " 'Original musical material from the thirteenth century' . . . "—S. Prokofiev, "Muzyka v fil'me *Aleksandr Nevskii*" ("Music in the Film *Alexander Nevsky*"), *Soviet Historical Film*, 27. **352** " 'The sounds of their horns' . . . "—*Ibid.*, 27. **353** " 'not when an accordion player' . . . "—Eisenstein, *Izbrannye proizvedeniia v 6-i tomakh (Collected Works in Six Volumes)*, III. Moscow, 1968, 582–83. **353** " 'Prokofiev's music is incredibly plastic' . . . "—Eisenstein, "Notes on S. S. Prokofiev," 488. **353** " 'found the third companion' . . . "—Eisenstein, *Izbrannye stat'i (Selected Articles)*. Moscow, 1955, 164. **354** " 'up to my ears' . . . "—P-Alpers, 432. **354** "Kataev was a 'safe' choice . . . "—Apparently, it was the influential Soviet writer Aleksei Tolstoy who originally suggested *I Am a Son of the Working People* to Prokofiev as a promising subject for an opera. **354** " 'very decisive, exact, abrupt . . . in the style of *Carmen*' . . . " and " 'I don't want that' . . . "—interview with Valentin Kataev, Peredelkino, February 1980. **355** " 'I want something different than he has' . . . "—P-Alpers, 432. **355** " 'Prokofiev was silent' . . . "—Leonid Lavrovsky, "Seif tvorcheskogo dara: iz vospominanii o Sergee Prokof'eve" ("The 'Safe' of Artistic Genius"), MDV, 514–15. **355** "admired the brilliant northern sunsets . . . "—LP, 205. **355** " 'To a ten-year-old schoolboy' . . . "—OP, 24–25. **356** "the premiere was a 'complete failure' . . . "— Richter, 458. **357** " 'Sergei Mikhailovich, you are a good Bolshevik' . . . "—Seton, 386. **357** " 'Despite a number of amazing moments' . . . "—Shostakovich-P, 255– 56. **358** " 'The Chicago music lovers are looking forward' . . . "—CSA, 1929, 1, 509. (Letters from Ephraim Gottlieb). **358** Prokofiev made numerous appearances in Moscow in 1939, including one at a special program devoted to Maurice Ravel, who had recently died. Prokofiev read an article he had written about Ravel and his music, calling him "one of the most important composers of our time." He stressed Ravel's influence on Russian composers, and the need to perform his works more frequently in the U.S.S.R. **359** " 'To write an opera on a Soviet theme' . . . "— Sergei Prokofiev, "*Semen Kotko*," MDV, 235–38. **360** " 'The work went at an intense pace' . . . "—Skorino, 301. **360** "He was also critical . . . "—*Meyerhold on Theatre*. Edited by Edward Braun. New York, 1969, 252. **362** "only a week before Prokofiev finished the piano score . . . "—OP, 25. **363** "In the huge volume of material . . . "—MDV. **363** " 'The theater named after the People's Artist' . . . "—

Serafima Birman, "On ves' otdal sebia muzyke" ("He Gave His Entire Self to Music"), MDV, 501.

CHAPTER 19

366 "One of her strongest memories of the summer of 1939 . . . "—MP, 393. **366** "One reliable Soviet source . . . "—from interviews in Moscow, 1980 and 1982. **367** "notably Victor Seroff . . . "—Victor Seroff, *Sergei Prokofiev: A Soviet Tragedy.* New York, 1969. **368** " 'a beautiful desert' . . . "—interview with A. Spadavekkia, October 1982, Moscow. **368,369** " 'It didn't seem to me that Sergei Sergeevich' . . . " and " 'My room was furnished' . . . "—Birman, 502. **369** " 'due to illness' . . . "—CSA, 1929, 1, 904. **370** " 'in all the squares and streets of Moscow' . . . "—OP, 21. **370** "According to Mira, Prokofiev began working . . . "—MP, 374. **371** " 'From the day of the first read-through' . . . "—Galina Ulanova, "Avtor liubymykh baletov" ("Author of My Favorite Ballets"), MDV, 432. **372** " 'Make do with what music there is' . . . "—Lavrovsky, 515–16. **372** " 'deviated somewhat' . . . "—SAB, 194. **372** " 'I know what you need—you need drums' . . . "—Ulanova, 433. **373** " 'understanding and sympathy . . . far from immediately' . . . "—Lavrovsky, 517. **373** "they came up with an anecdote . . . "—Ulanova, 434. **373** "they had to grope their way . . . "—LP, 208. **373** " 'countless curtain-calls' . . . "—Ulanova, 433. **373** " 'The success of *Romeo and Juliet*' . . . "—*Sovetskoe iskusstvo*, January 21, 1940. **374** " 'I was very surprised when I saw Prokofiev' . . . "—Ulanova, 435. **375** " 'This week you were to have conducted' . . . "—CSA, 1929, 1, 509. (Letters from Ephraim Gottlieb.) **375** " 'Serious musical people would gather' . . . "—Richter, 460–61. **376** " 'I was never especially close to Prokofiev' . . . "—*Ibid.*, 455. **377** "The Sixth Sonata is magnificent . . . "—Shostakovich-P, 256. **377** " 'in a permanently excited state' . . . "—LP, 209. **377** " 'We had to tone down the setting' . . . "—Skorino, 306–307. **377** " 'I don't think that any of my father's compositions' . . . "—OP, 25. **378** " 'will not be comprehensible to the masses' . . . "—*Sovetskaia muzyka*, No. 10, 1940. More than twenty years later, during the cultural "thaw" under Khrushchev, Soviet musicologist Marina Sabinina was able to point out that *Semyon's* real problem was being ahead of its time. Meyerhold's close association with the project also helps to explain why the opera was given such a cool reception in 1940. **378** " 'The evening that I heard *Semyon Kotko*' . . . "—Richter, 460. **378** " 'He had always been rather grim' . . . "—Interview with Alissa Shebalin, Nikolina Gora, September 1982. **379** " 'began to retell' . . . "—MP, 390. **379** "He had also been considering . . . "—N. Umnova, *Prokofiev's "Duenna" as an Operatic Spectacle*, 21. (Unpublished dissertation, Tchaikovsky Conservatory, Moscow.) **380** " 'In undertaking to write an opera' . . . "—"*Obruchenie v monastyre*" ("*Betrothal in a Monastery*"), MDV, 242. **382** "in the glittering hall named after his former professor . . . "—Glazunov had died in Paris in March 1936, after eight sad years of living abroad. **383** " 'Prokofiev arrived with his wife' . . . "—Richter, 462–63. **384** " 'Memories of our Paris life' . . . "—OP, 21. **385** " 'my wife' . . . "—MDV, 243. **385** " 'partly with irony and partly with respect' . . . "—interview with Oleg Prokofiev, June 1982.

CHAPTER 20

389 " 'On June 22, a warm sunny morning. . . . It was during these days' . . . " and " 'Soon afterward' . . . "—Sergei Prokofiev, "Khudozhnik i voina" ("The Artist and the War"), MDV, 243–44. **390** " 'We all shared one thought' . . . "—Lamm (2), 99. **391** " 'Sergei Sergeevich appeared in our compartment' . . . "—Lamm (2), 99. **391** " 'who retained all of her great artistic aura' . . . "—Prokofiev, "The Artist and the War," 245. **392** " 'A notebook of music paper' . . . "—Grabar, MDV, 495. **392** " 'All of us immediately noticed the significant change' . . . "—Lamm (2), 102. **393** " 'I read *War and Peace* with enthusiasm' . . . "—AB, 308. **395** " 'the numerous draft versions and plans' . . . "—R. F. Christian, *Tolstoy: A Critical Introduction*. Cambridge, 1969, 99. **396** " 'What is *War and Peace*?' . . . "—L. Tolstoy, "Neskol'ko slov po povodu knigi *Voina i mir*" ("A Few Words Concerning *War and Peace*") in *Polnoe sobranie sochinenii (Complete Collected Works)*. Moscow, 1955, XVI, 7. **397** " 'First, we would usually look over the text' . . . "—Anatolii Volkov, "*Voina i mir Prokof'eva: Opyt analiza variantov opery (Prokofiev's "War and Peace": An Attempt at an Analysis of the Opera's Versions)*. Moscow, 1976, 11–12. **397** "he managed to complete the first six scenes . . . "—See Robinson, *The Operas of Sergei Prokofiev and Their Russian Literary Sources*, Chapter VI. **398** " 'It seemed to me that bringing new and untouched Eastern folklore. . . . Write what you feel' . . . "— S. Prokofiev, "The Artist and the War," 245. **399** " 'simply monstrously, even "nightmarishly" interesting' . . . "—PM, 467. **400** " 'enormous impression on me' . . . "—Shostakovich-P, 256. **401** "In its compelling interplay . . . "—Delson, 209. **401** " 'We were all orphaned' . . . "—Lamm (2), 105. **402** " 'a hundred times worse' . . . " and " 'In Krasnovodsk it rained' . . . "—PM, 459–60. **402** " 'on the piano, on the floor' . . . "—Ulanova, 436. **402,403** " 'great freedom in all areas' . . . " and " 'I continue to regard the cinema' . . . "—PE, 279–80. **404** " 'understood each other almost without speaking' . . . " and " 'could never catch all the nuances' . . . "—B. Vol'skii, "Vospominaniia o S. S. Prokof'eve" ("Memories of S. S. Prokofiev"), MDV, 532–35. **404** " 'Here it should sound like a child' . . . " and " 'If the image corresponded well' . . . "—S. Prokofiev, "O rabote s Eizenshteinom" ("On My Work with Eisenstein"), MDV, 250–51. **405** "They advised him to 'strengthen the dramatic' . . . "—Mira Mendelson-Prokofiev, "Iz vospominanii" ("From My Memoirs"), *Sovetskaia muzyka*, No. 4, 1961, 103. **406** " 'Film work is interesting, profitable' . . . "—PM, 461. **406,407** " 'strengthening the film's patriotic resonance' . . . " and " 'It has moved once and for all' . . . "—S. Prokofiev, "S. S. Prokof'ev pishet muzyku k fil'mu" ("S. S. Prokofiev Is Writing Music to a Film"), *Muzykal'naia zhizn'*, No. 16, August 1983, 18–19. **407** " 'My method is more convenient' . . . " and " 'The spectator will leave' . . . "—*Ibid*. **408** "Prokofiev later used the pieces . . . "—Besides the waltz and polonaise that went into *War and*

Peace, the "Mephisto" waltz originally written for *Lermontov* also migrated elsewhere, reappearing in the Three Pieces for Piano (Op. 96) and in the Suite of Waltzes for Symphony Orchestra (Op. 110). **408** "Prokofiev the propaganda composer . . . "— See E. Vishnevetskaia, "Kinomuzyka S. S. Prokof'eva voiennykh let" ("S. S. Prokofiev's Film Scores of the War Years"), in *Iz proshlogo sovetskoi muzykal'noi kul'tury*. Moscow, 1975, I, 35–71. *Tonya* was never released—apparently the censors found it insufficiently realistic. Prokofiev reused its song leitmotif in his last opera, *Story of a Real Man*. *Kotovsky* was directed by Alexander Faintsimmer, the creator of *Lt. Kizhe*. *Partisans in the Ukrainian Steppe* was directed by the Ukrainian Igor Savchenko, and its score recycles music from the suite *The Year 1941*, *Semyon Kotko*, *Kotovsky*, and from Ukrainian folk songs. **409** " 'The opera provoked obvious interest' . . . "—Samuil Samosud, "Vstrechi s Prokof'evym" ("Meetings with Prokofiev"), SM, 116. **410** " 'It was intensely fascinating' . . . " and " 'He was alone' . . . "— Richter, 464–65. **410** " 'rather simple and worth much less' . . . " and " 'The important thing was to break the ice' . . . "—PM, 465 and 468. **412** " 'the electricity was turned off' . . . "—PM, 464. **413** " 'like shots in a film' . . . "—MDV, 661. **413** " 'extremely turbulent success' . . . " and " 'the composition seemed rather boring' . . . "—PM, 468–69. **414** " 'I am often thinking of you and your family' . . . "—CSA, 1929, 1, 702.

CHAPTER 21

417 " 'I found the enormous collective of the Kirov' . . . "—S. Prokofiev, "The Artist and the War," 248. **417** " 'It seems I'll be able to kill the beauty off' . . . "—PM, 470. **418** " 'as danceable as possible' . . . " and " 'Each character has his (or her) own variation' . . . "—S. Prokofiev, "O *Zolushke*" ("About *Cinderella*"), MDV, 250. **419** " 'The Prince mounts his throne like a saddle' . . . "—SS, 617, 1, 11. **420** " 'I wanted to convey the poetic love' . . . "—S. Prokofiev, "About *Cinderella*," 249. **421** "Prokofiev was using pieces of it . . . "—In 1942, Prokofiev arranged three pieces from *Cinderella* for piano as the Three Pieces Op. 95. *Cinderella* also provided music for several more cycles of piano music—the Nine Pieces from the Ballet *Cinderella* for Piano Op. 97 and the Six Pieces from the Ballet *Cinderella* for Piano Op. 102—and for the Adagio from *Cinderella* arranged for Cello and Piano (Op. 97-bis). In 1946, after the ballet's premiere, he also put together three symphonic suites from the ballet (Op. Nos. 107, 108, 109), and used three *Cinderella* waltzes in the Suite of Waltzes for Symphonic Orchestra (Op. 110). **421** " 'insufficiently represented in musical literature' . . . "—S. Prokofiev, "The Artist and the War," 243. **421** " 'perhaps inappropriate at the moment' . . . "—PM, 461. **421** " 'to sound in bright and transparent classical tones' . . . "—S. Prokofiev, "The Artist and the War," 248. **422** "flutists 'did not rush' . . . "—Richter, 467. **422** " 'enjoy a more full-blooded life on the stage' . . . "—Oistrakh, 452. **422** " 'had already paid him an advance of five thousand rubles' . . . "—CSA, 1929, 2, 358. **424** " 'unexpectedly released' . . . "—Samosud, 124. **424** " 'a couple of classical operas' . . . "—PE,

284. **425** " 'I'm taking advantage of this opportunity' . . . "—PK: to NK, October 20, 1943. **425** " 'Big changes have also taken place' . . . "—P-Alpers, 432. **426** " 'abrupt, but with a great sense of humor' . . . "—interview with Nina Dorliak, Moscow, October 1982. **427** " 'Everything happened very quickly' . . . "—Oistrakh, 452. **427** "The number of changes made in the flute part were 'minimal' . . . "—S. Prokofiev, "The Artist and the War," 249. **428** " 'wonderful—fresh, tasty, abundant' . . . "—PM, 473. **428** " 'completely helpless' . . . "—Khachaturian, 405. **428** "But some observers . . . "—See Schwarz, 233. **429** " 'On the edge of the village' . . . "—Dmitri Kabalevsky, "O Sergee Prokof'eve" ("About Sergei Prokofiev"), MDV, 415. **430** "On the last page of the score Prokofiev recorded . . . "—SS, 617, 1, 15. **431** " 'primarily lyrical in character' . . . "—S. Prokofiev, "The Artist and the War," 249. **431** Richter on the Eighth Piano Sonata— Richter, 466. **431** " 'very important not only for the musical material' . . . "—S. Prokofiev, "O moikh rabotakh za gody voiny" ("About My Works of the War Years"), MDV, 252. **434** " 'I'm busy now with work on my Fifth Symphony' . . . "—PE, 285. **434** " 'His hands dragged somehow' . . . " and " 'old-fashioned' . . . "— Richter, 465–66. **435** " 'The Great Hall was illuminated' . . . "—Richter, 470.

CHAPTER 22

439 " 'He lay completely motionless' . . . "—Kabalevsky, 420. **439** " 'I am aware and in complete agreement with' . . . "—PE, 285. **440** " 'animated conversation' . . . "—Kabalevsky, 420. **440** " 'An unusual holiday atmosphere reigned' . . . "—Samosud, 127. **441** " 'I'm not an agronomist's son' . . . "—MP, 378. **441** " 'one of the manifestations of the rare purity' . . . "—MP, 372. **442** " 'The air is marvelous, the food is tasty' . . . "—PM, 473. **442** " 'could not possibly. . . . He tried to work' . . . "—PE, 287. **443** " 'One would try in vain to get any information' . . . "—MP, 378. **443** " 'No one has hastened to shorten the War' . . . "—CSA, 1929, 1, 509. (Letter from Ephraim Gottlieb.) **443** "Cecil M. Smith . . . "—CSA, 1929, 1, 509. **444** " 'creative fertility of the years during the War' . . . "—CSA, 1929, 1, 702. **444** " 'There is so much I could and should tell you' . . . "—CSA, 1929, 1, 536. **444** " 'Happy you conducting American premiere' . . . "—telegram to Koussevitsky, November 6, 1945. (Music Division Archives, Library of Congress.) **444** " 'The *Ode* begins severely and solemnly' . . . "— S. Prokofiev, "About My Works of the War Years," 253. **445** " 'If he saw or heard a given theme' . . . "—Ulanova, 437. **446** "Prokofiev saw the production of *Cinderella* . . . "—Kabalevsky, 422. **446** "In *Pravda*, Shostakovich praised . . . "— *Pravda*, November 29, 1945. **448** " 'the cream of the Leningrad artistic intelligentsia' . . . "—Samosud, 134. **448** "had been performed at the Maly Theater fifty times . . . "—*Ibid.*, 139. **448** "Judging from Alpers's letter . . . it had become 'fashionable to praise and enjoy' . . . "—P-Alpers, 433. **449** " 'Sergei Sergeevich loved the *dacha*' . . . "—and " 'reading, looking over notes on chess games' . . . "— MP, 378. **450** " 'It seemed to me that on this occasion' . . . " and " 'Miaskovsky remarked' . . . "—Oistrakh, 452. **451** " 'I never worked with such passion' . . . "—*Ibid.*, 453. **452** " 'scum of literature' . . . "—Struve, 350–52. **452** " 'betrayed his ignorance of historical fact' . . . "—Swallow, 137. **452** " 'We committed a misrepresentation' . . . "—*Kul'tura i zhizn'*, October 20, 1946. (Translated by Marie Seton.) **452** "Because of the negative evaluation of Part II of *Ivan* . . . "— Prokofiev never managed to arrange the music from *Ivan* into a suite or cantata, as he had done with the music written for *Lt. Kizhe* and *Alexander Nevsky*. **453** " 'good poetic sense' . . . " and " 'Don't they understand' . . . "—Samosud, 146. **454** " 'one of Prokofiev's most radiant and buoyant works' . . . "—*Sovetskoe iskusstvo*, January 17, 1947. **454** " 'They stood next to each other' . . . "—OP, 27. **456** " 'you could set your watch by him' . . . "—Alissa Shebalin, interview. **456,457** " 'His secret wasn't only a brilliant command' . . . " and " 'And then suddenly he would whip his little notebook' . . . " and " 'tumultuous' . . . " and " 'As a result, the theatre's management' . . . "—Samosud, 145 and 149. **457** " 'stashed away in the desk drawer' . . . "—*Ibid.*, 150. **458** " 'I am prepared to accept the failure' . . . "— Kabalevsky, 424. **459** "that could be played by groups of student violinists . . . "— S. Prokofiev, "Povest' o chelovecheskom muzhestve" ("A Tale of Human Bravery"), MDV, 253. **460** " 'What united them was mutual admiration' . . . "—OP, 20. **462** " 'It is one of the most beautiful, most exalted' . . . "—cited in Schwarz, 213. **462** " 'It seems as though the two Prokofievs' . . . "—Nestyev, 398. **463** " 'In working . . . I strove to express in music' . . . "—S. Prokofiev, "A Tale of Human Bravery," 253. **463** "Prokofiev took great interest in this report . . . "—CSA, 1929, 1, 906. **463** " 'Prokofiev was always afraid that he was being overlooked' . . . "— Shostakovich, 37. **464** " 'huge number of books' . . . "—Nestyev, 403. **464** "more than twenty-three million copies . . . "—*Boris Nikolaevich Polevoi: Rekomendatel'nyi ukazatel' literatury (An Annotated Index of Sources)*. Kalinin, 30. **465** " 'not a single composer' . . . "—Semon Shlifshtein, *Sovetskaia muzyka*, No. 1, 1961, 26. **466** " 'I am dedicating my new opera' . . . "—S. Prokofiev, "A Tale of Human Bravery," 253.

CHAPTER 23

468 "But proof that it occurred . . . "—CSA, 1929, 2, 561. The marriage license is stamped: "11-A No.541637" and dated January 13, 1948. The document also states that Mira chose to take his name. Interestingly, the document reveals that Mira's father's name was Abram, although she went by the patronymic Alexandrovna. Perhaps he or she changed Abram to Alexander to obscure their Jewish origins. **470** "Under the reform of Soviet marriage law . . . "—M. G. Kozlova, who has organized and prepared for publication Prokofiev's archives at the Central State Archives, maintains that Prokofiev and Mira were unaware of the change in the law until around 1947 or 1948, shortly before they married. **470** " 'We had been married during the War' . . . "—Galina Vishnevskaya, 159. **471** " 'historical inaccuracies' . . . "— Schwarz, 214. **471** " 'formalist conspiracy . . . This version from Muradeli' . . . "—Shostakovich, 145. **472** " 'cannot appeal to the people' . . . "—Alexander Werth, *Musical Uproar in Moscow*. London, 1949, 61. **472** " 'artistic snob-bishness' . . . "—*Ibid.*, 72. **472** " 'Any listener will realize' . . . "—*Ibid.*, 83. **473** " 'Meeting upon meeting' . . . "—Shostakovich, 146. **473** " 'The attitude toward Prokofiev's music at that time' . . . "—Richter, 467. **474** " 'but have no basis in fact' . . . "—Schwarz, 218. **474** "He did send a letter . . . " and " 'The Resolution is valuable precisely in that' . . . " and " 'clear melodies and a harmonic lan-guage' . . . "—*Sovetskaia muzyka*, No. 1, 1948, 66–67. **474** Sources for the account of Lina's arrest include interviews with Prokofiev's acquaintances and colleagues in Moscow, interviews with Lina and Oleg Prokofiev, interviews with the staff at the U.S. Embassy in Moscow, and the version given by Galina Vishnevskaya in *Galina* (156).

CHAPTER 24

478 " 'Sergei Prokofiev's fate and art' . . . "—Ilya Ehrenburg, "On umel slushat' vremia" ("He Could Hear the Time"), MDV, 479. **478** "The musical model he was following . . . "—*Sovetskaia muzyka*, No. 1, 1948, 66. **480** " 'failing to convey a real sense of the people's life' . . . "—Nestyev, 404. **480** " 'As I was listening, I couldn't even recognize' . . . '—Samosud, 151. **481** "Kabalevsky went to console Prokofiev . . . "—Kabalevsky, 422. **481** " 'Formalism still lives in the music' . . . "—Schwarz, 229. **481** " 'had no decision-making power' . . . "—Samosud, 151. **482** " 'Don't despair after these failures' . . . "—P-Alpers, 434. **482** "In his account of their collaboration . . . "—Lavrovsky, 521. **482** "according to dates on the man-uscript score . . . "—P-Alpers, 443. **482** " 'Voices were raised sharply criticiz-ing' . . . " and " 'Why write ballets?' . . . "—Lavrovsky, 524. **485** " 'Good day, sir,' . . . "—Mstislav Rostropovich, "Vstrechi s S. S. Prokof'evym" ("Meetings with S. S. Prokofiev"), MDV, 471. **485** " 'tried to be like him in everything' . . . "—Vishnevskaya, 154. **485** " 'Man—that has a proud sound' . . . "—V. Blok, *Vio-lonchel'noe tvorchestvo Prokof'eva (Prokofiev's Works for Cello)*. Moscow, 1973, 45. **486** " 'my health is almost completely in order' . . . "—P-Alpers, 436. **486** " 'as insulted as it could possibly be. . . . All this didn't fit at all' . . . "—Richter, 468. **486** "Even so, he maintained the same strict schedule . . . "—Rostropovich, 477–78. **487** "Prokofiev was too sick . . . "—PM, 478. **488** " 'My health is behaving itself nicely' . . . "—P-Alpers, 439. **488** " 'It's a bright, simple, even intimate sonata' . . . "—Richter, 468. **488** "The history of the Sinfonia Concertante . . . "—Rostropovich gave the premiere of the Second Cello Concerto on February 18, 1952, in the Great Hall of the Moscow Conservatory, with Sviatoslav Richter conducting, and the premiere of the Sinfonia Concertante in 1954. Prokofiev was so inspired by his collaboration with Rostropovich that he began several other pieces for cello in 1952, both left unfinished at the time of his death: a Concertino for Cello for Orchestra and a Sonata for Unaccompanied Cello. **490** " 'But isn't the music too sim-ple?' . . . "—Kabalevsky, MDV, 423. **490** " 'a retrogression and not a step for-ward' . . . "—Olin Downes, NYT, April 22 and 26, 1953. **490** " 'As I work, I remember' . . . "—S. Prokofiev, "Vstrecha Volgi s Donom" ("The Meeting of the

Volga and the Don"), MDV, 257. **491** " 'strict to the point of severity' . . . " and " 'I don't think it is acceptable' . . . " and " 'At midnight we raised our glasses' . . . "— Mira Mendelson-Prokofiev, "Final Days," 283–85. **492** " 'deeply disappointed him' . . . " and " 'When I would ask him' . . . "—*Ibid.*, 287–88. **493** " 'Forgetting myself, I instinctively took hold' . . . " and " 'Sergei Sergeevich was still conscious' . . . "—*Ibid.*, 291–92.

APPENDIX I

SERGEI PROKOFIEV:

A CHRONOLOGY

1891   Born April 11 (April 23, New Style) at Sontsovka in the Ukraine
1900   JANUARY: first trip to Moscow and first introduction to opera
First opera, *The Giant*, composed
1901   DECEMBER: first trip to St. Petersburg
1902   JANUARY: introduced to Sergei Taneev in Moscow and begins serious study of music
SUMMER: begins intensive study at Sontsovka with Reinhold Glière
1904   AUGUST: moves with his mother to St. Petersburg and enrolls in the Conservatory
1905   Revolution of 1905 disrupts academic life at the Conservatory
1906   Begins study of instrumentation with Rimsky-Korsakov and meets Nikolai Miaskovsky
1908   Writes first symphony and piano pieces Op. 4, including "Suggestion diabolique"
DECEMBER 18: public debut at the Evenings of Contemporary Music with Op. 4 pieces
1909   Completes undergraduate studies at the Conservatory and begins graduate study
Diaghilev's Ballets Russes presents its first ballet, Nikolai Tcherepnin's *Le Pavillon d'Armide*, in Paris
Composes Op. 2 Etudes, Op. 5 Sinfonietta and First Piano Sonata
1910   FEBRUARY 21: Moscow debut and world premiere of First Piano Sonata
JULY 23: Prokofiev's father dies
Composes "Autumn" and "Dreams"
1911   Jurgenson publishes First Piano Sonata
Begins writing First Piano Concerto and *Maddalena*
1912   JULY 25: Performs world premiere of First Piano Concerto in Moscow
Writes Second Piano Sonata, Op. 11 Toccata and "Ballade" for Cello and Piano

1913   First trip to Europe; sees Ballets Russes perform in Paris
        Writes Op. 12 pieces and Second Piano Concerto
        AUGUST 23: Scandalous premiere of Second Piano Concerto at Pavlovsk

1914   Graduates from the Conservatory, winning the piano competition
        Travels to Europe and meets Diaghilev in London; Diaghilev commissions the ballet *Ala and Lolly* ("The Scythian Suite")
        Writes "The Ugly Duckling" and completes *"Sarcasmes"*
        World War I begins

1915   MARCH: travels to Rome to confer with Diaghilev, who commissions *The Buffoon*
        Composes *The Buffoon* and Op. 23 songs, completes "The Scythian Suite" and begins *The Gambler*

1916   JANUARY 16: premiere of "The Scythian Suite" in Petrograd
        Meets Meyerhold
        Composes Akhmatova songs (Op. 27)

1917   FEBRUARY: February Revolution ends Tsarist Rule and Provisional Government is established
        Completes *The Gambler*, "Classical" Symphony, First Violin Concerto, "Fugitive Visions," Piano Sonatas Nos. 3 and 4, and *Seven, They Are Seven*
        OCTOBER 25: October Revolution overthrows Provisional Government and Soviet state is established

1918   MARCH: the Soviet army withdraws from World War I
        APRIL: conducts premiere of "Classical" Symphony (No. 1) in Petrograd
        MAY 7: leaves Petrograd
        SEPTEMBER: arrives in New York
        NOVEMBER 20: performs at Aeolian Hall
        Meets Carolina Codina
        Composes "Tales of an Old Grandmother" and Four Pieces Op. 32

1919   Composes Overture on Hebrew Themes and begins *Love for Three Oranges* for Chicago Opera; begins *The Fiery Angel*

1920   APRIL: travels to Europe, where he renews contact with Diaghilev, who helps him rewrite *The Buffoon*
        OCTOBER: returns to the United States

1921   Travels to Europe for premiere of *The Buffoon* in Paris on May 17
        SUMMER: in St. Brevin-les-Pins, where he composes Op. 36 songs and completes Third Piano Concerto
        OCTOBER: returns to United States
        DECEMBER: premieres of Third Piano Concerto and *Oranges* in Chicago

1922 MARCH: leaves America, moving to Ettal, in southern Germany
1923 Piano appearances around Europe
Composes Fifth Piano Sonata and rewrites Second Piano Concerto
SEPTEMBER 29: marries Lina Codina (Llubera) in Ettal
DECEMBER: they move permanently to Paris
1924 FEBRUARY: birth of Sviatoslav
Composes Quintet Op. 39 and Second Symphony
1925 JUNE 6: Koussevitsky conducts world premiere of Second Symphony
in Paris
Composes *Le Pas d'acier*
1926 JANUARY: tour of the United States
Composes Overture for Seventeen Performers (the "American" Overture)
1927 JANUARY–MARCH: tour of the U.S.S.R.
JUNE 7: Premiere in Paris of *Le Pas d'acier*
Completes *The Fiery Angel*; revises *The Gambler* with Meyerhold's
help
1928 Composes *"Choses en soi,"* Third Symphony and *Prodigal Son*
DECEMBER 14: birth of Oleg
1929 APRIL 29: world premiere of *The Gambler* in Brussels
MAY 21: world premiere of *Prodigal Son* in Paris
AUGUST 19: death of Diaghilev
Revises Sinfonietta (Op. 5/48) and completes Divertissement
OCTOBER–NOVEMBER: trip to U.S.S.R.
1930 JANUARY–MARCH: tour of United States
Completes Fourth Symphony, First String Quartet and *On the Dnepr*
1931 Completes Fourth Piano Concerto, "Four Portraits and Dénoument
from *The Gambler*" and Six Pieces Op. 52
1932 Completes Two Sonatinas Op. 54, Fifth Piano Concerto and Sonata
for Two Violins
NOVEMBER: two-week visit to U.S.S.R.; invited to write score for
Lt. Kizhe
DECEMBER 16: world premiere of *On the Dnepr* in Paris
DECEMBER–JANUARY: tour of the United States
1933 APRIL–JUNE: extended stay in U.S.S.R.; completes film score for
Lt. Kizhe
Completes "Symphonic Song"
OCTOBER–DECEMBER: in U.S.S.R.; composes score for *Egyptian
Nights*
1934 APRIL–JULY: in U.S.S.R.
Completes *Lt. Kizhe* Suite, *Egyptian Nights* Suite, "Thoughts" and
Op. 59 Pieces

NOVEMBER–DECEMBER: in U.S.S.R.

1935 MARCH–OCTOBER: in U.S.S.R.
Composes piano score of *Romeo and Juliet*, Second Violin Concerto, "Music for Children" and Op. 66 songs
NOVEMBER–DECEMBER: tour of Spain, Portugal and North Africa with violinist Robert Soetens
DECEMBER: returns to Moscow to take up permanent residence there

1936 JANUARY–MARCH: tour of Europe
MAY: Lina Prokofiev moves to Moscow with their sons
Completes *Peter and the Wolf*, film score for *The Queen of Spades*, incidental music for Meyerhold's *Boris Godunov*, incidental music for *Eugene Onegin*, Russian Overture, Op. 73 Pushkin songs and *Romeo and Juliet* Suites
NOVEMBER–DECEMBER: tour of Europe

1937 JANUARY–FEBRUARY: tour of United States
Completes *Cantata for the Twentieth Anniversary of October* and *Songs of Our Days*

1938 JANUARY–APRIL: final tour abroad, to Europe and United States
Completes incidental music for *Hamlet*, film score for *Alexander Nevsky* and First Cello Concerto

1939 Completes *Alexander Nevsky* Cantata, *Semyon Kotko* and *Zdravitsa*
JUNE 20: Meyerhold arrested
Meets Mira Mendelson in Kislovodsk

1940 JANUARY 11: Soviet premiere of *Romeo and Juliet* at Kirov Theater in Leningrad
JUNE 23: world premiere of *Semyon Kotko* in Moscow
Completes Sixth Piano Sonata and *Betrothal in a Monastery*

1941 MARCH: begins living with Mira Mendelson
JUNE: Hitler's army invades U.S.S.R.
Sets aside *Cinderella* and begins *War and Peace*
AUGUST: evacuated with Mira to Nalchik
Completes Second String Quartet
DECEMBER: evacuated to Tbilisi

1942 JANUARY–MAY: in Tbilisi, where he completes first version of *War and Peace* and Seventh Piano Sonata
MAY: travels to Alma-Ata to work with Eisenstein on *Ivan the Terrible*
MAY–DECEMBER: in Alma-Ata; completes film scores for *Tonya*, *Kotovsky* and *Partisans in the Ukrainian Steppe*

1943 JANUARY–FEBRUARY: in Moscow
FEBRUARY–JUNE: in Alma-Ata; revises *War and Peace* and continues work on *Ivan*
MARCH: receives Stalin Prize (Second Class) for Seventh Piano Sonata

JUNE–OCTOBER: in Perm, where he completes most of *Cinderella* in piano score, and Flute Sonata

OCTOBER: returns permanently to Moscow

1944 Completes Second Violin Sonata (Op. 94-bis), Eighth Piano Sonata and Fifth Symphony

Premiere of Eisenstein's *Ivan the Terrible*, Part I

1945 JANUARY 13: world premiere of Fifth Symphony in Moscow

LATE JANUARY: Prokofiev falls, suffers a concussion and is hospitalized

MAY 8: German command surrenders

NOVEMBER 21: world premiere of *Cinderella* at Bolshoi Theater in Moscow

1946 JANUARY: Prokofiev receives Stalin Prizes for Fifth Symphony, Eighth Piano Sonata and Part I of *Ivan the Terrible*

JUNE 12: premiere of Part I of two-evening revised version of *War and Peace* at the Maly Theater in Leningrad

Settles in Nikolina Gora

Completes First Violin Sonata (Op. 80)

NOVEMBER 3: world premiere of *Betrothal in a Monastery* at Kirov Theater

1947 JULY: premiere of Part II of *War and Peace* at Maly Theatre is canceled

Completes Ninth Piano Sonata, Sonata for Solo Violin and Sixth Symphony

1948 JANUARY 13: marries Mira Mendelson

JANUARY–FEBRUARY: Soviet government launches harsh ideological attack on composers, including Prokofiev

LATE FEBRUARY: arrest of Lina Prokofiev

Completes *Story of a Real Man*

1949 Completes Cello Sonata

1950 Completes first version of *The Stone Flower*

1952 Completes Sinfonia Concertante and Seventh Symphony

1953 Dies on March 5

APPENDIX II

CATALOGUE OF

PROKOFIEV'S WORKS

(BY GENRE)

The catalogue includes only finished mature works. Dates are for premieres. Dates for Russian premieres before February 1, 1918, are Old Style.

I. DRAMATIC MUSIC
(Dates are for first staged performance.)

A. OPERAS

Maddalena. Op. 13. Composed 1911–13; only the first scene was orchestrated. Libretto by Magda Liven and Prokofiev, from Liven's play. Graz, Austria, November 28, 1981. (Orchestration realized by E. Downes.)

The Gambler. Op. 24. Composed 1915–17; revised 1927–28. Libretto by Prokofiev, from the novel by Dostoevsky. Brussels, April 29, 1929.

Love for Three Oranges. Op. 33. Composed 1919. Libretto by Prokofiev, from Vsevolod Meyerhold's adaptation of a play by Carlo Gozzi. Chicago, December 30, 1921.

The Fiery Angel. Op. 37. Composed 1919–27. Libretto by Prokofiev, from the novel by Valery Bryusov. Venice, September, 1955.

Semyon Kotko. Op. 81. Composed 1939. Libretto by Prokofiev and Valentin Kataev, from Kataev's novel *I Am a Son of the Working People*. Moscow, June 23, 1940.

Betrothal in a Monastery. Op. 86. Composed 1940–41. Libretto by Prokofiev, with verses by Mira Mendelson-Prokofiev, from the play *The Duenna* by Richard Brinsley Sheridan. Leningrad, November 3, 1946.

War and Peace. Op. 91. Composed 1941–52. Libretto by Prokofiev and Mira

Mendelson-Prokofiev, from the novel by Leo Tolstoy. Moscow, November 8, 1957. (Revised performing version in thirteen scenes.)

Story of a Real Man. Op. 117. Composed 1947–48. Libretto by Prokofiev and Mira Mendelson-Prokofiev, from the novel by Boris Polevoy. Moscow, October 8, 1960.

B. Ballets

The Buffoon (Chout). Op. 21. Composed 1915; revised 1920. Scenario by Prokofiev from folktales by Alexander Afanasiev. Paris, May 17, 1921.

Trapeze. (no opus no; music used in Quintet Op. 39.) Composed 1924. Scenario by Boris Romanov.

Le Pas d'acier. Op. 41. Composed 1925–26. Scenario by Prokofiev and Georgi Yakoulov. Paris, June 7, 1927.

Prodigal Son. Op. 46. Composed 1928–29. Scenario by Boris Kochno, from the Gospel of St. Luke. Paris, May 21, 1929.

On the Dnepr (Sur le Borysthène). Op. 51. Composed 1930–31. Scenario by Prokofiev and Serge Lifar. Paris, December 16, 1932.

Romeo and Juliet. Op. 64. Composed 1935–36. Scenario by Prokofiev, Sergei Radlov, Adrian Piotrovsky and Leonid Lavrovsky, from the tragedy by William Shakespeare. Brno, Czechoslovakia, December 30, 1938. (Leningrad, January 11, 1940.)

Cinderella. Op. 87. Composed 1940–44. Scenario by Prokofiev and Nikolai Volkov. Moscow, November 21, 1945.

The Stone Flower. Op. 118. Composed 1948–53. Scenario by Mira Mendelson-Prokofiev and Leonid Lavrovsky. Moscow, February 12, 1954.

C. Incidental music for dramatic productions

Egyptian Nights. (no opus no.) Composed in 1933–34 for Tairov's production at the Moscow Chamber Theater, which opened in December 1934.

Boris Godunov. Op. 70-bis. Composed in 1936 for Meyerhold's production of Pushkin's tragedy, which was never staged.

Eugene Onegin. Op. 71. Composed in 1936 for Tairov's dramatization of Pushkin's novel at the Moscow Chamber Theater; never staged.

Hamlet. Op. 77. Composed in 1937–38 for Sergei Radlov's production of Shakespeare's tragedy; opened on May 15, 1938, in Leningrad.

II. FILM SCORES

Lt. Kizhe. (no opus no.) Composed in 1933 for the film directed by Alexander Faintsimmer.

The Queen of Spades. Op. 70. Composed in 1936 for the film directed (and left unfinished) by Mikhail Romm.

Alexander Nevsky. (no opus no.) Composed in 1938 for the film directed by Sergei Eisenstein.

Lermontov. (no opus no.) Composed in 1941–42 for the film directed by Alexander Gendelstein. Unfinished.

Tonya. (no opus no.) Composed in 1942 for the film directed by Abram Room.

Kotovsky. (no opus no.) Composed in 1942 for the film directed by Alexander Faintsimmer.

Partisans in the Ukrainian Steppe. (no opus no.) Composed in 1942 for the film directed by Igor Savchenko.

Ivan the Terrible. Op. 116. Composed in 1942–46 for the film (in two parts) directed by Sergei Eisenstein.

III. MUSIC FOR SYMPHONIC ORCHESTRA

A. SYMPHONIES AND SINFONIETTAS

Sinfonietta in A Major. Op. 5. Composed 1909; revised 1914–15. Petrograd, October 24, 1915.

Symphony No. 1 ("Classical") in D Major. Op. 25. Composed 1916–17. Petrograd, April 2, 1918.

Symphony No. 2 in D Minor. Op. 40. Composed 1924–25. Paris, June 6, 1925.

Symphony No. 3 in C Minor. Op. 44. Composed 1928. Paris, May 17, 1929.

Sinfonietta in A Major. Op. 48. (Revision of Op. 5.) Composed 1929. Moscow, November 18, 1930.

Symphony No. 4 in C. Major. Op. 47. Composed 1930. Boston, November 14, 1930.

Symphony No. 5 in B flat Major. Op. 100. Composed 1944. Moscow, January 13, 1945.

Symphony No. 6 in E flat Minor. Op. 111. Composed 1945–47. Leningrad, October 11, 1947.

Symphony No. 4 in C Major. Op. 112. (Revised version of Op. 47.) Composed 1947.

Symphony No. 7 in C sharp Minor. Op. 131. Composed 1951–52. Moscow, October 11, 1952.

B. CONCERTOS

Concerto No. 1 for Piano and Orchestra in D flat Major. Op. 10. Composed 1911–12. Moscow, July 15, 1912.

Concerto No. 2 for Piano and Orchestra in G Minor. Op. 16. Composed

1913; revised 1923. Pavlovsk, August 23, 1913. Paris, May 8, 1924.

Concerto No. 1 for Violin and Orchestra in D Major. Op. 19. Composed 1916–17. Paris, October 18, 1923.

Concerto No. 3 for Piano and Orchestra in C Major. Op. 26. Composed 1917–21. Chicago, December 16, 1921.

Concerto No. 4 for Piano and Orchestra in B flat Major, for the left hand. Op. 53. Composed 1931. West Berlin, September 5, 1956.

Concerto No. 5 for Piano and Orchestra in G Major. Op. 55. Composed 1932. Berlin, October 31, 1932.

Concerto No. 2 for Violin and Orchestra in G Minor. Op. 63. Composed 1935. Madrid, December 1, 1935.

Concerto for Cello and Orchestra in E Minor. Op. 58. Composed 1933–38. Moscow, November 26, 1938.

Sinfonia Concertante for Cello and Orchestra in E Minor. Op. 125. Composed 1950–52. Copenhagen, December 9, 1954. (Based on material from Op. 58, this piece was briefly called the Concerto No. 2 for Cello and Orchestra, and was premiered in Moscow on February 18, 1952. Prokofiev then made further revisions and assigned the definitive title Sinfonia Concertante.)

C. Suites

"Ala and Lolly, The Scythian Suite" for large symphonic orchestra. (Arranged from music originally written for the unproduced ballet *Ala and Lolly*.) Op. 20. Composed 1914–15. Petrograd, January 16, 1916.

The Buffoon (Chout). Suite from the ballet. Op. 21-bis. Composed 1922. Brussels, January 15, 1924.

Love for Three Oranges. Suite from the opera. Op. 33-bis. Composed 1924. Paris, November 29, 1925.

Le Pas d'acier. Suite from the ballet. Op. 41-bis. Composed 1926. Moscow, May 27, 1928.

Prodigal Son. Suite from the ballet. Op. 46-bis. Composed 1929. Paris, March 7, 1931.

"Four Portraits and the Denouement from *The Gambler*," a symphonic suite for large orchestra. Op. 49. Composed 1931. Paris, March 12, 1932.

On the Dnepr. Suite from the ballet. Op. 51-bis. Composed 1933. Paris, 1934.

Lt. Kizhe. Suite from the film score. Op. 60. Composed 1934. Moscow, December 21, 1934 (radio performance).

Egyptian Nights. From the incidental music to the play. Op. 61. Composed 1934. Moscow, December 21, 1934 (radio performance).

Romeo and Juliet. First Suite from the ballet. Op. 64-bis. Composed 1936. Moscow, November 24, 1936.

Romeo and Juliet. Second Suite from the ballet. Op. 64-ter. Composed 1936. Leningrad, April 15, 1937.

A Summer Day, a children's suite for small orchestra. Op. 65-bis. Composed 1941. Moscow, 1946.

Semyon Kotko. Suite from the opera. Op. 81-bis. Composed 1941. Moscow, June 23, 1940.

The Year 1941, a symphonic suite for large orchestra. Op. 90. Composed 1941. Sverdlovsk, January 21, 1943.

Romeo and Juliet. Third Suite from the ballet. Op. 101. Composed 1946. Moscow, March 8, 1946.

Cinderella. First Suite from the ballet. Op. 107. Composed 1946. Moscow, November 12, 1946.

Cinderella. Second Suite from the ballet. Op. 108. Composed 1946.

Cinderella. Third Suite from the ballet. Op. 109. Composed 1946. Moscow, September 3, 1947 (radio performance).

Waltzes, a suite for symphonic orchestra. Op. 110. Composed 1946. Moscow, May 13, 1947.

Summer Night, a symphonic suite from the opera *Betrothal in a Monastery*. Op. 123. Composed 1950.

The Stone Flower, Wedding Suite from the ballet for symphonic orchestra. Op. 126. Composed 1951. Moscow, December 12, 1951.

The Stone Flower, Gypsy Fantasy from the ballet for symphonic orchestra. Op. 127. Composed 1951. Moscow, November 18, 1951.

The Stone Flower, Ural Rhapsody from the ballet for symphonic orchestra. Op. 128. Composed 1951.

D. OVERTURES, POEMS, DIVERTISSEMENTS, ETC.

"Dreams," a symphonic tableau for large orchestra. Op. 6. Composed 1910. St. Petersburg, November 22, 1910.

"Autumn," a symphonic sketch for small symphonic orchestra. Op. 8. Composed 1910; revised 1915 and 1934. Moscow, July 19, 1911. Petrograd, October 8, 1916.

Andante from the Fourth Piano Sonata, a transcription by the composer for symphonic orchestra. Op. 29-bis. Composed 1934. February 13, 1958.

Overture on Hebrew Themes, a transcription by the composer for symphonic orchestra. Op. 34-bis. Composed 1934. Moscow, November 30, 1934.

Overture in B flat Major ("American"); version for large orchestra. Op. 42-bis. Composed 1928. Paris, December 18, 1930.

Divertissement for Orchestra. Op. 43. Composed 1925–29. Paris, December 22, 1929.

Andante from the First String Quartet, arranged by the author for string orchestra. Op. 50-bis. Composed 1930.

"Symphonic Song" for large orchestra. Op. 57. Composed 1933. April 14, 1934.

Peter and the Wolf, a Symphonic Fairy Tale for Children, for narrator and large symphonic orchestra. Text by Prokofiev. Op. 67. Composed 1936. Moscow, May 2, 1936.

Russian Overture for symphonic orchestra. Op. 72. (Two versions.) Composed 1936 and 1937. Moscow, October 29, 1936.

Symphonic March in B flat Major for large orchestra. Op. 88. Composed 1941.

Ode to the End of the War for eight harps, four pianos and an orchestra of woodwinds, percussion and contrabasses. Op. 105. Composed 1945. Moscow, November 12, 1945.

A Festive Poem ("Thirty Years") for symphonic orchestra. Op. 113. Composed 1947. Moscow, October 3, 1947.

Pushkin Waltzes for symphonic orchestra. Op. 120. Composed 1949. Moscow, 1952.

A Festive Poem—the Meeting of the Volga and the Don for symphonic orchestra. Op. 130. Composed 1951. Moscow, February 22, 1952.

IV. MUSIC FOR INSTRUMENTAL ENSEMBLES

"Humorous Scherzo" for four bassoons. Op. 12-bis. Composed 1915. (Arranged from the "Humorous Scherzo" for piano of Op. 12.) London, September 2, 1916.

"Ballade" for Cello and Piano. Op. 15. Composed 1912. Moscow, January 23, 1914.

Overture on Hebrew Themes in C Minor, for clarinet, two violins, viola, cello and piano. Op. 34. Composed 1919. New York, January 26, 1920.

Quintet in G Minor for oboe, clarinet, violin, viola and contrabass. Op. 39. (Written to be used as the score for the ballet *Trapeze*.) Composed 1924. Moscow, March 6, 1927.

Five Melodies for Violin and Piano. Op. 35-bis. Composed 1925. (Composer's transcription of Op. 35.)

String Quartet No. 1 in B Minor. Op. 50. Composed 1930. Washington, April 25, 1931.

Sonata for Two Violins in C Major. Op. 56. Composed 1932. Moscow, November 27, 1932.

Four Marches for brass band, Op. 69. Composed 1935–37.

Sonata No. 1 for Violin and Piano in F Minor. Op. 80. Composed 1938–46. Moscow, October 23, 1946.

String Quartet No. 2 in F Major ("On Kabardinian Themes"). Op. 92. Composed 1941. Moscow, September 5, 1942.

Sonata for Flute and Piano in D Major. Op. 94. Composed 1943. Moscow, December 7, 1943.

Sonata No. 2 for Violin and Piano in D Major (composer's transcription of the Flute Sonata Op. 94). Op. 94-bis. Composed 1944. Moscow, June 17, 1944.

Adagio from *Cinderella*, arranged for cello and piano. Op. 97-bis. Composed 1944. Moscow, April 19, 1944 (radio performance).

March for band in B flat Major. Op. 99. Composed 1943–44. Moscow, May 14, 1944.

Sonata for Cello and Piano in C Major. Op. 119. Composed 1949. Moscow, March 1, 1950.

V. VOCAL AND VOCAL-SYMPHONIC MUSIC

A. ORATORIOS, CANTATAS, CHORUSES AND SUITES

Two Poems of Konstantin Balmont for female chorus and orchestra. Op. 7. Composed 1909–10. Petersburg, 1910.

Seven, They Are Seven, cantata for dramatic tenor, mixed chorus and large symphonic orchestra. Text from a poem by Konstantin Balmont. Op. 30. Composed 1917–18; revised 1933. Paris, May 29, 1924.

Cantata for the Twentieth Anniversary of October, for symphonic orchestra, military orchestra, orchestra of accordions, orchestra of percussion instruments and two choruses. Texts by Marx, Lenin and Stalin. Op. 74. Composed 1936–37. Moscow, April 5, 1966.

Songs of Our Days, suite for soloists, mixed chorus and symphonic orchestra. Op. 76. Composed 1937. Moscow, January 5, 1938.

Alexander Nevsky, cantata for mezzo-soprano soloist, mixed chorus and orchestra. Text by Prokofiev and V. Lugovskoy. Op. 78. Composed 1939. May 17, 1939.

Zdravitsa ("Hail to Stalin"), cantata for mixed chorus accompanied by symphonic orchestra. Russian, Ukrainian, Belorussian, Mordovian and other folk texts. Op. 85. Composed 1939. Moscow, December 21, 1939.

Ballad of an Unknown Boy, cantata for soprano, tenor, chorus and orchestra. Text by Pavel Antokolsky. Op. 93. Composed 1942–43. Moscow, February 21, 1944.

Sketches for the Soviet national anthem and the hymn of the Russian Soviet Federated Socialist Republic. Op. 98. Composed 1943 and 1946.

Flourish, O Mighty Land, cantata for the thirtieth anniversary of the Great October Socialist Revolution for mixed chorus and orchestra. Text by Evgeny Dolmatovsky. Op. 114. Composed 1947. Moscow, November 12, 1947.

Winter Bonfire, suite for narrators, boys' chorus and symphonic orchestra.

Text by Samuil Marshak. Op. 122. Composed 1949–50. Moscow, December 19, 1950.

Soldiers' Marching Song. Text by V. Lugovskoy. Op. 121. Composed 1950.

On Guard for Peace, oratorio for mezzo soprano, narrators, mixed chorus, boys' chorus and symphonic orchestra. Text by Samuil Marshak. Op. 124. Composed 1950. Moscow, December 19, 1950.

B. VOICE AND PIANO

Two Poems of Aleksei Apukhtin and Konstantin Balmont for voice and piano. Op. 9. Composed 1910–11. St. Petersburg, March 17, 1914.

"The Ugly Duckling" for voice and piano. Based on the fairy tale by Hans Christian Andersen. Op. 18. Composed 1914. Petrograd, January 17, 1915. (Also exists in a second vocal-piano version with a narrower tessitura, and in a version for voice and orchestra.)

Five Poems for voice and piano. Words by Valentin Goryansky, Zinaida Gippius, Boris Verin, Konstantin Balmont and Nikolai Agnitsev. Op. 23. Composed 1915. Petrograd, November 27, 1916.

Five Poems of Anna Akhmatova for voice and piano. Op. 27. Composed 1916. Moscow, February 5, 1917.

Five Songs Without Words for voice and piano. Op. 35. Composed 1920. New York, March 27, 1921.

Five Poems of Konstantin Balmont for voice and piano. Op. 36. Composed 1921. Milan, May 1922.

Two songs from the film *Lt. Kizhe* arranged for voice and piano. Op. 60-bis. Composed 1934.

Six Songs for voice and piano. Op. 66. Composed 1935.

Three Children's Songs for voice and piano. Op. 68. Composed 1936–39.

Three Romances on words by Pushkin for voice and piano. Op. 73. Composed 1936. April 20, 1937 (radio performance).

Three Songs from the film *Alexander Nevsky*. Words by B. Lugovskoy. Op. 78-bis. Composed 1939.

Seven Songs for voice and piano. Op. 79. Composed 1939.

Seven Mass Songs for voice and piano. Op. 89. Composed 1941–42. Nalchik, November 1941.

Arrangements of Russian Folk Songs for voice and piano (two volumes with six songs in each). Folk texts. Op. 104. Composed 1944. Moscow, March 25, 1945.

Two Duets, arrangements of Russian folk songs for tenor and bass with piano. Op. 106. Composed 1945.

VI. MUSIC FOR SOLO PIANO

A. SONATAS AND SONATINAS

Sonata No. 1 in F Minor. Op. 1. Composed 1907; revised 1909. Moscow, February 21, 1910.

Sonata No. 2 in D Minor. Op. 14. Composed 1912. Moscow, January 23, 1914.

Sonata No. 3 in A Minor ("From Old Notebooks"). Op. 28. Composed 1907; revised 1917. Petrograd, April 15, 1918.

Sonata No. 4 in C Minor ("From Old Notebooks"). Op. 29. Composed 1908; revised 1917. Petrograd, April 17, 1918.

Sonata No. 5 in C Major. Op. 38. Composed 1923. Paris, March 9, 1924.

Two Sonatinas. No. 1 in E Minor and No. 2 in G Major. Op. 54. Composed 1931–32. London, April 17, 1932 (No. 2 only).

Sontata No. 6 in A Major. Op. 82. Composed 1939–40. Moscow, November 26, 1940.

Sonata No. 7 in B flat Major. Op. 83. Composed 1939–42. Moscow, January 18, 1943.

Sonata No. 8 in B flat Major. Op. 84. Composed 1939–44. Moscow, December 30, 1944.

Sonata No. 9 in C Major. Op. 103. Composed 1947. Moscow, April 21, 1951.

Sonata No. 5 in C Major. Op. 135. Composed 1952–53. Revised version of Op. 38. Alma-Ata, February 2, 1954.

B. OTHER PIANO WORKS

Four Études. Op. 2. Composed 1909. Moscow, February 21, 1910.

Four Pieces. Op. 3. Composed 1907–1908; revised 1911. St. Petersburg, December 18, 1908 (No. 1 only). St. Petersburg, March 28, 1911 (complete cycle).

Four Pieces. Op. 4. Composed 1908; revised 1910–12. St. Petersburg, December 18, 1908.

Toccata in C Major. Op. 11. Composed 1912. Petrograd, November 27, 1916.

Ten Pieces. Op. 12. Composed 1906–13; revised 1913. Moscow, January 23, 1914.

"Sarcasmes," five pieces for piano. Op. 17. Composed 1912–14. Petrograd, November 27, 1916.

"Fugitive Visions," twenty pieces for piano. Op. 22. Composed 1915–17. Petrograd, April 2, 1918.

"Tales of an Old Grandmother," four pieces for piano. Op. 31. Composed 1918. New York, January 7, 1919.

Four Pieces. Op. 32. Composed 1918. New York, March 30, 1919.

Schubert Waltzes, selected and arranged in a suite for two pianos in four hands. (no opus no.) Composed 1918–20 (?).

Organ Prelude and Fugue in D Minor by Buxtehude, arranged for piano. (no opus no.) Composed 1918–20 (?).

March and Scherzo from *Love for Three Oranges*, transcribed by the composer for piano. Op. 33-ter. Composed 1922 (?).

"Choses en soi," two pieces for piano. Op. 45. Composed 1928. New York, January 6, 1930.

Six Pieces. Op. 52. Composed 1930–31. Moscow, May 27, 1932.

Three Pieces. Op. 59. Composed 1933–34. Moscow, 1935.

"Thoughts," three pieces for piano. Op. 62. Composed 1933–34. Moscow, November 13, 1936.

"Music for Children, Twelve Easy Pieces for Piano." Op. 65. Composed 1935. Moscow, April 11, 1936.

Romeo and Juliet, ten pieces for piano. Op. 75. Composed 1937. Moscow, 1937.

Divertissement, arranged by the composer for piano. Op. 43-bis. Composed 1938.

Gavotte (No. 4) from the music for *Hamlet*, arranged for piano. Op. 77-bis. Composed 1938. Moscow, November 22, 1939.

Three Pieces from *Cinderella*, arranged for piano. Op. 95. Composed 1942.

Three Pieces. Op. 96. Composed 1941–42.

Ten Pieces from *Cinderella*, arranged for piano. Op. 97. Composed 1943.

Six Pieces from *Cinderella*, arranged for piano. Op. 102. Composed 1944.

VII. MUSIC FOR OTHER SOLO INSTRUMENTS

Sonata for Solo Violin (or violins in unison) in D Major. Op. 115. Composed 1947. Moscow, March 10, 1960.

SELECTED
BIBLIOGRAPHY

I . SOURCES IN RUSSIAN
(Cited according to Library of Congress transliteration system)

A. Primary sources: books and anthologies (including articles and reviews written by Prokofiev, and Prokofiev's correspondence)

Krasinskaia, F. A., and Starodubtseva, M. K., eds. *Avtografy S.S. Prokof'eva v fondakh Gosudarstvennogo tsentral'nogo muzeia muzykal'noi kul'tury im. M.I. Glinki*. Moscow: Sovetskii kompozitor, 1977. 132 pp.

Nest'ev, I.V., and Edel'man, G. Ia., eds. *Sergei Prokof'ev 1953–63: Stat'i i materialy*. Moscow, Sovetskii kompozitor, 1962. 383 pp. Revised edition with some additional material published as *Sergei Prokof'ev: Stat'i i materialy*. Moscow: Muzyka, 1965. 398 pp.

Nest'eva, M., ed. *S.S. Prokof'ev: Al'bom*. Moscow, Muzyka: 1981. 158 pp.

Prokof'ev, Sergei. *Avtobiografiia*. Moscow: Sovetskii kompozitor, 1973. 704 pp. (A slightly more complete edition of this childhood autobiography was published in 1982, including twenty short chapters previously unpublished.)

———, and Miaskovskii, Nikolai. *Perepiska*. Moscow: Sovetskii kompozitor, 1977. 599 pp.

Shlifshtein, S. I., ed. *Sergei Prokof'ev: Al'bom*. Moscow: Muzyka, 1965. 232 pp.

———, ed. *S.S. Prokof'ev: Materialy, dokumenty, vospominaniia*. Moscow: Gosudarstvennoe muzykal'noe izdatel'stvo, 1961. (Second edition; first edition published in 1956.) 707 pp.

B. Primary sources: articles in collections (including correspondence)

Nest'ev, I., ed. "Neizvestnye materialy o Prokof'eve: Ob odnoi prervannoi druzhbe." *Istoriia i sovremennost'; Sbornik statei*. (Letters to Vernon Duke.) Leningrad: Sovetskii kompozitor, 1981, pp. 239–60.

Prokof'ev, Sergei. "Iunye gody." *Leningradskaia konservatoriia v vospominaniiakh 1862–1962*. Leningrad: Gosudarstvennoe muzykal'noe izdatel'stvo, 1962, pp. 60–68.

————. "Muzyka v fil'me *Aleksandr Nevskii*," in *Sovetskii istoricheskii fil'm: Sornik statei*. Moscow: Goskinoizdat, 1939, pp. 26–29.

————. "Pis'ma S.S.Prokof'eva—B.V.Asaf'evu." *Iz proshlogo sovetskoi muzykal'noi kul'tury*, 2. M. G. Kozlova, ed. Moscow: Sovetskii kompozitor, 1976, pp. 4–54.

————. "Pis'ma S.S.Prokof'eva k V.V.Derzhanovskomu." *Iz arkhivov russkikh muzykantov*, A. I. Volkov, ed. Moscow: Gosudarstvennoe muzykal'noe izdatel'stvo, 1962, pp. 93–118.

————. "Perepiska S.S.Prokof'eva s L.M.Glagolevoi." *Pamiatniki kul'tury: Novye otkrytiia*, V.A. Khalif, ed. Leningrad: Nauka, 1979, pp. 227–32.

————. "Pis'ma k V.E. Meierkhol'du." *Muzykal'noe nasledstvo*, Vol. II, Part 2. K. N. Kirilenko and M. G. Kozlova, eds. Moscow: Muzyka, 1968, pp. 214–31.

————. "S.S.Prokof'ev pishet muzyku k fil'mu." *Muzykal'naia zhizn'*, No. 16, August 1983, pp. 18–19.

————, and Alpers, V. V. "Perepiska." *Muzykal'noe nasledstvo*, Vol. I. L. M. Kutateladze, ed. Moscow: Gosudarstvennoe muzykal'noe izdatel'stvo, 1962, pp. 422–44.

————, and Shostakovich, D. D. "Vsegda dorozhu vashim mneniem." *Vstrechi s proshlym*, 3. M. G. Kozlova, ed. Moscow: Sovetskaia Rossiia, 1978, pp. 253–59.

————, and Ziloti, A. I. "Perepiska A.I.Ziloti s S.S.Prokof'evym." *Aleksandr Il'ich Ziloti: Vospominaniia i pis'ma*. Leningrad: Gosudarstvennoe muzykal'noe izdatel'stvo, 1963, pp. 255–60.

C. Secondary sources: books and collections

Asaf'ev, Boris. *Kriticheskie stat'i, ocherki i retsenzii*. Leningrad: Muzyka, 1967. 300 pp.

Astrov, Anatolii. *S. A. Kusevitskii: Deiatel' russkoi muzykal'noi kul'tury*. Leningrad: Muzyka, 1981. 191 pp.

Bazhov, Pavel. *Malakhitovaia shkatulka*, Moscow: Gosudarstvennoe izdatel'stvo khudozhestvennoi literatury, 1954. 600 pp.

Berger, L., ed. *Cherty stilia S.Prokof'eva: Sbornik teoreticheskikh statei*. Moscow: Sovetskii kompozitor, 1962. 314 pp.

Birman, Serafima. *Sud'boi darovannye vstrechi*. Moscow: Iskusstvo, 1971. 356 pp.

Blok, V. *Metod tvorcheskoi raboty S.Prokof'eva: Issledovanie*. Moscow: Muzyka, 1979. 143 pp.

————. *Violonchel'noe tvorchestvo Prokof'eva*. Moscow: Muzyka, 1973. 184 pp.

————, ed. *S.S. Prokof'ev: Stat'i i issledovaniia*. Moscow: Muzyka, 1972. 333 pp.

Del'son, Viktor. *Fortepiannoe tvorchestvo i pianizm Prokof'eva*. Moscow: Sovetskii kompozitor, 1973. 287 pp.

Eizenshtein, S. M. *Izbrannye proizvedeniia v 6- itomakh*. Moscow: Iskusstvo, 1968.

Fevral'skii, A. V., and Vendrovskaia, L. D., eds. *Tvorcheskoe nasledie V.E. Meierkhol'da*. Moscow: VTO, 1978. 488 pp.

Glebov, Igor' (Boris Asaf'ev). *Sergei Prokof'ev*. Leningrad: Triton, 1927. 38 pp.

Karatygin, Viacheslav. *Izbrannye stat'i*. Moscow: Muzyka, 1965.

Katonova, Svetlana. *Muzyka sovetskogo baleta: Ocherki istorii i teorii*. Leningrad: Sovetskii kompozitor, 1980. 296 pp.

Kholopov, Iurii. *Sovermennye cherty garmonii Prokof'eva*. Moscow: Muzyka, 1967.

Kremlev, Iurii. *Esteticheskie vzgliady S.S. Prokof'eva*. Moscow: Muzyka, 1966. 154 pp.

Liven, Magda Gustavovna. *Astorre Trinchi, Veselyi tovarishch, Maddalena*. St. Petersburg: Tipografiia glavnogo upravleniia udelov, 1905. 118 pp.

Martynov, Ivan. *Sergei Prokof'ev: Zhizn' i tvorchestvo*. Moscow: Muzyka, 1974. 559 pp.

Meierkhol'd, V. E. *V.E. Meierkhol'd: Stat'i, pis'ma, rechi, besedy 1917–1939*. A.V. Fevral'skii, ed. Moscow: Iskusstvo, 1968. 2 volumes.

———. *Perepiska V.E. Meierkhol'da 1896–1939*. Korshunova and Sitkovetskaia, eds. Moscow: Iskusstvo, 1976.

Morozov, Sergei Aleksandrovich. *Prokof'ev*. Moscow: Molodaia gvardiia, 1967. 278 pp.

Nest'ev, I. *Zhizn' Sergeia Prokof'eva*. Moscow: Sovetskii kompozitor, 1973. 662 pp. (Revised edition of the original 1957 version.)

Rogozhina, Nina. *Romansy i pesni S.S. Prokof'eva*. Moscow: Sovetskii kompozitor, 1971. 198 pp.

Roziner, Feliks. *Tokkata zhizni: Muzykovedcheskoe povestvovanie*. Moscow: Molodaia gvardiia, 1978. 205 pp.

Sabinina, Marina. *"Semen Kotko" i problemy opernoi dramaturgii Prokof'eva*. Moscow: Sovetskii kompozitor, 1963. 292 pp.

Savkina, N. P. *Sergei Sergeevich Prokof'ev*. Moscow: Muzyka, 1982. 143 pp.

Shlifshtein, S. I. *S.S. Prokof'ev: Notograficheskii spravochnik*. Moscow: Sovetskii kompozitor, 1962.

Tarakanov, Mikhail. *Stil' simfonii Prokof'eva*. Moscow: Muzyka, 1968.

Vasilenko, Sergei. *Balety Prokof'eva*. Leningrad: Muzyka, 1965.

Volkov, Anatolii. *"Voina i mir" Prokof'eva: Opyt analyza variantov opery*. Moscow: Muzyka, 1976. 134 pp.

Zil'bershtein, I. S., and Samkov, V. A., eds. *Sergei Diagilev i russkoe iskusstvo*. Vols. I & II. Moscow: Izobrazitel'noe iskusstvo, 1982.

D. Secondary sources: articles

Berezkin, Vladimir. "Na puti k Prokof'evu." *Sovetskaia muzyka*, no. 9 (Sept.) 1973, pp. 40–46.

Boganova, T. V. "O russkikh traditsiiakh v tvorchestve Prokof'eva." *Sovetskaia muzyka*, No. 8, 1959, pp. 76–83.

Dan'ko. Larissa. "Redaktsii *Duen'i*." *Sovetskaia muzyka*, No. 25, 1961, pp. 37–41.

Eizenshtein, S. M. *"Aleksandr Nevskii,"* in *Sovetskii istoricheskii fil'm: Sbornik statei*. Moscow: Goskinoizdat, 1939, pp. 14–25.

Gromov, V. "Zamysel postanovki," in *Tvorcheskoe nasledie V.E. Meierkhol'da*. Moscow: VTO, 1978, pp. 353–401.

Iarustovskii, Boris. "*Igrok:* Tragediia-satira." Part I in *Sovetskaia muzyka*, April 1970, pp. 103–14; Part II in *Sovetskaia muzyka*, June 1970, pp. 64–76.

———. "Prokof'ev i teatr." *Sovetskaia muzyka*, No. 4, 1961, pp. 66–80.

Krivosheina, N. A. (née Meshcherskaia). "Sergei Prokof'ev," in *Chetyre treti nashei zhizni*. Paris: YMCA-Press, 1984, pp. 53–64.

Lamm, Ol'ga. "Druz'ia Pavla Aleksandrovicha Lamma i uchastniki muzykal'nykh vecherov v ego dome (20-e gody XX veka)," in *Iz proshlogo sovetskoi muzykal'noi kul'tury*, 1. Moscow: Sovetskii kompozitor, 1975, pp. 72–103.

———. "Druz'ia Pavla Aleksandrovicha Lamma. V evakuatsii (1941–43)," in *Iz proshlogo sovetskoi muzykal'noi kul'tury*, 2. Moscow: Sovetskii kompozitor, 1976, pp. 99–109.

Mendel'son, Mira. "V Alma-Ate." *Sovetskaia muzyka*, No. 8, 1962.

———. "Iz vospominanii." *Sovetskaia muzyka*, No. 3, 1963.

Nest'ev, I. "O stile S. Prokof'eva." *Sovetskaia muzyka*, No. 4, 1946, pp. 10–26.

———. "V obshchenii s sovremennikami." *Sovetskaia muzyka*, No. 4, 1967, pp. 77–85.

Ordzhonikidze, Givi. "Prokof'ev v GABTe." *Sovetskaia muzyka*, No. 10, 1974, pp. 27–36.

Pokrovskii, Boris. "V rabote nad *Voinoi i mirom*." *Sovetskaia muzyka*, No. 4, 1966, pp. 55–58.

Rummel, I. "Iz istorii *Poruchika Kizhe*." *Sovetskaia muzyka*, No. 11, 1964, pp. 67–70.

Sabinina, Marina. "Ob opere, kotoraia ne byla napisana." *Sovetskaia muzyka*, No. 8, 1962, pp. 41–48.

Spadavekkiia, A. "Vstrechi s Prokof'evym." *Sovetskaia muzyka*, No. 3, 1958, pp. 59–64.

Vishnevetskaia, E. "Kinomuzyka S.S.Prokof'eva voennykh let," in *Iz proshlogo sovetskoi muzykal'noi kul'tury*, 1. Moscow: Sovetskii kompozitor, 1975, pp. 35–71.

Volkov, Anatolii. "Ob opernoi forme u Prokof'eva," in *Muzyka i sovremennost'*, 5. Moscow: Muzyka, 1966, pp. 74–117.

II. SOURCES IN ENGLISH

A. Primary sources: books and anthologies

Blok, Vladimir, ed. *Sergei Prokofiev: Materials, Articles, Interviews*. Moscow: Progress Publishers, 1978. 257 pp.

Prokofiev, Sergei. *Prokofiev by Prokofiev: A Composer's Memoir*. Edited by David H. Appel and translated by Guy Daniels. New York: Doubleday & Co., 1979. 370 pp. (Edited version of the 1973 Soviet *Avtobiografiia*.)

Shlifshtein, S., ed. *S. Prokofiev: Autobiography, Articles, Reminiscences*. Moscow: Foreign Lanugages Publishing House. 334 pp.

Savkina, Natalia. *Prokofiev*. Translated by Catherine Young. Neptune City, N.J.: Paganiniana Publications, Inc., 1984. 175 pp. (Translation of Savkina's *Sergei Sergeevich Prokof'ev*, with reproduced photographs and original documents.)

B. Primary sources: articles

Brown, Malcolm Hamrick, ed. "Prokofiev's Correspondence with Stravinsky and Shostakovich," in *Essays for Gerald Abraham*. Translated by Natalia Rodriguez and Malcolm Brown. Ann Arbor: UMI, 1985, pp. 272–92.

Prokofiev, Sergei. "I Shall be Classical in the Next Generation." *Europe, An American Monthly*, Vol. II, No. 4 (1936), p. 20.

C. Secondary sources: books

Balanchine, George. *Choreography by George Balanchine: A Catalogue of Works*. New York: Viking, 1984. 423 pp.

Brown, Malcolm. *The Symphonies of Sergei Prokofiev*. Unpublished dissertation, Florida State University, 1967. 518 pp. Available through University Microfilms International, Ann Arbor, Mich.

Buckle, Richard. *Diaghilev*. London: Weidenfeld and Nicolson,1979. 616 pp.

Braun, Edward. *Meyerhold on Theatre*. New York: Hill and Wang, 1969. 336 pp.

Duke, Vernon. *Passport to Paris*. Boston: Little, Brown & Co., 1955. 502 pp.

Evans, Robert Kenneth. *The Early Songs of Sergei Prokofiev and Their Relation to the Synthesis of the Arts in Russia, 1890–1922*. Unpublished dissertation, Ohio State University, 1971. 296 pp.

Hanson, Lawrence and Elisabeth. *Prokofiev: The Prodigal Son*. London: Cassell, 1964. 243 pp.

Haskell, Arnold. *Diaghilev, His Artistic and Private Life*. London: Gollancz, 1935.

Kochno, Boris. *Diaghilev and the Ballets Russes*. New York: Harper and Row, 1970.

Krebs, Stanley Dale. *Soviet Composers and the Development of Soviet Music*. London: Allen and Unwin, 1970. 364 pp.

Leyda, Jay. *Kino: A History of the Russian and Soviet Film*. New York: Macmillan, 1960. 491 pp.

————, ed. *Eisenstein: Three Films*. Translated by Diana Matias. New York: Harper & Row, 1974. 189 pp.

Macdonald, Nesta. *Diaghilev Observed by Critics in England and the United States 1911–1929*. New York: Dance Horizons, 1975. 400 pp.

Massine, Leonid. *My Life in Ballet*. London: Macmillan, 1968.

Nabokov, Nicolas. *Old Friends and New Music*. Boston: Little, Brown & Co., 1951.

Nestyev, Israel. *Prokofiev*. Translated by Florence Jonas. Stanford: Stanford University Press, 1960. 528 pp. (Translation of the 1957 Soviet edition.)

Percival, John. *The World of Diaghilev*. New York: Harmony Books, 1971. 144 pp.

Riasanovsky, Nicholas V. *A History of Russia*. New York: Oxford University Press, 1969. 748 pp.

Rimsky-Korsakov, Nikolay Andreyevich. *My Musical Life*. Translated by Judah A. Joffe. London: Eulenburg Books, 1974. 480 pp.

Robinson, Harlow. *The Operas of Sergei Prokofiev and their Russian Literary Sources*. Unpublished dissertation, University of California, Berkeley, 1980. 424 pp. Available through University Microfilms International, Ann Arbor, Mich.

Samuel, Claude. *Prokofiev*. Translated from the French by Miriam John. London: Calder and Boyars, 1971. 191 pp.

Schmidt, Paul, ed. *Meyerhold at Work*. Austin: University of Texas Press, 1980. 241 pp.

Schwarz, Boris. *Music and Musical Life in Soviet Russia*. Bloomington: Indiana University Press, 1983. 722 pp.

Seroff, Victor. *Sergei Prokofiev: A Soviet Tragedy*. London: Frewin, 1969. 384 pp.

Seton, Marie. *Sergei M. Eisenstein: a Biography*. London: Bodley Head, 1952.

Stravinsky, Igor. *An Autobiography*. New York: Norton, 1936. 176 pp.

————, and Craft, Robert. *Memories and Commentaries*. Berkeley: University of California Press, 1959.

Struve, Gleb. *Russian Literature under Lenin and Stalin 1917–1953*. Norman: University of Oklahoma Press, 1971. 454 pp.

Swallow, Norman. *Eisenstein: A Documentary Portrait*. New York: Dutton, 1977.

Taper, Bernard. *Balanchine: A Biography*. New York: Times Books, 1984. 437 pp.

Volkov, Solomon, ed., with Shostakovich, Dmitri. *Testimony: The Memoirs of Dmitri Shostakovich*. Translated by Antonina W. Bouis. New York: Harper & Row, 1979. 289 pp.

Werth, Alexander. *Musical Uproar in Moscow*. London: Turnstile Press, 1949.

D. Secondary sources: articles

Abraham, Gerald. "Prokofiev as a Soviet Composer." *The Music Review*, No. 3 (1942), p. 241+.

Belaiev, Victor. "Prokofieff in the U.S.S.R." *Christian Science Monitor*, April 9, 1927.

Brown, Malcolm. "Prokofiev's *War and Peace*." *Musical Quarterly*, July 1977, pp. 297–326.

Cooper, Martin. "Playboy or Prodigal." *The Listener*, February 16, 1961.

"Composer, Soviet-Style." Cover story on Prokofiev in *Time*, Vol. 66, No. 21 (November 19, 1945), p. 57+.

Downes, Olin. "Koussevitsky as a Magnetic Personality—Prokofieff and the Powers of Evil." *The New York Times*, June 15, 1924, Section VII, p. 5.

Layton, Robert. "*War and Peace* in London." *Tempo*, December 1972, pp. 50–51.

Lloyd-Jones, David. "Prokofiev and the Opera." *Opera*, August 1962, p. 513.

Lockspeiser, Edward. "The Unknown Prokofiev." *The Listener*, October 22, 1953.

McAllister, Rita. "Sergey Prokofiev," in Stanley Sadie, ed., *The New Grove Dictionary of Music and Musicians*. London: Macmillan, 1980. vol. 15, pp. 288–301. (Includes catalogue of works and bibliography.)

————. "Prokofiev's Early Opera *Maddalena*." *Proceedings of the Royal Music Association*, No. 96 (1969–70), pp. 137–47.

————. "Prokofiev's *Maddalena:* A Premiere." *Musical Times*, March 1979, pp. 205–206.

Mitchell, Donald. "Prokofieff's *Three Oranges:* A Note on Its Musical-Dramatic Organisation." *Tempo*, No. 41 (1956), pp. 20–24.

Nabokov, Nicolas. "Sergei Prokofiev." *Atlantic Monthly*, July 1943, pp. 62–70.

Newman, Joseph. "Prokofiev Admits Alien Taint to His Music, Thanks Accusers." *New York Herald Tribune*, February 19, 1948.

Payne, Anthony. "Prokofiev's *The Fiery Angel*." *Tempo*, No. 72 (1965), pp. 21–23.

Porter, Andrew. "Prokofiev's Early Operas: *The Gambler, The Love of Three Oranges*." *Musical Times*, No. 103 (1962), pp. 528–30.

————. "Prokofiev's Late Operas." *Musical Times*, No. 108 (1967), pp. 312–14.

"Prokofieff Finds Russia's Music Thriving." *Musical America*, January 10, 1930, p. 42.

Pugliese, Giuseppe. "The Unknown World of Prokofiev's Operas." *Hi Fidelity*, June 1966, p. 44.

Ramey, Phillip. "Sergei Prokofiev." Time-Life Records, New York, 1975.

Robinson, Harlow. "Can Soviet Leaders Learn to Love Prokofiev's *Oranges?*" *The New York Times*, April 12, 1981, Sec. II.

————. "Dostoevsky and Opera: Prokofiev's *The Gambler*." *Musical Quarterly*. Vol. LXX, No. 1 (Winter 1984), pp. 96–106.

————. "Fantasist: The Ballets of Sergei Prokofiev." *Ballet News*, May 1984, pp. 21–23 +.

————. "Love for Three Operas: The Collaboration of Vsevolod Meyerhold and Sergei Prokofiev." *Russian Review*, Vol. 45, No. 3 (July 1986).

————. "Prokofiev's 'Peter and the Wolf' is Fifty Years Old." *The New York Times*, November 10, 1985, Sec. II.

————. " 'The Most Contemporary Art': Sergei Prokofiev and Soviet Film." *Studies in Comparative Communism*. Vol. XVII, Nos. 3–4 (Fall/Winter 1984–85), pp. 203–18.

Slonimsky, Nicolas. "The 'Ugly Duckling' of Russian Music." *Christian Science Monitor*, January 27, 1945, p. 7 +.

Stockdale, Alan. "Prokofiev: Playboy of Modern Music." *Gramophone*, August 1939.

Swarsenski, Hans. "Sergei Prokofieff's *The Flaming Angel*." *Tempo*, No. 39 (1956), pp. 16–27.

————. "Unknown Works with a New Aspect." *Tempo*, No. 30 (1953), pp. 14–16.

Tempo, No. 20 (1949). Special issue devoted to Prokofiev.

Weinstock, Herbert. "Long, Twisting Road." *Opera News*, February 29, 1964, p. 9 +. (On Prokofiev's operas.)

INDEX

164, 173, 211, 231, 262, 293

London Symphony Orchestra, 164, 262

Love for Three Oranges (journal), 149, 296

Love for Three Oranges (Prokofiev), 16, 51, 83, 131, 148–56, 159–61, 164, 173, 190, 196, 204, 206, 209–10, 213, 214, 215, 220, 221, 240, 322, 332, 339, 359, 361, 379, 381, 419, 464, 479, 480
  literary source of, 148–49, 296
  march in, 17, 150, 201, 227, 271, 276, 356, 459
  popularity of, 148, 149, 150, 234, 454, 463
  premiere of, 145, 148, 168–69
  publication of, 175
  reviews of, 169, 187
  royalty in, 15, 49, 280

Lower Depths, The (Gorky), 195

Luke, Saint, 223–24

Lunacharsky, Anatoly, 137, 200, 204, 205

Lyadov, Anatoly:
  career of, 37, 66
  as Prokofiev's teacher, 35, 37, 43, 47, 49, 59, 71, 72, 84, 98

Lyubimov, Yury, 329

McCormick, Cyrus, 132, 135, 148

"Maddalena" (Liven), 81

Maddalena (Prokofiev), 68, 73, 75, 81–83, 85, 94–95, 102, 154

Mahler, Gustav, 59

Malachite Box, The (Bazhov), 482

Malevich, Kazimir, 4, 91

Malinovskaya, Elena, 252

Maly Theater, 396, 424, 441, 445, 447–48, 456, 481

Mamoulian, Rouben, 344

Mandelshtam, Osip, 91, 127, 336–37

Manuel, Roland, 163–64

March for Band (Prokofiev), 427

"March of the Trolls" (Grieg), 26

Maresyev, Aleksei, 465, 466

Mariinsky Theater, 16–17, 33, 48, 55, 65, 85, 91, 120, 121, 125,

145, 148, 184, 190, 216, 217, 223, 227, 252, 297
  Prokofiev's works performed at, 196, 204
  see also Kirov Theater

Marinetti, Emilio, 109

Marshak, Samuil, 341, 487

Marx, Karl, 338

Massenet, Jules, 26

Mass in C Minor (Mozart), 40

Massine, Leonid, 104, 113, 158, 162, 209, 210, 217

Matelots, Les (Auric), 187, 223

Matisse, Henri, 162, 460

Matyushin, Mikhail, 91

Maximilien (Milhaud), 261, 332

Maxwell, Elsa, 212

Mayakovsky, Vladimir, 3, 91, 92, 96, 136–37, 176, 226–27, 247, 270, 460, 487

Medtner, Aleksandr, 80

Medtner, Nikolai, 70, 80, 124, 201

"Memory of the Sun" (Prokofiev), 123

Mendelson, Abram, 365, 366, 385–386, 442, 448, 491, 493

Mendelson, Mari-Cecilia Abramovna "Mira," *see* Mendelson-Prokofiev, Mira

Mendelson-Prokofiev, Mira (wife):
  as collaborator, 367–70, 378, 380, 395, 397, 400, 408, 453, 464, 479, 482, 492
  courtship of, 365–68, 370–71, 378
  family of, 365, 366, 385–86, 442
  as librettist, 368, 378, 380, 395, 397, 413, 464, 479
  Lina compared with, 366, 367, 368
  on Prokofiev, 397, 442–43, 449
  as Prokofiev's biographer, 366, 368, 370
  Prokofiev's relationship with, 1, 2, 365–71, 378–80, 384–89, 390–393, 395, 397, 399–402, 408–416, 420, 421–22, 425–28, 430, 435, 436, 438–43, 445, 447–49, 453, 455–56, 460, 464, 466, 467–70, 471, 477, 479, 480, 482, 484, 486, 490, 491–93

Prokofiev, Sergei Alekseevich (*cont.*)
career of, 8, 10
character of, 9–10, 34
death of, 10, 33, 39, 41, 74–76, 187
family of, 9
politics of, 9, 14
Prokofiev influenced by, 9, 24, 393
Prokofiev's relationship with, 12, 74, 284
Prokofiev, Sergei Sergeevich:
academic education of, 13, 19, 22, 35, 38, 43, 55
on accessibility of music, 294–95
adolescence of, 22–30, 33–64, 66–76, 88
Anton Rubinstein Prize won by, 99
art songs composed by, 24, 53
autobiography of, 7–8, 14, 75, 94, 108, 127, 128, 132, 133, 135, 143, 151, 167, 173, 180, 187, 216, 229, 232, 272, 298, 368, 372, 492
automobile accidents of, 217, 236–237
automobiles owned by, 213, 217, 254, 333, 334
ballet as viewed by, 49, 66
ballets composed by, 2, 33, 47, 66, 116, 185, 226, 273–74
"battle of the pianos" won by, 99
biographies of, 366, 367
birth of, 8
bridge enjoyed by, 253, 254, 258, 264
as businessman, 70, 77, 80, 88, 103, 144, 159, 198, 242, 244
on California, 160
character of, 39, 50–51, 62, 75, 79, 89, 95, 99–100, 103, 107, 117, 147, 154, 174, 175, 181–182, 198–99, 217–18, 225, 231, 236, 239, 241, 242, 244, 248, 251, 253–55, 273, 275, 284, 295, 299, 308, 318, 319–20, 360, 368–69, 371, 372, 378, 383, 386, 392–93, 426, 428–29
chess enjoyed by, 13, 44, 62, 67, 165, 168, 172, 229, 254, 300, 304–305, 324, 325, 430, 442, 449, 461
childhood as viewed by, 7, 225, 306–307, 323
childhood of, 7–22, 393
as Christian Scientist, 39
citizenship of, 143–44, 197, 204, 206, 470
as collaborator, 28, 351, 353, 355, 359–60, 369, 371–72, 397, 404, 407, 484, 489
as composer, flexibility of themes used by, 221, 371
as composer, in childhood and adolescence, 12–13, 14, 17, 19, 21–24, 27–28, 38, 43, 47, 52–53, 56–58, 59, 62–63, 66–68, 69, 71, 73, 75, 192
as composer, speed of, 120, 123, 148, 224, 251, 261, 305, 351
on composition, 130–31, 327–28, 453, 492
on concerto form, 86
concertos composed by, 2, 77, 117, 262
as conductor, 53, 54, 71–72, 73, 78, 98, 114, 117, 122, 161, 162, 164, 230, 267, 293, 295, 332, 340, 342, 383, 400, 435–436
copyists used by, 194, 207, 214, 235, 340
dance forms in works by, 87, 420
as dancer, 46, 147, 374
death of, 1–2, 74, 493
description of, 8, 28, 35, 63, 95, 96, 107, 122, 145, 147, 161, 163, 175, 182, 183, 198, 206, 207, 253, 268, 289, 319, 334, 360, 368, 371, 426
diary of, 23–24
on dissonance, 243
eating habits of, 17, 43, 158, 251, 335
études composed by, 63, 68, 69, 78, 85, 110
evaluation of career of, 1, 2, 3
evaluations of talent of, 17, 19, 26,